# PLACING AESTHETICS

# PLACING AESTHETICS
## Reflections on the Philosophic Tradition

*Robert E. Wood*

*OHIO UNIVERSITY PRESS*
*Athens*

Ohio University Press, Athens, Ohio 45701
© 1999 by Robert E. Wood
Printed in the United States of America
All rights reserved

Ohio University Press books are printed on acid-free paper ⊗ ™
03 02 01 00 99    5 4 3 2 1

Library of Congress Cataloging-in-Publication Data
Wood, Robert E., 1934–
    Placing aesthetics : reflections on the philosophic tradition /
    Robert E. Wood.
        p.           cm. —(Series in Continental thought ; 26)
    Includes bibliograhical references and index.
    ISBN 0-8214-1280-9  (alk. paper).
    ISBN 0-8214-1281-7  (pbk. : alk. paper)
    1. Aesthetics—History        I. Title.  II. Series.
    BH81.W66      1999
    111'.85'09—dc21                                    99-27142
                                                       CIP

**Frontispiece.**   *Christus Africanus* by Robert E. Wood

*To Sue,*
*who, given but half a life, died at peace*

*and to Jim,*
*who, given two-thirds of a life, lived enough for three.*

# Contents

Abbreviations                                                                                    xi
Preface                                                                                          xiii


*I. Introduction: Fine Art and the Field of Experience*                                            1
    The Threefold Structure of the Field of Experience                          2
    The Manifold Forms of Art                                                  14
    A Preliminary Descriptive System of the Fine Arts                          18
    Phenomenological, Hermeneutic, and Dialogic Approaches                     30

*II. Plato*                                                                                       35
    Art in the Purged City                                                      36
    The Center of Order                                                         44
    Mimesis                                                                     50
    The Treatment of Art in the *Republic*                                      52
    The Ladder of Ascent to Beauty Itself                                       57
    *Response*                                                                  61
    A Brief Excursus: Plato and Wright on Architecture                          69

*III. Aristotle*                                                                                  71
    Meanings of the Term Art                                                    71
    Nature Illumined by Art: Plato and Aristotle                                75
    Art as Imitation                                                            77
    Division of the Performing Arts                                             82
    The Definition of Tragedy                                                   84
    *Response*                                                                  88

Contents

*IV. Plotinus and the Latin Middle Ages*                          95
    Plotinus                                  96
    Aquinas among the Latin Medievals         102
    *Response*                                111

*V. Kant*                                                         117
    *Critique of Pure Reason*                 118
    *Critique of Practical Reason*            123
    *Critique of Judgment*                    126
    The Beautiful                             128
    The Sublime                               136
    Art and Genius                            140
    Nature's Ultimate and Final Purpose       143
    *Response*                                145
    Epilogue: Hume's Notion of Aesthetic Community    152
    *Response*                                154

*VI. Hegel*                                                       159
    Hegel, Enlightenment, and Christianity    159
    The Starting Point of the Hegelian System 163
    The Development of the System             166
    The Nature of Art                         172
    The Basic Stages and Forms of Art         176
    *Response*                                182

*VII. Schopenhauer*                                               187
    A Synthesis of Kant, Plato, and the Indian Tradition    187
    *The World as Will and Representation*     189
    Aesthetic Experience and the Work of Art  194
    The Forms of Art                          196
    *Response*                                198

*VIII. Nietzsche*                                                 203
    Nietzsche's Horizon                       203
    Nietzsche's Aesthetics                    216
    *Response*                                223

*IX. Dewey*                                                       231
    Overcoming the Platonic Splits            232

# Contents

Overcoming the Cartesian Splits     234
Further Modifications of Traditional Notions     241
Dewey's Aesthetics     246
*Response*     257

*X. Heidegger*     *263*
Situating Heidegger     263
"The Origin of the Work of Art"     272
What Is a Thing?     274
Philosophy, Science, Art, and the Lifeworld     280
*Response*     296

*XI. Conclusion*     *303*
The Sensory Field     305
The Cultural World     310
Transcendence     319

*Appendix: On Sculptural Production*     *329*
Descriptions     329
Reflections     340

Notes     347
Bibliography     391
Index of Names     407
Subject Index     410

# *Abbreviations*

**Aquinas**
ST       *Summa theologiae*

**Aristotle**
*NE*       *Nicomachean Ethics*
*OS*       *On the Soul*

**Dewey**
*AE*       *Art as Experience*
*ExN*       *Experience and Nature*
FATE       "From Absolutism to Experimentalism"
*RP*       *Reconstruction in Philosophy*

**Hegel**
*ALFA*       *Aesthetics: Lectures on Fine Art* (Knox trans.)
*EL*       *Encyclopaedia Logic*
*HPM*       *[Hegel's] Philosophy of Mind*
*PR*       *[Hegel's] Philosophy of Right*
*PS*       *Phenomenology of Spirit*
*SL*       *The Science of Logic*

**Heidegger**
*BAT*       *Being and Time*
BDT       "Building, Dwelling, Thinking," in *PLT*
*EP*       *The End of Philosophy*
*IM*       *An Introduction to Metaphysics*
LH       "Letter on Humanism," in *Basic Writings*

| | |
|---|---|
| LP | "Language in the Poem," in *OWL* |
| MA | "Memorial Address" |
| NL | "The Nature of Language," in *OWL* |
| OWA | "The Origin of the Work of Art," in *PLT* |
| *OWL* | *On the Way to Language* |
| *PLT* | *Poetry, Language, and Thought* |
| *QCT* | *The Question Concerning Technology* |
| *WCT* | *What Is Called Thinking?* |
| *WP* | *What Is Philosophy?* |
| WPF | "What Are Poets For?" in *PLT* |

**Kant**

| | |
|---|---|
| *CJ* | *Critique of Judgment* |
| *CPR* | *Critique of Pure Reason* |

**Nietzsche**

| | |
|---|---|
| *BGE* | *Beyond Good and Evil* |
| *BT* | *The Birth of Tragedy* |
| *EH* | *Ecce Homo* |
| *GM* | *On the Genealogy of Morals* |
| *GS* | *Gay Science* |
| *TI* | *Twilight of the Idols* |
| *TSZ* | *Thus Spake Zarathustra* |
| *WTP* | *The Will To Power* |

**Plato**

| | |
|---|---|
| *Rep* | *The Republic* |
| *Sym* | *Symposium* |

**Plotinus**

| | |
|---|---|
| *Enn* | *The Enneads* |

**Schopenhauer**

| | |
|---|---|
| *EA* | *Essays and Aphorisms* |
| *WWR* | *The World as Will and Representation* |

# *Preface*

The origins of this book are multiple: a love of solitude, of woods and mountains and clouds and fields, of the changing moods on the surface of the water, of the play of light and deepening shadow on brush and timber in late afternoon; a love of the shape and color of bleached bones, slightly porous, dull white; a love of smooth, shiny stones and shells gathered along the shores of Lake Michigan and the Pacific Ocean; the experience of being arrested from time to time by the realization of my own mortality; a few fleeting moments of the sense of eucharistic presence; the experience of the look of the human other—the absence-in-presence of the conscious person in the sensory gleam of that most fascinating of objects, the human eye, whose presence announces an absence that is more present than all objects; the sense of the endless and the encompassing in the open expanses of Lake Michigan, the Mediterranean Sea, and the Atlantic and Pacific Oceans as well as in the contemplation of the starry skies above; the sense of the virtual omnipresence of life by its absence atop high mountains; the sense of austerity in the desert surrounding the Dead Sea viewed from Masada; the sense of the sacred in the foothills of Parnassus at Delphi; the sense of the presence-in-absence of those long dead at those same sites.

Then there was the reappearance of mortality in Rachmaninoff's *Isle of the Dead,* together with Arnold Böcklin's painting of the same title: the rhythm of the waves washing against the island's shores mirroring the even deeper insistence of the rhythms of life moving toward death, the stern announcement of necessity and the lyrical, serene voice of acceptance; the reappearance of bones, trees, and mountains in the paintings of Georgia O'Keefe and the sculpture of Henry Moore, and of cypress trees, fields, rocks, and stars playing in relation to houses and people in van Gogh; the intertwining of people and landscape in Brueghel; the starkness of Grüne-wald's crucifixion; the piercing presence of Zeus-Poseidon in the bronze attributed to Phidias at the Athens museum; the power of Michelangelo's Moses at San Pietro in Vincoli in Rome and of his David in the Accademia in Florence; the elegance of the bronze busts of Benin and the expressive-ness of the Yoruba *akuaba* fertility doll; the sense of cradling in the Piazza Navona in Rome; the soaring heights and rhythmic coordinations of San Pietro in the Vatican, Cologne Cathedral, St. Vitus Church in Hradčany Castle in Prague, and Notre Dame in Paris. Earlier there was the music of Tchaikovsky, Rachmaninoff, and Beethoven; then of Sibelius, Shostakovich, and Stravinsky; and later of Mozart, Bach, and Vivaldi: music of longing and striving, of the brooding presence of nature, of discordance and reso-lution, of joy and energy; but also the simple, serene but soaring spiritual-ity of Gregorian chant; and the mix of presence and loss in the nature poetry of Blake, Keats, Wordsworth, and Hopkins.

One semester I spent all my free time making my way through western Europe. In addition to traveling along some of the great rivers, lakes and mountains—on one occasion climbing the face of the Gaisberg outside Salzburg—time spent lingeringly contemplating the churches and galleries of the great cities gave me a special taste for sculpture, particularly bronzes. Upon my return to America I decided to enroll in courses on clay sculp-ture. Subsequently I produced about four dozen pieces, the best of which— appearing on the cover of this book—I finally had cast in bronze. In addition to an enhanced sensitivity to form and texture, this gave me an appreciation of the process of artistic production. I include in an epilogue a description of that process, along with some general comments on the nature of sculpture that I learned from working, viewing, reading, and re-flecting on the art form.

All these special attractions drew me initially to the philosophy of Henri Bergson, the subject of my master's thesis, grounded in intuition and open to the mystical; drew me to the erotic in Plato, to the mysticism of Plotinus, John of the Cross, and Therese of Avila; to Buber's philosophy of presence and dialogue, the subject of my first book; to the comprehensive dialectic of Hegel that attempted to encompass the whole tradition, with his massive work on aesthetics introducing us to the character of the Final and Encompassing; to the thought of Heidegger, who covered much of the same historical-philosophical ground as Hegel, but who was more sensitive perhaps to the basis of speculative thought in the lifeworld *(Lebenswelt)* and to its articulation in poetry, architecture, and painting.

My first book, *Martin Buber's Ontology,* explored the possibility of an integral mode of relation to persons, things, and the encompassing whole in a dialogic philosophy carried by a sense of presence and a deep awareness of the ineradicable pluralism of thought.[1] My second book, *A Path into Metaphysics,* presented a phenomenological, hermeneutic, and dialogic approach, reading select highpoints in the history of thought about the ultimate and the encompassing in terms of the governing élan of each thinker.[2] The book was guided by the conviction introduced by Bergson that the center of every great speculative thinker was "aesthetic," a governing sense of the whole that furnished a basic generative gestalt.

The present book, employing the same methods, advances more explicitly into that aesthetic center by attending to select high points in the history of philosophic thought on matters aesthetic and attempting to locate these considerations within the view of the whole advanced by each of the thinkers treated. In this process I attempt to show that the aesthetic is no mere icing on the cake but is rather the dynamic center of the whole speculative enterprise. Following John Dewey, I would claim that the aesthetic is integral experience; but integral experience, pressed to its ultimate depth, involves a sense of the encompassing whole. Hence I begin the treatment of each thinker with a consideration of the interplay of the central concepts of his view of the whole within which his explicit reflection on aesthetics is placed. Thus the title, *Placing Aesthetics.* I could just as easily have used the title *Metaphysics and Aesthetics,* but the term *metaphysics* is currently in disrepute in most philosophical circles, even in those Heideggerian circles where "the question of Being" as the question of the whole is alive indeed. And in that same Heideggerian line, I anchor my consideration in an attempt at a phenomenological inventory of the fundamental structures of the field of experience as a whole, features that pose the question of the whole and allow of alternative construals as to its ultimate character. It is within that field that I will find a central place for what I mean by the aesthetic.[3]

That phenomenological grounding will provide us with a point of departure for reading the tradition, beginning, not with opinions of thinkers, but with "the things themselves" as they are displayed in and through the approach of each thinker. This work is an attempt to root philosophy in the lifeworld and in its intensification rather than in an abstract flight from it, whether conceptual or mystical. Attention to things themselves will also provide the basis for an ongoing response to the thinkers with a view toward building an aesthetic that will, I hope, be less exposed to the partiality that frequently afflicts both piecemeal argumentation and wholesale "system building." I will attempt to gather together the basic results of my inquiry in the concluding chapter.

—The University of Dallas

# PLACING AESTHETICS
*Reflections on the Philosophic Tradition*

# I

# INTRODUCTION
## *Fine Art and the Field of Experience*

THERE IS SURELY SENSE to the notion that one ought to approach every study in terms of empirical acquaintance with the objects of the study. In fact, how else could one begin? Thus in approaching matters aesthetic, one should have firsthand acquaintance with art objects as well as with the beauties of nature and, if possible, with artistic practice. We are surely not exempt from that requirement. However, every study except philosophy begins with certain presuppositions which it is not the task of that study to analyze. Thus Euclidean geometry takes its point of departure from the possibility of beginning with sensorily given examples as instances of theorems that it then proceeds to prove by deducing the theorems from fundamental axioms. It is the function of the philosophy of mathematics to carry out a meta-reflection upon the framework presupposed by the mathematician. Thus arise questions about the status of sensa, of theorems, of the relation between sensa and theorems, of the nature of deduction, of the peculiar angle of abstraction taken by geometry vis-à-vis sensorily given objects, about the nature of mind and its relation to consciousness on the one hand and to organic functioning on the other, about the value of mathematical inquiry in relation to other forms of inquiry, and about the value of inquiry in relation to the totality of interests sustained by humans.[1]

The philosophic mode of inquiry begins with a meta-reflection upon what is presupposed in other areas of human experience with a view toward developing a sense of the whole of that experience and what it entails. Philosophy involves an exposition of the fundamental framework of experience as presupposed in all that we think and do. Its distinction from other disciplines that deal only with the sensorily verifiable does not lie in its being given over to "airy speculation" or unverifiable supposition. Philosophy rather deals with the fundamentally and comprehensively verifiable, with what essentially we cannot do without, and on that basis it supplies a critical assessment of the limitations involved in the abstractions with which other disciplines operate.[2]

So in approaching aesthetics we will begin, not directly with aesthetic objects, but with the overarching, always present, and immediately verifiable framework of experience within which the work of art, the aesthetic object in general, artistic activity, and aesthetic experience can be located. My contention is that not only aesthetic understanding, but all fundamental understanding must move in that direction. Of course there is very much understanding to be had without attending to that framework, as one can very fruitfully work for one's whole life in mathematics without once asking the philosophic questions involved in the discipline. And just as pursuing such questions will not necessarily make one a better mathematician but might even distract one from mathematics, so also taking this approach to aesthetics may have the same irrelevant or even counterproductive relation to aesthetic matters. I say "may" because it is possible that, as a result of such inquiry, one could become more profoundly related to one's own discipline—art or mathematics or any other field—indeed to one's own *Lebenspraxis* as a whole. Here so much depends on the continual coming and going between philosophical reflection and live involvement with the area in question.

## The Threefold Structure of the Field of Experience

Anything we do or undergo takes place within the overarching field of experience to whose fundamental structures we rarely attend but upon which we necessarily rest. The fundamental character of that field is one of intentionality, of which volitional activity is only the most obvious form. Intentionality involves the manifestness of objects in their apparent independence of our awareness. And by *objects* here I do not mean only impersonal things; I mean anything other than the center of awareness that can be present to awareness, whether persons or things or principles. Intentionality involves the simultaneous focal manifestness of the appearing things and (prefocally) of our own selves as subjects of awareness to whom things appear. The self involved here is not only or even not basically the empirically objective organic body that appears as such an object both to others and to oneself. It is rather the conscious center, the essential nonobject, the fundamental condition for the possibility of the appearance of any appearing thing, the point of origin or pivot around which the appearing world arranges itself. My own sensory objectivity is obviously rooted in the reality of my bodily being, but its appearance depends on there being a subject of awareness whose object it is. Objects are appearances "thrown over against" *(ob-jecta)* subjects who are "thrown under" *(sub-jecta)* the field of manifestness. The apparent independence of objects has to be understood as an independence in being but not in appearing. As Edmund Husserl, founder of the discipline of phenomenology we are here practicing, put it: Things are given *for us* (in terms of our conditions) as existing *in themselves* (independently of those conditions).[3] What appear are objects costructured in their appearance by what they are and by the structural conditions of the subject of awareness. It is the task of phenomenology to carry out and maintain a descriptive inventory of the essential features *(logoi)* of this field of appearing *(phainomena)* as a co-constituting relation of conscious subject and appearing objects.[4] However, the conscious subject tends to disappear from attention because of its natural directedness to another for which it functions as the locus of manifestness. Further, because of the dominance of empirical objectiveness, it tends to understand itself as another empirical object. But it is this nonobjectifiable subject of awareness that initiates responses that are intentional in the ordinary sense of the term (i.e., are deliberate). There are subdivisions of such deliberate intentionality, like artistic activity and aesthetic appreciation. But deliberate intentionality is founded upon the spontaneously functioning intentionality of the field of awareness wherein, like it or not, things present themselves.[5] Awareness by nature intends objects. Choice as deliberate intentionality is solicited by the prior presentation of those objects in the mode of spontaneously functioning intentionality. Artistic intentionality in particular is peculiarly and sensitively rooted in that prior spontaneously functioning intentionality and makes it manifest to the artist's audience.

Now the field of intentionality, as it presents empirical objects, has a threefold structure, which we will designate as sensing, interpreting, and presence-to-being.[6] The first level seems clearest—at least it is the most obvious. There are the ever-present sensa: colors, sounds, tastes, smells, and the various features linked to tactility: hard and soft, rough and smooth, heavy and light, hot and cold, dry and moist. Color seems to dominate insofar as it is always present in the normal waking world, whereas the other features are either recessive or variable. However, we could also say that sound dominates insofar as encounter with the speaking other is the primary focus of most of our lives, for which the visual furnishes the background. The world of art, at least in its nonverbal forms, articulates the field of sensa, but with a peculiar focus upon the visual and audile features—a peculiarity to which we will return later.

First then the sensory field. The status of the sensa is problematic. For one thing, even though we tend to think of them as the most concrete evidences, as we speak of them in this way they are presented in a most abstract way vis-à-vis our ordinary experience. For we do not normally see colors, but trees and sky, buildings and people, paper and computers. We do not normally hear sounds, but voices, traffic, drills, bells sounding, the wind blowing through the trees—that is, the sensa are already configured in terms of modes of taking them up interpretatively.[7] As Bernard Lonergan once remarked, what is most obvious in knowing—namely, the sensa—is not what knowing most obviously is.[8] What, more exactly, is the field of sensation, considered apart from our specifically human way of taking it up?

Comprehensively considered and in abstraction from the other two levels, it is a synesthetic-kinesthetic whole displaying an appearance, a synthetic phantasma, a showing focused upon the surface of things other than the perceiving organism. It provides a realm of appearance filtered in terms of the functional needs of that organism and thus shot through and brought to focus by desire.[9] To ground those claims, first of all, we have to consider that each of the senses has its own way of selectively responding to the total set of causal impacts made by the environment on the organism by producing its own distinctive appearance. A sensory power is a selective filter in relation to those causal impacts. There is a sense in which, as Nietzsche noted, what the senses provide is a lie.[10] The apparently empty space between my eye and the text being read we know by instrumentally unaided reflection to be full of dust particles and sounds. But experimental work shows that it is also full of air molecules and of radio and TV waves. It is replete with photons and, in fact, with irradiation from across the whole electromagnetic spectrum. But of course, to be able to see all that would make recognition of approaching obstacles or dangers, and food or mate or offspring, virtually impossible. Seeing at all, it would seem, necessarily entails not being able to see all that is present. The visual field is a luminous bubble blown by the nervous system making a certain type of appearance possible so that an animal being can have a functional space available to meet its needs. Correlative to that appearance is the rising up of desire that moves the seer in the direction of the organically desirable or away from the undesirable. Thus the functionally manifest space is not only sensory but also sensuous, evoking desire or aversion or felt neutrality. Second, in view of organic functionality, the seen plays in relation to the heard and smelt, and eventually and most basically, the touched and tasted, for its mode of appearance aims at satisfying the desire for food or mate, which have to be tactually apprehended to fulfill such needs.[11] The field of the senses is thus, as I have said, a synesthetic-kinesthetic whole of selective appearance shot through with desire and constructed to fulfill the needs of the perceiving organism.

But though it is a perceiver-dependent appearance and not the inner reality of what appears, yet in order to fulfill its function, the sensuous field cannot be entirely a lie. It does not provide pseudofood and -mate but real food and mate, though the fullness of either is cloaked by the interest-laden selectivity of the appearance. Through the regularity of sensuous appearance manifest over time, the sensuously given displays patterns, both of functioning wholes and of coordination between functioning wholes. In particular, those functioning wholes we call living appear as setting themselves off from the causal networks within which they are embedded, providing both the model and in our case the matrix for a rational system as a coherently functioning whole.[12] Animal organisms organize the materials drawn from their environs so that the sensuous plenum comes to manifestness to the perceiving organism through the organs thus created. The objectively observable, shaped into an organ system, provides the conditions for the process of observation itself, which completes the organic process. Providing an instance of a more general principle enunciated by Hegel, here objectivity is completed in subjectivity as the condition for the manifestation of objectivity.[13]

As it appears in the field of animal awareness, each part of an organic being, whether viewed from without or lived through from within, is not simply sensorily there in a positivistic way; more basically, it expresses something of the character of the living whole within which it operates. And in the case of animal organisms, their behavior expresses the inwardness of desire that surges up teleologically out of an organic base. The recognition of such expressivity in organically functioning wholes is the central aspect in the recovery of natural form from the tendency to reduce it to its elements.[14] Now, expression and the interpretation of expression belong together. But at the animal level the sensory surface of another animal expresses support for, or antagonism or indifference to, satisfying the desires of the percipient animal who is locked into the circle of those desires. The sensory surface furnishes the basis for an organic dashboard knowledge, a mode of display sufficient to learn what to push, pull, and turn in order to get the required output.[15] Rooted in organic purpose, sensation reveals, not full being but filtered-off appearance co-constituted by the character of the perceiving organism and the way things in the environment interact physically with that organism.

Now what I have presented thus far is analogous to a geometrical analysis, like the isolation of a plane or a line or a point from the three-dimensional solidity of the world of ordinary objects. As noted previously, the things of ordinary experience are not simply colors or sounds, but things being revealed (and concealed) in various ways. And that revelation is a function of the way they are taken up into the field of awareness. We have been taking them up here, not in terms of their sensory particularity, but in terms of their immediately given universal features. But let us leave aside this mode of taking up for a moment (it will be crucial for the arts) and attend to the third level—even more crucial for our understanding of aesthetics: what I have called presence-to-being.

If sensa seem the most obvious features of the field of experience, presence-to-being is the least obvious, but it is deeply tied to the peculiar implicitness of the subject of awareness. To cite Augustine in a different but closely related context, presence-to-being is *interior interiori meo*, inside my inside, "more intimate to me than I to myself."[16] The sensa anchor awareness in the constantly flowing Now. If there is an indeterminate depth of space surrounding the luminous bubble of sensory appearance Here and uncovered in scientific investigation, there is no less the indeterminate depth of time surrounding the Now of such appearance. Space and time present themselves as indeterminately spread in such a way as to encompass the whole of all possible sensory presentation, including the Here and Now. Like a geometrical theorem, though in a more basic manner (more basic because it grounds geometry and all other human endeavors), the presentation of space and time as indeterminate wholes has itself an atemporal character.[17] Now, to say of space and time that each *is* given as all-encompassing in relation to the field of sensory presentation, to say that the sensory field *is* a luminous bubble blown by the nervous system *is* to bring into play the notion of being, the participial form of the verb *to be*, whose third person singular form *is* "is." It is a notion that encompasses space and time, the things appearing in the sensory field and the self to whom all this appears. The notion of being is given as absolutely unrestricted, including in itself even the forms of non-being we find present in experience, such as the no longer and the not yet, the absent, privation, and the like. It includes everything within it and everything about every thing.[18]

We can see the all-encompassing character of the notion of being if we think of the principle of noncontradiction co-given with it. This principle grounds the possibility of predication and inference, and thus also our ability to bring the whirl of experience into a consistent world. We know ahead of time that everything encounterable or even thinkable is such that it cannot both be and not be at the same time and in the same respect. Identity of things with themselves and their identity and nonidentity with each other in terms of certain predicates allow judgments to come to stand firm and hold over time and make possible inference as a linkage between judgments on the basis of the identity or nonidentity of the terms of the judgment with each other. For example, my being the identical person I am throughout the changes of my lifetime, the enduring possibility of my behaving rationally, and the enduring groundedness of responsibility in rationality, indicates my essential responsibility for my actions. Expressed syllogistically: Every rational being is responsible; I am a rational being; hence I am responsible. Each of the three linked propositions expresses an enduring identity of meaning in each term—*rational being, responsible, I*—and between the terms in each proposition, so that through my identity as a rational being I am linked to being responsible. These processes of identification and inference allow us to build up the world of immediate dwelling (the *Lebenswelt,* or lifeworld) and ground the extension through scientific inquiry of the field of sensa on which we base the constructions of the *Lebenswelt.* Beginning with immediately given sensa and the principles of inference, we come to construct the worlds of meaning that we inhabit.[19]

We might get another handle on what presence-to-being involves by considering the fact of religions. Religions are answers to the question central to human existence: How do we fit into the scheme of things? Answers to that question found different ways of life and hold them in place. Concern for the all, for the total scheme of things is central to being human. That question tends to surface explicitly when some of our deepest expectations are shattered, for then we ask seriously and not as a matter of mere curiosity: What's it all about? Though the typically offered answers are plural and not all mutually compatible, the fact of those attempts still shows the commonality of the question. To be human is to be referred by nature to the whole of what-is in the mode of a question.[20]

The human being exists wakefully in the ever-enduring Now of sensory surface, directed by nature to the whole, but initially only in the mode of questioning, since the whole is at first only emptily intended.

Taking the point of view of the whole encompasses the whole of space and time and thus exhibits a Now *sub specie aeternitatis,* a Now that eternally encompasses the flowing Now of sensory experience.[21] The initial emptiness of our reference to the whole makes it necessary to construct worlds of meaning that situate the ever-given sensory Now within the encompassing whole to which we are directed by our nature. The play between the needs of our biological ground and the need we have for seeing something of the character of our relation to the whole places human beings before certain fundamental decisions. These decisions are both possible and necessary because our relation to the whole sets us at an infinite distance from the givens of biology and thus "condemns us to choose."

In our case, sexuality drives male and female together but also poses a problem not solved by sheer natural drive, namely, How shall we care for the offspring that emerge from that togetherness? Nature addresses humankind in terms of problems not solved by nature; nature presses human freedom for decisions. The cluster of decisions provided by humankind in response to this question constitutes the history of the institutions of marriage and child rearing. Feelings of possessiveness and power, grounded in nature but focused by the sedimentation of decisions we call institutions, cluster about mates and offspring to furnish a second level, beyond natural organic feelings, of felt reverberations in the presence of sensa.

The togetherness of the family makes collective the first problems posed by nature, namely, How do I get enough to eat and drink? and How do I protect myself against the threats posed by the environment? Actually, because human beings are not born even relatively self-sufficient but require years of care, these questions an individual might ask regarding himself or herself actually originate from the questions, How do *we* get enough to eat? and How do *we* protect ourselves against the environment? The sedimentation of decisions in this realm gives rise to the history of economic institutions. The plurality of humans poses the problem of how we relate to others in and beyond those relations of mate and offspring grounded in sexuality and eventuates in determinate social practices. Of course, involved in all of this is the problem of authority: Who makes the decisions? and How do we pass on the results of these processes to those who follow us? This introduces not only the dialectic between individuals and groups who are coexistent, but, perhaps even more powerfully, that between the live community and the tradition of folkways, the sedimented set of decisions, now become second nature, that have allowed the community to survive against the more or less frequent hostility of the environment, natural and social. The answers we give to the questions posed by nature and by our sedimented responses to nature are not just ad hoc solutions but involve the establishment of anticipated possible regularity of response that could apply anywhere and any time we meet the same situations. By our decisions we help establish or disestablish both individual and collective principles for action.

But the questions posed to our freedom by our nature in relation to the natural and social environment are not the only questions. Our nature as oriented toward the whole of being poses to us the basic question of the meaning of the whole as object of our deepest human desire. It may not be the most immediately overpowering desire; but the latter ultimately pales into insignificance without some sense of its relation to the whole. After the height of orgasm one could readily ask if it "means" anything. And ultimate meaning, we suggest, is a matter of seeing and indwelling in the belonging together of humans and other entities within the whole. So we not only have to make fundamental decisions as to how we are to respond to the basic questions posed by nature in the realm of practice, we also stand under the requirement of certain interpretative decisions regarding the meaning of each entity within the whole. That they are, in a sense, decisions seems clear from the fact that there is a plurality of them. Yet neither type of decision—interpretive and practical—can be simply arbitrary and unconstrained, since they will not hold over time unless they are in some way compatible with the totality of what is given, both in terms of the encountered and in terms of our own needs, individual and collective. They are deeply tied to the sedimented history of decisions of those long dead that constitute the institutions within which a We exists. Fundamental decisions are responses to directions we are invited to walk, presented by the concrete situation in which we find ourselves, insofar as such decisions involve our place in the whole scheme of things.[22]

It is out of this question about the whole that the most powerful and sophisticated of all institutions emerges, namely the institution of language. In the first place, that structure makes possible for each individual that is given in the sensory field to function as an icon of the whole. Further, the factual reoccurrence, spatially and temporally, of types, of kinds of entities mediates the mode of manifestation in the individual's relation to the whole. It is language that allows us to retain our awareness of types. And in its mediation, language functions fundamentally in opening up the space from which decisions come, the space of meaning that emerges from the wedding between immersion in the problems posed by the sensory Now and our fundamental reference to the encompassing whole of being. Focus upon the rude artifacts from prehistorical times that archaeologists discover often makes us forget that "primitive peoples" for millennia were developing that most sophisticated of instruments to which we are still necessarily beholden: language.[23] Language, incarnated in the flow of sound generated by our lips, gathers about the immediately given sensa the whole as known and as imagined and endows the objects presented with emotional reverberations of extreme depth and subtlety. It is upon these reverberations that the arts play.

However, over and above, and indeed, I would argue, at the basis of all our conceptual articulations, there is the depth dimension of our fundamental presence to Being, whose subjective correlate is what a long tradition calls the heart.[24] Now there are several meanings that cluster around the term *heart* in a way that is remarkably constant across cultures, Eastern and Western. One thinks initially of the blood pump in the center of the chest, a mechanism in principle replicable by a man-made mechanical heart. But that is an abstraction from a more primordial, lived sense of the heart as burning with rage or skipping a beat in love: heart as the center of our lived experience known first before any knowledge of physiological mechanisms. The term is extended to an object in expressions like *sweetheart* or *heart of my heart*. Finally, it has a transcendental extension in expressions like *the heart of the matter* used to signify the essential, the core (Latin *cor*). Heart in the second sense is that to which, in biblical terms, God speaks.[25] As such it is the center, the source and receptacle for all the other distinctively human functions. And it is that, I would claim, which art articulates: the desires of the heart as our most fundamental lived presence to Being.

Being as the concrete wholeness of things within the wholeness of what-is cannot be simply object of intellectual operations directed at the abstract universal. Judgment linking the universal to the particular depends on a totalistic sense of things, out of which emerges *phronesis*, or practical wisdom in the moral-political order, and taste in the aesthetic order. Both operate at the level of "the heart" and depend on a totalistic attunement. In actual experience, things and persons are not equidistant items of information appearing within the field of a detached, judging intellect; some stand out as arresting presences, drawing near, gripping us at the level of the heart, setting up a field of magnetic attractions. And fundamental frameworks of evaluation are not present as neutral alternatives; we indwell in such frameworks, we in-habit them. The arts articulate those modes of indwelling, those senses of presence. That is why it can rightly be said that one of the most direct modes of access to a culture is through its art forms. Art gives expression to what counts most, to lived principles, to cherished persons and things in a mode appropriate to those matters. Like religion, art speaks to the heart. And both are as deep as they reach into the whole of what one is. As Mikel Dufrenne remarks, "The depth of the aesthetic object is measured by the depth of the existence to which it invites us."[26]

Reference to Being, linked to consideration of the organically dependent character of sensory manifestness, pushes us toward a distinction between the field of awareness constituted by complex relations of manifestness between subject and object and the underlying subjects of being anchoring both subject and object of awareness. The subject of awareness is "tuned," disposed, and oriented to interpret and act in certain ways from beneath the field of awareness by reason of its being in a determinate world. It comes to understand itself not simply by way of introspection of present states but more deeply by reflecting on the patterns of action it engages in over time. The object of awareness, co-constituted by the organically needy and intellectually finite subject of awareness and the underlying subject of encountered being, expresses itself in the field of awareness—that is, it rises up into that field to announce itself as indeterminately exceeding the mode of manifestness it displays in that field. It has consequently to be interpreted as well as observed. There is thus a clear distinction between appearance and reality, where the latter is understood as the full being of what is and the former as an awareness-dependent display that both reveals and conceals full being.

Reference to Being, reference to the whole, places us always at an infinite distance, not only from what we encounter, but from our very selves. A perpetual distinction between I and Me emerges. *Me* represents the objectifiable aspects of myself, what I am at any given moment outside the fact that I am always, as *I*, projected beyond it. *Me* is the resultant of (1) my genetic endowment and biological unfolding; (2) my being assimilated to, while assimilating, the institutions of my culture, beginning with language and passing through all the regularities of thought, feeling, and behavior I have received and continue to receive through the imprint of significant others—parents, siblings, friends, teachers, spouses, media, and so forth; and (3) the history of my past choices, based on the possibilities opened up by the genetic and cultural determinants and sedimented in the habit structures that both bear me up as skills and weigh me down as compulsions. All of this is Me, which—though a variation on general biological and cultural themes—is the artist's material, peculiar to me, which I as center of awareness cannot but choose to shape. The choices I make on the basis of genetic and cultural endowments sink back into the darkness from which the tuning of the field of my awareness is accomplished: they determine my heart, the desire I have to be and to act in a determinate way, to allow some persons and things to draw near and others to recede, the motivational source on the basis of which I am inclined to choose the way I do. The heart is the zone of the Me closest to the I, "the real Me." But as set at an infinite distance even from my heart, I am enabled to assess my heart, to transform my motivational basis or allow it to be transformed by a "conversion." Ultimately, I am the artist of my own life, empowered and constrained in each moment by the material I have to work with. And the specialized skills I may master as an artist in shaping sensory materials may allow me to give expression to the total way I am tuned toward being, the depths of my own heart, in artworks that come to embody my own peculiar style of inhabiting the common world, the lifeworld of my culture.

The threefold structure of the Weld of experience gives us a "vertical" cross-section verifiable at any given moment. And though the framework is concretely filled by the peculiar way in which a given culture enters into a given person's pattern of choices, individual meaning occurs by way of how that individual is in time or how the relation between past, present, and future is achieved. There are many possibilities of being in time. One could perhaps develop a logical table of the various possible ways we can be related experientially to those three dimensions. One can be fixed on acting intensely by focusing on one of the dimensions. For example, one can be so fixed on the future that one rushes past the present and repudiates the past. As Henry Ford had it, "History is bunk!" since he was opening the future for, as Aldous Huxley put it, "the year of our Ford." Or one can be so fixed on the past as to suffocate the future and reject the present. As one of my superconservative Americanist colleagues remarked: "Nothing worthwhile was written after 1781." So one engages in reactionary politics. One can also learn to be "with it," in the flowing Now, plunging excitedly into "the latest." Or one can be dreamily related to a Romanticized past or a Utopianized future. Again, one can simply drift in the present. One can also take it as one's project to appreciate the aesthetic deliverances of the past by attending carefully to what appears in the present. But when this happens in disregard of the obligations one has to others—familial, civic, contractual—one is engaged in an irresponsible aestheticism, of which Kierkegaard gives the most powerful description in philosophic literature.[27]

Heidegger has called attention to a distinction between "average everydayness," the basis for our ordinary mode of being in time and dealing with one another, and "appropriated" existence (*Eigenlichkeit,* usually translated as "authenticity"—which has the unfortunate consequence of suggesting that average everydayness is "phoniness," which it most certainly is not, for Heidegger and in fact). In average everydayness there is a flattened, stereotyped, routinized sliding along in the present, filling in time with rootless chatter, the future appearing as object of curiosity, the past appearing ambiguously as something over and done with but also as operative in the present. In appropriated existence the present has a tensed character and we learn to tarry appreciatively alongside what is present by virtue of a dedicated project whereby we take over an inheritance in the light of our sense of destiny. How we project our future determines how we take over our past. In a conversion experience, we tell our story quite differently than we did before because its meaning changes and different aspects are focused and highlighted and different events are retrieved through the new way we project our future. Ultimately, the properly tensed and deepened relation to the present depends on how we take over our Being-toward-death, for that provides us with the ultimate term of our projects in time. For one who learns to accept the irremovable conditions of existence, running ahead toward one's own term opens up the preciousness of the time we have.[28] As Buber put it, for one properly disposed toward death, "The script of life is so incomparably beautiful to read because we know that death looks over our shoulder."[29] And, as Schopenhauer noted, if we did not have to suffer and die, the great questions of life would not so grip our attention and life itself would become slack.[30] Both Buber and Heidegger went beyond that to a sense of what we might call vocational awareness. That is tied in with how we conceive of our relation to the whole, the preoccupation of both religion and traditional philosophy. In that context, things step out of indifference and become significant presences; they speak to the heart.[31] Art draws upon this level of experience: in Dufrenne's words, just as in the case of the look of the human other, the work of art magnetizes the environment.[32]

Art itself appears within the field of awareness in terms of how both artist and audience take over their existence in time. Futurism, for example, completely repudiated the past, referring to "Pheidian decadence" and "Michaelangelesque sins."[33] The various forms of revivalism that dominated academic architecture in the nineteenth century looked exclusively to the past and were instrumental in initially crushing the emergence of new forms in figures like Wright, Le Corbusier, and Gropius.[34] But much of the works that followed in the International Style were focused exclusively on the present and repudiated all relation to past forms. In reaction, so-called postmodern architecture allows the reentry of past quotations into present work—though often only ironically.[35]

In order to set the general framework within which aesthetic experience occurs, I have considered the structures of the field of experience both "vertically," or as a cross-section, and also "horizontally," in terms of how we are in time. Let us now move more explicitly into the consideration of art.

## *The Manifold Forms of Art*

Ordinary language usage is part of the inheritance into which we enter by being born into a culture. It delineates sets of distinctions based on the distinctions and relations that appear interlocked in a real functional world. If we attend to the use of the term *art* in ordinary language, we see that it encompasses a great variety of senses, from the most comprehensive to the most specific. Each meaning can be understood in terms of its contrast with other meanings.

1. The first and most comprehensive contrast is that between art and nature. Nature provides the fundamental framework of our existence, not only in the sense of the cosmos in general and the biological environment in particular, but also in the sense of the basic structure of our distinctively human being that makes possible the peculiarly human manifestness of the biological environment within the cosmos and, as a consequence, the ability to transform according to our choices aspects of what is manifest to us. As I have shown, the structure of human nature is bipolar. It consists, on the one hand, of physiological functions that provide us, in common with other animal beings, the sensa in relation to our basic biological needs and those appetites that lead us to seek to satisfy those needs. On the other

hand, our natural structure also consists of the founding reference to the whole that sets off our distinctively human nature. On the basis of this originary human nature, we have to choose to direct our lives in terms of principles (i.e., ways of situating the Now in reference to the whole). Beyond the founding minimum of distinctive humanness as reference to the whole and by reason of that founding minimum which sets the basic direction for human existence, everything else that is distinctively human does not come into being by reason of nature but by reason of art in the broad sense of the word—that is, in terms of the modification of the naturally given through concepts that provide understanding of the given and thus determinate ways to reach goals for our striving. The whole of culture is thus arti-ficial in the literal sense; that is, it is made by art.[36]

It is important here to attend to the old Latin adage *Cultura fit secunda natura*, culture becomes second nature. Culture produces a set of spontaneities, felt responses to things and situations whose very mode of action is just like nature. This is one of the senses in which art "imitates" nature. One should think here especially of language, of which one becomes much more acutely aware when one enters a foreign country. Think of the distinction between "natural" and artificial languages. Both are actually artificial as created by human art, but a so-called natural language comes into existence over generations in response to all the claims of the natural and social environment. It takes one up into it as into nature; and of both culture and nature it is true that one can never provide an encompassing inventory.[37] This is linked to the fact that they are tied to the comprehensive set of ends embedded in the complex interplay of nature and culture that is the human person. Artificial languages are precisely surveyable because they are made by individuals to suit specific ends. And even within a "natural" language, one still speaks of an artificial style, one that is not based on a comprehensive "sense" of the region of which one speaks, but which operates in terms of rules and tricks that betray a lack of full indwelling, full presence. Fine art, the central object of our attention in this work, has a special relation to the comprehensive sense of indwelling.

2. Within this most fundamental distinction between art and nature, one can go on to distinguish, on the art side, between art (more narrowly conceived) and science. Whereas the theoretical function of science is to act as a mirror of nature, the function of art is to transform nature. But one has to bear in mind that the mirroring function has itself to come into being by the choice on the part of human beings to pursue a science of nature in the first place, by their art of choosing hypotheses and shaping

more comprehensive theories better suited than competing theories for explaining what is observed and for suggesting fruitful lines of research, by their art of active observation and experimentation, creating instruments to open further the secrets of nature, and by their choice to assimilate the tradition of scientific inquiry upon which they will build. Science as the completed manifestness of nature is the sought-for term of the art of inquiry. Thus there is not only a scientific knowledge of nature or a scientifically based transformation of nature, there is also a dimension of art within the practice of science itself.

Even the comprehensive distinction between art and nature is transformed when one attempts to understand nature in terms of art as shaping the environment. Both the Hebrew and the Greek roots of our tradition proceed on the basis of the metaphor of art. For the biblical tradition, in the beginning God created heaven and earth; in Plato's *Timaeus* the *demiurgos* persuades the chaotic receptacle of space and time to take on intelligible form.[38] For Aristotle, even though there is no conception of a fashioner or creator of nature but only of a divine exemplar, art nonetheless furnishes the basic analogue for understanding nature as involving in their togetherness the causal factors that are separated by the imposition of form upon matter by the human artisan seeking his own ends.[39] A nature is a form energetically shaping matter for the sake of achieving its own immanently given ends. That fundamental metaphor of nature, understood most basically in terms of art, operates throughout the philosophical tradition even up to and including the atheists Schopenhauer and Nietzsche.[40]

3. We approach closer to the fine arts when we distinguish, within the distinction between art and science, the art of shaping human life from the art of shaping the things of the environment. In this respect Aristotle distinguished *phronesis,* or practical wisdom, from *techne.*[41] *Phronesis* is "the art of arts," the art of the comprehensive shaping of human behavior that operates in the interplay between the political and the personal.[42] Although for Aristotle and the premodern tradition, the highest aspect of human life is the comprehensive mirroring of the order of things, which he called *theoria,* nonetheless, it is in one sense subordinate to *phronesis* as the art of the prudential arrangement of one's life in which *theoria* is the highest aspect.[43] It was Karl Marx who pointed out that in shaping nature we are simultaneously shaping ourselves by the act of producing, but we are also being shaped by the products in the act of using or observing them.[44]

4. The art of shaping the environment has two forms: that directed to-

ward forming things that are essentially means to something else and that directed toward forming things that are in some sense ends in themselves. The latter is the province of what in modern times we have come to call the fine arts.[45] But there are overlapping forms: architecture is the classical example, for it is essentially meant to serve the ends for which a given building exists; but as a fine-art form it does this by an aesthetic shaping of its materials. And, indeed, in all shaping of the environment for practical purposes there is the matter of good design. The peculiar togetherness of the sensory features, the aesthetic form, may be said to be the common focus of all the arts insofar as they are fine arts.

The following diagram summarizes the four distinctions I have just made.

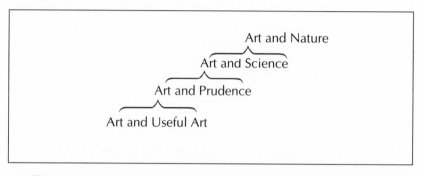

The term *art* is used in still another sense to describe the kind of institution in which a text such as this has been generated: a liberal arts school. In their origin, liberal arts were the arts of "the free man," of the leisure class not bound to the "servile" or "mechanical" arts. The former were divided into two sets: the quadrivium or "four ways" and the trivium or "three ways" which served respectively the theoretical and practical thrust of human existence. The trivium contained three arts: logic, or the art of valid thinking; grammar, or the art of correct expression; and rhetoric, or the art of persuasive expression, a fundamental art involved in the practice of political *phronesis*. *Art*, applied to the subjects of the trivium, has an instrumental sense: the arts of the trivium are useful for thinking, writing, and persuading.

The quadrivium (introduced in book 7 of Plato's *Republic*) comprised four mathematical "arts": arithmetic, geometry, astronomy, and music (understood as mathematical harmonics). *Art*, applied to the subjects of the quadrivium, seems a peculiar usage, for these subjects do not concern, like the trivium, how-to knowing. But they are understood as arts in the sense of being instrumental for the free operation of the mind, unconstrained by any other ends than purely theoretical observation. For Plato the quadrivium furnished ways to turn the soul from the realm of becoming to the realm of being, from the changeable to the eternal, freeing the mind from exterior demands to attend to what for him was its proper object.[46] As we shall see below, for Plato all arts are judged in terms of how they minister to that turn.

## *A Preliminary Descriptive System of the Fine Arts*

Understanding anything is a matter of seeing its relations to other things, showing how it is in some ways the same, in some ways different, as, for example, a human being shares properties with other material beings, with living things, with animals, especially the primates, but also has certain differentiating features.[47] "Basic" understanding of anything is a matter of seeing its most essential parameters in relation to the basic features of the encompassing field of experience. In this section I will focus in a preliminary way on the essential parameters of the various art forms in their togetherness. What I claim to do is to isolate some of the inescapable eidetic features of the world of art, features that are universal and necessary, that, like objects of geometrical proof, cannot be otherwise, but that, unlike geometrical proof, do not depend on postulates and abstract idealizations but on the immediate givenness of the regions of experience occupied by the fine arts. I will attempt to show some of the universal, essential, eidetic features involved in immediately given aesthetic particulars, just as redness and color and extension and quality, as universal forms, are found in red objects. The skeptic especially should note here the capacity to discern essential distinctions that are not matters of falsifiable empirical generalizations. One finds an immediate distinction between color as such and sound as such and is never tempted to mistake them. One finds too that color and sound are never presented to us nor are even imaginable except in a spatiotemporal context that indeterminately exceeds the immediate field of observation. There are eidetic constants in the interplay between awareness and its objects that transcend all opinions, personal and cultural, by making them possible.[48]

The field of the fine arts is the field of the senses—classically, not of all the senses, but only the fields of sight and sound. In common usage one does often speak of cooking or wine making or perfume making—although usually not of making love—as "fine arts" insofar as one develops forms that appeal to a palate capable of making fine discriminations in complex presentations of food or drink, or to a nose sensitive to subtle differences in aroma. One might well ask why these are not often listed under the fine arts in treatises on aesthetics, why the objects of seeing and hearing are the preferred locus of fine art.[49] From a purely aesthetic point of view, do the visual and audile arts not make the same appeal to a sensibility capable of refined discriminations in complex modes of presentation as do the culinary arts? What is there about seeing and hearing that sets off their field of operation from that of the other senses?

I would suggest, for one thing, that it has something to do with the fact that, in contrast with taste or smell or touch, which are "proximity" senses, seeing and hearing are "distance" senses. Taste and touch especially involve immediate contact with the object and thus a simultaneous somatic self-experience. Seeing and hearing operate over a significant distance and do not necessarily involve somatic self-experience. Under normal conditions of healthy functioning and of clear presentation of color or sound—where we do not have to strain to hear or see, are not pained by too much light or too loud a sound, or are not involved in some particular appetitive resonance—the appearing object fills the whole of our attention without a somatic self-experience. In this connection Thomas Aquinas speaks of sight as the most spiritual of the senses.[50] The distance involved, in sight especially, allows for the perception of unified wholes within the multiplicity of color presentation. And it is unified, sensorily manifest wholes or aesthetic forms that are the proximate and enduring objects of the fine arts. Functioning at a distance from individual somatic reverberations, sights and sounds are the focal points of a common world, a world we inhabit with others. As I noted earlier, sight dominates wakeful life as omnipresent, while sounds come and go. Nonetheless, because of the centrality of spoken language in our relation to the world and to one another, sound also has a centrality, but not so focally as sight. Hence we speak of all wakeful life through the metaphors associated with vision, as when we say, "See how this sounds or tastes or feels or smells, or how this geometric demonstration is carried out."

Sight displays aesthetic form in an immediately exemplary way. Colors, along with light and shadow, are set in tensive and harmonious relations of various sorts, playing within an overall spatial context of shapes that are spread out, discriminated, related, balanced, rendered rhythmic, and so on. Similarly, the temporality of sound admits of a unified togetherness through the diachrony of melodic lines and rhythmic repetitions and variations, and through the synchrony of harmonic relations. Furthermore, both the objects of vision and the objects of hearing admit of translation into mathematical ratios that virtually define what is meant by the harmonic, the proportionate, the rhythmic that constitute aesthetic experience. And in both cases, in the case of sights as well as of sounds, the capacity for unified togetherness allows for the expression of syntax and thus for reference to something other than sensuous surface. So the classical fine arts come to function as vehicles of expression of something other than sensuous surface through the peculiar shaping of sensuous surface. The harmonious play between the togetherness of sensory togetherness and referential togetherness constitutes the field of operation of aesthetic form.

One must note here, however, that the regular topographical transformability of a smooth surface admits of the tactual communication of language through Braille. But what would be the aesthetic shaping of a figure in Braille that would be the equivalent of painting or music? There is no publicly recognized Western art form dealing with the cultivation of tactility as there is for the gustatory and olfactory properties of things. Perhaps the *Kama Sutra* does this for the East; but the West has been too suspicious of sexuality to admit of a parallel cultivation for touch. And when we come to "high art," visual and audile arts take center stage insofar as they are tied to the communication, not simply of fine sensations, but of universally shareable meaning.

In religious liturgies—the Zen tea ceremony, for instance—an appeal is made to all the senses: seeing, smelling, hearing, tasting, the tactual cherishing of the utensils. Pre-Reformation Roman and Greek Christian liturgies used richly brocaded vestments, elaborately decorated liturgical vessels, music (vocal and instrumental, usually the organ), incense, bread and wine, set within elaborate architectural enclosures containing statuary and icons. Liturgical procession and drama alternated with sacred reading and oratory. The liturgies drew upon all the senses and artforms to convey a sense of the Holy recollected through the recounting of primordial religious history. But in either case, smelling and tasting are not highly cultivated, and tactility plays at best a very small role, purely subsidiary—perhaps in the handshake or embrace of peace. However, in the film *Babette's Feast* (*Babettes Gaestebud*, Danish-French, 1987), the heroine is presented as an artist who makes a sacrament of love out of a connoisseur's feast of food and wine, drawing together the assembled community whom she serves in such a way as to break down the barriers that separated them and to bring the event to culmination in celebratory dance. The movie recalls followers of the Reformation, whose bleak life involved only one aesthetic form, sacred music of the plainest sort, to the community-building power of the aesthetic sensuousness involved in pre-Reformation worship.

As I mentioned above, within the field of sensory operation there are two fundamental parameters necessarily involved: space and time. The fine arts settle into the various features of space and time by themselves and in relation, appealing to seeing and hearing either alone or together. Seeing color and shape has a special (but not exclusive) relation to the articulation of space, while hearing sound focuses and articulates time. But the situation is complicated by the fact of language. Though rooted in the here and now of sensory presence through sound patterns in speech or through visual patterns appearing in a text, language nonetheless has as its essential function to relate the here-and-now sensorily appearing individual things to the encompassing whole. The word as the sensory index of the universal concept is a kind of flight from the Now, grounded in the Now, a breaking out of the ever-flowing luminous bubble of sensory presence. The linguistic fine arts play in relation with the other fine art forms in a kind of complementary tension as primary carriers of the referential function of the mind.[51] But in addition, language contains the potential of music and dance in sonority and accent.[52] And so we can develop a preliminary descriptive system of the fine arts based on three parameters: space, time, and language, as they enter into the sensory field. Note that, as preliminary and descriptive, this systematic presentation does not broach the evaluative questions of good and bad art, high or low art, nor any possible expressive hierarchy within the arts. (See diagram on the following page of the basic relations between the art forms briefly discussed below.)

As a matter of fact, it is language that, allowing us to locate any encountered object and any experience within the space of a meaningful world, opens up the field for all the arts. So let us begin with the linguistic fine arts. Prose is the literary form closest to ordinary language. It occupies a range from a page of information, which operates in the visual field, to storytelling, which, like poetry, is meant to be heard. In between, arranged in an order of more naturally proximate to less naturally proximate to art, are forms like the novel, the biography, the historical essay, the philosophical dialogue, the treatise, and the scientific paper. All of these transcend the everyday use of language and become literary prose insofar as they take on aesthetic form, the latter genres lending themselves less to that form than

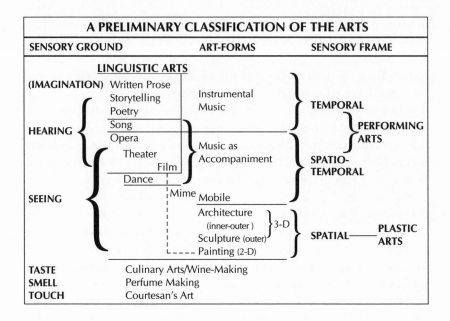

the former. An illuminated medieval manuscript or an illustrated page on one of Blake's poems or E. E. Cummings's arrangement of print in representational visual form seem calculated to work at the visual level the way melody works in relation to lyrics.

With the linguistic arts there is always a tension with the sensuous. At the level of written prose, immediate sensuousness has become wholly subordinated to the imaginative performance that the text leads us to undertake. A novel is not in the written text any more than the cake is in the recipe or the sonata in the musical staff. The written text is a series of directives for imaginative (or, in the case of music and theater, for physical) performance. The medium here is the imagination itself. Nonetheless, imaginative reconstruction or imaginative performance is a kind of second-order sensuousness that in principle can draw upon all the senses in literary description, only now transplanted from direct encounter into visual instructions for re-presentation in imagination.

Poetry is closer to sensuousness than storytelling and, a fortiori, than written prose, for poetry is meant to be heard, even though the invention of writing allows it to be read silently and thus only to be seen. But as read silently, its referential function takes over almost completely and its anchor in the sensuous is atrophied. Storytelling or dramatic reading entails the dynamics of speech: pacing, volume, expressiveness. But more than does storytelling, poetry accentuates the sonorousness of language. It sets up rhythms and rhyme schemes, it employs alliteration and attends to the interplay of various sound possibilities. Originally meters and rhyme schemes may have been mnemonic devices to help the minstrel, but over time the sonorousness takes on greater significance, perhaps initially by association with the accompanying lyre. On the side of reference, poetry creates metaphors that reconfigurate the way things appear by recontextualizing the reference of the words, thus drawing upon novel associations to create a distinctive mode of presence. In its focus on sound relations, it functions to anchor language in the extended Now of living experience, from which we are prone to take flight into a world of imaginative or theoretical abstraction. As such it is related to song; and indeed, as in Homer, the function of the poet is to sing of heroes.

The art that isolates sound is instrumental music. It employs various features of the world of sound: tones and beats woven into a combination of melodies and rhythms, playing in relation to each other in harmonies and expressed in the timbre of various instruments. The first of musical instruments is the human voice, usually employing poetically shaped lyrics in song, in which the modulations of sound are even more emphasized than in poetry by itself. As employed in ordinary communication, language is an instrument wholly taken up in reference; it virtually disappears from focal awareness as does the baseball bat when we focus upon hitting the ball. But poetry sets up tension between sensuousness and reference. In song, musical accompaniment further accentuates the sensuousness. In opera, the lyrics often seem to furnish a mere occasion for the vocal elaboration of sound. In modern jazz, the development of "scat singing" plays with the various sound possibilities of the voice without employing them at all in the directly referential function they have in language.

Theater gathers together sights and sounds over time, with painting furnishing the backdrop and the enactment of the drama through words and deeds providing the focal point. The whole human body, together with its oral linguistic possibilities (from the latter of which dance abstracts), is the instrument of the art. Setting that to music leads to the idea of opera as the *Gesamtkunst*, the totalizing art, theoretically elaborated and actually practiced by Wagner. Set in the grandeur of the opera house, orchestral sound, lyrics, costuming, stage setting, and dramatic action (at times also involving dance) combine to present a single spatiotemporal, sound-and-color impression embracing a whole world of meaning. In a Wagnerian opera the natural tension between the sensuous form and the referentiality of language is resolved in the direction of the sensuous, where the "sea of harmony" is said to generate the text as well as the action. Wagner saw opera as performing the same liturgical function as ancient dramatic presentation, drawing upon all the artistic means to bring about a sense of participation, through the polis, in a cosmic whole.[53]

Film is *the* contemporary art form. It is wholly dependent on contemporary developments in technology. Film recording of motion and coordinated sound recording are very recent inventions. There is also the technology of special effects, which is increasingly more sophisticated. But film is the contemporary art form in another sense. It provides the most readily accessible presentation of all the art forms simultaneously. It functions, in a manner similar to opera, as a *Gesamtkunst*. It requires the cooperative artistry of script writers, actors, directors, camera operators, editors, costume makers, makeup artists, special effects experts, set-designers, musicians, and recording experts.[54] But in film the music is clearly accompaniment and thus strictly subordinate—unless the film is about musical performance. So much is that the case that I cannot recall movies that do not have musical accompaniment; even more, I am not usually aware at all of the musical soundtrack. However, the difference between action accompanied and not accompanied by music was demonstrated graphically in the PBS tribute to composer-director John Williams where a scene from *Jaws* was shown without and then with his accompanying musical score. The difference in emotional impact was amazing.

Of course, film, like painting and its allied arts, is two-dimensional. In terms of actual viewing, however, it creates a three-dimensional experiential world. In this it is closest to theater, except that in film the visual aspect takes on a much more powerful role, since the camera focuses for us by choosing the frame, the proximity or distance of the visual point of view, and, by fading the background, the focus itself. This focusing makes the viewer much more passive than in theater. Hence a greater immediacy and thus broader mass appeal is established. Furthermore, the camera can change settings immediately and range widely within a given setting, and can include flashbacks and superposition.[55] Film, in addition to popular music, with its relative lack of sophistication, is the art form most suitable to a mass democratic audience. Filmed opera expanded its possibilities when it moved from the visual-audial recording of stage performances (reaching a certain high point in Ingmar Bergman's work) to performances in real settings that gave the camera and the performance greater space in which to operate (e.g., *Carmen*, featuring Placido Domingo, 1984). In theater the word is the primary focus, standing in necessary tension with the visual enactment. Of course, both art forms can approach either end of the tension between the visual and the linguistic, between action and dialogue. Some films (e.g., *My Dinner with André*, 1981) give primacy to the dialogue, while some theater performances bring the action into greater prominence—though the dialogue still remains the center of the latter art form.

Considered in terms of their media, written prose, storytelling, poetry, song, and music in general are strictly temporal arts. Outside of written prose, the other art forms listed occupy the temporal field of sound. Written prose is a second-order art form, defocusing the immediately sensuous written page in order imaginatively to reconstruct the whole field of space-time sensuousness as displaying the context for the interaction of the characters. Opera, theater, and film are spatiotemporal arts since they appeal both to the space-and-time-occupying field of vision and to the time-occupying field of sound, the latter both in musical form and in linguistic form. There are also other forms of spatiotemporal art, such as dance or the mime that, like untitled instrumental music, are nonlinguistic. Beyond observable movement in space—a feature it shares with mime—dance introduces a further parameter insofar as it is usually linked with sound through music, thus bridging not only space and time, but also sight and sound. Mime and dance occupy two ends of a continuum of relation between reference and aesthetic form, while they stand over against acrobatics. Mime is wholly absorbed in reference ("imitation" as mirroring). Dance approaches mime when it is primarily referential (though always in the context of establishing a rhythmic whole), but dance can also operate in the free elaboration of form without reference. Dance is usually accompanied by music, or at least by the beat of a drum, the clapping of hands, or the stamping of feet, and thus appeals both to hearing and seeing, though the primary focus is seeing. Dance, whose material is the mobile possibilities of the body as a whole, has to be one of the primordial art forms. Perhaps it initially entailed communal coordination of movement through a simple common beat or rhythm associated with tasks that required cooperative effort, and then opened out into the possibility of complex movements of extraordinary grace achieved only with difficulty by individuals and groups, as in the development of ballet. Acrobatics stands over against both mime and dance in that it expresses nothing but exhibits the body reaching certain goals.[56] All the forms we have considered thus far are performing arts, in which temporality plays a central role. Each must

25

be considered both from the point of view of the audience and from the point of view of the performer.

Let us consider next the plastic arts, which shape things in space. Chronologically, the first form is probably architecture, which is rooted in the biological need we have for protection from the elements. It shapes materials into a three-dimensional functional form.[57] As a fine art it attends to the articulation of space, and does that not only by providing certain boundaries and thus enclosing space. It also sets up an environmental space, alternating between focus on the vista and focus on more intimate places, gathering and opening for inhabitants and visitors the natural environment as well as the environment constituted by buildings already in place. It attends to the play of light and darkness at different times of the day and in different seasons. It attends to the appearance of different textures and colors under those conditions. It gathers all this together in such a way as to present a unified whole to one who walks around and through a building. Finally, it carries out this shaping process in such a way as to provide an environmental feel that suits the activities people will undertake in and around the building. It does all this as a functional form insofar as the formation of space inside and out fosters rather than inhibits what is to be done in and around the building. Allied to architecture would be the arts of interior decoration and landscape gardening, as well as the arts of design in furniture and utensils. Of all the art forms, these would seem to have the least overt referential function; they anchor us solidly in the Now of sensuous presence. And yet, especially in religious architecture, they are able to shape space in such a way as to communicate a sense of the sacred and the transcendent. Architecture is also linked to sculpture and painting by providing niches and walls for statues and paintings and to musical performance and drama by providing the space for performers and audience.

I will discuss sculpture more fully in the appendix. At this point I will anticipate only a few of its eidetic features. Traditionally it shapes only three-dimensional surface and thus, by disregarding the spatial interior, attends more one-sidedly to the three-dimensional whole than does architecture. It also tends to employ one material, like clay or wood or marble or bronze. But modern sculpture approaches architecture aesthetically—though not functionally—as it employs different materials in various combinations and opens up the interior of its materials through holes and hollows. It employs various textures and colors and sets up a play between light and shadow. The sculptural object occupies space and sets up a tension within the perceptual field between its own space and the surrounding space. One could indeed refer to architecture as a form of sculpture, as sculpture linked to utility. One could also speak of sculpture as a form of architecture, as architecture freed from utility.[58]

Grounded, like architecture, in functional need, but annexed in a sense to sculpture, clothing design comes to take on the form of a fine art. It both reveals and conceals the mobile three-dimensional human form and has its own decorative surface elaboration. Taking off from that is the art of jewelry making as a miniform of sculpture, usually "abstract," in which the quality of the materials is part of the central focus.

There is a form of plastic art (plastic in the extended sense of shaping visible materials) that works in a more abstract medium than architecture or sculpture, namely painting, together with those similar fine art forms like drawing, printmaking, and photography. They employ the abstractness of two-dimensional surface, establishing the play of color and shape, although in the case of black-and-white drawing or photography, they approach abstraction from all color. (Here I consider both black and white from a nontheoretical, wholly experiential point of view as the absence of color: black because our dominant experience of it is in the absence of light, where no colors show; white because it is usually that on which we begin to lay color on canvas or paper.) Representational forms of painting give the illusion of a third dimension; attention to surface texture gives a real three-dimensional character to a painting. The latter moves toward relief sculpture, which is a transitional form between two-dimensional and three-dimensional forms, from etchings to high relief. It is perhaps not without significance that the terms *art* and *artist* are used paradigmatically of painting and the painter, for it is in painting that the immediacy of integrated wholes is given all at once, whereas the architectural and sculptural wholes can be given only through moving in and around the three-dimensional forms. Painting (with its cognate forms) presents a standing Now as nothing else can do.

In terms of actual viewing, the arts of the two-dimensional surface approach a certain abstraction from time, since everything is present at once to the viewer. However, one must at least move one's eyes from point to point in order to enrich one's perception of the overall gestalt, and thus time necessarily enters in, not as simple endurance in the Now, but as continual change of focus. The arts that shape three-dimensional space add an indeterminate number of perspectives for viewing and require successive movements not only of our eyes but of our whole physical being as we move around and within the work. Architecture, insofar as it involves the changing play of light and dark through different seasons, may also be considered a temporal art: though the building does not change, its mode of presentation does. Perhaps one might say the same about sculpture. But painting and its allied art forms require optimal lighting conditions and thus are only accidentally temporal. The invention of mobile sculpture simultaneously occupies space and modifies that occupation through time; but it also allows stationary viewing, since it moves and thus does not require our whole body to move in order to grasp its overall gestalt. It is thus a spatiotemporal art.

In attending to any of the art forms, what is required is always what one might call imaginative performance, which is one reason I began my preliminary classification of the art forms with written prose, which most obviously demands such performance. The printed text provides the most idealized form of the act of attending operative in all art forms, even in the most immediate form of the two-dimensional plastic arts, as an act of imaginative performance. Reading a novel is the clearest case of taking the text as a set of recipes for imaginative construction. The author does not lay out a wholly complete world, no matter how detailed his descriptions, but indicates, through his linguistic constructions, a kind of core object around which we have to construct our own imaginative variations.[59] It requires a developed imagination to perform in response to the imaginative possibilities laid open on the printed page by a master novelist. When a novel is turned into a film, the imaginative possibilities are focused and rendered explicit in a single way. That is why a film version of a great novel is so disappointingly reduced compared to the richness of our imaginative performance in reading it. We might extend this observation to all the art forms, even to that which seems to be most explicit, namely painting. One must learn to "perform" the painting through gathering the details together, but also through indwelling in its immediate felt texture in order to reach the total gestalt. No art form lies open to immediate experience without some type of imaginative reenactment.[60]

At this point it would be fitting to follow a bit further the tension between linguistic reference and sensuousness in the arts. Consider the difference naming makes in how we attend to the sensuous. Arthur Danto tells the fictitious story of two artists, each of whom was commissioned to do a mural in a new science building. One mural was to be given the title *Newton's First Law*, the other *Newton's Third Law*. As it happened, each artist produced exactly the same painting: a single black line running straight across the white wall parallel to the floor and about a third of the way up from the bottom of the wall. But the titles make one attend to the same sensuous configuration differently. In the first case, following the inertial law that a body in motion will stay in motion in a straight line unless acted upon by an outside force, the line on the wall appears as a line segment tracing the path of motion of a projectile through space. In the second case, following the law that for every action there is an equal and opposite reaction, the line is a division between two white masses pressing against one another. Danto goes further: a physically identical painting might also be entitled *Sea and Sky at High Noon*. In another example, Danto suggests considering two possible titles for a painting that shows the sun shining from above on a landscape where a farmer is plowing his field while, in the lake below, two legs are shown of a figure splashing into the water. One would look at the painting differently if it were entitled *Work and Play*—or, as it actually is— *The Fall of Icarus*, by Brueghel.[61] Further, to take a musical example, would anyone think of the sea at sunrise or at high noon or in a storm if Debussy titled his work *Opus 34* instead of *La Mer* and gave no programmatic subtitles? Untitled paintings or instrumental music or purely abstract untitled sculpture represent attempts to attend to the pure aesthetic form without focusing on any direct reference. But then, as Henry Moore observed, there are always felt reverberations of forms and colors derived from past associations on which the abstract artist draws for at least an indirect kind of reference.[62] Pure aesthetic forms, scrubbed clean of all overt reference, nonetheless are peaceful or agitated, joyful or sad, strong or languid, and so on. As Aristotle observed of instrumental music, such forms produce states of mind similar to those obtained in the context of their real counterparts and are thus "the most imitative of artforms."[63] And because such forms appear in a field of awareness circumscribed by the lived disclosure of space and time as a whole, and, indeed, of *the* totality of meaningfulness, of "the world," works of art articulate a sense of indwelling in the whole; they establish a world. But, as Heidegger observed, it is language that opens up the space of such a world in the first place.[64]

One could draw up a scale of art forms, from those in which aesthetic form is purely subordinate to reference, to those in which overt reference disappears from purely aesthetic forms. At the level of dominant reference we would have, as a measure, the philosophic treatise in which no attention whatsoever is given to literary form. Then, as we enter the sphere of the aesthetic, we would have philosophy presented in dialogue form with judicious employment of drama, imagery, parable, and myth, as in a Platonic dialogue, or history written with great literary polish and descriptive power.

At a level next to that we would have the novel; then poetry in which the play with the possibilities of sound combinations takes a more dominant role; then song in which aural forms are still more dominant; then instrumental program music, then music with referential titles, and finally music with only genre and chronological series titles, as Sonata in G Minor, op. 4.

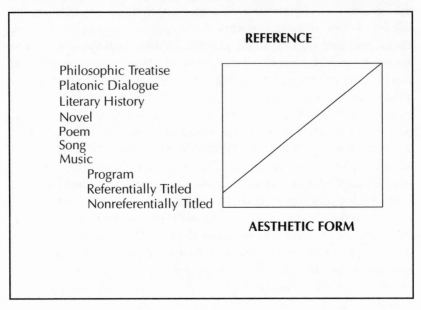

One could take art forms like painting and sculpture and show a similar scale exhibited by individual works within each of the forms, from the dominantly referential to the dominantly aesthetic-formal. Walter Pater once remarked that all art seeks the status of music.[65] Overtly referential or not, art forms bring about distinctive moods by reason of their organization of the sensuous. Like music, all art speaks to the heart and thus affects the emotional wellsprings of action, inclining us to act in the direction of the ways we are moved. That is why Plato and Aristotle spoke of the ethical character of music.

## Phenomenological, Hermeneutic, and Dialogic Approaches

The preliminary laying out of the field of experience for a discussion of the fine arts that I have just completed made use of a phenomenological method. Phenomenology is a permanent prolegomenon, acknowledged or not, to any philosophy. Phenomenology is, to begin with, descriptive explication of the essential structures *(logoi)* of the various modes of appearance *(phainomena)*, various relations of manifestness between conscious subjects and their differing types of objects. The sensorily given precisely as sensory, even though the most obvious aspect of manifestness, is only a starting point for knowledge, since to know something means to grasp it "as" something. To grasp something "as" something here is to bring to bear upon the sensa universal meanings expressible in words. What I have attempted is to lay out some of the fundamental eidetic features, the immanently present universal forms of the general structure of the field of experience and of the various aspects of the sensory domain within that field insofar as these aspects are the field of operation for the fine arts. I would claim that most of what was presented was not simply my opinion but inescapable eidetic features involved in the arts. In that sense I would claim to have presented features even more necessary than Euclidean geometry because they are immediately given features of the objects of experience presupposed in doing geometry or any thing else, whereas Euclidean geometry, resting on those features, operates in terms of abstract, idealized reconstruction of the quantitative aspects of the sensorily given.

But not all grasping of something "as" something is a matter of phenomenological description—that is, description of the immediately appearing, the immediately given. Very much of it is a matter of hermeneutics, a matter of interpreting the sensorily given, as the sciences furnish various interpretations (theories) of the nature of matter or of life, or as in everyday life we attempt to interpret the signs of someone's behavior in order to understand her basic character.[66]

The hermeneutical moment in this study is really twofold. On the one hand I am aiming at a philosophy of art and beauty, and thus must not only describe what occurs in the encounter with beauty and art and in the production of fine art; I must also furnish a comprehensive interpretation of the whole field of aesthetic phenomena. The development of that task is tied to the second hermeneutical aspect of my study, which lies in my major methodological decision, namely to approach the construction of an aesthetics through the study of a select portion of the great texts in the philosophy of art and beauty throughout the history of Western philosophy. The meaning of these texts does not lie on the surface. Philosophy is the attempt to think critically and comprehensively about the ultimate framework of all our dealings; and, since we are by nature referred to being, that involves thinking comprehensively about the whole of what is. That means that each concept cannot be understood until we see how it is related to all the basic concepts of a given philosophy. For example, even something so apparently self-evident as the meaning of the term *body* cannot be taken in identically the same way in the works of every philosopher, even though the starting point in the sensory givenness furnishes a point of reference for the more comprehensive meanings advanced by different philosophers.[67] Thus in my approach to each of the philosophers, I will not begin immediately with what they have to say about matters aesthetic, but with an interpretation of their comprehensive view of things within which we can begin to see the fuller significance of their aesthetic claims.

The second hermeneutical aspect leads to a third methodological factor, the dialogic. The structure of the field of experience gives us a common point of reference for all discussion provided both in the sensorily given and in the grounding reference to the whole of being. Every great philosopher has attempted to break through the sedimentation of meaning furnished by the cultural shaping he has received in order to get back to the basic phenomena and to construct his interpretation from there. But no constructive interpretation has ever been able to win over all intelligent, well-informed, diligent, and honest inquirers. Rather than allowing us to rest content with a selection of that which suits our own preferences and thus to fall into either a closed-minded dogmatism or an equally comfortable relativism, our founding reference to being pushes us out of the comfort of both dogmatism and relativism. It demands a dialogism, an entry into genuine conversation aimed at a more encompassing disclosure that will display the limits of our chosen views and thereby allow us a better grasp of the encompassing whole. It requires that we take a stand, that we judge as well as interpret the meanings of others, but also that we stand ready to be judged in terms of the possibly greater adequacy of those other views.[68] But we have the best chance of being less inadequate if we attend to the insights, both as phenomenological observations and as hermeneutic recommendations, offered by the great minds who have gone before us.

❧ ❧ ❧

In concluding this introduction, let me lay out the path I will follow in this work. I will focus on certain central figures in the history of the philosophy of art and beauty. Among the Greeks I have selected Plato and Aristotle as by far the most outstanding, ground-breaking thinkers. Through his impact on Plotinus, Dionysius, and Augustine, Plato (whose works— except for the first third of the *Timaeus*—were unavailable before the Renaissance) indirectly influenced the thought of the Middle Ages and directly, through the translation of his works by Ficino in the fifteenth century, impacted upon the Renaissance. But it is surprising, especially in view of the unsurpassed beauty of the architectural achievements and the spiritually lofty Gregorian chant of the Middle Ages, that none of the major thinkers had much to say about art and beauty. And though the translation of Aristotle's works in the twelfth and thirteen centuries decisively shaped every phase of thought in the High Middle Ages, this was less so through his *Poetics*, his single sustained work on matters aesthetic (and that dealing with one artistic mode, namely tragedy). My approach to the Middle Ages will be more diffuse than the approach in the other chapters. Beginning with Plotinus, whose mode of thought decisively affected subsequent thinkers, I briefly consider Augustine, Dionysius, and Albertus Magnus, articulate the metaphysical frame that fused the Aristotelian and Platonist modes of thought in Aquinas, and conclude with Bonaventure.

The name *aesthetics* emerged as the term for the philosophy of art and beauty in the eighteenth century in the work of the German philosopher Alexander Baumgarten. At the same time the British tradition of taste developed. I will treat the latter in my discussion of David Hume's essay "Of the Standard of Taste," as an epilogue to an aspect of the German tradition which gained its first powerful expression in Immanuel Kant's *Critique of Judgment*. After Kant we have the rich development of the German philosophical tradition, which had a great deal to say about the arts. I will discuss the views of Hegel, Schopenhauer, Nietzsche, and Heidegger. I also include a chapter on John Dewey, one of America's greatest philosophers, who stands in the tradition of Hegel, but turned in a more empirical, pragmatic, and open-ended direction, for whom, nonetheless, the aesthetic is absolutely central, the aim and measure of all experience.

Throughout I will draw upon the structures I have explored in this introduction and work toward building a more comprehensive aesthetic by ending each chapter with an appreciative and critical response. In the conclusion I reflect somewhat systematically on the ground I have covered.

# II

# PLATO

IN MY TREATMENT OF Plato, the first of the great philosophers to address matters aesthetic, I begin to flesh out more fully the framework considerations I have offered in the previous chapter by an interpretation that builds a whole world of meaning, encompassing every aspect of human existence. There is a sense in which one might say that Plato's philosophy is essentially an aesthetic. Beauty plays a central role in his thought, though he has some harsh things to say about its appearance in art. However, in spite of the latter, his own works exhibit an artistry unmatched in the history of philosophy. The use of images and parables, the development of myths, the delineation of characters, the drama of their action and reaction in relation to the themes under discussion, and the overall structuring of the dialogues are neither pleasant accompaniments to philosophical argumentation nor irritating distraction therefrom. Though argumentation and rational construction are crucial to philosophy, they are essentially in a relation of mutual dependence upon a fuller sense of participation in life that affords the starting point, gives the basic insights about which we argue and from which we construct our theories, and finally, provides, in the holistic feel for things (the "lived aesthetic") that it involves, the basic test of all comprehensive claims.[1] Rational development stands in a dialectical relation with the heart as the felt residue of an interplay between a tradition and the individual thinker that provides our basic orientation toward things.

The key texts on beauty are in the *Phaedrus,* and especially in the *Symposium.* The key texts on art—and indeed on the pivotal ideas in Plato's thought—are in the *Republic,* which stands at the logical and chronological center of Plato's written work. The core idea of the latter dialogue is justice, but the key to understanding justice is understanding the relation between the city and philosophy. In that relation, beauty and art play an important role.

It may seem odd to begin a treatment of aesthetics with notions like justice, the city, and philosophy. Today we are used to a division of labor, with specialization even in "philosophy." We have fallen into that habit because of the astonishing success, both theoretically and technologically, of scientific method, which operates by specialized division of labor. Alexander Pope said, "Know then thyself, presume not God to scan; / the proper study of mankind is man."[2] Today thinkers have gone further: they would say that the proper study of humankind is bits and pieces of nature. In what many today call philosophy, we find a family resemblance to what the ancient tradition called philosophy. Then philosophy was "love of wisdom," where wisdom was understanding something of how we humans fit into the total scheme of things and how we might come into proper relation to the whole in our lives. It involved conceptual analysis and argumentation, but always within the overall matrix of the pursuit of the wider, more comprehensive vision—indeed, a vision governed in Plato by growth in a pervasive sense of awe before the strangeness of our situation.[3] In philosophy today conceptual analysis and argumentation conducted within regional specializations are the norm. In the more ancient view, represented in its first most powerful form by Plato, adequate understanding of any region involved understanding its place in the whole. Corollary to this is the view that each basic concept implies all the others. As Hegel later put it, "The truth is the whole."[4] I have begun this text by staking out the structure of the field of experience as it opens out to the whole of Being. I have gone on to locate art within that whole and to delineate the field of art by an analysis of the sensory fields and the spatiotemporal framework within which they operate. Following out that structure, I will approach each thinker by locating art and beauty within the whole of his thought. And that means seeing the place of the aesthetic within the whole of human life. Let us then take this approach to Plato's aesthetics.

## Art in the Purged City

In the *Republic,* Socrotes, Plato's spokesman, focuses on justice. After an introductory skirmish in which conventional ideas of justice (giving to each his due; giving benefits to allies and harm to enemies; and obeying the laws made in the self-interest of the stronger) are tested in a preliminary way by locating them in broader contexts to show their implications, and after the sources of those conventional ideas are explored, Socrates proposes to examine the justice of the individual in terms of the justice of the city.[5] He proceeds to do so by constructing several strata of a city, beginning with that involved in the provision of food, clothing, and shelter by a simple division of labor. Socrates calls this "the true, the healthy city." It is a city centered on health: it supplies basic biological needs. There is an additional aspect to this level: the citizens also sing hymns to the gods.[6] Here the aesthetic dimension, embodied in music, is subordinated to a sense of the sacred. Music emerges beyond biological need in conjunction with our metaphysical reference to the whole, since the gods are exhibitions of the community's sense of "the meaning of it all." Perhaps it is a "true and healthy city" because it satisfies not only biological need, but also metaphysical need, which is linked to the need for togetherness with others as simultaneously rooted in biology and in the metaphysical. Such a city would provide psychic health as well as health of body. It is a "true" (*alethes,* unconcealed) city in the sense that it is the most immediately manifest, though not the most developed. But it is unclear what Socrates' understanding of the status of the gods was at this level. At the third level of the city Socrates constructs (and which we will shortly consider), the gods are trimmed down to being projections of civic ideals. Are the gods here at this first level projections of the citizens' togetherness in their feasting and thus in their provision of biological necessities without further ideals? Whatever their putative status, the gods do exhibit a first articulation of our metaphysical need.

The citizens here are presented as moving out of this level by a desire for luxury: "sweetmeats and soft couches."[7] The promotion of luxury also introduces us to a surplus need, beyond biological necessity, that is distinctively human. It is the need for beauty, exhibited in the first city as subordinated to worship; but here it seems to be detached from any other consideration. Chefs, pastry cooks, cosmetologists, fashion designers, and musicians fill the city. No distinction is made between the cultivated satisfaction of biologically rooted appetites and the occurrence of a distinctive aesthetic experience. Culinary art and the art of the beauty parlor are placed on the same level as the art of music. What seems to stand at the center of the luxurious lifestyle is feeling good, having pleasurable sensations, being titillated, having goose bumps, feeling chills running up and down our spines. One remains locked within the immediacy of biologically based satisfaction, culturally stimulated and provided.[8]

Now, the first level of the city is described as the true and healthy city, but also as "a city for pigs," who have only biological needs to satisfy. Glaucon, who makes the observation, overlooks the hymns to the gods—although perhaps he understands them only too well at this level. This first level has a natural measure: what is required for biological well-being. But on the second level, where humans are driven by the desire for luxury, there is no natural measure. Because we are by nature not only rooted in biological appetites and sensations but also, at the other pole of our being, referred emptily to the whole, the play between these two poles in the field of awareness can lead to the indeterminacy of biological satisfaction, which we can endow with the character of the absolute and pursue measurelessly. At the cutting edge of our being we are indeterminate, forced by nature to choose our way and select our measure or go on and on endlessly and ultimately meaninglessly, now this way, now that. The city can consequently become measureless, bloated, feverish. People seek more and more as they are introduced, by those who would profit by them, to appetites they did not know they had. The city would seem to have undergone a fall from primitive simplicity, based on natural need, into measureless self-indulgence. But since human nature is not merely biological, and since the desire for beauty is distinctively human, the fall into the search for luxury is, so to speak, a fall upward. One cannot understand the peculiarly mixed character of this paradoxical upward fall until one grasps more fully the character of humanness which will also open up the possibility of another understanding of the divine. Plato introduces us to that bit by bit through a kind of dialectical inversion of the desire for luxury brought about by the logic of its own development.

Since the immediate environment cannot supply enough, the citizens of the bloated city begin a program of expansion. For this they need an army that also protects them, not only from the greedy eyes of outsiders but also from each other. It thus keeps order within the city. The introduction of an army involves the introduction of another lifestyle: a disciplined lifestyle that rises above the soft hedonism that drives the luxurious city. The discipline consists of gymnastics and music. Gymnastic exercise produces hardness and endurance, but, pursued one-sidedly, it also fosters brutality and insensitivity. It is offset by training in "music" which, without gymnastics, fosters softness, but which, together with gymnastic, tempers or tunes the dispositions.[9] Later, in Plato's *Laws*, the Athenian stranger discusses gymnastics as a form of dance and thus as an art form itself.[10] Dance is a fusion of gymnastic and music in which the whole body is the instrument. The perception thereof is visual for the observer but kinesthetic for the performer. The stranger focuses on the latter and stresses its effect in rendering the psyche graceful, rhythmic, orderly.

But returning to the discussion in the *Republic:* so that the "guard-dog" trainees do not prey upon the citizens, they must be trained to think in terms of dedication to the city as a whole.[11] The vehicle of such training is "music," understood basically as instrumentally accompanied poetry. That involves two components, beyond the relatively fixed character of the givenness of unconscious biological processes and corresponding to the two trainable aspects of human existence: psychic disposition and intellectual focus. Psychic disposition is trained here by the blend of gymnastic and music mentioned above. However, it is also affected by the aesthetic character of the visual and auditory ambiance. The cultural environment of visual and audile products that surround the citizenry from birth ought, says Socrates, to be characterized by grace, harmony, good rhythm. Socrates refers here to such visual products as paintings, clothing, utensils, furniture, and buildings.[12] It is important to notice that it is not the pictorial quality of paintings that is at stake here—how they mirror the outer world, as Socrates will ask us to think of them in book 10.[13] Linked with architecture, furniture, clothing, and utensil design, paintings are considered here in terms of their purely aesthetic properties. Design must consider not only function (although in book 10 Socrates does claim that form should follow function); design should also follow beauty.[14] The latter, however, should not simply be superadded to the former in an external way; rather beauty should support and flow from function. A culture that focuses exclusively on functional products without concern for the aesthetics of good design is a fractured culture: its world is either un- or anti-aesthetic (though maybe the former is impossible—"He who is not with me is against me")—or such a utilitarian culture, though having a place for beauty, separates art from the everyday.[15] The dispositional impact is what concerns Socrates here.

In the second book of his *Laws,* Plato has the Athenian stranger reject as senseless, along with the display of virtuosity for its own sake, tune and rhythm without words.[16] And in his *Republic* "melody *(harmonia)* and rhythm *(rhythmos)* will depend upon the word *(logos)*."[17] *Harmonia* referred to the relation between tones over time (hence "melody" in more modern terms), *rhythmos* to the beat found also in dance, and *logos* to the referent.[18] So it would seem that direct representation is what is important. Yet the stranger also says (and Aristotle will pick up on this) that all music is representative and imitative.[19] What does a tune on the lyre or the harp "represent" and "imitate"? Instrumental music, like the dance, can cover the ground between a rhythmic mime on the one hand and the elaboration of the synchronically and diachronically patterned togetherness of sensory elements on the other. Aristotle will suggest that the latter imitates character *(ethos)*. And that implies different moods and dispositions: happy or sad, vigorous or languid. But in the *Laws* the Athenian stranger insists on the association of the tunes and rhythms with the word. Association with the word will dominate until the eighteenth century, when musical forms will emerge whose only overt association with words will be a title indicating the genre (fugue or concerto, for example) and a chronological listing (opus 4).

In the *Republic*, Socrates advocates the same qualities in the audile modalities of music as he did in the plastic arts. Hence he calls for the repudiation of "Dionysian" music, which leads to high stimulation and wild abandon. He advocates "Apollonian" music, which fosters a sense of good order, grace, harmony, due proportion.[20] (In modern terms, one might think of acid rock versus Bach.) Notice that these are the same characteristics of good design in the plastic arts. Furthermore, the very timbre of different instruments tends to Dionysian or Apollonian effects. He thus advocates the lyre, the zither, and the shepherd's pipe, but not the "polyharmonic instruments," especially the flute,[21] the former set having a more calming effect, the latter one more exciting. (In contemporary terms, one might consider the effect of the electric versus the acoustic guitar.) Again in the second book of the *Laws,* the Athenian stranger returns to the discussion of Apollonian and Dionysian music, only here he says that the gift of Dionysus must no longer be condemned without qualification, for the music of Dionysus helps reduce the natural frenzy of youth through the imparting of rhythm.[22] Through music, Socrates says, good rhythm and harmony (or their opposites) sink deeply into the soul and affect our disposition to behave. And precisely because music affects the psychic disposition so profoundly, changes in the basic forms of music are linked to changes in political regimes.[23]

Socrates gives no further direct description of the properties he wishes to see promoted by art. They seem to be features which we have to learn to recognize by contrast with their opposites. He lists *eulogia*, or fine language; *euharmostia*, or easiness of temper; *euscheymosuney*, or gracefulness or good form; and *euruthmia*, or rhythmic order.[24] Fineness in language would seem to have to do both with conventional associations and with sound, though the two may not coincide. (Respondents who did not know English once selected "cellar door" as the most euphonious expression in a long list with which they were presented.) *Euharmostia* has affinities with harmony, and harmony implies the unity of parts such that all of them belong together, with all incongruities removed. Gracefulness involves the smooth transition between each aspect, primarily in temporal terms, but applicable also to spatial transitions. That which is graceful displays a kind of effortlessness, a lack of strain or tension. A grace is a gift, and gracefulness in performance is a matter of aligning oneself with one's gifts so that, as it were, "it" operates in me rather than "I" operate. Rhythm is the regular repetition of a pattern within a margin of variations, literally taken in the temporal order of sound, but transferable to spatial pattern as well. Order is the opposite of randomness; it obtains when there is a governing principle. In Greek all the terms are preceded by the prefix *eu-* which means "good." While each musical piece must have order, harmony, and rhythm so as to be something other than noise, only the graceful piece exhibits the dignity Socrates is intent on promoting at this point in the dialogue. Such grace seems to be the result of shaping by deliberate control based on thinking in terms of the unity of the whole polis. That is what *eu-* implies here. Art forms are to be promoted that open the psychic disposition to comprehensive rational shaping in terms of the needs of the polis.

There are three levels of human existence involved here. At the unconscious biological level, we have a natural model of a rational system: the harmonious synchronic and diachronic functioning of a complex multiplicity of parts—a fairly adequate description of health. Plato frequently uses the healthy organism as a symbol of psychic well-being—though it is much more than a symbol, being a lower-level phase of a complex psychosomatic unity.[25] At the basic level of psychic experience we have our emotions and their dispositions affected both by physiological state and the impact of past and present conscious life. Plato calls for measures to effect their harmonic tuning so as to produce a kind of prerational rationality. He says that such tuning will provide a fit matrix that will recognize and welcome fully reflective reason when it dawns.[26] The minimum presence of reflective reason awakens through the presence of the word. It is here that poetry plays a key role, for the poetic word not only opens up the world for reflective intelligence, it simultaneously provides it body and location in the lived world through the rhythmic and harmonic shaping of sound.

The referential function of the word is employed at this level of the exposition to furnish models of civic exemplarity for the military trainees.

Notice that it is not truth that is the issue here. One does not tell tales of the gods that speak of unseemly conduct (e.g., Zeus overthrowing his father, Cronus—"even if it were true.").[27] Furthermore, one does not present heroes trembling in fear at the imminent prospect of death, not to would-be soldiers.[28] Furthermore, one does not present the gods as changing forms, appearing in dreams and visions. Any kind of opening to what transcends the city is closed off. No revelation or special intervention is allowed. This referential level is the level of *musike* Plato has Socrates purge first, and he spends the most time with it. I have reversed the emphasis, stressing the consideration of aesthetic form apart from overt reference, because I believe that is, indeed, Plato's main intention here. The purgation of the referential function of literature is done with Adeimantus as interlocutor, an adamant, no-nonsense man—no laughter in *his* city—who wants to make rules to keep the citizenry in order. And the city Socrates builds for him allows no entry of revelation into or exit of human aspiration out of the city. It is not Adeimantus but Glaucon who is Socrates' interlocutor in moving from the healthy to the luxurious city, in discussing the aesthetic side of the purgation of the arts, and, later, in opening up Eros for Beauty Itself, which transcends the city. With Adeimantus, Socrates plays "moralist" of civic exemplarity, projected as protected cosmically by the gods; but with Glaucon, he works at tuning the dispositions that open out beyond the city to the whole and the Source.

Visual and audile art play an important role in the shaping of psychic disposition. Through connection with the word, the intellectual level of our being is given shape directly. Through music and visual art (and at this point "nonrepresentational" visual art in clothing, utensils, buildings, and furniture) one reaches what is announced as the (somewhat surprising) aim of education at this level: the appreciation of beautiful things.[29] The announcement of the aim is surprising because of the stolid emphasis on reference and moral exemplarity and the apparently—but only apparently— secondary character of aesthetic form. In a curious passage that indicates the several levels on which Plato moves here, he has Socrates speak of putting the guardhouse at the highest point of the city; but he goes on to say that that is the "fairest" sight, and further that they ought to put their guardhouse in music.[30] Everything turns on tuning the psychic disposition through harmonic visual and audile art in tandem with the formation of conscious human commitment to the city as a whole.

Having constructed a three-level city, Socrates parallels it with three levels of the soul: a desirous, a spirited, and a rational level, paralleling the majority of the population pursuing healthy and luxurious needs with the desirous level, the military with the spirited level, and its leadership with the rational.[31] He goes on to locate what came to be known as the cardinal virtues (meaning the hinges—from the Latin *cardo*—of fully functional human life), setting them in relation to each of the psychic levels, finding justice in the condition for the operation of each level: justice consists in each level performing its proper function, or doing its own thing.[32] That involves subordination of the desires to the rational level, which has concern for and knowledge of the whole of the city. A city so ordered is beautiful, a *kalipolis;* and that is rooted in the right ordering of the soul, paradigmatically in the rulers.

But it is crucial to understand what this implies, since the nobly disposed youths Glaucon and Adeimantus, who are Socrates' primary interlocutors, seem content with the city built up to the end of book 4 that harmonizes the soul in itself as a mirror of the harmony of the city. However, such a city is essentially faulty, since it recognizes no dimension of the soul that transcends the power of the polis. The text makes clear the insufficiency of the account, since Socrates says so several times.[33] But the interlocutors—and, I fear, too many readers, Karl Popper in particular—forget the caveats and consider the purged city to be Plato's realistic proposal.[34]

Something curious takes place in the dialogue at this point that is crucial to understanding Plato's thought. Socrates speaks as if he had finished with his argument, showing justice in a city and a soul that had been so structured that each part performed its proper function for the good of the whole and so that the harmony of each soul mirrored the harmony of the city as a whole. He is about to consider forms of order that deviate from the order he developed thus far—in effect skipping what turns out to be the very heart of the dialogue.[35] But his interlocutors are especially interested in one of his proposals. In order to foster the soldiers' identification with the city, Socrates had suggested two methods for breaking down preoccupation with narrower concerns: the elimination of private property for the higher classes, since such property tends to make them each preoccupied with themselves, and with the establishment of a community of wives and children, so that they would not be preoccupied with, or unduly favor their own families to the exclusion or diminishment of the interests of others within the city. All would be one family.[36] The interlocutors are interested in the community of wives—I suggest as a measure of sexual liberation. For Socrates proceeds to frame his response to their interest within two other claims whose connection with that interest is not immediately apparent. One is the claim (treated before he responds to their question) that women and men are equal, the other that philosophers should be kings.[37] I suggest that Socrates aims at a purging of their veiled erotic interest by suggesting the equality of women to men, in direct contrast to their subordination as mere sexual objects. But I also suggest, in view of the fact that all this is expressly constructed as an image of the soul, that what had been left out is the feminine dimension of the psyche: its receptivity to that which is above. Socrates says that thus far we have had the male drama; now begins the female drama, the drama of Eros.[38] However, he goes on to play to the erotic interest of his audience by proposing that the most valiant warriors will get the best mates and that those who are retired would be able to "frolic" with whom they pleased.[39] He introduces the notion of philosopher-king by describing him as a peculiar erotic type. In contrast to the lovers of beautiful things (and remember that the appreciation of the qualities of beautiful things, as distinguished from their titillating effect "in us," was the culmination of education for the warriors), philosophers are described as "lovers of the vision of Beauty Itself."[40] And what they do when they are "turned out to pasture" is "frolic" with the Ideas![41] What is going on here is an attempt at elevating the notion of beauty even further than it had been in the purged city. Socrates does so by considering it as the goal of Eros.

We are now at the heart of the dialogue, at the heart of Plato's understanding of beauty, and at the heart of Plato's philosophy as such. In the following, what may seem a distinctively nonaesthetic excursus will provide us with a further articulation of the ultimate framework constitutive of human experience, within which the nature and role of aesthetic experience and its objects—and indeed of any human experience and its objects—can be properly understood.

## The Center of Order

A line has been drawn between beautiful things and Beauty Itself. The duality this introduces is further articulated by the proclamation (without initial grounds) of the notion of the Good, which is placed on the side of Beauty Itself. The side of beautiful things is developed by an analysis of the three factors necessary for the visual perception of such things: visual object, eyeball with the power of seeing, and light source that makes seeing possible. That threefold structure furnishes an analogy of the Good that functions as metaphorical light source for the intellect, allowing it to ap-

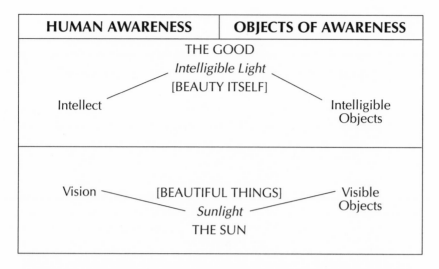

prehend "intelligible objects."[42] But once again, that is merely proclaimed, not grounded. The grounding occurs in the process of developing the Line of Knowledge in two directions. On the one hand, there is a horizontal division between the two regions named by the distinction between beautiful things and Beauty itself and initially articulated by the distinction between the two triplets paralleling physical vision and intellectual insight; on the other hand, there is a vertical division between human awareness and its objects.

Socrates asks us to take a line, dividing it by any proportion and dividing its segments, in turn, by the same proportion.[43] The upshot of such construction is found to produce a line divided into four portions such that the two central portions turn out always to be equal to one another. One could test this inductively by trying different proportions, such as 3:1, 2:1, or 10:1. But one could also "demonstrate" the more general theorem involved in such construction: *any* proportion used to divide a line and to subdivide its initial divisions yields a fourfold division such that its central portions are always and everywhere equal. When you are able to demonstrate that and reflect on what you have accomplished, you become aware of a basic distinction in experience between the particular visual object, drawn on paper and seen in the light by the eye, and the theorem, which is understood and demonstrated to apply to *all* lines constructed in the manner suggested: it is understood by the intellect "in the light of the Good." We have advanced in the articulation of the original line drawn between beautiful things and Beauty Itself. We are pointed, by the relations that obtain between the

| THE GOOD (Beyond *"ousia"*) | | | |
|---|---|---|---|
| **STATES OF MIND** | | **OBJECTS OF MIND** | |
| *Noesis* $\Big\{$ | EPISTEME<br><br>DIANOIA | FORMS $\Big\}$<br><br>MATHEMATICS | *Ousia* |
| *Doxa* $\Big\{$ | PISTIS<br><br>EIKASIA | THINGS $\Big\}$<br><br>"IMAGES" | *Genesis* |

things we see, to a region of meaning that both appears in such objects and stands beyond them through its capacity of being present in *all* like objects. We arrive thus at a distinction in our own self-understanding between sensing and intellection.

The line drawn is a visual given. Reflection upon it leads us to the non-visually given (because universal) theorem that it exemplifies. Doubling reflection back upon that distinction leads us to understand the subject-object framework within which mathematical understanding occurs: the play of the fourfold of universal and particular, intellection *(noesis)* and sensation. Mathematical understanding leads us out of the cave of our sensibility and opinions, allows us to cross the Line to the region of intelligibility, which displays meaning in the sensory and measures our opinions about that meaning. Reflection upon the framework of mathematics is no longer mathematics but philosophy. Playing upon the double character of the Line, taken literally as exhibiting a theorem and taken figuratively as exemplifying the structural levels of the field of experience, and then reflecting the Line back upon itself, Plato locates mathematical understanding *(dianoia)* at the third level of the Line. Philosophic insight *(episteme)* is located at the fourth. The emptiness of the philosophic level is filled, at least partially, by the structures of the Line, the play of the fourfold, now understood, at least in a preliminary way.

One might ask where metaphoric reflection falls on the Line. I would suggest it falls at the third level, with mathematics as the object of *dianoia*, or insight *(noia)* through images *(dia)*. Plato names the lowest level of the Line—where we think in terms of, and are imprisoned within, sensory images—*eikasia* or knowing "icons." He also has a more extended notion of "image," which includes "images of justice in the lawcourts," where an "image" is an opinion *(doxa)* held without sufficient grounds. Plato himself constantly practices a *dianoetic eikasia,* a formation of sensory images—in the context within which we are working, the image of the divided Line correlated with the complex imagery of the Cave—which releases us from fixation on "images," whether in the realm of sensation proper or in the realm of opinions, by fixing our minds on the intelligible. Plato thus shows in practice the basis for the connection of the arts with wisdom.

But we have not yet arrived at an understanding of the Good and thus of Beauty Itself, the reason for offering the articulations thus far. By reflecting on the visible line and by reflecting on that reflection, we have arrived at a general articulation of the ultimate subject-object frame that makes mathematics, and indeed any level of understanding, possible: the play between sensible and intelligible and, correspondingly, between sensation and intellection. Socrates invites us to carry reflection one step further: to reflect on what makes the framework itself possible. The Good, he says, makes possible the mind, its intelligible objects, and both the ability to understand as well as the truth or unhiddenness *(aletheia)* of the objects.[44] At the very basis of what-is as a whole there is a mutual referredness of mind and things: things are intelligible and mind can understand. That must have a ground. Note that, because what is at stake in understanding is, initially, the instantiability of a theorem in an indefinite number of instances, wherever in time and whenever in space they might be found, the whole of the spatiotemporal universe is pregiven as a field for intellectual operation. The whole is somehow precontained in the reference of the mind which is thus sprung out of the Now of sensory presence. In the light of the openness of the whole we come to understand any particular. That is why the Good is called the principle of the whole.[45] As principle of the whole, it is not simply the principle of the intelligible but of the visible as well. Since this is the case, a reflection that follows the Line of Knowledge toward the Good will view the Line as the ascending curve of a circle that arises from the sensory toward the top, where we find the Good, which then, as principle of the whole, curves back to the beginning in the sensory to bind the whole together. This, we suggest, is why Plato employs imagery and story: they bring us back to where we always already are: this world here and now present in the sensory field, but illumined by the changeless field of the intelligible, at the summit of which is the Good, whose shining is Beauty Itself.[46]

There is this further consideration. When we come to understand (i.e., to demonstrate a geometric theorem), we proceed from a limited number of axioms, guided by a principle of unrestricted scope, the principle of non-contradiction, which allows us to deduce from that limited number of axioms, not only the theorem in question, but also the whole of the geometric region it inhabits. The relative fewness of the axioms generates the vast complexity of the theorems in a kind of cascading order of complexity. The employment of the principle of noncontradiction provides unity in that complexity by giving it coherence. What might have otherwise been scattered observations and isolated generalizations takes on the unity of a coherent scheme. If one reflects further upon the relative fewness of the axioms, one is led to ask whether that multiplicity might itself be located within a larger context and thus whether the different regions of experience might not be unified by appealing to a single principle, which we might then project as "the One." Plato calls this "the upward way," while deductive mathematics follows "the downward way."[47] Metaphorically speaking, it is "in the light of" our search for that One, drawn by the directedness of the mind toward the whole, that we are led to apprehend more and more of the coherence of the whole field of experience and its objects. The shining of that One, i.e. its functioning as ground and term of our search, generates the manifestation of the coherence of what is and draws us upward toward the fuller manifestness of that coherence.

We should note, however, that the "upward way" from mathematics toward the Good only covers part of the total field illumined by the Good. There is the whole dimension of psychic life, the locus of the display of the cosmic order which includes that life as its own inwardness. Once again, it is story and imagery that bring us to understand that life.

The Line presents us with a primal division within human experience between (1) what is first approached as the realm of the visible and (2) the realm of the intelligible to which Plato introduces us, first by mathematical reflection, then by reflection upon the subject-object framework presupposed by mathematics, and finally by reflection upon that reflection. Placing them in juxtaposition, we can discern some of the opposing predicates of the two realms: the visible is composed of sense-perceptible particular actualities presented in the here and now of bodily immediacy which have come into being, are subjected to change, and eventually pass out of being.

The mathematical theorem presents itself as both independent of and as extending to all its particular instances, actual or possible, throughout the whole of spatial and temporal relations. Though it came into awareness at a certain point in the history of culture, may have come to be known at a certain point in the reader's history, and may, through recursion to barbarism, pass out of awareness generally some time in the future, the theorem still presents itself as having always been true and thus as itself transcending change and thus also transcending spatio-temporal location and the conditions of its own knownness by a human. Nonetheless, its truth is resident in the particulars that are its instances. There is thus an identical core of meaning that can exist in a universal, atemporal mode or in a particular mode, immanent in a here and now. The understanding of bodily particulars would thus seem to involve two principles: (1) a principle of intelligibility in accordance with which the theorem is true of that particular, and (2) a principle that allows the multiplication of the principle in many times and in many places. Plato calls the former an idea, or *eidos* (Form); he calls the latter "the Receptacle" *(hypodoche)*, "the nurse of becoming," or what more recently Whitehead, following Plato, relates to the restless matrix of space-time.[48] It is as if the Receptacle were a flowing river on whose banks stood a tree. The wavelets make possible the multiple and transitory mirrorings of the tree as its image is held for a split second and in different ways by each of the wavelets. The flowing realm of space-time Plato refers to as the realm of *genesis* or Becoming; the intelligible realm he calls *to on* or *ousia* or Being, and the Good as source is considered to be "beyond *ousia*."[49] Becoming is made possible and thinkable by the ingredience of Being into the nonbeing of the Receptacle, of intelligibility into the flux. Time is the flowing of an ever-moving, unextended Now from the no longer to the not yet; space is the existent emptiness in which such flowing occurs. Space-time is existent negativity, a kind of nonbeing complex entering into the constitution and togetherness of the things that are—or perhaps better, within which spatio-temporal things are. Thus perceptible things are "mixtures of being and nonbeing."[50] By contrast, each changeless Form just "is" and does not come into being, change and pass out of being. This provides us with some of the essential eidetic features constituting the subject-object framework of our experience. In our Introduction we have attempted to fill in some of the eidetic features of the appearance of aesthetic objects.

The mathematical introduction to the region of intelligibility is relevant to the notion of Beauty since it leads us to understand Beauty Itself as related to the One radiating the light of intelligible coherence upon the whole. The mathematical approach is also relevant to the notion of Beauty in a way more directly tied to our sensory experience, for the mathematical is harmonic, proportionate, orderly, coherent. But Beauty at all levels is the harmonic: beauty of body, beauty of psychic disposition, beauty of mind, beauty of the belonging together of sensuous display and intelligible grounding.

## Mimesis

At this point we are able to consider one of the central notions of Plato's aesthetics: the notion of mimesis, or imitation. Following the lines we have considered thus far, not only mathematical objects but things in general as we encounter them (and we ourselves insofar as each of us is one of those things) are viewed as "images" or imitations of pure Forms in the flux of the Receptacle. Reflection upon the Line of Knowledge provides a mimetic vision of the entire universe of experience: a hierarchy of image-imaged relationships. At the very bottom are shadows, reflections, and dreams: all parasitic upon the things whose shadows, reflections, or images they are.[51] But all three of these types of images image the sensory surface, which has a subjective-objective structure (i.e., an image structure in relation to the underlying material things). Sensa are relations of things to our senses, relations of manifestness that, like the horizon and the perspectives of the object appearing within the horizon, are not there without the co-presence of things and a perceiver. The things so present exceed their manifestness within the circle of sensation.

Further, the reality of physical things whose external images appear in mirrors and dreams and are observed by us, is an "image" of the Forms. The mathematical level of the Forms is approached through images, beginning with figures drawn. The philosophical level transcends the pictured. And the whole region of Forms finally mirrors the One by exhibiting the unity of multiplicity that we call coherence. Even the region of Forms, though stable, involves nonbeing by participating in the Form of Otherness that accounts for the plurality of Forms. Just as Form mirrored in the negativity of the Receptacle (space-time) grounds physical things, so the One mirrored in the negativity of the Form of otherness grounds the region of Forms.[52] Thus the whole of reality has a mimetic structure as each lower level images the next higher level. That means that each level both exists in itself and has, as its ontological deep structure, its participation in the higher levels.

The process is complicated by the fact that human beings, who by their nature belong to the region of Being as well as to that of Becoming *(genesis),* introduce a whole new set of images that we call culture, within which art appears. Culture is not only the set of artifacts that fill the sphere of sensa; it is also the "images of justice in the lawcourts,"[53] the interpretative structures that position us in the whole and link the ever-present Now of sensory immediacy to the whole in the mode of revealing and concealing. No way of understanding discloses the final character of reality as a whole and of ourselves within that whole. We become explicitly philosophic when we become aware of our directedness toward the whole. And yet for Plato *philo-sophia* can never become *sophia.* We can never look directly at the Sun (Good) else we would go blind. We are cautioned in Plato's *Laws*: "Let us not make darkness at noon by attempting to stare at the sun. Let us rather contemplate it in its images."[54] And those images are not simply the images provided by nature as sensa; they are, more deeply, the poetic images that provide us with our lived sense of the whole. Together with the sensa, such interpretive images help to weave the web of *doxa,* the field of immediate presentation of ourselves and the things with which we are engaged, constituting the collective mode of inhabitance that we call our world.

As a further delineation of the notion of imitation, Plato in his *Sophist,* in the context of a discussion of sculpture, distinguishes two forms of imitation, eikastic and phantastic.[55] The former presents an ikon, an exact and proportionate likeness of the original, the latter a phantasm, a distortion adjusted to the position of the perceiver to make the statue appear in the true proportions of the original. Such was the practice of Greek sculptors and architects. Huge statuary that would be seen only from the ground level was constructed with the upper parts proportionately larger so that they would appear proportionately normal from the ground. Socrates seems to be condemning the latter, but in fact he consistently practices phantastic imitation in adjusting his discussion to the character of his interlocutors, making the dialogues pedagogical studies of the blocks that stand in the way of the ascent of the soul. Hence his "poetry."

We should take note here of Socrates' distinction between "imitative" and "narrative" modes of poetic presentation in the *Republic.*[56] In the latter, author and narrator make clear, when they are describing something, that they stand at a distance psychically from what they narrate. What this means we can see by contrast with "imitative" presentation, where author and narrator pretend they are what they narrate. They imitate or mirror the object by giving the illusion of the object itself. An imitative narrator acts out what he describes by pretending to be Achilles or making sounds like a horse braying. An imitative author hides himself behind his writing.

Acting out, says Socrates, produces in the soul the disposition of what is imitated. Hence one may safely imitate the virtuous, but not inferior things like women in various emotional states or evil men or madmen or artisans or the sounds of animals or of other things of nature. He expressly includes in this prohibition imitating one overtaken by love. And given the high place assigned to Eros in the *Symposium* and the *Phaedrus*, one can again see the confining horizon within which this part of the dialogue occurs. Eros as the depth dimension of the soul is viewed as something lowly, belonging, from the perspective of the totalitarian city, to the lowest level of the soul, the desirous part.[57]

Reading the whole as an image of the soul, perhaps we are to understand the need to transcend the situation where we are mirrors of our social environment without attaining to that centeredness of existence that allows us to speak on our own. Further, it is at least curious that Plato's practice in the very section in question is to present his extremely controlled construction as if it were a direct transcription of Socrates' actual conversation. Plato clearly "imitates" rather than "narrates." Why? Because what he has to say here is confined within the perspective of the city, where one does not speak fully on one's own by basing himself on transcendence of the dominant opinions, reaching to the primordial evidences from which the opinions could be properly assessed.

Once we understand something of the depth dimension of the soul opened up by the center of the dialogue, we understand that the basic orientation of the soul to the whole cannot be contained within the city. Doing justice to the soul involves creating conditions for the possibility of its opening out to the whole, transcending not only the lower levels of bodily based desires, but also the limited tasks and basic opinions of the city.[58] A philosophy that understands that can also engage in the production of the seductive surface of art because it knows the antidote to that form of seduction that locks us into the sensory surface and the appetites correlative with it but also and simultaneously locks us into our socially conditioned presuppositions.[59]

## *The Treatment of Art in the* Republic

With that as a general background, we can now look to book 10 of the *Republic*. There, having completed the basic argument of the work on the superiority of justice—understood as ordering the soul in its directedness toward the whole—to injustice as the opposite, Socrates returns to a discussion of poetry, followed by a discussion of the rewards of justice in this life and the next, and capped off by the poetic creation of a myth of the afterlife. In the purged city, poetry is the chief element undergoing purgation. Here at the beginning of book 10 poetry is not purged but seemingly relegated to the lowest fringe of human experience. Yet it appears at the very end of the work in the myth of Er that Plato poetically concocts. It is this apparent contradiction that we have to understand.

Socrates considers poetry in book 10, not in terms of its support for the training of the military (the premise under which he operated in books 2–4), but for its truth-value. Remember, at the earlier stage truth was set aside in favor of civic exemplarity. "Don't tell tales of the gods engaged in unseemly conduct, *even if they are true!*" Approached now in terms of its truth, poetry, having passed through an analysis, in the middle of the work, of the truth of the soul as the soul's direct and evidential relation to truth transcending and thus ever in tension with the demands of the city, is compared to painting. And painting itself, as we noted earlier, is compared to a mirror held up to the sensory surface of things.[60]

The comparison with painting is seriously defective in terms of Socrates' own observation in the second and third books of the *Republic*, where what was important about painting was not its mirroring quality but its design properties. What makes a good painting is not that it is an exact likeness but that the frame is so selected that the space and the light and shadow are aesthetically distributed and the colors play in proper relation to one another so as to establish an overall organic presentation pervaded by a mood appropriate to the subject depicted. In the second book of the *Laws*, besides knowledge of the thing imitated and the correctness of the likeness, the excellence of the execution is an essential ingredient of any critical judgment.[61] Excellence of execution concerns the *how* of presentation, which is just what the passing reference to painting in the earlier part of the *Republic* entails. I suggest that in *Republic* 10, Socrates is deliberately downplaying art, focusing on its mirroring function in order to bring us, who have been exposed to a preliminary uncovering of the full dimensionally of psychic life as the locus of the manifestation of the truth of the whole, to bring us to reflect more deeply on the positive significance of art.

This is supported by the fact, already alluded to, that Socrates says that he would be willing to admit poets into the state if only a case could be made for them.[62] And he further points out that even though poets water our passions and aid their growth, thus diminishing our rational powers, we can attend to poetry without harm "if we know the antidote." I suggest that the antidote lies, not in the absence of passion in favor of a cold rationalism, but in the dialectical relation between Eros and Logos. Following the ladder of ascent to the beautiful described in the *Symposium* (something I will shortly treat), the space for the operation of reason is opened up and oriented beyond the cave of culturally mediated sensibility and beyond the limited constructions of reason toward the whole and its source. Thus the whole realm of poetic operation can be developed in such a way as to draw so-called reason on to greater and greater adequacy. One could then understand why Plato's own poetic work concludes the dialogue, which otherwise comes down so hard on poetry.

In the myth of Er Plato poetically concocts a story of the afterlife which becomes a paradigm for Virgil, Dante, and Milton. A fictitious world is created where *doxa* is removed and the soul is judged nakedly, not being clothed in the exteriority of appearance to others.

But to return to the linkage of the opening discussion of book 10 to the Line, in book 10 Socrates hearkens back to the Line and speaks of three levels: there is the thing made by man, say, a bed; there is, second, that to which the maker looks, the Idea of a bed ("made," Socrates says, "by god"); and there is the image of a bed made by the painter.[63] The middle level (the god's Idea) belongs on the upper part of the Line, on the side of Being; the types occupying the extremes in the verbal description belong below the Line, on the side of genesis, or Becoming, the painting occupying the lowest level. In the second book of the *Laws* Socrates calls attention to the possibility of a thousand representations of the same object available to sight, since spatially a given object affords an indeterminate number of perspectives.[64] A painting thus presents an extremely limited selection from the real multiplicity of aspects available.

We might note here that perspectivity, and thus an essential reference to the position of the viewer, is an essential feature of visible objects. Not the display of things in themselves, but of things in relation to the perceiver is what characterizes such evidences. A painting replicates one such subject-related perspective. Hence, in the *Republic*, the painting is located "three degrees removed from reality." This does not simply mean that it is an image of an object that imitates an Idea, since that gives us three levels and hence only two degrees. A painting is an image of an image (visual perspective) of a full object, which itself is more than the sum total of visible aspects, having also audile, tactile, and other sensory, as well as nonsensory, aspects that "imitate" the appropriate Idea. Plato gives no attention here to the peculiar focus a painter can give to an object that makes the Idea more clearly present than the thing's visible surface alone does. Plotinus, and later Schopenhauer and Hegel as well as Heidegger, will pick up on this and claim that the artist stands at the level of the Idea and thus a work of art can be higher than the natural sensorily given.[65] Martin Buber will observe that the artist is faithful not to appearance but to being, enhancing the expressivity of the appearance so that it more clearly displays the invisible interior.[66]

One wonders how serious Socrates is about the Idea of the bed as made by god. One would have thought the Idea was made up by the artisan. In the *Parmenides* Socrates agrees that his notion of Ideas is meant to cover things like justice or wisdom. He is not sure about natural species, and he is positive that there are no Forms of ugly things.[67] If no natural species are Forms, it would seem that the Ideas of human artifacts would also not be Forms. However, they are a function of the divine element in us, our intellect, that which we distinguish by reason of its being the locus of the manifestation of atemporal objects, objects that transcend the here and now of their instances.

Further in the discussion in book 10, Socrates makes a parallel distinction of three levels when he links the maker of a horse's bridle, the user of the bridle, and a painter of a picture of the bridle.[68] Here the user is the measure for the maker and occupies the same place as the god who "made" the Idea of the bed. This suggests that "the god" is the divine element in us that ought to govern the animal in us. He speaks in this connection of the world of the painter as not only three degrees removed from reality, but also three degrees removed from "the king" (i.e., the self-governing power in us).[69]

But all three images—the picture of the bed, the picture of the bridle, and the two-dimensional mirroring of the surrounding world—suggest a very peripheral role for imitation. Applied to poetry, we have the poet who learns to produce perspectival illusions, lacking the crucial depth dimension, of the solid activities in which humans engage—just what Plato has Socrates do in books 2 through 4!

A passage in Plato's *Sophist* delineates two forms of making, divine and human.[70] Each type divides into a form of reality and the corresponding form of an image of that reality. Thus a god makes physical things and their images in shiny surfaces, their shadows, and their appearance in dreams. As a craftsman, the human artisan makes artifacts and, as an artist, paintings of the artifacts. In the latter case, we have the same distinction as in book 10 of the *Republic*.

A passage in the *Gorgias* distinguishes among the human arts the arts of appearance or "sophistical arts" and the arts of reality.[71] As I noted in the introduction, human artifaction can be understood in a broad way to include arts like cooking, gymnastic training, and legislation. Socrates considers both arts of the body and arts of the soul. Regarding the body, the restaurant and the beauty parlor provide pleasure and cosmetic beauty, while medicine and gymnastic provide health and the natural bloom of a vigorously trained body. The "sophistical arts" give the appearance of beauty and the good; the arts of reality produce real physical beauty and real physical good. Regarding the soul, sophistry proper, along with poetry, are said to manipulate appearance, while, by contrast, wise legislation and philosophy foster real psychic development.

It might be possible to link up the consideration of "divinely made" dreams with the sources of inspiration tapped by the artist. In the *Phaedrus*, Socrates speaks of divine inspiration and of divinely inspired art, which seems to be distinguished from "imitative" art, the practitioners of which he places far down on a hierarchy of character types.[72] The divinely inspired artist not only has technical knowledge, but also *enthusiasmos*, that surplus spark of divine inspiration which, unlike *techne*, the artist cannot give himself.[73] But maybe we dismissed too readily the "divine" making of the Idea of the bed. Like artistic inspiration, the idea of an artifact "just comes," like a dream, to the first one to think of it. So a "god" (read: nonempirically present source of inspiration) creates in the artisan (at least in the first one who thought of it) the Idea of the bed.

Nonetheless, the difference between the two modes of inspiration—that of the creative artisan and that of the creative artist—is vast. The artisan qua artisan creates a form that is directed exclusively toward use, so that the artifact, so to speak, disappears from the focus of awareness in its functioning. In bed one might sleep or daydream or make love: in all three cases, the bed is not focal but purely peripheral to the field of awareness. (The selection of a bed for an example, followed by the example of the bridle, may not be incidental to the attempt at purging Eros that goes on in the *Republic* as well as in several other dialogues.) The artist, on the other hand, and even the artisan insofar as he is an artist as well, produces a work characterized by aesthetic form. Here the object does not disappear from or recede to the periphery of attention insofar as one is in the aesthetic mode. The well-formed object is precisely a significant presence, a focal object characterized by beauty.

## The Ladder of Ascent to Beauty Itself

The *Republic* can be understood as an attempt to purge the luxurious love of beauty that possesses Glaucon and those like him. The dialogue begins with Socrates and Glaucon headed "up to the city," when they are arrested by the threat of force on the part of several men whom Socrates has to persuade to let him and Glaucon continue their journey up to the city. The dialogue consists in persuading the actual city to let Socrates conduct, up to "the city laid out in heaven" and constructed in words, the Glaucons of this world,[74] those with a "musical and loving nature," as the *Phaedrus* puts it.[75] The actual conduct of the discussion is itself calculated to lead to that heavenly city. Glaucon moves the action out of the first city dedicated to physical well-being by his remark that it is "Pigsville," without "sweetmeats and soft couches" (i.e., distinctively human luxuries).[76] The purged city is introduced in a discussion with Adeimantus, who seems content with not telling the full truth about the gods because his vision is limited to the city; but Glaucon enters again when it is a question of the purely aesthetic (as distinct from the referential) features of *musike*.[77] Glaucon appears further as chief interlocutor when the study of the Good is introduced as rooted in the love of Beauty itself.[78] The discussion of the Line is meant to teach us how to move up the ladder of different levels of experience toward the vision of the Good itself, which is either identical with or closely related to Beauty Itself. The same ladder is discussed within the context of a much more explicit treatment of the notion of Eros in the *Symposium* as the teaching of Diotima on the ascent to Beauty. Diotima, a female, appears near the end of a male—indeed, male homosexual—discussion of Eros.[79] Again, first the male, then the female drama.[80] In both cases, the female drama far outstrips the male. Let us turn our attention then to Diotima's speech.

Diotima had proclaimed the fundamental character of Eros to be a desire of the mortal for the immortal aroused by a beautiful form and leading to productive activity.[81] This is clear enough at the level of sexual Eros, not indeed in the immediacy of the experience thereof, but in the inner directedness of its consummation to a term that outlasts both the momentariness of the experience and, in the normal course of things, the mortality of the couple. Sexual Eros produces offspring who produce offspring who produce offspring, and so on, as the establishment of the "immortality" of the species in time. This is true of animal organisms—indeed, of all organisms—in general.

Human Eros is cut into by the peculiar structure of the field of human awareness as open, beyond the Now of animal awareness, to the whole. Thus human beings are driven by a desire to become immortal through the recognition by others, present and to come, of their immortal deeds and works in battle, in sport, in art and literature, in the founding of institutions. These Diotima calls "the lesser works of love." There are also "the higher mysteries."[82] We enter into the latter by a definite progression that begins with the arousal of desire for one bodily being. The heightened state tends to produce "winged words" as the one in love bursts into poetic apostrophe. By a natural dynamic, the feeling of love tends to suffuse everything, so that the world itself seems beautiful. Again, in the course of development, such a state is gradually transformed into love for the beauty of the person that shines through the exterior. Here the sensory presence, especially of the eyes, "the windows of the soul,"[83] display the real presence of the consciousness of the other. And one may be led to see past, and thus reduce to the peripheral levels of our awareness, an otherwise uncomely exterior when the beauty of the person shines through.

Thus far everything seems to jibe with the ordinary course of experience. But Diotima seems to take an unanticipated leap when she claims that the next step is to learn to love the beauty of laws and institutions. However, the leap is reduced when we think of what tends to produce beauty of character. We realize that it is good upbringing, being shaped by the long accumulation of reinforced choices that constitute a tradition. One "falls in love with," becomes attached to, commits oneself to a tradition that has that power precisely because one is concerned with shaping and sustaining the beauty of souls. One becomes a "patriot."

This kind of natural dynamic of love still occurs "under the line," "inside the Cave," in history. If nature is a repetitive mirroring of the atemporal Forms, history is an ever-shifting approach to, and a falling away from an ideal arrangement in which reason governs prudentially, increasingly aware of the overarching order within which human life occurs and ever open to, and critically appreciative of, possibly higher forms of inspiration. In both cases, there is a measure, the discernment of which gives rise to the various sciences of nature (physics, biology), of the soul (psychology), of the virtues (ethics, politics), of being itself (metaphysics). Plato's *Statesman* delineates two types of measure: the quantitative and the qualitative. The quantitative concerns number (the abstract), length, breadth, and depth (the spatial) and the swift (the temporal), while the qualitative concerns the mean *(meson)* between excess and defect, the fit *(prepon)* in terms of preparedness to act, the opportune *(kairon)* in terms of the temporal rightness of action, and the due *(dikaios)* in terms of the obligations involved in action.[84] The quantitative appears initially as value-free measure, the qualitative as measure of value. However, the two types of measure overlap. In organisms, quantitative measures in spatial proportions and temporal rhythms are crucial to the qualitative well-being of the organism; and in works of art, spatial and temporal distribution according to ratios are constitutive of the aesthetic. Aristotle will remark that a well-formed drama is like an organism, in which everything is there that needs to be there to bring about the aesthetic effect and nothing that is there is such that its absence would not deter from the overall effect.[85] Here we have the idea of a mean between aesthetic excess and aesthetic defect. The differing modes of knowing are thus all concerned in some way with measure.

The pursuit of the sciences is an ever-developing process in which the underlying universal coherence is increasingly laid bare. The manifest togetherness of the Forms presents us with a deeper level of beauty, more stable than the ever-shifting, but law-governed realm of nature and the rise and fall of order in human history measured by the science of the human soul as the place of the cognitive display of cosmic order. The passion for such pursuit follows from the natural openness of the mind for the whole. It culminates in a vision of what Diotima calls Beauty Itself, which is presented in such a way that, far from being a mere analyzable concept that can be captured in a definition, it is the radiance of that which, as the One/Good, gathers the whole into unity and, being glimpsed as final object of human Eros, gathers the soul together into unity. Understanding human Eros in this way, we can see that, following the distinctions discussed in the *Symposium,* there is a pandemian or "common" and a uranian or "heavenly" Eros, and hence a higher and lower Dionysian function in Plato's thought.[86] In the fuller Platonic conception, the Apollonian level of *nous* rises out of the common Dionysian level, drawn on in its constructions by a heavenly Dionysian level of sublimated Eros. The purged city of the *Republic* is an Apollonian construction without the heavenly Dionysian and hence is a level of totalitarian closure and tyranny, subjecting the soul to complete subservience to the city and desublimating its fundamental human Eros. In a fuller view of Platonic thought, the last word belongs to a Dionysian height.

Now, just as we might have thought that we had left behind the world of the senses in passing outside the Cave, over the Line, from Becoming to Being, Socrates speaks, in the *Phaedrus,* of the privileged character of Beauty. Of all the Forms, it is the only one that is "perceptible by the eyes," a Real Presence, directly discernible and not merely inferentially available, in sensorily given things.[87] What has been going on is not at all a flight from the body and its senses, a disincarnation, but the hollowing out of an un-fathomable depth behind the sensory surface of things. Most especially, in the interpersonal context within which the *Phaedrus* is cast, the eyes of the other are the expressive media of the depth of the person and of the prepersonal depths of Eros for the Good that founds all personhood. In friendship, the deepest sense of the presence of Beauty Itself is found.[88] But this also raises the problem, treated in *Greater Hippias,* of the relation between "inward" beauty of character and outward display.[89] The beauti-ful ballerina who sadistically beats her grandmother comes to mind: beauty of external form set in motion through graceful action coexists with a character capable of doing ugly things. But that ugliness is also displayed in sensuous exteriority.

Amid all this talk of beauty, what has been said about that which is rec-ognized in all these stages of recognition? What is this feature called beauty? What are its properties? *Greater Hippias* proposes the notion of the appropriate *(to prepon)* as instanced in elements in relation to their context.[90] It raises the problem of the link of beauty with the useful. One must dis-tinguish the usefully appropriate from the aesthetically appropriate. But the *Republic* indicates that beauty in all things follows function.[91] Beauty thus has something to do with the way things appear functionally together in experience. In the *Republic,* as we saw, Socrates recommended being sur-rounded by works of visual and audile art that were characterized by grace, harmony, good order, good rhythm, good proportion. The "good" in all this is something directly perceived and is related as object to the right ordering of the soul, which subordinates the biologically grounded ap-petites to the ordering power of intellect and which aims intellect at an open search for the comprehensive order of things to which we are essen-tially directed by nature. Hence the togetherness of sensory surface sets up reverberations in all the other dimensions of our being, so that one can be led from the harmonious, graceful, well-proportioned, well-ordered togetherness of sensory surface to the perception of similar properties at progressively higher levels and vice versa. The mimetic structure of being, opened up in its multidimensional character by the pedagogy of the Line, is what makes possible this marvelous ascent. It is an ascent grounded in the look of the other, the encounter with which is developed in depth by sharing the pursuit of exploring and indwelling in the broader context of institutions, of nature and of cosmic ground, the direct relation to which constitutes the depth of being human.

Philosophy as introduced by Plato is love of the vision of the whole, aspiration toward which generates authentic human existence. Philosophy lives out reflectively the fundamental structure of the field of human experience. Unlike the poetic and religious modality of relation to the whole, philosophy is not simply inspired and proclamatory; it is also systematic, dialogic, and self-critical. It tests the adequacy of putative visions of the whole by their capacity to take into account all the features of the field of experience in their togetherness laid out in the reflective development of the Line. Yet by reason of its own essential incompleteness, it is open to poetic vision and, in philosophers like Plato, even generates its own poetic vision. It grows when it learns to respond to the admirable and the awesome. It is linked intimately to the arts and is anchored most especially in the beauty of the other person.

☙ ☙ ☙

## Response

How has this investigation of Plato aided our inquiry into aesthetics? First of all, it has developed, through his treatment of the Line of Knowledge, our understanding of the field of experience. What we can learn in a special way by beginning with Plato is how to approach any study within the context of the whole and thus to understand how regional specializations get carved out from the whole of experience. Plato is the unsurpassed philosopher of experience as he is also the dialectical explorer of alternate ways of configuring the whole of being to which experience always refers without possessing it in any final way. That totalistic concern looks to the effects of the aesthetic region on integral psychic functioning and thus lays the basis for the possibility of an ethical critique of art that is significantly more than a desire to stay within the mores of a community, since it involves the possibility of a critical assessment of those mores as well.

The Line of Knowledge presents, in its incipient analysis of sensation on the one hand and of the One/Good on the other, a developed version of the biological-ontological frame I have laid out in the introduction. Principle of the whole, the One/Good/Beautiful is the ultimate term of human Eros. I called the principle Being, though Plato had Socrates say that it is "beyond *ousia*," beyond beingness as involved in the intellect-Form correlation, and thus beyond the distinction between subject and object. I referred to our orientation toward it at first simply as "reference to Being," though I finally associated it with "the heart." Plato names our orientation Eros, the mortal's desire for the immortal that belongs to all the living. Eros concerns how we are related to time, which, together with space, is the enduring framework of all experience. As organisms we unfold, endure, and decline, exhibiting a definite temporal pattern from birth to death. As alert organisms, the effects of past experiences lead to routinized associations and responses. Also as alert organisms, our erotic desire leads, without our necessarily knowing it, to the transcendence of death in passing on our genes in our offspring. As humans our language gives expression to our capacity to isolate and relate recurrent types *(eide)* that we know to apply to all times and places where individuals of the type can be encountered. Space and time as a whole thus come into our purview; hence the "deathless" order of natural occurrence is capable of being made more explicit and refined in the sciences. On account of this apprehension of *eidos*, we are able to run ahead of our current and past organic situation and anticipate our term. Noting this distinctiveness, the Greeks referred to us as the mortals. Even though all living things die, we alone live out of an anticipation of our own term. Hence Eros and *Thanatos*, together with Logos as linguistic incarnation of the apprehension of the order of *eide*, belong inseparably together in human experience.

Current attacks on "Platonism" and "essences" in terms of "the theory-ladenness of perception" and "the deferral of presence" have to come to terms with Plato's observation that all arts depend on the recurrence of *eide*. Their recognition distinguishes the bungler from the expert. We might locate that in a more primordial region, that of life itself. The critics have to eat, and eating is a recognizably recurrent need for *all* organisms. It depends on the ability to distinguish the edible from the inedible, the noxious from the nonnoxious, the nourishing from the nonnourishing. The "theory" that accompanies and structures perception here is that of life itself. Here, in living form, there is the likewise currently odious "hierarchy" of functions, with the controlling center in the nervous system and lower and higher centers of integration in the structures of the brain, from the reptil-ian, through the mammalian, to the fully human cortical structures. These are some of the *eide* differentiated by physiological research. They rest on other *eide* ferreted out by physics, beginning with the periodic table. It is knowledge of further recurrent structures that makes possible complex building tasks and the "hi-tech" culture we live in today. As in Plato, recog-nition of recurrent *eide* makes possible all the arts. Nonetheless, it is impor-tant to observe that the *eide* we come to know are *eide* of appearance, of modes of presentation and not of final ontological depth—a knowing Plato sees as reserved "for the gods." Kant, Nietzsche, and Heidegger will un-derscore that with differing degrees of success.[92]

The reflective power of intellect as the capacity to apprehend univer-sal Form directs Eros, oriented at the biological level toward a temporal mirroring of the eternal, to the direct display of the unchanging and thus "immortal" order governing the temporal. Or perhaps it is better to say that intellect, drawn on by Eros, is able to clarify to itself what it is that all life seeks. This places an aesthetic principle first: the totalistic desire of the heart for the total-real. One should note here that the emphasis on Eros moves beyond a "merely intellectual" relation to a more "totalistic" rela-tion, a relation of "the whole person," of which Augustine will later make much. It is the relation of what I have called "the heart," and of which the biblical command, "Thou shalt love the Lord thy God with thy whole heart," is the most revealing instance. In Plato there is thus a link between "insight" into intelligible relations and "vision," which reverberates through-out the whole of experience. There is thus always a "visionary" aspect to Platonic "intellectualism" that brings philosophy into close proximity to the arts. This is a connection reinvoked more recently by Heidegger.

This relation, I suggest, is why the philosopher is presented by Socrates first of all as the lover of the vision of Beauty Itself. That also recurs to the opening line of the first work in Western metaphysics, Parmenides' *Peri phuseos,* where "the steeds that bore me took me as far as my heart could de-sire," up from the realm of the mixture of darkness and light to the blazing light of the identity of Being and thought.[93] Since such "vision" transcends subject and object, it goes beyond the detachment of intellect into a par-ticipative identity with Being Itself.

The polar tension between our ontological reference, on the one hand, expressed in the notion of the Good together with its subjective correlate, human Eros, and, on the other hand, our biological ground, which generates the field of sensa together with the appetites correlative with it, sets up the tension between appearance and reality. Biology gives us our first access to things, a field of "images," of appearance relative to our biological needs. In my reading, the initial emptiness of our metaphysical Eros leads to the construction of cultures as ways of situating the here and now of bodily appearance within the Whole by means of the apprehension of universal Forms. But cultural constructions are plural, because, I would claim, culture rests on the *perspectival* apprehension of Forms or on different interpretive interweavings of nonperspectively apprehended Forms. And precisely because of that perspectivity, culture in turn produces a second level of appearance, for example, "images of justice in the lawcourts," which open up certain possibilities of thinking, feeling, and acting, but which thereby close off deeper and, finally, normative possibilities for assessing the cultural images. Images articulate the very way things are present to us. The founding distance of humanness provided by reference to the totality via the notion of the Good as principle of the whole makes possible the re-formation of what is given by nature, not only to satisfy the demands of biological nature, but also to indicate, through aesthetic form, the way we are situated in the Whole. In this way, appeal is made to the whole of human experience, to our sense of participative identity with the Whole.

The Line of Knowledge, I claim, provides us with the irremovable and nonperspectival frame of human experience that, in turn, furnishes the fundamental orientation from which cultural images can be assessed. Each level of the Line exhibits a fundamental eidetic structure that, as apprehended, provides the initial filling for the fourth level of the Line, the meta-level of philosophic reflection on the other operative levels of experience. Hence the space between the always-present sensa and the One/Good is not entirely empty. The distinctions between sensing and the sensa and between the intellect and the intelligible are cut across by a distinction between subject and object on the one hand and between universal and particular on the other. Finally, the distinctions are surmounted by a principle of unity which grounds the play between all these distinctions and which is the ultimate term of inquiry.

Reflection on the status of sensa as images derived from biological interaction allows us to see that by themselves they are mute without our taking them up interpretively, without reading them as signs of expressive wholes that are not only expressive of their ontological ground in the togetherness of the Forms, but also, in the case of the other sensorily presented human being, expressive of the depths of psychic life. In the human case, a gap opens up between the beauty of the person and the character of its sensory display. And the beauty of the person, in turn, rests not only on subjective, purely idiosyncratic qualities, but on instantiating noble institutions in its behavior, displaying love of the beauty of cosmic order in its speech, manifesting Eros for the Good in its look.

The beauty recognized in sensory form in general instantiates laws of proportion, harmony, grace. And the creation of beautiful sensory form in the arts expresses the artist's apprehension of the universal harmonic. As the human psyche is displayed in its sensorily given behavior—in overt action, word, and look—so is it displayed in its own artifacts as sensorily available. If we can have disordered souls, we can have disordered and disordering artifacts. Expressive of a disordered psychic life, such artifacts tend to produce disorder in their observers. Our current culture furnishes a powerful demonstration of this claim.

Plato makes a clear distinction between what I have called aesthetic form and reference, between the harmonic shaping of sensory materials and the display of something other than the shaped object. He analyzes its operation in poetry, where he criticizes the civically undesirable things represented and the musical forms (rhythms and harmonies), modes of presentation (narrative or imitative), and instrumental timbres as well as musical styles (Dionysiac and Apollonian) through which the represented objects are presented. The fundamental Apollonian-Dionysian distinction is based, at one level, on the natural distinction between the biological pole and the possibilities for understanding and shaping that emerge from our ontological pole as initial empty reference to the whole. But at another level, the Dionysian rises from the lowest level of the soul toward the transintellectual One as object of complete Eros. At the highest level, Platonic thought is Dionysiac, erotically drawing us beyond Form to the Source, in continuity with the Eros that arises at the physiological level as a desire for eternity. In the *Republic,* Plato overtly places Eros at the lowest level of the soul, but covertly presents it as the vehicle of philosophic ascent to the Good. In the *Phaedrus* and the *Symposium* it overtly functions as the vehicle of ascent, but it is occasioned by the attractiveness of the human form. One might ask for the relation between the perception of art objects and the ascent made possible through Eros aroused by the perception of the human form. Plato advocates Apollonian style in all the arts by reason of its ability to bring harmony—and that means "rationality"—to the psychic field. How does that play in relation to the "madness" of Eros? In the *Republic* the philosophic type seems to furnish the *Aufhebung*, the sublimated synthesis of these two features, simultaneously Apollonian and Dionysian. Harmonic shaping is furnished by the Apollonian ambiance of the polis and thus has in principle a public character. Erotic attraction is in principle private, transcending the polis in its lower forms by recurring to the animal base and in its higher forms by philosophic ascent. In and through the aesthetic harmonization of Glaucon's soul, the sublimation of interpersonal Eros can lead out of the Cave and toward the heavenly city.

Plato further clarifies the distinction between aesthetic form and reference when he recommends being surrounded from birth to death by artifacts—and he lists buildings, furniture, utensils, and clothing, as well as paintings—that have the requisite rhythmic and harmonic properties without directly representing any object. Note here that painting is considered, not as in book 10 of the *Republic* in terms of its mirroring function in making perspectivally manifest the exterior of a body, but in terms of its presentation of aesthetic form. It is in this that he lays the basis for the later focus on pure aesthetic form, originally in music, but also in painting and sculpture. But for Plato, music without words is meaningless, and so he cancels on the one hand what he opens on the other. Mikel Dufrenne speaks in this regard of the representational prejudice of classical aesthetics and carries on his discussion in terms of the expressivity of aesthetic form.[94] Plato's own treatment of Beauty Itself as a real presence in beautiful things points in the same direction, though in thus addressing the topic, he links such perception to erotic arousal in the presence of the beauty of a human body, not to the contemplation of artistic objects. Shorn of his heavy representational and interhuman erotic emphasis, Plato's observations about Apollonian aesthetic properties and the real presence of Beauty Itself in beautiful things could be considered the charter for abstract art.

Note also that rhythm and harmony are transferred from the musical arena, where they qualify sound, to the plastic, spatial arena, where they qualify visual objects. In both instances, through the plastic and the performing arts, music and harmony sink deeply into the soul. It is important to underscore this insight because it is so often overlooked in those who claim that Plato was basically hostile to the arts. In fact, Plato was more sensitive than most to the power of the arts. He thereby sought, not to oust them, but to employ them to bring what I have called prerational rationality to the soul, to shape the emotional wellsprings of action and attention in such a way as to foster the eventual emergence of an explicit rational pattern of experience, "with eyes fixed on the whole,"[95] aimed at that which exceeds it as principle of the Whole. By *rational pattern* I mean a whole style of attending that is capable of weighing and measuring both quantitatively and qualitatively, that is habituated to being intelligently alert to all the relevant parameters of a situation, that is aimed at the whole of reality within which human activity occurs, that is capable of attending to the long range as well as to the immediate, and that is capable of dispassionate assessment because it is moved by passionate (i.e., emotionally totalistic) commitment to the undisclosed Whole. Aware of the undisclosed Whole, philosophic Eros is capable of being sustained by an enduring awe that, far from being extinguished, is deepened as it understands more and more of the fuller context within which everyday awareness occurs.[96]

In fitting artistic activity and appreciation into that larger context, Plato treats various art forms in different ways. His major focus is on *musike* as instrumentally accompanied poetry. But he also treats sculpture, painting, dance, architecture, and manufacturing design in general. And whereas, regarding painting, his major focus in the *Republic* is on its mirroring function, he also treats it in passing, as we have noted, in terms of its purely aesthetic form. But he tends to subordinate aesthetic form to intellectually apprehensible meaning: he has one of his characters in the *Laws* claim that instrumental music without words is meaningless. He likewise has some significant things to say about the dance as a form of gymnastic for the soul. His focus here is not on the audience but on the performer. And here the object of the dance is not so much to train the body as it is to tune the soul, not only making it able to bear up under hardship, but also making it graceful, rhythmic, and harmonic. Indeed, all the art forms are considered in terms of their effect in tuning the soul so that it welcomes reason. For Plato beauty in everything turns on use, upon the proper functioning of the entity in question. So also, the beautification of the human being turns on health of body and soul, the latter being advanced by the perception of beautiful forms.

In Plato, beauty itself is extended from sensuous form to psychic disposition and from there to the objects of scientific treatment, not only the objects of mathematical harmonics that govern what is seen and heard, but also the objects of the philosophic sciences of psychic life, of ethics as its proper attunement, and of metaphysics as the unveiling of the harmony of the whole physical-psychic cosmos and perhaps of its Source. Beauty as a transcendent Form is privileged in that it appears in the sensory field itself as exceeding the locus of its manifestation, as being both in and beyond the beautifully seen (or heard) object. Plato thus points to a peculiar experience of transcendence that gives a curious flavor to all he writes, but which experience is implicit in, and the ground of, the fascination that sensuous beauty exercises on us all.

Beauty is that which binds the whole together: universal Form and particular instance, intellectual apprehension and bodily resonance. The abstract reflective movement out of the Cave of sensibility and culture into the sunlight of intelligibility involves, as its necessary complement, a recuperative, concretizing reflection that binds the two realms of our experience together. Art, made reflectively aware by philosophic reflection of the fundamental parameters and basic direction of psychic life, is able both to set in motion the ultimate deepening of the lifeworld and to bring to significant, participative presence the intellectual depth carved out by philosophic reflection. But even further, in its intuitive flashes of insight into the character of the whole, art gives rise not only to critical assessment on the part of philosophy, but also to further possible rational development.

It is on the basis of these sets of connected insights that Plato is led to the censorship of the arts and thus to infringe on artistic freedom, the one unexamined absolute of the current artistic community. That community seems to embody Plato's notion of democracy, where freedom to do what you want is the central value and where every other value depends on the choice of the individual, who is in principle free from all binding norms. Art gives expression to such free individuality and creates whatever communities happen to gather around the idiosyncrasies of expression that emerge. Tradition, order, rule, law—all represent limitations on artistic freedom. We are in a similar cultural position as that encountered by Plato. And his response to the situation is applicable to our own: the intrinsic nature of psychic life, oriented toward the whole and capable of rational ordering of its own life in attunement to the cosmic order, provides the measure for the intrinsic value or disvalue of all cultural products. Do they open out psychic life in such a way as to allow it both to exercise rational judgment and to draw upon its total Eros for the whole, or do they in some way inhibit both aspects of psychic development? Several things are rejected in principle: abandonment to biological appetites, total and uncritical immersion in culturally biased projects, and a rationalism that fails to recognize its own need to transcend itself in our passion for the whole to which our experience of the beautiful leads us.

Plato provides for us a rich harvest of aesthetic insights that move beyond the narrowness of art for art's sake into the breadth of art for the sake of the expanded, deepened, and harmonized human soul, attuned to the fineness of sensory surface expressive of the character of the whole and aware of unfathomed depths.

🌿 🌿 🌿

## A Brief Excursus: Plato and Wright on Architecture

Locating beauty in the relation of form to function, Plato anticipates one of the fundamental principles of the mode of architecture represented in the twentieth century by Frank Lloyd Wright. Wright rejects the "pictorial view" of art that has dogged the tradition, just as Plato rejects "imitation" as holding a mirror to sensory surface.[97] The shape taken on by a work of art is that dictated by its function, just as in the case of any living form.[98] It is this that has been reborn in the industrial arts in the design of ships, airplanes, locomotives, and automobiles.[99] The more functionally adapted, the more streamlined and thus beautiful the objects appear. Architecture ought to translate this into the nonmobile forms of buildings: the form, stripped of all mere superadded decoration and rendered simple,[100] is determined by what is to be done in and around the building and thus by the essential human values involved.[101] Furthermore, as in things of nature, the form should also be adapted to the environment within which it essentially stands, expressing its belonging to the earth, and indeed, to this piece of earth, this peculiar environment.[102] To that extent, it is important for Wright to stress an intense appreciation for the qualities of the materials involved.[103] Furthermore, and as essential to his conception of *organic architecture*, there is a stress on the peculiarities of space, both inward and outward. A building is not walls and ceiling; it is the space these carve out.[104] In this stress on appreciation of materials, on the nature of space, and on belonging to a peculiar environment, it is not so clear that Wright would find an ally in Plato, for Plato most often seems more interested in the way out of the Cave. Where he is more like Plato is in his view of music as sublimated mathematics, furnishing him an image of architecture as similarly constituted.[105] Here both the mathematical and the sublimational are essential. And this is directly parallel to Wright's view that life itself is sublimated machinery, a mechanism that transcends itself. Mathematics and the machine are dead and spiritless, but they are the body in which the spirit realizes itself. Functionality is essentially linked to the character of the human spirit, whose inner experience is expressed in art and in religion, both of which exhibit a sense of the Whole.[106] The architect must therefore know something of the intrinsic order of the universe.[107] But where Wright would no doubt again stand strongly opposed to Plato is the low level at which Plato places democracy. Distinguishing with Plato liberty from license,[108] Wright nonetheless calls for and develops an architecture that is expressive of the democratic spirit in, among other things, his underscoring of the individual Usonian house on its own private acre.[109]

# III

# ARISTOTLE

## *Meanings of the Term Art*

T HE APPROACH I TOOK in the introduction to locating fine art in the broader scheme of things human was basically Aristotelian. Let us review it at this point. I took an inventory of the uses of the term *art* in ordinary experience, ranging them in a hierarchy of broadest to narrowest usage and setting them in a system of contrasts. At the broadest level art is contrasted to nature. Aristotle expands on that by providing an insight into the nature of a nature: a nature *(phusis)* is a principle of motion and rest, of development and completion, that is intrinsic to a thing.[1] Natures head in their own directions or tend to endure in states toward which they have tended. A nature so conceived provides the frame within which art occurs.

Art is that which depends on choice.[2] Everything distinctively human has its origin in art in this broadest sense. Human nature is part of the frame of nature, since it involves a givenness that does not depend on human choice for its form, and that givenness involves structural features corresponding to tendencies to act along certain lines. Human nature involves a tension between two given factors: a biological-sensory factor and a factor of transcendence or of initially empty reference toward the whole of being. As Aristotle put it, "the human soul is, in a way, all things."[3]

The biological factor is comprised of basic vegetative processes, processes of anabolism and catabolism, of growth and sustenance, and of reproductive tendency.[4] Over and beyond that, it involves the level of sensory wakefulness and thus of the sensory manifestness of things. That manifestness takes place within the Now of the perspectives set up by our bodily position, by the limited thresholds of our perceptual organs, and by our organic needs. For Aristotle the sensa are the activations of the perceptibility of things in relation to the activation of the perceptual powers of the perceiver—indeed, in a relation of "intentional identity." ("The sensible in act is the sense [power] in act.")[5] As the horizon of vision and the perspective appearance of a material thing within that horizon are not absolute features of "the world outside," but conditions of manifestness relative to a biologically based percipient, so also with the sensa that appear within such perspectives. Such appearance is locked into the flowing Now but anchors all our wakefulness.

Our knowledge of the factor of transcendence has its root in the fact that we judge whatever we confront in that sensory field in terms of meanings that refer to all actual or possible instances of those meanings, whenever in time and wherever in space they might occur, even in such elementary sensorily focused experiences as seeing this page "as white." The whole of space and time is marginally pregiven as a term of reference for our judgments. But the judgments center on the employment of the notion of being whose reference is absolutely unrestricted. The judgment that something "is" such and such involves a reference to the wholeness of what is judged and to the encompassing whole that includes it, the one judging, and everything else as well. The way the human soul is all things is, initially, by way of empty reference. But it is precisely the emptiness of that reference that makes it necessary to choose how we are to work at uncovering that whole and how we are to arrange our lives so as to come to terms with the tasks imposed by our nature and the conditions of past choices, both our own and those of the tradition that bears us. Human nature is precisely that nature that has to choose to create culture. And since cultures are choices based on a necessary partiality in the manifestness of what-is and of all the parameters of our own being, they are necessarily plural and, alas, probably necessarily or at least contingently antagonistic.

There is then an art of producing culture in general. We might say that distinctively human nature is culture-producing nature, nature that operates by art, nature that produces forms. That includes the art of creating institutions—social, political, economic, educational, religious—that form a way of life. The art of producing culture also includes bringing theoretical knowledge *(theoria)* into being, the aim of which is the contemplation of the invariable, the frame of nature within which decisions are made.[6] Knowing how to introduce variations into nature presupposes knowing something of the invariants of what nature provides.

Under the narrower heading of art, as contrasted with *theoria*, Aristotle contrasts making *(poiesis)* with doing *(praxis)*.[7] The habit of the latter is prudence or practical wisdom *(phronesis)*, of the former it is art in a still narrower sense *(techne)*. *Techne* shapes something external; prudence shapes our own habits, individually and collectively. *Techne* thus falls under practical wisdom and is governed by it. Aristotle calls practical wisdom, in the broader usage of the term *art*, "the art of arts."[8] It is the habit of alert, intelligent focus on all the relevant parameters of our lives in the concrete situations in which we find ourselves. As a "habit" it is far from a dull routine, for it is concerned with building and breaking as well as sustaining routines, as the situation might require, in order to keep intelligently alert to the demands of changing contexts in the light of the naturally given human ends. It is a *hexis*, or habit (Latin *habitus*), or a "having," the fundamental way we possess ourselves, guided by the priority of concretely alert intelligence.[9] One way of looking at good or bad habits is in terms of whether we "have" ourselves (e.g., in skills) or whether we are "had" (e.g., in addictions)—although there is a fusion of the two, having and being had, in a passion for excellence, possessing ourselves in being possessed by what is worthy in itself.[10]

The "habit" of art in the narrower sense of *techne* is similar to the habit of practical wisdom. It is intelligent alertness to possible gestalten *(logoi)*, forms that can be brought into being externally. Aristotle defines *techne* as a habit (i.e., a mode of self-possession) concerned with making *meta logou alethou*.[11] We can see to what extent translation is interpretation by considering some possible renderings of this phrase. One is "involving a true course of reasoning";[12] another, "with true reason";[13] and again, "a rational quality . . . that reasons truly."[14] Antecedent to these we have Aquinas's *recta ratio factibilium*, "right reason regarding what can be made."[15] Interpreting what is involved in "a rational quality" or "right reason" and close to the phenomena of actual artistic production would be "according to the manifest togetherness of things." *Aletheia*, usually translated as "truth" and understood as correctness or rightness, actually involves a coming into presence of a form. Literally it means unconcealment.[16] *Logos*, rooted in *legein*, to gather, to read, involves a togetherness, a set of connections. The Latin *ratio* comes directly into English as *ratio*, or a set of relations, and indirectly as *reason*, which is actually a matter of seeing the peculiar relations that constitute things. Art is thus the habit of seeing connections for making. Reasoning is involved, but it is seeing that togetherness that is crucial. Elder Olson suggests that art involves a peculiar sort of hypothetical reasoning that works from whole to parts: granted a given whole, the idea of a possible form to be made, one proceeds to figure out how to bring it into actual materials.[17] So art involves two features: (1) a manifest togetherness, an idea as a possibility for shaping, and (2) a figuring out of the steps required to bring it into being. Aristotle will indicate something of the basic character of the manifest togetherness operative in one of the art forms in his *Poetics*, parts of which we will consider later.

Art as *techne* is often divided into useful and fine art, though the division overlaps in certain cases: for example, in the case of good design in architecture, utensils, furniture, clothing, and so forth, which Plato has Socrates advocate in the *Republic*. But the ancients had no significant distinction between useful and fine art. The fine is a desirable quality of whatever has been made, no matter how utilitarian. For Aristotle as well as for Plato, both aspects, the fine and the strictly utilitarian, are useful in effecting the tuning of psychic disposition. The good and the beautiful tended to coincide.

Almost all of Aristotle's aesthetic remarks turn on production and the character of the products. However, he makes observations in relation to temperance that have significant implications for aesthetic appreciation. Temperance *(sophrosune)*, he claims, is rooted in *sodzousa ten phronesin*, keeping your head, being able to direct yourself thoughtfully, preserving practical wisdom.[18] He notes that intemperance, as a matter of excess in sensuous indulgence, is not located in seeing or hearing, the typical "aesthetic" senses, nor, for that matter in smelling or even in tasting as such. One cannot be overindulgent in looking at paintings or sculptural pieces or the beauties of nature. Nor can one be overindulgent in hearing music or appreciating odors or developing a cultivated palate for food or wine. Intemperance, he notes, can be present in these matters only indirectly insofar as, in effect, the vegetatively based desires are involved (i.e., the desires linked to nourishment and reproduction). Here we can be intemperate by destroying our bodily base, clouding our ability to direct ourselves intelligently, and failing to attend to the fine qualities of things. Aristotle locates the problem of intemperance in tactility, though even here he refers to refined pleasures such as massages and warm baths, which, apart from other possible connections, pose no direct problem for temperance. He shows by contrast what an aesthetic experience is by noting that a dog loves the sight and smell of a rabbit, but only in connection with his desire to eat.

Kant will refer to a similar phenomenon in his often misunderstood notion of "disinterested satisfaction," which he connects to an "unconstrained favoring."[19] One is not forced by antecedent organic need to attend to the object. One attends freely to the fine qualities of the thing's presentation.

## Nature Illumined by Art: Plato and Aristotle

As I also noted in the introduction, the broad contrast between art and nature is not the last word. Both Plato and Aristotle, and later, Kant, Schelling, Schopenhauer, and Nietzsche, use the analysis of art to illuminate nature. For Plato, according to the mythos of the *Timaeus*, nature itself is the product of divine art: the cosmic demiurge looks to the eternal Ideas and persuades the Receptacle, the restless chaos of space-time, like the artist's clay, to take on intelligible form.[20]

Aristotle approaches nature differently, but takes his point of departure from an analysis of *techne*. He distinguishes four types of explanatory factor, four distinct strands, four "causes" or "(be)causes" *(aitiai)* that answer the question, Why did this occur? The artist is the one who brings about the work of art by his action: he is what comes to be called the efficient cause *(arche)*. He works in terms of an idea that he intends to realize for a purpose that may or may not coincide with the work of art (e.g., he intends the work in order to pay his bills). The goal, posed initially as a creative idea, together with the purpose, are spoken of as the final cause, or *telos*, that for the sake of which something happens. The stuff the artist works with is the "material cause" *(hule,* lit., wood) which helps determine the quality of the finished product. Finally, the idea as realized in the material is the "formal cause" *(morphe,* lit., shape, and *eidos,* or intelligible look). The efficient and final causes are here "extrinsic causes" vis-à-vis the work of art. The material and formal causes are, by contrast, "intrinsic causes."[21]

Now artifaction *(techne)* occurs within the framework provided by nature *(phusis)*, both the nature of the materials and of the artist himself as a product of a natural process. The artistic form, though ultimately immanent in the natural material, is imposed on it. The material itself has a natural form that is intrinsic to it and nonimposed. It developed as a process of nature. Its immanent natural form is a certain proportion of elements, describable in a formula *(logos)*.[22] The elements—fire, air, earth, and water—are determinate forms that are subjectible to change. The basis of that subjectibility to change is what Aristotle calls *prote hule*, or prime matter, a pure potency, not empirically observable the way the elements are. It functions the way Plato's Receptacle functions, as a principle of both change and the multipliability of Form in a plurality of instances throughout the appropriate places and times.

The artist himself has a nature, the biological-transcendent, culture-creating nature described above. That nature is understood by Aristotle in terms of the immanentization of all four causal factors. The material cause involves the elements, but shaped through a developmental process by the psyche as entelechy, a self-formative principle that has its end within itself *(en telos echeia)*.[23] The biogenetic process involves the gathering of the elements into organs that are the instruments *(organoi)* for the activation of the psychic potentialities. The process heads toward the fully functional adulthood of the organism. Organs exhibit the same structural principles as the whole organism. The eye, for example, involves certain proportions of the elements "informed" by the unseeable power of seeing, both of which—observable organ and power of seeing—are fulfilled in actual (unseeable) seeing as the goal of the biogenetic process.[24] In the human case, the sensory furnishes the materials to be penetrated intelligently for the purpose of knowing and acting as a higher, ultimate goal, or telos (e.g., to understand the eyeball as an organ governed by the power of seeing). The psyche is the immanent formal, efficient, and final cause that gathers the material elements about itself; the psyche is the immanent artisan of its own developed nature as enmattered form.

Once again, then, as in Plato, art furnishes the starting point for the analysis of nature. However, in Aristotle's case, there is no external divine artisan, only immanent natures seeking their ends and shaping materials for realizing those ends. An Aristotelian god is a Pure Exemplar for those natures, a kind of telos rather than an agent. The world goes on because each nature seeks to be as like the divine as its nature allows: in the case of all material things, being in its proper place; in the case of all living things, being fully actualized and being immortal through reproduction; in the case of all animals, being aware and experiencing satisfaction; and in the case of all humans, being present to themselves as possessing cognitively the intelligible order of things.[25] Later, in Schelling, the underlying Artist is considered to work like the human artist, out of the inspiration of his unconscious and out of a need to discover himself in his creation. In Schopenhauer, as in Nietzsche, the underlying Cause, the One, is entirely blind, completely unconscious and brings forth the world by necessity; it should thus no longer be called God or a god.[26]

## *Art as Imitation*

As did Plato, Aristotle speaks of art as imitation. Art is related to nature not only for its materials but also for its forms. The form manifest for making "imitates" natural form. Here, however, *natural* has an extended meaning that includes every given, natural or man-made. Art has its origin in a native tendency to mimic that is found especially in children and is the chief means by which they learn. Children imitate their parents and thus learn to speak and behave in conventional ways. They imitate animals and even inanimate things and thus come to have an empathetic sense of the world. And humans learn not only by producing imitations, but also by attending to them. However, even when we do not recognize the object imitated, we naturally delight in the qualities of the presentation: the colors, the rhythms, the harmonies.[27]

Aristotle here distinguishes clearly the mirroring, referential function of art from the aesthetic form of the vehicle of reference. This form is found in the peculiar togetherness of the elements of the sensory presentation, its design properties. As in Plato, there is some question about how that last tendency might be annexed to imitation. Recall, Plato criticized the poets first of all in terms of verbal reference: they should not provide bad civic examples. He went on to consider types of melody and rhythm, the timbre of instruments, and the modes of presentation (narrative or dramatic). The consideration of melody, rhythm, and timbre turns more on the question of sensuous form. Plato, for one, called for a certain type of sensuous form, one exhibiting good (read: Apollonian) design properties in clothing, buildings, and utensils that are not themselves "imitations" but realities in their own right. If we consider instrumental music (untitled), we have *the* nonrepresentational form of art. But, Plato noted, through rhythm and harmony of sensuous form, the disposition of the soul is profoundly transformed.[28]

Aristotle picks up the same notion in his distinction here between imitation as a means of learning and delight in sensuous form as the twin origins of art. In the case of imitations that are to be considered artistic, fully aesthetic form must combine reference (imitation in the more obvious sense—i.e., as representation) and sensuous form, so that the latter is suitable to the former. But the notion of sensuous form as distinct from reference also has an imitative role for Aristotle. In what surprises modern readers, who would expect exactly the opposite, music, he says, is the most imitative of art forms. What it imitates is ethos, usually translated somewhat one-sidedly as "character."[29] Character involves that preconscious directedness of our dispositions out of which we spontaneously act: the sum total of our habits as they rise up to the level of felt tendency to act. Ethos as feeling and mood is what Aristotle has in mind with his remark on music's imitative character. Plato had spoken of the need for a blend of gymnastic and music in order to establish a kind of prereflective rationality of disposition. The organism itself was for him a model of a rational system: the coherence over time and space of a complex multiplicity of factors. It furnishes, according to Aristotle, an invariant ground for our action. Above it rises what he calls the ethos level, the level of emotions persuadable by reason that establishes character.[30] Plato refers to the same level as that of the desirous and the spirited parts of the soul. Harmonious sensuous form linked with reference into a full aesthetic form balances that dispositional ground and thus establishes another mode of rationality at this prereflective level of felt disposition. When fully reflective rationality begins to dawn, it will find a welcome matrix in such a disposition. For Aristotle, as for Plato, music, whether linked to the word and thus to overt reference or not, in its purely aesthetic modality produces harmony or disharmony in the psychic disposition to act.

We might note that music is not reduced to the causal factors involved in wave production. Like all sense qualities, for Aristotle, as for Plato, sound comes into being only in relation to perceivers, though that does not make it "merely subjective." It is a relation of manifestness of things to perceivers, establishing a novel "between" that overrides the modern subject-object dichotomy.[31] According to the latter, sound waves produce inner, subjective effects contained within the nervous system of the perceiver, leaving the problem of how we get to know the "objective" sound waves.[32] For Aristotle the imitative character of music lies in the effects it produces: feelings like those given by nature or culture (e.g., sorrow, joy, placidity, love, vigor, wrath). It is thus not the sound as such that is imitative but the emotional reverberations it sets up "in" us. Aesthetic form produces surrogate emotions. I should note, as Heidegger will later, that emotions, like observable sensory features of things, are not simply inner subjective experiences but ways in which we participate in the "life" of other entities, persons, or things—the way we are attuned to them. Emotions *(ethe)* are ways of opening onto the world, ways of disclosure.[33] What they disclose, I would claim, is the "inwardness" of the other, its wholeness, its surplus beyond what we cognitively apprehend, the mystery of its being, which is the way it belongs to the totality. But then, of course, we would have to consider emotions, not as raw animal feelings, but as distinctively human ways of feeling, rooted in an animal base but modified in terms of our founding reference to the totality as mediated by culture. Considering this dimension of aesthetic form, of the mode of presentation involved in all art, Walter Pater would later remark—as I noted in the introduction—that all art seeks the status of music as sheer play with the rhythmic and harmonic combinatory possibilities of its sensuous medium.[34] But both Plato and Aristotle note that such play produces states of mind like those produced by both natural and nonartistic cultural situations. It is these states of mind that art imitates.

Aristotle further remarks that art in general partially imitates and partially completes nature.[35] There are several ways in which this seems to occur. First, recalling that *techne* covers both useful art and what we today would call fine art, we could see art as an extension of the powers of human nature. The invention of tools in general enhances the powers nature already provided to humans. Aristotle notes the physiological inferiority of humans—animals have claws and wings for fight and flight. But humans have also by nature that peculiar relation of intelligence and hand—that "tool of tools"—that allows art to supplement what we lack by nature.[36] But specifically in fine art, there are at least four ways in which art goes beyond what is given by nature. First, in that it involves an exploration of the possible, art exhibits an understanding of the universal, that which would be the same under similar circumstances. Aristotle sees art as thereby more philosophic than history, which only presents the actual.[37] The materials of such exploration, however, are those provided by human experience, which is thus "imitated" by art but also surpassed in the direction of the possible. That gives a kind of generic sense of artistic imitation and completion that is realized in different ways. Even in the most fantastic fiction (e.g., in the Hobbit stories of Tolkien) the author works in a way analogous to the geometer. Once the characters and setting are laid down, the novel proceeds like a kind of deduction from these premises. It fails if it does not adhere to its premises. And what appears through such constructions are universal truths about human experience. In the Hobbit stories, you come into the presence of quest, honesty, the omnipresence of evil, and the like; and your understanding is thereby enriched in a concrete way. Indeed, the exploration of the fictively possible frees the universals immanent in human experience from the contingencies of their usual instantiations in order to allow them to stand forth more clearly.

In a second and more specific sense, art partly imitates and partly completes nature in that some forms of art present men, not as they are, but as they should be: art presents the obligatory. Aristotle reports here on Sophocles' claim.[38] Of course, one could say that art imitates (i.e., represents) nature as both the possible and the obligatory. Here *nature* is not in contrast to *history* but includes all actual occurrence. But in neither case does art merely reproduce surface, as Plato's mirror example might suggest. In Aristotle's sense, the representation of the possible and the obligatory would be a "completion" of nature, which is partially imitated in the construction of the work of art because the basis for the construction lies in knowledge of actual human life. The possibility art explores here is the moral ought.

In a third sense of imitation and completion, expressed in Schopenhauer and found originally in Polyclitus's Spearbearer (the *Doriphoros*) as a canon for treating the human body sculpturally (a sense Aristotle does not directly treat), art discerns certain ideal tendencies in actual physical forms and gives them embodiment in a work.[39] The actual human body could be considered the way a geometer considers actual triangles. Actual triangles can be compared as more or less adequate approximations to what is mentally projected as perfect triangularity. So Polyclitus, basing his work on the comparative study of actual human proportions running in tandem with a doctrine of certain harmonic proportional relations, projected an ideal human form for sculptors. The possibility art explores here is the physiological ideal, which Kant will explore in another way under the notion of "the ideal of beauty."[40]

The exploration of the moral ought and of ideal physiological proportions parallels the emergence of geometry as the projection of ideal figures and Plato's deliberately parallel projection of ideal humanness and of typical deviations from that ideal, both based on the hierarchy of human psychic structure. One might say that what is typically Greek is the power of this ideal-typical projection in geometry, in ethics, in sculpture, and in poetry.

In a fourth sense of imitation and completion, which gives the generic difference in the exploration of the possible that fine art explores, Aristotle calls attention to what we might call the *organicity* of the work of art, perhaps *the* defining criterion of art. An organism is a complex, integrated whole, a coherently functioning, harmonic system, each part of which requires all the others. So the organic character of a work of art means that each part ought to be such that its elimination would affect the fundamental character of the work. If the elimination of a part makes no essential difference to the character of the work, the part is aesthetically superfluous. If something essential to the character of the work is missing, there is aesthetic defect.[41] During the Renaissance, Alberti reformulated this principle for architecture.[42] By the criterion of organicity, most of what occurs in an actual event would be left out of its retelling in a story. In storytelling one picks out only the details that are relevant to the overall development of the story line. Actually mirroring the events dramatically would take as long as the events. Telling all the details of the events would be interminably longer. There are an amazingly complex set of factors existent and happening each second in an interpersonal exchange. Most are not relevant to the story. The attempt at full mirroring would be tedious rather than artistic. (Consider here the implausibility of the basic premise of the film *The Truman Show*.) The same could be said of a painting or a sculptural piece. The artistic sense of form is a peculiar capacity for abstraction from the actual even in strictly representational art. But then we are back to the consideration of aesthetic form playing in tandem with imitative reference. The peculiar togetherness of sensuous form in the case of untitled instrumental music and the peculiar togetherness of aesthetic form and reference in the representational arts is what is distinctively artistic. That togetherness has the character of organicity. The ability to grasp and bring into being gestalten having that character, making according to such a "manifest togetherness," is fine art. Such art thus imitates nature's productive organicity, rooted in and thus corresponding to the organic rhythmicity of human existence.

Aristotle gives piecemeal reference to the modes of imitation in different art forms. Music, as I have already noted, imitates character, which is the sum total of our dispositions to act. Music gives us dispositional states similar to their real counterparts. The difference, of course, lies in the non-real character of the musical context. By that I mean that through performance a different world is added to the world of everyday experience. Music might induce longing or exultation or brooding depression or peacefulness, or any other mood whose real objects are not present. There is no beloved or victory or defeat or quiet achievement; but we are given to feel as if there were such in our lives. This is true whether the music in question is purely instrumental and without a title, is titled or, indeed, is fully "referenced" by accompanying a text. Drama, instrumentally accompanied or not, imitates character (again ethos), but character as interplaying with character through action and diction, in deeds and words.[43] I will return to that when I deal with Aristotle's analysis of tragedy, below.

By contrast with music, Aristotle claims that painting does not imitate ethos but only gives signs of it.[44] What it might imitate (i.e., mirror) would be sensuous surface, which might be adequate in the case of landscape, though here too, as in the case of photography, what makes it aesthetic is not exactitude of representation but frame and balance of shapes and colors, light and dark. The immediacy of musical experience reproduces the dispositional state underlying the surface portrait. The immediacy of a portrait reproduces surface but expresses the inwardness of disposition. What is peculiar here is the notion of sensuous surface because, in the case of the human being especially, its very character, particularly as found in the face, is to be expressive of inward, psychic disposition. It is modern Positivism that scrubs the surface clean of all expressivity and claims to find in sensuousness referred to sensuousness the whole meaning of things as far as our access to them is concerned.

## Division of the Performing Arts

In the beginning of his *Poetics*, Aristotle locates his chief subject matter, which was to be drama, both tragic and comic, within a division of the performing arts.[45] The basis for the division seems to lie in some of the basic characteristics of language, namely reference as carried by rhythmic and sonorous qualities. If we concentrate on rhythm alone and develop it, we have the basis for dance. If we isolate sonorousness and rhythm, we have the basis for instrumental music. Exclusive concentration on reference leads to ordinary prose, where sensuous form is lost in the reference. The process of learning to speak is parallel to learning to swing a golf club: one forgets about the club, indwells in it the way one indwells in his own body, and focuses attention on the ball. So in ordinary prose the words are defocused in terms of the what they make manifest. Finally, if we attend simultaneously to all the features—reference, rhythm, and melody—we have the basis for poetry. Here the reference is fully embodied in such a way that the rhythmic and sonorous qualities built into or accompanying the reference come into greater prominence and bring the referent into fuller presence. Think here of the difference musical background makes to a suspenseful or romantic movie. The fit between the visual presence and the musical background enhances the character of our participative presence. It is in such a context that drama, whether comic or tragic, fits.

Poetry for Aristotle's purposes in the *Poetics* is divided into serious and comic, and the former into epic and tragedy.[46] Epic and tragedy are differentiated in several ways. Epic presents a series of incidents covering a long time span, whereas tragedy focuses on one event, usually within a single day. Epic is narrated, while tragedy is enacted or "imitated." Epic is presented in a single meter, tragedy in several. Aristotle considers comedy a species of the inferior, indeed of the ugly, dealing with characters lower than the average type, whereas epic and tragedy deal with the higher character types.

In his *Politics* Aristotle discusses three roles for music: *paidia,* or amusement useful for relaxation (e.g., sleep, drink, and dancing); *paideia,* or education in virtue through pleasure in excellence; and *diagoge* and *phronesis*—a seemingly odd conjunction, since *diagoge* means a course of life or even pastime, though its linkage with practical wisdom places it significantly above *paidia.*[47] Amusement can be both relief from toil and a harmless end in itself. In its latter function, it is suited to the ends of human life. But beyond that, music contributes to ethical formation, for "virtue consists in rejoicing and loving and hating aright" and music produces those dispositions in us. It creates enthusiasm and sympathy and thus aids in developing the power of forming right judgments. It is in this context that Aristotle remarks that music is the most imitative of the arts as far as the fostering of ethos or felt disposition is concerned.[48] This is possible since the soul is, or at least possesses, harmony.

Now, his focus is on hearing the music, not playing. He regards the latter as fit only for slaves, and the higher class should only learn to play enough to be able to judge the performance of others. But whether as performer or member of an audience, one should be so cultivated as to be able to feel delight, not only in common music, which slaves, children, and even some animals can appreciate, but also and especially in "nobly beautiful *(kaloi)* melodies and rhythms."[49] Instruments that require great skill, such as the flute and the harp, should not be part of *paideia* because practice in these instruments takes too much time away from higher things. Besides, the flute is too exciting and one should only listen to it as furnishing relief from the passions—presumably part of the relief from toil referred to earlier. For Aristotle, the other problem with the flute is that one cannot use the voice with it, which seems related to what Plato had one of his characters advance in his *Laws,* namely that music without words is meaningless.

## The Definition of Tragedy

Aristotle defines tragedy as "the imitation of an action that is serious or heroic *[spoudaios]*, complete, having magnitude, in dramatic not narrative form, using language with pleasant accessories, to arouse pity and fear with a view toward their purgation."[50] I have already spoken of imitation. Let us focus first on action *(praxis)*. Analytical philosophy distinguishes and relates action and motion.[51] When my hand goes up, there is motion governed by mechanical laws. It may or may not be action, depending on whether it gives expression to the human life of meaning that animates the purely physical. Peter Sellers's Dr. Strangelove (in the film of the same name, 1964) deliberately restrains with his left hand his right hand's tendency to go up automatically in a *Sieg heil!* salute. The former is action, the latter mechanical motion—though, since Sellers is imitating the character, the depiction of pure motion is also action. Action is the level of meaning embodied in but surmounting the level of physical laws. Such action, however, is typically interaction between people, so that meaning here exists in the interplay and not in some purely private interiority.[52] One attends from one's own body to the other person(s) and the goals we share or about which we struggle. In either case, action takes place in a shared world of meaning. It is the realm of interaction with which tragedy deals.

The Greek adjective for "serious" or "heroic" *(spoudaios)* describes one of the characteristics that sets tragedy off from comedy. This may be linked to Aristotle's observation that tragedy deals with characters above the ordinary—hence "heroic." The nature of the seriousness is further specified by the emotions of pity and fear that are aroused by tragic performance. The interaction imitated constitutes a single action capable of being excised from the (fictional) whole life spans of the agents involved. As an action it itself has an organic wholeness: a definite beginning and a definite end tied to the beginning, not just chronologically but in terms of meaning.[53] The transition from one to the other constitutes a coherent singleness in spite of the multiplicity of its episodes.

*Teleios* (completeness) is from *telos* (goal), underscoring the direction of a process that furnishes its final explanation. The fully functional adult organism is the telos of the biogenetic process brought about by the psyche as *entelecheia* (having its end within itself). That is why a good "imitation" is "like an organism."

The reference to magnitude *(megethos)* is explained in terms of the ability of the ideal spectator to take in the object as a whole. Aristotle links that with beauty as relative to the perceiver, appealing to spatial size to illuminate the temporal. Too minute a creature cannot be appreciated, nor can that which is of vast size (he suggests something like 1,000 miles long).[54] So the beauty of a drama stands between too short and too long, relative to the ideal spectator. Here we have an anticipation of an aesthetic distinction Kant will make central to his analysis: the distinction between the beautiful and the sublime. The beautiful is rooted in forms we can take in, the sublime in those that exceed our capacity.[55]

The qualification "in dramatic not narrative form" underscores the simultaneous appeal to the eyes and the ears in dramatic performance, as distinct from the purely auditory appeal of narration, though obviously one might listen to a reading of a drama or actually read the work silently to oneself—a more modern practice, especially fostered by "speed reading." Dramatic performance gives a more holistic imitation than does a reading—something that Plato has Socrates repudiate at one stage of the analysis in the *Republic*. In fact, Socrates repudiates even dramatic reading, insofar as the reader enters into the characters and becomes (at least a verbal) actor.

The discussion of language focuses on the particular embellishments of language proper to poetry. But it is located in a more elementary analysis of language. Aristotle presents a hierarchical list of the aspects of language taken up into discourse.[56] First of all, like an organism, spoken discourse has its elements *(stoikeia)*, based on the sonorous possibilities of the human oral cavity: vowels and consonants (which "sound together with" —*con-sonare*—the vowels by "clipping" them in various ways). Their elementary combination yields syllables. Thus far the analysis is phonological. Next we reach the semantic level, the level of meanings. At the lowest level of meaning we have what the medievals will call the syncategorematic units which work together with *(syn)* the categories. Aristotle lists articles and "joints" (the latter have never been clearly identified). The categories or basic predicates are the lexical units of atemporal nouns set into temporal contexts by verbs. Nouns and verbs together are subjected to inflection *(ptosis):* declensions (persons and cases) and conjugations (tenses, moods, and the like). The analytical hierarchy brings us to the sentence *(logos)* as the locus of realized meanings.

As Plato presented us with a preliminary eidetic analysis of poetic *musike* (reference, manner, rhythm, melody, style, and instrumental timbre), so Aristotle presents us with a preliminary eidetic analysis of spoken language. In this treatment of the relation between the physical components of sound and the intentional components of meaning we find a direct expression of the body-mind relation—indeed it is one enactment of that relation. As in the organism visible material is gathered in such a way as to be expressive of the underlying psyche, so in language the physical vehicle, organized and inhabited by the soul, is subsidiary to the expression and reception of meaningful discourse as contact of mind to mind. But in poetry, mind and body, meaning and sound, are joined through the mediation of sound elaborated by musical harmony. Here soul in the full sense joins together intellect and body.

But all this is preliminary to the treatment of linguistic embellishment, Aristotle's primary focus here. He calls again for the mean, this time between the clarity of ordinary prose and the elevation of ornamental language: poetry needs the right mix of the two, both in order to contact ordinary meanings and to support the sense of elevation above the ordinary in the heroic characters presented.[57] Metaphor receives special attention here as the peculiar *alethes logos,* the special manifest togetherness that is the mark of genius *(euphuia).*[58] Hitting upon the novel expression that combines sameness and difference in such a way as to heighten the presence of the object, lifting it out of everyday manifestness, is one of the chief attributes of poetic *techne.* The pleasant accessories to language might also include musical accompaniment, used primarily in the choral odes that separate the various dramatic episodes.

The arousal of pity and fear with a view toward their purgation *(katharsis)* gives the main effect as well as the final purpose of tragedy in Aristotle's treatment. He explains this in his *Politics* by reference to certain religious rituals.[59] The sacred melodies induce frenzy, which releases the participants from the governing power of emotions like pity and fear. Their souls, he says, are lightened and delighted. Similarly, tragic performance provides an innocent cathartic pleasure. Here Aristotle seems to oppose the position advanced by Socrates in the *Republic* that the theatrical experience of emotions makes us all the more subject to them, and being subject to emotions makes it more difficult to discern the truth.[60] According to Aristotle's reading, the experience of a tragic performance does the opposite. And perhaps it does so by way of inoculating us against their absolute sway so that we might see clearly and judge rightly: we get a taste of pitiable and fearful situations, experiencing emotions that (as Aristotle said of music in general) "hardly fall short of the actual affections"—all the while knowing that the situations contemplated are fictional and thus not at all threatening either to the actors or to the audience. But there is further—though Aristotle does not mention it in the *Poetics*—the contemplation of the noble discussed in the *Nicomachean Ethics*.[61] Nobility is measured by how the character bears up under adversity. The release from pity and fear clears the ground for "the understanding of the universal" with regard to human action available through the poet's vision of the noble character and its dramatic enactment.

There is a second teleological element involved in Aristotle's treatment of tragedy. The art form has a historical genesis that has developed over time to reach what Aristotle calls "its natural form."[62] Tragedy begins in the Dionysiac religious festivals that consist in drinking and dancing to frenzy. The dancers form a circle, which constitutes a sacred space cut off from the secular everyday world. They represent satyrs—half-goat, half-human—brought to a state of high sexual excitement by the rituals. These goat songs *(tragoidiai)* gave the name to tragedy. At the beginning of the songs, and sometimes also between them, the leader recited stories of gods and heroes. The stories came to take on central importance. Aeschylus, the first of the great tragedians, diminished the role of the chorus, established the centrality of a single story, and brought two major actors onto the stage formed by the choral ring. Sophocles added the third character, along with scenery. For Aristotle, that brought tragedy to its fully mature natural form. Once brought to that level, it can fill its cathartic function most fully. What is curious about the claim to a natural form here is the apparent assimilation of culture to nature. Aristotle also speaks of different types of meter as naturally fitted to different forms of poetry.[63] In the interplay between various human faculties lie distinctive natural possibilities that require a fairly long cultural evolution, often spanning many generations, before they reach maturity. Such is the case likewise with the sciences. Given Aristotle's commitment to the eternity of species, for him humankind always existed and thus must have lost and found the sciences and the arts again and again.[64] That leads him to the position that mythology is decayed philosophy (or, alternatively, that philosophy is sublimated, purified mythology). Given evolution and given the development of science and technology as well as the emergence of different artistic genres and styles since Aristotle, one would have to extend considerably his notion of nature as applied to culture.

But to return to tragedy: Aristotle applies his form-matter analysis to it, distinguishing material parts, formal parts, and the overall form or 'soul' of tragedy as a third sense of telos.[65] The material parts are analogous to our own bodily components: they are the prologue followed by the first choral ode, called the parode, followed by the episodes of the play that are separated by various odes, culminating with the exode as the chorus leaves the stage.[66] The formal parts are—all but one—like our various functions, some more basically physical, some more basically psychological. They are mythos, character, thought, diction, melody, and spectacle.[67] *Charakter* is literally the stamp given to a person by antecedent conditions, internal and external. It involves the person's felt disposition to behave. Here it refers to the whole psychophysical agent whose deepest dimension is thought embodied particularly in diction, but also in visible action. Melody and spectacle provide support and setting for the action that occurs in the interplay between these components. But the animating principle, that which draws the whole together into unity, the "soul" of tragedy, is the mythos. Sometimes *mythos* is translated as "plot"; but plot is too skimpy a notion, a mere skeleton, as it were. Like psyche, whose work it is, mythos here is no disembodied abstraction, but the togetherness of the psychophysical whole, articulated down to its least member. The real dramatic art is the ability to see and display the organic togetherness of all the components, rhythmically paced, rising to the essential turning point, and unraveling to its organic conclusion in such a way as to arouse pity and fear in the audience and leave the spectators purged so that they might be able to contemplate the universal truths of the noble in action.

## Response

Aristotle's genius lay in his ability both to discern fine distinctions within the region of experience and to develop the inferences to what might stand beyond that field as its ground. He knew how, in Plato's terms, to carve along the joints of any region he explored and thus to distinguish regions for further exploration in the specialized sciences.[68]

Though, as basically a biological thinker, he was particularly intent on exploring the sensorily given, nonetheless, the sensorily given is always linked to the fact that the explorer, the human soul, "is, in a way, all things" (i.e., is always referred, beyond the sensory as such, to the totality within which the sensory is to be located). Aristotle exhibits the same basic structural analysis of the frame of human nature I presented in my introduction. Biologically based sensa he views fundamentally as relations of manifestness between a needy organism and a material being in the environment. But in the case of human awareness the sensory is found within a mind referred to the whole. That involves being able to take the sensory as the expressive indicator of the ontological depth of the sensorily given thing; and that, in turn, involves apprehending the intelligible, universal form as the proximate ground of the peculiar mode of sensory givenness in each case; that, finally, involves the apprehension of Pure Form as Self-Thinking Thought, as the self-presence of Form toward which all sensorily given being aspires as Primal Exemplar of actuality, eternality, and joy in the self-presence of the Whole. By reading the sensorily given in terms of its own expressivity based on the human reference to the Whole, Aristotle is able to locate wholeness, as with Plato, in the One/Good, which all things imitate. But, beyond Plato's own "idealism," Aristotle develops an idealism that reads the One/Good as the self-presence of Form. In the world we occupy, self-presence, in its various modalities, is not immediately given, but is the term of process. The sensorily given and we ourselves as correlate to it begin more as ordered bundles of active potentialities aimed at their integral actuation.

In that ultimate context, art is viewed, along with nature, as a source of coming into being. I have followed Aristotle's divisions in my introductory treatment of the various meanings of the term *art*. After being set over against *theoria* as the mirroring of the eternal order, art as *techne* is subdivided into the overarching political art of shaping human life (within which falls everything humans bring into being) and the art of shaping the environment. Aristotle enables us to extend the analysis of artifaction to an understanding of the nature it presupposes: the nature of the artist as a human being and the nature of the materials shaped. Based on a causal analysis of what is involved in artifaction, both the nature of the materials and the nature of the artist are viewed as form given to antecedent materials. In living things this takes place according to a teleological hierarchy of levels in which the lower levels are presupposed and subsumed by the higher, and in which the lowest is a level of pure passive potentiality to be shaped, at the antipode to the full actuality of Self-Thinking Thought.

Art in general is a possibility of human nature that supplements that which nature, both inside and outside us, provides. It involves the apprehension of a gestalt as a possibility for shaping and apprehension of the steps needed to bring it into being. More specific factors are involved in bringing particular art forms into being. In poetry, the focus of Aristotle's aesthetic analysis, he points to the sensitive, indeed even ecstatic character of genius (literally the ability to stand outside oneself) needed to indwell in the characters in order to give expression to the ethos or inward disposition expressed in their gestures, but also to see unusual sameness in differences that lies at the basis of the invention of one of the chief vehicles of poetic expression: the metaphor. And the general capacity involved in poetic creation is the capacity to grasp and form the plot as the concrete integral togetherness of all the factors involved in a piece, the vital soul of dramatic art, a concrete instance of the principle of organicity.

We might pursue here Aristotle's causal analysis of artifaction. Having distinguished the causal factors is one thing: material to be shaped, actual shaping, form to be brought into being, and reason for the shaping. The clarification of how they actually function is another. What is the relation between the extrinsic formal cause (the artist's idea) and the material cause (the stuff to be shaped)? That depends in part on the status of the idea. Perhaps at times it comes full-blown into mind, as Mozart is said to have conceived some of his pieces.[69] At other times it may come to clarity after a more or less lengthy process of playing with the idea in mind. Again, it may begin only as an impulsion, a sense of direction that grows and comes to fuller clarity as one works with the materials.[70] The measure of a mind here, as in any other region, is the quickness with which it comes to see the whole, to grasp significant unity in what otherwise would be a scattered multiplicity, to envisage form.

Furthermore, the relation of the idea to the materials is different in different art forms. In the plastic arts it is often the case that the materials talk back in the process of formation. In sculpture, shaping one way limits the possibilities for the next step; and especially with wood or marble, there is necessarily a process of discovering the limits as one uncovers the grain in the process of working the idea into the materials. In painting, laying on one color sets up tensions with other colors. Even in drawing, a line charges the space in which it is drawn and thus sets aesthetic limits to the next step. And in the creation of characters in the novel, their initial delineation leads them to object to any attempt to force them in a direction contrary to their constitution. Sensitivity to the play between the given and achieved factors on the one hand and the aura of possibilities in their significant relations on the other is crucial to every process of artistic shaping.

One might also inquire into the source of artistic ideas. How much is technical skill involved, how much a certain natural giftedness? To be a musical composer, one needs a developed sense of musical form and a fertile sense of novel possibilities similar to what is involved in a more restricted way in musical performance. A musician may learn to play according to a metronome; but unless one advances beyond that level, one never plays with the dynamics born of real human-felt inhabitance of a piece expressed in the right combination of louder and softer, faster and slower execution as they are relevant to the aesthetic unity of the whole piece. One arrives at that level only by being open in the moment of execution to the reception of whatever gifts one might have for musical performance. There is then the possibility of "inspired" playing that participates in the "vision" of the composer.

Aristotle, I said, exhibits a fine capacity to carve the field of experience and what it implies along the joints provided by nature. He is a master of analytic divisions. He locates poetry, the object of his one major treatise in aesthetics, within a division of the performing arts, which he seems to derive from, or at least relate to, aspects involved in linguistic expression: sonorousness, rhythm, and reference. Rhythm is the basis of dance; linked with sonorousness, it is the basis for instrumental music; both linked with reference, the basis for poetry. In discussing poetic diction, he analyzes language, as a specific instance of the body-mind relation, down to its physical units in the elements of sound and up to the various levels on which meaning enters into sound, culminating in the unity of discourse with felt inhabitance created in a poem. Aristotle thus not only situates poetry within the larger frameworks of the other arts and within a preliminary investigation of the nature of language, he also locates both within the still larger framework of human structure as referred to the cosmos that has been our primary focus from the very beginning.

He positions the tragic art within a division of poetry and analyzes it into its parts, both formal, pervasive parts, and material or sequential parts. As Plato provided us with the beginnings of an eidetic analysis of music, so Aristotle provides us with a parallel eidetic analysis of tragedy and, indeed, of language arts. He draws the whole together by an encompassing definition that finds its soul in the plot and its end in the catharsis of the audience. Unfortunately, Aristotle says very little about catharsis. And focus upon it leads to the absence of any reference to what many testify to in the experience of tragic drama: spiritual illumination. Perhaps purgation receives what seems to be a disproportionate emphasis because the passions stand in the way of facing, clearly and rationally, the tragic situation. But given Aristotle's powerful theoretical interests, one would have thought that the dimension of insight would have been central to his consideration here. One has to dredge them up by his introductory and undeveloped notion that poetry is more philosophical than history because it explores the possible and thus involves knowledge of the universal. However, perhaps the two aspects—spiritual illumination and purgation of pity and fear after their evocation—might be linked by the following observation. It is one thing to develop devices for arousing passions (one thinks of many of Stephen King's writings and the movies based on them); it is another to produce a work characterized by organicity. Following tragic art involves apprehending the organic gestalt of the emplotment. (One misunderstands the character of this apprehension in confusing it with being able to give the bare bones of a "plot summary." Paul Ricoeur understands better, I think, when he views emplotment, "the soul of tragedy" for Aristotle, as the whole organically functioning piece.)[71] Apprehension of the emplotment of a work encompasses and situates the experiences of pity and fear that follow from the artist's employment of the appropriate devices. Tragic depth follows from the depth of the apprehension expressed in the emplotment. One can be thus simultaneously purged and illumined by attention to the tragic performance. Consideration of the *Ethics* suggests that what emerges from tragic performance is the contemplation of the noble exhibited in the character's ability to bear up under extreme adverse conditions.

In focusing on tragedy, Aristotle shifts the focus of aesthetics from beauty and the Eros correlative to it to the horrible and the emotions of pity and fear aroused by it. Plato favors Apollo, but it is an Apollo as sublimated Dionysus, joyous and exultant in creating. Aristotle, one would have to say, favors a sober Apollo—all clarity, all order, but won by staring the Dionysus of destruction in the face. Distanced objectification of the horrible wins release from the disorienting emotions it evokes in order to allow us to contemplate the noble.

Aristotle's discussion of music is limited, even within the *Poetics*, where it seems to be confined to a consideration of meters. He does discuss its use in the *Politics*, but fails to attend to the way in which it aids in intellectual cultivation, which he only mentions. And he presents a challenge to the view that music is abstract as distinguished from imitative by claiming that music is the most imitative of the arts. In direct contrast to painting, which Plato presented in book 10 of his *Republic* as a clear example of mirroring, Aristotle considers music to imitate ethos or state of mind or mood by producing it in the audience, whereas painting can only give an exterior sign of such mood. I could, however, apply the same reasoning to painting and suggest, as Plato did in his passing treatment of it in the purged city, that the rhythm, harmony, play of colors, and distribution of forms likewise perform such "imitation" by evoking a mood appropriate to what is represented in "representational" painting or, just like purely instrumental music, evoking a mood without representation in "abstract" painting. I have cited Walter Pater's remark that all art seeks the status of music. It is remarkable how this runs like a refrain through modern artists. Kandinsky saw abstract art operating like music.[72] Gauguin claimed that color, like music, was able to express the inner force of nature by representing a mood rather than an object.[73] August Endell remarked that nonrepresentational art "can stimulate our souls as deeply as only the tones of music have been able to do."[74] Matisse claimed an analogy between the living harmony of colors in a painting and the relation of sounds in musical composition.[75] In Feininger, music suggested the rhythmic organization of his paintings.[76] It has also been suggested that in Art Nouveau generally, the symbolic power of the line corresponds to the melodious role of sound in Symbolist poetry.[77] Finally, Frank Lloyd Wright, as noted above, saw both music and architecture linked mathematically, while Schlegel saw architecture as "frozen music."[78]

In his treatment of tragedy, Aristotle introduces—though not by name—the central aesthetic notion of organicity by which we understand the mean between the extremes of aesthetic excess and aesthetic defect. Aristotle notes—and we should extend his observations to all art—that a tragedy should be so constructed that, as in an organism, nothing essential to its total operation is lacking and nothing is present that could be omitted without affecting that operation. Such organicity belongs both to the "soul" of the work's reference and the "body" of its sensory presentation in their integral togetherness as a unified meaning. In Kant this property will be located, along Aristotelian lines, in the *form* of the work of art.

Organicity relates human fabrication to the order of living things. In a sculptor like Henry Moore and an architect like Frank Lloyd Wright, living form is the archetype. In Kant, the origin of genius is spirit as animating principle of the creative faculties, producing vital works and evoking a sense of distinctively human life in the audience. (But we will see later that Kant has not the same relation to nonhuman life forms as Moore or Wright or Aristotle.) Kandinsky, the "inventor" of nonrepresentational painting, saw his very abstract work as preserving something of nature's organic growth.[79]

It is here that we might press a bit further into the basis for the two origins of poetry Aristotle suggests: the natural desire to imitate, through which we humans learn, and an innate appreciation for harmonies and rhythms. Through the first we are able to exist as political animals—that is, as sensate beings with biological survival needs whose empty reference to the whole is filled through our introduction into the sedimented words and deeds, thoughts and actions, interpretations and choices of others that constitute the whole we call our culture. It is here that our imitative tendencies help us to learn the culture. But that is set on a biological base; and the biological is a matter of inner rhythms and overall harmony of rhythms and functions correspondent with an environment characterized by rhythms and attunements—by the alternations of day and night, by the changes of the seasons, by the phases of the moon, by the lapping of the waves and the patter of the raindrops. For our own survival, our biorhythms must be attuned to the rhythms of the world surrounding us, a world of which we are an integral part. And yet, because we are referred to the whole, we can back off from biological need and let ourselves appreciate the rhythms and harmonies that surround and comprise us at our basic level. We can also learn to produce works that have rhythmic and harmonic properties and bring them into organic unity. Such works are "fresh," "live," "vital," "organic," as distinguished from those that are "stale," "dead," "mechanical."

In general, Aristotle provides us with sober, workmanlike analyses. There is no hint of something like Plato's passionate fascination with beauty. In fact, Aristotle says very little of beauty beyond limiting it to what a human can take in (between the petite and the monstrous), relativizing it—in the case of human beauty—to different ages of human maturing,[80] and listing (without explanation) the properties of order *(taxis)*, due proportion *(symmetria)*, and definedness *(horizmenon)*.[81] It would seem that for Aristotle, the aesthetic is a subordinate region within the larger whole of the human project, while for Plato it is the very center of that project.

Nonetheless, for both thinkers—as for all thinkers up to the nineteenth and twentieth centuries—art is not a region that exists for its own sake. Everything experienced, art included, is for the sake of enabling the human being to become better attuned to the cosmic order, following out the basic orientation of humanness toward the totality. But art's special role is to locate that orientation in the here and now of bodily presence in the world of the senses and thus to allow us to participate in that world more fully.

# IV

# PLOTINUS AND
# THE LATIN MIDDLE AGES

THOUGH THE ARTISTIC PRACTICE of the Middle Ages was unparalleled, especially in the construction of the cathedrals that housed magnificent sculptural and pictorial works and were filled with the haunting sounds of Gregorian chant, it might not be too far off the mark to claim that, from the point of view of aesthetics (i.e., reflection on the nature of art and beauty), the thought of the Middle Ages was essentially derivative. Indeed, among the major thinkers, the great philosopher-theologians, besides citation and paraphrase of traditional sources, one finds very little sustained treatment of aesthetic matters, and almost nothing of any significance with regard to works of art. The one exception was the notion of divine beauty and the corresponding development of the transcendentality of beauty. Treatment of beauty was largely a matter of commenting on Dionysius, an early-sixth-century Syrian monk who leaned heavily upon pagan neo-Platonism. In the ninth century Scotus Eriugena developed a system of thought heavily dependent, in turn, on Dionysius. And in the High Middle Ages, commentary on the Dionysian corpus, begun in the ninth century with Scotus Erigena, attained new life with Albertus Magnus, who was followed in this by his pupils, Thomas Aquinas and Ulrich of Strasbourg.

The major texts dealing with aesthetic themes have been collected, like a series of pre-Socratic fragments, in Tatarkiewicz.[1] However, the difference between these and the earlier fragments is that they are found in whole texts and operate out of a deliberate attempt to gather up and arrange positions handed down from previous ages.[2] The dominant philosophical framework for the Middle Ages was Neoplatonic, developed especially by Plotinus, and mediated by Augustine and Dionysius. And so we begin with a treatment of Plotinus, the prince of Neoplatonists, who created a bridge between Plato and medieval thought.

## Plotinus

Some six hundred years after Plato, Plotinus attempted to provide a systematic account, in treatises arranged in groups of nine (hence called *The Enneads* or *The Nines*) of the themes treated dialogically, dialectically, and hence nonsystematically by Plato.[3] It is Plotinus's philosophy that provided the categories through which the Christian church interpreted the biblical tradition, all too often in a dualistic, otherworldly direction. As Thomas Aquinas pointed out, such a view posed great problems for understanding the central New Testament teachings of the Incarnation of the Logos, the sacramentality of Christian worship, and the final Resurrection of the Body.[4]

In Plato's development of the Line of Knowledge, the question of the status of the intellect was left open. Where do we stand when we each ascend beyond the privacy of our sensations, feelings, and preferences and become the subject whose correlate is the eternality and necessity presented paradigmatically in mathematics? Later, the medieval Muslims, Avicenna and Averroës, would speak of the one Agent Intellect in which we all participate.[5] Thomas Aquinas, basing himself on the observation that it is each of us individually who understands, labored strenuously against this conception; but he retained a residue of it in his notion of the agent intellect in each of us as "a certain participation in the divine light."[6] Later still, Schopenhauer would speak of becoming "the one Eye of the world" in contemplating the "Platonic Ideas."[7] And Hegel would speak of God coming to His Self-awareness in human beings through the development of scientific, philosophic knowledge.[8] Earlier, Augustine held that we are within the Logos when we grasp intelligible form.[9] In this they follow Plotinus, who held that we are able to stand within the World Mind, the Logos, which contains the intelligibility of the whole.[10]

Plotinus goes further in the direction indicated in Plato by what, in his *Republic*, he calls the Good as the ground of intellect and intelligibility, beyond subject and object. As noted earlier, Plato also has Socrates refer to it as "beyond *ousia*," usually translated as "beyond being." This becomes a staple in the Neoplatonic tradition and is made much of today by Emmanuel Levinas.[11] However, *ousia*, the term that, in Aristotle, was subsequently translated as substance, should, I suggest, be translated here as beingness. Plato refers to the Good as "the most manifest region of being" *(tou ontos to phanotaton).*[12] I would maintain that being *(to on)* is all-encompassing, for being is everything about everything, outside of which is absolutely nothing. It includes the realm of genesis, with its modes of relative nonbeing (pastness, futurity, potentiality, privation, absence), the realm of the *ousia* or beingness of beings (their intelligibility as correlate to intellect), and the Good as source of both *ousia* and *genesis.* What is important here is the testimony to a region beyond both what the senses can apprehend and what can be grasped by the abstract, conceptual, universalizing operations of the intellect. It is correlate to Eros as the desire of "the whole person."

In Plato the Good as the One, immediately irradiating the splendor of coherence upon the Forms, is, more profoundly, the principle of the whole. Its being "beyond," its utter transcendence, is at the same time its complete immanence. That is why the ascent from the Cave involves the return to the Cave: the One as *arche tou holou,*[13] as principle of the totality, circles back beneath the surface of the Cave images. If the Receptacle stands beneath things as the principle of their being spatiotemporal individuations of universal Forms, the One stands "beneath" the Receptacle just as it stands "above" the Forms. It is as Beauty that the One is a Real Presence in sensorily given things, healing the *chorismos,* the gap between the Forms and the sensory appearance.

The Good as the One is manifest in the peculiar experience of unity that we call the mystical, an experience described in similar terms in the East and in the West: "I and the All are one," "Atman is Brahman," "God and the soul are one."[14] Porphyry, Plotinus's biographer, reports on Plotinus's claim to have been drawn four times out of ordinary experience and into an ecstatic experience of unity with the One.[15] This gave him a peculiar appetite for being "alone with the Alone."[16] For Plotinus, following Diotima in Plato's *Symposium,* this One radiates itself in all things as Beauty, as the coherence, the harmony of each and all.[17] The initially experienced intoxication associated with sensory surface is suffused with a sense of the ultimate expressivity (i.e., the symbolic character of all things as mirrorings of the One in multiplicity). The sensory surface is therefore not simply color and pattern, but colored pattern illuminated by a underlying depth. For Plotinus there is nothing beautiful that does not express something more than beautiful.[18] Even Beauty Itself, irradiating all Forms and all things, which participate in and thereby express their Forms, is an expression of the One beyond.[19]

Focusing on beauty in all its forms and levels, Plotinus argues against a common ascription of symmetry to things as a necessary characteristic of beauty by pointing to symmetrical things like an ugly face that are not beautiful. Rather than symmetry, Plotinus argues for "dominance by form" as the essence of beauty in all its types; and by that he means unification, coherence, harmony of parts, the mirroring of the One in the manyness of matter, of functions, of concepts, but also simple instantiation of form. Full penetration by pattern, total unification, absolute coherence is, I suggest, precisely what Aristotle meant by the property I have described as organicity.[20] But there is also the simplicity of color with its luminosity (Plotinus uses the example of gold). Luminosity is the irradiation of the One, a surplus beyond pattern that makes pattern accessible. It bears witness to a "more" than what can be discriminated and united in intellectual operations, which stand at a distance from a given object. The beautiful object stands out from others as an arresting presence. It involves a participatory relation that overcomes the distance of subject detached from object in analytical and synthetic operations. Intuition of the Idea in relation to the sensory object that expresses it is participative presence.

For Plotinus, the Logos or World Mind flows out from the One as illumination from the source of light.[21] In so proceeding it can only go into multiplicity, first in the founding distinction of subject and object, and then in the progressive complexification of the realm of Idea-objects from unity to multiplicity.[22] From the realm of the Logos flows the World Soul as the last emanation within the eternal Trinity, turned, as creative power, toward the world of individual spirits. Eventually the One generates material multiplicity like light dispersing itself into darkness. Matter is the ultimate opposite of the One as the dark principle, the principle of dispersal, multiplying individuals under the same Form at different times and places, forcing the enmattered forms to struggle to develop themselves and maintain themselves and eventually to lose hold of themselves as they finally sink into the dispersal of the elements they employed in securing their peculiar and precarious hold on existence.[23] The material world came into being as a prison for the pure spirit, who falls from a higher realm so deeply that it forgets its own belonging to the supercelestial realm within the bosom of the divine Trinity.[24] Nonetheless, in order to be, things must mirror the

One and thus contain within themselves degrees of unification at various levels, answering to the level of the hierarchy of being they each occupy.

The hierarchy of beauties described by Diotima can then be meaningfully understood as more intensive and, at the same time, more comprehensive levels of unification. According to Plotinus, the perception of such intensive comprehensiveness, and thus also of sensuously formed objects as expressive thereof, depends on the achievement of a more intensive unification of our own individual lives, awakening from our fall into matter.[25] Even though at one level our intellect remains with the Logos, nonetheless we begin this life "sunk in matter," unconscious, floating in the darkness of the developmental processes of the embryo. As human form comes to dominate physiologically, awareness emerges as a stream of urges and impressions that are gradually shaped through the acquisition of language and patterned responses developing into motor habits. Such shaping is the aim of Plato's "primary education." The explicit intellectual pattern emerges later through the ability to con-centrate, literally to be at the center with something, to pull oneself together out of the flowing distractions of appetites and contingent impressions coming from the environment. Such concentration emerges more comprehensively in the philosopher. It is surmounted by an even more concentrated mode of existence when the higher Dionysian, mystical pattern emerges: that of participative knowing that co-implicates awareness and its object—only here subject and object are not only united as two in one; they are for Plotinus one and the same.[26]

But since not everyone can participate in such deep unity, then not everyone can attend to the deepest expressiveness of sensory surface. This is transparently clear in relation to the written and spoken word. But it is also the case with regard to the immediacy of sensuous form, whether visual or audile. In high art, the sensuous togetherness of form plays in relation to the depth of its capacity to express the profundity of things apprehended and given shape by the artist for the properly integrated receptivity of the perceiver.

Furthermore Plotinus, in keeping with Diotima's teaching in Plato's *Symposium,* also remarks that one cannot expect to reach the higher levels of contemplation unless one learns to contemplate the beauties given through sensation.[27] Ascending the Ladder of Beauty involves a turning around of the soul, wallowing in the pleasurable sensations occasioned by the sensorily given, to appreciate the beauty of individual sensuous forms themselves. The soul must be purged of its own self-indulgent proclivities, which

scatter its attention. Passing through the sensory surface to the person encountered and expressed in that surface requires an even deeper conversion; and moving beyond to the historic formative powers shaping personal
being, a conversion still deeper. As one moves more deeply within, one is
able—in a metaphoric inversion that always seems to accompany the
metaphor of depth[28]—to ascend to higher and higher levels of illumination. More inward power of concentration is required to grasp the eidetic
invariants that generate the observable particulars, and more power still to
bring the plurality of Ideas into the light of unity. But most of all, the deepest purgation is required to be drawn up into identity with the source of intelligible light: the One itself. This pattern, derived from Plato, becomes
the classic pattern for the "three ways" of the spiritual life in the Middle
Ages: the purgative way, the illuminative way, and the unitive way.[29]

The summit does not lie in becoming a spectator, but in having beauty
penetrate the whole soul so that contemplation turns into vision. Self-
knowledge becomes one with oneself.[30] Knowledge, even of oneself, loses
the external character of what we usually call knowledge and becomes
participatory, at one with the known, and thus self-knowledge and other-
knowledge at one. Ordinary separations—knowledge from participation,
knowledge of self from knowledge of the other—are here one.

Plato has Diotima claim that the highest level is the vision of Beauty
Itself, suggesting an ascent away from the sensuous starting point. However, Socrates in the *Phaedrus* claims that, of all the Forms, the privilege of
Beauty is that it is perceptible through the eyes as a "real presence" in
beautiful things. Plotinus similarly claims that, for one who has mounted
up to the higher levels, the sensuous surface is like the face of the beloved
which expresses, for one who loves, the depth of the beloved.[31] So there is
a kind of dialectic of an inward-upward move, beyond the Cave of culturally mediated sensibility, playing in tandem with a return to sensibility,
which is now participated in as expressive of the depth of Final Reality.
The move inward and upward carves out for the mature an infinite depth
beyond sensory surface in which the immature are fully enmeshed.[32]

Along these lines, even though Plotinus's remarks tend to devaluate the
material world more deeply than some of the things Plato has his characters utter, Plotinus reverses the order of value in Plato's discussion of the
arts in *Republic* 10. Things, Socrates says, are images of Ideas and our sensations are perspectival images of things, whereas art, like a mirror, gives us
images of those images, "three degrees removed from reality." For Plotinus,
following Plato's remarks about inspired art as distinct from imitative art,

which mirrors sensory surface, the higher forms of art proceed from an apprehension of the generative Ideas.[33] Things are expressions of the World Soul working the potential chaos of matter into meaningful expressions of the unity of the Ideas. The high artist grasps the Ideas, not simply as static, atemporal unities, but, allied to the World Soul, as creative forces.

Schopenhauer will later distinguish the *unitas post rem*, a unity following the presentation of an entity, a reconstruction by analytical and synthetic intellectual operations of the *unitas ante rem*, the generative unity of the Idea that produces its instances in an atemporal vertical causality intersecting the horizontal temporal causality exhibited in observed antecedence and consequence.[34] So it seems that in Plotinus the Ideas themselves are not static forms, as they appear to be in Plato's dialogues when he takes his point of departure from mathematical form; they are generative forces. This is how artistic intuition apprehends them, since such intuition is essentially generative, essentially tied to the possibility of working the form into the externality of matter. For Plotinus, then, art imitates nature, not by reproducing sensuous surface, but by grasping her mode of production.[35]

Yet, because material embodiment is viewed as a fall of the soul, Plotinus considers art in the mind higher than its artistic expression in an actual work.[36] Boethius will mediate such a view to the Middle Ages in his remark that musical theory is more excellent than musical sound.[37] This is linked to the view that for an artist—Plotinus speaks specifically of the sculptor—the form is in the mind and not in the material.[38]

But even in the mind, the idea of the work is an idea expressed in images. This entails a link between imagination and intellect that parallels the link between sensation and imagination. For Plotinus imagination has two faces.[39] On the one hand, it stores and recombines the images received through sensation. Now sensation does not give us the thing in its ontological depth; it presents us with the surface of the thing appearing within the thresholds set up by our bodies and answering to our organic needs. However, art that proceeds out of the apprehension of nature's creative Ideas is no mere mirroring of that surface but an expression of the depth apprehension; hence the appearance of new images not simply derived from sensory surface.

Plotinus has astonishingly high praise for the power of images. He underscores the pictographic character of Egyptian hieroglyphs as transcending the discursiveness of propositions and expressing insight into the "wisdom of nature" that roots its creation of multiplicity in unity. Contemplation of the Forms is not consideration of propositions but experience of creative powers.[40] Grasp of Form is grasp of the expressive power of images, and is hence a creative intuition, an apprehension of the possibility of the transformation of sensory surface to express creative depth.

If the work of art, through the Idea it instantiates in its own creative way, brings us to the beauty of the One as the final object of human Eros, it is also linked with an intellectual "aesthetic" that is attuned to the togetherness of the Forms. All speculative thought is rooted in such an "aesthetic," a sense for wholeness that resists analytical dissolution and compartmentalization while recognizing the essential though subordinate role of analysis. Even speculative construction rests on the transconceptuality of the ultimate depth, correlate to the whole person. Every beauty stems from what is beyond and gives expression to a surplus that irradiates the conceptual work as it irradiates the work of the artist.[41]

## Aquinas among the Latin Medievals

Plotinus, as I have said, supplied the basic Neoplatonic philosophical framework for medieval interpretation of the scriptural tradition. Augustine remarks that very much of Christianity was in the Neoplatonists: Trinity as the One/Father producing the otherness of the Logos/Son, from which flows the World Soul/Spirit, followed by Creation, Fall, and Return of creatures to God. But Augustine further remarks that there is one central omission: that the Logos became flesh.[42] The claim that, minus this exception, much of Christianity is in Neoplatonism is an ambiguous claim, since the essence of Christianity is the incarnation and bodily resurrection of the Logos. Nonetheless, it was especially through Augustine in the West and Dionysius in the East that Neoplatonism entered into the Middle Ages.

Augustine's *Confessions* records the journey of a soul initially caught up in "fleshly beauty" and "worldly eloquence," converted first to Neoplatonism and then to Christianity. He laments: "O Beauty, ever ancient, ever new! Too late have I known thee!"[43] For he sought it in sensuous charms and warm embraces—he wallowed in the "seething caldron of unholy loves" in Carthage and had an illegitimate child (Adeodatus, "gift of God") by one of his mistresses—only to find that the Beauty he sought was not there. Following the Diotiman ladder of ascent in experience, turning within and upward, he came to a vision of Beauty Itself beyond all things. His personal experience thus gave him an ambivalent relation to physical beauty and also to art forms. Hans Urs von Balthasar speaks of an Augustinian "nervousness" regarding the senses.[44] In the *Confessions* Augustine acknowledges that he struggled with the issue of having music banned from the churches because it is so sensually enticing; but then, recalling that he had been moved to tears by music after his own conversion, he acknowledges that it might be an aid to "the weaker soul."[45]

Beauty in creatures he sees, in keeping with the Platonic and Aristotelian conceptions, as linked to objective properties rooted in form.[46] Following the *Book of Wisdom*, he identifies the properties as *modus, species, et ordo*—that is, measure or proportion, form (or type or even appearance) and order as ordination to an end.[47] These properties produce a concordance of parts to constitute a single unified whole.[48] This measured whole mirrors, in Platonic fashion, the realm of eternal numbers.[49] However, Augustine adds a new twist to aesthetic considerations: integral to the unification peculiar to beauty is an opposition of contraries that produces aesthetic tension.[50] Though Augustine stresses the objective properties, he also speaks of the beautiful as suiting our nature (i.e., as proportioned to or harmonious with our faculties)[51]—a position that Aquinas, following Aristotle, will stress as well. And anticipating a distinction Kant will later make, he also distinguishes beauty from *suavitas* (pleasantness or agreeableness) by distinguishing (differently than Kant) the perception of visual qualities from the perceptions of the other senses.[52]

Following Plotinus, Augustine claims that the artist must know the ideal form he wishes to embody and that his giving body to the form inevitably involves an inferior realization.[53] At best, when they are not the object of vain curiosity, the arts can assist in turning the soul inward and upward and thus away from the senses, for the goal of human existence is "spiritualization." Having to work through sensory imagery in order to communicate is a result of the Fall.[54] Such an attempt is justified ultimately under the aegis of charity,[55] but it amounts, in the words of Robert O'-Connell, to "an array of mud-huts, slapped together from the soul's own 'ruins.'"[56] In a comprehensive and critical—though not entirely unappreciative—study of Augustine's reflections on art, O'Connell summarizes Augustine's attitude toward artistic work, an attitude that will fatally stamp medieval thought: "Superbia, pride, the restless, 'curious' desire to be engaged in action, the arrogant will to construct a temporal imitation of the eternal world of beauty, the dissipation, literally, 'spilling forth' of its interior riches in a flight further and further from the divine to the outermost reaches of 'lesser and lesser' being—all the key elements of Plotinus' description in *Ennead* 3.7, of the fall from eternity into time are firmly in place."[57] Augustine seems to have had no sensitivity to painting, for he makes little mention of it. Indeed, he viewed both painting and the theater as species of lying.[58] And in his treatment of music, he is only concerned with rhythm (governed by number), the least sensuous of the features of music.[59] We have already taken note of his hesitation even to allow music in church. On the other hand, Augustine himself was a consummate rhetorician, as exhibited especially in the beauty of his *Confessions*. At times he displays an appreciation for the various marvels of human productivity, but then reminds himself and his readers that they are, after all, a result of the Fall into the body.[60] One of the results of the Fall is that we are immersed in the part and fail to see how it fits into the whole so as to constitute the poem of the universe.[61] This is one of the most fruitful aesthetic observations Augustine has made.

Dionysius—now called Pseudo-Dionysius because he passed himself off as Dionysius the Areopagite, disciple of St. Paul, even though he lived several centuries later—developed a *pankallism,* a vision of all things as manifestations of divine beauty.[62] Beauty is a transcendental property belonging to all things by reason of their participation in Beauty Itself, a real presence in beautiful things, as in Plato's *Phaedrus*. For Dionysius, beauty *(kallos)* is derived from calling *(kalloun),* whereby the divine calls things to itself and to their place in the order of things. This call has two aspects: beauty functions as formal cause in giving things the being they have, but it also functions as final cause, which establishes in creatures an Eros for Beauty. Hence, as correlate to *pankallism* we have a *paneroticism,* the universality of desire that draws the creature to its source. In calling things to their place, Beauty thereby communicates the harmony of brightness of all things which flashes like light.[63] Two properties are linked together here: consonance and splendor, or harmonious relation between parts and a surplus "shining through" of what expresses itself from beyond the perceptible relations. Dionysius stressed the transcendence of the infinite divine in relation to everything positive we can say about the divinity. The last word about God is that we cannot say about God. He is essentially hidden, a mysterious Source: He is "beyond being."[64]

In a way reminiscent of Heidegger, Dionysius claims that Being itself, which Balthasar reads as equivalent to Aquinas's *esse commune,* is "the first of all the creatures," essentially other than all beings, which share in it.[65] Balthasar further suggests that this notion designates "the space of the spiritual life," a life that entails dwelling in the sense of totality and encompassment as the mysterious depth from which all things come and which ultimately mediates our lived relation to God.[66] The manifestation of harmonic properties in creatures is irradiated from within by the presence of the final mystery, giving to the perception of beauty a certain haunting character that takes us out of the everyday and suggests the presence of infinite depth. But as in Plotinus, the apprehension of the Beautiful and Good and One and the Same as such is made possible by the soul's entrance into itself from things without, being collected into unity.[67] Read in isolation from other counterbalancing tendencies, this carries out the Platonic-Neoplatonic tendency of shutting out the world of the senses in order to move "within" and "above." But read in a broader context, as I have already suggested, it carves out an experiential depth-dimension beyond our surface relation to all things, so that everything we encounter becomes sacramental, a theophany, a manifestation of the presence of divine Beauty.[68]

In the 1240s Albertus Magnus lectured on Dionysius's *Divine Names* to an audience that included Thomas Aquinas.[69] In *De pulchro et bono*—an opusculum formerly ascribed to Aquinas—Albert laid stress on terms that describe the surplus of beauty over goodness as a light, a shining, a radiance, a splendor, an incandescence, a resplendence, a lightning *(fulgor)*, a superfulgence, a *claritas* (linked to *clarus*, "famous," parallel to Greek *doxa* as "glory"), a supersplendence rooted in the substantial form.[70] In an otherwise austere scholastic presentation, this piling up and even manufacture of terms to describe a single property is indeed remarkable. Albert is clearly struggling to give expression to a surplus in the experience of beauty beyond the analyzable properties to which it might otherwise be reduced. In the expression *splendor formae* this luminescence is linked to proportion and consonance, which are understood as a relation of aspects within the object. But whatever the identifiable ratios involved, *splendor* is a surplus property. And in the Dionysian context, it is understood as the directly perceived expression of the depth of divine mystery irradiating all things.

Thomas Aquinas, according to Etienne Gilson one of the greatest arrangers of ideas in the history of thought, gathered up and synthesized what was available of Western intellectual tradition up to his time in the light of the newly available Aristotelian corpus, itself available until then only in fragments.[71] Aristotelian at the level of natural philosophy, assimilating the act-potency, substance-attribute, form-matter analysis of nature, and viewing the human being, not as a spirit externally related to matter, but as an essentially incarnate spirit, Aquinas was nonetheless Platonist at the deepest levels. Here the doctrines of participation, the divine Ideas, creation, and immortality were assimilated into the Aristotelian view.

The key concept of Aquinas's thought, his distinctive contribution, was the way he understood the distinction of essence and *esse,* originally introduced by Avicenna: as the most fundamental realization of the act-potency relationship, where *esse* is "the act of all acts," "form even with respect to substantial form," and essence is the receptive potentiality that limits the degree to which an entity is.[72] *Esse,* to be, is basic act, in every case individual; it is distinct from the limitation provided by a given essence. *Esse* is, however, by nature unlimited, so that its factual limitation in the beings of experience requires a Ground Whose Essence does not limit but is identical with His *Esse,* Who therefore cannot *not* be. Such a Ground is not in the deepest sense a once-upon-a-time Starter of the world-process, but—whether Starter as in Plato or Nonstarter as in Aristotle—a perpetual Source of being. Finite things are thus not simply initially but, more deeply, enduringly related to their infinite Source. As unlimited *Esse,* God is thus wholly other than all creation, utterly transcendent. However, as Source of being for creation, God is pervasively immanent in every creature, "more intimate to me than I to myself," as Augustine expressed it,[73] for without His constant creative sustenance and all-penetrating awareness, no finite thing can be at all.

In the Dionysian line, Aquinas developed a "negative theology," a theology of limits to conceptual comprehension. As infinite and one, God is beyond the limitations and distinctions with which our finite intelligence operates. For Aquinas we can infer the existence of Pure *Esse* and the presence of those attributes required for creation (power, wisdom, goodness, unity, infinity), but we cannot understand the infinity of the mode of existence and the identity of these attributes with one another in the infinite Ground. Hence inference has to be complemented by negation. For Aquinas our last word about God is that we do not comprehend God. But, by reason of the structure of creation, creatures express the presence of the ultimate unencompassable mystery of God to those sufficiently attuned to the depths.[74]

This provides the first division in the hierarchy of being: God as pure *Esse* unlimited by any essence, Whose essence is to be; creatures whose essence limits *esse,* participating in being in various degrees. The degrees are determined by the dominance of form over matter. Living beings are a step above the nonliving because of the unitary assimilation of the elements by the activity of their psychic form seeking its own ends. Beings that are aware are capable of "assimilating" the forms of other things "without the matter." Intellectual beings assimilate the same forms as purely sentient beings, without matter but also without the individuating conditions of matter, so that intellectual knowing is universal, laying the basis for language and for the sciences. Embodied intellectual beings, human beings, are hierarchized according to whether they live at the intellectual pole of their being, ultimately dwelling in the presence of God. And beyond humans are pure forms, angelic intelligences, each a distinct species rather than a variation on a species theme as individuated by matter.[75]

This view of hierarchy sets the framework for the doctrine of the transcendental properties of being, various aspects that display the richness of the *esse*, the to-be of things. Unity, thinghood, otherness, truth, and goodness are the properties laid out in the famous list in Aquinas's *De veritate* (1.1). Their historical origin lies in Plato's dialogues. They apply according to the formula: whatever is, insofar as it is, is one, good, and so on. The qualifying "insofar as it is" indicates the essentially hierarchical character of being. Enmattered beings are developmental, each beginning as a center of active potentialities and following a pattern of development until it reaches the fully adult actualization of those potentialities, so that the actual state is higher than its potentiality. And the potentialities are hierarchized according to the transcendence of matter involved: sensory operations are higher than unconscious physiological processes because they transcend their own material boundaries, while intellectual operations are higher than the sensory because, in the apprehension of the universal, they transcend the individuating conditions of matter and thus the immersion in the here and now present in both unconscious physiological processes and sensory apprehension. In this view, then, some things "are" more than others; and all "are" at some time more than they "are" at others. Accordingly, insofar as an entity actualizes its basic potentialities and occupies a rank on the hierarchy of types, it is unified, "thingly," other, intelligible, good.

Beauty does not make the list, but the elements are there for its inclusion. Aquinas, following Aristotle, sees beauty as involving a relation between knowing and desire. His description—*pulchrum est id quod visum placet: beauty is that which, when seen, pleases*—is not particularly helpful since truth also pleases; but that characterization does stress the appetitive response, the felt relation to the subject. For Aquinas, beauty brings the appetite to rest in the object.[76] There is thus a more holistic relation than in a purely intellectual act. In the definition, *visum* here might be taken, in the line of ordinary language, as analogously extended to all wakeful states: "*See* how this sounds, how this tastes, how that feels, how it smells; *see* the line of proof in this demonstration."[77]

Aquinas notes with Aristotle the peculiarity of human sense perception: only humans can come to delight in the beauty of sensible things in themselves and not simply in connection with their function in keeping us alive.[78] This could be understood in two opposed ways: on the one hand, the simple enjoyment of feelings produced by objects—which is characteristic of Plato's luxurious city; on the other, the appreciation of the sensory features of things themselves characteristic of Plato's purged city. There seems to be no clear discrimination of these two possibilities here.

We might note in this context Aquinas's view that sight is the most "spiritual" of the senses because it is filled with the object.[79] Contrary to touch, the lowest of the senses in Aquinas's estimation, in the sighting of the visual object qua visual (except in the case of the feeling of strain involved in an excess of brightness or darkness in the medium) there is no simultaneous experience of one's own body, which may distract attention from the characteristics of the object. However, the arousal of bodily feelings may accompany the sighting and thus deflect attention from the object to the feelings. Vision thus provides a kind of anticipation of the objectivity of intellect and points in the direction taken by Kant's emphasis on the "disinterested satisfaction" involved in aesthetic perception.[80]

This might be the place to note a shift from Cassiodorus, for whom all the senses perceived beauty,[81] to Aquinas, who restricted perception of beauty to sight and hearing,[82] and Thomas Gallus, who distinguished the higher senses of sight and hearing, which are annexed to the intellect, from the other and lower senses, which are annexed to affection.[83] Aquinas in the text cited claims that sight and hearing are maximally cognitive and that their objects are the only ones considered beautiful, in direct contrast to the objects of touch, taste, and smell. Even today, ordinary usage does not call the feel of velvet, the taste of wine, or the aroma of perfume beautiful—maybe exquisite, delicate, delightful, or fine, but not beautiful.

In considering what it is about the *visum* that pleases, Aquinas lists, without showing their interconnections, three properties of the beautiful.[84] The first is integrity or perfection, having all aspects together, being completely formed, a notion implicit in Albert's emphasis on form. The second property is Albert's feature of due proportion or consonance, which Aquinas considers in two different ways: the way Albert understood it, as a relation of one quantity to another,[85] to which Aquinas adds Augustine's observation of the relation to our cognitive power[86]—which itself parallels Aristotle's claim that beauty is relative to our capacity to perceive. Aquinas maintains that the senses are a kind of *ratio* or "reason," and that is the basis for our delight in the ratios of things: things beautiful by reason of the relations of their parts are suited to our own sensory faculties, which consist of corresponding ratios. The third property is Albert's *claritas*, which, as we have noted, carries more than the English *clarity*, including parallels to Greek *doxa*, which involves the notion of glory. Hence some translate it as "splendor" to maintain the connection with Albert's *splendor formae*. Jacques Maritain for one reads *claritas* as a kind of surplus of intelligible light available through the senses and lost when one turns from sense to abstraction and reasoning.[87] All three properties are associated with the notion of form,[88] picking up on Albert's notion of *splendor formae*.

Attempts have been made to correlate these three properties with the transcendental properties of unity, goodness, and truth respectively and then to import Bonaventure's notion of beauty as the fusion and seal of the transcendentals.[89] However, as I have noted, beauty did not make Aquinas's famous list of the transcendentals in *On Truth* (1.1). This may partly be explained by the close association the medievals saw between beauty and goodness viewed as perfection,[90] though, as I have noted, Aquinas claimed that beauty adds to goodness "a certain relation to the cognitive power." Qualifications such as *certain* are open invitations to interpretative ventures. In view of Aquinas's description of beauty as that which, when seen, pleases, the "certain relation" might be that of providing pleasure in the viewing. However, perfection or integrity is only one of the three features Aquinas offers and thus the identity of beauty and goodness as perfection cannot be sustained. Presumably there are completed entities—one thinks of some insects—that are not well proportioned, and presumably also some well-proportioned and completed entities through whom the splendor of the form does not shine. Beauty would require all three and to that extent would not be transcendental. Again, since proportion on Aquinas's reading involves, following Aristotle, a proportion to our powers, Umberto Eco suggests a further argument that beauty cannot be transcendental.[91] For Aquinas, since the mind is referred to being, both of its powers, intellect and will, entail the manifestness of the transcendental properties of truth and goodness respectively. One only has to distinguish sensory and ontological beauty to free the transcendentality of beauty. In his treatment of the Trinity, Aquinas correlates the three properties of beauty with the Word and thus locates beauty within the heart of the divinity.[92]

Eco notes that the weakest element in medieval aesthetics is its theory of art, which is essentially a theory of craftsmanship. For Aquinas art is, directly translating Aristotle, *recta ratio factibilium*, a phrase usually itself translated as something like "right reason regarding things to be made."[93] Eco goes on to say that the medievals had no notion of the creative power of art.[94] But Aquinas's borrowing of the revised notion of imitation from Plotinus contained that potential: art imitates nature, he says, in her manner of production.[95] This could be allied with the Aristotelian notion of the organicity of the work of art: as nature produces objects having the character of the integral togetherness of all its parts, so also art can come to produce artifacts not resembling any exterior form of entity, but possessing the crucial factor of organicity, thus providing distinctively human "growths."

Aquinas viewed the arts as inferior to intellectual communication. Artforms are superficial, standing on the empirical surface.[96] Poetry is *infima doctrina*, inferior teaching, having a defective mode of truth, but useful, as are all the arts, for communicating something of truth to the uneducated.[97] Furthermore, arts are considered inferior to the extent that their practice involves greater implication in the body[98]—an odd view for someone who fought for the Aristotelian notion of psychophysical holism against the dominant Neoplatonic dualism.

It is in the thought of Bonaventure, Aquinas's contemporary, that beauty not only takes on the character of a transcendental, but takes center stage as the final transcendental. Balthasar considers Bonaventure to be the high point and last glorious development of a sapiential theology, of monastic wisdom, rooted in *gustus experimentalis*, an experiential tasting of ultimate things.[99] The root of his theology is an experience of being overpowered by the fullness of reality,[100] an ecstatic *excessus*.[101] The key concept is *expression*:[102] creatures express God because God internally expresses Himself in His Son,[103] and each creature expresses itself to perceivers as an interior light shining in the exterior.[104] Again according to Balthasar, of all the medieval thinkers, Bonaventure had a most positive assessment of sensory knowledge and delight, wherein our grounding and enduring experience of expression is found.[105]

Bonaventure adopts Augustine's discussion of *modus, species,* and *ordo,* which he understands as expressing respectively the existence, the relation to other things, and the relation to its end of any creature.[106] It is the treatment of *species* that is particularly helpful, for it concerns especially the relation of manifestness, on account of which one of the terms used for beauty is *speciositas*. *Species*, before it becomes the word we define as "type," is appearance, relation to apprehending power, manifestness, display.

Beauty is the optimum mode of display. On the one hand we have the manifestation of the ordered character of the sensorily given, on the other the shining through of signification, ultimately of the presence of the divine. The one factor concerns the delight in apprehension, the other the delight in judgment. Because of the Fall we tend to be caught up in the first and are unable to read the language of creation. Anticipating Galileo, but with an entirely different sense of "reading," for Bonaventure nature is a book written by God and addressed to human beings; Scripture teaches us how to read it,[107] but only the mystics are proper readers.

Being drawn out of ourselves by beauty at all levels, we experience the integration of the transcendentals, for "beauty encompasses every cause"[108] and is the seal on the transcendentals. Bonaventure associates unity with the Father, truth with the Son, and goodness with the Holy Spirit, but beauty is their circumincession.[109] Insofar as all things mirror the Trinitarian ground—as traces in subhuman things, as images in humans, and as likenesses in perfected humans—beauty shines forth in them. The centrality of beauty in Bonaventure generated his fear that the "sapiential" center, the experiential "tasting" of ultimate things, was disappearing from theology in favor of the analytical and constructive rationalism of the Scholastic movement. "Splendor" began to disappear from view. Rationalism drives out aesthetics.

So the medieval thinkers were preoccupied with beauty primarily as an attribute of the divine and as a manifestation of the divine in the beings we encounter. But they did very little to advance the understanding of artistic production or appreciation. God, and nature as the manifestation of God, were more fundamental to the concern of the philosophers, who operated under the aegis of theology.

## Response

The culture of the Middle Ages stood in a constant tension between what it saw as the fact and implications of God's own Incarnation and the tendency toward disembodiment and otherworldliness coming out of pagan gnostic or Neoplatonic "saints." Following Plato's ascent out of the Cave of *doxa*, Neoplatonism developed severe ascetic practices linked to a real contempt for "bodiliness." So as not to be undone by these pagan "saints," Christians tried to outdo them in the severity of their asceticism and in their expressions of contempt for "the flesh." So, one finds in monastic literature reference to "filthy matter" close by reference to "filthy womanhood." This was assimilated into a tendency to establish first-class and second-class citizenship in the church: first-class belonged to those who have "renounced the world" with vows of poverty, chastity, and obedience, concessionary second-class to those who accumulated property, married, and made their own basic decisions. Not the family but the monastery was viewed as the cradle of Christian existence.[110] Even in Thomas Aquinas, who established an Aristotelian—and thus psychophysically holistic—hermeneutic of the biblical tradition, the practice of the nonverbal arts was a lower form of existence precisely because they involved greater implication in the body.

However, as in Plotinus, ascetic practice provided interior distance that allowed the surface of the sensory world to be reconfigured as the face of the Beloved One, so in the monastic tradition, for the soul purified of its bodily desires, the world was sacramental, a theophany, a manifestation of the presence of God precisely in and through its beauty, as we find in Francis of Assisi's *The Canticle of Brother Sun*.[111] As we will see, even in that most powerful anti-Platonic, anti-Christian thinker Friedrich Nietzsche, a measure of asceticism is an essential moment in the deepening and integration of any human life.[112] Here belongs Augustine's observation regarding our all-too-common tendency to immerse ourselves in the immediate and lose sight of the whole. For Augustine, this is part of the danger of the attractiveness of sensory beauty. It can too often stand in the way of our apprehension of the total "poem of the universe." However, deep art can have the opposite effect than that of which he warns us: it can draw us in and through the transformation of sensory surface to a sense of the encompassing whole.

I should underscore here the central image of light and the related terms *splendor, radiance, brilliance, shining*. With regard to the human face, it is when the face is most expressive of the depth of the person's joy that we speak of a radiance. Here we should assimilate Plotinus's way of speaking of the whole of the sensory surface as "the face of the beloved" (i.e., of the Origin Whose depth that surface expresses for one sufficiently attuned). This is in line with Plato's observation that Beauty Itself and not just the proportionate beauty of beautiful things is visible, shining through visible things. Here too belongs the Judeo-Christian notion of the *kabod*, the *doxa*, the glory of God as something seen.[113] One way in which this is represented artistically is by the halo surrounding the head of the saint or by the golden background commonplace in sacred icons. Vincent van Gogh thought that the radiance and vibration of colors paralleled the function of the halo in displaying eternity in the work.[114] The beautiful sensory surface is both harmonically proportionate in its parts and expressive of an ultimate depth. This state of affairs corresponds to the founding structure of distinctively human nature as biologically rooted, metaphysically referred field of awareness. There is, then, a sense of completion—or of glimpses of completion—in the epiphany of the brilliant.

Here also belongs the Plotinian, Dionysian reading of Plato's "beyond *ousia*" as a feature of the One that bears witness to a depth of experience transcending the analytic and synthetic work of what we have come to call intellect. There is an experience of wholeness aligned with the fullness of Being that cannot be adequately expressed conceptually nor met with sensorily. Yet, evoking the Eros of "the whole soul," it leads to comprehensive, constructive speculative vision and artistic fabrication. The constraints of conceptual construction are expressed in Dionysian and Aquinian apophatic or "negative" theology, which is a theology of limits. It lays the groundwork for a rereading of the role of the perception and creation of beauty that points beyond rational construction to being apprehended by the mystery of wholeness.

Here again belongs Dionysius's notion of Being which Balthasar links with Aquinas's *esse commune* and calls "the space of the spiritual life."[115] It is a complete encompassment and depth enclosing and surpassing every actual creature. It corresponds to Heidegger's notion of Being. According to Balthasar, it disappeared from theology after Bonaventure. It became the abstract, indifferent, empty notion of Being, Nietzsche's "last trailing cloud of evaporating reality."[116] The way back into the ground of spiritual life, the ground of all rational construction, thus the ground of metaphysics and theology, is the way of meditative dwelling with the whole of one's being in the encompassing mystery that grants what is given for human existence. It is the arts that can lead us to that way of thinking.

There is another aspect of Plotinus's thought that merits appropriative development in aesthetics. Reversing Socrates' judgment in the *Republic* that art mirrors surface, Plotinus, we noted, claims that profound art reaches to the generative Idea. Following our interpretation of Aristotle, we might inquire in this context whether there are not two distinguishable kinds of intuition here: the grasp of ideal form and the grasp of the steps needed to give the form material existence. The latter is tied to the development of motor habits correlated with knowledge of the properties of the media. The sensuous surface thus has to be seen, not simply in terms of the sensory togetherness of colors or sounds, but as *expressive* of underlying

Ideas operating as creative forces. The high artist is one who can grasp the universal forces and give them expression in his reformation of sensuous surface. This is in the line of Aristotle's observation that art partly imitates, partly completes nature. It is, indeed, reflected again and again in the work of modern painters, sculptors, and poets. Buber speaks of the artist as faithful, not to appearance, but to being.[117] Kandinsky, like Plato and Hegel, sees our routine relationship to things as losing touch with their inner nature.[118] The abstract artist awakens us to the real core of things hidden in the everyday. Henry Moore spoke of the inner forces evoked by the sculptor.[119]

I should comment here on Plotinus's notion that the form of the sculpture is not in the stone but in the mind of the artist. This may be true of clay (and also of paint and sounds), but it is not true of stone or wood. Plotinus's view is in direct contrast to Michelangelo, for whom the form is in the marble and the task of the artist is to find and release it. In his pessimism regarding the embodied condition, Michelangelo was deeply influenced by Neoplatonism, yet as a working sculptor, he appreciated the formal character of his material. Indeed, it seems that the notion of form imprisoned in marble was for him a symbol of the human condition.[120]

The monastic spirit that in Bernard of Clairvaux protested against the sumptuousness of the churches still fed the spirit that generated those same churches. The sense of harmony and proportionality throughout the sacred buildings, of gracefulness exhibited by the Gothic vaults, of the subtlety and splendor of color and light in the stained-glass windows, of playfulness and dignity in the transformed shapes of nature and humankind that decorated the facades and occupied their niches, the sense of the calm but dynamic, serene but soaring sonority of the Gregorian chant that filled the dizziness of the ascending spaces: here was, in its own way, a culmination of aesthetic sensitivity and mastery of media. Everything conspired to draw the heart in and through the transformation of materials to a sense of the splendor of the encompassing divine. A whole worldview gains presence and embodiment in such glorious works of art. A definite conception of our relation to the whole fills the empty space of our founding orientation to the whole, placed solidly on the earth of our biologically mediated encounters, but fills it in a way that transcends the detachment and abstraction of its intellectualized expression. Here the arts function at the center of a lifeworld that answers to the deepest desires of the human heart.

The High Gothic cathedral was all light and verticality. It spontaneously drew the heart upward to look to the source of light. It contrasts with the strong horizontality of the Greek temple and Wright's notion of the building belonging to the earth. Plutarch claimed that we learn speech from other humans and silence from the gods.[121] Silence, entering into building, opens us to what is above. Sacred architecture mediates the above and the below, setting our aspiration to the sacred onto the earth.

But one must ask what the medieval philosophizing theologians added intellectually to the understanding of this lifeworld beyond that presented by the pagan forebears. Practically everything said in these matters is a repetition of what the pagans have said. Only the ontological context is deepened, and that is significant gain indeed, though not directly for aesthetic theory.

# V

# KANT

ONCE ON IMMANUEL KANT's tombstone stood the words, "The starry skies above, the moral law within."[1] They are taken from the closing paragraphs of his *Critique of Practical Reason,* the second work in his critical project. The beginning of the quotation reads: "Two things fill the heart with ever new and increasing admiration and awe *[Bewunderung und Ehrfurcht]*. . . ."[2] The starry skies above are the object and model for mechanistic science. In Newtonian mechanics the laws that govern the stars govern all terrestrial motions as well. It was such knowing that furnished the exemplar of knowing analyzed in the first part of Kant's critical project: *The Critique of Pure Reason.*[3]

To determine the nature, limits, and interrelations of human powers, Kant attempted a systematic critical assessment, in turn, of the capacities of knowledge in the theoretical order—of willing-action in the moral order, and of feeling linked to judgment in the order of aesthetics and organics. "The moral law within" is the object of the second critique, which concludes with the sentiment of admiration and awe cited above. In the third critique, *The Critique of Judgment,* awe before the starry skies combines with awe before moral law to produce the feeling of the sublime.[4] In the presence of the overwhelming size of the starry skies we experience the dual emotion of sensing our own insignificance—hence the component of *Furcht,* or fear—and overcoming it with a sense of the sublimity of our own minds and their moral destiny—hence the component of *Ehre,* or honor, in *Ehrfurcht,* or awe. Checked initially by the sense of insignificance, powerful vital emotion bursts forth in the feeling of awe, which entails an emotional uplift. Among other things, the *Critique of Judgment* focuses attention on the sublime, the experience of which underlies the entire critical project. Awe before the starry skies and awe before the moral law combine in the aesthetic experience of the sublime. Like Plato's, Kant's philosophy is carried by the aesthetic.

## Critique of Pure Reason

In the first critique Kant introduced what has been called "the Copernican revolution in thought."[5] In astronomy Copernicus introduced the first revolution, contending that the spontaneous and ever-verifiable view of the motion of the sun around the earth is an appearance set up by the position of the observer and that the true view is the motion of the earth both around the sun and on its own axis. This accounts for the apparent view by situating it within the new context—an extremely important general methodological point.

Kant made a similar move with regard to the nature of human thought in general: he made the "transcendental turn," transcending or going beyond the traditional focus on objects to which humans have to adjust in knowing, and attending to the conditions in the knower to which appearing things have to adjust in order to appear and which thus limit our cognitive access to things.[6] He is guided here by the hypothetical distinction between an intellect that knows things exhaustively because its thinking makes them to be (an *intellectus archetypicus*, namely, God)—analogous to an artisan who in the practical order knows the form of the things he fabricates because such knowing is the origin of the form—and the human intellect, which, in the theoretical order, is receptively related to the impact of things upon our sensibility.[7] Because of the latter, we have to build up over time—over millennia—our knowledge of things. Hence Kant's fundamental distinction between *noumena* (correlate to Greek *nous*, intellect), which are things-in-themselves as completely transparent intuitive projects of a hypothetical divine, creative knowing and *phenomena* (from the Greek *phainomai*, I appear), which are things-for-us as ob-jects of finite, bodily situated, and thus discursively knowing sub-jects. Things that appear not only set conditions for our knowledge but have conditions set for their appearance by the structure of human receptive knowing.

We begin the knowing process in the mode of sensibility, passively being affected by things. Colors, sounds, smells, tastes, heat and cold, texture, and pressure are effects in us of what are in themselves physical transformations. Thus light, shining on a visible object, is partially absorbed, partially reflected; propagated through space, it enters the eye by passing through the pupil and the lens; it projects an inverted image of the object on the rods and cones of the retina, setting up electronic impulses that are carried by the optic nerve to the visual center in the back of the brain, where the color pattern is effected in the field of awareness. We thus begin our experience, not with things "out there," but with their effects "in" ourselves.[8] It was modern scientific experiments in physics and physiology that led to this view.

So the first conditions that have to be met for objects to appear are determined by the physiologically receptive apparatus that sets up certain thresholds within the field of sensory awareness governed by biological need. The apparatus, together with the incoming impulses, produce color as a subjective experience. There is no color apart from this process, though there are things and wave propagation—or so we think. But as Berkeley pointed out, if the only access we have to things and wave propagation is through subjectively experienced sensory qualities, these things are as subject related as are the sensory qualities.

Now there is also no immediate appearance of color apart from the experience of spatial location. And every spatial location is experienced in such a way as to be located in turn within an indeterminate spread of space beyond the horizon experienced in any given appearance of, for example, a color pattern. Space as a whole is co-given by an immediate intuition as the context for experienced spatial locations.[9] Similarly, nothing appears, whether outwardly or inwardly, except it appears in time, which is likewise co-given with any experienced temporal span as indeterminately exceeding what is experienced in time past, time present, and time to come.[10] The intuitions of space and time as invariant *forms of sensibility* are immediately co-given with—for Kant actually projected on—any experienced object. They are something like rose-colored glasses, which necessitate that everything we see appears rosy. The difference is that the forms of sensibility are inborn, like having rose-colored lenses in our eyeballs by nature. For Kant this accounts for the peculiarity of geometric demonstration that must have overwhelmed the Greeks when they discovered it. One can know a priori, without looking at all the instances, that certain theorems are necessarily true of *all* like objects in space, whenever and wherever we find them. One can further determine, without looking at *any* instances, that certain theorems follow, via the axioms of the geometric system, from other theorems with absolute necessity and can be subsequently observed to hold empirically. Plato thought that this introduced us to a noumenal realm of universal Forms according to which such objects have been made. Kant suggests that it introduces us to the inner optics of our own mental forms, within which every object has to appear.[11] Geometry is human and not at all divine knowing. It unpacks the implications of the forms of our mind. "Whenever" and "wherever" are a priori: we live out of relation to the whole of space and time.

There is a second level of a priori forms or lenses through which the world comes into explicit human focus for us. Space and time are empty as encompassing but individual wholes. But the second level of forms are empty as abstract universals: they are the categories of the understanding.[12] They furnish the principles for sorting and ordering the constant subjective flux of sensations into an objective and thus in-principle intersubjective world of coherent and enduring objects. The mind is not simply passive to sensations: it works them up into a world of meaningful objects through the employment of its innate principles.

In developing his system of categories Kant takes his cue from formal logic, which does not belong to the character of things but to the way the mind sets about thinking about things. It furnishes mechanisms for working out implications and inferences that, apart from the materials they are given to work with as starting points, yield only validity and not truth. Truth depends on the character of the starting points. And so we need a logic supplementary to formal logic, which is the logic of implication and inference; we need a transcendental logic of reference that yields the experiential starting points. Kant takes the table of types of judgment from formal logic and develops from them a table of categories of reference.[13] Basically they are arranged around the general headings *quantity, quality, relation,* and *mode,* which will appear throughout Kant's work, furnishing the basis for a systematic inventory of aspects of whatever objects he will treat. The most important aspects are found under the heading of *relation*: substance-accidents, cause-effect, and reciprocity. All objects appear, in and through the variations of their sensory accidents, as relatively independent and enduring functional wholes, as substances linked in causal chains of antecedence and consequence, and as involved in reciprocal relations with their contemporaries. Affording principles for sorting and organizing our sensory experience, such categories are always filled in our wakeful life.

In addition to these transcendental concepts there are empirical concepts like dog, tree, and cloud. In both cases there is the contrast of the sensory individuals and the universal concepts. For Kant the bridge between them is afforded by the imagination—"an art hidden in the depth of the soul"—which provides examples of empirical concepts and schemata of the categories. In the latter function such schematizing always involves some temporal feature: substance is endurance through time, causality antecedence and consequence in time, and so on.[14]

Through the operation of the categories via the imagination, experience comes to take on the character of a single whole of phenomena, of appearances. If all appearances are appearances *of* something—albeit for Kant an unknowable thing-in-itself—they are also always appearances *to* someone. In some way co-perceived or ap-perceived with whatever appears and yet ever transcending the sphere of objects and the formal and categorical conditions making objectivity possible, there is what Kant calls the transcendental unity of apperception, the "I think" that must accompany any representation.[15] It is always an "I" that takes up things through the functions described.

Beyond the categories employed by the "I think," there is a third level of a priori forms of the mind, corresponding to our reference to being as reference to the totality: the ideas of reason.[16] Kant uses the term *Vernunft* (reason), in contrast to *Verstand* (understanding employing the categories), to indicate the drive toward totality as the background or horizon against or within which all experience occurs. Based on three different ways in which we are related to the totality, reason operates with three totalizing ideas: the ideas of World, Soul, and God. The idea of World, or the cosmological idea, constitutes the horizon of all our attempts to build up and extend our understanding of what is given from without. It is a lure that draws us on in an ever-broadening but never-ending process toward completion of our knowledge of the cosmos. The idea of Soul functions in the same way regarding our attempts to understand our inward life, the life of consciousness. Finally, the idea of God functions as the Plotinian One, ground of the differentiation of experience into outward and inward, as that which, if known, would unify all our experience. It would make the universe to be a uni-verse, turning the plurality of experiences toward unity, displaying the ultimate coherence of all things. Contrary to the categories of understanding, which are always filled in ordinary experience, Ideas of Reason can never be filled by any experience or concept.

Kant's analysis begins with the streaming plurality of sensations as the lowest level; it terminates in the idea of the unity of the whole in the One.

In between, functioning in relation to the lowest level of enduring plurality in sensory givenness, we have the unfolding of more comprehensive levels of unification employed by the "I think" via the work of the imagination: the forms of space and time, the categories of understanding, and the ideas of reason under the One Being. This enables Kant to account for the various sciences that have emerged and developed since the time of the Greeks. Geometry, as the first science, has its origin in the a priori form of space; and mathematics in general unfolds different modes of possible spatial and temporal interrelation.[17] Formal logic emerges from analysis of the structures of implication and inference operative in geometry but extended to all experience. Physics operates out of a combination of mathematics with the categories, especially the notion of causality as necessary sequence of antecedents and consequents. Kant understands causality here in the manner of Newtonian science, where the whole state of the universe at a given time determines the whole state at a subsequent time to yield the Clockwork Universe. It is a world of universal determinism.[18] These stable and developing sciences clue us in to the responsible use of the mind in coming to know. Such use consists in unpacking and interrelating the forms of the mind with the sensory appearance of things. In this Kant insists that "thoughts without [sensory] intuition are empty; [sensory] intuitions without concepts are blind."[19] Only their interrelation yields responsible knowledge.

Then there is metaphysics, the putative queen of the sciences, which claims to know the fundamental principles of being, to be able to leap over the horizons established through patient work in other disciplines and to operate in the region of pure reason. Looking over the history of metaphysical thought and comparing it with formal logic, mathematics, and mathematical physics, we see that metaphysics, far from presenting itself like they do as a stable and developing science, appears as one great battlefield of contending factions.[20] Kant attempts to show that we are so related to the totality that there is no way of resolving the fundamental conflicting views that necessarily emerge from our position in relation to the whole. Thought that moves in this region necessarily generates irresolvable antinomies: for example, that the world had to have a beginning, as Bonaventure for one argued, since, among other things, there would have to be in any now an actual infinity of immortal souls that is being added to constantly;[21] or that the world cannot have a beginning, the opposite of which Aristotle called ridiculous, since the eternity of time follows from the nature of time as moving synthesis of the before and after in the now.[22] Aquinas recognized the antinomy and claimed that the issue was in principle undecidable by reason and can only be known by revelation.[23] Kant goes the round of such antinomies.[24]

Kant then attacks the alleged crown of metaphysics, the proofs for the existence of God. He discusses three possibilities: one is based on a particular experience—that of goal directedness; a second is based on experience in general; and a third is based on abstraction from all experience—which he calls the teleological, the cosmological, and the ontological proofs respectively.[25] The cosmological proof, if it proves, proves only a first cause without being able to determine its features. The teleological proof, again if it proves, proves that the causation involved entails intelligence, which—as Hume noted—could be plural, demonic, or value-indifferent, given what is given in experience. For the first two to work as proofs of an infinitely perfect God, Kant claims they need to invoke the ontological argument, an argument first advanced by Anselm and here given the name by Kant. It is based on the logic of the notion of being *(ontos)*. The notion of perfection, of fullness of being, is that than which no greater can be conceived; that which is outside merely being thought about is greater than what is merely thought about; hence the notion of perfection or the fullness of being contains the note of existing beyond merely being thought about.[26] But, Kant observes, as did Aquinas before him,[27] that this attempt supposes an unwarranted move from the necessity of thought to the necessity of existence. Hence all the proofs advanced ultimately do not prove in any necessary way but at best provide ways of making final sense of things. They are, in contemporary terms, hermeneutic rather than metaphysical.

The upshot of this analysis is that in this life our cognitive faculties are not made for insight into things-in-themselves. Responsible thinking resists the temptation to eschew patient, cooperative work in the established sciences and to leap beyond the horizon to the ultimate in the employment of "pure reason" (i.e., reason operating without the check of experience).[28] Our knowing is and will remain, in Nietzsche's terms, "human, all too human."

## Critique of Practical Reason

Cognitive experience is not our only experience. We also have the experience of being obligated, of having responsibility thrust upon us and of realizing that we are able either to assume the obligation or to abandon it.

This obviously raises the problem of how this is possible, given the absolute determinism of the Clockwork Universe. Kant refers to the experience of freedom involved in moral action as "the sole noumenal fact."[29] The entire analysis of the first critique yielded a world of phenomena, of appearance made possible by the character of our faculties. If the world *appears* as determined, that still leaves open the possibility that noumena, things-in-themselves, might not be so determined.[30] And our moral experience presents us with a demand for freedom as responsible self-determination.

Now this relation between freedom and obligation may seem unusual to most people, who see freedom as the ability to do what they like. But what we like is determined by antecedent conditions, beginning with native physiology and psychology and interplaying with cultural shaping. Liking is a welling up of feeling that can be explained deterministically. The experience of obligation awakens us to the possibility of not being determined by our spontaneous likes and dislikes but of determining ourselves over against them, of shaping and directing them through choices based on judgment.[31]

On the other hand, what is required for genuine moral behavior are criteria for assessing our own likes and dislikes as well as the obligations that a given society imposes on its members. Here Kant introduces what he calls the categorical imperative, which he contrasts with a hypothetical imperative.[32] The latter takes the form of an if-then proposition: *If* you wish to achieve X, *then* do Y,—basically, If you wish to be happy do X and avoid Y. By contrast, the categorical imperative poses no conditions but sets an absolute obligation. It takes several forms in Kant's articulation, three of which are particularly illuminating. The first, "So act that your principle for action can be made a norm for all humankind,"[33] is rooted in the universal orientation of the mind. The universalizability of our maxims is what is called for here. The second formulation, "Treat humanity, whether in yourselves or in others, always as an end and not simply as a means,"[34] looks to that same capacity to operate in terms of the universal (which he here calls our humanity) as significantly more than a mere means to the efficient gratification of our appetites. It is this which gives an inalienable dignity to every human being. The third formulation, "So act as if you were legislating for a kingdom of ends,"[35] looks to the togetherness of all humans as ends in themselves. Worked into the concrete, this involves the obligation both to the ongoing rational development of our faculties and to ongoing benevolence toward other persons in assisting their development.[36] Such principles allow us both to put our appetites in order and to judge the obligations laid upon individuals by a given social order, for the cannibal might feel obligated to eat the heart of his enemy and might experience extreme feelings of guilt if he chose not to, even though the practice involves the most extreme instance of treating a human being as a mere means and in no way as an end.

Morality involves not just acting *in accord with* such principles, it also involves acting *because of* such principles. One could, for example, act honestly and, like Ben Franklin, consider such action as the best policy; but one could also do so, not because of the moral obligation involved, but because people will trust you and therefore give you better business deals so you can make more money and thus gratify yourself more effectively. We might also follow moral rules, not because they are what we as humans ought to do, but because we wish to obtain some reward or to avoid some punishment.

But to operate in terms of such principles is to be involved in a struggle with our appetites and with those who refuse so to operate. Often those who strive to live up to such principles encounter great difficulty and are far from experiencing happy fulfillment, whereas those who fail or refuse often experience ease and contentment. For Kant this argues for postulating (not conclusively proving) the immortality of the soul so that there could be a coincidence between happiness and deservedness to be happy met with so infrequently in this life. Such coincidence Kant calls the *summum bonum,* in an anthropological transformation of the medieval concept, which applied to seeing God Himself.[37] Achievement of the human *summum bonum* also furnishes the basis for arguing to a Being Who can read the innermost movements of the human heart to see whether one has acted inwardly *because* of the moral order and not simply externally *in accord with* that order. It demands something approaching omniscience and omnipotence together with a sense of ultimate justice in One Who would be able to bring about the required coincidence. Beyond a first principle or a finite, plural, and morally indifferent cause or causes, the moral order implies all that we have come to recognize as God: omniscient, omnipotent, all-just creator and judge.[38] Freedom in relation to the deterministic World, the immortality of the Soul, and a moral God, inaccessible in a purely theoretical way, return as conditions for the moral order. Our shipwreck in the theoretical order points to the real purpose of our faculties: moral action in this world.[39]

The analysis of the first two critiques brings into focus a problem to which I called attention earlier, one of the deepest problems confronting reflection on the place of science in the modern world: the problem of the relation between determinism and freedom. Kant presents us here with two separated realms: determinism operates at the level of phenomena, of things appearing under conditions set by our faculties; freedom as rational self-determination implies transcendence of the phenomenal order. The question is how they are related. It is the third critique that attends to that interrelation.[40]

## Critique of Judgment

We reach the heart of the present exposition, the work in which the felt tonality, the aesthetic feeling of awe that governs the critical project is given its due. Its title does not immediately suggest its contents. The introduction presents judgment as the link between the universal concept and the experienced individual, a function previously assigned to the imagination. Kant goes on to distinguish two forms of judgment: determinate judgment and reflective judgment.[41] In the determinate judgment the universal is given and judgment subsumes the individual under it, as in the general operation of the categories as fundamental a priori; in the reflective judgment, the individual is given and the one judging seeks the universal under which that individual can be placed. It is reflective judgment that is Kant's focus here, and that in two specially chosen domains: the aesthetic and the teleological.

In the first critique Kant presented the principles for establishing objectivity in experience, for moving from a subjective "rhapsody of impressions"—presumably the situation of the infant—to an intersubjective world of coherence and consistency.[42] But those principles provide nothing of the *kinds* of objects that can so appear. For that we have to look to the regular collocations of sensations within the conditions of objectivity. When we pay attention to what is thus given, two orders jut into prominence: aesthetic objects (whether works of art or things of nature, whether evoking the experience of beauty or of sublimity) and living forms in their logically hierarchical relations of genera and species.[43]

The key experience is our awareness of our ability to transform nature through concepts, which is Kant's definition for art in general, whether that of the plow maker or of the sculptor.[44] It seems not accidental but fitting that the discussion of art appears in the center of the work, with the notion of genius occupying the exact center because this provides the analogue for a series of reflective judgments that attempt to make comprehensive sense out of what is given in experience.[45] For Kant they amount to projecting onto nature itself our experience of operating according to pre-conceived goals. Thus when we attend to living things, we see that, though they cannot violate the laws of mechanics, they operate in a way that we can only understand on an analogy with our own transformative activity. Thus we introduce, in addition to mechanism, the notion of teleology, or operation in terms of a prior conception *(logos)* of a goal *(telos)* we seek. Living forms display themselves *as if* they were operating on some such grounds when they form themselves through the articulation of their or-gans as instruments for the realization of vital purposes and when they search outside themselves for food, drink, and mate.[46]

In the second book of his *Physics* Aristotle makes the same move.[47] From an analysis of artefaction as externally imposed form caused by an artisan operating on some material in terms of a preconceived goal, Aris-totle internalizes formal, final, and efficient causes in the psyche, the basic formal and self-forming principle of living beings orchestrating material elements to suit its natural purposes.[48] Kant's contention is that, though this is our only way to make sense out of living forms, it is a projection, not an insight into the metaphysical constitution of things. Organisms act *as if* unconsciously they were operating like we do consciously. (Since *logos* suggests conscious conception, instead of teleo-*logy*, theoretical biologists today have introduced the term *teleonomy*, where *nomos* refers, not to a con-cept, but to a law of goal seeking.)[49] Kant thereby moves us both backward, behind modern mechanistic physics, to an earlier view of nature, and for-ward to the biological views of the twentieth century. Thereby he also points out a large region in which mechanisms are naturally taken up into purposes, smoothing the way for thinking of human self-determining free-dom as able to operate in the universe described in physics by subsuming its mechanisms under human purposes.

The second region where Kant projects human purposiveness is the aesthetic region. In beautiful forms and in situations evoking the feeling of the sublime, it is as if nature were so arranged as to bring about the pe-culiar feelings that indicate the presence of such forms and situations.[50] Of course, in the case of artistic forms, nature *is* rearranged for that pur-pose, only in that case the artist does not operate entirely in the same way as the plow maker. The production of artistic forms requires genius, the gift through which, as Kant has it, "nature gives the rule to art."[51] It is his or her inborn nature even more than it is mastery of certain knowable techniques that makes the artist. In really inspired art, the artist has no awareness of the wellsprings of his or her novel ideas. Here again, as in the case of natural beauty, it is as if nature, working through the artist as the source of inspiration, had the purpose of bringing about the peculiar aesthetic feelings. Indeed, for Kant it is inspired art that sensitizes us to the beauties of nature.[52] It is as if through the artist nature is teaching us to appreciate her own beauties. We retain something of this insight when we refer to a scene or a person as being "pretty as a picture." Kant thus speaks of the whole aesthetic region as exhibiting "purposiveness without a purpose"—that is, appearing as if it had a purpose without our being able definitively to assign a real purpose, as we can in ordinary human activity. So the general concept arrived at by reflective judgment for thinking both the organic and the aesthetic regions is "purposiveness."[53] Pleasure itself—aesthetic or otherwise—Kant understands as the sign that a purpose has been fulfilled.[54] That is what gives unity to what otherwise seem to be two unrelated regions.

Besides the regions of natural organic form and aesthetic form, there is a third region where Kant deals with purposiveness. Considering the whole of nature as a purposive system, Kant finally projects the notion of God as a divine artist operating through ideas of species and ultimately through the overarching moral idea, creating an arena for the development of human faculties through the work of culture under the moral law. The notion of an ultimate "technic of nature" in a divine moral Artisan will thus draw the whole critical work of reason into unity with itself.[55] But, note well, it is only in the mode of "as if." This is the way to make sense out of the whole of our experience, but it does not guarantee that this is the way things as a whole finally are. We are still in the realm of phenomena. Our awareness is always "human, all too human."[56]

In the aesthetic region Kant focuses on two distinguishable objects: the beautiful and the sublime. I will deal with each in turn.

### The Beautiful

Kant's analysis of the beautiful exhibits two basic movements that are clarified by his distinction between free and dependent beauty.[57] Free beauty is pure (i.e., abstracted from all admixture of concepts); dependent beauty involves a relation to concepts. Kant begins with an analysis of free or pure beauty, separating beauty from features with which it is for the most part mixed and therefore often confused. There is the empiricist confusion of beauty with what simply produces agreeable sensations; there is the rationalist confusion of beauty with perfection, whether physical or moral, measured by some conceptual and therefore intellectual standard.[58] While, more often than not, agreeable sensations and concepts of what a given object ought to be accompany beautiful objects, for Kant these features do not constitute their beauty. We have then first to separate out beauty from its usual accompaniments and view it by itself; then we have to fold it back into its relation to its usual accompaniments. Pure beauty is trivial beauty, yielding only aesthetic surface; it is literally super-ficial. Kant uses as examples of pure beauty flowers, bird plumage, and seashells in the natural order and arabesque drawings (wallpaper design) as well as musical fantasias (without words) in the artistic order.[59] Nontrivial beauty is dependent beauty, requiring the unity of aesthetic surface with concepts expressing something more significant, especially in what Kant will term the Ideal of Beauty (of which more later).[60]

Kant begins his aesthetic with an analysis of free beauty. He arranges his analysis around the four basic genera of logical judgments I have mentioned earlier: quality, quantity, relation, and mode. Schopenhauer considers this exercise a procrustean bed, where the given has to be either stretched or chopped off to get it to fit into the forms of the first critique.[61] Jean-François Lyotard suggests that the exercise is intended to show the uselessness of the direct application of the categories: the aesthetic given escapes the logic of the categories and produces "logical monsters."[62]

Beginning with *quality*, he notes that the judgment of taste involved in the perception of the beautiful is based on a feeling of pleasure and is thus subjective. But aesthetic pleasure is a peculiar sort. Our bodily pleasures are what he calls "interested": feeling has to do here with how the object can be used.[63] As Aristotle noted, the hound loves the look of the hare, but only because it is potential food.[64] And whatever pleasure we might find in the good is likewise "interested," though in a different way. Aesthetic pleasure is, by contrast, "disinterested," a feature of a state of mind in which we attend, Kant says, not to "existence," but only to the sheer appearance of the object.[65] By the term *existence* Kant presumably here refers to such features as the process of the coming to be of the object or the causal consequences that follow from the reality of what appears as well as the real substructure of the object. In the case of food, one of the features of existence is that it will be consumed to nourish the body; in the case of an art work—for example, a painting—there is the chemical composition of the gesso and paint as well as the nature of the canvas and the support of the stretcher. None of this is a matter of direct aesthetic concern. Aesthetically we contemplate the beauty of an object's display without concern for any such "existential" features and therefore "what we can get out of it." We thus obtain "disinterested pleasure." One could profitably consider here the difference between an aesthetic and an erotic satisfaction in attending to nude statuary. Detached from the compulsion of our own bodily appetites and from all desire to subsume the object under our projects, we are able to give the object what Kant calls free favoring, treating it for its own sake. Here one needs to distinguish a focus on one's own feelings from a focus on certain features of the object. Hence, even though distinctively aesthetic feeling is the first criterion of the presence of the beautiful,[66] Kant will swing attention from the peculiar pleasure involved in aesthetic perception to the object of such perception. He will attend to what he calls the "form" of the object.[67]

The feeling involved is variously described as one of harmony, of enlivening, and of free play—all attributed to the peculiar relation between imagination and understanding.[68] *Harmony* by itself suggests something static—and this seems to be the way Schopenhauer was to understand it. But *enlivening* and *free play* suggest something more dynamic. Unfortunately, Kant does very little to elaborate on these features. In his discussion of art, he notes that a symbol creates an indeterminate set of associations governed by their harmonizing with the disposition proper to a given form, so that the mind is set in motion to move freely among these associated images and—presumably—among the concepts that might be associated with them. There would then be a certain creative moment even in the reception of the beautiful object, so that, as one commentator suggests, the meaning of free play is creativity.[69]

The judgments listed under quality in logic are affirmative, negative, and infinite, where *infinite* combines the affirmative and the negative, negating the negation to arrive at a new affirmation.[70] Perhaps that is what disinterested satisfaction involves: the positivity of interested satisfaction from the point of view of the perceiver involves the negation of the object's independence; but the aesthetic stance of "unconstrained favoring" negates that negation, allows the object to present itself "for its own sake" and thus provides a higher level of positive subjective satisfaction, not limited by the object's subordination to need.

Under the heading of *quantity*, Kant speaks of the judgment of taste as providing a "subjectively universal" satisfaction.[71] A satisfaction focused on the beautiful appearance for its own sake and not generated by any individual interest on the part of the viewing subject raises one above the peculiarities of one's private subjectivity, but not in the way a concept does. The universality involved is not objective but subjective: it lays a claim upon all human beings to respond to the beautiful object, which is itself not a universal but a distinctively individual object.[72]

The formal logical categories under the heading of quantity are: universal, particular, and individual, where, once more, the third synthesizes the first two.[73] A particular merely instantiates the type that is a universal over against the particulars that fall under it. An individual is such that in it the type is not only instantiated but fully realized. In the aesthetic object, the universality of the claim of beauty has a peculiar fulfillment, making the beautiful object a distinctive individuality. Furthermore, Kant focuses on the universality of the claim that the distinctive individuality of the aesthetic object makes: that all should respond to it appreciatively. Here we must distinguish between "I like it" and "It is beautiful." The former might refer to the merely agreeable, and regarding that one might say: "Different strokes for different folks." But the latter appeals to all observers.[74]

In connection with this Kant distinguishes the charm of particular sensory features and the form exhibited by the beautiful object. Compare a melody played on a violin with the same played on a tuba. The differing instrumental timbres might appeal differently to different people, depending on what pleases them. More, or even most, people might prefer the violin. But it is not the sensory mode as such that, according to Kant, constitutes the beautiful; it is the *form* of the melody. To prefer the sound of the tuba to that of the violin is not a defect in the perceiver; but to fail to appreciate the beauty of the form *is* considered a defect. The beautiful is such that all *ought* to appreciate it. The sensory charms, which strike different persons differently, merely serve to bring into focus the form, which all should learn to appreciate as the sameness in the difference.

It is in this context that Kant also disallows the entry of an explicit concept into the aesthetic judgment qua aesthetic. As we noted in the first moment, the judgment of taste with regard to the beautiful is based on a peculiar feeling, not on a concept, not even the concept of perfection, otherwise we would have an intellectual and not an aesthetic judgment.[75] But for Kant there is ultimately an *implicit* concept involved, since the judgment is an interplay of the universal and the particular.[76] In fact, for Kant it is the judgment that generates the aesthetic feeling.[77] As I indicated previously, that feeling he identifies as one of harmony in the free play of the relation between imagination and understanding.[78] That relation is the form of judgment, the form of the togetherness of the faculties required for any judgment: imagination to synthesize the manifold of sensations, understanding to provide the concept for that manifold.[79]

There is not a little ambiguity in Kant's formulations. On the one hand, in the initial moment, the judgment of the beautiful is based on a feeling; on the other hand, the feeling is based on a judgment. Judgment involves a certain detachment, a holding one's own in the face of the given, and yet the experience of the beautiful involves being taken by the form of the object, which demands unconstrained favoring. On the one hand, the experience involved is that of the form of the judgment; on the other, the form of the object. The whole region involves a certain tension of opposites. What is involved in each of the features indicated is the reciprocal emergence of judgment and feeling, of detachment and attachment, of the form of the judgment and the form of the beautiful thing. But Kant gives the priority to the judgment because it alone releases us from "constrained favoring" and allows us to let the object be itself.

Free play suggests not being bound by the ordinary operation of judgment. Kant claims that an aesthetic idea gives rise to much thought without being fully determined to one thought.[80] A beautiful work is overdetermined: it sets the cognitive faculties in peculiar motion to play within certain limits. This relation of free play is the ground of the claim to universality, for it is that which makes any knowing and any distinctively human communication possible: that imagination as the faculty of gathering up sensations harmonizes with our faculty of providing universals fit for understanding such a gathering. According to Kant, the feeling of the a priori form of the judgment as the harmonic relation between imagination and understanding is what is evoked by and reciprocally tied to the coming into focus of the form of the beautiful sensible thing, produced in works of art through aesthetic ideas.[81] And just as Kant speaks of the form as the play of figures in space or of sounds in time,[82] so the form of the judgment to which it corresponds involves the free play of the cognitive faculties. Play, whether of figures or of cognitive faculties, indicates a freedom from domination by purposes, appetitive or moral. The aesthetic is a space of fully free activity, though finally it is tied in several ways to our ultimately moral destiny. But it is the reflective distance afforded by this relation between the universal and the particular that pulls us out of the merely private subjectivity of the life of the senses and allows for the universal communicability of aesthetic feelings.[83]

Eventually Kant identifies the implicit concept involved in the judgment of the beautiful as that of the supersensuous ground of experience (presumably the same as the notion of the noumenon, or thing-in-itself), an indeterminate concept of reason that can never be filled.[84] Indeed, it is that concept that gets differentiated, by reason of the relation of exterior and interior involved in all experience, into the ideas of World and Soul on the one hand and the idea of God as ground of their relationship on the other. There is then a reference to the noumenal that provides the peculiar attraction of the beautiful, though for Kant, and contrary to Plato, this noumenal cannot itself appear. And since our fundamental relation to the noumenal is moral, Kant ultimately aligns the beautiful with the moral, not as a means thereto but as a symbol thereof.[85] The beautiful has its own constitution, and it is only when we attend to it as such that it can function as a symbol. Thus even colors come to take on the qualities of human action: bold, soft, stately, and so on.

The presence of the indeterminate concept of the supersensible as the horizon of all human wakefulness allows Kant to solve what he calls the antinomy of taste, which arises when we reflect on the aesthetic[86] One side of that antinomy is expressed in the often-quoted proverb *De gustibus non disputandum* (regarding taste there ought not to be dispute).[87] The other side of the antinomy is the factual dispute that goes on throughout the ages. Insofar as the dispute claims to rest on determinate concepts from which one could rationally argue, for Kant dispute is beside the point, for the judgment of taste rests on a feeling and not a determinate concept. Nonetheless, by reason of its alignment with the indeterminate concept of the supersensible, taste generates dispute because there is a universal claim made in the attribution of beauty. The *de gustibus* proverb applies to the agreeable, to our attention to sensuous charm rather than to beautiful form. Beautiful form evokes the harmony of the cognitive faculties and refers, beyond this, to the indeterminate concept of the supersensuous, which receives determination through the moral order.

Dependent beauty ties the beautiful thing to determinate concepts of what a thing ought to be and thus to the notion of perfection. In this connection Kant introduces the so-called Ideal of Beauty, which he locates in the depiction of the idealized form of the human being as morally expressive.[88] In this case the beauty of the form is tied to its expression of something not directly perceptible by the senses, a state of mind. When the moral state of mind finds a bodily display in a form that itself constitutes a norm for the species, we have the Ideal of Beauty. State of mind and state of sensory display have to be proportionate to one another for ideal beauty to be realized. However, for Kant, as distinct from Plato, the moral state of mind is not itself beautiful but is only said to be so by metaphoric analogy. The Ideal of Beauty is the result of a conceptual amalgam of two distinct but related regions: sensory exteriority and moral inwardness.[89]

In discussing the expressive fusion of a moral state of mind with a species norm, Kant suggests that one arrives at such a norm—remember it is a norm of display—by a kind of superimposition of experienced forms of the same kind until an average form is delineated. It suggests a type, an aesthetic idea with which nature itself can be thought to operate in producing the inexperienceable substructure in the thing that will display itself in approximation to that norm.[90] Given Kant's description here, the art that carries the ideal most fully would be sculpture and, to a lesser extent because limited to two-dimensional presentation, painting. The other art forms would seem to be excluded.

In his analysis of the judgment of the beautiful, under the genus of *relation*, Kant refers to the feature of what he calls "purposiveness without a purpose," something we have already considered: beautiful objects appear when the perception of their form brings about the free play between imagination and understanding, *as if* nature had produced beautiful forms for that purpose.[91] It is helpful to recall the categories Kant located in the first critique under relation: substance-accidents, cause-effect, reciprocity.[92] The notion of purpose gathers them up in the notion of an organism, governed by purpose, reciprocally cause and effect of itself, whose accidents, caused by the substance, cause the substance itself to become actual.[93] That notion, as we have already noted, locates the beautiful, together with the organic, in the larger view of purposiveness.

Under the genus of *mode* Kant calls attention to the peculiar necessity attending the judgment of taste. Under the logical genus of mode are the categories of actuality, possibility, and necessity, together with their opposites.[94] For Kant it is possible for any representation to be bound up with pleasure. A pleasant representation actually produces pleasure. But an aesthetic representation has a necessary reference to pleasure.[95] There is an appeal to a kind of necessity in the form of an obligation laid upon all humankind to attend appreciatively to what can be designated as beautiful. Being able to do this involves the development of a *sensus communis*, a common sense.[96] This common sense is to be distinguished, on the one hand, from the kind of understanding common to a given community regarding proper operation in that community (better called common understanding). On the other hand, it is different than the Scholastic *sensus communis*, the single root of the sense powers that allows us to integrate their differing objects into a single phantasm, making possible the appearance of a given individual or type in and through the multiple perspectives afforded by the operations of each of the sense powers—a notion derived from Aristotle.[97] As contrasted with common understanding and Scholastic common sense, an aesthetic common sense is a kind of ideal to be striven for: a capacity to judge beautiful objects built up through attention to the classical models that have emerged and stood the test of time by their continued ability to draw the attention of sensitive and reflective individuals throughout the ages.[98]

This does not mean that the past furnishes the unalterable set of rules for judgment and operation in the present, as certain neoclassical critics would have it. Proper attention to the classics involves the ability to contact the same sources of judgment and activity that the original geniuses contacted in the production of their works. They teach us how to see and, if we also are gifted with genius, to create works that are both original and exemplary.[99] For Kant there is no substitute for direct encounter with the beautiful, for direct experience of form without having to appeal to explicit criteria. There is here a kind of aesthetic autonomy parallel to moral autonomy. One has to learn to see for oneself. Rules derived from past experience or from what others—especially the experts—tell us can get in the way of being open to the emergence of novelty in the work of genius.

Kant attempted to analyze the necessity he saw in judgments of the beautiful which is indicated in the difference between the two claims "It is beautiful," which testifies to a peculiar subjective feeling of any properly disposed spectator in its presence, and "I like it," which testifies to a subjective but also merely private state in relation to what I find agreeable. The former requires cultivation of attention and is based on a judgment; the latter has the character of undisciplined immediacy. That cultivation is made possible by attention to the classics. Particular claims we might make could be mistaken and we are given pause by appeal to the community, living and dead, of the cultivated judges. However, the ultimate appeal has to be, not to that community and its judgments, but to one's own direct perception. What they say has to be validated directly by each, so that the community's judgment might be shifted by a single perceiver getting that community to see what it otherwise missed in the object. There is thus a pivotal relation between judgment and perception here. According to Kant, the feeling the cultivated observer has in the presence of the object is precisely a feeling of that harmonious relation between understanding and imagination involved in all judgment. This might be why those who are so cultivated tend to be those who are involved in professions and who are regularly called upon to use their judgment in often novel ways in their professional work.[100]

## The Sublime

In terms of the historical genesis of the third critique, the notion of the sublime was added to the project.[101] Kant himself refers to it as an appendage *(Anhang)*.[102] In Lyotard's reading, through the notion of the sublime, "the teleological machine [the attempted gathering together of reason in the notion of cosmic purpose] explodes." Rather than bringing reason into harmony, the sublime exposes the "spasmodic state" critical thought experiences when it reaches its limit, the "principle of fury" as the demand for the unconditioned, which the critique restrains.[103] This, however, seems extreme. Reference to the totality coupled with the notion of the *summum bonum* and of immortality introduces a principle of hope to which, in my reading, the experience of the sublime bears witness.[104]

However, Kant's own later insertion into the plan of the third critique and his designation of it as an appendage seems to challenge our interpretation of the sublime as the dispositional ground of the critical project as a whole. This seems strange, since he had already written *Observations on the Feeling of the Beautiful and the Sublime* during his precritical period (1764).[105] What is crucial is that, in the text from the second critique cited in the introduction to this chapter, he highlighted the disposition of awe accompanying the contemplation of "the starry skies above and the moral law within" without designating it explicitly as the sublime. In the third critique, the *Bewunderung und Ehrfurcht* provoked by the starry skies above and the moral law within, supreme instances of the objects of the first and second critiques respectively, are focused on both regions together, as the overwhelming magnitude of the distance between us and the stars schematizes the superiority of our ultimately moral relation to the totality. The cool feeling of *Achtung* or respect in relation to the moral law is turned in the direction of an emotional, stirring experience on the occasion of encountering something overwhelming in the outer world. In Kant's analysis, what overwhelms us in nature threatens our empirical insignificance: the stars make us appear tiny indeed. As the Psalmist says, "When I look at the heavens, the work of your fingers, . . . what are human beings that you are mindful of them?" But what follows is significant for Kant's analysis: "You have made them a little lower than God. . . . "[106] An instrumentally aided empirical inspection linked to calculation and scientific theory shows us as flyspecks on the surface of this flyspeck we call the earth. But our founding mental reference to the totality places us infinitely beyond even the largest conceivable finite extension and power. The initial emotional putdown brought about by the empirical consideration checks and dams up our spontaneous feeling of life. An awakening to the incomparable character of our own mind releases the dammed up feeling to produce a feeling of exaltation. This analysis lies at the background of Rudolph Otto's notion of the Holy as the *mysterium tremendum et fascinans*—the mystery that simultaneously repels and attracts us, that causes us to tremble in fear and to be bound to it in fascination.[107] Such an experience requires a certain level of mental cultivation to resist the purely negative feeling produced in us by nature's magnitude. The savage cowers in fear; one who has been awakened to the transcendent character of the human mind is in a position to experience the sublime.

The sublime exhibits the same four moments as the beautiful (disinterested satisfaction, subjective universality, purposiveness without a purpose, and necessary satisfaction), but it has another basis.[108] However, whereas the beautiful involves the feeling of harmonious interplay between understanding *(Verstand)* and imagination, the sublime involves a tension between imagination and reason *(Vernunft)*. Through the emergence of beautiful form within the space created by distancing oneself from the pressure of need-based perception, imagination and understanding experience their harmonious relation; we find ourselves at home in the world. But if beauty involves loving something without interest, sublimity involves esteeming something *against* sensory interest.[109] The deep background of psychic harmony in tune with the appearing environment lies in being pried loose from any being-at-home by reason's horizonal reference to the totality. Mind is directed to an unreachable beyond. As Lyotard would have it: "The absolute is never there, never given in a presentation, but it is always 'present' as a call to think beyond the 'there.' Ungraspable, but unforgettable. Never restored, never abandoned."[110] This creates a fundamental tension within the human being, an irremovable *Widerstreit*. Paralleling Derrida, Lyotard speaks of it as the *différend*, that which is different than anything that falls within the field of our experience and must be permanently deferred in coming to presence. Lyotard makes this *différend* the center of his thought.[111] This both wounds imagination as the faculty of presentation by the essential nonpresentability of the encompassing Beyond and gives imagination an extension it would not otherwise have by luring it into the construction of symbols. The sublime *(das Erhaben)* performs an *Aufhebung* of imagination, both canceling it and taking it up.[112] It generates alternative traditions in the history of art such as Mannerism or the Baroque or Surrealism, which embody an aesthetics of excess, and Suprematism or Abstract Art in general, which embody a minimalist aesthetic, both standing over against classical representationalist realism of the beautiful. This embodies the basic controversy between the Moderns and the Ancients, between "an aesthetic of 'presence' and the pagan poetics of good form," between the presence-in-absence of an unreachable (because infinite) encompassment and the full-bodied observation of familiar objects idealized.[113] In the Chinese tradition, we have the alternation between the Confucian focus on being together with others in familiar society and the Taoist belonging to the mysterious cosmic whole.[114]

Kant actually refers to three types of sublime experience. The two that are focal in his exposition appear on the basis of nature in relation to cognition and desire respectively; the third appears in relation to persons. Regarding the cognitive side of reason there is what Kant calls the mathematical sublime, an instance of which is the starry skies above. The experience of our own insignificance in this instance is linked to our ability to think beyond any given magnitude of the encompassing totality. From the point of view of understanding, this introduces us to a *progressus ad infinitum,* which Hegel will later designate as "the spurious [or bad] infinite."[115] However, what is at stake in relation to reason is the ability to think *the absolute totality* as the substrate underlying all experience. Reason runs ahead of the *progressus* of understanding to encompass it absolutely—though only in thought.[116] The empirically based experience of being *abgestossen* (repelled) joins with the reflectively based experience of our relation to the totality, to which we are simultaneously *angezogen* (attracted). This is the fundamental experience of the antinomic character—not simply of the *thinking* of the totality, but of the *existence* of human reality manifest to itself experientially as held in the tension between the at-home and the Beyond.

But the experience of the "mathematical" sublime, the sublime in relation to quantity, has a higher finality in relation to the desire of reason, which is the will. For Kant human reality does not culminate in the contemplative or theoretical but in the practical. The antinomies of theoretical reason block the way of theoretical completion but point to "the sole noumenal fact" of freedom under law, which leads into the immortality of the soul and the divine as omniscient, omnipotent, and just judge. The mathematical sublime is surmounted by the dynamically sublime, manifest in the encounter with the overpowering aspects of nature, nature under the aspect of causality.[117] In relation to the storm at sea or the tornado, what is threatened is not only the sense of one's significance in the massive order of space, but one's very existence. One is reminded of Pascal's reflection on the human being as a "thinking reed" that a mere vapor can destroy, but whose whole dignity consists in thought.[118] But for Kant thought itself points to an awareness of the ultimate superiority of our moral vocation.[119] For Kant, then, nature in these displays is not sublime; sublime in the proper sense of the term is our vocation as possessors of reason. Nature's display only serves as a symbol of this distinctively human superiority.[120] It would seem to be another way, beyond the beauties of nature and art, in which we gain some indication that "we are meant" by the world process, that we are in some sense the purpose of what appears in the world. Only in this case, the tendency of the beautiful to make us feel at home in the world is unsettled by our ever-unfulfilled reference to the undisclosed totality.

However, in addition to his major focus on objects occasioning the feeling of the sublime, Kant's discussion of the sublime in his General Comment on aesthetic judgments also focuses on persons and thus slides over into sublime dispositions. He includes enthusiasm as an affective straining of our forces by ideas that establishes a powerful and permanent disposition. Among the Jews, in their prohibition of graven images, that very negation in relation to the infinity of God produces a most exalted feeling of the sublime. But because enthusiasm deprives the mind of its ability to engage in free deliberation about principles, it falls prey to fanaticism, which substitutes ferment for insight and easily slides into superstition. For Kant, every vigorous affect is sublime. He mentions here anger and indignation, which lead us to overcome powerful resistance. But more sublime is the noble character pursuing its principles with vigor and without affect. Among the sublime dispositions Kant also includes isolation from society, provided it rests, not on misanthropy or anthropophobia, but on ideas that resist our sensible interest—indeed, any case of setting aside our own needs for the sake of principle Kant regards as sublime.[121] It would seem that in art the presentation of such a disposition in an ideal human form is what the Ideal of Beauty is all about.

## *Art and Genius*

As I have already indicated, art plays a pivotal role in the third critique. If we conceive of nature as divine art, ultimately as the work of a divine moral Artist working in the way in which a human artist operates with aesthetic ideas, we can bring the initially segregated realms of mechanistic nature and moral freedom into relation. We can thus bring the three regions of reason—cognitive, moral, and aesthetic—into harmony.

As I have said, for Kant genius is the inborn character through which nature gives the rule to art. His point is that genius does not operate according to explicitly known rules—or rather, though certain rules (e.g., those of technique or genre) might be implicitly operative, the distinctive character of genius is the emergence of something original, which then may be shown to exhibit rules. Like Aristotelian *phronesis*, genius in its exemplary originality is primordially rule generating rather than explicitly rule following.[122] Similarly, Giordano Bruno had maintained, in his "Discourse of Poets," that poetry is not born in rules, but rules in poetry;[123] in the 1750s in England, Joseph Warton and Edmund Young advocated a total rejection of rules in art, whether technical or aesthetic rules;[124] and what was at stake in the *Sturm und Drang*, which had swept Germany during the time just before Kant was writing his third critique, was the proclamation of the absolute radicality of genius, breaking with the past and establishing the new.[125]

In the creation of beautiful art—and it is the rendering rather than the theme that makes it beautiful—the same harmonious interplay of imagination and understanding that takes place in appreciation also takes place. But whereas appreciation is animated by the work, creation is animated by the emergence of inspiration, the fruit of "spirit" *(Geist)* as origin of aesthetic ideas.[126] Spirit for Kant does not seem to be another faculty but refers to the unknown source "in nature" that inspires as the animation of all the faculties. The ancients referred to muses or angels; Kant refers to spirit as nature giving the rule without specifying what that nature is. It is another case of a situation in which it seems "as if" there were a purposive agency operating from behind the phenomenal screen inspiring the genius to original creation.

But originality is not sufficient, for one can produce original nonsense. Rather, originality has finally to be subjected to the judgment of taste cultivated, as in Hume, by a study of the diversity of classical pieces in diverse genres and styles, a taste that has learned to discern aesthetic form and to be ready for the emergence of yet-to-be classical pieces. Genius also involves mastery of a medium in order to give body to the spirit.[127] In this way genius produces works of exemplary originality. Genius thus consists in the animation of the harmonious interplay of imagination and understanding by spirit as the source of aesthetic ideas that, linked to the judgment of taste, result in the emergence of novel works, styles, and genres that become exemplary for others.

Kant's analysis involves certain inversions of the notion of the matter-form relation as it obtains in art. On the one hand, mastery of a medium provides the material that is informed, animated by genius. But, on the other hand, genius also provides the material that is formed by taste. There is involved here a reciprocity between tradition and innovation in the relation between craft and genius on the one hand and in the relation between taste and genius on the other.

Kant goes into some detail in describing what he means by an aesthetic idea. It is the inverse of a rational Idea which, as I have previously indicated, is a concept for which no intuition is adequate, an open, horizonal concept that functions as a lure for further exploration. World, Soul, and God are the basic ideas of reason. As I suggested earlier, they articulate the founding notion of being in terms of the bifurcation of experience into empirical object and conscious subject governed by the drive for their common ground. An aesthetic idea, by contrast, is an intuition of the imagination for which no concept is adequate. An aesthetic idea gives rise to much thought without any thought being able to encompass it. Both types of ideas are similar in their calling for some kind of elaboration, the rational calling for experientially grounded conceptual filling, the aesthetic for further interpretive articulation.[128]

Kant deals with such ideas as they cluster around objects of pure beauty and of dependent beauty. Music, untitled and unaccompanied by program or text, is a prime example of pure beauty. Paralleling Aristotle, Kant sees it as a kind of language of the affections; but, beyond Aristotle, he sees it as giving expression to an indeterminate whole of an incredible wealth of thought.[129] One can see it in this way by linking it to the indeterminate concept of the supersensuous Beyond, which lures understanding toward comprehensive rationality. In this he prefigures and probably gives rise to Schopenhauer and, following him, Nietzsche, both of whom consider music as the expression of final ontological depth.[130] In the Pythagoreanizing line of Plato, Kant goes on to link music with the mathematical study of harmonics.[131] Nonetheless, he seems to backtrack on these suggestive notions by claiming that music is the lowest of the art forms, easily sliding into the merely agreeable and doing least for informing the mind. In this it is the polar opposite of poetry, the most informative of all the arts.[132]

When we come to dependent beauty, Kant sees the role of aesthetic ideas as that of providing symbolic schematization for rational ideas.[133] Thus, for example, Plato's Myth of Er, Dante's *Divina Commedia*, and Milton's *Paradise Lost* give symbolic expression to the ideas of the afterlife, of final judgment, of heaven, hell, and purgatory, all of which are morally important but cognitively empty. We can know nothing definitive about the afterlife, but we can make meaningful practical postulates that can be brought closer to us by means of imaginative symbolization. But even in relation to actual experience, art can give such things as love, death, and envy such expression as to bring them significantly closer to us than any theoretical consideration can. Artistic presentation thus sets the mind in motion, thinking more deeply about actual experience and pondering the larger implications of experience, all the while deepening our sense of presence.[134]

Kant discusses both the beautiful and the sublime in terms of the relation between imagination and the higher faculties of understanding and reason: the beautiful produces harmony in the relation between imagination and understanding; the sublime produces tension between imagination and reason. In the case of understanding within the cognitive field, imagination is, first of all, a retentive and synthesizing faculty, gathering about a single object present in the sensory field other experiences of the same sense at different times and of different senses at the same and at different times, furnishing thereby the sensory manifold that the concept is meant to comprehend.[135] In relation to the concepts generated therefrom, imagination likewise furnishes schematic examples as bridges between a given manifold and the concept. More deeply, imagination furnishes the temporal schemata that build the bridge from the pure concepts of the understanding (the categories) to the individual given in the field of sensation. Thus the category of substance is schematized as endurance through time of an entity in and through the variation of its accidents, while the category of cause and effect is schematized in terms of the temporal antecedence and consequence of linked substances in a regular way.[136] But in the aesthetic field, imagination provides the symbols that give fuller presence to the things we already know and that also bring us into a meaningful but noncognitive relation with rational ideas of the afterlife like eternity, heaven, hell, purgatory.[137] Imagination thus plays a key role in the life of the mind.

Kant presents a possible division of the arts based on the notion of art as expressive of aesthetic ideas.[138] Expression involves articulation, gesticulation, and tone. Under articulation he locates poetry and rhetoric, the basic linguistic arts. Under gesticulation we find arts of sensible truth and of sensible illusion. The first includes architecture and sculpture, providing us with three-dimensional real things; the second involves representational painting, which provides an illusion of three-dimensionality, but also (somewhat surprisingly) landscape gardening. Included in the arts of tone are music, which provides sound-tones, and nonrepresentational painting, which furnishes visual tones. Then there are mixed forms: drama is rhetoric combined with pictorial exhibition; song is poetry combined with music; the play of sound and of figures is dance; all these forms are combined in opera.

Kant goes on to provide a judgment of the relative worth of the individual arts, assigning poetry the highest value since it is the most communicative. Instrumental music is assigned the lowest level, shading off into the merely agreeable and furnishing a mere mood, for example as background for a dinner party. He does not assess the other art forms in between these two extremes.

## Nature's Ultimate and Final Purpose

The aesthetic, I said, is set within the larger context of an attempt to bring nature and freedom together via the projection of the notion of purposiveness onto nature in various ways. From an aesthetic point of view Kant looks at nature as if it were oriented in a threefold manner: (1) toward bringing about the harmony of the faculties in the presentation of the beautiful, whether directly in natural phenomena or indirectly through the natural inspiration of genius; (2) toward awakening us to the sublimity of our own calling in the presentations of overwhelming magnitude and power; and (3) toward easing the transition between our biological responses to the sensorily given and our moral obligation by teaching us a disinterested relation to the sensa.[139] In the latter way, beauty becomes a symbol of the morally good.

From the point of view of organic phenomena, Kant projects purposiveness into things, not in relation to us, but in relation to the ends they seem to seek. Thus we can only make sense out of living processes if we consider them as seeking their own growth, sustenance, and reproduction —though we have to subtract from such seeking the state of awareness involved in our own deliberate seeking.[140] In sexual reproduction we have to think of the function of each of the sexes as aimed at the other by nature. And when we consider the variety of species, we see them linked in what appears to be a systematic way, where minerals function as nutrient for vegetative life, and plants in turn as food for herbivores, which, in their turn, are food for carnivores.[141] But all of them are material for humans, who have the distinct capacity to set goals and impose them on the rest of nature. The conditions for the possibility of setting and carrying out goals involve two components of culture: a culture of discipline that clears the space for those functions by learning the control of appetites, and a culture of skills that enable us to reach the goals most efficiently. The basis for this process is civil society as a condition of freedom under law, where each person's pursuit of goals is checked by denying infringement on all others' similar pursuit.[142] It is as if nature had in mind this capacity to project and reach goals in orienting all other presentations of both natural and cultural development to this as its ultimate end. But even beyond this, for Kant there is a final end, an end that does not need anything else as condition, and that is the moral end: acting in accordance with the categorical imperative.[143] That points us ultimately beyond the phenomenal world in which we live to the noumenal realm as our final destiny. And it is here that we reach consideration of the Cause of all as a moral Artist-Artisan, arranging nature as an arena for human moral activity.

Kant links the aesthetic to our moral destiny in several ways. First, there is the distancing from appetite involved both in aesthetic and moral experience. Second, there is, linked to this, the aesthetic symbolization of the moral, first by that very appetitive distancing, but also by natural forms spontaneously taking on moral qualities like the stateliness of trees or the purity of snow. Third, there is the Ideal of Beauty as the presentation of the human form displaying moral action. Fourth, there is the awakening to our moral destiny through the experience of the sublime. Finally, there is the formation of aesthetic community based on the imperative of favoring the beautiful, the respect for aesthetic autonomy in allowing direct encounter with the form of the object as the final criterion for judgment, and the study of the classics as the vehicle for developing aesthetic perception.

Understanding, which was the core of the first critique, points to a supersensible substratum of appearance that is wholly indeterminate; judgment provides the possibility of determination by intellectual power; and reason provides the determination through moral law. Judgment thus occupies the point of transition from the concept of nature (as appearance) to the concept of freedom (as "sole noumenal fact").[144] The whole region of reflective judgment—the beautiful, the sublime, and the organic—points to the possibility of the insertion of causality through concepts into the mechanical world of nature and thus serves to bring together the fractured halves of the field of thought brought about in the first and second critiques.

## Response

Kant's approach to aesthetics is set within the context of his own critical project. Within that project it is aimed at unifying the antithetical regions of mechanically necessitated knowing and moral responsibility grounded in human freedom. And it carries on that operation by an analysis of the power of judgment linked, at first in a seemingly implausible way, to the experience of pleasure. The complication of the context makes difficult a critical assimilation to our own aesthetic project. The difficulty is eased a bit by reason of the common phenomenological ground of our introductory approach and Kant's attention to the modes of givenness of aesthetic objects.

One of the most serious difficulties is the apparent arbitrariness in the first critique's limitation of "theoretical knowledge" of causality to mechanical causation. In the second critique Kant is driven to acknowledge the "causality of freedom," and in the third, the reciprocal relation of cause and effect in the self-causation of organic process.[145] It seems more reasonable to begin with the full phenomenology of causation and view mechanical causation as the lowest level, clearly subsumed under organic causation (e.g., in our own eating), with both mechanical and organic causation in turn subsumed under causation-through-concepts in human choice (e.g., to eat in a elegant manner or to fast).

Kant's phenomenology of feeling focuses on four distinctively different kinds of feeling: of the agreeable (sensation), of the beautiful (taste), of the sublime (awe), and of the moral (respect).[146] The two feelings occupying the center in our list are the center of Kant's analysis in the third critique, while the two modes flanking the center are means of contrast.

We thought we detected a parallel distinction between the agreeable and the beautiful in Plato's distinction between the objects of attention in the luxurious and the purged city. Luxury moves beyond the biologically necessary, the healthful (which governed the first city), in the direction of measureless self-indulgence. What would satisfy such desire is the reformation through human ingenuity of what is given by nature. Here the criterion seems to be what will produce positive somatic reverberations. The emergence of artistic form here is not for the sake of the appreciation of the form itself, but for the sake of the gratification it produces. Reading this situation in terms of the Cave allegory: in the luxurious phase we are chained to the cave of our own sensory appetites, for whose gratifications new industries are created. But the aim of the purged city is the turning around of the soul, and its education at this level is said to culminate in the appreciation of beautiful things. Appreciation here is a state of soul attuned to the things themselves in their display, while luxurious gratification seeks merely a pleasing state of the organism.

Kant's distinction between the beautiful and the sublime parallels the distinction implicit in Aristotle between the aesthetic of the beautiful in music and painting and that of the horrible as represented in tragedy. The sublime is occasioned by that which threatens our existence. For Kant, the horrible or the ugly as represented in art contains beauty in its mode of treatment. The artist does a "beautiful" (read: excellent) job of representing the horrors of the crucifixion.

Kant focuses his insights within the broader context of his analysis of the general conditions for objectivity functioning in a biologically receptive knower who begins with being-affected sensorily and learns, through a priori principles, to separate out the merely subjective from the intersubjective elements in the stream of bodily impressions and to stitch them together into a coherent world of appearance. Aesthetic objects appear within such conditions for objectivity and are especially able to affect pleasurable responses. For Kant it is the character of the sensory as such that produces agreeable or disagreeable sensations, since we are not photo- or audio-receptors but needy organisms shot through with desires. And though there are general tendencies for certain sensa to produce similar pleasurable reactions in large numbers of individuals, there is no universal necessity in such reactions. Strawberries taste good to most people, but are not similarly pleasing to all. (Note, however, that pleasure in taking in nourishment and in sexual activity is a necessary accompaniment of these activities, given their linkage to natural organic ends.) However, the very capacity we have to objectify—to set out sensations over-against *(ob-iectum)* the subjectivity of the self in judgment—makes possible our attending, through the given sensa, to the form of the togetherness of the sensa, the configuration of sensory features. A certain reflective distance is established as one focuses attention on the character of the thing's presentation. Reflective distance is distance from one's own organic need, so that one is free to attend, not to the satisfaction the object produces, but to the form of the object. Kant calls such satisfaction "disinterested," "unconstrained" by need, able to give "free favoring."[147] Nietzsche scoffs at the notion of "disinterest" in the presence of the artistic nude.[148] But if a nonhomosexual male might appreciate Michelangelo's *David* in a nonsexual manner, so also might a heterosexual female, as a heterosexual male might learn aesthetic appreciation of Bernini's *Madame Canova*. And, indeed, one's appreciative response to one of Cezanne's paintings of fruit might not be one of drooling in hungry anticipation.

"Disinterested" attention does involve a satisfaction, though one that is fixated on the qualities of the object rather than on the satisfaction itself. In general, our reflective distance and our capacity to understand rather than simply undergo sensations make it possible both that we deliberately eat for nourishment and have sexual relations for procreating as well as that we are able to separate the pleasures found in both from their natural ends and cultivate them explicitly. Puritanism would find the latter morally reprehensible. But deliberate cultivation is not submission to appetite; it is another expression of rising above animal proclivity by shaping it. Kant locates aesthetic satisfaction in what he calls the harmonious free play of the cognitive faculties, namely, imagination and understanding. It quickens our sense of distinctively human life—not our animal life sunk in itself, wallowing in its own gratifications, but our cognitive life, rooted in our ability to make good judgments beyond merely felt preference. Thus there are two directions pleasurable experiences can take: the direction of our own organic reverberations and the direction of objects. Attention to the latter in the form of display they take in the sensory field awakens us to our distinctive humanness.

But a genuine aesthetic favoring likewise does not essentially involve the employment of concepts, such as "rules of taste" or concepts of physical or moral perfection, that would supposedly determine what the object ought to be. Furthermore, aesthetic judgment abstracts from what Kant calls the "existence" of the objects, which I understand to be their substantial underpinning and causal context, both in terms of their origin and their consequences as physical things. Aesthetic judgment attends only to their sheer display in the sensory field—that is, their relation to a bodily situated perceiver.

The object of aesthetic experience is the form or the mode of presentation, the how of an object's presence to our perception. It is reciprocally tied to the experience of the form of the judgment, the harmony of the imagination and the understanding. Mikel Dufrenne suggests that aesthetic form is actually composed of several factors in a progression: contour, the unity of the sensuous qualities, the unity of meaning, the unity of style, the unity of spectator and work.[149] "The form is less the shape of an object than the shape of the system which the subject forms with the object" founded on "the logos of feeling."[150]

Kant's connection of the aesthetic with the teleological in the third critique as a whole invites comparison between notions of form in both cases. In living form we have the presentation of a functional whole whose sensory display is expressive of its own striving to reach its ends. In the aesthetic realm, form might be isolated apart from what it expresses—though in art it always in some way expresses the aesthetic idea of the artist, even in the most abstract forms, like untitled instrumental music. But form most often accompanies and thus expresses its referent.

In the visual realm, Kant sees form primarily in the pictorial line, with color a mere pleasant accompaniment that, unless it operates to make the line more focal, is an aesthetic distraction. Here he is opposed by turn-of-the-century notions like those of Cezanne, who saw painting as an essential synthesis of line and color.[151] Cezanne remarked, "Form is at its fullest when color is at its richest."[152] Matisse likewise considered color harmonies as the primary form of painting.[153]

Having separated aesthetic judgment from both "interest" and "concept," Kant goes on to fold in both. Thus his first step is to separate out the genuinely aesthetic from other factors that might be confused with it. Then he can more safely relate it to those separated factors. He does this by a distinction between free and dependent beauty. As examples of the former he focuses on things like bird plumage on the one hand and arabesque drawings on the other. However, what we experience here is only trivial beauty. This first move seems to place Kant against the tradition rooted in Plato's Ladder of Beauty and having the greatest impact on the Middle Ages. In

Kant's view, the beauty of the person, of the laws that form persons, the beauty of the sciences, which study the principles of cosmic harmony as well as the principles for judging the adequacy of human laws, and "the vision of Beauty Itself" do not involve literal instances of beauty but metaphoric extensions. As far as the "beauty of the sciences" is concerned, even the conceptual study of harmonics is not the study of beauty but of extractable relations considered apart from the aesthetic experience. Kant suggests we should call mathematical demonstrations (as we often do) elegant rather than beautiful. For him, beauty strictly speaking lies in the form present in sensory display. However, Kant's notion of dependent beauty allows for some extension in the expressivity of the presentation in relation to the inwardness of character realized in his Ideal of Beauty.

"The vision of Beauty Itself" in Plato and the carryover of that into Plotinian mysticism and medieval notions of divine Beauty—making allowance for the differences in these assimilations—does claim to have an experiential basis. Augustine picks up on the Platonic-Plotinian line in his exclamation in the *Confessions* where, referring to God, he exclaims, "O Beauty ever ancient, ever new! Too late have I known Thee!"[154] Here we have an essential transformation of the pagan experience, which spoke in terms of encounter with an encompassing region or a type or principle. The Augustinian and subsequent medieval assimilation involves the experience of the presence of a Person. Why would Plato call the vision he speaks of one of Beauty Itself and why would the Christian tradition speak of divine Beauty? Kant speaks here of the danger of illuminism, fanaticism, and superstition, short-circuiting the hard labor of the intellect in favor of supposedly privileged intuitions.[155] But the real question is what we make of the experiences to which these various traditions bear witness.

However, there is a Kantian parallel to the experience of Beauty Itself or Himself in the experience of the sublime. Sensorily appearing objects of great magnitude of size and power provoke a feeling of awe. Such feeling expresses the antinomic sense of both insignificance and exaltation, since, though our bodies are tiny and impotent in the face of such magnitudes, our intellects can think beyond any magnitude and our wills are called to a realm transcending the whole domain of the sensory. For Kant, strictly speaking, nature is not sublime; it is only our reason, practical and theoretic, that is so. The experience of the sublime, which I have claimed, grounds the whole critical project, is a mode of *self*-discovery. Kant's interpretation parallels the anthropological reduction he performs in the notion of the *summum bonum*. As I noted previously, whereas for the tradition in general and for the medievals especially God is the *summum bonum*, for Kant the *summum bonum* is the coming together of happiness with deservedness to be happy (by reason of consistently acting from moral principle) for which God functions as means. (No matter that this seems to violate in the highest instance the categorical imperative to treat the person as an end and never simply as a means.) However, Kant does claim that the experience of the sublime can schematize for us such notions of the wrath of God.[156] He further claims that there is no more sublime poetry than the Hebrew, which bases itself on the essential unrepresentability of Yahweh and that it is that very unrepresentability that can evoke the most profound feelings, which, unchanneled by rational considerations, can erupt into the wildest fanaticism. Here Kant is clearly working with what I have initially described as the emptiness of the notion of Being and is recommending how to understand its all-encompassing character. He clearly seems to recognize the functioning of Platonic Eros, born of poverty and plenty and thus always empty, always longing, having designs upon absolute plenitude. Only he keeps turning it back upon itself rather than bringing it into relation with that nonobjective Object, transcendent of the Enlightenment's Supreme Being, which no concept can encompass. Contrary to Kant, the sublime typically does not involve a focus on ourselves but on our sense of the Beyond, which is expressed in encounters with overwhelming magnitude and might, a Beyond that draws us and gives us a sense of belonging to it. I suggest that Kant turns the experience back to humanness because of the way he understands autonomy.

Kant's ethics involves the rational individual being absolutely self-determining, completely autonomous. This, in turn, involves a certain distancing from any mode of being drawn by inclination, and thus the appearance of being antithetical to any notion of grace. However, in the notion of genius we see an area in which the notion of grace appears: genius is that power through which nature gives the rule to art. Certain individuals are gifted in being able to act beyond rules in such a way as to be both original and exemplary, not so much following rules as generating rules. In Kant such grace functions in establishing aesthetic community, binding humans together synchronically and diachronically through the communication of that which would otherwise seem purely private, namely, the inwardness of feeling.

Art likewise teaches us to view the beauties of nature. The Alps appeared merely tedious to the pragmatic Romans, who saw in them obstacles to their imperial and engineering ambitions until Petrarch's poetry began to teach people to see them otherwise.[157] Even Winckelmann, the originator of a renewed appreciation for the originality of the Greeks in art over against what were subsequently viewed as the merely derivative Romans, found the Alps a bore.[158] The same was true of Rousseau's *Reveries of the Solitary Walker* in relation to the pragmatic tendencies of the age of Enlightenment: Rousseau reintroduced an aesthetic appreciation for mountains.[159] Thus through the work of genius both art and nature serve to bring our cognitive faculties into harmony and thereby to bring us more in harmony with each other. By drawing upon the study of the products of genius throughout the centuries, Kant assimilates Hume's standard of taste: the dialogic community of critics whose taste is honed on the study of classical forms.

The genius works through aesthetic ideas, the intuition of forms for shaping materials. Such ideas thereby give rise to much thought in their viewers without any particular thought being adequate to encompass the works. In this way aesthetic ideas obversely parallel rational ideas, which can never attain to intuitive filling. But in this way also they "schematize rational ideas" by giving them body, presenting them in such a way that they "draw near" and are more present. Consider here Plato's Myth of Er, Dante's *Divina Commedia*, Milton's *Paradise Lost*. But aesthetic ideas can also bring human traits closer to us: love, death, virtue—perhaps not closer than an actual experience of them in our own lives and in the lives of others, especially those close to us—but closer than the mere thought of them, no matter how carefully worked out conceptually. It is in effecting this "sense of presence" that art is most effective. And it is in this that we come to *realize* what we might already *know*.

Dufrenne suggests that such "realization" is the work of imagination, which "gives full weight to the real by assuring us of the presence of the hidden and distant."[160] In Kant the link with the noumenal is the link with what is in principle hidden and ultimately distant from all our determinations. Looking forward to Heidegger, I contend that the notion of Being opens up the notion of the encompassing and unencompassable to which we are essentially referred, the mystery that surrounds the dashboard of both our everyday and our scientific dealings. The depth of our lives pivot about the extent to which we live out of a sense of the hidden and distant.

## Epilogue: Hume's Notion of Aesthetic Community

Central to Kant's aesthetics is the notion of aesthetic community, built out of the study of classical models. Kant does little to develop this notion. But in the epoch immediately preceding Kant's, David Hume, in his short essay "Of the Standard of Taste," offered a penetrating analysis of the way aesthetic community comes to be formed. Since the reflections are independent of the foundations in his general philosophic approach, being based rather on more commonsensical discussions, I append a brief discussion of this work.

Hume's "Of the Standard of Taste," which Peter Kivy, with justification, regards as "the most mature aesthetic document to come out of the British Enlightenment, and one of the few real masterpieces of which the philosophy of art can boast."[161] In this essay Hume comes to terms with the key problem involved in the adage: *De gustibus non disputandum.*[162] One should not dispute about taste—because, apparently, different people have different tastes. How then even speak about a standard in this realm?

Hume begins by noting the often observed—because readily observable—differences in taste, and even goes on to deepen the case by noting the less obvious differences that underlie apparent verbal agreements. In this he is much like Alasdair MacIntyre today (an editor of Hume's moral writings very likely clued to the notion by Hume), who argues a similar thesis in *Whose Justice? Which Rationality?*[163] This plurality of taste is so, Hume claims, because beauty is not a property of things but a relation to the mind.[164] (Of course, strictly speaking, in Hume's general philosophy, everything experienceable is a relation to—literally, in—the mind.) In spite of that, he goes on to suggest that some standard could be developed. It turns out that the "standard" is a dialogic community of cultivated observers.

One way of reducing the plurality is to point to differences in native capacities: on one end of the scale some have sensory deficiencies, and, on the other, some possess an uncommon delicacy of taste or imagination. Hume calls attention here to two characters in Cervantes's *Don Quixote* who were able to detect the most subtle iron and leather flavors, unnoticed by most others, in a cask of wine. Though taste is a subjective being-affected, it yet has a kind of objectivity because it is related to certain constancies detectable by more common means—in this case a key with a leather thong attached to it found at the bottom of the cask when the cask was emptied. The two characters' taste provided a standard for others less sensitive to the properties in question.[165]

In the case of works of art, granted a certain basic sensitivity, nonetheless a certain cultivation is also required. Hume wants to find the equivalent of the leather-thonged key and thus another medium to defend the immediacy of cultivated sensibility. One has, first of all, to learn the purpose of a given art work; then one has to attend to the coherence (consistency) of the whole in view of its purpose; and, finally, one has to observe how its design properties serve that purpose. In order to be able to achieve such perception in any given situation, one has to attain to a serenity of mind, free from all agitation, along with an ability to recollect past experiences that clue one in on how to attend to a given piece and provide one with the means for assessment. These conditions make possible the final condition: a careful, undistracted attention to the object given.[166] In this process one moves from simple immediacy of response through reflective distance to a mediated immediacy.

Granted such attention, Hume goes on to note how cultivation could then expand on native sensitivities. One who practices an art is in a better position to appreciate its qualities than one who does not. Presumably the practitioner has a better understanding of both the materials and ways of construction so as to be better attuned to the way these appear in the finished work. But Hume's notion of practice here seems to refer more to the practice of reflective attention rather than the production of art works. One who, in addition, contemplates the plurality of works and styles, past and present, in a given species of art is in a better position than one who merely practices his own style or attends to only one style. Further, one who compares species of art and degrees of excellence in each species is more likely to have better judgment than one who does not. Such a one operates within a more expanded field of awareness and can appreciate diversity. Again, one who returns to a work again and again is able to judge and thus appreciate better than one who attends to only a single superficial viewing. A work of art is a complex unity-in-multiplicity such that every aspect cannot be taken in during a single limited period of attention. And a classic is, by definition, that which merits continually renewed attention by reason of providing renewed satisfaction by many people in different epochs and by the same person at different times. But in order to attend properly to a work, in any given context one must have serenity of mind, a recollective state, and a proper focus on the object.

Note here that the study of art forms takes its point of departure from the preexistence of models of excellence in each form. A traditional canon guides the development of taste.[167] What one learns by this study is, negatively speaking, freedom from confining prejudgments in order to let a given work work upon him. Through the cultivated contemplation of a plurality of arts, genres, styles, and degrees of excellence, such a critic, far from being locked into the past, learns openness to the different, to the new. All this puts the critic in the position to make personal judgments, to articulate them verbally, and to test them against the judgments of similarly culti-vated critics. Relation to other critics involves the analysis of components and the synthesis of those components into a whole, the translation of cul-tivated perception into language, and the explicitation, defense, and trans-formation of criteria. It is the joint verdict of critics so operating that constitutes for Hume the standard of taste.[168] The standard of taste then involves a peculiarly qualified dialogic community.

Hume is quite aware of the fragility of such a standard, though he claims that, when one looks over the history of thought, one finds that it is more stable than theology or even than science. Plato, Aristotle, Epicurus, and Descartes successively yield to each other, but Terence and Virgil still hold sway. There will, however, always be differences in preference owing to differences in individual constitution, in age, and in moral and religious commitments.[169] Nonetheless, the cultivation of taste along the lines sug-gested will mitigate the differences in judgment. Indeed, one might learn to recognize degrees of excellence in a genre or a style without any great per-sonal love of that genre or style. Granted also those differences that are ir-removable, the dialogic community of critics should also have a measure of tolerance for diversity within limits.

Hume claims that such a process would lead to a knowledge of the rules that define the limits of diversity.[170] Unfortunately, "Of the Standard of Taste" provides little specific guidance in this regard beyond a few com-ments on what is good and what is bad in Ariosto's work: good are force and clearness of expression, readiness and variety of inventions, natural depiction of the passions; bad are improbable fictions, mixture of comic and tragic styles, lack of narrative coherence, and continual interruption in narration. Hume says no more about these features than simply listing them.[171]

## Response

Taste is a peculiarly modern phenomenon. It seems to go back to Re-naissance *gusto,* a notion promoted by Balthasar Gratian. In contrast to simple liking or disliking, taste is a capacity that requires cultivation. It involves rising above one's own proclivities and those of one's contemporaries, selecting and rejecting in a way that produces overall harmony.

It seems to me undeniable that, in addition to aesthetic preferences based on uncultivated proclivities, the cultivated study, along the lines suggested by Hume, of the full range of art works and types judged excellent throughout the ages opens one to qualities to which one would otherwise have no access. An aesthetic canon is capable of freeing one from one's own idiosyncrasies and from the prejudices of one's epoch or group. But one has to learn to move beyond mere acquaintance with and thus ability to talk about past works, to a sensitivity to the qualities of their real presence.

The canon is an indispensable aid in the cultivation of such taste, and gender ought have nothing to do with it. If it were possible, it would almost be better not to know the first names of a given artist, for it is not simply a question of the work of white males—or of males of any color—but excellence of aesthetic form playing in tandem with depth of reference that are worthy of consideration here. The works that exhibit such excellence and depth are those that have continued to appeal, throughout the ages, to sensitive, informed, reflective, and critical observers.[172]

Hume's skeptical empiricism lessens the scope of his own appreciation. Above all, his reductionist assumptions about human mentality (thought as the little agitation of the brain)[173] disallow his following out what is involved in his observation about the encompassing darkness surrounding the island of light provided by sensations. We are aware of the Beyond—indeed, as I have attempted to show throughout, everything distinctively human is based on the fact that we are directed, though by nature only emptily, to the totality via the notion of Being. Not being by nature directed beyond the empirical circle, the animal evidently experiences no lure of what lies beyond its current functioning. Hume's own claims about the essential character of sensations and the acute discrimination of types he makes throughout presuppose an ability to be beyond the Now of sensory impression by eidetic insight which situates the given in the whole of space and time as the field of possibility for the individual instantiation of the types. This presupposes the prior givenness of that field as the condition for the possibility of the apprehension of types. Cultivating the reference to Being as the ultimate condition for this possibility involves a sensitivity to the mystery of wholeness in each appearing thing, and especially in the self as the locus of the revealing/concealing of the Whole. The attempt to articulate that sensitivity has been the role of the arts from time immemorial. Lack of such sensitivity involves an essential closure to the deepest work of the works of art that come to us from the past. Hume has lost that sensitivity, and in this he is paradigmatic of much of modern taste.

Hume thought that the community he described could develop "rules of taste." It was just such rules that governed late-nineteenth-century academic art, against which all twentieth-century movements in art were directed. The rules became a procrustean bed rather than a framework within which possibilities could be explored. Kant will release the first great protest against such a conception. The study of the classics is essential but not so that we might practice servile imitation. Rather, we should learn to contact the same creative source—*die ewige Anfang*, the eternal beginning, as Schelling would have it[174]—in order to bring forth or recognize works that are both original and exemplary.

One of the problems one has to encounter in dealing with the nature of taste is the variability it has shown throughout the ages, not only in the obvious area of clothing styles, where the present style is king, but also in the shifts in appreciation that occur in aesthetic communities. The Renaissance and the Enlightenment viewed the Gothic cathedrals as irrational monstrosities,[175] expressions of the irrationalism of the Dark Middle Ages, while poets like Goethe set in motion a Gothic revival[176] and historian-architects like Viollet-le-Duc even went so far as to claim and demonstrate that the Gothic cathedral showed an immense rational mastery.[177] Frank Lloyd Wright condemned the architecture of the Renaissance as inauthentically derivative from Roman and Greek forms, which he also viewed negatively, along with the eclecticism of later nineteenth-century building practice; but he had high praise for Mayan, Egyptian, and Japanese architecture.[178] Futurist Umberto Boccione spoke of "Phidian decadence" and "Michaelangelesque [*sic*] sins,"[179] while Henry Moore favorably annexed both Phidias and Michelangelo to their more overtly powerful antecedents, going back to Assyrian, Babylonian, Egyptian, and Mayan sculptural forms.[180] Gaugin and Picasso introduced an appreciation for what was previously considered primitive barbarism.[181] The 1913 Armory Show in New York, which displayed paintings from Europe since the turn of the century, produced strong negative reaction from the critics, only for the works to become standard museum pieces.[182] In its premiere performance, Stravinsky's *Rite of Spring* almost caused a riot and the composer had to leave through a window, even though the piece has now become part of the standard repertoire of the symphony orchestra. Shakespeare himself had been in eclipse during the Enlightenment as a kind of undisciplined barbarian until Addison began to rescue him and Dr. Johnson sprang to his defense. Futurist Carlo Carra, in a complete reversal of traditional aesthetics, went so far as to advocate a need for inner disharmony brought about by new forms.[183] Taste clearly swings in all the arts.

What is positive about the current situation is that, through the invention of what André Malraux calls "the museum without walls," namely the art book, people have access to the art of all the world.[184] Hitherto one had continuing access only to what was in one's own collection or in the local museum and had to remember what one had seen elsewhere. In the case of the visual arts, one can follow Hume's admonition significantly further than he and those prior to recent times were able to do and learn to appreciate the beauties of the widest possible variety of genres and styles. In the case of literature, we are in a position to extend the canon to the founding texts of East Asia in India, China, and Japan. One is not then tied in, as tends to be the case with clothing styles, to the current, but can range over all of human history.

Hans-Georg Gadamer noted a distinction between taste and fashion. Fashion is simply what is currently in, and will soon be out: for example, the best-seller in literature, the latest rage in clothing styles, the most recent school of philosophy. Taste involves, negatively, a certain distancing from one's own uncultivated proclivities and from what surrounds one in the present, a distancing brought about by attention to a wide range of artifacts available from the past. Positively, taste involves a holistic sensibility, also made possible by that distance, which allows one to select or forego what the present offers as that can or cannot be assimilated into a sense of wholeness.[185] In a era when the decontextualization of choice has rendered individual "freedom" an absolute and all standards are rejected, it is crucial to learn to expose oneself sensitively and reflectively, along the lines suggested by Hume, to the wide variety of exemplars made available by modern methods or reproduction in order to learn what harmonious sensibility has meant in differing contexts. For what is at stake is not simply individual preference but integrated or disintegrated living. Goethe remarked that the greatness of a nature is shown by the capacity to absorb the greatest multiplicity without suffering disharmony. In today's situation of pluralism, the need to cultivate such integrated personality is greater than ever before in history.

# VI

# HEGEL

## Hegel, Enlightenment, and Christianity

A FIRST APPROACH TO G. W. F. Hegel may be taken in terms of a comparison between two ideal-typical positions: what I will call the Enlightenment heritage and Orthodox Christian Theology. The approach is ideal-typical in that it develops in terms of a projection of certain tendencies in different thinkers that are viewed as heading toward an ideal term that may be held *in toto* by none of them, but that illuminates tendencies in them all. And I want to approach the three positions—Enlightenment, orthodox Christian, and Hegelian—in three areas: theology, anthropology, and Christology. I take this approach partly because it allows us to fill in something of the thought movements to which we have paid insufficient attention, but which are required by an overview of the salient points in the whole of Western thought; but mainly because it is particularly illuminating with regard to Hegel. Some of the typical contemporary rejections of Hegel have the same basis in the Enlightenment as some of the typical rejections of orthodox Christianity (which is not to say that Hegel was entirely orthodox).

In the Enlightenment theological heritage, there is the tendency to consider God as a separate entity, absolutely one and apart from things, in a manner one might envision the separation of one atom from another in Greek atomic theory. Creation is the fashioning of preexistent material by this God as a Divine Architect or Watchmaker.[1] In the area of anthropology, there is a tendency to view the human Spirit as spatially locatable, inside the head. Locke's view comes to mind: awareness as a dark, empty chamber into which light enters through the slits of the senses.[2] Spirit is considered as either separated from the brain, as in Locke's "inner chamber," or identical with it, as in Hobbes's or La Mettrie's materialism or Hume's phenomenalism.[3] In either case, experience is something subjective that occurs inside the head as an effect of exterior causal processes, which tend to be viewed as so all-encompassing that even so-called free acts are explained in terms of antecedent causal processes. On the social level, there is social atomism. Paralleling methodical procedure in classical physics, society is considered in terms of its ultimate constituents, isolated individuals, starting from which we attempt to construct a comprehensive view of society through the positing of a founding contract between those isolated individuals.[4] Original innocence belongs to human nature, which becomes corrupted through social structures.[5] The Good Life is viewed as satisfaction of appetite and thus as freedom from pain. Medical research aims especially at the latter, technological advancement in general at the former.[6] Humankind progresses in enlightenment as we learn the mechanisms of nature and use them for our benefit (i.e., the procurement of pleasure and the avoidance of pain).[7] If we wish to retain Christianity in such a view, Christ is viewed as the good man, the moral exemplar.[8] Grace, if considered at all, is conceived of as an outside aid in reaching the Good Life.[9]

If we compare this set of related views with an ideal-typical analysis of orthodox Christian theology (at least pre-sixteenth-century orthodoxy), we find a significant contrast on all scores. Many of the things for which people blame Hegel are actually closely related to the claims of this traditional Christian theology. Among other things, Hegel is trying to give a conceptual transcription of that theology. He claims that Christianity has revealed the basic truth; but he also claims, following Lessing, that revelation was not rational when it occurred (it was received from without and not at all understood in its basic grounds), yet it is directed toward our rational comprehension.[10] Thomas Aquinas says something similar in his *Summa theologiae* where he talks about things that are available through philosophic inference as well as through revelation. Aquinas includes in the latter such things as the existence of God, those of His attributes inferable as the causal grounds of the objects of experience, and the natural moral order, specifically the Ten Commandments. They were revealed, according to Aquinas, because they are necessary for proper human behavior, but they can only be discovered through reason by thinkers of significant capacity, with great effort, over long stretches of time, and with significant admixture of error. But once given, such truths can be underpinned and fully integrated into our lives by reaching them through the extensions of our experience by means of the work of reason. However, there is a limit: for Aquinas some truths—those that are not inferable as causally implicated in what we can experience—can only be known through revelation.[11] That includes the central Christian dogmas of the Trinity, the Incarnation, and the nature of the Sacraments. Hegel, on the contrary, acknowledges no limits: we can give a conceptual transcription of revelation that makes sense out of it (i.e., integrates it into our experience as a whole) and that likewise makes sense out of the entire history of Western philosophy.[12]

In the orthodox Christian theology I am considering, the first truth is that God is Trinity.[13] This is one of the things that Aquinas places beyond the scope of reason's power of inference. Not so for Hegel: God as sheer identity, the One as First Principle, is dead; God as Trinity, as identity-in-difference, is alive, a moving Ground, the very paradigm of Reason.[14] In the traditional teaching, common to both Plotinus and Augustine, God "others" Himself in the Logos, which is the basis for the outpouring of the otherness of creation.[15] The Logos precontains all the ways the Father/One can be mirrored outside the Godhead in creation. The Holy Spirit is the union of the otherness of the Father and the Logos-Son. Being is trinitarian in its ground. These were some of the basic truths, essential to Christianity, that Augustine claimed to find in the Platonists.[16] In traditional orthodox Christology, the Logos was made flesh in Christ, who was not only the good man, the holy rabbi, the great teacher, but God in his otherness.[17] Only the Logos, as the internal otherness of the Father, could enter into the otherness of creation.[18]

In creating, God does not simply remain separate, but, by reason of the fact of perpetually giving complete being to creation, He is, in the words of Augustine, nearer to creatures than they are to themselves.[19] God, being absolutely infinite as the ground of the total being of the finite, is more transcendent than the Watchmaker God of the Enlightenment, who fashions matter separate from Him, or, for that matter, more transcendent than the finite, noncreating, exemplar divinity of Aristotle. At the same time, He is more immanent than in either view as the Ground of being of all that is, having to sustain knowingly and freely all that is. God is not simply Fashioner but Creator, not simply giving form and furnishing exemplarity, but also giving full being to all outside Himself.[20]

And only humanness, as sole locus of openness to the Infinite in material creation, constitutes the external condition for the possibility of being assumed by the Logos in the God-Man.[21] Humanness is understood as the image of God and is thus not wholly locked up in the finite, but is finite-infinite, finite having designs on the infinite. The human being as the image of God consequently involves a view of Spirit that is not simply identical with the body, nor simply contained within the head or even totally within finite conditions. The human being as aware and responsible, having intellect and will, is openness to the totality of Being.[22] However, historically human beings are in a darkened condition brought about by an Original Fall that is passed on to the whole race.[23] This transmission is linked to the fact that a human being is not an atomic individual, but is intrinsically social, and, indeed, as believer, a member of the Mystical Body of Christ, the Incarnate Logos. That is not intended merely as a metaphor but as an ontological reality.[24] There is an internal connection between all believers, who share in a common life, the life of grace, which is not only an outside aid but, more deeply, a participation in the divine life, the indwelling of the Trinity in our own togetherness as a community of love. Love as the bond of the Spirit in the community is an identity-in-difference: not simply an external connection or an interior merging, but the fostering of difference by identifying with it and discovering one's own identity in the process. This becomes the formula for Being itself. God is an identity-in-difference as divine Love; so also with God and creation, Spirit and body, individual and community—they are intelligible as identities-in-difference, each dyad in its own way. God is love. Trinity expresses that: the Spirit is the bond of love between the Father and the Son, Who are other than one another and yet are united in the deepest and most complete manner possible.[25] That has implications for thinking about interpersonal relationships.

The trinitarian structure of identity-in-difference is the logical "genetic code" for all reality. Creation is God's own othering for Hegel—though this is far from being orthodox. In orthodoxy the Trinity is complete before creation, needing nothing outside Itself. God creates out of love and out of choice to share divine goodness.[26] In Hegel, by contrast, God is empty possibility developing out of the empty notion of Being and requiring, needing instantiation in the concrete realms of Nature and History.[27] For Hegel, God *needs* creation and *must* create. Creation for orthodoxy is *other than*, not the *othering of* God. The latter is, in orthodoxy, the Incarnation. Further, the point of creation is that God be manifest in knowledge and love, and in orthodoxy the Incarnation is the in-principle final manifestation of God that is completed in fact through the completion of history.[28] Finally, in Christianity one does not flee from pain but, when it is inevitable, embraces it, not masochistically but by identifying with Christ on the Cross, Who asked precisely not to have to undergo it—though one finds it difficult to resist seeing masochism in much of the spiritual tradition. It is through His suffering and death that His Resurrection and consequently our redemption occurs.[29]

There is clearly a vast difference between the Enlightenment heritage, which we all share rather spontaneously and are inclined to defend "rationally," and the Christian tradition, which Hegel attempted to interpret rationally in the modern era. He claimed to be an orthodox Lutheran to the end of his life, but the claim has been challenged (in different ways, based on differing interpretations of what he actually did).[30]

## The Starting Point of the Hegelian System

Hegel is the great synthesizer, who sought to contain the entire philosophic tradition, with its Greco-Roman and Judeo-Christian sources, in a single system of astonishing power and insight. There is a very real sense in which he establishes a persuasive synthesis of Parmenides, Plato, and Aristotle, mediated by the dominant symbols of Christianity and grounded in the turn to the subject focused in a special way in Descartes.

Parmenides opened Western metaphysics with the proclamation of the identity of thought and being and presented a claim to knowledge of the essential features of being. He described a goddess revealing to him that "'It is' and 'It is not' is not." He proceeded to a conceptual analysis that removes all elements of nonbeing ("It is not") from the notion of being ("It is"). If we perform that analysis, being shows itself as changeless and absolutely one: changeless because change involves the nonbeing of the no-longer and the not-yet in the never-finally-there of the moving Now; absolutely one, and not a one of many that is itself composed of a multiplicity, because any one among many is *not* the others, and any one composed of multiplicity is such that one aspect is likewise *not* the others.[31] However, for Hegel, as for Nietzsche, such being is not the fullness of reality but "the last trailing cloud of evaporating reality."[32]

If we think how we might arrive at such a notion starting from the things of experience, we might set in motion a sorting process that, by leaving aside concrete differences, arrives at progressively higher order (i.e., more universal, more encompassing) logical classes. Beginning with the multiplicity of actual people, we leave aside the many interesting things that distinguish each of them to arrive at the notion of humanness, which is their common identity. Thinking in terms of the next wider class, we arrive at the identical notion of animal, which leaves aside the concrete differences between the various species of animals, humans included. Moving further upward and leaving progressively more aside, we arrive at the identical notion of organism, and further still at the notion of body. Finally, in the Aristotelian line, we reach the category of so-called substance (*ousia*, beingness), which includes the bodily and the mental.[33] Going back to the concrete things from which analysis began, we are able to sort out common features in all substances: quantitative features such as weight or extension, qualities such as sensory features or powers or habits, relations of various sorts, including the spatial and temporal, actions and passivities and the like. The features fall into the general notion of attributes (*symbebekota*, things that are "yoked together" with the basic beingness of things). Substance and attributes are described as being-in-itself and being-in-another respectively: a substance, such as a person or a tree, exists as self-grounded ("in itself"), in opposition to the features of things, such as their color or height, which exist only in and on the basis of the things that ground them. Hegel takes us one step further: leaving aside the "in itself" and the "in another," we arrive at the pure notion of being. Since (as we followed in the line of substance) every logically higher order, i.e. more inclusive category, can be inclusive of broader ranges of things only insofar as it leaves aside more and more differentiating aspects of those things in order to concentrate upon commonalities, the last move, isolating the notion of being from the two modes of being-in-itself and being-in-another, leaves us with a notion that is completely empty. Hence it turns out to be identical with its opposite, nothingness or nonbeing. But then, far from being changeless, as Parmenides claimed, such a notion is identical with becoming or process, for, as Plato indicated, process is the mixture or synthesis of being and nonbeing: being no longer what it was and not yet being what it is to be.[34]

Here we find Aristotle's notion of *phusis*. The notion of being is not only the empty notion of process; it is also all-encompassing, for outside being there is nothing. Hence the empty notion of being strains toward its own unfolding in the totality of the concrete universe. Being has an erotic structure in the Platonic sense of the term *erotic:* it is emptiness that has designs on plenitude. But in contrast to Plato, it is the Eternal having designs on the temporal for Its fulfillment. At the same time, Parmenides' claim that "thought and being are one" gives the telos to the process: being in its inner nature is directed to manifestness, is intrinsically related to Spirit and is completed in being understood.[35] So, it would make no final sense to have a world in which Spirit did not appear. Hence the embarrassment that surfaces today in the all too common epiphenomenalist notion of spirit that is left over once we turn over all explanation in the sciences to observation and mechanism. In such a view, spirit as awareness is a residual by-product of the nervous system that is able to do absolutely nothing, not even practice science.[36] Its functional place is taken by brain mechanisms; its appearance is undeniable, but also inexplicable because—by hypothesis—totally inactive. It is the locus of a wholly passive display of part of the workings of the nervous system. But if nature can be understood, so, contrary to the epiphenomenalist, can the locus of its manifestness, namely human understanding. And nature comes to fuller manifestness when we understand that it strains to produce, in increasingly more complex and centralized animal organisms, the conditions for its own progressive manifestation. It is this link between being and manifestness that sets the immediate context for Hegel's view of art. Far from being irrational, such a view leaves no dangling irrationals such as appear in that scientific view that leaves out conscious Spirit, except as functionless epiphenomenon.

Being-Nonbeing-Becoming constitutes the first triad of Hegel's System and exhibits the kind of formulaic structure that Fichte had described as thesis-antithesis-synthesis.[37] The synthesis is called *Aufhebung*, an ordinary German term that can mean three apparently quite different and even opposing things: cancellation, preservation, and elevation. The notion of Becoming cancels out the one-sidedness contained in the notions of Being and Nonbeing, preserves what is seen in each of them in isolated fashion, and elevates the insights contained in them to a new and higher level of mutual compatability.[38] In a sense this is the strategy for approaching any great thinker in the history of thought. What we have to realize is that each classic has a hold on something of crucial significance, else it would not have continually drawn the attention of those who think seriously in these matters. But thinkers hold opposite views. What is seen by a given thinker? Preserve that. What is one-sided about the understanding of what is seen? Cancel that. How can we put these two insights together and do justice to what is seen in them singly? The Spirit drives in this way over time through all partialities to a more comprehensive understanding of things: generating positions, evoking counterpositions and finding higher syntheses.

When we arrive at the empty notion of Being we find something that is there for Spirit as something manifest to us. So going back to Parmenides, the first great metaphysician, there is a sense in which thought and being are one. The question is, in what sense are they one? At least in this sense, that being is there for manifestation to Spirit and that manifestness is an identity-in-difference. We stand over against what is being revealed to us; it is being manifest precisely as it is and where it is, other than us; but it is also "in" us as our knowledge. Thus there is also a kind of identity: what is called in the Scholastic tradition an intentional or cognitive identity. Knowing is, in Scholastic terminology, being the other as other.[39] Being other is change; knowing is being *the* other, precisely as it is other than the consciousness to which it is manifest. Thought is not just present to itself in blank self-identity. The whole of being is there for manifestness; the point of being is to be there for manifestness.

So what we get in the Parmenidean formula on the identity of thought and Being is a statement of the fundamental teleology of the process of reality. The reality process is not simply that of empty Being trying to become fully what it can be—though that is the case; it is, more fundamentally, Being as aimed at creating the conditions for its being fully manifest by producing the conditions for the locus of manifestness: human existence.

## The Development of the System

Nature strives to produce from itself complex and centralized organic structures that culminate, on one level, in the animal senses, which manifest aspects of the environment relative to the needs of the organism; but on another level, there is a leap to another genus when fully reflective Spirit appears. The human Spirit is the goal of nature's own hierarchical process that strives for its own manifestations.[40] Spirit working at the manifestations of nature is the history of thought. The history of the uncovering of nature is the history of the uncovering of that which aims at producing Spirit. And that uncovering is only possible through the production of culture in the broader sense: language, family, economy, political organization. The aim of political organization is ultimately to make possible the display of the whole.[41] In this sense Hegel is continuous with the line from Plato and Aristotle to Aquinas. The highest activity in this universe of physical reality is contemplative thought, speculative thought (from *speculum*, the mirror, the "spectacle"). The ultimate aim of thought is to mirror the whole: the Spirit is, in this way, all things. At the base of things, thought and Being are one in intention; thought and being strain toward becoming one in actuality as the telos of things.

Nature elaborates for itself *in concreto* what that Logos system is in itself and *in abstracto*.[42] Here Hegel is in the line of Plato, Plotinus, Augustine, and Aquinas: the Logos precontains the ways in which the infinite divine can be imitated in the finitude of nature. The One, for Hegel an empty primordial process, spills over into the multiplicity of intelligible principles that constitute the Logos system, the system of possibilities for the One to be realized in multiplicity. The Christian thinkers had put together Platonism and the prologue to St. John's Gospel: In the beginning was the Logos, *with* God and *as* God, through Whom all things were made and Who was the Light illuminating all men. Within the Trinity, the Logos is the othering of the Father that makes possible the otherness of creation and the entry of God Himself into that otherness in Christ the God-Man. The task of the sciences is to uncover the Logos-system mirrored in things. But in Hegel, the Logos-system consists of mere possibilities for existence. He calls it "God in Himself."[43] Reversing Plato, the Ideas are not real being from which things instantiating the Ideas in space and time are derivative and secondary;[44] rather, following Aristotle, things are real being *(prote ousia)* and the universal Ideas are being in a secondary sense as the fulfillment of concrete things in their intelligible manifestness to Spirit.[45] Abstract universals are intelligibilities actualized by the Spirit in its relations of manifestness to things. In the Aristotelian view, "the intelligible in act is the intellect in act."[46] So for Hegel the Logos-system needs Nature and the emergence of Spirit out of Nature in order that the Logos become actual. Hence the Trinity *requires* spilling over into creation because in Itself It is only an intelligible system of possibilities.[47]

For Hegel, the first triad, Being-Nonbeing-Becoming, spills over into a second, Essence, and is related to it as inner to outer insofar as intelligibility involves a move from surface to depth.[48] The two are joined synthetically by the Notion *(Begriff)*, in which the show of the process occurs, although at this stage it is the notion of the show, the concept of manifestness, not the manifestness itself. Real manifestness requires concrete Nature worked up to the point of humanness. The inner is transformed from intelligible interiority to conscious interiority. And the latter is not a withdrawal from the publicity of things, but the locus of their manifestness. The actual Spirit is the place where the manifestness of the whole occurs. Here is a retrieval of Parmenides' "Thought and being are one" and Aristotle's "The soul is, in a way, all things."

Within the context of the Logic we find the grounds for correcting what is perhaps the most frequent misunderstanding of Hegel's System. Those grounds lie in Hegel's demonstration of—paradoxically expressed —the necessity of contingency. When the System—the necessarily coimplicated structures of Logic, Nature, and Spirit—spills over into spatiotemporal existents, it enters into the realm of vast contingency. For Hegel there is no way one could deduce—Laplace-like—the position and velocity of any particle in the universe or the coming into being of any particular entity or the vast plurality of species. These all belong to the empirical realm, replete with contingency, that is the domain of continuing empirical scientific exploration. The System claims to present the necessity of the coming into being of just those general levels of actuality—physical, living, animal—requisite to the emergence of the human Spirit.

Spirit in its actuality is a product of Nature, indeed the goal of nature. Spirit has its other, namely body, as a moment of outwardness required for the emergence of Spirit.[49] Spirit needs the sensorily given other to come to apprehend the intelligible inwardness revealed and concealed in the sensory surface. But such surface can only be manifest through the bodily organs. (Here we begin to see the location and glimpse something of the role of art.)

The manifestness of the whole is the Notion of notion or the Idea fully returned to itself in comprehensive thought.[50] Hegel uses the image of a tree to give a graphic conception of the main lines of his System. The first triad of the Logos gives what we might today call the basic "genetic code" and the Logos system constitutes the seed. Nature is the tree ramifying into its various branches according to the logical genetic code. The Logos-system is being-in-itself, or potentiality; Nature is being-outside-itself, or spatiotemporal existence; and Spirit in its history is being-in-and-for-itself, or actualization, being returned in manifestness to the Logos-system. Spirit divides into three forms: Subjective, Objective, and Absolute Spirit. Subjective Spirit is the bud on the tree of life; Objective Spirit the flower; Absolute Spirit the fruit, the telos of the tree. Subjective spirit divides into three again: anthropology, as the physical articulation of the organism, grounds phenomenology, or the realm of the appearance of things and persons to awareness and thus of an inwardness that makes manifestness possible; both are surmounted by psychology, which comprehends the subjective conditions for intelligent fashioning and intelligible manifestness.[51] The ultimate distance from the Now (which Hegel calls "negative," or "formal freedom") afforded by our reference to the whole makes possible both freedom of choice in the practical order and intelligible manifestness in the theoretical order.[52] Freedom of choice introduces a vast level of contingency, in and beyond the contingencies of Nature, of arbitrariness, irrationality, and also of creativity characteristic of humanness. The structures displayed at this level are the conditions for the possibility of the next two levels: Objective and Absolute Spirit.

The essentially embodied Spirit is, to begin with, merely Subjective Spirit, merely the basic set of human potentialities in concrete individuals. It requires Objective Spirit—that is, the development of the objectifications of thought in institutions, habits, customs, ways of life, traditions, in order that, through time, Spirit might come more fully to itself through the growing manifestness of the whole. (Here we begin to see the role of tradition in the development of the conditions for art.) Subjective Spirit does not develop its potentialities without a social matrix, which is the objectification brought about by past and present human subjects. One does not arrive at even a rudimentary self-consciousness without the presence of the human other, threatening or confirming.[53] But that does not occur without a developed institutional matrix, beginning with the institution of language. Objective Spirit is the other in relation to the Subjective Spirit, the instantiations of which—human individuals—stand in dialectical relation to one another. The development of Subjective Spirit is thus not only dependent on society, but also on history.

History itself has a goal. Not all people are on the same level except as Subjective Spirit, which, from the point of view of the telos, can participate in history further as it unfolds. Social, political, and economic institutions become, in a sense, more rational over time, not only in the sense of becoming more subjectable to calculation, but also in the sense of becoming more articulated and more understood, providing more amplitude for the exercise of individual choice, and, above all, coordinate with and supportive of the growing manifestness of the intelligibility of the whole of Being. Intelligibility and freedom develop because intelligence objectifies itself more and more through history.[54]

One has to understand here another of Hegel's oft-quoted and mostly misunderstood claims: "The rational is the real and the real is the rational."[55] That has to be related to his claim to the necessity of contingency in nature and to both contingency and irrationality brought into being by human choice in history. It has also to be related to his teleological view of nature and history. "Real" translates *wirklich,* which indicates the reaching of a goal, the actualization of a directed potentiality. The rational is what has reached its fulfillment. What has not reached it, though factual, is not real or actual and thus irrational. In this context, also note Hegel's seemingly arrogant claim that if the facts do not measure up to the Concept, so much the worse for the facts. All that means is that if a fertilized ovum develops into a functionless cripple, so much the worse for the factual cripple; if a functional adult fails to become mature, reflective, and responsible, so much the worse for the factual adult; if the factual arrangements in a society fail to evoke or tend to block the emergence of mature, reflective, and responsible citizens, so much the worse for the society. The cripple, the immature adult, and the repressive society are all factual but "unreal." The task of thought is to penetrate through the contingencies and irrationalities to detect the underlying rationality operative in nature and in history.

Objective Spirit is, again, divided into three: the abstract sphere of right,[56] the inner sphere of "morality" *(Moralität)* or conscience,[57] and that which puts the two together, the concrete ethical community (*Sittlichkeit,* from *Sitte,* customs, the concrete ways of life for a people).[58] Ethical life, in turn, exists along three levels: family, civil or contractual society, and the state. They are related in the following way: Family is immediate and concrete, growing up spontaneously through time out of natural sexual and consequent parent-child relations.[59] Civil society is the abstract and mediated level of contract based on the modern notion of abstract rational individuals taking initiative and entering into contractual relations.[60] Ethical life is the encompassing concreteness of a given society bonded together by customs and group feeling. Modern civil society drives a wedge into traditional society, opposing it as the explicitly rational over against the spontaneous and traditional, but grounding the possibility of an enriched ethical community realized in the modern state. Led by patriotic feeling, we are willing to sacrifice our private interests and our very lives for the good of the more encompassing whole.[61]

Now we should underscore, contrary to an army of critics beginning with Kierkegaard, that Hegel's view does not involve the swallowing up of the individuals but rather their location within a vision of the whole. Furthermore, the development Hegel envisions is rational precisely insofar as it advances in maximizing opportunities for individual choice—of occupation, marriage partner, religious affiliation, speech, assembly, and the like—though within the structures that make possible "substantial freedom" (i.e., identification with family, state, and God), and ultimately making possible "absolute knowledge" as the comprehensive view of the whole.[62] Even then, what speculative knowing comprehends is the moral necessity of a community, rooted in the inwardness of the presence of the divine Spirit of love revealed historically through Christ. Such community is characterized by its awareness of the necessity of each—whether at the level of taking responsibility for oneself or at various hierarchical levels for the community—to choose a course of action existent within contingent contexts and generative of consequences that cannot be fully envisioned—hence the necessity of the fallibility of choice. But by reason of being bound to the community, there is also the necessity of offering grounds for the course chosen and being open to correction by others. By reason also of the bond of the community, there is the correlative need for forgiveness for mistaken choices. Absolute knowing is the manifestation of the necessary interrelatedness of categories, which culminates in the coming into being of such a fallible, dialogical community bound together by the spirit of sharing in the divine.[63]

For Hegel the coming into being of such a community and its development through time according to the lines of the System follows Christ's pronouncement that "it is expedient for you that I go [from you into heaven]. If I do not go the Spirit of the Father will not come. When he comes he will teach you to worship in spirit and truth."[64] Spirit reaches its deepest inwardness by appearing in bodily presence and withdrawing therefrom into inwardness and encompassment of all bodily presence. We will see this theme developed especially in the coming into being of the Gothic cathedral.

Objective Spirit is not the goal but merely the flower that precedes the goal. The final fruit of the tree of Being is the realm of Absolute Spirit or Spirit absolved from the mere abstract possibility characterizing the Logos-system considered by itself, the concrete but non-self-present realm of Nature, and the conscious but finitely bounded realm of human awareness constituting history prior to the emergence of the Hegelian System. Through history Spirit returns to itself. This occurs first in the realm of *art*, where the Absolute is displayed in sensory form; then in the realm of *religion*, where the turn within, to the heart, is accomplished. The process is completed by the comprehension made possible over time through the development of *philosophy*.[65] We will return to art shortly.

The mode of interiority that rises above art is religion, which gives expression to the human heart's rising up from the everyday to the encompassing eternal.[66] But religion thinks about the absolute in pictorial terms: God is a father, the Logos a son, the Spirit a dove.[67] In the development of theology, it thinks conceptually, but only with the static, regional abstractions *(Vorstellungen)* of the understanding *(Verstand)*, not in the developmental and comprehensively related categories *(Begriffen)* of all-encompassing Reason *(Vernunft)*. One has to give the conceptual cash value of the pictures and life to the abstractions through philosophic comprehension, which thus rises above religion, moving even more inward because it reaches the very inwardness of Spirit.[68]

Philosophy begins in Parmenides with the notion of Being and the proclamation that thought and Being are one.[69] But this occurs at the beginning only abstractly and apart from the world of our everyday experience. It has to descend into the world to comprehend it totally. Its in-principle comprehension is displayed in the System we have sketched. Such a system not only comprehends the main lines of Nature, it also, and especially, includes the main lines of History. For Hegel, the divine Spirit operates even more in History than it does in Nature.[70] Providence governs what occurs, driving toward the full disclosure of the meaning of the whole. But History, like Nature, is no serene unfolding of a harmonious whole: it involves the pain of struggle and destruction, even at the level of the history of philosophy. However, in and through the cross of contradiction, suffering, and destruction, the meaning of the whole is progressively displayed.[71] For Hegel, art is a critical dimension of that display.

## The Nature of Art

Rather than focusing on the transcendentality of beauty in which natural beauty has a central place, as in the Platonic and medieval traditions, Hegel focuses on art. The beauty of nature for Hegel is a mirror of human moods and is in itself too indeterminate for a science of beauty.[72] Subhuman nature cannot exhibit the kind of unity capable of expression in a single form such as we find in human beings precisely because in humans Spirit as such is active.[73] And even the human being, enmeshed in "the hunger of Nature" and "the prose of everyday life," is not capable of exhibiting the full ideality of Spirit.[74] Art, on the other hand, has already passed through the medium of Spirit, which allows for a more determinate conceptual treatment and thus stands on a higher level than the beauty of nature.[75] In fact, art allows for the possibility of the presentation, not only of surface beauty, but of ideality, and that because it is the expression of Spirit.[76] What appears in art is like the human eye, in which the unity of the whole behind the surface is expressed. The whole is concentrated in the external show.[77] In art we are detached from the limited manifestness characteristic of animal desire and human need and have returned to ourselves as free spirits in our proper infinity. Art shows the inner repose of the human spirit, even in the midst of outward tensions; it exhibits the ideality behind the surface show. In a lyrical line anticipating Nietzsche, Hegel remarks: "Even in the expression of suffering the sweet tones of the plaint must penetrate and clarify the sorrows, so that it continually may seem to us worth all the suffering to arrive at such sweetness of plaint in its expression. And this is the sweetness of melody, the singing of every kind of art."[78]

Hegel begins his introduction to the study of art by confronting various views. One view considers art something frivolous, mere phenomenal froth covering the deeper things of life. By contrast, Hegel notes that in art people have given expression to some of their deepest insights.[79] He thus pushes beyond Kant's initial concentration on taste in relation to sensory surface (arabesques, bird plumage, and the like) as "free beauty" and follows the direction indicated by Kant's "ideal of beauty" in that form of "dependent beauty," which is the human being acting under moral laws. Taste, says Hegel, only deals with the surface.[80] We must press beyond to that which is expressed in the highest forms of art: the noblest ideals and the deepest insights of humankind.

Another view, encountered in the tenth book of Plato's *Republic,* claims that art by its nature deals with a medium of mere exteriority, surface, even deception and is thus unworthy of serious study. Hegel counters with the claim, backed up by and central to his System, that *appearance is essential to being* and that the appearance of things in art is more revelatory of the heart of things than the surface nature presents in ordinary experience.[81] Art is born of Spirit, and that alone places it higher than all of prehuman nature.[82] Indeed, one might say that the manifestation of Spirit is itself the meaning of nature: when Spirit manifests itself, nature gains something of its own telos. But art in its higher forms doubly manifests Spirit: it displays

Spirit's insight into that which stands beyond the sensory surface and thus beyond subjective Spirit. Indeed, even and perhaps especially as mediated by common interpretation, objects in the lifeworld close off more of their underlying meaning than they disclose. That spontaneously appearing surface, product of the interplay between animal senses and cultural interpretation, is more deceptive than the higher forms of art, for it presents itself as final "reality," though it is merely mediated surface. It is a hard rind through which thought must penetrate to reach toward the depths it conceals.

While accepting the view that art gives expression to deep insights, others think that the aesthetic is still a dispensable coating on the ideas, like sugarcoating on a pill.[83] But for Hegel art effects a mediation between abstract ideas and presence in the sensory environment. In art the spiritual is sensualized and the sensuous spiritualized.[84] Art "consists precisely in the reciprocal relation, affinity, and substantive fusion of significance and form."[85] However, having its origin in insight that is one with the emotions of its creator, it attains to an alien existence in its expression in the work of art that calls for a return to the Spirit through the work of appreciative, and eventually of comprehending, thought.[86]

The ground of the work of art is the insight of genius who needs technical ability to translate his insight into external form.[87] Those who place nature higher than art on the grounds that nature is God's creation, which we cannot rival, fail to see that God operates in human beings as well—and even more deeply. It is He who inspires the genius with ideas which rise above mere nature to manifest its significance as the matrix for spirit.[88] Through such manifestness nature itself comes to fulfillment. The work expresses both its subject matter and who the artist himself is. If the work that emerges from such inspiration is great art, it is purged of all that is merely idiosyncratic both in the object and in the vision of the artist.[89]

Hegel confronts various views of the purpose of art. One is that art imitates nature. If that is understood to mean copying the sensuous surface, Hegel considers it superfluous when successful, since nature does a far better and more consistent job of creating that surface—and here Hegel agrees with the critics who hold to art's essential superficiality. Even in the case of Zeuxis, who painted grapes so realistic that doves pecked at them, creating illusions is not a very exalted business. For Hegel the invention of hammer and nails was far more important. If the imitation is to rank as fine art, the object and the mode of presentation must be beautiful. And in visual presentation, the frame must be so selected as to present a well-proportioned use of space. Further, the object also must undergo transformation from a mere natural fact to something expressive of spiritual life. So art must elevate its object from the everyday to the ideal.[90] And even further, some arts are not given over to such imitation as their essence: consider especially architecture and music. However, natural shapes constitute an indispensable foundation for art, from time to time rescuing it from the stiffness and staleness of convention into which it often falls. Yet such imitation is not the end of art, only a sort of beginning.[91]

A second view of the aim of art is that it is to arouse the heart to sympathize with the whole range of human feelings. But these feelings are both good and bad, noble and ignoble, based on insight and based on illusion. Art would thus only serve to magnify the inner contradictions from which we all suffer. Thus the question emerges of the unity to be attained in this vast welter of conflicting feelings aroused by art. One suggestion, related to Aristotle's notion of catharsis, is that art's end is to mitigate the fierceness of desires. It does this by giving us the distance afforded by objectification. We do not simply live in our passions: we observe them in the objects of art. The talk about "oneness with nature" in feeling is mere barbarism: art dissolves that oneness and makes us more human—in other words, more in possession of ourselves as rational agents by granting us distance from nature, which is itself a lower phase of being.[92]

And we have to go further since the view in question still does not separate the pure from the impure in passion itself. Art is thus said to aim at moral instruction as its essential end. Art has been in fact the first instructor of a people, not only for moral purposes but also in terms of general worldview.[93] But considered this way, art seems superfluous coating on what is available prosaically in its full truth. Form and content are separated into the delightful, which is inessential, and the didactic, which makes the work of art a dispensable means. The sensuously individual and the spiritually general become external to one another.[94] In the context of the time in which Hegel wrote, which is still in many ways our time, the conflict between the polarities of existence was especially stark. In the dominant Kantianism, the moral realm, which in one view it is art's sole task to teach, is based on a separation of will from impulse, whether noble or ignoble, and denies their reconcilability. But the conflict extends further to the more general conflict between essential reality and actual existence, between abstract law and individual phenomenon, between reason and sensory experience, spirit and matter.[95] Kant both heightened the antitheses, especially in his view of morality, and provided, in his third critique, the basic direction for their overcoming. Hegel sees in the Kantian notion of purposiveness the notion that reconciles the universal and the particular since the encompassing end subsumes the particular parts and phases of a biological process and since, in the work of art, the concept is wholly united with the aesthetic form. Correspondingly, in our aesthetic perception understanding and sensibility are fused.

In Hegel's view, art's fundamental mission is to reconcile these antitheses. Thought, by reason of its empty orientation to the whole via the notion of Being, sets up an abstract realm in opposition to the sensuously given immediate. It is art's mission to heal the rift thus generated. Art ought to be "generality made absolutely individual and sensuously particularized."[96] It is not fundamentally subservient to moral instruction or, indeed, to education in basic worldview. It has its end in itself: to reveal the Absolute in sensuous form, to display Spirit as the encompassing ground and telos operative here and now in the sensuous display of the natural materials reshaped by genius in such a way that the Ideal wholly penetrates all the details of the presentation. Here Hegel expressly puts forth the school of Phidias as an exemplar of ideal presentation.[97] One should note that the fundamental character of the re-formation of the sensuous material is historically correlated with the character of Spirit's awareness of the Absolute. This yields several different stages in the development of art.

## The Basic Stages and Forms of Art

As Hegel sees it, there are three stages in the history of art: symbolic, classical, and romantic. They are based on three relations of art forms to the idea of art as the display of the Absolute, the meaning of the whole, in sensuous form.[98] To begin with, Spirit is present to the sensuously given Now against the background of the whole of being that is initially present as empty intention. Spirit strains to give sensuous expression to the empty whole that appears as the mysterious Beyond. Spirit does not grasp the character of the whole but only stands before it in awe. This gains expression first of all in the monstrous, the huge, the distorted and strained—but also in the simple reproduction of the everyday (a cat, a lion, a beetle, an ibis) as containing some feature symbolic of the Beyond. All this is characteristic of what Hegel calls the *symbolic* stage of art, as it appears, for example, in the ancient Egyptians, Hindus, and Chinese. Its basic vehicle of expression is found in architecture, which deals with massive forms, many of which are not directly imitative of nature but symbolize (i.e., suggest) the strangeness of the mysterious Beyond: the overpowering massiveness of the temples appearing in all ancient empires, the geometric perfection of the Egyptian pyramids, the distortions of sculptural forms on Chinese and Indian temples.[99] Yearning, fermentation, mystery, and sublimity are characteristic of this stage.

The second relation of Spirit to the sensuous as the display of the Absolute occurs in *classical art* when Spirit begins to grasp the inner intelligible nature of reality and the adequate natural expression of that inwardness in the human body as Spirit's own natural otherness. Classical art reaches its high point in Greek classical sculpture, where the ideal proportions of the body—freed from the blemishes of factual contingency—give expression to the repose of Spirit in its inwardness as perfectly united to its exteriority. At the end of the development of Greek thought in Aristotle, the divine Spirit is viewed as finite unitary ground and center of all. Leading up to that we have the notion of the divine split into various divinities that are, in fact, projections of human powers.[100] Greek sculpture presents that finitely understood divine in human form as the statues of the gods. The human body is that sensuously appearing form naturally suited to the expression of finite Spirit. Consequently, this is the stage in which art is wholly adequate to the conception of the divine reached up to that point. Viewed in terms of its highest mission, this is the high point of art, which is identical with a religion of art: it is the classical phase of art. At this stage of human penetration into the encompassing Beyond, art is the vehicle for relating us adequately to the Absolute conceived as finite Mind.[101]

In Christianity both the encompassing infinity of God and human identity with that infinity are manifest. The sensuous as finite presentation is consequently inadequate in principle to give sufficient expression to it. As a result, the classical stage is left behind and we reach thereby what Hegel calls the *romantic* stage of art. The term *romantic* here does not refer simply to the period from the end of the eighteenth to the middle of the nineteenth centuries in the West. It refers to the art that emerged after primitive Christianity—the art that appeared beginning in the Christian Roman Empire. Perhaps one should read the term as *Roman*-tic. In this phase there is a return to the symbolic insofar as the infinity of the divine Beyond cannot be adequately expressed in the sensuous the way finite divine Spirit can in the gestures of the human body. But there is an advance insofar as the Beyond is no longer empty nor full in its finite viewing; it is manifest as Infinite Spirit.[102] Art in this phase is art transcending itself into inwardness and a sense of grounding encompassment.

In one—of many—of his most disputed phrases, one that especially drives art lovers to paroxysms, Hegel speaks here of "the end of art." One fails to note the qualification: "in its highest mission."[103] Once Christianity announced the infinity of God, art was no longer the adequate instrument for that communication. By contrast, at the level of comprehension of the Beyond as finite Spirit reached by the Greeks in the classical age, art became fully adequate to giving expression to such a view, since the human body's external show *is* the natural expression of Spirit. That is what made it classical in the sense of unsurpassable in its type. Religion and art were then capable of identification. But with revealed religion, art could no longer carry on the highest mission because the finite sensuous and the infinite Beyond are not commensurable. Hence the end of art in its highest mission. But Christianity opened up art to a greater range of thematic explorations because of its announcement of the identity of the divine and the human, so that anything in which humans took an interest became expressions of the divine in some way. Hence when modernity opened up the centrality of subjectivity implicit in Christianity from its inception, artistic activity, especially in painting and music, burst into full flower.[104] Hegel went on to claim that, even though its highest mission is a thing of the past, achieved in the classical age of the Greeks, in the future one could expect art to develop different modes of technical elaboration.[105] But the great modern flowering of art has occurred simultaneous with the development of modern philosophy, which culminated in the ultimate inwardness of final intelligible manifestation in the Hegelian System.

The romantic phase is especially characterized by its emphasis on the heart, as in Pascal's expression, "The heart has its reasons, of which 'reason' knows nothing."[106] In Hegel such "reason" is *Verstand*, while *Vernunft* as the faculty of totality deeply involves the heart. One of the fundamental imperatives of human existence is the unity of heart and head. Hegel speaks of "the possibility of a culture of the intellect which leaves the heart untouched . . . and of the *heart without the intellect*—of hearts which in a one-sided way want intellect, and *heartless intellects*—[which] only proves at most that bad and radically untrue existences occur."[107] Religion has its locus in the heart as articulated in terms of our founding openness to the totality. The properly attuned heart is rendered intuitive to all the nuances of any region of thought or practice, and indeed to everyday existence as a whole.[108] Heart is "concentrated individuality" whose special form is genius.[109] It is on this that the arts are based, and it is to this that the romantic phase of art is particularly attentive.

The romantic phase is expressed especially in painting and music. Here physical dimensionality begins to disappear. In painting it is reduced to a two-dimensional surface, to which the viewer has to add the third dimension through his imaginative vision, supplying for the intrinsic deficiency of the medium but adding inwardness thereby.[110] In music we have a complete abstraction from three-dimensional palpability in the concrete presence of sound, which Spirit has to continue to gather since sound rapidly disappears as it moves through time.[111] But music is not mere registration of sound impressions; it is, as Aristotle noted, productive of ethos, the inward dispositions of the heart. These art forms become progressively central vehicles of expression as the basic Christian view pervades institutions, especially flowering in modernity, when subjectivity, inwardness, freedom take center stage. Music is the art of inwardness; and as it develops in modern times into "absolute music," detached from any attempt to portray or imitate, it corresponds to the formal freedom of the abstract ego, which simultaneously surfaced in modern politics. "For musical expression therefore it is only the inner life of soul that is wholly devoid of an object that is appropriate, in other words, the abstract personal experience simply. This is our entirely empty ego, the self without further content."[112]

On the other hand, with Christianity there is a peculiar emphasis on the work of the Spirit as establishing community. Hegel lays great emphasis on community. Absolute knowing, I suggested above, develops the categories that show the teleological completion of the world process in the fallibilistic, dialogic community of confession and forgiveness within the larger structures that expand the arena for individual choice and responsibility while anchoring the individual solidly in family, in state, and in the divine. The enlarged arena for artistic creativity is addressed precisely to that community. And yet Hegel claims that the most suitable subject matter for artistic treatment is taken from the heroic ages—either the early phases of civilization or those transitional phases when an old order has crumbled. It is in these times that order rests on individual virtue and not on an articulated set of laws and practices, as in the modern state. Here it was that the meaning of the whole could be concentrated better in a single figure.[113]

Poetry is a peculiar art form that appears centrally in all three historical phases—symbolic, classical, and romantic—through which art passes.[114] Poetry is able to abstract completely from all direct sensuous mediation in order to appeal directly to the imagination, the central organ of art in all its forms and phases. Thus it uses either sound or written language, being, in a sense, indifferent to either.[115] Nonetheless, Hegel does note the peculiar relation to sound that constitutes poetry—meter, rhyme, alliteration, and the general harmony of sounds—that effects a reconciliation between meaning and sensuousness that Hegel considers to be the mission of all art.[116] In Hegel's treatment of the beauty of art, he actually spends the most time describing the content most suitable for epic and dramatic poetry: the heroic individual in a definite situation, full of conflict. And in dealing with particular art forms, he devotes by far the most space to poetry.[117] By contrast, sculpture and painting are extremely limited in their ability to depict situation and character.[118]

Poetry takes three forms: the universal art of epic, which presents the encompassing community; the individual art of the lyric, which gives expression to individual inward sentiment; and the reconciliation of universal and individual in drama. But the latter goes beyond the other two forms insofar as it gathers together all the other art forms. Aimed at performance, it is both visual and audile; developed as language, it is the bearer of articulate meaning; accompanied by music, dance, and set, and contained within an architectural setting, it is, indeed—to employ a term soon to be made popular by Wagner—the *Gesamtkunst,* the totalizing art form.[119]

Though certain art forms take center stage in each historical phase of development in art history, nonetheless, the advancement of spirit in penetrating the character of the Encompassing leads to the further development of the specific art forms. This is especially the case for Hegel in architecture. Although it carries the highest mission of the spirit at the symbolic phase in expressing the apprehension of the divine as empty and mysterious Beyond, architecture reaches its own perfection only at the romantic phase, in the Gothic cathedral. Romantic architecture, found in the Gothic, is especially well suited to express the turn within and the upward soaring of the spirit to the Infinite through the sensuous and beyond the sensuous.[120] And so in the romantic we have a return to the symbolic, not because the Beyond is dark, but because its infinity is revealed as Infinite Spirit, as I have noted previously. In Gothic architecture the community is set apart from the outside world and through plastic, musical, and poetic forms, in tandem with the upward movement of the architectural interior, the community together is drawn beyond the sensuous.

Poetry is peculiar, since it has a certain independence from the three chronological phases through which the other art forms develop.[121] This is perhaps linked to its basic operation in the medium of imagination, where it becomes the basic vehicle of religious expression.[122] All art in its earlier forms is linked to religion. Thus epic is the linguistic art, which reaches perfection in an early phase of a culture. And lyric and drama reach a certain high point as well in the classical age, though the modern age seems to have surpassed that period in these forms (e.g., in Shakespeare and in the Romantic lyric poets).[123] And though poetry is surpassed in philosophy and Romantic poetry in Hegelian thought, nonetheless it remains the province of poetry—and indeed of the arts in general—"to translate speculative thought into terms of the imagination, giving a body to the same in the sphere of intelligence itself."[124]

Considering the highest function of the arts as the revelation of the divine, Hegel sees architecture as providing the setting for the god who appears in sculpture. He further sees the arts of painting, music, and poetry, which call for completion in the observer-hearers, as informing the community within which the Spirit dwells.[125] Formed by the community, the individual is most its own self in liturgical communion with others—except when raised to the level of totalistic philosophic comprehension on the basis of that communion. But maybe even philosophy is completed in oral communication with the community.

The different aspects in the development of the Spirit are coordinate with one another. The great forms of symbolic art emerge on the basis of a society settled in some way by law and written records in the Oriental empires of China, India, Assyria, Persia, Babylonia, and Egypt.[126] The arts develop as religious expressions on the basis of awareness of the existence of the encompassing All and our special relation to it, but also on the basis of ignorance of Its nature. Thus politics, art, religion, and reflective thought emerge as coordinate forms of the Spirit.

At the next level, Greek institutions in the classical age, though based on a slave substratum, recognize the freedom of the citizens.[127] That makes possible free inquiry and thus the rise of philosophy as self-critical and systematic thought. As a consequence, the Encompassing is no longer seen as empty mystery but as that which is coordinate with reflective thought—ultimately, in Aristotle's God, as Self-thinking Thought. The "other side" of sensory immediacy and everyday functional attention is thought. Classical art gives expression to that in the statues of the gods, finding that sensuous form fit by nature to express finite Spirit, namely the form of humanness.

Christianity, in proclaiming the identity of God and Man in Christ, set in motion a political process that culminates in modern institutions that recognize the freedom and dignity of all humans.[128] In proclaiming the Infinity of God, Christianity also reduced art to a secondary role because its media are no longer adequate to the message.[129] Christianity also, through its Logos doctrine, opened the way to absolute Idealism in philosophy. But, in initiating the romantic phase in art, Christianity indirectly opened art to all that is of interest to human beings.

## Response

I have devoted what some might regard as an inordinate amount of space to my sketch of the Hegelian System. But it was necessary in view of Hegel's claim that the truth is the whole, and that only by seeing the whole can we grasp the fuller significance of the parts. It also provides us with a way of looking back on the historical ground we have covered in its fullest context. Art, as a part, must be seen in its relation to the whole. I am partial to that view and partial to very much Hegel has to say. Such partiality dictates the general form of my work, which covers select highlights in the history of aesthetics, but does so by locating the aesthetic within the overall context of each philosopher's thought. Further, however, I attempt to carry on thereby not merely a series of reports on particular thinkers, but a series of developing reflections on the nature of art and beauty. The play between the thinkers furnishes the means by which, in and through and beyond the "opinions of the philosophers," certain features of the aesthetic realm itself come to be displayed.

Perhaps the central feature of Hegel's thought is his focus on appearance and on its mode of completion in art. Plato tends to treat the realm of appearance *(doxa)* as an obscuring of the Idea; Kant, as an occlusion of the noumenal; and some common interpreters of modern science, as an inexplicable, functionless epiphenomenon that percolates out of the workings of the nervous system uncovered in natural science. For Hegel, being reaches its telos in appearance and one of the highest modes of that telos in art. We are not inexplicably caught in appearance; it is rather appearance that explains the point of the mechanisms of nature. Everything preconscious in nature is simply the condition for the possibility of consciousness and therefore of its own manifestness through the inquiry initiated by consciousness.[130] As in Plato, so for Hegel there *is* an obscuring of the Idea in everyday awareness—the appearance of "the hard rind of nature" tied to the functional adjustment of the organism to its environment and of the individual member to its own limited projects and to society; but it is in art that such obscuring is overcome by clarity. Art is the appearance of spirit and, in its highest forms, not simply, as in everyday behavior, the display of limited intentions, but, as in religion and in philosophy, the mediated display of an apprehension of the meaning of the Whole.

The appearance of the meaning of the Whole in limited forms is one of the most important insights developed in this work. Plato initiated this with his notion of the epiphany of Beauty Itself as the display of cosmically encompassing plenitude in beautiful things. Beauty is spoken of as the only Form perceptible with the eyes; all the other Forms require a turn within and above, away from the sensorily given which reminds us of this Other. On the contrary, we are talking here of a Real Presence in things and not of a reminder in things that leads us away from the reminder to the Presence. In this regard, Hegel claims that it is art that "heals the rift" created by reflection between the encompassing Beyond and the here-and-now present sensorily given. Plato's focus in this regard is not on art but on natural beauty, and, most particularly, the beauty of the human form as object of Eros.

For Hegel the beauties of nature are insufficiently determinate to serve as objects of a science of beauty. Nature mirrors back to us our own moods, which are themselves indeterminate in relation to the clarity of the Concept. Because art has passed through Spirit, it is placed on a higher level than all nature. But passing through Spirit means ultimately being in proximity to the Concept. Nature by itself is more distant from the Concept, but has Concept as its own teleological ground. Nature points to humanness as its completion and humanness, in turn, points to the Concept as *its* own completion.

But there is a sense in which the works of Spirit can themselves constitute a screen between Spirit and its reference to the whole. There is the vanity of "culture" (better pronounced here as "culchah"); there is the "world," which the New Testament says we are not to love. In the Stoics, in Francis of Assisi, in Chinese Taoism, and in Rousseau there is a movement "back to nature" that has its roots in this observation. Nature itself is the whole or the expression of its Origin and civilization is a movement *contra naturam*. Martin Buber distinguished between form and object in relation to works of culture, a distinction that is a subspecies of his distinction between I-Thou and I-It relations. Object appears within networks of identification and use constituting the everyday appearance of things; form appears when the object is haunted by a sense of encompassing mystery and transforms our relation to everything.[131] A work of art may be object of art-historical analysis, exhibition of the psychology of its author or the sociology of the author's general situation; but its fundamental work is addressing the viewer as a significant presence beyond all objectification. Hegel is not unaware of something like this: as we have noted, he speaks of the "hard rind" of the everyday appearance of things; he also speaks of a rising up of the heart, the center of feeling, out of the quotidian to a sense of the eternal and encompassing; and he claims that in art we find a healing of the rift between the sensory surface and our enduring, founding reference to the whole. But it is art and not the immediate appearance of nature that seems so to function for him. Yet in common with those movements and thinkers I have mentioned, in Hegel the return to nature breaks through the staleness of culture to stimulate the development of new artistic forms.

As the preface to this work indicated, my own sense of things is deeply saturated with the sense of prehuman nature in its glorious, haunting, mysterious encompassment. I see the recurrent movement against civilization and back to nature as a healthy corrective, but also as an equally one-sided view of our relation to nature. With Hegel, I see human nature as a part of nature, above "nature" in the limited sense that dualisms have assigned to the term *nature*, and the telos of subhuman nature. Human nature is creative in relation to prehuman nature outside and inside itself, but in such a way as to be able to bring that nature to its own unfolding. Art is a wedding between Spirit and nature in which Spirit finds itself and its own history at one with nature. Back to Nature movements tend to leave no place for history and the works of Spirit; certain humanisms view nature only as adversary. In the line of Hegel, I see the relation as dialectical. As in Kant, art sensitizes us to the beauties of nature while aligning us with our moral task; but it also opens us up to what I would regard as the ultimate point of morality: the appreciation of Being, relishing the role of each type of entity and each individual within the Whole as the basis for appropriate action. Such appreciation avoids what would violate the integrity of each thing and promotes its fullest unfolding within the order of the whole.

There are several meanings of the term *nature*. One is sensory surface —that in which Impressionism often seemed to take exclusive delight. Another is that which is the depth generating that surface. Great portrait artists are interested in such a nature in individuals. A subset of that meaning of nature is that of an archetype expressed in an individual of a species. Classical and neoclassical art was interested in that meaning of nature. Leonardo calls for drawing to attend to the forms displayed immediately in the surface.[132] It is this that Hegel recommends as a rejuvenating sense for even the most abstract forms of art. Henry Moore advocated the same attention. But Moore looked for formative powers beneath the surface.[133] Frank Lloyd Wright suggested a similar move for architecture. But architecture is peculiar in that it must attend to the structural principles of natural forms under penalty of collapsed structures. It is linked to nature more directly than any other art form. Architecture requires engineering knowledge of physical principles. But beyond this, for Wright, it requires the study of living nature in order to learn how to establish, through building in and with the environment, an organic whole.[134]

Hegel's work in aesthetics displays a keen awareness of the eidetic features of each artistic genre, but he is especially focused on the way in which each feature is related to the communication of meaning, which can eventually be sublimated into the conceptual system. However, contrary to Kierkegaard, the individual—person, work of art, or natural thing—is not "swallowed up" in the System. It is rather located than swallowed, directed than coerced. The universal *requires* its instantiations. And in the case of things human—persons and works—freely choosing individuality is central. Works of art, individual lifestyles, cultural worlds are not mere expressions of subjective idiosyncracies nor simply means for grasping abstractions but the rich ways in which the power of the universal is displayed. The System sets the frame for the appearance of human creativity. One measure of the rationality of the political system is the development of opportunities for choice and thus for creativity.

In response to the further Kierkegaardian critique that philosophers construct huge thought castles and dwell in miserable shacks nearby, a central tenet of Hegel's thought is the notion of dwelling and its locus, the heart. In the heart is the possibility of healing the rift set up by the abstractive work of mind between its own work and the Now of our encounters. Indeed, that the work of reason penetrate to the heart is a central Hegelian imperative. But the work of reason is not restricted to its deliberate phase in philosophy: before it rises to explicit conceptual manifestation, it is already operative in nature and history generally, and specifically in the life experience of a community and of those on the leading edge of development. In my introduction, I emphasized the heart in connection with reference to the totality via the notion of Being. The heart is the center of the Me from which the I as reference to totality stands initially at an infinite distance. The central human task is to bring the heart into coincidence with that founding reference. In that task the arts play an essential role by establishing significant presences. Hegel has the distinction of bringing both the arts and the notion of the heart to the center of the human-cosmic drama.

Kant noted that we can only understand what we make, displaying the essentially manipulative character of Newtonian science;[135] but his complementary view of the appearance of the purposive in life forms and in art forms was linked to a sense of the unencompassable noumenal. Giambattista Vico noted the same basic constructive-noetic principle and then claimed that, since we have made history, that alone is what we can understand.[136] Hegel, in effect, linked the three principles—the constructive-noetic, the teleological, and the historical—by viewing nature and history as constructed by Spirit for the purpose of manifesting to itself its own nature as rising out of nature and history as its own preconditions. Both Kant and Vico displayed a sense of awe before the encompassing as final mystery. For Hegel, it would seem that, although the "rising up of the heart from the quotidian to a sense of the eternal encompassing" is the enduring ground of philosophic comprehension and that the healing of the rift between the eternally encompassing Beyond and the flowing sensuous Now is the perennial task of art, the sense of mystery seems to evaporate in conceptual comprehension.[137] And for us that is a great loss.

# VII

# SCHOPENHAUER

## A Synthesis of Kant, Plato, and the Indian Tradition

ONE WAY OF LOOKING at Arthur Schopenhauer's thought is to view it as a synthesis between Kant and Plato (together with Plotinus) on the one hand and the Indian tradition on the other. Schopenhauer's early work *On the Fourfold Root of the Principle of Sufficient Reason* was straight Kantian analysis.[1] Recall in Kant the three levels of form, which function as filters or glasses through which the world of appearance is constituted. The first level is that of the forms of sensibility—space and time—which furnish the encompassing frame of all appearance; the second, the level of the categories of the understanding, which sort the flow of experiences and form them into a world of consistent objects; and the third, the level of the ideas of reason, which set the goal of unifying experience as a whole through time. All these are functions of the "I think," the transcendental unity of apperception whereby all experience is unified by the coperceived I as conscious self-employing of the categories of the understanding and striving toward the systematic unity of the whole.

Now in *On the Fourfold Root of the Principle of Sufficient Reason*, Schopenhauer develops the foundations for the various sciences along Kantian lines, resting on the distinctions just recalled. Mathematics is rooted in the forms of sensibility. Natural science is based on the operation of the categories of the understanding, specifically causality. Reason is the ground of logic through which we attempt to establish consistency throughout the whole of our experience. And if we consider the human subject, not only as a center of knowing but also as a source of feeling and of action or willing, we have the basis for the humanities. Everything has a sufficient reason, an explanatory ground; but the explanations are different because of the different regions of experience. In each case, providing a reason consists in establishing relations. However, Schopenhauer does more than merely repeat and amplify Kant.

I said that Schopenhauer's thought could be understood in terms of a kind of fusion between Kant and Plato together with Plotinus. In Plato there is, on the part of the knower, the realm of *doxa*, of opining-appearing, which is, ontologically, the realm of genesis, or Becoming. This is intersected and surmounted by the realm of Being, of *ousia*, locus of the Ideas or noumena (objects of *nous*), which are eternal and universal. They, in turn, are surmounted by the Good, which is also the One, irradiating the Beauty of coherent manifestness on all below it. When we analyze particulars as intelligible particulars—things that can be understood (and being able to be understood means being able to be exhibited as instances of universal meanings)—we require two basic principles: a principle of intelligibility, which comes to be called form, and a principle of both mutability and the multipliability of the same form at different places and times and for different durations. Plato names the latter principle the Receptacle *(hypodoche)*, which Whitehead calls "the restlessness of space-time." Aristotle terms it *prote hyle*, or prime matter. Matter so understood grounds both space and time. Spatiality involves having parts outside of parts and thus mutability, the capacity to come apart, and consequently also temporality. Reality as we see it in individual things is a mirroring of changeless and universal principles in a changing and manifold matrix. Matter is thus also spoken of in medieval times as the *principium individuationis*, or the principle of individuation. Schopenhauer uses this expression to refer, not to matter, but to matter's derivatives, space and time together.[2] The principle operates to reflect and multiply what he calls Platonic Ideas. For Schopenhauer, Platonic Ideas specifically include the Ideas of animal species.[3] It is these and other natural forms that are filtered through the *principium individuationis*, so that sensorily given things are expressions of their corresponding Platonic Ideas, jutting into the net of phenomenal relations explored by the sciences with their sufficient reasons. But for Schopenhauer, as for Plato, the Ideas in turn are expressions of something more primordial.

## *The World as Will and Representation*

Schopenhauer's main work is *The World as Will and Representation* *[Vorstellung]*. Following Kant, his claim here is that the world as we experience it is not noumenal reality, but our representation of that reality. In its actuality it is, first of all, the direct expression of Platonic Ideas that present themselves in and through the phenomenal realm analyzed by Kant. We have to think here of Kant's third critique, *The Critique of Judgment*, in relation to the first critique. *The Critique of Pure Reason* analyzed the conditions for the possibility of objectivity, of intersubjective verifiability, of thinghood, as distinguished from merely subjective, private, personal experiences. The analysis does not determine what *kinds* of things appear objectively. Kant notes that the appearances of things are capable of being arranged in hierarchies of genera and species, as if Nature met the mind's need for logical order halfway by providing such appearances. Nature can be viewed as if a Divine Artist arranged matter into organic forms, giving expression to His intuition of the specific aesthetic ideas. For Schopenhauer, fortified by the development of German Idealism from Fichte and Schelling to Hegel, the "as if" is lifted: the kinds of things that appear *are* expressions of Platonic Ideas. Each individual is an expression of an ideal form of the species whose perfection it strives to reach, hampered by the complexity of the material conditions of the instantiation of the form. Here Schopenhauer sets himself in opposition to Positivism, according to which the knowable is the sensory in the regularity of its sequences. Hume was the great early modern proponent of this position: we exist, he said, within the great sea of surrounding darkness, inhabiting a small island of light, which is the realm of sensory impressions. He admonishes us to forget about the surrounding whole and to pay attention to surveying and extending the island of light so that we may learn to harness it to our purposes. Auguste Comte gave the name Positivism to this position.[4] The optometrist practices it when he measures the eyeball. But when he does so he abstracts from the fundamental expressivity of the eye. Driven by the will, he views only those aspects of the phenomena that serve our purposes.[5] Schopenhauer, following Kant's third critique, reintroduces the notion of the expressivity of all phenomena that allow for contemplation detached from the interest of the will.

As I have said, what are expressed in experience are Platonic Ideas passed through the *principium individuationis*, which is the realm of the Kantian forms of sensibility (space and time). But the Ideas, in turn, are expressions of what stands behind or above them. In Plato/Plotinus, Ideas are expressions of the One. In Schopenhauer it is not clear whether both the immediately experienced individuals and the Platonic Ideas are the realm of phenomena or whether the individuals are phenomenal and the Ideas noumenal. However, it is clear that both are the world as representation. Whether, like the immediately sensed individuals, they are relative to our modes of understanding and perception, Platonic Ideas give expression to what underlies them. In Plotinus it is the One, in Schopenhauer it is the Will.[6]

Schopenhauer goes back to Kant here and the idea expressed at the end of the third critique that freedom is the sole noumenal fact, where freedom for Kant means our capacity to direct ourselves by our own will over against our being directed by our inclinations, by our passions, by the law-governed movements of our nature. Schopenhauer accepts the will as the escape hatch from the phenomenal, governed by the *principium individuationis*, to the noumenal. However, will is now understood as desire, not as transcendence of desire. Everything phenomenal is expression of underlying desire. Thus the bodily organs express their corresponding desires: the mouth is hunger and thirst incarnate, the sexual organs incarnate Eros.[7] Conscious desire emerges out of a more primordial process of natural desire that Schopenhauer terms Will. Escape from desire transcends the principle of individuation and leads to the notion of a universal subject, as in Plotinus's World-Mind. Basing himself on the mystical experience of identity with the One, Plotinus in effect raised the question implicit in Plato and taken up by the medieval Arabian thinkers and by the German Idealists: where are we and who are we when we rise above the privacy and individuality of our feelings and opinions and are able to uncover the universal, public necessities of science? How can a private interiority uncover a public exteriority, an individual come to know a universal, a temporal being contain an atemporal truth? The answer given in Plotinus and followed in the traditions cited is, in Schopenhauer's terms: when we reach the level of Platonic Ideas we become the World-Mind, "the single eye of the world" as subjects of will-less contemplation, since we have to suspend the peculiarities of our own desires to let what-is appear "for its own sake."[8] In aesthetic contemplation what we apprehend is the Platonic Idea expressed in the individual contemplated.

Plotinus saw his view of things as similar to that of the Hindus. So did Schopenhauer. In the Hindu view the surface of things, the everyday world of experience, is Maya, the veil of illusion, cloaking the basic truth that underlying everything is Brahman, the One, identical with Atman, the Self. Our immersion in the everyday world causes us to lose sight of that and to believe that plurality, difference is fundamental.[9]

But now comes the most decisive thing for Schopenhauer. The ultimate character of the single underlying Will has to be read in terms of what gives expression to it in the sensory surface. If we follow the ancient tradition, the world is a harmonious totality that expresses the One, which is the Good. But if we look carefully, we see conflict, tragedy in the world: "nature, red in tooth and claw," as Tennyson put it.[10] Species are so constituted as to prey upon species. Beneath the tranquil meadow happily reflecting the light and warmth of the noonday sun in early spring, insect preys on insect while the hawk circles above seeking her prey and we sit tranquilly by nibbling on a lamb-chop sandwich. The eternal slaughter goes on. Human history itself is the history of fragile periods of peace strung over continually potential and, all too often, actual war and devastation. Disease, decline, and dissolution follow the bloom of youth. Pain, physical and psychological, dogs conscious existence at every step. As one drooling inmate of Peter Weiss's *Marat/Sade* has it, "Man is a mad animal. . . . I've helped commit a million murders. . . . We few survivors walk over a quaking bog of corpses always under our feet. . . ."[11] In Tennessee Williams's *Suddenly Last Summer,* the poet around whom the play centers wandered one summer day onto a beach in which sea turtles had laid their eggs. At a given time each year, the female turtles slowly crawl up out of the sea. Each laboriously digs a hole in the sand and deposits up to two hundred eggs in its nest. After covering the eggs, she drags herself, exhausted, back to the sea. The sun incubates the eggs, and over time the sand begins to move and then to boil as the tiny turtles hatch, emerge from the sand nests, and instinctively start to make their way to the sea. But beforehand, birds of prey have begun gathering on the cliffs nearby, watching for the first signs of the hatch. When the newborn turtles commence their dash to the sea, the birds swoop down, turn them over, and make a feast of their entrails. The devastation is mighty, and only a small number of the hatchlings make it safely to the water—only to be confronted by the predators of the sea. Of the original two hundred little turtles, one or two from each nest survive to carry on the perennial process. And the poet said, "Suddenly last summer I saw the face of God."[12] Down on that beach, he saw that God was intrinsically vicious. This is at the heart of the Schopenhauerian vision: the underlying ground that all things express is not ultimately the Good/One/Beautiful or the loving Father, but a single, vicious, self-contradictory Will. This is a complete reversal of the traditional view. Schopenhauer would say that it is rooted in a willingness to view reality on its own terms without the possibility of mythological consolation. "God" is actually blind, indifferent, intrinsically conflicting underlying Will spewing up a world that expresses His reality.[13]

The conflict and tragedy that afflicts the external world, both in the relations of natural species and in the relations between people as individuals and as communities at various levels of comprehensiveness, is also found within each of us as the conflict between our animal natures and our higher aspirations. If we escape serious disease and natural disaster, we are constant prey to inward tensions, rarely achieving inward peace.[14] If we could see psyches rather than bodies, we would see something that would resemble Napoleon's army retreating from Moscow: beaten, bruised, battered—an eye missing in one, an arm or a leg blown off in another, crawling, hobbling, painfully attempting to make our way home. And in the end we are food for worms.

Here we can see a kind of sea change in the whole tradition. A completely different sense of the underlying realm emerges. In Hegel, the underlying Spirit was good, but it developed through contradiction and suffering, rising out of its initial emptiness and blindness. In Schopenhauer, the underlying Will is full but blind, causing suffering in what it produces. It is itself not fulfilled but canceled in those who learn to rise above it.[15] Here Schopenhauer turns to the Indian tradition again. He moves close to the thought of the Buddha, who proclaimed the Four Noble Truths. The first is that reality is suffering. The second is that suffering occurs because of desire. The third is that one can gain release from suffering by "the blowing out of desire," the achievement of Nirvana. The fourth is that Nirvana is achieved through the Eightfold Path, beginning with right speech and right occupation and culminating in right meditation. The idea is to attain release from the anguish that afflicts us because of the structure of desire: only the saint attains salvation. And it is along these lines that Schopenhauer understands the Christian asceticism of Meister Eckhart, Angelus Silesius, Bonaventura, Madame Guyon, Johann Tauler, and the New Testament itself.[16]

Schopenhauer picks that up and weaves it into his peculiar combination of Kantian and Platonic/Plotinian themes. His claim is that the underlying reality expressed in the phenomenal order is intrinsically self-canceling, not only in terms of species biting into species because of their basic constitution, but also and especially because of our own basic internal organization that produces psychological tensions, particularly that between the higher aspirations and bodily desires. And the bodily desires themselves are so constituted as to produce the deceptive satisfaction we call pleasure. We are often and foolishly tempted to identify such pleasure with the good. However, it is intrinsically related to pain, not only by producing phenomena like the proverbial hangover after a night of revelry, but also by way of opening up the pain of longing after its temporary satiation. Pleasure itself is simply momentary release from such pain and has no status apart from it. Once satisfied, it only rests for a while and then the pain begins all over again. One way of obtaining release from the will is in aesthetic contemplation, freed of desire.[17] Another is in sympathetic identification with the sufferings of others—not simply human beings, but also other living things as well. Attention is defocused from our own desire and attached to the sufferings Will produces in others.[18] Here we have a seeming recurrence to a basic Hindu notion involved in the ritual formula *Tat tvam asi*, "That art thou," giving expression to the experience of the basic identity of all creatures.[19] But, by reason of the intrinsically conflicting character of Schopenhauer's Will, sympathetic identification is not because of the substantial identity of all things with Brahman, but because of the sage's nonidentity with the One/Will through detachment. Here we have a parallel to the Compassionate Buddha, who, in the Hindu line, learns identification with the suffering of others.[20] Such a one stands above being immersed in the natural struggle of species and of individuals within species expressed in our appetites: he learns to feel for and with others. But the Buddha teaches only release from suffering, not identity with final reality, about which he offers no doctrine.[21] For Schopenhauer identification would seem to have no metaphysical grounds. Rather, he argues for a self-imposed nonidentification with the Will, about which he has a definite doctrine: it is the origin of suffering and destruction as well as of delight and creation. The highest way of escape for Schopenhauer is the achievement of Nirvana, the final aim of the Buddhist way of life.[22]

I underscore that this is not (as in Plotinian and Hindu, as well as in Christian, mysticism) becoming identified with the Will that underlies everything, but precisely becoming detached from it, since It creates suffering in and among Its individuated expressions. Mystical union with the One is definitely not the aim of Schopenhauer's teaching because the underlying One is not good. The task is to get away from It, to blow out the desire that immerses us in It.

## Aesthetic Experience and the Work of Art

Aesthetic experience, like sympathetic identification with others and the achievement of Nirvana, is a means for release from the Will. In aesthetic contemplation the bodily desires are stilled for a moment.[23] Here Schopenhauer follows Kant again: the basic characteristic of aesthetic experience is disinterested satisfaction, a release from bodily based desire in order to let the sensory surface appear in its own integrity. But for Schopenhauer it is not simply the sensory surface in its formal properties that is the object of contemplation. More fundamentally, it is the Platonic Ideas expressed in that surface. For Schopenhauer as for Plotinus, though atemporal, the Idea is not simply the finished form of a developmental process, but includes as well the stages of the process, for the Idea is not simply archetype but generative form.[24] For Schopenhauer, all things are beautiful in their own way, but the things that stand out and arrest us in their beauty are the things in whom their Idea is most visible. In the aesthetic experience of such objects, one becomes the will-less subject of contemplation. Though in this way one attains release from the intrinsic contradictoriness of Will as it appears in us, aesthetic contemplation only releases us for a time. Sympathetic identification as a basic disposition endures over time, but still involves care. Radical release only occurs in the achievement of Nirvana. But aesthetic experience, owing to its more frequent occurrence, helps us to understand the ultimate possibility: final release from the Will.

As did Kant, Schopenhauer considers genius to be the source of art.[25] But he also extends the notion so that it is required for any aesthetic experience, though to a lesser degree in appreciating than in originating the work of art. Genius is the capacity for objectivity, for letting the thing stand out in its own right and not simply as subsumed under our needs.[26] Ordinary experience likewise presents the surface of things through the filters of the *principium individuationis* and the categories of the understanding. In ordinary experience the Platonic Idea is distorted. Creative genius runs ahead of such experience and grasps what nature is stammeringly trying to say.[27] Bringing it forth in a work of art, genius in effect exclaims to nature, "This is what you were aiming at!" That is one way of understanding Aristotle's claim that art partly completes, partly imitates nature. Similarly, perceptive genius, present in various degrees in all of us, discerns through aesthetic experience the presence of the Platonic Idea in such works and in those things of nature where it is most evident. However, the depth of the work is not only what is given to the senses; that must be "born in the imagination of the beholder, though begotten by the work of art."[28] Schopenhauer here anticipates Dewey and Heidegger, who claim that the work of art is what it does to the beholder. I will return to this shortly when I talk about the various art forms.

Ordinary knowledge, subservient as it is to our will, to our striving to live and to satisfy ourselves, and scientific knowledge, an extension of ordinary knowledge indirectly related to that same striving, are governed by the principle of sufficient reason and yield up to us only knowledge of relations, not of things-in-themselves.[29] Such knowing is linked to the ongoing "horizontal" series of causes and effects in space and time. We are driven to such knowledge by our own needs, revealing that about things which allows us to transform them for our purposes. But such knowing is also shot through by the Platonic Idea as a "vertical" component, an eternal ingredient entering into the ongoing flux of events.

It is crucial here to follow Schopenhauer's distinction between concept and Idea.[30] The former we have readily available in ordinary and scientific language in our terms for species and universal forces. But this only gives us the *unitas post rem*, the unity after the thing, affording concepts that yield no more than we put into them. They are our constructs. An Idea, on the other hand, is a *unitas ante rem*, a unity eternally antecedent to things, a Plotinian creative force of which things are the expression. Following Kant's notion of aesthetic ideas, they are intuitions to which no concept is adequate. They are apprehended by the artist, but not in an abstractly universal way, the jejune way of concepts. They are apprehended in individual objects of perception as creative forces expressing themselves in those objects.[31]

Again, as did Kant, Schopenhauer distinguishes the experience of the beautiful from that of the sublime. He does so by way of the latter's naturally hostile relation to the human will: the objects that occasion the experience of the sublime are those natural things that threaten to crush us by their overwhelming power or remind us, by their immensity, of our own bodily insignificance. In the perception of the beautiful, the will is spontaneously removed and pure knowledge gains the upper hand without struggle. In the perception of the sublime, such knowledge is gained only by a forcible breaking with the will. Schopenhauer goes further, presenting us with levels of the sublime from those close to the beautiful to those most far removed, based on the threat to our existence posed by the object. The beauty of light shining on a cold wintry day presents "the faintest trace of the sublime in the beautiful," since we are aware of the threat to life that the bitter cold presents. The silence of boundless uninhabited prairies under clear skies furnishes a second example, forcing us out of our usual relations and needs. The desert, removed from those organic forms that sustain our life, is more sublime still. Then there is nature in turbulent motion against which we are forced to struggle—especially when the turbulence is large-scale. Here we have the full impression of the dynamically sublime. In a different way, the mathematically sublime appears in the spatial and temporal immensity of the known universe as well as in the towering character of architectural monuments, where the insignificance of our own size is brought home to us in a powerful way. Finally, the sublime also appears in a character who has learned to view things, even those inimical to himself, in an objective manner. Here one who can contemplate the sublime becomes himself sublime.[32]

In addition to the two aesthetic modes Kant distinguished—namely, the beautiful and the sublime—Schopenhauer further distinguished the graceful and the characteristic. Beauty has a spatial, grace a temporal character. Grace has to do with movement: with smooth transitions among coordinated parts. But grace presupposes beauty: a well-formed body is a prerequisite for graceful activity. The characteristic has to do with human beings, the one case where the individual stands out from the species and has its own "Idea." A portrait artist in particular tries to capture what is peculiarly characteristic of that individual—whether it be beautiful or graceful or not.[33] So with Schopenhauer we get four distinct aesthetic categories, and not simply the classical two, traceable back to Longinus's discussion of the sublime.[34]

## *The Forms of Art*

Like Hegel, Schopenhauer refers to the various art media, all of which are such that they require completion in the imagination, for exact depiction of individuals, as in a waxworks reproduction, reveals only individuals and not the Platonic Idea.[35] Recall the two-dimensional depiction of three-dimensional objects in painting (Schopenhauer adds the linear sketch thereof in drawing); recall also the restriction of space to the point of abstract motion through time that constitutes the medium of music; recall finally the relative indifference to visual or audile medium in poetry (and, indeed, in all verbal expression). Schopenhauer adds sculpture to the list with the observation that painted statuary is far inferior to the bare marble of a Grecian statue precisely because the former leaves less to the imagination. He praises the infallible Greek aesthetic sensibility that observed this rule, not knowing that the statues were originally painted. (Of course, that does not alter his principle.)

Attend next to the specific functions of each of the art forms. Among them, pure instrumental music has a privileged place. All other art forms give expression to Platonic Ideas: at the lowest end, architecture expresses the struggle between gravity and rigidity and between light and shadow;[36] at the highest level, the struggle between persons and between Fate and humanity finds expression in tragedy. Drama is the most perfect expression of human existence.[37] Schopenhauer sees the individual human being as presenting the highest Platonic Idea, suggesting an ideal of each human expressed (e.g., in portraiture), but also a hierarchy of humanness embodied in individuals. The novel at its best is most revelatory of the inwardness of the individual. The height of that artistic genus is found in *Tristram Shandy*, *La nouvelle Héloïse*, *Wilhelm Meister*, and *Don Quixote*.[38] Music, however, reaches beyond the Ideas to that which they themselves express: the Will. Music is the language of desire. It reaches into the heart of things and expresses the continuing alternations between conflict and resolution. Here we have the basis for the Wagnerian conception of music. The word itself is a secondary expression of the emotions expressed in music.[39] But Schopenhauer also opposes in advance the Wagnerian conception of opera as totalizing art *(Gesamtkunst)*. He goes so far as to say that "pictorial," or what comes to be called program, music is in principle objectionable and that opera, by piling up the means to aesthetic enjoyment, confuses and barbarizes music. It is "an unmusical invention for the benefit of unmusical minds," making them less receptive to "the sacred, mysterious, intimate language of music."[40] Music reaches to the heart of things. Parallel to that, the deepest dimension of the self is the heart, of which the intellect and its prose is the expression.

Seemingly along Hegelian lines, Schopenhauer says that philosophy is related to the arts as wine to grapes.[41] However, philosophy itself has to be understood as ultimately intuition into the heart of things and not simply conceptual understanding. The latter only presents the *unitas post rem*, the unity we are able to construct after the fact, so to speak, semiartificially building up out of scattered pieces that which is essentially unitary. Intuitive philosophy reaches the Platonic Idea as the *unitas ante rem*, the unity that generates the thing and that can only be grasped by artistic, that is to say, generative insight. There is a sense of the generative and unitary ground of the object contemplated. Here Schopenhauer again draws upon Plotinus, who claimed that the artist reaches to the Idea, which the thing expresses and the mirror only superficially represents. Indeed, as I already remarked, for Schopenhauer the artist grasps that which Nature is only stammeringly trying to say and proceeds to say it better. One thinks here of Aristotle's notion that art partly imitates, partly completes nature. Presumably philosophy rests on the same intuitional capacity, but brings the multiplicity of such intuitions to some final intuitive synthesis.

## Response

One of the chief claims of Schopenhauer is the distinctiveness of music vis-à-vis the other art forms. He picks up on Kant's observation that music is the language of affections, which gives rise to the aesthetic idea of an indeterminate whole of an immense wealth of thought. But he reverses Kant's assessment of its value, which was based on the dimming of the priority of verbal-intellectual manifestness evident in poetry. For Schopenhauer, music gives direct expression to the encompassing Will while other art forms point to it indirectly by expressing the Platonic Ideas, which, in turn, are expressions of the Will. The metaphysical claim parallels the Neoplatonic notion of the relation between the One and the *Nous*, locus of the cosmic Logos. The One is beyond the Logos, transcending every distinction, including the distinction between subject and object that frames the region of the Logos. There is a distinctive relation to the One: a non-dualistic experience of identity beyond concepts and words. In orthodox Christian theology the Logos, though one with the Father in a unity closer than any other mode of unity, is other than the Father, being His mirroring in otherness. In a direct parallel, for Schopenhauer the Will lies beyond the Platonic Ideas which are its expression. At the level of art, music provides the mood, which generates the word and thus mirrors the world process. Interestingly, this reverses the understanding, common in the Christian tradition, of the priority of the word, both in terms of the creation story in *Genesis*, where God's speech is the origin of things, and in the prologue to John's gospel, where it is announced that in the beginning was the Word. This also goes back to Plato, for whom—at least in the *Laws*—music without words is nonsensical, suggesting a merely supportive role for music. It is found also in neoclassical aesthetic. Surprisingly, on this point Schopenhauer's view seems more in keeping with the trinitarian doctrine of the Origin beyond the Word. Obviously different, however, is Schopenhauer's reversal of traditional value, finding in the ultimate Ground—because of suffering, struggle, and death in its expressions—a repelling rather than an attracting source. Contemplation through music, rather than uniting us to the grounding Will, frees us from it.

As we have previously noted, the position on the priority of music over the word is opposed by Gregorian chant, in which, following the prologue to St. John's gospel ("In the beginning was the Word"), music is essentially subordinated to the word. Schopenhauer would probably say that even such a view betrays itself when it musically elaborates the Alleluia at great length after the sufferings of Lent, an emotional breakthrough revealing something of the real underlying character of things. Hegel likewise sees music as an intermediary form of art, leaving exterior form behind and straining toward the interiority of poetry. Poetry itself approaches philosophic prose as the highest manifestation of the ultimate depth of interiority, which music only expresses inadequately. Schopenhauer reverses that: the word is derivative and essentially inadequate expression of that which music alone most fully expresses.

In poets like Schiller and Poe, a "musical mood" gives rise to the poetry. Poe, for example, discusses the origin of "The Raven" in the attempt to express the feeling of sadness. He searched for a word that would best express that and arrived at *nevermore*. Lenore, night, the black raven, and so on followed therefrom.[42] Dufrenne speaks of "an atmosphere" that crystallizes into a represented world. He insists that "it is on the basis of music that one must understand the realism of the representational arts, not vice versa."[43]

One serious ambiguity in Schopenhauer's general view is the conflation under the term Will of the appetites we share in common with the animals and our possibility of acting over against those appetites, and then his projecting into the Ground of being the blindness of those appetites over against the principles we consciously select as the bases for our choices. There does not seem in general to be an explanation for how we are able to put ourselves in a position to transcend "the will" (as appetite) except through the active cooperation of our "will" (in traditional terms, as ability to choose over against our appetites), which is aligned with our capacity for insight. Nor does there seem to be an explanation of how the arts emerge, which allow us to transcend our ground in the Will through contemplative distance. In Kant it is as if the ground of things through the genius aimed at bringing us above our appetites in aesthetic contemplation and thus bringing us halfway to the moral state of the organization of our appetitive life to support our respect for Humanity in ourselves and in others. In Schopenhauer, by contrast, the emergence of the arts seems groundless. It just happens that the Will produces an open field that transcends its own unconscious aims through conscious contemplation.

There is also a tension in his account of our relation to others. It is the same capacity of rising above the self-centeredness of appetites that makes possible both aesthetic contemplation and identification with other beings who are suffering. But in aesthetic contemplation we are detached from the objects of contemplation, whereas in sympathetic identification we are united. Again, no ground for the possibility of such identification seems forthcoming.

To switch to a positive note, Schopenhauer's focus on the negative factors in the world and in our self-experience is a realistic corrective to an all too idyllic notion of the harmony of nature. But unlike Hegel, who takes account of the power of the negative as a conceptual translation of the Christian focus on the Cross, Schopenhauer provides no resolution outside of escape, while Hegel, following the Christian tradition, links the negative factors with an invitation to move to a more encompassing view of things and thus to a richer and deeper life. Schopenhauer in a sense returns to elements of the Greek approach to tragedy—a return that forms the point of departure for Friedrich Nietzsche.

In his view of pure beauty, Kant set in motion a view of art that focuses on aesthetic surface to the exclusion of all other reference: art for art's sake was the result. However, Kant himself considered pure beauty only for the sake of isolating the strictly aesthetic moment as object of conceptless disinterest before he folded back in both concepts and interests. In this way he was able to move from a trivial surface aesthetic to what one might call a depth aesthetic. It is the depth aesthetic that interests Schopenhauer, especially in assimilating Kant's notion of aesthetic ideas to Platonic Ideas as the archetypes of natural species and as the special objects of art. Here he brings to the fore the key notion of the *expressivity* of sensory surface that was implicit in Plotinus especially. Indeed, in the Neoplatonic line, sensory surface is expressive of ontological depth in the individual, which is expressive of the even deeper realm of the Forms, which, in turn, are expressive of the ultimate One. One must distinguish here the surface copier, who exhibits fine hand-eye coordination and who was, for the most part, rendered superfluous by the camera, from the visionary artist, who, grasping the underlying generative Form expressed in individuals, transforms surface to express depth. But as we distinguish different Forms, we must realize that the human is a peculiar Form. An individual human is not simply an instance of a general archetype. Oriented toward the level of the universal, humans must choose what they are to be, individually and collectively. Hence every human is unique in a way that no other instance of a species is unique. And the more profound the level at which the individual operates, the more unique his or her existence. Hence for Schopenhauer there is opened up for the artist the possibility of apprehending and giving expression to the peculiar idea of an individual human, especially of the great individual. Such an individual would more adequately express the One that is expressed in everything—only for Schopenhauer the One is contradictory, whereas the fully achieved individual human would be harmonious. Schopenhauer even confesses the inadequacy of his view when he suggests at the very end of his magnum opus that there might be something positive corresponding to his negative notion of nirvana as the essence of sainthood.[44]

Schopenhauer followed the example of Kant in developing a view of hierarchy among the arts. For Schopenhauer the hierarchy is rooted in his metaphysics and thus is based, not primarily on aesthetic form, but on reference: there are corresponding levels of depth within the arts. First of all there is the hierarchy of types of referents, from the depiction of landscape through animal forms to human forms. Since humans are the highest types and tragedy reveals the essence of things, tragedy is the highest art form depicting types. Then there is the transcendence of music beyond those types to give expression to the Will, which all types express, each in their own ways. Apart from the hierarchy of reference, in its aesthetic form architecture displays an aspect of universal struggle at the level of the lowest forms: the struggle of gravity and rigidity on the one hand and of light and darkness on the other. Architecture and music bear witness to the fact that even aesthetic form is, in its own way, referential. And in this we return to Aristotle. But one must ask why it is that, though struggle often is an explicit theme, whether directly referential in tragic drama, or indirectly in musical tension, nonetheless, the aesthetic experience is one of resolution and harmony, producing disinterested calm. And beyond this, not every referent treated aesthetically exhibits struggle—perhaps the majority of thematic works do not—so that Schopenhauer seems to skew his theory by selectively attending to works and aesthetic forms that fit his theory.

We should note here Schopenhauer's departure from Kant on the notion of the sublime. Where Kant maintained that what we call sublime objects are really only occasions which remind us of our own sublimity,

Schopenhauer does not depart from ordinary usage: what is sublime is what is hostile to our desire. But then how does one distinguish between the threatening and the sublime unless it be in our regarding of it?

Schopenhauer will be aligned with Nietzsche in pushing for a priority of music over the other art forms. In this he is in opposition to a line that begins in Plato and goes through Kant and Hegel. Plato had said that music alone without lyrics is meaningless; Kant had placed music at the bottom of the hierarchy of the art forms because it is basically an art of the agreeable, not of the beautiful or sublime, giving us least information about what is; Hegel is said to have had little sympathy for orchestral music.[45] In all three cases, it seems that a view of the superiority of reason is the reason. On the other hand, in Plato I have attempted to show that there is a priority of Eros that leads reason, constantly incomplete, to transcend itself; and in Kant it is clear that reason points beyond that which we can conquer cognitively in the phenomenal order.

# VIII

# NIETZSCHE

## Nietzsche's Horizon

ONE MIGHT SAY THAT the founding experience of Friedrich Nietzsche's philosophy is the experience of the death of God. It is announced, like Plato's thought, in poetic form through the Parable of the Madman in *The Gay Science*. Nietzsche describes a madman who lit a lantern in the morning hours and went in search of God, like Diogenes, who claimed that the light of day was not sufficient to reveal an honest man. The madman's audience of unbelievers mocked him, asking whether God had gotten lost or emigrated. The madman proclaimed that God was dead and that he and they together had killed Him. He wondered at the power that made this possible, for the act was equivalent to drinking up the sea of meaning within which we swim, wiping away the horizon that locates us, unchaining the earth from the sun, which, holding us in place, illuminates us. And with that act there is no longer any absolute direction, no up or down. We stray as through an infinite nothing, feeling the breath of empty space, the chill that sets in without the sun, the darkness. God is dead and is in the process of decomposition. Yet people are still oblivious to it. It takes time for the stench to reach their nostrils. They have not yet attained the ears to hear the proclamation of the event. The madman, realizing he had come too soon, threw down his lantern, and its flame was extinguished. But he went about the churches, tombs of the dead God, singing: *Requiem aeternam deo.* Eternal rest unto God![1]

Nietzsche here hearkens back to Plato's *Republic* and the notion of the Good symbolized by the sun.[2] That dialogue attempted to determine, by its argument, its structure, and its action, an absolute "up" and "down" for human existence. It begins "down in the Piraeus" and goes down further in reflection to Hades, from which it rises through the construction of several levels of a city until it reaches the highest level that is drawn "out of the Cave" upward to the sunlight of the Good. Inside the Cave is the realm of matter and change, of nature and history; outside the Cave is the realm of Forms, eternal measures, universal and changeless, illuminated by the unifying power of the One/Good. This constitutes one of the two roots of the Western tradition. The Judeo-Christian tradition is the other root, gathering all explanation and all aspiration into Yahweh/God. The two roots, Platonic and Hebrew-Christian, came together in Patristic theology and governed together the entire Western tradition until relatively recently.

Today, in the era of deconstruction, there is no longer any sun, any single center of reference. There is a pluralism in principle, with not even the dream of a totality or of any kind of a fundamental principle or foundation, any kind of ultimate point of reference. There is no longer a measure, no up or down. And what follows from it is an experience of emptiness.[3]

If we look back over some of the thinkers from the modern era I have covered in this text, we see a transformation of the Platonic-Christian center. In Kant we see the beginning of an inversion of the tradition in this sense, that the *summum bonum*, the highest good, is not God as it was for the medievals or, in a sense, for Plato (insofar as the Agathon functioned as the highest end). Rather, for Kant the *summum bonum* is the coming together in a human afterlife of happiness and deservedness to be happy for which God is the guarantor. It is not God that we seek, but our own final happiness.[4] Correlative to this, the aesthetic experience of the sublime is transformed from that which pulls us out of ourselves and might become symbolic of the divine, to that which reminds us of our own sublimity.[5] In the ancient-medieval tradition seeing God is our final happiness.[6] In Hegel the notion of the divine is the notion of an eternally antecedent realm that by itself is mere possibility. For Hegel what we call God in the Christian tradition is, before creation, possibility of realization. God is unconscious or not fully self-conscious and comes to consciousness in Nature and in History, which are His own self-unfolding. When we say that God realizes Himself in the realization of full humanness, we are saying in effect that God is nothing but humanness fully realized, as Feuerbach and the other

Left Hegelians realized. Feuerbach saw in the statement that God is all-knowing, all-powerful, all-wise, all-just, and all-loving a projection of the immanent ideals of human existence, the approach to which is the meaning of Nature. Nature's meaning is to produce human beings whose own significance lies in reaching asymptotically toward complete knowledge, complete control, full wisdom, justice, and love. These are all human characteristics drawing us into the deep future of fuller humanness. In the notion of God we have an alienated projection of such ideals. We are driven toward such projection because of the ignorance, impotence, foolishness, injustice, and lack of love that afflicts human history and that alienates us from our true essence as humans. The ideals are given with human nature as the kind of being that is open to the Whole, aiming at the Whole in the modalities of knowing, acting, and feeling.[7] In Schopenhauer the underlying is also unconscious, but the character of the underlying is no longer good. The ground of things, the Will, is intrinsically contradictory. And if that is God, He is not to be loved but avoided. One should flee from such a God. Here we have a complete reversal of the tradition on that point. And coming off of Schopenhauer we have Nietzsche.

Nietzsche expressed mixed feelings at the discovery of the death of God. There is a kind of sadness, a feeling of emptiness, a sense of what he calls nihilism that follows from the realization of the death of God. In high culture, the very function of God has been transmuted, then negated, then reversed. There is nothing that takes the place of God: there is no measure, no final up or down anymore. The place defined by the Platonic Good that was taken over by and melded with the Hebrew-Christian God is now no longer occupied—indeed the very existence of the place is in question. There is no ground for values; there is a nothingness of values, a value nihilism.[8] This first vision of nihilism brings about a kind of emptiness and despair. What gave meaning to the earth, the holy, the sacred, is no longer seen as a viable option.

One who stands outside the prevalent sense of rationality seems, by comparison, to be mad. Nietzsche himself is the madman, yet one who comes too early. It takes a long time for corpses to decay and for their stench to reach the nostrils of the many. Nietzsche claims, in effect, to have a better nose than most: he can smell the decay of the flesh of the divine. In another place he says that great deeds take a long time before they are heard; the deed of the killing of God may take a hundred years before it will be heard.[9] Almost a hundred years later, on the cover of *Time* magazine, the organ of proclamation to the many, there appeared the question, "Is God Dead?"[10] It brought to light the discovery that Nietzsche had sniffed out in the third quarter of the nineteenth century.

But though on the one hand there is a feeling of emptiness, on the other hand there is the notion that we have to become gods ourselves to be worthy of the deed. And there Nietzsche finds the basis for a certain kind of exultation: the sea is open, the horizons free;[11] we can ourselves become the sun.[12] The very context within which this appears, *The Gay Science,* is a book about learning how to laugh and dance—and that not in oblivion of the negative factors of existence.[13] Quite the contrary. There are many such factors, as Schopenhauer never tired of pointing out and as Nietzsche was not afraid to face. But in spite of that, for Nietzsche life is indescribably fertile, creative, rising up again and again in new forms, in spite of the conflict and destructiveness that stands internal to its very character. Rejoicing in the creative upsurge of life is the exultant side in the discovery of the death of God.[14]

This turns upon realizing that the place of the Good as the origin of the realm of Being in Plato's view and in the Christian tradition is itself nihilistic. There is thus a second and deeper kind of nihilism. In the first type, there is sadness at the disappearance of that which defines ultimate meaning for most people and has defined it throughout Western history: the Good/Yahweh/God. But for Nietzsche this is itself a deeper form of nihilism: the very place of value is nihilistic. The reason is that Plato has to posit another realm in order to find worthy the realm in which we live, the realm of becoming, of embodiment—or better, *because* he finds life unworthy, Plato posits another life. In fact, according to Nietzsche, the Platonic-Christian view is a derogation of, a blasphemy against this life, a slur upon existence, for it claims that the only thing that gives meaning to this life is something beyond it and that this life is consequently a shadow life, life in a cave, a valley of tears.[15] For some of the early Christian Platonists, like Origen, the realm of matter existed because Adam and Eve, who were pure spirits, fell; and their fall generated this world as the land of their exile.[16] For Gregory of Nyssa, the sexual origin of life is the result of the Fall.[17] Nietzsche reports Pope Innocent III's repetition of Augustine's judgments on the "filth" of human origins.[18] This life, this world is a dark place, a bad place. We do not belong here. We should keep ourselves safe from its allurements and pray that we get out of it as soon as possible. But woe to those who are happy, rich, talented, successful, famous. Blessed are the downtrodden, the poor, those at the bottom, the worst.[19] Christianity becomes Platonism for the people,[20] a way of reconciling oneself to the negative factors of existence—as well as a convenient prop for political establishments, a civil religion that keeps control over the many.

Nietzsche takes the Platonic-Christian teaching on the afterlife as a slur on this life, a saying No! to life: "I had always sensed strongly the furious, vindictive hatred of life implicit in that system of ideas and values. . . . Christianity spelled life loathing itself. . . . A hatred of the 'world,' a curse on the affective urges, a fear of beauty and sensuality, a transcendence rigged up to slander mortal existence, a yearning for extinction. . . ."[21] Nietzsche wants to affirm against that the exultation of existence, joy in the rising of life in spite of destruction and pain. Life is inexhaustibly good. Say Yes! to it![22] Life is constant process, constant metabolism and catabolism. It is like a flame that is constantly being fueled. Platonism proclaims the superiority of fixity—in effect, of deadness—and thus is the extreme opponent of life. Platonism really consists in a set of abstractions made from the flux of life. Thus there is nihilism in the very way the value question is posed in the tradition.

Whatever the grounds offered, Nietzsche notes an intrinsic order to life itself. Rank and hierarchy are intrinsic to being. There is a higher and lower: higher men and lower men. There is a kind of natural morality, which Nietzsche calls master morality, in which the operative terms are *good* and *bad*. They basically mean competent and incompetent respectively. Name any kind of functional capacity, including sainthood, and you have rank: there are those farthest removed from it, those who most deeply epitomize it, and many grades scattered in between. Artist, athlete, chemist, entrepreneur, financier, philosopher, saint—any individual who aspires to instantiate any one of these types can be shown to occupy a rung on an empirically discernible hierarchy relative to others who perform the same function, a hierarchy intrinsic to the very nature of things. Master morality is an order in which the omni-competent are on top because they ought to be there, and those on the bottom belong there because they are incompetent.[23]

But historically there came a slave revolt in morality and a reversal. Good and bad are inverted into a corresponding evil and good.[24] Nietzsche has in mind the Sermon on the Mount with its woes to the rich, the happy, the laughing, and its blessings on the poor, the sad, the mourning.[25] Evil are those who are proudly exultant in their success and superiority. Good are those on the bottom. In proportion as one has less one is to be rewarded hereafter; in proportion as one has more, one is to be deprived. The last shall be first and the first last. Many of these things in the Christian bloodstream are rooted in ressentiment: those on the bottom resent the fact that they are on the bottom and desire the fall of those on top.[26] Nietzsche presents an amalgam between the slave revolt and Platonism in his view of Christianity as Platonism for the masses. Down here, in this life, we have the rich and the poor; there, in the afterlife above, the rank is inverted. Those who proclaim this view attempt to uproot their ties with this life through vows of poverty, chastity, and obedience, to become disembodied, otherworldly spirits who hate the body and this "land of exile," this "vale of tears." But those who proclaim this also hold the greatest power over those whom they persuade.[27]

The upshot of the slave revolt is, in secularized terms, democratic socialism—socialism where everybody works for everybody else, and democracy in which every man is equal. That leads to a flattening out of all hierarchy, in particular the financial hierarchy, and is rooted in resentment of any kind of natural superiority. Democratic socialism is secularized Christianity, which continues the inversion of the natural, master morality.[28] Nietzsche calls for a transvaluation of values, an inversion of the slave inversion, getting back to the natural order of intrinsic rank and hierarchy.[29]

Natural order is governed by what Nietzsche called Will-to-Power, a variation on the Schopenhauerian theme of Will as fundamental ground, as comprehensive basis expressed in each entity. Will-to-Power is the world "viewed from the inside."[30] Nietzsche was stimulated by Schopenhauer, but went beyond Schopenhauer. Nietzsche's development led him to stress creativity, the origin of form and the self-surpassing involved in creativity. It becomes difficult to see in Schopenhauer any ground for creativity if art, like religion, is essentially life denying. In the notion of the Will-to-Power, Nietzsche preserves the continuity of the realm of art, and indeed of culture as a whole, with the realm of nature. And, contrary to Schopenhauer, he celebrates both.

Will-to-Power is *Wille zur Macht*, where *Macht* is rooted in *machen*, to make, so that Will-to-Power should be understood as will to create.[31] Such a will-to-create produces ever higher forms—that is, forms with ever more developed capacity to create unity in ever more complex multiplicities. Life is a matter in each instance of gathering power to itself, of appropriating the nonliving and the living, but also of creating beyond itself on the basis of that gathering of power. We kill plant and animal life to permit the expansion and sustenance of our own power. Life in each case destroys in order to build and, through reproduction as well as in the formation of culture, to create beyond itself, exulting in such creation.

Going back to Heraclitus (but also to the Old Testament *Book of Wisdom*),[32] Nietzsche views the operation of the Will-to-Power as play—according to Eugen Fink, the central concept of Nietzsche's philosophy.[33] The notion stresses unpredictability and transsubjectivity, the latter in the sense that in play the individual subject is not in full control but is rather dependent on the direction the total play complex takes.[34] Will-to-Power has consequently to be understood in an individual case as knowing how to let oneself be taken, to go along, as well as to take whatever control is possible in order to achieve form. This links with Nietzsche's later emphasis on *amor fati*, the love of one's fate, the lot one is given, the hand one is dealt— in Heidegger's terms, one's *Geschick*, one's destiny following one's *Geworfenheit*, one's thrownness.[35] As Fink puts it, world-play involves the "cosmic agreement *[Einklang]* of man and world in the play of necessity."[36]

The human being stands at the top of the hierarchy of forms that emerge from the world-play. The tradition stemming from Platonism seized upon the work of intellect and will as the directive center of consciousness and claimed the alien descent of the intellectual-volitional subject from another realm, a fall into the body with its passions. Nietzsche deconstructs the notion of subject so conceived, displaying the complexity of the "simple" act of willing[37] and calling attention to the operation of instinct in the life of "intellect."[38] He constantly refers to the whole human being as "physiological" and as a play of forces.[39] But on the other side of such relocation of the subject of awareness within the transformed physiological context there is the exaltation of the creative type, that is one who requires discipline, bringing the chaos of passions into order, "chaining the dogs in the basement," gaining simplicity by keeping the most extreme opposites in tension, ideally without effort, extending the temporal horizon of one's awareness through holding himself to long-term projects, gaining power over himself, and becoming—like Goethe, Nietzsche's lifelong model[40]—a whole person. Such wholeness is measured by the extent to which one can contain multiplicity in unity,[41] learning to "'live resolutely' in wholeness and fullness of being."[42] Far from dissolving the human being into the play of forces that are factually operative in him, far from exalting self-indulgence in one's passions as the exhibition of the "free spirit," Nietzsche saw his free spirit as just the opposite.[43] It is the lower types—and this includes too many who claim descent from Nietzsche—that wallow in the "liberation" of passions. Nietzsche's aim is "to make asceticism natural again."[44] This is an indispensable condition for "the higher men."

One of the higher levels on which the will-to-power operates is that of a political state as the fusing together of multiplicities of different individuals and groups over long periods of time.[45] The most powerful way in which that is achieved is not by means of weaponry, which conquers only the body, but by means of the conquest of the soul through the bestowal of comprehensive meaning. This is the work of "the higher men" who embody more fully the most fundamental metaphysical ground, which is the Will-to-Power. They operate in Hegel's realm of Absolute Spirit: artists, philosophers, and saints.[46] Who are some of the higher men? Lao-tzu, Confucius, Buddha, Socrates, Jesus, Muhammad, Shakespeare, Goethe—all of them poets of a sort who create a comprehensive form of life that governs billions of people for thousands of years. They create the horizon of meaning within which the many come to find meaning, whatever their hierarchical rank otherwise. All life—and thus all human life—needs a horizon within which to live.[47] One cannot live with unlimited horizons. Human beings need a "ring of myths" that give the stamp of eternity to the quotidian, providing a creative womb for those who operate within the ring.[48] We human beings, however, are peculiar in that we are always pushed to create limited horizons and to strain at their edges, so to speak. We have to create culture whose fundamental structures lie in the definition of the horizons of meaning, within which everything else occurs. The great religions do precisely that through their founders, the great creative types, those who embody the Will-to-Power most deeply.

One problem with modern democratic socialism is that it does not promote the higher men but, as noted above, flattens out natural rank and hierarchy.[49] Democratic socialism produces what Nietzsche calls "the last man," who "invents happiness" (i.e., a universally available, easy gratification that the technological system produces for the many).[50] It is supposed to give meaning to the earth, but ends in recurrent boredom and the need for constant novel stimulation. The last man loses the meaning horizon provided by the higher men and falls into meaningless distraction. The higher type is the meaning of the earth through his ability to create a horizon of meaning that is existentially compelling, that grips his followers, who freely adhere to his message.

The higher men are not hedonists but disciplined types, often ascetics of the most rigorous sort. This seems to be out of step with Nietzsche's notion that life itself is the ground of meaning, for asceticism seems to express a denial of life. Nietzsche distinguishes the ascetic *ideal*, which is life denying, from asceticism as a natural condition for all higher creativity. In any case, we would have to get beneath the various meaning structures in order to understand what it is that produces them (i.e., life in its creative upsurge). Discipline, especially self-discipline, is the indispensable condition for an enduring form of life.[51] But even further, the life-denying forms of life are also expressions of a way of giving meaning to life creatively. This leads the great creative one to form illusions.

Illusions, however, are not necessarily bad; they are often life sustaining. "Truth" (i.e., the claim to ultimate meaning) is the lie we need in order to live.[52] Truth is the creation of a horizon of meaning that defines the ultimate meaning structure for those who come to exist under it. An analogue to this—and more than an analogue, another expression of the character of life—is animal perception. Perception is a "lie" that is needed in order to adjust to the environment. In ordinary experience, it looks like the space between my eyeball and this book is empty; it feels like the desk is smooth and stable. As a matter of fact, the space is full of unobserved entities and the desk is rough and in constant agitation at the subatomic level. Perception simplifies and gives the illusion of fixity and stability in order that the organism be able to adjust to its environment and thus survive. Perception is a "lie" invented by life to promote life.[53]

Project that into the distinctively human realm. Not only is there the initial lie that perception itself creates for us, but also the "lie" that characterizes each of the meaning systems. Each poses itself as absolute and encompassing; and yet by the very nature of the case, each is only a perspective.[54] Whatever it discloses, it simultaneously closes other ways of ultimate conception. But that again is a lie needed in order to allow people to grow up and adjust—a kind of second womb created by culture. The horizon of meaning is a "lie" created by life through the higher types. Nietzsche is here paralleling Plato, who in his *Republic* has Socrates observe that, in teaching children, the rule is, "The false before the true."[55] To begin with, we tell children fables, fairy tales; later we go on to the true picture—Nietzsche would say, the adult tissue of lies that has us in its grip as our way of coping with life. Indeed, for Nietzsche, "in art the lie becomes consecrated, the will to deception has good conscience at its back."[56]

There are several further remarks on truth we should consider here. One is Nietzsche's claim that we have art lest we perish from truth.[57] The truth here is that of the true horrors, the suffering and destruction endemic to life at every level. I elaborated on that a bit in the previous chapter on Schopenhauer. Life is truly like that—no "lie" involved. Nietzsche even claims that the measure of character is how much of such truth one can bear.[58] The second is that dedication to truth leads to the canceling of

Christianity—and indeed of theism, unmasking what the genealogy and history of Christianity reveal: resentment of the gifted and successful, contempt for the earth, self-contempt, and the operation of power.[59] But, third, Nietzsche sees—and this is one of the most difficult things to construe credibly—belief in truth itself as something to be overcome.[60] One aspect of this is his frequent equation of truth with Platonism—that is, with acceptance of "another world" of fixed and eternal forms and the corresponding dualism of soul and body.[61] It is that which he calls metaphysics and which falls to perspectivism and "physiology." Even science involves such Platonistic faith. As a counter to this Nietzsche suggests that truth is a woman;[62] and woman he sees as surface, lightness, delighting in appearances,[63] also as given to seduction,[64] but as the very image of mother earth, of life itself.[65] Here is where, facing the truth of the horrors of existence, one sees in art, with its preoccupation with surfaces and the beauty of appearance, an overcoming of "truth"—both in the sense of creatively coming to terms with life and in the sense of repudiating the Platonism of another and better world. The ultimate conclusion to the faith in truth is that appearance, "the lie," is divine.[66] Ultimately, Nietzsche claims, art is worth more than truth.[67] It is in this connection, he says that life requires truth and deception,[68] and by that I would understand the recognition of perspectivity, afforded by the artistry of life, which reveals and conceals. Finally, he claims that the will to truth is a mask for the will to power.[69] This should at least lead the inquirer to ask, In what is *my* will to truth rooted? Is it a desire to be able to tell others what to do? Is it a way of calling attention to my superiority, attracting the attention of others like the little boy in knee pants reciting his repertoire of nursery rimes to the oohs and ahs of the adulating adults? But Nietzsche evidently has something further also in mind: truth in the service of life.[70] In his early work he praised truth only as connected with justice and thus repudiated the search for trivial truths, which afflicts the scholar.[71] What enhances one's capacity to do, to create, to produce something beyond the perishing moment of pleasure or pain? Is it the fact that he who does "the truth" enters into the light?

The higher types are all, in a sense, artists: they create out of inspiration. And the definition of horizon they create is great insofar as it comprehensively unifies the multiplicity of things actual in a culture. This requires attunement to the materials available at the time, a sense of all the parameters of existence that are operative in the culture, and creation of comprehensive form, which takes account of and fuses that multiplicity. There are more powerful and less powerful definitions of horizon. But the greater visions create forms of such power that the "lie" lasts for thousands of years in binding a people together. Perspectival disclosure holds people under its sway for millennia as the putative absolute disclosure of final meaning (the very definition of ultimate horizon). But the meaning systems eventually come apart as time moves forward and we await the bringer of new meaning, the creator of a new horizon that can bring together and put the stamp of eternity on the plurality of directions functioning in a culture.[72]

Socrates created what we recognize as the philosophic type that came to play a central role in Western culture to this day.[73] But that type so conceived is rooted in a contempt for the earth. It is a high type because of the power it has exhibited: it touched a nerve in human existence and led to a form that lasted for millennia. People recognized it and responded by saying, "Yes, that makes sense; let's live that way"—and they continued to do so throughout the centuries. But there are plural ways of horizon definition. The latter is both arbitrary and not: arbitrary in that there is a decision involved, but not arbitrary in that, if it is profound it will last, if superficial it will fade.

The very way the definition of the horizon has occurred historically through the great higher types is such as to be by and large one that is still nihilistic. One needs to get beneath that to see that life itself is the ground for the creation of these forms. Life itself is the fundamental value. What Nietzsche calls us to do is to say Yes! to life.[74] We have to realize that we do not cognitively possess the whole, and the manifestness of the whole is rooted in the myth of a knower before whom the whole is manifest. There is no uncovering of the whole, but there is the uncovering of horizons that are more or less adequate. Thus we have different perspectives. But it is life, the will to create, that surges up in the higher types and leads them to form the horizon within which the many come to exist. There is no need for metaphysical justification that appeals to another life, to Being apart from Becoming; life in its creative upsurge is justification enough.

Consider a football stadium and see the definition of existence it represents: "Sunday observance," which gives meaning to the drabness of the workweek, identifying with the "saints," seeing the battle of "good and evil," and finding a center of meaning without needing any further metaphysical ground. (As I look out my office window at Texas Stadium, home of the Dallas Cowboys, I see Revival Tent Architecture.) People find significance through activity governed by the creation of an arbitrary set of rules that are rigidly enforced. If someone does not follow the rules, they spoil the game for others. There is nothing in the nature of things that says we have to play this game or play it with these rules, since rules are made up and continually modified. Generalizing that: the game of human life is operative at the level of problems posed by nature, such as the need to eat and the need to take care of the relation of the sexes because of the offspring that emerge from that relation and the need to find a way to make these decisions collectively. The problems posed by these needs can be solved in terms of different games: different economic games, different social games, different political games. But all this also can be, has been and *must be* encompassed and given ultimate horizon by some system of ultimate meaning. It is important to have rigid rules and adhesion to those rules, but not such that they cancel out powerful urges. Urges ought rather to be channeled. So we get the powerful instincts of athletes channeled and honed along certain lines determined by rules. The rules allow them to concentrate their powers and to find significance in that concentration, celebrating the upsurge of life. But there is no one, encompassing, *natural* societal form, no one defining horizon: they are all artistic fabrications on the part of great creative geniuses. One of those geniuses was Socrates, another was Jesus, but there are others. We do not need metaphysical justification appealing to another life, to Being apart from Becoming, for this exhibits contempt for life. Life in its own creative upsurge is justification enough. Nietzsche calls upon us to celebrate life: not to say No! like the otherworldly ascetics, but to say Yes! to being as it is.

The top of Nietzsche's natural hierarchy is what he calls the Overman *(Übermensch)*. Nietzsche says that man is a rope stretched from ape to Overman.[75] Man is a transitional species, suggesting something in the future. The Overman, he says, is the meaning of the earth.[76] The Overman and what he calls *the higher men* are related to one another.[77] The higher men— like Homer, Socrates, Moses, and Jesus—have been the most powerful definers of the ultimate horizon in our tradition. But they were all under the illusion that they were taking heavenly dictation, that some divine entity or its emissary—a muse or an angel—was whispering in their ear.[78] With the experience of the death of God, the essential ingredient in the prevailing definition of the horizon can no longer hold. Enter the "free spirit," the spirit of the higher men become fully self-conscious, aware of its historical self-alienation in Absolute Spirit.

Nietzsche has Zarathustra, the inventor of dualism, repent his error through the "discovery of solitude," thus freeing the human spirit.[79] On the mountaintop he encountered, not a higher entity or its emissary, but rather absolute solitude. There was no one besides himself. That discovery makes possible the emergence of the Overman. Like the higher men, he will appear unpredictably and will create the horizon of meaning for the many; but, unlike the higher men, he will be free of the illusion of divine inspiration. That does not mean he will be free of inspiration—quite the contrary: he remains, like all great artists, a medium, a mouthpiece for overpowering forces.[80] Ideally for Nietzsche he will be—in another variation on a Platonic theme—a saint-emperor, "the Roman Caesar with Christ's soul."[81] He will not proclaim another life tied in with contempt for this life. He will teach us how to celebrate this life, how to laugh and dance. He will teach the Gay Science.

Three fundamental concepts interplay in Nietzsche's understanding: the Overman, Will-to-Power, and Eternal Recurrence of the Same. The Overman expresses the Will-to-Power as the will to create form, which occurs in terms of the Eternal Recurrence of the Same. The latter is Nietzsche's way of coming to terms with the two worlds of Platonism and thus of the tradition where Being lies beyond Becoming. For Nietzsche, Eternal Recurrence installs Being within Becoming.[82] Eternity lies inside Becoming and not outside it. There is something in the very character of life, expressed in joy, that seeks eternity. In one of the middle chapters of Nietzsche's major work, *Thus Spake Zarathustra*, there is a song for whose stanzas the concluding verse is: "All joy seeks eternity, seeks deep, deep eternity."[83] That is in a sense a retrieval of Diotima's claim in the *Symposium* as to the nature of Eros: the mortal seeking the immortal, the temporal seeking the eternal.[84] Procreation is the establishment of eternity in time. The eternal repetition of the same is, for one thing, the eternal proliferation of individuals under a given species. This is in Aristotle as well as in Plato, except that for both there is a claim to something superior beyond time: Self-thinking Thought, Pure Form as the Unmoved Mover in Aristotle[85] and the realm of Forms surmounted by the One/Good in Plato.[86] Within time Eros constitutes that in the perishable which surpasses perishing. But for Plato as for Aristotle, that is because the perishing seeks to emulate that which stands eternally beyond time. Nietzsche, however, seeks to install the eternal within time in the self-surpassing creativity of life's Eros.

There are various ways in which Nietzsche talks about eternal recurrence. In *The Will to Power*, posthumously published, he speaks of eternal recurrence as a kind of scientific hypothesis.[87] The basis for it is the supposition of a finite number of entities in the universe and an infinity of time. Given that, the combinatory possibilities will have to repeat themselves again and again. We have to think about eternity seriously in this context. There is an example in the Hindu tradition about the duration of the fundamental unit of time, the kalpa: if a bird drags a piece of the finest silk over the highest mountain peak once every hundred years, a kalpa is the time it would take to flatten that mountain. That constitutes but one unit, like a single second, in the eternity of time itself.[88] If the thought of infinite empty space brought Pascal up short,[89] the thought of infinite time should do so as well. Given that, all combinations would seem to have to repeat themselves eventually.

The doctrine of Eternal Recurrence is also the basis for a kind of categorical imperative to prevent the Overman from complete arbitrariness in his creation of form. In the first announcement of Eternal Recurrence in 1882, Nietzsche says something like: So create that you can will what is created to reoccur forever and ever.[90] In a sense that is equivalent to thinking in Christian terms about heaven or hell. Whatever path we choose in life will be with us forever. Nietzsche proposes the equivalent within time. One wonders how literally the teaching is to be taken, and whether it is itself not a kind of myth directed at the problem of the temptation to absolute arbitrariness in the Overman's creative activity. It gives an infinite weight to each decision.

However we understand Eternal Recurrence, for Nietzsche nature strains to gather power that unifies otherwise independent centers of power. In human form, it strains to produce political states that unify human beings. But states have as their own telos, and thus as the ultimate goal of nature, the production of the artistic genius, who gives meaning to the togetherness of humans in a state. And for Nietzsche, the highest artistic creator is the tragic artist who reveals to us something of the real character of existence.[91]

## Nietzsche's Aesthetics

In his posthumously published notes titled *The Will to Power,* Nietzsche remarks that hitherto reflection on art has been largely restricted to "woman's aesthetics," which he identifies as emphasis on the recipient, the perceiver of the art work.[92] His own focus is on the creative aspect, the origin of the work of art, the creation of form. One of the features of form creation lies in bringing to some kind of interpenetration two facets of human existence. The first is the upsurge of instinct that Nietzsche names Dionysus and the other is the urge toward form that he calls Apollo, given prominence in his first work, *The Birth of Tragedy out of the Spirit of Music*, a work in which all the major themes of his thought are prefigured.[93] The Dionysian represents the forces of the unconscious that find expression in orgiastic religious experience: drinking, singing, and dancing to intoxication, being caught up in a kind of mass emotional infection in which the participants experience an immersion in the Great All, of which each individual is an expression. The principle of individuation is lost sight of, not simply for the sake of an escape from routine but by way of a religious sensibility that seeks a lived relation to the Whole. The Apollonian impulse runs counter to this: it is characterized by clarity, order, restraint, harmony. If the Dionysian principle is analogous to intoxication, losing oneself in a whirl of religious enthusiasm, Nietzsche likens the Apollonian principle to a dream where the individual figures stand out. The Apollonian provides the eternal in the realm of appearance while the Dionysian speaks out of the inexhaustible depth of the noumenal.[94] The roots are clearly Schopenhauerian: the underlying Will expresses itself in Platonic Ideas, which, in turn, are expressed in the phenomenal order by passing through the *principium individuationis*. But there is also a more sober Greek parallel in the notions of *peras* and *apeiron*, limit and the unlimited.[95] The turn Nietzsche gives it is the focus on the human instantiation of the notions.

Though in the beginning of *The Birth of Tragedy* Nietzsche speaks of two origins operative in the arts—the Apollonian "dream" state as the origin of the plastic arts and epic, the Dionysian state of "intoxication" as the origin of music, song, dance—nonetheless, ultimately the two are fused and the whole Apollonian realm is understood as a projection of the underlying Dionysian.[96] As regions of art forms, both have their origin in psychic states that break with the everyday world and in which something other than the controlling ego is operative in us. But beyond nature's production of these states in the ordinary individual, there is nature's production in the artist, which leads to reconfigurations within the everyday world that put us in contact, not simply with private psychic states, but, more important, with what we might call encompassing powers of being. The Dionysiac is a single, underlying creative totality, a sea of energy that expresses and limits itself in clearly definable Apollonian forms. In Dionysian experience, "the spell of individuation is broken, and the way lies open to . . . the innermost heart of things."[97] In the experience of tragic art we become "one with the primordial joy in existence," in spite of fear and pity aroused by struggle, pain, and destruction.[98]

The Apollonian is expressed among the Greeks in the Homeric gods, clearly individuated types that stand over against the Dionysiac nature forces. Mythically, the rule of Zeus, king of the Olympians, comes about through the overthrow of his father, Cronus, who governed the age of the Titans. The Titans as savage, monstrous nature forces are overcome by the more humanized Olympians.[99] Nietzsche goes back to the story of King Midas, who confronted the satyr Silenus and asked what the greatest thing in life might be. Silenus responded: The greatest thing is not to have been born; the next greatest is to die as soon as possible.[100] Life is terrible under the governance of the nature forces, under all those aspects on which Schopenhauer focused our attention. But after the age of the wisdom of Silenus, the Greeks created the Olympians. This allowed them to live in spite of the terror of existence, in such a way that, with Homer's Achilles, one would rather be a serf in this world than a king in the underworld.[101] The artist Homer created the illusion of the Olympians, which allowed the post-Homeric Greeks to celebrate this life rather than, following the wisdom of Silenus, to flee from it. Nietzsche's claim is that the fusion of the Dionysian and Apollonian forms was achieved in Greek tragedy, where "Dionysus speaks the language of Apollo; and Apollo finally the language of Dionysus."[102] This echoes Schiller's unity of the sensuous impulse and the form impulse in the play impulse.[103] Its major message is that, in spite of the destruction of the tragic hero, life is superabundantly fertile.[104] Here Nietzsche opposes the Aristotelian view, "half-medicinal, half-moral," of the aim of tragedy as purgation from the sway of the emotions of fear and pity and yet aligns himself in his own way with the Aristotelian view that poetry is more philosophic than history, allowing us to grasp the universal—even though the character of the universal and the nature of the grasp differs substantially from Aristotle's view.[105]

As in Schopenhauer, great plastic art presents to us representatives of regional forms precisely as representative (i.e., as types); music presents to us representatives of the creative source itself. In poetry the two are fused insofar as "the musical mood" generates the word (Nietzsche cites with approval Schiller's observation on his own poetic practice).[106] But it is in Greek drama and in Wagnerian opera that we arrive at a *Gesamtkunst* where the body of the actors and dancers become the primary instrument.

It is important to stress that the fusion works a transformation of both Apollonian and Dionysian forms. The individual is not a dreamlike flight from reality, nor is he or she swallowed up in the Dionysian. Rather, the individual stands out as an expression of the underlying Dionysian and becomes sublime rather than horrible,[107] appearing "surrounded with a higher glory."[108] The individual becomes a symbol of the underlying Dionysian and does not stand simply in a truth relation to what it expresses, but rather exists sui generis.[109] At the same time, the art form transfigures everyday life. As Richard Schacht has it, "Dionysian reality is sublimated and Apollinian ideality is brought down to earth. Both meet on the plane of individual human existence and yield a transfigured representation of it in which the conditions of human existence are at once preserved and transformed."[110]

Emphasis on the Dionysian sea of energy and the shattering of the principle of individuation appear again later in Nietzsche's work in his deconstruction of the ego, the subject, into a play of forces held together by a grammatical fiction.[111] The creative one becomes a channel through which the Dionysian announces itself in the emergence of form from the potential chaos of forces. As we have noted, such creativity presupposes a prior organization of one's life, a certain asceticism of instincts, and thus—paradoxically—control by the "grammatical fiction." And creativity is both grounded in and produces a system of control, a tradition of shaping. For Nietzsche, "every mature art has a host of conventions as its basis. . . . Convention is the condition of great art, *not* an obstacle."[112] The controlling ego is resituated, not only in relation to its own instinctual life, but also in relation to its historical context—the two dominant aspects evoking *amor fati*.

Contrary to modern dogma, for Nietzsche the true artist is not one who expresses his peculiar subjectivity. One might think such of the lyric poet in particular. But for Nietzsche, subjective art is just bad art.[113] For one thing, art is not merely subjective, idiosyncratic "expression."[114] As Nietzsche said, great art, like language, rests on "a host of conventions." Furthermore, the true artist is "the medium through which the one truly existent subject celebrates his release in appearance."[115] The true artist speaks universally because he is a channel for the underlying encompassing ground, which Nietzsche, in common with the Idealist tradition, here identifies as *subject*. However ambiguous that might be in this context, it will be clearly superseded in *The Gay Science* by the announcement of the death of God and his repudiation of all "metaphysical consolation" in his 1886 "Attempt at a Self-Criticism" directed at *The Birth of Tragedy*.[116] That does not involve repudiation of inspiration. In *Ecce Homo* Nietzsche says: "one accepts, one does not ask who gives," for there is no Who, only the enigma of visions and inspiration.[117]

The origin of Greek drama in the Dionysiac rituals actually locates "the spirit of music" first in the dance, because it is the dance circle that was the prototype of the stage, setting off the sacred from the profane. The rhythmic movement of the body is the basic instrument in the expression of personal participation in the primordial power of being, recognized as primordial and all-encompassing—hence something more than mere privatized—or even socialized—intoxication, whether in the individual or in the mass emotional affection of a group. The original Dionysian dance circle survives as the chorus. The chorus creates a sacred space within its circling dance. Through the revelry and frenzy of the dance, the image of the god appears in their midst and is embodied in the leader of the chorus, who eventually dons a mask of Dionysus. The characters of tragedy come out of that original form. They are rooted back in a kind of Dionysian sea and yet emerge as clear characters occupying the region of Apollo.[118]

For Nietzsche, the high point of the Apollonian-Dionysian fusion occurred in the tragedies of Aeschylus and Sophocles. But then came Socrates and with him Euripides, his putative disciple. Socrates introduced the philosophic type, who corroded the tragic synthesis. "Aesthetic Socratism" arose: to be beautiful (and good and true) is to be a matter of clear knowledge.[119] Dionysian rapture is smothered by the cold blanket of Socratic reason. According to Nietzsche, Euripides never understood the Dionysian depths of his predecessors: in place of the large mythic figures of earlier tragedy, Euripides presents us with the ordinary man. Life is flattened to the everyday. The Dionysiac becomes "fiery emotions," and the Apollonian "clear ideas." Here we have a psychologistic reduction of the larger cosmic-religious function of the notions in Aeschylus and Sophocles.

According to Nietzsche, aesthetic Socratism moves in that direction: the theoretical type that Socrates introduces is interested in the unveiling of nature and in the cast off garments; he loses the great artist's interest in the hidden depths.[120] When that attains to one of its consequences, we then hear talk of "Greek cheerfulness" (Heiterkeit: cheerfulness, serenity, clearness), which is actually a species of superficiality without any awareness of the metaphysical depths plumbed in pre-Euripidean tragedy.[121] Art eventually becomes froth, the bubbly exterior of life, with nothing of its relation to the cosmic depths. One has to think that observation in relation to Nietzsche's other claims regarding art's celebration of surface. Is it that Platonism is surface, seduction, appearance, and that tragic art creates an appearance that tells the real truth?

"Greek serenity" seems the equivalent of Schopenhauerian aesthetic contemplation as the stilling of the will. Heidegger for one thinks that Schopenhauer's interpretation of Kant's "disinterested satisfaction" was based on a misunderstanding that became the standard interpretation of Kant. Heidegger sees Kant as actually closer to Nietzsche: "disinterested satisfaction" is "unconstrained favoring."[122] Schopenhauer's view of art as pointing toward the blowing out of desire was the main thing that set Nietzsche in opposition. For Nietzsche art is not a narcotic or a flight from life but the stirring and rapturous celebration of life.[123] Where Schopenhauer advocates saying No! to life because of the immense suffering it inflicts, Nietzsche advocates saying Yes! to it in spite of suffering and because of the rapture of creativity in the will to power. But then Nietzsche notes that the function of art depends on the character of the perceiver: one who is overwrought because of desire seeks the stilling of Will; one who is languid requires stimulus.[124]

Nietzsche was particularly concerned with the "Alexandrianism" that stemmed from the introduction of the theoretical type. In the transition to the Hellenistic age, whose center was Alexandria in Egypt, the scholar replaced the creator. An essentially shrunken creature in Nietzsche's view, the scholar confines himself to a small circle of soluble problems.[125] Nietzsche was particularly sensitive to the difficulties this entailed since he studied classical philology in an era when the aim of classical study was shifting— and precisely along Alexandrian lines. Up to that point it had been *Bildung*, the shaping of human life through the study of the classics. Now it was becoming *Altertumswissenschaft*, the science of antiquity, the objective determination of facts with no concern for the comprehensive shaping, through such study, of the ones who read the classics.[126] Granted, *Bildung* still operated within the general horizon of Platonism and Christianity; but it also operated within a horizon that informed life with comprehensive meaning. As in Alexandria, the modern scholar becomes a specialist. Nietzsche's project was to consider the scholar in terms of the artist and the artist in terms of life.[127]

For the Nietzsche of *The Birth of Tragedy* at least, the German tradition provided the basis for a Greek Renaissance that went back to the Dionysiac origins. This moves beyond the Apollonian classicism admired by Winckelmann, who had reawakened appreciation for the Greeks where the Renaissance doted on the Romans. One line of this further recovery moves musically from Luther through Bach and Beethoven to Wagner.[128] The other moves philosophically from Kant to Schopenhauer. Both limited the operation of logic to phenomenality and opened the way to a wisdom beyond logic.[129]

The whole, nature and society together, is a kind of aesthetic phenomenon. The great artist is life itself. As its darling, life produces those higher types that, as in Kant, are the geniuses through which nature gives the rules. And these higher types come to define the fundamental forms of life, the fundamental games that constitute cultures. For Nietzsche some of the greatest works of art are the Jesuit Order and the Prussian Officers Corps—scarcely something his contemporary Dionysian followers would approve.[130] For such works to succeed there has to be "the will to tradition, to authority, to centuries-long responsibility, to *solidarity* between succeeding generations backwards and forwards *in infinitum*."[131] This is what is involved in the instinct for institutions eroded by the rise of democracy and liberalism. Today, "that which *makes* institutions is despised, hated, rejected. . . ."[132] However, this stands in tension with Nietzsche's praise of "the will to be oneself, to stand out—that which I call *pathos of distance* [which] characterizes every *strong* age."[133] As I have indicated previously, for Nietzsche this entails, in each individual, a will to "compel the chaos that is within to take on form,"[134] to have the hounds in the basement quietly chained, to enjoy the clear air at the top storey as a condition for all great productivity.[135] The aim is ultimately "the grand style," to become simple, logical, even mathematical, to become law, holding together opposites without tension, and thereby taking up becoming into being.[136] The tension entails distinguishing the herd from the masters. But even the master's will to stand out entails respect, even reverence for their real equals and thus a real ability to discern quality.[137] The ideal of mastership in the Overman involves, as we noted before, "the Roman Caesar with Christ's soul."[138]

Nietzsche returns to the more comprehensive Greek meaning of art expressed in Aristotle's description of politics as the art of arts. Art in the narrower sense is not the locus of aesthetic detachment; rather it gives the umbrella of meaning within which such enduring lifestyles can succeed by receiving ultimate legitimation. But art in the narrower sense also sets such meaning systems upon the earth of bodily encounters. Of course, cultures are in conflict; but that produces conditions for the creation of new forms, keeping us from falling back into a general slackness as Hegel also maintained. Life goes on, continually spewing out new forms in nature and in history. To identify with it is not only to accept the inevitability of conflict and destruction, but, even more so, to exult in life's boundless creativity.

## Response

Nietzsche's work might be viewed as parallel with Kant's sublime: threat to life producing exultation. The tame aesthetics of Schopenhauerian-Kantian "coming to rest" in the detached contemplation of beautiful form is set aside. Schopenhauer's understanding of the sublime is itself based on detached contemplation, the sublimity of detachment measured by the degree of potential threat to one's own life exhibited by the sublime occasion. In contrast to the beautiful, which brings us to rest (though in the quickening of the feeling of distinctive human life in the free play of the relation between understanding and the imagination in the capacity to make a judgment), Kant's understanding of the sublime links it to an upsurge of emotion, of the feeling of life—and here Kant sees life not in its distinctively human form, but in the general form of living existence—in the face of occasions that would threaten it. For Nietzsche tragic performance brings us face to face with the destructive power of the Dionysian, but evokes exultation in the Apollonian creativity of that same power instantiated by the tragic artwork itself, and not simply by what it represents. Nietzsche's scorn for "disinterested satisfaction" understands it the way Schopenhauer understood it, as on the way toward the "blowing out" of desire. Nietzsche fails to attend to the context of Kant's understanding of that expression. For Kant art has its origin in genius, in the work of spirit, which animates all the faculties; it has its immediate terminus in a work characterized as fresh, vital, organic, in contrast to the dead and mechanical; and it effects a quickening of the sense of distinctively human life. The difference between Kant and Nietzsche lies more in how they view that stimulation of the sense of life. For Kant life here lies in the capacity to make good judgments; for Nietzsche it is closer to the religious "enthusiasm" and "illuminism" Kant repudiated: a kind of cosmic intoxication. This brings us back to Nietzsche's proximity to Plotinus in the transcendence of Eros over nous.

In assigning priority to the Dionysian dance circle, Nietzsche retrieves and develops a suggestion present in Plato, the only other thinker I have treated—and the only other major philosopher of which I am aware—who gives a major role to dance among the art forms. And, as in Nietzsche, dance for Plato is linked to a certain priority of music among the art forms. Remember that in the *Republic*, Socrates joins together music and gymnastics as the instruments of the first stage of *paideia*—initially as ways of tuning the soul and the body respectively, but eventually as cooperative in tuning the psyche in the balanced tension between softness and hardness of disposition. In the *Laws* the gymnastic required is dance, which imparts order to the chaotic flux of emotion in the life of the young. Note that dance here is a kind of psychotherapy, a moral tool for tuning the dispositions, not, as in Nietzsche, a way of participating in the depths of the cosmos.

Socrates said that through music order and harmony sink most deeply into the soul. What are we to make of those "depths"? Are they to be taken as real and not just metaphorical opposites to "the heights" gained by going out of the Cave of temporality and sensibility and ascending to the region of pure intelligible light, the light of Beauty Itself? Are "the depths" the region of the emotions tied to the organism? In the *Republic* bodily based feelings occupy the lowest (deepest?) level of the psyche and include hunger, thirst, and Eros. However, we know from the *Symposium* and the *Phaedrus* that Eros is exalted into relation with the region of the eternal as the intermediary, tying the temporal and the eternal, the very realm in which philosophy operates, so that the depth of Eros is the vehicle of aspiration toward the heights. Without Eros reason becomes calculation in the service of one's own egoistic ends or, at best, in service to the city. It is that Eros which reappears in Nietzsche.

Plato extends the harmonic tuning of the psyche achievable by music into the region of the spatial arts, surrounding the psyche from birth to death with artifacts—buildings, furniture, utensils, clothing, paintings—having the properties of order, grace, harmony, proportion. We have several times noted Walter Pater's remark that all art seeks the status of music —that is, an ordered aesthetic totality, representative or not. As such, other arts have the same effect as music in effecting an emotional tonality. Here we see an antecedent to Nietzsche's "grand style." Nonetheless, such rhythmic tuning through seeing and hearing is all in the receptive mode. Plato adds another dimension in dance, an active mode, a performance mode in which the body as a whole is the instrument. Kinesthetic feelings, feelings of the balance of our own bodily movements, join the feelings that come through the eye and the ear. Nietzsche reinstates and recommends such aesthetic priority.

In Plato, the upward ascent of the soul involves the prior harmonizing of the emotional life so that, with the emergence of the rational pattern of experience, which seeks to unveil the cosmic harmony, it will find a welcome matrix in the already rationally ordered psychic life. Yet, as I have said, the dance and the music that bring about that order do not seem to involve the display of the primordial and all-encompassing as they do in Nietzsche.

In Plato the ultimate aim is to harmonize the whole human psyche, whose basic nature is philosophic—that is, occupying the region between the eternal and the temporal as the mortal having designs on the immortal, in the mode of rational exploration and rational ordering of life as a whole within the never fully revealed cosmic Whole. Rationality is led by Eros, which might be understood participatively as the complement to noetic detachment. It is in this direction that Plotinus takes us: the One/Good/Beautiful as correlate to Eros is that with which we are finally to be identified in the field of awareness in its mystical completion. (Doesn't Plotinus also speak of the Dionysiac here?) But that mystical moment is the anchor of a fully rational life that orders the life of the body and the world around us and that alternates between the discernment of rational order and participation in the Source.

This is both near and far in relation to Nietzsche. For him the desideratum is "the grand style": compelling the chaos that is in us to become form, giving the stamp of the eternal on the quotidian linked to an exultant sense of participating in the creative-destructive cosmos. And achieving that involves a certain asceticism of the instinctive life so as to achieve a clear sense of things. But whereas in Plotinus this is tied up with a certain contempt for things and a desire to be with that which lies beyond it all, in Nietzsche it is linked with the affirmation of this life and a repudiation of claims to an absolute transcendent. Nietzsche sees a close relation between the two: affirmation of a transcendent is linked to contempt for this life.

A professor of ethics at a secular university found it astonishing that his avowedly Christian students regularly announced that they would have no reason to be moral if there were no God who would punish and reward them for their deeds. Should it not be the other way around: finding something about the intrinsic value of life leads us to the affirmation of God? (I take this to be what is at stake in Dostoyevsky's *Brothers Karamazov*.) In fact, if we look at what Plato does in the *Republic*, we see that he develops the argument about the nature and superiority of justice over injustice explicitly, *without* any appeal to the gods or an afterlife. The Ring of Gyges has the function of making one hypothetically disappear from men *and gods*, so that thoughts of external rewards and punishment do not enter into the heart of the argument.[139] In considering what the nature of justice is and whether it is better than injustice, all we would have to deal with would be the intrinsic order or disorder of our own experience. Plato pulls us away from that which too many people today consider the indispensible ground of ethics: a divine Legislator, Judge, Rewarder, and Punisher in a life hereafter. Plato temporarily puts that in brackets. When the argument is completed, he restores the appearance to others: over the long haul, even in this life, the truly just man is found out, as is the truly unjust; and in the afterlife, it is likely that rewards and punishments will be justly administered.[140] But this restoration of the external appearance *(doxa)* of the soul is precisely superadded, not constitutive of the intrinsic grounds of moral action. For Plato, contrary to many of his followers, especially many of his Christian followers, the right way is immanent in life itself. But even so, the way Plato establishes the right order is by appealing to the realm of Being and the Good, which stand outside the realm of time and life. In virtue of this we tend to view ourselves dualistically as souls separate from bodies, imprisoned in our bodies and thus in our passions. And our aim is thus disembodiment.[141] Hence Nietzsche's critique of Platonism in favor of life. However, there are countervailing texts in Plato. *Phaedo* appeals to the psychological blocks that feelings arising from the body set in the way of the emergence of a concentrated rational pattern of experience; but the *Timaeus* presents the basis for an ontology (as distinct from a descriptive psychology) of the body as the house of the soul (i.e., the place where the rational soul is at home in the cosmos).[142]

Contemporary enthusiasts for Nietzsche heed his emphasis on standing above the herd and his praise of the creative individual without attending equally to his attack on private subjectivity and his reading of great art as expressive of the concrete universality of encompassing life. Along with this goes his emphasis on the need for discipline—for a measure of asceticism, for a chaining of the dogs in the basement of one's life, for a measure of chastity, humility, and poverty—as a condition of creativity. There is as well his stress on tradition as a general condition and of artistic convention as a specific condition of artistic creativity. These are measures that "Dionysiac artists" in the twentieth century have ignored, often invoking the authority of Nietzsche.

One major criterion of form creation is efficacy, the pragmatic test, something like a scientific theory. The theory is regarded as true insofar as it is not only able to take account of known regularities of nature, but is also fruitful in suggesting lines of experimentation that uncover more and more of the context of nature. However, the theory is discarded insofar as a more comprehensive theory arises that unifies the lines of research achieved and going forward at a given time, suggests further lines of exploration, and is able to do justice to the anomalies that resist penetration under the older theory.[143] Something analogous to this takes place at a more encompassing level in the comprehensive horizons of meaning, which deal, not simply with one aspect of experience, but with whole ways of life that have, ingredient in and grounding them, definitions of the umbrella of meaning, of what finally counts, what is finally "up" or "down" for human existence. The creation of meaning systems has to be fruitful in bringing about the possibility that various subforms of human life, different types of functions and personalities come to live under these umbrellas. There is something about them that is true the way a scientific theory is true: it is not finally but hypothetically true, contextually true, perspectively true. It discloses certain facets of the surrounding world and allows for certain connections to emerge in our experience without being the final disclosure. As you get one scientific theory substituting for another, so you get various religious and philosophic systems contending with and often driving out others. Only in that case we have a tendency to settle down in one or another without the drive beyond emerging in so central a fashion as we have in the scientific tradition. (Perhaps the inherently ongoing, self-corrective character of science ought to be present also in the philosophic tradition. Dewey, as we shall see in the next chapter, calls for an application of the scientific method so conceived especially to ethics.[144] But this is largely not the case, because philosophy has tended to model itself on the absoluteness of religious claims. One might wonder whether that absoluteness is tied to the fear both of chaos that ontological openness sets on an animal base and of the ultimate emptiness correlated with that very openness.) The more comprehensive character of the horizons of meaning lies in their opening out perspectives not only theoretically but also practically and aesthetically: paths for thinking, doing, and feeling. But none of them are anything but perspectives, and to that extent they are all "lies," but are also disclosures as well. Heidegger will pick up on that: Being reveals and conceals itself in all the philosophies that have emerged in such a way that none has been able to drive the others out.[145]

The will-to-power is the will to create beyond the level at which one exists. The criteria for creation lie in the fusion of complexity. The more comprehensive and powerful the unification, the higher the type of horizon creation.[146] Ultimately and ideally it would seem that the highest form would be one in which every individual would find a way of tapping his or her potentialities consonant with the unity of the whole. This would seem to be the final projection of form, which comes to terms with all the life forms present. Whether or not that is possible is a question. To create a perspective is to load the dice in one or the other direction. Creating conditions for the emergence of certain lifestyles inhibits the emergence of other forms. The predominance of a disciplined lifestyle inhibits the emergence of a loose, self-indulgent form and vice-versa. In individual lives, the nature of decision is not only to cut off deliberation about possibilities, but also to cut off all those possibilities except the lines opened up by that on which we actually decide. Choosing one way allows one to tap potentialities unavailable without commitment to that way; but that means that other possibilities have to lie fallow. The pursuit of one is the exclusion of the others. A society likewise cannot choose to foster equally all styles of life but only a limited set of forms compatible with one another. If we try to let all forms go forward simultaneously, chaos results. The context within which all forms, and especially all higher forms (i.e., more complex forms, having more prerequisites for their achievement), would be inhibited.

The choices that have been made historically involve an elite class that depends on a slave class. Whether they are called slaves in some direct way or are slaves indirectly—Marx's "wage slaves"—there are people who have to be at the bottom, an essentially servile class.[147] Whether they are given greater latitude one way or another, there has to be some class at the bottom that makes possible an elite from which the Overmen can come—except in democratic socialism, in which meaning dies because of antipathy against any elite. The highest elite are the creators of comprehensive meaning, the supreme artists. What I want to stress first of all is the parallel between such meaning creation and scientific procedure. Traditionally, meaning systems have been viewed statically. Scientific procedure suggests that we consider them dynamically. But I also want to stress, along with Nietzsche, a certain priority of the aesthetic. It is exemplary unification of mind and feeling, of sensibility and intellect, of individual and group, of the Now and the Whole. It binds together what the priority of abstractive intellect takes apart. It teaches us "how to dance," a celebratory fidelity to the earth, a paean to creation.

For Nietzsche art is produced by nature and functions both as supplement to and overcoming of nature.[148] This is linked to Nietzsche's various statements about truth. Platonistic eternal, nonperspectival Truth is out: it is a lie concocted to help us deal with suffering. A true life is one of "fidelity to the earth." There is also truth in the service of life as distinct from the collection of trivial truths. Wisdom is higher than such truth seeking. Further, the truth is that life is full of horrors, but also that it is indescribably fertile, creative. To be creative is thus to be true to life. For Nietzsche, finally, art is worth more than truth—either Platonistically conceived or, more truthfully, in terms of the horrors and the trivialities we find in life. But art is most fully true to itself when it stems from and exhibits a unified life, a life in which reason, will, and sensibility are one, in which the theoretical is united with the practical.

One of the deep problems with Nietzsche is the status of his own claims. If all is perspectivism, how can we know that? And does he really want to say that the deepest truths, both in the theoretical and the practical order, are merely perspectives? I have tried to maintain throughout this work the proximate and enduring priority of the structures of the field of experience that give us the conditions for possibility of our perspectival construals of the character of the Whole to which the deepest structure of the field of experience emptily points. The skeletal framework of the field of experience and what is implicit in that recognition can be animated by different worldviews. But that very fact, linked to our directedness by nature to the whole, entails a heuristic and dialogic imperative to remain open to what is other than what presents itself within the perspective we currently occupy. Finally, all that we deal with appears within the perspective of human, all too human awareness and is linked to the fostering of that distinctive form of life.

# IX

# DEWEY

OUTSIDE OF HEGEL AND Schelling, there is no major philosopher who has devoted as much attention to the aesthetic or given it as central a role as John Dewey. This may come as a surprise to some. In their standard two-volume survey of American philosophy, Elizabeth Flower and Murray Murphey do not even mention Dewey's *Art as Experience,* in spite of their relatively extensive period-by-period, work-by-work survey of his publications.[1] And yet for Dewey the aesthetic furnishes the basic measure of everything human.

The centrality of the aesthetic is linked to the centrality of experience, for in Dewey's view, the aesthetic is "experience in its integrity."[2] Attention to the features given in experience returns us from the region of ultimate ontological construals, which is a battlefield of contending views, to that which is always already there when we set about to think. To the extent that he makes this turn, Dewey exhibits many parallels with the phenomenological orientation of this book.

Though he falls, with C. S. Peirce and William James before him, in the general line of American Pragmatism, Dewey's basic position is more accurately described by what he calls *Instrumentalism,* which indicates the fundamental character of an idea.[3] Generally speaking, the common view of the nature of an idea in the tradition has been to conceive of it as either an intrinsic and higher reality (e.g., Plato and Hegel) or a mirror of such, whether relatively clear (Aristotle) or initially distorted by the medium (Locke). In any case, according to Dewey, for the tradition generally an idea is essentially retrospective, related to the past, to what has been; the idea is to that extent essentially a priori.[4] In contrast, Dewey himself, reflecting on the function of modern scientific ideas, sees an idea as essentially prospective, future oriented, tied in with our action on things in experimentation and modified or rejected in terms of testable consequences. This view is related to his general strategy of trying to overcome the dualisms that occur within experience and that tend to be canonized by philosophers, especially those that are introduced in the Platonic tradition, which turns on the status of the Idea. The tendency toward dualisms is exacerbated in modern times by Descartes, who in some sense falls within the Platonic line. For Dewey it is the aesthetic which finally heals all such splits, for the aesthetic, as I have said, is experience in its integrity.[5]

## Overcoming the Platonic Splits

The basic split in the Platonic tradition is that between Being and Becoming, the stable and the changing, the eternal and the temporal, to which we have access through the distinction between Ideas and the things that mirror them.[6] To recur to things noted in my first historical chapter, for Plato the Idea is superior since it does not come into being and pass out of being, though it may come into awareness and pass out of awareness. *Idea* is a technical term that does not cover any "bright idea" I might happen to have, but rather indicates something essentially objective that the mind sees or mirrors when it is properly attentive. Take, for example, the geometric demonstration that the internal angles of a triangle are equal to 180 degrees. When seen, it shows itself to have a kind of atemporal validity, to have been true even before it was seen. Thus an Idea in the technical Platonic sense is not a subjective state of mind, although some of the things *we* call ideas are subjective states of mind. A Platonic Idea is an eternal truth over against the plurality of instances that mirror it in the changing context of the world of nature as well as in the changing character of human culture and human individual minds. Culture and the minds that carry it may be such that a given Idea never enters into their field of awareness or, having entered, has passed out of it; but the Idea remains an eternal measure of the things that instantiate it and the minds that mirror it. This sets up a basic split between the eternality of Ideas on the one hand, and the temporality of things and empirical states of awareness on the other.

Parallel to this is a split between mind and body. Mind as intellect discovers itself only when it pulls itself away from its bodily involvement and is able to concentrate, to "become a center together with" the object on which it centers its attention. In order to achieve this it has to pull itself out of the flowing distractions of its bodily existence.[7] A split between mind and body thus follows the split between Idea and thing. On the Platonic reading, both of them are expressions of the split between Being and Becoming. The Idea always "is," as compared with the things of our ordinary focus, which at one time were not, at one time will not be, and, when they are, are always such that they are no longer what they were and not yet what they will be. Their mode of being is one of becoming, and their degree of being is the degree to which they realize the fullness of their type.

Linked to the mind-body split is the split between reason and emotion. In the *Republic*, Plato has Socrates present Eros, together with hunger and thirst, at the lowest level of the soul (*epithumia*, desire) and criticize art for watering the desires rather than drying them up, as is required for the emergence of the rational from the biological pattern of experience. Along Pythagorean lines, the *Phaedo* has Socrates present the bodily desires as virtually the tomb of the rational soul.[8] These positions are the ancestors of Stoic *apatheia*, or lack of passion, and parallel Buddhist nirvana, which gained Western expression in Schopenhauer's philosophy.

The split between mind and body, linked to the separation and superiority of the Idea over the thing, leads to the priority of *theoria*, or the contemplative life over the realm of praxis, which puts us in contact with the grubby things of material reality.[9] The latter is the sort of thing with which the slave class, along with their immediate overseers, is preoccupied, but from which the lords are removed. Theory and practice are split off from one another and each is located in a different stratum of society. An elite class is ideally given over to the higher pursuit of *theoria;* those less gifted intellectually and dispositionally engage in the workaday world for the sake of the elite's leisure to pursue contemplation.[10] This view is maintained even in the synthesis of Christianity and Greek thought in Thomas Aquinas.[11]

We can see then that these various splits are systematically connected with one another and follow from a certain quite natural conception of the status of an Idea. Dewey offers a counterposition to this conception. As I indicated earlier, rather than being a mirror of an eternally existent order, for Dewey an idea is essentially an instrument fashioned for a purpose. It arises when we face problems posed by the relations we find in our overall social and biological environment while carrying on the tasks involved in living our lives. By reason of the continually shifting character of the environment and our relationship to it, our ideas are always capable of change —indeed, must change or suffer the penalty of diminished effectiveness in carrying out our life tasks.[12]

Natural science presents us with such a conception of an idea: it operates by hypothesis, which is retained insofar as it is fruitful in bringing about an expansion of our awareness and control through continued experiment; it is modified or discarded when it does not. Contrary to the basically retrospective, backward-looking character of the Platonic Idea, Dewey's conception of an idea is, as I already remarked, essentially prospective, future oriented. Contrary to the eternality of the Platonic Ideas, in Dewey's view ideas are necessarily capable of transformation over time. Dewey's conception does not place us in the state of contemplative inaction, but calls for bodily action on the environment in the form of experimentation. It does not fortify us in our complacency but establishes a methodically self-corrective process. Stimulated by the environment and calling for action, such an idea integrates thought and action, mind and body, organism and environment, thus overcoming many of the splits that have afflicted the history of thought, especially since Plato.[13]

## *Overcoming the Cartesian Splits*

But there were several distinctively modern splits that emerged in the sixteenth and seventeenth centuries and which both added to and reenforced the Platonic splits that lay in the deep structure of Western history. The Reformation that arose within Western Christendom in the sixteenth century led not only to the breakup of Christendom as a social-political system, but also to a lengthy period of bloody religious wars. Out of that experience emerged the search for a new ground of human togetherness independent of religious belief: a separation of church and state, the tolerance of competing belief systems and the pursuit of value-free natural science tied to the transformation of the environment to serve the more obvious aspects of human well-being. It was the way this new science was conceived that produced a new set of splits within experience.

That science had its first philosophical grounding in René Descartes, who reduced the world to two sets of differing substances: extensive material substance, exhaustively treatable by quantitative methodology, and thought, the whole field of awareness, considered as spiritual substance.[14]

Natures other than human were reduced to mechanisms without aware-ness, and human nature became what Gilbert Ryle later called "the ghost in the machine."[15] Entailed in all this was Galileo's way of conceiving a dis-tinction between primary and secondary qualities. Based on discoveries in physics and physiology, the measurable properties were considered to be-long to material things as primary qualities, while the sensory features, con-sidered secondary and derivative, were located within—in the literal sense of the term *within*—the human perceiver as subjective effects of the pri-mary qualities belonging to the object. Color, for example, was an effect in-side the head—and, following casually thereupon, inside awareness—of the agitation of the retina by light waves.[16]

Descartes arrived at this view by beginning with a methodic doubt in order to sort out levels of certitude within experience. The upshot of his employment of that doubt was the indubitable self-presence of awareness to itself expressed in the famous *Cogito ergo sum.*[17] The problem that gener-ated was the problem of how to get out of the initial confinement of the *cogito.* That problem was directly connected with the way, following Galileo, Descartes conceived of the distinction and relation of primary and sec-ondary qualities. If we have initial access only to our own being-affected in the form of colors, sounds, and the like, how do we come to know the pri-mary qualities and things external to us?

Methodic doubt is an intellectual invention aimed at sorting out levels of certitude in experience. The everyday world is subjected to such theo-retical doubt by noting the occurrence of illusions in waking experience and of dreams while sleeping. In the latter case we have as vivid a sense of reality as in wakefulness. The Chinese Taoist sage Chuang Tzu once dreamt he was a butterfly, but then awoke to find he was still Chuang Tzu. He then reflected that he might really be a butterfly dreaming he is Chuang Tzu.[18] Finding no absolute certitude in that direction, Descartes turns next to mathematics, only to undermine the absolute character of the certitude available therein by appealing to the admittedly wild hypothesis of a hypo-thetical evil genius tinkering with awareness to make it *think* it has certitude. Then Descartes presents his basic discovery, the Archi-medean point of his thought: even if such a wildly hypothetical being were constantly deceiving me, he could not deceive me about one thing: my self-presence in the act of being deceived. *Cogito ergo sum* I think, therefore I am.[19] No matter what I am thinking about, no matter how deceived I might be with respect to that object, I am indubitably present to myself while I think. So indubitably is this true that any attempt to doubt it exhibits it, for to doubt is a mode of thinking, which necessarily involves self-presence. And so there is an intellectual Archimedean point around which everything can be made to pivot—or better, from which one can move the world intellectually, reconstructing our understanding of things through the employment of rigorous method.

But notice that this *cogito* is, to begin with, disengaged from its embodiment. Descartes eventually canonized such disengagement by claiming that a human being is really two substances: a thinking substance—the mind—and an extended substance—the body—with nothing in between.[20] There are thus two regions and two kinds of entities with only external—though "intimate"—connection between one another, a ghost in a machine. The machine notion prefigures the way modern science has gone on thinking about the body, in principle explicable in terms of mechanical laws. Then there is the ghostly thing haunting the machine, an angel or a devil, or a merely epiphenomenal ethereal thing that does not appear in the observable mechanical context, namely thinking (Descartes's generic term for the whole field of awareness).

From this position, Descartes attempted to work his way out to God as truthful Creator of the mind and thus as guarantor of truth when the mind seeks it in responsible, i.e. methodologically certified, ways.[21] Then Descartes returned attention to the external world. The latter is shorn of the colors, sounds, tastes, smells, and tactile features that it has in everyday experience: they are merely subjective qualities as effects of physical processes. The external world delivers its secrets through mathematical physics, which separates the quantitative causes from the sensory effects.[22] The self-enclosed mind is a subject initially separated from its deceptive everyday objects as well as from its body, which is the source of the original deceptions. The outer world and the body within it return in methodically purified form as objects of mathematical physics and the criteria for distinguishing wakefulness from dream or illusion in ordinary experience are found in implicitly employed principles of coherence and consistency (prefiguring Kant's position, which I have briefly discussed earlier).[23] The initial state of being locked up inside our own minds, dealing only with the subjective contents of our personal experience, is a peculiar modern legacy picked up by Empiricism and by Kant. In Descartes, the ontology of matter has to develop in correlation with observation and experimentation in the sensory field to discover which of the possibilities of mechanical sequence compatible with first principles has been realized in fact.[24]

The initial disregard of the senses is linked with the enduring downplay of the life of feeling, which is tied in with our intimate association with the body. This sounds like the Socrates of the *Republic,* but not like the Socrates of the *Symposium* and the *Phaedrus,* for whom there are deeper, more metaphysical dimensions to the passionate life. And so we have again the emphasis on a fundamental split between reason and emotion and an implicit rendering of the whole aesthetic region as peripheral and merely decorative.

At the same time, this self-involuted intellect, shorn of all passion, seeking certitude through careful methodological procedure, methodically cut itself off from the context of the tradition in which it exists, viewed as a source of confused and conflicting interpretations. Hence we have a psychological foundation and reinforcement for a social atomism: the individual, the self-initiating, self-sustaining, self-made person who is the arbiter over the whole tradition, reconstructing the world of knowledge and action from his own internal resources.

Another distinctively modern split occurs, based predominantly on Cartesian foundations: the fact-value split. The world turns out to be a set of mechanically governed facts shorn of intrinsic value. This is tied to the elimination of substantial forms and consequently of teleology in nature, a position that can be traced back to ancient atomism.[25] Things are the result of the accidental shuffling of particles; they are not "headed in the direction" of actualizing the potentialities of their natural forms. In the dominant tradition from Plato and Aristotle through the Middle Ages, there are grades of excellence in nature based on a hierarchy of substantial forms and on the degree to which individuals of a species fulfill the nature given by their substantial forms. Value is coterminous with the fulfillment of a thing's natural goals and with the place a thing occupies in the hierarchy of being. All this disappears with the emergence of modern physics: in place of a hierarchy of natures seeking their ends, we find colorless, odorless, valueless matter in motion according to fixed mechanical laws, with phenomenal organisms appearing like froth spewed forth by the ocean waves. Absent from this view were Aristotelian natures, formative principles organizing material for the sake of realizing their own natural ends. Nature eventually became "the clockwork universe," a single whole composed of atomic particles combining and separating according to invariant laws. Learning those laws enabled us to transform materials for our purposes, making us "masters and possessors of nature."[26]

Reinforcing the Platonic dualisms, there are thus several peculiarly modern dualisms: of mind and body, of subject and object, of fact and value, of individual and community, of past and present. Descartes's methodic doubt pried him loose from bodily sensations and passions and from traditional modes of understanding and behavior—precisely Plato's cave of *doxa*. The method placed him at one remove from things and persons, having immediate access only to his own consciousness, the famous *cogito* from which we have to reason our way to the world outside. The physical world is stripped of the colors, sounds, tactile, gustatory, and olfactory features that are now located in the mind as effects of the measurable features that inhere in the single property of *extension*. Extension, in turn, operates according to invariant mechanical laws to yield a clockwork universe. Primary qualities take center stage, secondary qualities are reduced to subjectivity, and all Aristotelian forms as final causes, and thus as values—or what Dewey will call tertiary qualities—have been banished.

Dewey attempts to overcome the splits that have their origins in the Platonic and Cartesian traditions, on the one hand by his instrumentalist theory of idea (which I have already briefly discussed) and, on the other hand, by his biological theory of mind. The biological theory of mind, derived from Darwinian impulses and mediated through the work of William James, erodes the Cartesian model in that awareness is displayed as a function of the broad context of physical-physiological interaction on which awareness itself rests.[27] Awareness is possible only within a biological matrix that involves the habitual storage of routes of response to the impact of the environment on the organism. This region of response constitutes a kind of iceberg from which consciousness emerges as its tip. Consciousness itself, though essentially future oriented at the level of intelligence, is intelligible both in terms of its grounding in past interaction routes, and also in present interplay with the environment, only part of which is ever manifest in the present—indeed, only a part is *ever* manifest, even in science.[28] In this process the conscious mind does not display itself as an entity but as a function that, though pivotal in our lives, is linked to the massive set of habit structures that are continuous with the motor routes that our "body" has inscribed within it. For Dewey, awareness itself is a flickering process over against the more enduring aspect of mind that is empatterned in the "meat." Mind is enduring in the sense that my knowledge and my skills remain "in my mind" even though they are for the moment out of my awareness. Awareness itself flickers in the sense that its "light" goes on in the morning and goes out at night, occasionally dimming and brightening in between.[29] Awareness is thus not identical with mind but is its cutting edge, the relatively self-directive aspect of mind. In this way, Dewey thinks, much along the lines of Aristotle, of a psychophysical whole that is itself a node of partially manifest interaction with the environment.

But, as in Aristotle, all this is not viewed as a purely internal matter, not simply a private, inward, enclosed state—which is the tendency in modern accounts of experience, beginning with Galileo and Descartes and going through Locke and Berkeley to Hume and Kant. Experience in that tradition is a self-enclosed effect of physical causation, giving us the problem of how we get outside to know other persons and things—indeed, to know the physical causation that produces sensation in our subjective privacy. It is the Cartesian problem in empiricist terms. For Dewey, interaction-based awareness brings us outside our privacy into the manifestness of the world, as we will see in Heidegger as well.[30] Experience in general is not an internal occurrence but the transformation of physical interaction into participation in what lies without.[31] Interaction is what occurs in photoelectric cells, computers, and robot mechanisms. But experience is heightened vitality that involves being taken, beyond both the spatial internality of the impact of the environment on our organism and the privacy of our internal sensations, into active and alert commerce with the world. At its height experience signifies complete interpenetration of self and the world of objects and events. Though based on physical interaction, experience is much more. It attains a certain height in those all-encompassing emotions that bring us outside ourselves and into deepest communion with things, the emotions upon which great art develops.[32]

To say that the Cartesian mind-body split is overcome by a biological theory of mind does not mean that for Dewey we are "meat" and nothing but meat (even though, in many prevailing accounts, perhaps coexistent with an epiphenomenal awareness). Dewey is in some sense close to Nietzsche's "physiology" here, which, as Heidegger explains, has to be understood in a manner quite different than in modern biological thought. The latter is fundamentally "meat" analysis and presupposes the Cartesian split that allows us to prescind from awareness in the living being and treat the body as a meaty mechanism. But the body is not simply something externally observable; it is, more fundamentally, something I as a conscious-unconscious entity *live through*. This position is basically Aristotelian in that we are not composed of mind *and* body but are each a psychophysical whole comprised, in Aristotle's terms, of soul and body as a form-matter or act-potency relationship. For Aristotle, the very structure of the body *is* the soul in one of its moments of activation. The soul builds up its own body as an instrumental complex in order to allow the higher powers of the soul, the powers of sensory and eventually rational awareness, to emerge. In this view there is no inner spiritual substance somehow linked to an outer physical substance. There is but a single entity that is multilayered and in which the very character of the "physiological" (in the modern sense) is the condition for the possibility for the development of the higher levels. Something like this Dewey, along with Nietzsche, is also after.

Taking it further, mind is functionally embedded in a material matrix that is not fully nonmind. By reason of evolution, "matter" itself is that which, through complexification and centralization, becomes actually what it is potentially: enminded and aware. The typical way of understanding evolution misses this feature of matter because it operates under the Cartesian split. It continues to think comprehensively in terms of mechanical explanation based on visual observation for which awareness—visual or otherwise—is an embarrassing epiphenomenon. Explanation proceeds from the lower, earlier, less complex to the higher, later, more complex. For Dewey, resisting the Cartesian split, there is a co-modification of the ideas of "mind" and "matter" such that deeper explanation proceeds from the later forms to grasp what is merely potential in the earlier. Emergent evolutionism encompasses and situates mechanistic evolutionism. "Matter" is a relatively unintegrated state of what in integration is the ground for the emergence of the manifestness of things.[33] As Schelling put it, working along similar lines, mind-body duality is the ground for the manifestation of mind-body unity.[34] In this (as in several other matters) Dewey is not so far from Hegel. "Mind" is the meaning of "matter."

Here Dewey also attempts to overcome the fact-value dichotomy that runs through modern thought from its inception. Mind possessing ends is no stranger to nature, and nature as manifest to mind exhibits culminating phases, aesthetically displayed in the appearance of form. There is value as soon as there is life, which involves not mere mechanical sequence but patterns of development, processes leading toward an end.[35] Dewey thus in effect reintroduces Aristotelian substantial form as entelechy, the actualization of ends immanent in its initial stages. Only, beyond Aristotle, such forms are not eternal; they are temporary solutions to problems posed by the environment for the realization of the comprehensive goals of life.[36]

At the same time that Dewey overcomes the split between mind and body, he also overcomes the split between individual and society-tradition.[37] Tradition is the deep past and the society the residue of the past in the present. Mind is conditioned by that matrix. We are not brought up as rational animals. Rational animality is a goal, not only for individuals in their upbringing to adulthood, but also for society. We are assimilated to a society in such a way that the societal structures enter into the rhythms of our being, into our feelings about things, our spontaneous responses, our patterns of thought. We are conditioned and relatively determined by the whole fabric of interaction with the biological environment as well as with our parents, siblings and the people with whom we associate as we continue our lives.[38] Philosophies themselves are emergents out of this kind of matrix and tend to be justifications for it as a prior sense of the Whole that guides our philosophizing.[39] One constructs arguments for his prior sense of the Whole and against its opponents. If the arguments fail, the vision is not abandoned; one makes up other arguments. Prior to reflectively rational articulation is societal articulation. Not that awareness is simply a pure reflex of the society—a typical Marxist view.[40] The situation is rather dialectical or interactional, in which the individual is the cutting edge of the modification of the tradition on the basis of the tradition, just as awareness is the cutting edge of the modification of previous habit structures in the individual.[41]

If we attend to the fully concrete context within which we operate, we find that a global rejection of tradition is impossible because tradition has entered into the concrete fabric of our being. We might reject some dominant strands of a tradition, as Dewey himself rejected his own religious upbringing; but we are still necessarily enmeshed in countless other strands, beginning with the language we employ. There is no comprehensive handling of all the concrete factors of our existence. We as conscious agents always remain carried more or less—"thrown," as Heidegger for one will strongly emphasize. But part of our task is to become more extensively aware and thus more intelligently self-directive, individually and societally. Education for Dewey is thus not simply initiation of students into the societal way of doing things, into the tradition. More fundamentally, it provides the conditions to make intelligence emerge more clearly in the operative life of the society as the responsible cutting edge of the tradition.[42]

## Further Modifications of Traditional Notions

Linked to the Platonic view of things is the notion of the One/Good as the final cause of everything. All things aim at a single end. Against such a view, Dewey first observes that, by reason of evolution, there are not simply fixed ends for species. Complex interactional situations pose new problems solved often by the coming into being of new species. Ends are thus ends-in-situation or ends-in-view.[43] Secondly, Dewey proposes an ultimate and irreducible plurality of ends among human beings: different people in society seeking different ends, with intelligence operating in order to bring about those ends, formulating ideas, checking their experienced consequences, and modifying them in the light of those consequences. The plurality of ends is worthwhile promoting: business, art, farming, sports, engineering, and so forth.[44] Dewey finds criteria for distinguishing such examples from the ends most people would call criminal by following out the conditions for the possibility of intelligently creative cooperative existence. But for Dewey it is not the case that we can set up a hierarchy among these pursuits: they are simply different. Intellect functions as an instrument to bring about and modify the character of the many ends to which people find it worth their while to dedicate their lives.

But if we think solely of a plurality of ends, we have the grounds for chaos. One of the necessary conceptions is that of the creation of a social whole out of that plurality. That is where the development of social ethics comes into the picture.[45] One way to work this out is to conceive of society as oriented around a single end and enforced by a single body of power and opinion. But for Dewey a better way—better because it is closer to the actual character of life—is to draw upon the operative intelligence of the various interests, formulating organizational ideas and testing them out in the arena of social action in a kind of democratic process operating through rational debate tied to actual practice.[46] As in natural science, so also in society: we ought to have an experimental method in ethics and politics. The social whole has to be continually reconfigured to take account of emergent and divergent interests and of more extensive knowledge of the actual context of our operations.[47]

When Dewey eschews fixity of ends, he seems to be thinking more of strategies or rules. But even evolution has certain "fixed ends": growth and sustenance of the individual organism and reproduction of the type. What is not absolutely fixed are the strategies and transformations that have to be changed to realize those ends. We might call this more generalized level of ends "meta-ends." Dewey himself maintains several such ends. He sometimes says that "the only fixed end is growth."[48] However, in organisms one has to distinguish healthy and cancerous growth. Healthy growth involves harmony among various components heading toward and sustaining the fully functional adult form of a given species. Human growth heads toward some kind of psychic balance, but also one that is rich in proportion to its ability to contain within itself variety-in-unity.[49] For Dewey, association of people is the condition for the possibility of the emergence of distinct individuals with rich experience. The state is the widest coordinating agency measured by how it elicits intelligently responsible, creative, and cooperative individuals, and individuals are measured correspondingly by how they act intelligently, responsibly, creatively, and cooperatively.[50]

Full integration at the human level is aesthetic integration, the integral togetherness of all the parameters of experience. Thus, as we have indicated before, the aesthetic is the real meta-end. How it is achieved in multiple circumstances always involves some kind of transformation. Crucial to achieving aesthetic integration is the emergence of the pattern of intelligence, one of the fundamental ends of education. Intelligence is the capacity to make explicit what is implicit in ordinary experience, to analyze and synthesize, to grasp the possibility of achieving significant integrations, to apprehend consequences, and thus to move from spontaneous emotional prizing to thoughtful appraising. Intelligence is the cutting edge of conscious mind.[51]

Growth under patterns of intelligent aesthetic integration has conditions for its possibility. Health is one; self-restraint sufficient to apprehend clearly and shape significantly is another; courage and persistence in carrying through what intelligence projects is a third; initiative, learning, sensitivity, balance of interests are also entailed. However, a human being is no isolated monad but is dialectically tied to a definite community shaped by a specific set of traditions. Relatedness to others and thus obligation is ingredient in humanness; hence wide sympathy, justice, and friendship are essential to integral humanness; democratic society follows from respect for individuals and their ends.[52] By the time we ferret out these conditions, we see that we are to a large extent back on the territory mapped out long ago by Plato and Aristotle. We also see that one essential difference is the Christian addition of the dignity of individuals developed along distinctively modern lines in terms of enlarging the scope for freedom of choice, as Hegel pointed out.

Thus we see that there are several related meta-ends in Dewey's thought, expressed in several fixed criteria: the criterion of growth, the intellectual criterion, the moral criteria—individual and social—all integrated into the aesthetic criterion. Integral experience intelligently achieved in the relation of individuals in society working toward richer and deeper integrations: this is the comprehensive meta-end that guides Dewey's thought. He installs us in life more sensitively and more intelligently. And in this process he is especially concerned with appreciation of the everyday world, the cave of *doxa,* and the concrete complex of problems people of all sorts have to face in that world. He is concerned to focus on the kind of knowledge required to come to terms with that world and the way that occurs individually and socially.

There is a consequence for educational theory that follows from the Platonic notion of idea but that is not necessarily Platonic. There is a tendency to think that, by reason of knowledge already being there in some eternally valid and unshakable way, all that teachers have to do is pass it on through lectures and writing. Learning is a process in which the teachers who have such knowledge hand it over to the students, who receive it passively. By contrast, Dewey conceives of education as an interactive process in which the ideas of the teacher, which are largely residues of the past, are challenged and modified in terms of the interaction that goes on with colleagues and the students. In this way, school is not simply a preparation for life, but is itself a slice of life wherein interaction dominates and ought to dominate.[53]

Dewey's notion of education is often misunderstood as overly tolerant and permissive, aimed at a pragmatism understood as a kind of grubby materialism seeking "success." But for Dewey education is first of all a societal affair; society has a stake in how it educates its children. Education ought to draw upon the initiative of the students, but it should also constantly shape them through the teachers, whose end is both to mediate the tradition and to bring about the increasing emergence of intelligence, creativity, and cooperation in what tend to be animal or socially reflexive centers of action. Society is measured by its capacity to produce from within itself individuals who are creative and take intelligent initiative in such a way as not simply to foster their own ends, but to pursue the common good of the society. But the common good of society always has a stake in promoting creative individuals. The individual and social poles interpenetrate in the work of intelligent construction.[54]

Another split that tends to arise in the context Dewey is dealing with is that between the sacred and the profane. The sacred is contained spatially within churches and is pursued temporally on the Sabbath; the profane is temporally the workaday week and spatially the world outside the churches. Outside our minimal sacral activity lies the worldly activity with which we are predominantly preoccupied, alternating between work and leisure. On Dewey's reading the sacred has been separated off from its origin in the character of civic togetherness. Athena was a projection of the experience of the Athenians as to the sacredness, the inviolability of their common bond. She expressed and celebrated the sacred character of that bond by embodying the common ideals of the citizenry, but was no real entity that stood beyond that togetherness. Here Dewey parallels Feuerbach in his notion of God as a projection of the ideals of humanness—only the Greek gods were not perceived as alien but as immanent. The sacred is initially discovered in the promises people make to one another and in their togetherness as generations bound by group piety. The sacred is not simply end, but both end and means.[55]

Parallel with this is the split between the world of art and the workaday world. Art is set in museums; the workaday world is one in which—if one conceives of the sacred and the beautiful as in some sense ends—we develop as pure means in order to arrive at the leisure to pursue the things that are considered ends in themselves: aesthetic, intellectual, or religious goals. If the world of everyday work is mere means, then aesthetic and religious values tend to disappear from it and we get the antiaesthetic, all-too-secular environment of the modern factory. But for Dewey, art, like the sacred, ought to penetrate the workaday world, bringing the experience of those who operate within it to a greater integration.[56]

Here Dewey resists the notion, deeply embedded in the tradition, that some things are mere means and other things simply ends. Education is thought of as securing the means for the work world, while the work world is means for aesthetic, intellectual, or religious ends. For Dewey means and ends interpenetrate, so what is from one point of view an end is also a means and vice-versa.[57] As education is both preparation for life and a slice of life, so the aesthetic, the intellectual, and the religious are both ends within life and, when bound together with the workaday world, means toward fuller life.

Dewey is dispositionally opposed to any splits, which he sees as rooted in departing from the wholeness of experience. They have institutional expressions and epistemological and metaphysical defenses. We have to lead all these things back to their origins in experience to discover where the splits occur in order to bring about their overcoming. In this he follows an Hegelian model of overcoming antitheses through the detection of identity in difference. Throughout, the antithetical relations are transformed into dialectical relations of mutual interpenetration: ends and means, mind and body, body and environment, society and individual, the current state of society and tradition, theory and practice, sacred and profane, education and life, and finally, the aesthetic and the workaday. We will now turn to a fuller consideration of that final and central relation.

## *Dewey's Aesthetics*

Current practice, reinforced by a long tradition, places art on a pedestal, locating it high above ordinary life and viewing it as one of the exalted ends for which the workaday is mere means. For Dewey, it is precisely this exaltation and separation that stands in the way of understanding art.[58] Its causes lie in modern developments: consider the rise of nationalism and imperialism—for example, Napoleon's filling the Louvre with the spoils of war and thereby removing art works from their original location in the life of a people; consider capitalism, which promoted the private collector; consider the development of industry, which pushed the artist aside into a ghetto of individualistic "self-expression" apart from community functions; finally, following from all this, consider art theories, which emphasize the purely contemplative aspects of an art so separated from the rest of life, especially those theories that focus on form apart from matter. [59] Dewey's aim, as we said, is to reverse this separatist tendency and to reconnect art with its origins in human life as a whole.[60]

As we have pointed out, in spite of his overt rejection of a single end, for Dewey the aesthetic is, in a sense, the goal of the development of individuals and societies. The aesthetic measures everything else. Indeed, Dewey goes so far as to say that art is "the complete culmination of nature."[61] The aesthetic is experience in its integrity, as distinct from what happens in science or philosophy. The latter always involve second-order developments in relation to even ordinary experience because they are *features* of experience, *aspects* of experience. A scientific statement *points to* an experience, but an aesthetic statement *constitutes* an experience, a special experience that brings together all the facets into an integral whole.[62] Individual lives and institutional arrangements are measured by Dewey in terms of their ability to support that kind of experience.

The end character of the aesthetic follows the notion of natural form as the integral functioning of all the rhythmic processes that constitute the life of an organism.[63] But the aesthetic end is not apart from the other things we do, including the *pursuit* of aesthetic ends. Nor are other things mere means to this more exalted end. As we have said, for Dewey nothing should be treated as mere means, since that leads to an un- and antiaesthetic treatment of the development of means. If one thinks interactively or dialectically, the ends-means relation ought not to be conceived of in this one-way manner. In some sense the means ought to be ends, and the ends means. For Dewey, corollary to this is the imperative, which we have seen first enunciated by Plato, that art ought to pervade the instrumental world of everyday life. One of the problems of modern society is the way in which ugliness suffuses the workaday world, especially in the factories, where, during Dewey's time, most people worked. The unaesthetic and antiaesthetic character of the working situation results from viewing that context as one of pure means for some other, perhaps more exalted, ends. The individual workers are seen as means for the profit of the owners and vice versa. The work itself is considered a means for each of them being able to purchase certain goods in the context of their leisure—whatever the character of those goods may be. In the case of most people, the purchasable goods involve some kind of sensory gratification as escape from the ugliness of the everyday world. As Marx observed, in the modern factory system, men tend to feel at home in their more animal functions: eating, drinking, having sex; whereas in their distinctively human function of transforming the world by praxis, they are alienated by the work situation.[64] If ends and means ought to influence one another reciprocally, the aesthetic as well as the intellectual and the sacred ought to pervade the workplace. In Dewey's view, aesthetic resolution of the conflicts that emerge in the intersecting rhythms of life at certain moments, though a kind of overarching meta-end, is itself a means, providing us with an exemplar to help us work at such resolution with different materials when dispersal necessarily sets in. Learning aesthetic perception teaches us how to go about any other facet of life that we would otherwise tend to treat as mere means. Dewey thus finds the distinction between fine arts and useful arts wrongheaded. "It is this degree of completeness of living in the experience of making and of perceiving that makes the difference between what is fine or esthetic in art and what is not. Whether the thing made is put to use, as are bowls, rugs, garment, weapons, is, *intrinsically* speaking, a matter of indifference." In fact, art is "useful in the ultimate degree" when it contributes to "an expanded and enriched life."[65]

Originally, the aesthetic served a fundamental function in the life of a people. It was not a separate region of museums or concert halls where one goes to look at or listen to something called art that is largely the concern of an elite class that cultivates a special attention on special days, just as originally religion itself was not simply something participated in on the Sabbath, but something that pervaded the life of the people. All the higher-order "ethereal things" were grounded in the life of the people. Those who built the Parthenon built it, not as a "work of art," but as a civic commemoration to serve a civic function.[66] And the people who build and are served are not some kind of aliens fallen from a higher realm into the context of natural processes but are continuous with the rhythmic processes of nature itself. The aim of Dewey's aesthetic is to recover contact with experience in its integrity.

Dewey's integrating move focuses first on reconnecting the aesthetic to its origins in natural rhythms, those involved in the activity of the human organism—inhaling and exhaling, the systolic and diastolic rhythms of the heart, the cadences of walking and of repetitive action upon the environment, the rhythms of waking and sleeping, hunger and satiety, work and rest, birth and death—as well as the rhythms observed and adjusted to in nature outside the organism—the action of the waves, the ebb and flow of tides, the alternation of day and night, the phases of the moon, the changes of the seasons, the rhythmic patterns of color in animal markings and bird plumage. The organism itself is a balance of rhythmic functions interplaying with the rhythms of the environment, standing in tension with it, falling out of phase and coming into balance through adjustment. Emotional tension develops and is satisfied in this coming into rhythmic balance. Here is the natural germ of aesthetic experience.[67] Rhythm in general is "ordered variation of manifestation of energy."[68] It is "rationality among qualities."[69] Central to these observations is the notion of organic form, the unification of rhythms centralized in the organically based field of awareness.[70] "Underneath the rhythm of every art and of every work of art there lies, as a substratum in the depths of the subconsciousness, the basic pattern of the relations of the live creature to his environment."[71]

And as I noted earlier, experience in general is the transformation of physical-physiological interaction with the environment into conscious participation in it. We are brought out of privacy into the publicity of the outer world. The founding vehicle of this process is the operation of the sense organs.[72] They are the means of being outside oneself, and any derogation of the senses puts us out of contact with real things. As Dewey has it: "Oppositions of mind and body, soul and matter, spirit and flesh all have their origin fundamentally in fear of what life may bring. They are marks of contraction and withdrawal. . . . The unity of sense and impulse, of brain and eye and ear exemplified in animal life [can be] saturated with conscious meanings derived from communication and deliberate expression."[73] That unity of sense and impulse saturated with conscious meanings derived from human communication is the goal of art, in which meaning penetrates into the sensory. Consciousness adds regulation, selection, and redisposition to sensory elements.[74] The process culminates in full interpenetration of animal and human in the joy of aesthetic experience, which is to be distinguished from pleasure found in our animal functions. Though the latter is by no means to be despised, joy is distinguished from pleasure by the wholeness ingredient in it.[75]

Besides the integration of sensation and impulse with distinctively human meaning, there is the further integrative feature found in the fact that, although in art works one or the other senses is primarily operative, the experience itself is synesthetic. The visually perceived surface, for example, is suffused with tactual qualities, and what we hear calls forth visual and tactual experience. This is so because what we perceive are not isolated "inner sensations" but qualities of things that function as magnetic poles, drawing together our various experiences upon the things, making perception not an instantaneous snapshot, but a process developing in time.[76] Because of this synesthetic character of perception, Dewey resists divisions of the arts in terms of distinct sensory fields and spatial or temporal modes, such as I have offered in the introduction—at least insofar as they lead us to think of isolated sensory fields rather than of synesthesia.[77] But it is obvious that in the various art forms, different senses take the lead. What Dewey underscores is that the other senses are still implicitly operative in the field of awareness, in which one element is focal.

Reflection on the process of deliberate artistic transformation of sensory materials eventually leads to the idea of art as "the greatest intellectual achievement of humanity," the idea of being able to shape the whole of human existence in terms of ideas.[78] Among the Greeks, the notion of art extended beyond what we have come to call both fine and mechanical arts and applied even more deeply to the art of shaping human life as a whole. As we have noted, Aristotle called *phronesis* the art of all arts. Dewey expressly appeals to the Greek *kalos-kagathos,* the beautiful and good (which Britishers sometimes translate, characteristically, as "the gentleman"), a fusion of ethics and aesthetics, establishing proportion, grace, and harmony in human conduct.[79] Rooted in such a holistic form of life, poetry, art, and religious feeling spontaneously flower.[80] Dewey extends the notion of art as aesthetic process so far as to say that the intelligent mechanic who takes pride in his work and takes care of his tools is engaged in an artistic activity.[81]

Experience, I said, was pivotal for Dewey's aesthetics. Art is that which celebrates those moments in the stream of experience of which we can say that it was "an experience": *that* party, *that* trip, *that* day. Dewey elaborates on the characteristics of those special moments: "Every successive part flows freely without seam and without unfilled blanks in what ensues. At the same time there is no sacrifice of the self-identity of the parts. . . . [There is] a unity constituted by a single quality that pervades the entire experience in spite of the variation of its constituent parts. This unity is neither emotional, practical nor intellectual, for these terms name distinctions that reflection can make within it."[82] The pervasive quality lies at the center of what makes experience aesthetic.[83] Here Dewey notes several times the aesthetic quality of real intellectual activity. It is guided by a sense of the region within which it operates, the "aura" in which facts and theories swim. There is an emotional attraction for certain ideas.[84] Hence the term *beauty* has been applied both to sensuous charm—within whose region Kant restricts the use of the term—and to the harmonious proportion of parts, the latter of which encompasses both the sensuous and whatever else we may focus attention on.[85] (The exclamation "Beautiful!" spontaneously arises in the excellent execution of a play in football or the successful liftoff of a rocket.) But the difference between intellectual and aesthetic or artistic experience is that in the latter the pervasive quality is found in the very medium of expression, so that art mediates this quality from which intellectual expression—even though rooted in such quality—abstracts.[86] It is this quality that leads in the construction of the art object to the selection of some items and the rejection of others. It binds together the various elements into a living whole rather than a mechanical and artificial construction. In spite of the emotional character of this pervasive character, Dewey considers it a mistake to hold that the content of art is emotion. Emotions, like sensations, are "intentional," are *of* or *about* something; and it is our relation to the "something" that art is all about.[87]

Dewey further adds that in the special experiences within which art is rooted, time is brought to a kind of unity: the past reinforces the present and the future quickens what now exists to give a sense of fulfillment.[88] The moment of which we can say that it was *an* experience can be excised from the flow of life because it has a certain unity in itself. These observations directly parallel features of Aristotle's description of the exemplary work of art having the property of aesthetic organicity. Aristotle spoke of tragedy as having a beginning, middle, and end, not simply in terms of chronological succession but in terms of meaning, so that it begins in order to reach an end, and the middle is the meaningful transition between the beginning and the end. The whole constitutes a unity that is like a living organism, such that each part requires all the others, none is intelligible without the whole, and none may be eliminated without damaging the character of the whole. According to Dewey, that organic property is derived from those moments of each of which we can say that it was *an* experience.

Consider the hunt. The narrative art begins in recounting experiences such as this, creating overall qualitative unity, leaving aside irrelevancies, which, though required for human experience to be such, are not necessary to the story—otherwise the storytelling would take infinitely longer than it took to live through the event. The aesthetic enters into the character of experience, but it is concentrated, focused, and refashioned in story to make it the subject of an art form.[89] "[T]he work of art . . . , just because it is a full and intense experience, keeps alive the power to experience the common world in its fullness. It does so by reducing the raw materials of that experience to matter ordered through form."[90] In this way all art is "abstract," distilling the aesthetically relevant from the aesthetically irrelevant in nonartistic experience. But even abstract art has a limit as art: unless it is to lapse into the purely private, it must still present common qualities found in experience.[91] Abstract art is not the antithesis to nature but a mode of its fulfillment. What stands in antithesis to nature is "arbitrary conceit, fantasy, and stereotyped convention."[92] Many forms of "realistic" art are not truly naturalistic because they reproduce details while missing their moving and organizing rhythms, which may indeed be picked up in "abstract" forms of art. Naturalism, in Dewey's sense, is the escape from convention to perception insofar as convention hampers genuine attending. As in Plato's Cave and Hegel's hard rind of everyday surface, for Dewey art involves the breaking of stereotypes to arrive at more careful attention to what is there.[93] Ordinary experience typically involves mere recognition and set responses; it does not linger over its objects long enough to let experience of them develop to some sense of completeness. Art teaches us how to let our experience develop to its integral fullness.[94]

Aesthetic form is realized through achieving "the completeness of relations within a chosen medium." However, contrary to intellectual modes of interrelation, relations within an artistic medium are dynamically interactive. Indeed, in keeping with the grounding of the artistic in the natural, form is found in *"the operation of forces that carry the experience of an event, object, scene, and situation to its own integral fulfillment."*[95] Precisely because aesthetic experience is developmental, the formal conditions of aesthetic form are continuity, cumulation, conservation, tension, anticipation, and fulfillment.[96] It would seem that such an analysis is derived from the performing arts; but Dewey applies it to all the arts. In the plastic arts, as I noted in the introduction, the eye has not only to take in the total gestalt, it has to traverse the piece from aspect to aspect and from these aspects to the overall gestalt as a deepening and enriching process. Here Dewey seems to follow the same lines as Plato, transferring the rhythmic, harmonic qualities found in music to the plastic arts.

The abstraction of the aesthetically relevant from the aesthetic clutter of everyday or even extraordinary experience and its concentration into form is ingredient in the expression of an artist. In this regard Dewey devotes special attention to the notion of expression.[97] The mere giving way to an impulsion, like sneezing for example, does not constitute expression in the aesthetic sense. Such an act is expressive, not in itself, but in the interpretation of an observer. Expression, like impulsion, does involve an urge from within; but, Dewey says, "it must be clarified and ordered by taking up within itself the values of prior experience before it can become aesthetic expression. And these values are not called into play save by objects in the environment that offer resistance to the direct discharge of emotion and impulse."[98] Three things are thus involved in artistic expression: an impulse, a conscious drawing upon prior experience, and interaction with materials to be shaped in terms of a knowledge of the techniques of shaping. Expression is rich in proportion to the depth of the impulse, the breadth of prior experience, and the mastery of the medium. The impulse is that which generates the "pervasive quality" that guides all artistic production. Prior experience "thickens" the character of present involvement, beyond what is immediately given; it mediates our relation to the fuller context, which makes the immediately given—say a static thing visually appearing from a single fixed perspective—not only sensorily present but meaningful.[99] Indeed, it is past experience that creates "the aura and penumbra in which a work of art swims"—a favorite metaphor of Dewey's which he applies also to the peculiar emotional tonality of ideas for one who really can advance them.[100] The mastery of a medium involves a real love of the qualities of materials and an experimental spirit intent on exploring the expressive capacities of a given medium.[101] It also involves a measure of resistance to our designs by the materials, without which we would not be challenged to develop—a specialized application of a general feature found in the relation of the live creature to its environment. Indeed, the evolution of technique is linked to the emergence of new kinds of experience.[102] Without the mastery of materials, expression is clearly hampered: it becomes discharge or exhibition rather than expression. Without reflective drawing upon rich experience, there is no significant compression that grounds significant expression. In the interplay between the emotion that initiates and guides the process, a kind of Aristotelian mean is required: too much emotion disturbs recollection and technical mastery, too little emotion leads at best to a formally correct but sterile product.[103] With the unity of profound impulse, broad experience, and mastery of materials—through a Wordsworthian "emotion recollected in tranquillity"[104]— both the material environment and our own experience come to take on significant lived form.[105] But even here, in the process of expression, the originating emotional impulse itself undergoes transformation. This marks the difference between immediacy and refinement. In that process things in the environment come to function as "metaphors" for the generating emotion, as in a poem skylarks, stars, the moon, still ponds, and rushing torrents come to stand in relation to love, and love itself is refined in a relation beyond animal immediacy.[106] In that process, though "realistic" objects might enter into an art piece, they enter purged of their aesthetic irrelevancies and transformed.[107] Here we see the basis for the possibility of a difference between the artistic treatment of a nude and a pornographic treatment: brought into relation to the totality of elements that compose a picture animated by an impulse other than lust, "realistic" associations are downplayed in the art piece and another mode of appreciation emerges.[108]

Regarding the "work" of art, Dewey holds a similar position to that which we have met in Schopenhauer and will meet again in Heidegger. The work of art is not the art product, the objective thing, but the experience it effects.[109] So understood, the work of art, to begin with, is perception. The objective thing is the agent of the perception. For Dewey the inadequacy of many theories of art lies in their confining attention to the art product, which is separated from the conditions of production, often taken out of the context in which it was originally meant to operate, and considered apart from experience. But experience is the origin and end of the art product. There is, however, no univocal experience of a given work. It provokes different experiences in different people, different epochs and in different encounters by the same person, including the artist. Though, in the case of the plastic arts, the product retains its identity (except for the natural wear of time), it generates indeterminately many different experiences of itself.[110] In the case of the performing arts, each performance is different, a variation on the identity of the score or script. (However, modern duplicating techniques in audio and video recordings have enabled us to replay past performances, to hear or see identical versions of the same performance at different times and in different places. The performance becomes a kind of "universal" instantiated in different spatiotemporal instances.)

Aesthetic viewing is not a matter of mere passivity. The work of the art product also involves the working of the perceiver. In reading a novel the reader uses what is written as a recipe to perform an imaginative construction. The result is as rich as the constructive imagination of the reader. The same might not seem to be the case with regard to a painting. There the object is present to direct frontal viewing. Nonetheless, as we observed several times, the perceiver has to learn to move from an initially apprehended gestalt in order to focus on particular aspects and back again to the whole so that the richness of the piece has a chance to do its work in a continuously spiraling process.[111]

Crucial to Dewey's view of aesthetic perception is an initial being-seized by a pervasive quality intuitively apprehended. Its parallel on the side of artistic creation is the impulsion of "the musical mood" that Schiller indicated as generative of the words of the poem (and, as we noted, he was followed in this by Nietzsche). Indeed, like Walter Pater, Dewey considers "an harmonious ensemble in any art" to be "the musical quality of that art." Discrimination of parts comes after the intuitive seizure, but the parts must be distinguished as belonging to the pervasive quality that animates them. Aesthetic perception is a matter of learning to be apprehended by an integral whole, an exemplary togetherness of aspects that evokes the togetherness of all the aspects of experience, within which intellectual discrimination plays a subordinate role. But it is reflective discrimination that learns to distinguish between being the victim of cheap theatrical tricks that might arrest attention by shocking or horrifying and being in the presence of genuine aesthetic quality.[112] Furthermore, one learns to discriminate the mechanically repetitive rhythms in certain forms of popular art, especially music, from the more complex vitality produced by higher art forms. Dewey singles out gospel hymns, as governed by an external and imposed rhythm, that are correlated with the relatively impoverished sentiment they invoke. Richly aesthetic rhythms sum up and carry forward rather than simply repeat. Variation within an integral whole producing tensions and leading to culminations of experience is central to works that become classic. One is able to grasp a symmetry in which the whole is seen to "hold together within itself the greatest variety and scope of opposed elements."[113] On the other hand, Dewey views such culmination as simultaneously "leading to a new longing," so that "the completeness of the integration of these two offices [of accumulation and anticipation] . . . by the *same* means . . . measures artistry of production and perception."[114]

That brings us back to the discussion of form and reference and the relation of sensory surface to the theme treated in that surface. In the case of purely decorative art, we would seem to have a case of superficiality in the literal sense: setting upon the surface. But as Plato noted, even without explicit reference, art forms having properties of grace, harmony, and proportion sink into the depths of our souls and produce like properties in us. The "superficial" in this region is the vehicle for the profound insofar as it reaches into the emotional depth of the soul. This is especially the case with music, which, in its nonprogrammatic, nonverbally tied form, affects us most deeply. But more fully referenced art pieces can do their work as we come to understand more fully the context of their reference. This does not mean that the work furnishes an occasion for reverie or free association. In order for the work of art to do its specific work, whatever connected meanings we discern have to find their place in the sensuousness of the mode of presentation so that there is a complete fusion of reference and form as we are brought out of our privacy into the world of aesthetic objects.[115]

But the work of art is, beyond the immediate experience, its impact on how we conduct our lives. This brings us to Dewey's observation, following Shelley, that poetry affects that which produces morality, namely our whole sensibility. Art civilizes, not in the sense of domesticating, but in the sense of deepening our sensitivity. Poets for Shelley are the founders of civil society, "the unacknowledged legislators of mankind."[116] Imagination is the chief instrument of the good. It develops our ability to put ourselves in the place of others and it makes us more alert to the actual context in which we are called on to operate. As Dewey has it, "Art is more moral than moralities, for the latter either are or tend to become consecrations of the status quo, reflections of custom, reinforcements of the established order. The moral prophets of humanity always have been poets, even though they spoke in free verse or by parables."[117]

Dewey presupposes that, in human life as in life in general, fixity is only and ought to be only relative—especially in institutions, customs, and laws.[118] In his view, one ought to learn to grow constantly, expanding and unifying experience, coming to terms with all the relevant parameters functioning in experience—which involves constantly moving beyond where one has been to broader, deeper, and more integrated experience.

Transformation is always called for, at some times more than at others. And that involves the imaginative capacity expanded by art.

The common enjoyment of works of art is the sign of a unified collective life, but the work of the art product is also the bringing about of such a life. Art both forms and gives expression to something beyond the quirks of a "sensitive and creative individual"; it forms and gives expression to the togetherness of a community, bringing together people who would otherwise be apart.[119] The work of art thus overcomes the opposition of individual and universal, subjective and objective, freedom and order, which has captivated the philosophic tradition, by binding them together.[120] Dewey pushes the expansiveness and unifying power of art into the appreciation of cultures foreign to ours, the main access to which we have through their art. Art is a kind of universal language because it arises from the universal fact of encounter with the rhythms and energies in the active interchange of the live creature with its environment. It thus builds communicative bridges within a given community and allows access to what is foreign.[121]

Finally, one must distinguish significant levels of aesthetic depth, culminating in a sense of the universe itself made available through art. As Dewey says, "The sense of an extensive and underlying whole is the context of every experience and it is the essence of sanity."[122] Meaninglessness lies in isolation from that encompassing Whole. The work of art brings into focus not only the quality of being an integral whole but also of belonging to a larger, all-inclusive Whole, which is the universe in which we live. Religious experience accompanies intensive aesthetic perception precisely as this feeling of the universal Whole. For Dewey this is "the mystical" in the positive sense of the term. In a profound work of art, "we are, as it were, introduced to a world beyond this world, which is nevertheless the deeper reality of the world in which we live in our ordinary experiences. We are carried out beyond ourselves to find ourselves."[123]

This goes back to Aristotle: the human soul is, *in a way,* all things; and to Parmenides' claim that thought and being are one. A powerful work of art brings us into a concrete sense of the enveloping whole, present, and manifest in the particular—which is quite close in many ways to Plato's notion of Beauty as the radiance of the One really present and perceptible through the eyes—and Hegel's notion of beauty as the Absolute manifest in sensuous form. If the aesthetic is the basic measure and meta-end in relation to everything else in human life, the range of the aesthetic reaches from the superficial to the profound. The final measure would be how we grow in the sense of the depth of the Whole behind the surface of the present, with alert sensitivity to the features of the here and now.

Dewey contrasts two views of how this sense of the depth dimension arises: one, presumably Platonic, is that is descends from above; the other—his own—that it arises from below by assimilation and transformation of the rhythms involved in the interaction of the live creature with its environment. For him there is no ultimate adjudication between these two views: one is left with a choice. But the choice he makes is tied deeply to the sense of alienation and the fracturing of integral experience that has dogged the Platonic view and led to a mysticism of flight from the here and now.[124] As in Hegel, it is art that mediates between our bodily-sensory insertion into the here and now and our founding reference to the Whole.

## *Response*

There are several parallels between Nietzsche and Dewey that lead into the aesthetic. Both Dewey and Nietzsche are attempting to overcome the Cartesian splits but also the Platonic tradition that lies at the larger cultural background. Both of them are in some respects close to an Aristotelian conception that involves a "biological" theory of mind. (Note that Aristotle's treatment of the soul appears in his general treatise in biology, *On the Soul*, which is the theoretical part for which such works as *The Parts of Animals* and *The History of Animals* supply the empirical part.) The priority of Becoming or process over Being is also common to both Dewey and Nietzsche. That is also an Hegelian thesis: Being is Becoming (which is likewise true for Aristotle at the level of *phusis*). A third parallel is their common rejection of anything that transcends nature. Both of them view the notion of a transcendent God as rooted in a condition of contempt for life on this earth. A fourth parallel is the priority of aesthetics in human life. For Nietzsche life is redeemed aesthetically. It is aesthetic creation that allows us to live with the terrors of existence by carrying the Dionysian upsurge of nature into the creation of dynamic form. Art is the full meaning of nature. There is a fifth parallel: contrary to Schopenhauer, both Nietzsche and Dewey view art as emotionally moving. However, for Dewey art at the same time produces an ordering of the emotional response through our being drawn out to appreciate the character of the art object. This is not that far from Kant insofar as "disinterested satisfaction" allows for "unconstrained favoring" of the object and the resultant pleasure is an experience of the quickening of life. But for Kant that means the quickening of

the distinctive human capacity to judge in the free play of the relation between imagination and understanding. This is not a matter of emotion, of
a being drawn out of the whole person in relation to the object, for Kant
restricts that to the effect of the sublime brought about by a tension between the finitude of the imagination and the infinite orientation of reason. For Kant the experience of the beautiful is rather one of harmony,
thus giving rise to Schopenhauer's view of the aesthetic as akin to the more
advanced "blowing out of desire" in Buddhist nirvana.

Thus although, like Nietzsche's, Dewey's thought appears as a challenge to the tradition of philosophic thought, it is in many ways continuous
with that tradition, especially in its Aristotelian and its Hegelian forms. But
that is only in keeping with his overall strategy of overcoming splits. In this
case, the old and the new interpenetrate. As I have indicated, Dewey's
thought is Aristotelian not only in its "biological" holism but also in the priority of *phronesis* as directedness through intelligent alertness to all relevant
parameters of the concrete environment. But Dewey's thought is Aristotelian without the fixity of species, the priority of *theoria* and its correlates, Self-thinking Thought on the one hand and elitist society on the
other. Dewey's thought is Hegelian in his dialectical style of resolving antitheses, in its capacity to come to terms with an evolving universe, but also
in his emphasis on the sense of the Whole functioning as the background
of all experience and as the explicit focus of certain moments of aesthetic
experience. But his thought is Hegelian without the notion of the Absolute
and thus without an absolutist reading of art, religion, and philosophy.
Ideas are not ends but instruments. It is the idea of art that gives us the
model for all human operation.

I am dispositionally favorable to Dewey's overall philosophic strategy
of tracing dualities back to their origin in the field of experience and turning them, as in Hegel, from dualities into dialectical relations within an
overarching whole. Art in particular has tended in modern, especially post-
Kantian, times to occupy a separate region, unconnected with other regions of human experience. Kant himself performed a theoretical kind of
surgical separation in his first two critiques, severing the region of knowing
from the region of moral responsibility. And, in his attempt in the third critique at healing the rift he had created, Kant compounded the splits initially by separating aesthetic form from its relation to biological appetite on
the one hand and rational conception on the other. Though he went on to
reconnect the aesthetic with both poles of our being and to use it as a
hermeneutic model for understanding the character of the Whole as the

product of divine art, in the course of the nineteenth century aesthetic thought often tended to follow his initial move of separating the aesthetic and hence produced the movement of "art for art's sake."

Dewey himself attempted to link the aesthetic to the other facets of human existence, so that the aesthetic would pervade the whole of human life. This is actually an old Platonic theme: from birth to death the citizenry should be surrounded by objects—clothing, buildings, utensils, furniture, paintings—that have the properties of order, grace, harmony, proportion. Ideally such an environment tends to produce the same qualities in the emotional lives of the citizenry. And such prereflective emotional rationality creates a fit matrix for the development of reflective rationality that extends such sensibility to the cosmic Whole.

Kant also viewed the aesthetic as an integrating center in the field of human experience; but his mode of integration is significantly different than Dewey's. For Kant the aesthetic lifts us off of our animal relations and ultimately sets us in relation to the moral order. For Dewey and for us, esthetics has its origin in the live creature's relation to its environment. Embued by nature with rhythmic sensitivity, human beings, by reason of their primordial distance from the immediacy of the sensorily given and the appetites linked thereto, are capable of choosing to transform themselves and their environment rhythmically: dance and song as well as poetic storytelling modify the natural temporal rhythms, and the design of utensils, clothing, housing, and furniture, which use decorative elaboration of utilitarian artifacts, as well as self-decoration through tattooing or other cosmetic devices, modify natural spatial rhythms and harmonies.

Drawing upon the rhythmic relation of the live creature to its environment, art provides a level of access, a kind of language, that cuts across the Babel of tongues found throughout the earth. One can come to a kind of direct access to the generative sensitivity of foreign culture. While we could grant that, nonetheless, it is the fusion of form and substance, of sensuous shaping with reference that leaves such access largely at the level of suggestion, for it is the mother tongue that gives expression to the deeper meanings that contextualize what is directly accessible. If we recur to Danto's discussion of Brueghel's *Fall of Icarus* cited in the introduction, we see that one ignorant of the language and mythological tradition would only have access to "work and play on a summer's day." And that would be far from what is actually "in" the painting.

By reason of their founding reference to the whole, human beings must take up the sensorily given interpretively and thus deepen the natural reference to biologically functional surface by divining the ontological depth. The primary vehicle of this interpretive movement is language that prearticulates the character of the whole, linking given particulars to their kinds and fitting their kinds into a world of meaning. In functioning through language as carrier of the referential feature of human artefaction, ideally the rhythmic modification of materials fuses with reference to constitute a single whole. Dewey contrasts this fusion of the referential function and the aesthetic function, which we have seen distinguished from Plato onward, with the purely referential function of ordinary language and of the specialized languages of science and philosophy. The latter *refer* to experiences, while the art object *constitutes* experiences; the prosaic functions *re-present* things, while the aesthetic functions *present* things; the former operate in absence, the latter in presence. However, presence here is not a matter of sheer immediacy. The art object passes through the mediation of the artist's own past experience and evokes the mediated response of aesthetic perception. Like Schopenhauer before him and Heidegger after, Dewey properly distinguishes the art object from the *work* of art, the physical reality from the experience it evokes. However, Dewey does not understand by this that the art object functions as an occasion for reverie; rather, he maintains that the experience evoked brings us out of ourselves and into an enriched contact with the environment. He emphasizes what phenomenologists call the *intentionality* of emotions, their referredness to that which lies outside the inwardness of the experience, their capacity to disclose something beyond the privacy of the individual perceiver.

Perhaps most significantly, Dewey testifies to the extent of that disclosive capacity when he calls attention to the sense of an enveloping whole, the wholeness of the universe itself, that is often evoked by the work of art. Here we meet with a theme I laid down in the beginning and have followed throughout the course of this study: that the field of human experience is ultimately referred to the whole of being as one of its poles, while anchored in sensory presence as another. In the work of art there is an intensified sensory presence of a unique individual that, at the same time, functions as a vehicle through which we gain an intensified sense of the Whole, within which it and we as perceivers exist.

The meeting and indeed fusion of these two poles of the field of human reference deepens our sense of presence and transforms our relation to everything. As Dewey puts it, art affects that which produces the moral order: our sensitivity to things. This is a different route within the aesthetic arena to Kant's moral end. The work of art not only can bring about a peculiar experience in relation to an individual object, it can also transform most deeply the substratum of all experience as referred to the whole. Thinking about art can thus lead to comprehensive thinking about the whole of human experience and the whole of its field of reference. More than that, however, as in Hegel, art is capable of healing the rift that thought produces between itself and the sensuous givenness of our life-world. Indeed, for Dewey and in fact, the way it treats aesthetic experience is a peculiar measure for the adequacy of a philosophy, provided one understands the aesthetic as stretched along a continuum from sensory surface to encompassing depth.[125] But once we do that, we are in essential continuity with the tradition we have been examining from Plato onward.

Dewey contrasts two incompatible views of the origin of art, with no means for adjudication between them other than choice (viz., the notion that beauty "descends from above" or that it "arises from below"). But one wonders how far apart they really are, at least at one level. The crucial factors are: (1) that there is an encompassing depth beyond sensory surface, (2) that, correspondingly, human reality is a reference to that encompassing depth, and (3) that there is a mode of access to it that takes place in sensory presence rather than in mere re-presentation. "Descent from above" and "arising from below" may be two metaphoric ways of speaking about the same kind of experience. If we talk about the real presence of Beauty Itself in beautiful things discernible through the eyes as in Plato or the presentation of the Absolute in sensuous form as in Hegel, how different is that from the sense of a world beyond this world as the depth of this very world to which Dewey calls attention? But where the crucial difference finally lies is in the experience of being addressed by a personal encompassing Ground, as in the biblical tradition and in contemporary thinkers like Martin Buber or Emmanuel Levinas. It is in terms of such an "aesthetic" that medieval thinkers assimilated the Platonic tradition into the biblical tradition of personal address. And it is in such aesthetic that we are essentially interested. A Deweyan approach anchors the aesthetic most firmly in this world, in the world of biological existence, and, with Nietzsche, admonishes those who would despise this world, to remain faithful to the earth which, having created, Yahweh saw as good.

One could go quite far in paralleling the ancient tradition with Dewey's sense of the nonfixity of particular ends and his implicit notion of a series of meta-ends encompassed by the aesthetic. We find a kind of Deweyan meta-end in Plato's notion of the Good, which involves the notion of oneness to be mirrored creatively in our individual and collective lives in different contexts as one comes to terms intelligently with the concrete. Aristotelian *phronesis* as the capacity to achieve the good situationally is precisely the habit of forming and breaking habits intelligently, with full alertness to the requirements of situations and the general (meta-)ends of humanness. It is a habit of not falling into habits in the sense of unintelligent fixed routines incapable of being modified without great difficulty. The achievement of *phronesis* is possible only if we have some control over our passions, and that is why temperance and fortitude are required. The structure of the virtues in their togetherness are not rule governed but rule generating. And though the aesthetic accent is not so pronounced and central in Aristotle as in Dewey, flexibility and intellectual alertness in relation to the given environment put us quite close to Dewey's peculiar aesthetic. The general Greek ideal of the *kalos kagathos,* the beautiful and good person, is something to which Dewey makes explicit appeal.

The fixity of meta-ends in spite of Dewey's preference for change and relativity has its parallel in Dewey's notion of ideas. It cannot account for itself (i.e., for the fixity of the notions of idea and intelligence). We might note here, with Lonergan, that everything is subject to revision except the conditions for the possibility of revision.[126] In prehuman life the meta-ends of growth, sustenance, repair, and reproduction are realized in changing contexts to produce the evolution of species. In human life, growth tied to the emergence of intelligence taking the lead in establishing integral experience for creative and cooperative individuals are the fixed meta-ends operative in changing contexts. So also, reflection on these processes presupposes fundamental conditions for reflection aiming at the display of the general and concrete character of the Whole within which we are operative.

# X

# HEIDEGGER

## Situating Heidegger

FROM MARTIN HEIDEGGER'S FIRST major work, *Being and Time*, his thought has focused on the notion of Being, but the method of his approach was phenomenology, the method characterizing my own introduction. Heidegger's approach falls in the line of his teacher, Edmund Husserl, the founder of Phenomenology. Husserl understood Phenomenology to be comprehensive philosophy; it is at least permanent prolegomenon, acknowledged or not, to any philosophy. Phenomenology comes from two Greek terms, *phainomenon*, appearance, and *logos*, essence. Phenomenology is a comprehensive descriptive inventory of all the essential ways in which appearance—that is, presence to consciousness—occurs: direct evidence in sensation, imaginative presentation, recollection in memory, judging, inference, willing, desiring, feeling, presence to oneself as conscious, "apperception" of other persons, and so on.[1] Phenomena are appearances, modes of manifestation, always involving particular modalities of awareness at their base, always involving a conscious subject related to a manifest object. Consciousness itself is the intending of those modes of manifestness: such intentionality is the basic feature of awareness. All consciousness—deliberate or not—intends, that is, points toward and thus manifests some object. Further, human awareness always involves an eidetic component, an element of universality. The sensorily given "this" is always seen *as* something: as a tree or a dog or a book, which notions apply, beyond "this," to all actual or possible instances of the type given in this instance. The universal feature is usually emptily intended and only partially filled. A tree is a whole, only aspects of which I concretely know. Microbiology and physics press at a more complete filling of what a tree is, but not necessarily all that any given tree is. The whole of treeness is revealed and concealed in what we actually know of trees. Introduction of other conscious entities complicates the analysis by *appresenting* the other's awareness as a kind of absence in the fullness of sensory presence.[2] The consciousness of another is co-given expressively with the givenness of positively identifiable sensory features, but not at all in the way colors and sounds are given. Each science operates in terms of a certain angle of abstraction from the ever-pregiven, all-encompassing *Lebenswelt* or lifeworld of meaning and inhabitance built up out of the interrelation of human beings over countless generations. Phenomenology aims at sustaining a systematic inventory of the lifeworld. But all science and the lifeworld itself are subjected to a process of historical sedimentation whereby the basic phenomena are covered over by the mediations of a tradition. Tradition works with words and, through words, with ready-made concepts whose origins in direct experience and whose limitations are no longer thought. One can repeat the words; further, one can learn something of their meaning; further still, as in every science, one can even carry on deductions from ready-made concepts which, by reason of their founding—though abstract—relation to their origins in lifeworld experience, have functional consequences. But none of these abstract processes gets us back to the originary phenomena to which phenomenology leads us.[3]

Historically Husserl goes back to Kant and to Descartes. The latter made the fundamental discovery of the *cogito* and the multiple realm of "seeming" that is its enduring correlate. But he did not pursue the fruitfulness of the "seeming" theme, preferring to follow the direction of theoretical reconstructions.[4] Kant distinguished phenomena and noumena and thus, according to Ricoeur, founded phenomenology.[5] Contrary to Descartes, he resolutely confined his attention to phenomena, but nonetheless remained under the influence of the theoretical abstractions of Newtonian cosmology.

Heidegger has significant relations to all three thinkers. Husserl gave him his point of departure: phenomenological inventory. Heidegger's first and most famous book, *Being and Time*, was dedicated to Husserl. Heidegger devoted several books to the study of Kant: *Kant and the Problem of Metaphysics*, *What Is a Thing?*, and *Phenomenological Interpretation of Kant's Critique of*

*Pure Reason.*[6] The first highlighted the significance of time and imagination; the second opened up considerations that would lead, in other writings, to the priority of the work of art; the third, an earlier lecture course, lays the background for the ontic-ontological distinction. However, for Heidegger phenomena are not thereby cut off from noumena, but provide us with various revealings—and concealings—of the being of things.[7] Such revealing and concealing follows out Husserl's distinction between empty intentions and their partial filling on the one hand, and his *Lebenswelt* analysis on the other.[8] Radicalizing Descartes and Husserl, Heidegger attempted to find—in the words of one of his essays—"The Way Back into the Ground of Metaphysics."[9] In this connection he introduces a basically Kierkegaardian distinction between abstract thought, with which philosophy has always been engaged, and concrete dwelling. Abstract thought sets things at a distance, splitting subject from object. Especially in Descartes and the modern tradition stemming from him, the subject-object split becomes a separation: we begin, according to these thinkers, inside the private chamber of our awareness and are confronted with the problem of winning our way out. For Heidegger, on the contrary, we begin as being-in-the-world—that is, as indwelling, inhabiting a world, built up through a tradition, where we are "outside" our privacy and close to persons and things.[10] We have to pry ourselves loose deliberately from such involvement to arrive at the artificial problem of a separate *cogito*. Furthermore, the world we inhabit is not simply a physical cosmos, but, more deeply, a world of functional meaning prearticulated for us by the work of prior generations. Such a world is made possible by the fundamental character of humanness, which Heidegger calls *Dasein*, often hyphenated as *Da-Sein* to indicate Heidegger's particular emphasis. *Dasein* is the "there" *(da)* of Being *(Sein)*, the place where the whole of what is is disclosed as a matter of question, for which the various worlds of meaning provided by different cultures and different epochs are the putative answers.[11] A cultural epoch entails, beyond implicit phenomenological description, *interpretation* of what underlies the directly available and how that fits into the Whole. Hence phenomenology turns in a hermeneutic direction.[12] Here Heidegger supplies underpinning for Nietzsche's observations on the essentially interpretive, perspectival disclosures of the meaning of the Whole provided by the "higher men," that is, the artists, philosophers, and saints.

Descartes had reversed the medieval notions of subjectivity and objectivity. For example, in Aquinas objectivity is an aspect of things related to the abstracting attention of cognitive subjectivity: objectivity is the face things present to finite cognition—their "over-againstness" *(ob-iectivitas);* and both cognitive subjectivity and objectivity rest on the more basic "subjectivity of being" in both knower and known. At the basis of there being subjects of awareness and their objects, there are subjects of being, namely human beings and things, only aspects of which we humans know. Heidegger underscores the indeterminate receding of the subject of being in whatever we encounter as it rises up to present to us an object, an aspect, relative to our awareness. But, especially in his early classic, *Being and Time,* he emphatically underscores the noncoincidence of human reality with awareness and indicates, with the notion of *Dasein,* the full being of humanness, which tunes the field of awareness. Such full being is biologically grounded, culturally fashioned being-in-a-world with others determined in its essential features by those long dead. The Greek notion of *charakter* or "stamp" indicates the preconscious determination that "tunes" the subject of awareness, inclining it to see and act along certain predetermined lines. In-habiting a world is being so spontaneously tuned. The reflective *cogito,* the methodically controlling "I," emerges out of such a matrix. It was this especially that attracted Heidegger to Aristotle's ethics and its requirement of the prior shaping of one's ethos through the right upbringing.[13]

Attend at this point to our original view of human nature. Human nature involves a biological ground that gives us the ever-present sensory surface yielding aspects of things in the environment related to our biological needs. The sensory circle reveals something about things, but it conceals much more. And, as Nietzsche remarked, the way it reveals is "a lie," fundamentally misleading if we take it alone as revealing of the way things finally and fully are. On the other hand, human nature involves a transcendent direction: it operates in terms of the notion of being; it involves openness to the totality of each being within the totality of what is. This is the old Aristotelian notion that the human soul is, in a way, all things, and the even older Parmenidean notion that thought and being are one—something to which we have constantly recurred in this book and to which Heidegger gave renewed attention. Being is not simply minimal being outside nothing, but everything about everything, because outside being there is nothing at all. Being as a whole, however, is not known but is referred to by the character of what we are: openness to the totality. Openness to the totality and, for us, the initial emptiness of the totality outside of the positive presence of sensa, requires that the immediate presence of these sensa be brought into interpretative relation to the Whole. Such a bringing of the sensory surface into relation with the Whole necessitates the development of culture. Culture is the establishment of a world of meaning that is not simply a theoretical way of looking (this, after all, came very late in human history), but is a way of being for a people, a lived-in, dwelt-in sense of the Whole involving modes of thought linked immediately to modes of operation. Thought, feeling, and action are interpenetrating elements involved in the inhabitance of a world. Inhabitance, or dwelling, is crucial here. To in-habit, as Dewey also observed, is to become habituated in a certain way, to have a way of standing toward things as a quasi-permanent orientation. This involves an opening up of the totality from a certain perspective. It involves the Whole coming out of its initial concealment into a disclosure of meaning within which we can come to formulate propositions and check their correspondence with experience. Correctness of representation or correspondence to what is opened up depends on a prior opening up of a sense of meaning of the Whole within which propositions can be formulated. Any given opened-up totality is, however, only one way of disclosure: it is essentially perspectival manifestation of the Whole. For everything revealed there is the underside of concealment. What we are dealing with finally is orientation toward the absolute mystery of Being, which always lies beyond any rational mastery.[14]

In this respect, consider science as a kind of progressive, ongoing, self-corrective way of thinking about the world, no state of which is definitive, but each state of which shows something of the character of what is, though never in such a way as to include the Whole exhaustively. But science is a limited theoretical project, resting on the more encompassing project, which is that of being-in-the-world, inhabiting the world. The scientist, before, during, and after his acting as a scientist, belongs to a culture, shares its lifeworld. *World* here does not mean physical totality but world of meaning, as in the classical Greek world, the primitive Christian world, the twentieth-century Western world, the ancient Egyptian world, the Chinese world. These are ways of disclosure, primarily practical, governing in a global fashion how we conduct our lives. Heidegger underscores the dominance of world disclosure in the expression "the world worlds": rather than being at our disposal, world does something to us; it holds us in its grips and discloses/closes our fundamental possibilities.[15]

At its deepest level, such a world of meaning is governed by the fundamental meaning of the term *Being* operative within it.[16] Thus for Heidegger, the history of Western thought is essentially the history of the notion of Being. Heidegger calls attention to "the ontological difference" between Being *(Sein)* and beings *(Seienden),* which includes entities and their beingness *(Seiendheit)* or the principles that constitute them as beings—the latter subdistinction found, for example, in Plato's distinction between things in the realm of genesis and being, which lies in their Forms. Being for Heidegger is that which grants access to entities and their principles. It is correlated with the fundamental structure of humanness as *Da-Sein*, as openness to the Whole. However, the Western tradition focused attention on entities and principles and failed to attend to that which granted them. For all its focus on the beingness of beings, it is characterized by the for-gottenness of what Heidegger names Being. Furthermore, it is governed throughout all its variations by the Greek experience of Being as standing presence. What is is Now, exemplified particularly by Plato's notion of Form, but opened initially by Parmenides. This sets Being in opposition to becoming, to appearing, to thought, and to the ought, which are, in differ-ent ways, other than Being so conceived. The Being of the things we en-counter and of our own selves lies in unchanging principles.[17] But what governs *that* distinction is the experience of Being as standing presence.[18] For Heidegger, Being as what makes possible the distinction between forms/principles and things needs to be rethought in terms of how time enters into that conception, how the Now dominates, but also how the Now is itself constituted by retention of the past and protention of the fu-ture, two notions to which Husserl gave close attention.[19]

The interplay of the three temporal dimensions focuses on "presenc-ing" as the way in which things draw near to us and thus engage us. The essential dimension in this presencing process is the future. How I draw up my past and thus stand in the present depends on how I am related to my future. If my fundamental project is amassing a fortune, the study of meta-physics, though perhaps required by a particular curriculum, is not some-thing to which I would be inclined to be deeply present, for it is hard to see how such could contribute to my fundamental project. If, however, I un-dergo a conversion and project my future differently, I will look at my past differently and tell a new story about my life, for different things will jut into significance and others sink into indifference. I might even come to find the study of metaphysics worthy of my sustained attention. The depth and quality of my relation to the Whole might take center stage and my plutocratic project might then sink into indifference or become trans-formed into a means for philanthropy. Modern science emerged when a different "ground plan of nature" was projected, a non-Aristotelian view of what was henceforth to count as nature: there are no longer natures seek-ing immanent goals, but a single Nature, a world machine built from elementary particles combining and separating according to fixed mechanical laws. Under that projection very much of the mechanisms of nature have been uncovered, but, among other things, at the price of the separation of fact from value and the concealing of the process of revealing itself.[20] And at the most fundamental level, the way each of us relates to the ultimate future of the end of our being-in-the-world, our own death, determines how we are present to all our projects. Among the ancients, humans are characterized by being "the mortals"—not simply because we will die (that is true of all living forms), but because we live out of an *anticipation* of our not-being-in-the-world. How we face that ultimate term—embracing it or fleeing from it—determines how we are present in any given Now.[21]

For the most part we live in an "inauthentic"—or better, "unappropriated" *(uneigenlich)*—mode, determined by what "they" say, what "they" are doing, what is "in." Our past enters into how we are present, but in a way that is ambiguous with regard to what is really disclosed and ambiguous with regard to what *I* determine and what is determined in me by my tradition. Our future is an object of curiosity: we are attracted by this and that prospect, but we run from the thought of our ultimate term. We huddle together in the present, filling the time with endless and meaningless chatter as we wait to die—a thought from which we flee into chatter and busyness.[22] What awakens us to "authenticity" and allows us to appropriate for ourselves what is available is letting our own death enter into our lives as a "real presence." It can then happen that, in a "moment of vision," our mortality lays hold of us. Pried loose from our unappropriated belonging to the "they," we are enabled resolutely to engage in projects lived within their ultimate temporal perspective. The unsettled character of our being-toward-death opens up a pervasive and irremovable anxiety as our own being-toward-death has to be understood in terms of our being toward the Whole expressed in the notion of Being itself as the revealing-concealing of the Whole.

This is most basic for Heidegger. Any disclosure of the Whole is simultaneously a concealing of what does not show itself within the way of revealing characteristic of a given world of meaning. Hence the finitude of any given world, and hence the notion of the historicity of Being itself.[23] Hans-Georg Gadamer suggests that Heidegger's basic contribution was to shift phenomenology from concern for the given to concern for the hidden.[24] In this regard, the historicity of Being is linked to Heidegger's notion of essence. Contrary to the Platonic tradition, essence is no atemporal endurance, definable once and for all. It is rather endurance through time, displaying itself now this way now that. The display is essentially connected with the perspectival character of the disclosure of the whole. This means that thought has to be essentially historical.

In working through the historical character of the manifestation of Being, Heidegger follows Kierkegaard's distinction between thinking and dwelling by distinguishing two modes of thinking: one is "representative-calculative"; the other is "meditative," thinking as dwelling.[25] The former constructs and is ultimately governed by the will-to-power, to cognitive or practical mastery. The latter "lets things be" in appreciatively dwelling on them. Representative-calculative thinking devises methods and makes progress.[26] Meditative thinking follows a way and returns recollectively to where we always already are. The former operates in absence; the latter in presence. The former speaks to what we have come to call *the intellect*, the con-centrated point detached from our whole mode of indwelling; the latter speaks to *the heart*, the core, the center of our being and ground of thinking, acting and feeling, which articulates our mode of indwelling.[27] Parallel to the distinction between these two modes of thinking is Heidegger's distinction between two modes of truth, linked to two Greek terms, *orthotes* and *aletheia*. The former, coming into English in such terms as *ortho-doxy*, or correct opinion, is truth as correspondence between mind and things that attains to correctness of representation. For Heidegger truth as correctness is essentially derivative from the more primordial notion of truth as *a-letheia*, or un-concealment. The formulation of propositions and their being checked against the availability of evidence both presuppose the prior opening up of a space of meaning. The term *un-concealment* calls attention to the link between revealing and concealing and embodies the notion of direct presencing. Correct propositions which correspond to what is are derived from the coming to presence, out of concealment, of what is, in such a way that what is manifest remains rooted in the mystery of what is and will remain concealed. *A-letheia* is linked to *lethe*, unconcealment to the essentially concealed. *Dasein* has an essential stake in how its relation to the *lethe*, the hidden mystery of Being, is preserved.[28] This is intimately linked to the role of the arts.

There is a further Heideggerian thesis connected with this: the priority of language. Before our employment of language in addressing others, language addresses us: "Language speaks."[29] Language is not a mere instrument by which we give expression to fully formed thoughts. Rather, language, which we first learned functionally as children, has us in its grips, prearticulates our world of meaning in the mode of indwelling, and makes possible our discovery of what we think. Language primordially gives rise to thought. Functioning in our lifeworld, language is like our own body: we presuppose it in thinking how and what we think. As the ground of our being-in-the-world, language is the ground of our essential historicity. Language, history, *Da-Sein,* along with the founding structure of our own embodiment as an expression of our belonging to nature: together they constitute the framework that supports the field of explicit awareness.[30] All that we do within that field can never overtake and encompass the framework that makes it possible. *Orthotes* can never overtake *aletheia,* for the latter is the condition for the possibility of the former, not vice-versa.

The history of Western thought is in part the history of the notion of truth. For Heidegger, it begins among the Greeks as *aletheia,* but focus shifts permanently to *orthotes.* As a variation on that theme, with Descartes truth becomes certitude: the presence of things is transformed in accordance with our methodologically purified representations. In more recent times, certitude gives way to what Heidegger calls *enframing (Gestell):* the approach to things as "standing reserve" *(Bestand)* for our projects.[31] This describes the nature of modern science as in essence technological. Given the dominance of this mode of revealing (experimental science as the exclusive way of revealing), we tend to view ourselves as photoelectric cells, computer brains, robot mechanisms. Much is revealed in this approach, but what is essentially concealed is the very character of revealing.[32] Awareness is ignored or explained away or admitted as an embarrassingly functionless epiphenomenon.[33] The world that emerges in this way is increasingly planned for efficiency, but it is no longer a world in which we can fully dwell. As a consequence, though it becomes increasingly "rational," it also becomes increasingly meaningless in the holistic sense: the world is no longer our dwelling place. But the technological view was already prefigured in the way in which Plato conceived Being as Form, object of an intelligible look, functioning as plan for the demiurge to fashion material for his purposes.[34] And that view set itself up in direct opposition to the arts. Plato considered the arts as the primordial articulation of the Cave, the sheltering, confining semidarkness, semilight of the lifeworld. The origin of philosophy is the battle with poetry.

At this point, then, we turn to the arts. Heidegger reinstates the battle between philosophy and poetry; but rather than subordinating poetry to philosophy, he almost tends to the opposite. "Poetry" articulates being-in-the-world, which guides the way of philosophy. For Heidegger, the arts provide "the saving power" in the epoch of enframing. The arts operate in the meditative mode of "letting things be," rather than dominating them conceptually and practically. It is within the modality of the sensitive dwelling afforded by the arts that we can learn to await the new advent of meaning in the era of the darkening of the world expressed in "the flight of the gods, the destruction of the earth, the transformation of man into a mass, the hatred and suspicion of everything free and creative, the pre-eminence of the mediocre."[35]

## "The Origin of the Work of Art"

One of the chief statements of Heidegger's aesthetic views is his "Origin of the Work of Art," written in 1935 and 1936.[36] It would be helpful to begin at the end of this rather convoluted essay, wherein the notion of origin tends to be lost sight of, and work backward. There, at the very end, Heidegger remarks: "The origin of the work of art,—that is, the origin of both the creators and the preservers, which is to say of a people's historical existence, is art. This is so because art is by nature an origin, a distinctive way in which truth comes into being, that is, becomes historical."[37]

There are several things here that require expansion. First of all, the work of art is not fundamentally and properly the thing that stands there, but rather is the work it does. Heidegger's thought parallels Dewey's and Schopenhauer's in that respect. What stands in a museum and is dusted by the cleaning personnel is something at hand, like a table or a mop board or a shelf. It is labeled as a work of art, but that is a kind of extrinsic denomination. For Heidegger, it is largely a work that was; now it is a labeled, locatable, viewable, dustable object.[38]

Second, the work of art does not simply involve an isolated genius creator and a small coterie of preservers; it involves a way for a people, the world of a people. Art is a way in which the world is exposed. This remark is tied to a view of personhood as necessarily embedded in a tradition or a complex web of traditions. If we regard ourselves as self-made individuals, it is only possible on the basis of having been shaped and sustained in a certain way by a peculiar tradition. Preservers are those who are brought through the work, in an uncommon way, into a world of common inhabitance.[39]

Third, art is the setting-into-work of truth.[40] What is truth? For Heidegger, as I have said, there are two senses: the ordinary view and a more profound view. Truth as correctness of representation is derived from *aletheia*, unconcealment, which has, as its other side, concealment. We indwell in the Whole in the modality of a world that furnishes the meaning field within which things are accessible and within which we come to formulate and test our propositions for their (orthotic) truth. In Heidegger's view, world is more in being than any of the things that are. It is not merely the collection of things present-at-hand nor a merely imaginative framework added to such things. It is neither "objective facts" nor "subjective construals" nor theories about the facts. World is something more than the tangible and perceptible in which we think we are at home.[41] Here we must recall again that in our ordinary wakeful life we are not dealing with sensations but with things, in the disclosure of which sensations are subsidiary. Sensations by themselves are abstractions from the concrete reality of things: they are the vehicles of our access to things, not the typical focus of our attention. And we have access to things through the mode of disclosure of the Whole that has us in its grips antecedent to reflective thought. Art is one of the origins of the disclosure of a world. It is the setting into a work of the truth (i.e., the disclosure of a world). The art work is a peculiar kind of thing that opens up the space of a world and does so for its preservers. Through this disclosure, truth becomes historical—that means it becomes effective, operative. It is that which, before people come to think about it, has them in its grips.

The historicity of truth also means perspectival disclosure of the whole and thus involves struggle among various modes of putative final disclosure. Those raised Christian will be Christian before they even come to think about it. Those raised in the modern world spontaneously come to think about the world scientifically: they are held in the grip of a mode of revealing that is characterized as technical, calculative. Within contemporary people these two modes of revealing, Christian and scientific, are involved in some sort of tensive relation to one another. They inaugurate a struggle for dominance as the primordial mode of revealing. But as perspectival, the modes of revealing are always tied to concealing, to the Not *(das Nichts)*, the Nothing in relation to the world of disclosure.[42] Because we are gripped by the scientific mode of revealing—a relatively recent phenomenon in the history of mankind—we can come to do science without necessarily reflecting on the peculiar angle of abstraction afforded by that particular way of coming at things. We take it to be simply definitive, *the* way of revealing—until we think about it. What grounds the scientific mode of revealing? Once we press that we see that we need something more than science as observation and theory: we need, to begin with, a phenomenological reflection on the mode of revealing that characterizes the scientist himself and that rests on the broader context of the scientist's inhabitation of a common world. He talks to other people in ordinary language; he lives with his family; makes political and moral decisions, decides to devote himself to science, and maybe even prays—not on the basis of his science, but on the basis of the disclosure of the lifeworld out of which science comes as a peculiar kind of abstract angle. The notion of a world becomes crucial as a way in which the historical existence of a people is established. The work of art is a way in which that world is set up.

But art is only one of the ways. Others include the action that grounds a political state, the experience of the nearness of the divine, essential sacrifice, the thinker's questioning of being.[43] The latter is Heidegger's own direction: making us see the hidden in what we think is clear and definitive, the mystery that is involved in the everyday, and the antecedent decisions, most of which each of us has not made, which are involved in the way in which we come to think, act, and feel. Science is not an original opening out of truth, but the extension of a domain already opened up, the discovery of the right, the correct within the more primordial establishment of a horizon of meaning.[44]

One would have to ask here how these various ways of opening out of the whole for dwelling are related to one another. Heidegger does not explicitly deal with the question when he presents this list. However, if we return to his consideration of art near the end of the essay in question, we will see aspects of a possible answer. Art is essentially poetry, of which poesy (or poetry in the usual sense) is only one expression. However, poesy is a privileged mode because it is *the* language art and language is the primary articulation of our mode of being in the world. All the other arts take shape in the space opened up by language.[45] So also political founding, essential sacrifice, experiencing the presence of the divine, and the thinker's questioning of being are all rooted in the poetic art. In seeming agreement with Dewey, who follows Shelley: the poet is the unacknowledged legislator of mankind.

### What Is a Thing?

Moving on from the end of "The Origin of the Work of Art," let us consider its overall structure. It has three parts whose topics overlap:

Thing and Work

Work and Truth

Truth and Art

We have looked at the relation of truth and art. Let us consider the relation between thing and work. Heidegger spends a great deal of time discussing the notion of "the thing" here and elsewhere. As we have already noted, he has an entire book dedicated to the question *What Is a Thing?* as well as a shorter essay titled "The Thing."[46] The essay under consideration here focuses once more on that notion. Nothing would seem more obvious and less problematic. But it is the obvious that is the aspect of experience we least think about. Our ordinary modes of thought are actually past decisions—the decisions of those long dead—over against other possible decisions: they conceal as well as reveal. And Heidegger tries to get us to question our ordinary conceptions in order to understand their modes of concealment. Heidegger tries to approach the work of art from the beginning of the essay in terms of the notion of the thing, since the work of art is one of the things that we meet.

As noted above, the cleaning personnel in the museum dust the statue, the frame of the painting, the door, the mop board: these are all equally things from the point of view of the duster. Heidegger focuses on three traditional conceptions of the thing that are all correct (orthotic), but none of which is fundamental.[47] There is the Aristotelian notion of the thing as the bearer of properties, the Berkeleyan notion of the thing as the unity of the sensory manifold (i.e., the togetherness of the multiplicity of sensory features); and there is, again, the Aristotelian notion of formed matter. For Heidegger, all the notions are too general to come to terms with the peculiar thinghood involved in the work of art. The first involves the notion of at-hand *(vorhanden)* objectness, which places the thing too far away from the immediate involvement required by the work of art.[48] Furthermore, it parallels the subject-predicate structure of sentences and leads us to question whether linguistic structure mirrors the structure of the thing or whether we read linguistic structure into the thing. The second notion actually brings the thing too close to our bodily being in the sense that it is reduced to its effect relative to our senses. The sensory surface is entirely subsidiary in our ordinary dealings with things where we hear, not auditory phenomena, but fan motors, planes overhead, voices, doors slamming, and the like. Third, the notion of formed matter does not apply primarily to things but to equipment. In the second book of Aristotle's *Physics,* where the form-matter relation is discussed, Aristotle begins his analysis by talking about equipment as the occasion for reaching the notions of form and matter.[49] Aristotle makes no distinction here between the making of a piece of equipment and the making of a work of art. So the form-matter distinction is itself too wide to deal with the thinghood of the work of art—and also too narrow for the notion of thing itself.

In developing his own approach, Heidegger views the thingly character of a thing as turning upon its belonging to the Earth.[50] Here *Earth* does not mean a chemical mass located in the solar system. Earth is rather the self-closing, purposeless bearer of things in our world, a bearer that is set in opposition to the openness of the world of a people. The conflict of World and Earth appears in the figure of the work of art and reveals the nature of equipment and things as such. Heidegger uses van Gogh's painting of a peasant's shoes as an example. The shoes are equipment used by a peasant woman. In their daily use they disappear from attention. This is what Heidegger means by the ready-to-hand character of equipment. When they are not in use, they are set aside in their ordinariness, perhaps to become simply present-at-hand, describable scientifically. But in the painting the belonging of the shoes to the world of the peasant woman and to the earth of her dwelling are manifest.[51] Van Gogh's mode of treatment brings that world to presence in a way that the objectivity of observation, whether through a casual glance at the shoes in the corner or through careful inspection, could never do. The latter modes yield facts, data; the former brings to presence, restores "being" to things.

Heidegger distinguishes in this respect the ready-to-hand, the present-at-hand, and the work of art. In *Being and Time* Heidegger talks about a hammer as that which fits into a context of operations in the world of the carpenter.[52] It is not simply its being at-hand as a thing that can be sensorily described which manifests it as hammer; it is its having a function, the context of which has to be already disclosed, which allows us to identify it specifically as a hammer—that is, a tool used primarily for pounding and extracting nails. One who has no knowledge of the world of the carpenter will only be able to describe the thing at hand without having access to what it is—like many primitive artifacts that are found in museums of fine art today. This parallels the scientific approach to organic bodies, which are alive with sensuous and rational life but which are treated in biology solely in terms of their sensorily descriptive properties. When we understand things we bring to them something more than their immediately verifiable properties. When we live with things, the functional context is disclosed.

It is the work of art that sets that functional context more deeply into the character of Earth and the character of World. In the work of art,

World is manifest as a world of inhabitance and Earth as native soil. Native soil is not something a chemist could ever analyze. Native soil is revealed by the peculiar sense of being at home that opens up when we inhabit it for some time. There is a kind of nostalgia experienced by remembering the smell of burning leaves in autumn up north back in the 1950s, linked to long walks, the chill in the air after early frost, raking leaves after school, and awaiting a supper of hot homemade soup with your family before getting down to homework and anticipating a well-deserved rest. Inhabitance of a world, a way of being, effects the sense of native soil. It is in the work of art that World and Earth are brought together focally.

Earth is "the unpurposed self-closer." Earth resists disclosure as a mystery of darkness for what we have come to call intellect. We describe its properties and break it apart to carry on the description. But that is always treating it in terms of its "for-us" (i.e., in terms of its relation to our senses). That makes possible what Owen Barfield describes as "dashboard knowledge," which allows us to manipulate the surface in order to get our desired responses, but which leaves hidden and forgotten the final depth of things.[53] In itself, Earth withdraws even as it juts up into the field of sensation. The claim that Earth is "unpurposed" suggests the elements that enter into the form of living things. Living things can be understood up to a point in terms of their telos. By contrast, Earth is simply there, in itself without a purpose, but capable of being taken up into the purposes of the living, prehuman as well as human. Earth is simply there in its supportive opacity. And even the things that are alive cannot be fully understood in terms of purpose. Heidegger likes to quote Angelus Silesius, who said: "The rose is without a why."[54] Why are there roses? Who knows? Furthermore, there is something unexplainable about the way in which earth displays itself in terms of sensory properties. Why should it be the case that having the kind of "meat" we do involves the disclosure of colors or sounds? Why should disclosure be tied up with "meat"? Earth itself, which enters into the rose and into the meat of our own bodies, is ultimately purposeless in itself.

In the work-being of the work not only is equipment manifest in its belonging to world and earth, but other things too are so manifest. The ordinary comes to take on an extraordinary character as we recognize it, so to speak, for the first time. The depth of meaning involved in belonging to a world of dwelling and the rich sensuousness involved in belonging to native soil meet in the coming to presence of a work of art. In the work of art, contrary to the character of equipment, the sensuous is not subsidiary, disappearing in its function; it enters into the focal character of significant presence.[55]

Heidegger highlights the feature of *polemos*, or struggle, brought about by the work of art, the aesthetic tension to which Augustine called attention. The work appears as a gestalt, a form that bears the tension between Earth and World. But here the tension between Earth and World involves the tension between a tendency to concealment and a tendency to unconcealment respectively, only Earth is the essentially concealed that rises up to partial manifestness in sensuousness, and World is the opening up of paths for thinking, acting, and feeling that contains the partial concealment of its own possibilities. World disclosure opens up a future whose actual texture and concrete disclosure of new possibilities is not revealed. The work of art as a form establishes that tension and thereby provides an aura of meaning, a measure of "world space" in which the everyday appears as extraordinary.[56]

In Heidegger's later work, Earth is absorbed into World as one of the regions that constitute the Fourfold of the World.[57] *Earth* again has to be understood here, not as a location in the solar system and not as a chemical mass, for these are abstractions from native soil, from the sensuousness of rhythm and melody that sound in our words, from the radiance of color, from our own lived embodiment. It is part and parcel of our speaking that it rises up from the sensuousness, the "earthiness" of language, not as that which we control with full deliberateness (we know how artificial "studied" style is), but as that which grows up in us. It is in the latter that Earth appears primordially as Earth. Language that rises up poetically from this Earth is foundational natural language, of which ordinary language is a sedimented resultant, and scientific and philosophic languages, flattened out abstractions. World that includes Earth so considered is a world for dwelling. That is why a scientific world is uninhabitable. That is why contemporary literature is filled with the experience of alienation. Insofar as the world we live in is increasingly and totalistically a technologically reconstructed world, it is not a world that brings us to ourselves. It is a world in which presences have become increasingly absent. Inhabitance shrivels through the priority of the work of the reflective *cogito*, that has forgotten the soil in which it is rooted.

Earth always interplays with the second region, Sky, as the open expanse that allows Earth to appear and that sets the measures for our time on earth, generating the days and the seasons. It encircles our lives and by its vastness gives us a sense of our smallness and our simultaneously belonging to that vastness, which animals could not notice. It is the region of Kantian awe: "the starry skies above."

Mortals are the third world region. We humans belong to the earth: we come from the earth and are made of the earth. The human (Latin *humanus*) is humus, earth as soil. Biblically, human beings are made from the slime of the earth, or from its clay. Earth in turn flowers forth in our speech and in our art. But we also return inevitably to earth. We are mortal. That, however, does not mean simply that each of us will one day fall apart, decaying into the earthly elements of which we are composed—though that is also correct. Much more basically, we humans are "the mortals"—those who live out of an awareness of having to die and are likewise distinguished as the ones who speak. Death and language belong together. One for whom the Whole is opened up through language is one who lives out of an awareness of the whole of its temporal span and thus out of an anticipation of the temporal termination of its being. Mortals are speakers, for whom therefore there is language, for whom the wholeness of their own being as stretched from birth to death is opened up by a rebound from both terms and becomes the echo chamber of the Whole.

Called out from Earth and living under the Sky, Mortals take the measure of their being from the Gods, the fourth world region. Gods here are to be taken as messengers of what is highest, sources of inspiration regarding those things that set the measure, the Sacred, the inviolable. As Mortals are linked to the Earth, so are Gods linked to the Sky, to that above us which measures us, which reveals what is most high, which encompasses us with its vastness. For Heidegger, the Gods are linked to the dimension of concealment manifest as such—as essentially concealed, by the Sky, which presents an essential unreachability. It is the domain of the hidden God.

World is, for Heidegger, the interplay of these four regions: Earth and Sky, Mortals and Immortals. The peculiar character of the interplay differs in different cultures, and indeed in different epochs within a culture. That is why manifestness is essentially historical. *Seinsgeschichte*, history of Being, is the essentially perspectival, essentially mutable, essentially temporal opening up of the Whole.[58] When the four regions play together in our silent listening, when we are not intent on mastery, but are open, meditatively, thankfully letting things be manifest, the poetic word arises. With this word things become significant presences, and with this play of things and word, world comes to hold sway.

What then is a thing? Thing is that which assembles the Fourfold and which is assembled by the Fourfold. The German for "thing," *Ding*, originally meant "assembly." Heidegger parallels that with the Greek term *logos*, especially as it appears in the fragments of the pre-Socratic philosopher Heraclitus. *Logos* as the gathering performed by the word is the origin of our term *logic* as the kind of gathering we call reasoning, but it is ever so much richer. Logic cultivates the sphere of what is opened up and is thus derivative of that which opens up a region. *Logos* is related to *legein*, which means to read but also to gather; it also applies to that which is read, namely the word. (*Logos* in the prologue to John's Gospel is translated as "Word.") According to Heidegger, for Heraclitus *logos* is primarily the gathering together of the Whole in things that occurs when the appropriate word arises.[59] That gathering together of the Whole, for which humanness *(Da-Sein)* furnishes the locus, is the opening out of a world for a people. In one of Heidegger's most difficult yet more compressed and revealing statements: "If we let the thing be present in its thinging from out of the worlding world, then we are thinking of the thing as thing."[60] The disclosure of thing and world is reciprocal. It is not something we do but something done to us: things "thing" us by "thinging" (i.e., gathering a world); world "worlds" by holding us and things together, presenting things in a way that has us in its grip. The play of thing and world in the clearing granted to *Da-Sein* comes to pass in and through the poetic word. And such a word stands at the origin of every work of art.

Art, in revealing the fundamental character of the thing as an assembling of the whole for dwelling, leads us back from the abstract one-sidedness of science, the all-sided abstractness of philosophy, and the partiality of all our particular interests to the wholeness of meaning. Art brings us from our various modes of absence and imposition to the presencing of the Whole in the sensuously present. It teaches us to "let things be"; it speaks directly to the heart, the center of thought, action, and feeling; it teaches us meditative rather than simply calculative and representative thinking. It brings us back to the ground of metaphysics: it articulates our sense of Being as the whole within which we come to find our own wholeness.

## Philosophy, Science, Art, and the Lifeworld

I will draw together many of the themes I have articulated, expand some of them, and bring them closer to us by considering six ways of life focused throughout Heidegger's work.[61] This will highlight what being-in-the-world involves as the ground of metaphysics and will bring to light the central role of the artist-poet, reinvoking Plato's battle between philosophy and poetry for primacy in articulating the lifeworld. For Heidegger philosophy does not stand above poetry, as it does for Plato; rather philosopher and poet "occupy twin peaks equidistant from the valley" of everyday life.[62] I will call these ways of life that of the peasant, the artist-poet, the philosopher, the scientist, the man on the street, and the thinker. The peasant and the contemporary man on the street exhibit ways of life that have to be constructed out of Heidegger's concerns, but they throw light on the other ways of life. They help illuminate what being-in-the-world entails. The first two ways, that of the peasant and that of the artist-poet, the latter furnishing the framework of meaning for the former, antedate the emergence of philosophy as a design on the Whole and continue as possible ways thereafter. The way of the scientist as specialist follows the emergence of philosophy and that of the contemporary man on the street follows from the technological impact of science on society as a whole. The way of the thinker is poised somewhat ambiguously between philosophy and poetry. The peasant, the artist-poet, and the thinker operate in the medium of the lifeworld and thus fall on the side of poetry in the historic battle between philosophy and poetry. The philosopher, the scientist, and even the man on the street suffer from a certain abstraction from the full medium of experience. I will treat them in what is, for the most part, a kind of chronological order and conclude with some comparisons between them.

*The Peasant.* I use the term *peasant* to refer to those like Heidegger's Schwarzwald neighbors, for whom he exhibits the greatest respect. The peasant world is the world of Heidegger's own origins and the chosen milieu within which he primarily thought. So respectful was he of those who dwelt in this world that he asked and followed the advice of one old farm neighbor when he received a call to come to teach in Berlin in the early days of the Nazi regime.[63] The peasant represents a mode of being-in-the-world largely untouched by philosophy, science, and modern technology, but not by poetry in the large sense of the term.

The peasant (German *Bauer*) lives in an order of building *(bauen)*—that is, both cultivating and constructing—for the sake dwelling or inhabiting (becoming habituated to and familiar with) his world. At his best, he treasures things through thinking meditatively (i.e., recollectively, appreciatively). He learns to let things be present, making their claim upon him.[64] He is engaged in his daily tasks, where things appear in equipmental contexts.[65]

Undertaking those tasks, he dwells on the earth as his native soil, under the sky. He allows the alternation of night and day and the cycles of the seasons to govern his life. He entrusts his crops and cattle to the earth and cultivates them.[66] He has a place in his home for a reminder of death: the *Totenbaum,* the niche awaiting the corpse of the next family member to die.[67] There is also a place near the common table: the *Herrgottswinkel,* the Lord God's corner, surmounted by a crucifix.[68] The peasant heeds the announcements of the Most High, the inspirations that give him fundamental orientation in life, mediated by his own religious tradition.[69] He walks over the bridge that blends into the banks and is surmounted by a statue of a saint, a bridge that becomes a living image of his own transition from mortal to immortal shores.[70] He respects the ways passed down to him from ancestral times into which he initiates his own children.

Solitude is an essential part of this life. It affords the power of "projecting our whole existence into the vast uncommonness of the presence of all things."[71] The *Bauer* lives out a sense of the environing Mystery, from which everything arises into his field of awareness.[72] One who dwells thoughtfully in this element knows how "to receive the blessing of the earth and to become at home in the law of this reception in order to shepherd the mystery of Being and watch over the inviolability of the possible."[73] He comes to know the ancient *phusis* as "the arising and receding of all that is present in its presencing and absencing."[74] He gathers things into his heart in respectful repose.

The key notion here is the heart, the old Anglo-Saxon word for the thinking of which is *thanc.*[75] It is not a merely emotional but an essentially dispositional notion. It is the region of our basic stance toward what is, inclining us habitually to attend and act in certain directions. It is tied essentially to gratitude, to appreciation, to thankfulness. It treasures past blessings and hence is essentially linked to memory. Memory, in turn, is originally tied to the holy and the gracious, the inviolable which grants the poetic inspiration.

Heidegger refers to the characteristic activity of the heart so conceived as *das andenkendes Denken,* thinking that recalls, or meditative thinking.[76] Such recollective thinking is the supreme thanks. It evokes devotion.[77] Recollection and devotion, turned in gratitude toward what has been granted and devoted to acting in accordance with it, gathers time together and in so doing deepens present being by providing it with the ultimate lived context of the Mystery. Since it rests on the structure of *Dasein* as relation to the Whole, such thinking reaches out most fully to the outermost limits as well as to the most inward—that is, it develops a sense of the encompassing whole of what is, while simultaneously reaching inward to what is deepest in *Dasein*.[78]

Meditative thinking is not given to abstraction and logical arrangement. It thinks in the medium of the lifeworld, in the mode of dwelling, of inhabitance. Such meditative dwelling is a mode of thinking that belongs to humankind as such and is distinguished from the modes of thinking characteristic of specially talented types: mathematicians, scientists, philosophers, theologians.[79] Heidegger attests that his own philosophic work "belongs right in the midst of the peasants' work," rooted in the Alemannian-Swabian soil.[80] So much is that the case that he reported in a letter to Gadamer that the *Kehre*, the turn in his thought from *Dasein* to Being, "came to me in a rush"—*Ereignis*-like, event-like—as he returned home to Freiburg and the Black Forest and began "to feel the energy of his old stomping ground."[81] We should take that claim with the utmost seriousness.

Among contemporary intellectuals, it is precisely this that has been the object of resistance, even ridicule. Heidegger's background and chosen milieu incline him toward what is regarded as the closed society of the peasant, an anti-intellectual society, suspicious of strangers, resistant to the other, the outsider, opposed to the city, to democracy, debate, compromise, to technological and scientific advance, the components of the chosen milieu of modern intellectuals. What surfaces here is an essential tension between freedom and *pietas*, reflected respectively in modern society and its intellectual apologists on the one hand and, on the other, in Heidegger's peasant society and the apologetic ingredient in his own thought. *Denken als Danken* (thinking as thanking) is the reinvocation of ancient *pietas*, given expression in Aristotle, in Cicero, and in Aquinas,[82] as an attitude of gratitude for gifts that is rooted in a sense of an indebtedness that cannot be repaid, for the gift provided is the whole context of one's life. *Pietas*, exercised toward one's family, toward the tradition, and toward God, involves the recognition of the origin of all of one's real possibilities: the family brings one into being and provides (expressed in Greek) one's *charakter*, one's fundamental stamp, mediating the ways of one's community, which afford the concrete possibilities for any effective action, suffused with a sense that the whole context—one's own being included—is provided by the divine. Modern freedom had to fight an uphill battle against such *pietas*, which tended quite naturally to hold one in thrall to the given economic-social-political order.

Hegel's work may be viewed as an attempt to establish ancient *pietas* within modern civil society based on individual freedom of inquiry and operation.[83] Heidegger's work—at least at a fundamental level—reinvokes such *pietas* against the civil society of his contemporary critics. And it is in the element of *pietas* that poetry especially operates.[84]

*The Artist-Poet.* Even living in the way described, the peasant, like everyone, falls into a mode of everydayness, into the "they," the anonymous "one."[85] Mystery tends to disappear. Routine and surface come to dominate as things become flattened out. It is the artist, and especially the poet, who provides what Heidegger refers to as a "world space" in which the mysterious depth of the thing announces itself as emerging from and as sheltered within that which encompasses everything.[86] Indeed, the peasant moves in a world opened up by the creative ones, basically the poets and the founders.[87] One should think here of the role the biblical authors play in providing for the West the ultimate framework and feeling for the world. In the light of the poetically achieved world space everything is taken out of the commonplace; in Heidegger's terms, it receives its "being."[88]

The artist-poet struggles with everyday appearance, fights the battle between World and Earth, establishes figure in the rift between the two, and thus opens up the "inwardness of things."[89] In the 1930s especially, the *polemos* of Heraclitus tends to take center stage: struggle, battle, the praise of the strong.[90] But it is not the physical strength exhibited in overpowering others that is involved here; it is the spiritual strength to win back a sense of the depth that surrounds us from the tendency toward superficiality in everyday appearance. The struggle is essentially with such a fallen appearance for the sake of "being" as depth and as encompassing in relation to the everyday surface.[91]

Humans learn to dwell when they stand in the play of the fourfold of Earth and Sky, Mortals and Immortals. It is the poets who initiate that dwelling. Through them we learn to liberate the Earth from domination; welcome the Sky, which guides the seasons; hold ourselves ready for the announcements of the Immortals; and lead other Mortals toward their authentic death.[92] Things *are* in Heidegger's sense, they have their being, they appear charged with significance, as they gather a world of inhabitance. In so doing they "thing" us—they lay hold of us and gather us together insofar as we are available to "let them be." Things are not simply passive to our projects; they can also take hold of us, absorb us, magnetize our attention. And they can so "thing" us insofar as world "worlds" (i.e., insofar as an encompassing way of thinking, acting, and feeling has us in its grip), for things appear meaningfully present as they stand in webs of meaning relations that ultimately stretch to the Whole. It is paradigmatically in art that things come to "thing" us and world comes to "world" us.[93]

The artist as shaper of materials—of sound, of paint, and of glass, of stone and wood, clay and bronze—depends on the most primordial of artists, the poet, who gives shape to language, which opens up the Whole. Language gives expression to the *Logos* which gathers a community over time as it gathers together the coming to presence of the Whole for the community.[94] Poetry creates the primary music that sets linguistic meaning upon the earth of sonority. Within the space of its meanings all other art forms come into being.[95]

Art in general operates in the same medium of meditative dwelling charactertistic of the peasant, who takes things to heart, who is thoughtful. *Mnemosune*, memory as devotion, is the mother of the Muses, but also the daughter of Sky and Earth.[96] Thinking that recalls is the origin of poetry.[97] It proclaims the Holy, which, for Heidegger, is ancillary to consideration of the divine. The Holy, announced by the poet, is a dimension of encompassment and demand that calls for devotion. Only in letting things be—devotedly, thoughtfully—can the true sense of the divine dawn.[98] Great art occasions such thinking for a community. Great art is grateful letting be.

The dialogue that Heidegger conducts between thinking and poetry focuses on the nature of language. Language is the element in which we live, the relation of all relations, the openness in which everything appears.[99] As Heidegger sees it, in a reversal of what one might have thought, everyday language itself is flattened-out poetry.[100] We tend to see things differently because we live off an inheritance of the view of language that goes back at least to Aristotle, according to which language is an instrument we use to express previously complete thoughts.[101] Poetry would then be a kind of ornamentally embellished ordinary language. But for Heidegger, following a line of thought that appeared earlier in Heraclitus's notion of the logos, it is language that first addresses us.[102] And the vehicle of that primordial address is the poet who hears that logos. The poet gains entrance into the relation of word and thing.[103] The Aristotelian view is correlated with the view of truth as *orthotes*, whereas the poet opens up truth as *aletheia*. In the "needy time" wherein we live, a time of the flight of the gods, several poets—in particular Friedrich Hölderlin and Stefan George—turned to the nature of language.[104]

Heidegger spends a good bit of time in two different pieces meditating on the final line of George's poem "The Word": "Where word breaks off, no thing can be."[105] Poetry allows the thing to *be*—that is, to emerge into appearance *(bhu-)*, to come alive *(es)*, to enter into a world of dwelling *(wesan)*.[106] Reflecting these Sanskrit roots of the Indo-European conjugations of the forms of the verb *to be* (German *bin, ist, wesen;* English *been, is, were*), Heidegger's apparently idiosyncratic usage squares with those sedimented meanings long since forgotten in the common notion of being as being-outside-nothing—for Nietzsche, "the last trailing cloud of evaporating reality." It also parallels George's peculiar usage in the passage cited. The poetic word permits the thing to enter into a world of human dwelling. And dwelling is entering into the play of the Fourfold.[107]

The thinker, Heidegger says, thinks Being, whereas the poet names the holy. But the George passage seems to suggest that it is the poet who names Being. In the *Letter on Humanism*, Heidegger sets up a kind of order: thinking of Being is a prelude to thinking the holy, which, in turn, opens up the divine; this then allows us to think what God might be.[108] So we have what Heidegger would call "a calculative ordering": Being, the holy, the divine, God. To the thinker he assigns the task of bringing about a relation to the first, beyond the region of things and their principles dominating Western philosophy and science. To the poet he assigns the proclaiming of the holy. He plays on terms for wholeness, the healthy, the hale, healing, linked to *das Heilige*, especially in Rilke. The divine is the region of the immortals, the messengers of the Most High. In George, word breaks off when it returns us to the soundlessness of the pealing of silence, wherein healing occurs.[109]

As the art of language, poetry creates the context for all the arts. For Sophocles' *Antigone* chorus, the human being is the strangest *(deinotaton)* of all the creatures on earth, who creates cities and ways, but is essentially without city or way.[110] For Georg Trakl, the poet is called apart so that the stranger finds a home on the earth.[111] Every poet speaks out of a single center that remains unsaid.[112] Trakl's center, according to Heidegger, is the notion of *Abgeschiedenheit*, that apartness of the poet from the everyday that makes possible the creation of a home on earth.[113] Such being-at-home involves a sense of nearness (neighborliness). At its most authentic, neighborliness happens through the poet preserving farness in a creative tension between opposites that gives a depth to our experience.[114] We must distinguish modes of nearness and farness: (1) at the personal level, certain persons and projects are "near and dear to my heart"; (2) as an abstraction out of that comes the measurable nearness and distance of the sciences; and (3) at the root of both is the way the whole appears as measure of the near and dear. At the latter level we have the coincidence of nearness and distance in the mystery of encompassment involved in being, awareness, language, history, nature. Poetry gives expression to our relation to the mystery.

Though poetry is rooted in *mnemosune*, it is yet attentive to destiny, which comes from the future.[115] As we already noted, in ancient mythology, *mnemosune*, in turn, is the daughter of earth and sky. For Hölderlin, as a student of classical Greece, earth and sky form the site of the wedding feast of gods and men to establish the fourfold.[116] The play of the Fourfold, which brings things to presence, is set in the relation between past and future. As we noted before, for Heidegger the past comes to us from the future.[117] In "authentic" existence, the relation between the three temporal dimensions is tensed: the present takes on depth when the emergence of a project allows us to take over the past as the history that leads to the project. The fully tensed relation to time provides a sense of destiny, a kind of vocational awareness, a sense of a life project to be achieved. But this occurs in such a way that one is not simply looking past the present and thus is unable to tarry with things. On the contrary, the deepest tarrying with the present occurs through the activation of the other two temporal dimensions, with the priority of the future as vocation.[118] This frees us from an irresponsible aestheticism. The poet who becomes the vehicle for this sense of destiny is thus no dandy tarrying at the fringes of a culture but is rather one who establishes its basic sense of being.[119]

In a needy time, to be a poet is to attend, singing, to the traces of the fugitive gods.[120] The poet attends to the holy, which forms the basis or provides the element for the epiphany of the divine or the Immortals as messengers of the Most High, or of God Himself. Is the holy then the togetherness of the Fourfold? But in relation to humanness, Being precedes the Holy. Thinking of Being does not operate as song. It is song that would establish relation to the Earth. The medium of poetry and of the arts in general is sensuousness, belonging to the Earth. Earth flowers from the mouth of the poet (Hölderlin). Song is that flowering as the celebration of existence.[121] Singing and thinking are twin stems in the neighborhood of poetry.[122]

Rilke adds another dimension that runs along the lines of Heidegger's central preoccupation. Rilke's central image of the "globe of being" as the integral totality of things is parallel to Parmenides' thinking of Being. Rilke distinguished the center of this globe as encompassing, other than all objectification, and corresponding to the heart, the inner dimension of human dwelling. In such dwelling pain, love, and death belong together. Loss of the center involves a fracturing and a loss of that belonging together. Afflicted by care because of death and pain, we create security for ourselves through objectification; yet we are thereby removed from the center, the boundless and open, which is beyond all security. An eye on the integral Whole may allow for a transcendence of technology through formative power.[123] Heidegger's observations on technology have one of their roots in his dialogue with Rilke. Generally, in the later Heidegger the poets become his chief interlocutors, for he attempted to find the way back to the ground of the metaphysical tradition, which opened modern science and thus contemporary technology. That ground lies in the sense of Being corresponding to our mode of dwelling, whose center lies in the heart. It is the formation of the heart that is the task of the arts in general, but of poetry in particular.

*The Philosopher.* Philosophy is a distinctively Greek phenomenon. For Heidegger, as for Hegel, there is no non-Western philosophy but only a certain family resemblance to philosophy *stricto sensu*.[124] Philosophy emerges in the West in the train of Anaximander, Parmenides, and Heraclitus, who were primordial thinkers and not yet philosophers—indeed, at least for the Heidegger of 1951, they were too great to be philosophers.[125]

Philosophy has what we might call its proto-origin in a poetic-intellectual experience of Being in Heraclitus and Parmenides as emerging into presence, which they termed *phusis*, whose stems stress emergence *(phuo)* and manifestness *(phainomai)*.[126] Plato and Aristotle focus on the "what" in what emerges into presence, but the coming to presence is itself unfocused.[127] The "what" is idea or *eidos*, the intelligible look, the face things present to intellectual looking, the ever-Now, always already there, perpetually standing intelligible.[128] Here we see what Dominique Janicaud has described as "the transition in metaphysics from Being-present to Being-essential."[129] The distinction between Being so conceived and beings who appear as its instances still occupies, in Heidegger's view, the level of beings *(Seienden,* as things and principles) and does not rise to the level of Being *(Sein)* as that which grants the distinction.

However, in his reading of Plato and Aristotle, Heidegger claims that for them, as the first philosophers, philosophy still plants its roots in awe; it feeds on astonishment before the mystery of the Whole and grows in such astonishment as it carries on its essential questioning.[130] It is led to ask about the most fundamental things, to unsettle all the settled so as to get to the roots of things. Like art, philosophy too creates so much world space that in its light even the ordinary appears extraordinary.

But just as in art what comes to be is subjectible to the everydayness that flattens out all appearance, so also with philosophy. The astonishment allied with the peculiar coming to presence of that which is given for thought disappears and one falls into argumentation and construction far removed from fundamental awe. The passing on of problems within a given horizon fails to think the unconcealed horizon in relation to the concealed encompassing out of which it comes. Philosophic problems are subject to what Heidegger—perhaps thinking originally of the Sophists, but not only of them—calls "the cheap acid of a merely logical intelligence."[131]

The history of philosophy, precisely as metaphysics, becomes the history of the forgottenness of Being as mysterious encompassment coming to presence in what it grants for thought. But though there is a reigning forgetfulness from the very inception of philosophy as metaphysics, nonetheless, metaphysics is not false or wrong.[132] But unless it is led back to its own ground, what is essential to *Dasein* is lost. And that entails a relation of philosophy, through thinking its ground, to the arts.

*The Scientist.* For Heidegger science operates in the conceptual space opened up by philosophy.[133] Scientific thinking is derived from philosophy.[134] But the development of the sciences is their separation from and completion of philosophy.[135] Science always and necessarily operates on the basis of what is manifest in the lifeworld, but only insofar as that has been transformed by conceptual transcription. After distinctions have been conceptually inventoried, specializations can be cultivated that are no longer concerned with their origins or their relations with one another. Just as one can operate within the functional circle of the everyday world, unaware that, as Kierkegaard put it, "we float on waters 70,000 fathoms deep," so in science we can master cybernetic functions without ontological meaning, without questioning the framework of manifestness within which science itself occurs.[136]

Scientific specializations emerge in the wake of Plato and Aristotle.[137] But distinctively modern science emerges through a distinctive projection of the ground plan of nature that sets it in decisive contrast to the Aristotelian view, which it supplanted. For Heidegger, this is not necessarily a progression *tout court*—although there is clearly a progressive manifestation of features of nature under the modern paradigm. What holds sway in modern science is the essence of technology, a view made thematic in Nietzsche, for whom being itself is will-to-power.[138] Nature is made over into what it has to be in order to be progressively controlled, assimilated into our projects. In the Galilean-Newtonian view, there are no longer natures seeking to actualize their forms; there is only Nature, a single system of colorless, odorless, tasteless, soundless, valueless, irreducible elements located in an empty container space and, simultaneously, in a flowing, riverlike time, combining and separating according to invariant laws.[139] As a consequence, from the point of view of science, natures can thus no longer be violated. Aristotelian natures, substantial forms each seeking their respective *teloi* are considered mere phenomenal appearances of what has been called the dance of the atoms. And learning how they dance without us enables us to becomes conductors of the dance. In this way, for Heidegger, things lose their "being" and become data.[140] But for Heidegger also, this was already prepared for when Plato thought the Being of beings as intelligible looks that were archetypes for divine production.[141]

In the first emergence of modern science, we have the age of the world picture: Nature is the in-principle viewable. But then, with twentieth-century physics, nature disappears into the objectlessness of standing reserve: *Gegenstand* becomes *Bestand*, standing-over-against becomes standing-at-hand.[142] In contrast with Nature for the peasant, modern Nature is placed under demand, no longer entrusted with sustaining us and our works. Standing within Nature, attuned to its essential rhythms and fitting human projects within it, the peasant is disposed by a basic *pietas* for the Nature God or the gods have provided. In contrast, in the modern disposition, humanness stands over against Nature, which it summons to appear in such a way as to provide maximum yield for humanity's projects: Nature is a field for the operation of unbounded human freedom. Rather than the shepherd of Being, modern man seeks to become the lord and master of Nature.[143] Held in the grips of the scientific-technological way of viewing, we allow no other view of Nature to stand. People look to science to decide on the place of human being in the Whole and to set the standards for human decision.[144] Much is revealed, but what is concealed is revealing itself, and thus *Dasein*, as the locus of manifestness.[145]

Though a scientist may, as a reflective person, shift into the philosophic mode, science does not, as science—indeed, cannot as science—think its own presuppositions, its own rootedness in the structure of *Dasein;* hence science is in the dark regarding its own nature.[146] In Heidegger's not too rhetorically wise way of putting it: "Science does not think."[147] Its thoughtlessness regarding its own encompassment is rooted in its essential one-sidedness.[148] And the great danger that attends this movement is that *Dasein* itself will disappear into the standing reserve: human beings will themselves become simply on hand for the projects of some Overman.[149]

*The Man on the Street.* Human reality as *Dasein* is thrown being-in-the-world, on account of which we are always inauthentic in the sense of not being fully self-possessed, being in the grip of a world articulated long before we entered on the scene.[150] But there is a massive difference between the world of the peasant and the world of the contemporary man on the street. The inauthenticity of the peasant was still the expression of a world that had a place for the essential things he could thinkingly take to heart. An essential part of his world was the heeding of the poets—again, consider here the biblical authors.

The contemporary man on the street is held in the grip of the same mode of revealing characteristic of modern science as its technological essence has come to clearer focus. Scientific technology holds sway; and for it there is no longer any room for that which falls outside the scope of its methods, for action not guided by its attitude of dominance, hence for the Holy, which places its demands on us.

In lines reminiscent of Nietzsche's about the last man,[151] Heidegger speaks of the devastation of the earth as the condition for a guaranteed high standard of living and happiness for all, leading to the "high-velocity expulsion of Mnemosyne,"[152] of meditative thinking, of thoughtful recollection attuned to the Holy. For Heidegger we live in a time of "the darkening of the world, the flight of the gods, the destruction of the earth, the transformation of men into a mass, the hatred and suspicion of everything free and creative."[153] The sense of history vanishes (one recalls Henry Ford's famous remark: "History is bunk!") and the boxer (or today the multimillion-dollar athlete) is hero. Devotees of speed and of time-saving devices, we seem to have no time.[154] If we think of the Whole at all, we think of it in scientific-technological terms. The arts are pleasant diversion, entertainment, prettification—not manifestations of the fundamental. The Holy, which great art proclaims, has disappeared from our purview. For Heidegger "perhaps what is distinctive about this world-epoch consists in the closure of the dimension of the hale [*das Heiligen*]."[155]

Modern humanity is essentially homeless.[156] It has lost the element in which *Dasein* by nature lives. Even the contemporary farmer no longer lives in Nature as the ever-environing, nurturing Whole, unencompassable by science. Technology in the form of radio and television invades his silence and prevents his meditative thought.[157] Language as simultaneously the home of Being and the dwelling place of humankind degenerates into an instrument for communicative purposes[158] and further into "a mere container for their sundry preoccupations."[159] Without the sense of Being, humankind is like a fish out of water.[160]

*The Thinker.* Given what Heidegger understands by thinking, logic is not, as logicians claim, the requisite thinking on thinking.[161] In fact, if we cannot think beyond logic, we are left with the previously designated "cheap acid of a merely logical intelligence." And science does not "think." Both science and logic cultivate a domain already open. Thinking is concerned with coming back reflectively upon that opening.

Heidegger regularly refers to philosophers as thinkers, in contrast to scientists, who are said not to think insofar as philosophy deals with the frameworks presupposed by science. Socrates, for example, is the purest thinker of the West,[162] and Nietzsche is a great thinker.[163] Aristotle, Plato, and Kant are thinkers.[164] Presumably philosophy has to do with conceptual elaboration, construction, and argumentation as a means of working out that thought. But Heidegger also distinguishes philosophy, which is in essence metaphysics, from thinking, which concerns the ground of metaphysics and thus enters into proximity with the element in which the arts live.[165] As we have noted earlier, for Heidegger, Heraclitus and Parmenides were thinkers but were of too great stature to be philosophers. Here, from Socrates to Nietzsche, something essential loses focus. Metaphysics is the ultimate conceptual framework presupposed in all our dealings, scientific and otherwise; but its practitioners do not think that which it itself presupposes, the way Being itself comes to presence. Metaphysics thus contributes to the forgottenness of Being—indeed, because it is considered the most fundamental form of thought, it is the major culprit in the occlusion of Being that holds sway in Western philosophy and science.[166]

Because philosophy, observing and inferring, operates from out of the perspectives granted in each case but does not think the granting, the history of philosophy calls for a "destruction,"[167] a dismantling *(Abbau)* of "representations that have become banal and vacuous,"[168] a desedimentation that leads back to the ground of original givenness, originary coming to presence. This allows one to stake out the positive possibilities of the tradition. Such a process involves an overcoming *(Überwindung)* of metaphysics. Heidegger insists that the destruction or overcoming of the history of metaphysics is not its elimination because metaphysics is not false or wrong.[169] He later admitted that the term *destruction* had lent itself to a misunderstanding "of insuperable grotesqueness."[170] He rejects as superficial an interpretation that would, as Janicaud puts it, "consist in setting oneself against metaphysics, in rejecting it as an opinion, or else in dismissing it as a discipline now obsolete. Metaphysics is less overcome than assigned to limits."[171] In fact, for Heidegger metaphysics belongs to the nature of humanness—presumably, like science, available in principle to any fully capable human.[172] "Even overcome, metaphysics does not disappear. It returns in another form and maintains its supremacy."[173] As Joan Stambaugh observes, "overcoming" metaphysics signifies not elimination but incorporation.[174] Heidegger says that what is involved is "neither a destruction nor even a denial of metaphysics. To intend anything else would be childish presumption and a demeaning of history."[175] In this sense, overcoming is related to authenticity, in which, instead of taking for granted and going along, we each appropriate and thus take radical responsibility for the "inauthentic," which is our irremovable ground as the prior genetic and cultural shaping we have and must have received. According to Jean-François Mattéi, deconstruction is "the *return* toward the original site of metaphysics in order to appropriate it within its own limits and to prepare a new beginning."[176] Thought climbs back down from metaphysical abstraction into the nearness of the near.[177]

Furthermore, in Heidegger's view, each philosophy, which is at base metaphysics, is inexhaustible. "Overcoming" metaphysics is transforming it by replanting it in the soil in which it originated, the soil of fundamental awe.[178] But this requires a loosening up of the soil. In what does this loosening up consist? Heidegger uses another metaphor here: it involves attempting to "get into the draft," which draws the thinker, guiding him in his conceptual articulations.[179] Concepts have to be brought back to their origins in the lifeworld. Rootless elaboration of problems that follow from previous formulations, argumentation of positions pro and con, construction of explanations, elaboration of systematic connections: all this philosophic work has to be led back to its origins, not simply in specialized experiences, but in the encompassing field of the lifeworld, which, above all, includes our orientation toward the Whole.[180]

We accomplish this leading back by thinking the unthought, presumably the lifeworld payoff, the deepening of the sense of real presences, for thinking takes place in the medium of the lifeworld,[181] as Heidegger identifies the locus of his own thinking in the lifeworld of the Swabian peasant. In leading the conceptual apparatus back to the lifeworld, we see that, primordially considered, philosophy is lived correspondence with the Being of beings.[182] But then, without some form of such correspondence, we would not be able to speak: the Whole has to be opened up in a certain way through language. However, for Heidegger, philosophy—adequately understood—is *fulfilled* correspondence.[183] Presumably, in maintaining some distinction between philosophy and primordial thinking, the fulfilled correspondence is not simply the demonstrable circle of concepts, but the experiential filling of that circle, the rising up and return of conceptualization to the sense of holistic attunement to the Whole, revealed and concealed in and through the peculiarity of a given philosophic circle of concepts.[184]

The thinker's task is to make clear the perspectives we occupy in relation to the encompassing mystery. In so doing he operates within the element thematized by the artist-poet but also implicitly constituting the lifeworld of the peasant. Thinking, Heidegger says, is "memory, devotion and thanks," features that characterized the meditative taking to heart of his peasant friends.[185] "Thinking" operates prethematically in the peasant, the artist-poet, and even in the philosopher. But it is not attended to explicitly in any of them. That is the task for what Heidegger comes to call, paradigmatically, the thinker. He is ultimately "the shepherd of being,"[186] one who cares for the presencing in what is present. Heidegger uses another metaphor: he is the one who "works at building the house of Being," the house that is language.[187] He builds linguistically by setting language into the element in which it lives.[188]

In this regard, Heidegger's understanding of Parmenides is central. He focuses particularly on two Parmenidean dicta: *to gar auto estin noein te kai einai,* usually translated as, "Thought and being are one";[189] and *chre to legein te noein to eon emmenai,* often rendered as, "One should both say and think that being is."[190] Thought in its primordial sense is the place where the sense of the Whole opens up. It *is* this opening up. Early Heidegger calls this place *Dasein,* human reality as the "there" of the dawning of the meaning of Being *(Sein).* The thought of Being is the being-taken by that meaning, being attuned to it, living in it. *Noein,* thinking, is taking to heart, which is letting be; nous is the *thanc.*[191] Taking-to-heart allows the presence of what is present to make its claim.[192] "Apprehension [*noein*] is the happening which has man."[193] Taking to heart presupposes the gathering *(legein)* performed by language that lets things be present in the way they are present. Linguistically mediated manifestness precedes taking to heart as letting lie before. But it also follows as safeguarding in the gathering of what is taken to heart.[194] The two together, *legein* and *noein,* rooted in language and the heart, show what thinking is.[195] Letting-lie-before corresponds to the theoretical moment, but taking-to-heart fulfills our belonging to Being. Philosophy and its development in the special sciences is aimed at conquest, possession. Philosophy as fulfilled attunement to Being sets the conceptually elaborated within the framework of fundamental awe attuned to the encompassing mystery, out of which all that comes to presence comes to presence. It is finally a mode of letting be, which is a mode of being possessed.[196]

Contrary to what it might seem from very much that Heidegger says and from much that his readers draw from him, he is not calling for a repudiation of technology, of science, or of metaphysics.[197] They are part of the history of what has been granted to us. What is needed is a "friend of the house of Being" who, as he says, "in equal manner and with equal force is inclined toward both the technologically constructed world-edifice *and* the world as a house for a more original dwelling," one who is able "to re-entrust the calculability and technicity of nature to the open mystery of a newly experienced naturalness of nature."[198]

*Conclusion.* The thinker, the artist-poet, and the peasant operate out of meditative thinking. Each has a peculiar sense of the environing mystery to which we essentially belong—belong, that is, as called upon to be aware of it and to listen for the essential claims it makes on us. But each operates with a different vehicle: the thinker operates negatively in the sphere of concepts, loosening them to get a sense of the unsaid draft that draws on the philosopher; the artist-poet operates in the medium of what is most immediately insistent in the lifeworld, sensory manifestness, within the context of a lived sense of the Whole. The artist-poet, by bringing sensuousness, earthiness to focal presence, works to win back the sense of the whole and thus the depth of each least thing from the flattening out that tends to constitute everyday appearance. The paradigmatic peasant occupies the sphere of everyday experience pervaded by tasks but knows the nearness of the environing mystery, which he takes to heart. Peasant, artist-poet, and thinker—they are all friends of the simple who have experienced its quiet force.

In a sense counterpoised to these are the philosopher, the scientist, and the contemporary man on the street. The former operates constructively in the sphere of the concept, feeding off fundamental generative intuitions that produce encompassing frameworks. The modern scientist operates as a specialist out of a peculiar, more encompassing framework that transforms Nature into what it has to be in order for us to manipulate it. The contemporary man on the street is the recipient of the scientific-technological framework, which tends to drive out of consideration other modes of revealing. The latter two types—scientist and man on the street—are in principle, insofar as they think exclusively in the dominant framework, alienated from the element proper to humankind, the element of meditative thinking. The philosopher seems to be a transitional figure. He thinks in terms of the presuppositions of science and the lifeworld, but he fails to think the mystery in the element proper to it because he is dominated by the thought of Being as standing Now. Insofar as he is an essential thinker, he is sustained by fundamental awe and lives in a deepened presence of the Whole appearing in all things; but apparently, qua philosopher, he does not *think* that off which he lives. In attending questioningly to the ground of metaphysics, Heidegger has performed an essential service: in the words of Janicaud, he "has altered the light in which the landscape was bathed."[199]

Getting back behind what holds sway in Western thought from its inception leads to the possibility of a second beginning. It leads into the element in which the arts operate. It could provide, in the darkened era in which we now live, the "saving grace," for the reinvoking of a lifeworld, like the lifeworld of the peasant, which has a place for the Holy. However, such a reinvocation can occur only in relation to the context of scientific-technological orientation, which is the dominant mode of revealing granted to us today. In the element of the lifeworld we can relearn how to correspond to the mystery that surrounds us. In this element we can learn a mode of thinking other than the representative-calculative mode that currently dominates us. We can learn again meditatively taking to heart. And in this task the arts and thinking on the arts take the lead.

## Response

Heidegger has provided much of the orientation that guides this text. In particular, the distinction between two modes of thinking, representative-calculative and meditative—and, correspondingly, the distinction between the intellect and the heart—has been pivotal. These parallel sets of distinctions are crucial in approaching the different roles in human life of the sciences (taken in a broad sense that includes philosophy) and the arts.

Representation *(Vorstellung)* abstracts from our coimplication with things and persons, from our participative presence, where we find ourselves involved with what is other than ourselves; it places them before our minds *(vor-stellen)*, at a distance; it re-presents them. Even in the presence of things, it abstracts from their presencing, the way they lay hold of us. Such representation makes calculation possible. In the broad sense Heidegger uses the term, calculation involves the ordering of things, placing them in frameworks, outlines, schemata. Mathematical calculation is only one form of calculative thinking in this sense. What is crucial is the underlying stance involved in these two aspects of what we have come to call the work of intellect. Based on abstraction from the claim beings have on us in our total life situation, in the *Lebenswelt*, we are enabled to arrange things to suit our projects, theoretical or practical. In its extreme form, representative-calculative thinking creates the *Gestell*, the enframing that turns all beings, not only into objects *(Gegen-stände)* set over against us in function of our abstract representations, which allow them to appear in a certain manner, but (more radically, though along the same lines) such thinking turns things and persons into a reservoir of resources *(Bestand)* for our technological transformation along whatever lines we will. This is the situation in which we now find ourselves, the world we inhabit or the world that is uninhabitable, the mode of manifestation that has us thoughtlessly in its grip.

Meditative thinking *(das andenkendes Denken)* is thinking which returns us to where we already are, to the lifeworld, to our co-implication with things and persons, to participative presencing. Meditative thinking learns, not to master calculatively, but to let persons and things be present. It learns to let them draw near, lay hold of us ever more deeply. Meditative thinking "treasures things in the heart"; it is essentially appreciative thinking, thinking as thanking. It is attuned to our essential giftedness, our having been granted what and who we are and thus our place among things. Meditative thinking belongs, not simply to intellectually gifted types (as representative-calculative thinking belongs to mathematicians, scientists, philosophers); it belongs to human beings as such. It naturally expands to the essential space of *Dasein:* attending to the announcements of what is highest through what the Greeks called Muses and the Hebrews, Angels, the sources of inspiration speaking through the poets and prophets; recalling our essential mortality, the necessary closing off of all our possibilities for being in the world, thus bringing our life as a whole into focus and allowing at the same time for the deep and essential to come into focus over against the superficial and accidental; attending, finally, to the enduring presence of the sensuously given, our root contact with beings, framed by earth and sky. And precisely because it is called upon to heed whatever might emerge as an indication of the Most High, meditative thinking is aware of the finiteness of its apprehension and is thus attuned to the vastness of what is hidden behind all that is manifest. It learns to let whatever appears be ever more deeply present as the announcement of the ultimate encompassing Mystery to which we belong essentially as humans.

Now that space of meditative thinking is, for Heidegger, the space in which the arts operate. It is the space belonging to the heart, the core, the unifying center of humanness, whose correlate is significant presences drawing us into and beyond the whole of beings as the Mystery at the heart of Being. If intellectual thinking re-presents in absence, meditative thinking operates in presence; it presents. The medium of intellectual thinking is the language of prose in which the medium itself disappears in its function of revealing abstract meaning. The medium of meditative thinking is the language of poetry, in which the medium, coming into focus qua sensuous, places us upon the earth. It corresponds to and deepens our dwelling, our inhabitance of the lifeworld. Poetry opens the lifeworld to appreciative thinking as it opens the space within which the other art forms operate.

In the line of Heidegger, Dufrenne insists that the "objective world" is founded upon the world of inhabitance, which is, first and foremost, a world of feeling. Even science is possible only by reason of a certain sympathy for the subject matter.[200] Feeling is thus not merely something private, merely subjective; it manifests something of the Being of things. Above all, it is capable of showing "the mysterious splendor of being which precedes men and objects," a splendor on which primitive religions rest and which the arts at their highest evoke.[201]

Like Dewey, Heidegger distinguishes the empirically present art product from the *work* of art. The latter involves for Heidegger the opening up of a world for dwelling. The form of the work appears only insofar as we are taken up in the struggle between World and Earth, or, as Heidegger later puts it, in the play of the Fourfold. However, the works we find in museums are typically works that *were*, for the character of the world that produced them is long gone. This raises the problem of what he calls the preservers. And by this he does not mean those who practice the technique of art restoration, for these only preserve the art product. How do we relate to works that have been?

Consider a work of art intended to give expression to the depth of religious experience; consider a loving treatment of the Madonna and Child. An animal looking at the painting presumably sees only visual patterns without connection to biological needs and thus the picture appears in a mode of indifference. The aesthetically and religiously uncultivated viewer sees a picture of a woman holding her baby. The aesthetically sensitive see an organized framing of a richly textured surface of color relations and of the play of light and shadow appropriate to the display of the relation of mother and child. If not believers, they might still gain a sense of the fulfilling character of the way of life associated with what is depicted; but they might not be moved to accept it as true. As Hegel remarked, though we can appreciate the beauty of a Medieval or Renaissance work depicting the Madonna and Christ child, we no longer bend our knee because we stand at another level in the development of the human Spirit.[202] George Santayana spent his last years in a convent in Spain, not because he believed in Catholicism, but because he found the whole ambiance most beautiful.[203] Along the same lines, Walter Kaufmann bemoaned the fact that religion, which had produced some of the greatest works of art known to humankind, was essentially a thing of the past. For Kaufmann the regret was not that the moribund religions furnished a right relation to things as that they generated such incomparably beautiful art, the likes of which we will probably never see again in a world from which the sacred has virtually disappeared.[204] In contrast, religiously sensitive viewers see a holy picture that might not only touch them deeply but also reinforce their commitment to a whole way of life associated with that Mother and her Child. They stand, not in the mode of "as if" in the presence of an aspect of a charming story; the work of art helps them to realize what they already accept.

But insofar as epochal transformations of the horizon of meaning entail translation of a faith tradition into a different mode, believers too stand in relation to past art works as works that were. There is a sense in which, just as the teachings of the faith require a reinterpretation as we gain distance from the epochs within which beliefs have been formulated, so also the expression of the lifeworld of faith requires new artistic mediation in different epochs. But both a faith hermeneutic and novel art work are deepened insofar as they are related in a mode of critical retrieval to the works that were.

With Nietzsche and Dewey, Heidegger senses the endangering of the lifeworld that emerged with the emergence of philosophy in Plato. The lifeworld for Plato is the Cave of sensibility and of tradition; its architects are the poets, its decorators the other artists. From the time of Plato onward, philosophy and its saintly followers have been all too inclined to contemn the world of the senses and thus the arts. Christianity, breathing deeply the vapors of disembodied spirituality and otherworldliness generated by the pagan gnostic and Neoplatonic saints, became, in its institutionalized form, "Platonism for the people," as Nietzsche remarked. It inclined toward a view of first-class and second-class citizenship in the church based on the degree of remotion one achieved from one's bodily experience. Sexuality above all was strongly suspect and almost condemned, allowed as an instrument of procreation but begrudgingly accepted as a result of the Fall. But the central doctrines of the Incarnation and Final Resurrection of the Body exerted a countervailing power and the arts were assimilated to the liturgy of the pre-Reformation church. The church of the Reformers paradoxically reinstated sexuality by eliminating celibacy as an ideal and contemned the arts, while simultaneously purging churches of all art except music, which operates with the least material medium.

With Nietzsche and Dewey, Heidegger sees the arts as articulating our belonging to the earth, though in no case is it a matter of collapsing humanness into bodily encapsulation, where aesthetics is simply a matter of fine, physiologically internal feelings. For all three art takes us out of such an enclosed self; and in the great work of art something of the character of both sensorily present things and the whole in which they are installed is displayed. For Nietzsche eternity is installed in time; for Dewey the encompassing Whole is revealed as the depth behind the sensory announcement; for Heidegger the Whole is opened up as a world for human dwelling under the measure of the Most High. Art sets us on the earth as it brings near the meaningful character of the Whole. And yet, whereas Nietzsche and Dewey eliminate anything beyond the world as it now is, for Heidegger a Transcendent is still an open question philosophically and an essential space is created for theophany. That is his historical mission and his essential grandeur as a thinker.

Aside from the fact that the restoration of the thing rather than encounter with the human other is the center of his focus, one thing for which Heidegger could be faulted in his meditations on art is the absence of any discussion of the temporal arts—and that despite the centrality of the notion of time for his thought about Being. Perhaps, however, there is a connection between his neglect of reflection on the human other and his ignoring of dramatic art, in which the person is the center. But what about music, the pure articulation of time in and through sound? About that he says, to my knowledge, absolutely nothing significant. I find that astonishing. Van Gogh's painting of a pair of peasant's shoes, the Greek temple, and nature poetry or poetry about poetry are his primary focus when discussing the arts. Why this fixation on things? Why this neglect of the person? Why this ignoring of music?

Recall especially the close connection discerned by Plato and Aristotle between music and morality, with music sinking most deeply into the soul and affecting our disposition to behave. If language gives focus to our felt dwelling in the world, music presents the tonality of that very indwelling. Aside from architecture, which is the pervasive art form in every civilization, and film, which is the distinctive art form of our culture, music pervades our culture as it did no other. But one has only to scan the radio channels surrounding any of our large cities to find one or perhaps two classical channels. The dominant music forms today both express and give shape to the felt tonality of dwelling in the world of the twentieth-century West. And those musical forms, along with the culture they articulate, are rapidly spreading throughout the world. When I was in Germany during the fall of the Berlin wall one of my expatriate American colleagues remarked: "You can't stop rock and roll!" That is worlds removed from the culture articulated by Bach, Mozart, Vivaldi, and Beethoven. The world of enframing is a world expressed by a music of a self-indulgent wallowing in uncultivated feelings. But music itself expresses most deeply our mode of being in time.

# XI

# CONCLUSION

IN CONCLUSION, LET ME summarize, clarify, and extend my leading contentions, focusing discussion on the interrelation of form and what I am
calling *the aesthetic center.*[1] In so doing, I will rehearse the primary evidences
on which I have rested throughout. I have been developing a series of related theses: first, that human nature is culture creating, condemned by its
nature to giving form, to shaping by choice, in itself and its offspring, the
potential chaos that ontological openness sets on an animal base; second,
that the region aesthetics addresses is the heart as the developed center between intellect, will, and sensibility, whose correlate is significant presences;
and third, that aesthetic form plays a significant role in shaping that center.

As my most fundamental point of departure, I have maintained that
the field of experience is by nature bipolar: on the one hand there is the
ever present and fully actual field of sensa, which rises up out of our desirous organism in interaction with its environment; on the other hand
there is the empty reference to the whole of what is via the all-inclusive notion of being, which sets us at an infinite distance from that environment.
That is the founding structure of what Hegel called Subjective Spirit. The
distance established by reference to the Whole poses for us by nature a
twofold task: linking the biologically given plenum with the emptily given
Whole through eidetic description and interpretation, and choosing to act
among the possibilities provided by the given and our understanding of it.
As interpretations and choices play in relation to the biologically given over
time and the empty space between the sensuously manifest Now and the
Whole gets filled with what we call culture in the widest sense of the term,

felt proclivities develop so that some features in that total field of awareness draw near and become significant presences while others recede into relative indifference. We have come to call the capacity for interpretation *intellect*, and the capacity for choosing, *will*, while the region of felt proclivities and significant presences has been named the *heart*. It is in this latter region that we find the aesthetic.

The dominant tradition underscores moral and intellectual development. Most people have emphasized the moral and downplayed the intellectual, while academics have emphasized the intellectual. In theological circles there has been a stress on the primacy of orthodoxy; in the last half of the twentieth century, there has been a counterstress on the primacy of orthopraxy.[2] However, theologian Hans Urs von Balthasar has called attention to the priority, going back into the Old Covenant and still present centrally in theology until the end of the thirteenth century, of what we might call—following the orthodoxy and orthopraxy emphases—orthoaesthetic, a right sense of things, a right modality of felt presence.[3] Orthoaesthetic plays in relationship to both intellectual and practical operations; and, in fact, the intellectual and the practical are, for the most part, rooted in and sustained by the aesthetic. Interestingly enough, in this emphasis theologian Balthasar parallels many of the observations advanced by secularist John Dewey. As we have seen, for Dewey the aesthetic is integral experience. It provides the sensibility that generates moral rules and practices and suggests comprehensive interpretations. It opens out into a sense of the depth of the world surrounding the pragmatic surface of experience.[4] This region of integral experience is, again, what I am calling the heart. I have attempted to show throughout how the aesthetic operates at the center of the thinkers we have considered.

In this conclusion I want to treat the aesthetic at three levels: the sensory field as the primary field for the operation of the arts, the field of culture, which provides the world of meaning brought to expression in the arts, and the all-encompassing field opened up by our reference to the whole. These correspond to Heidegger's notions of Earth, of World, and of Mystery as they come to presence in the work of art and address the heart.[5] In my reflections I am following Heidegger's *Schritt zurück*, a reflective step back, from philosophy as generally practiced, into "the ground of metaphysics" in our mode of being present to things. And, in the Heideggerian manner, the focus on "the things themselves" has allowed us to mine the tradition of thought in such a way that certain conventional ways of understanding are loosened up by being brought back to their founding modes of givenness, thereby uncovering alternative lines of thought. Hence the approach I have taken—appearances to the contrary notwithstanding—involves not simply reporting the opinions of philosophers nor an eclectic sampling of various positions, but the extraction of the phenomenological yield from the ore of each system, attempting to show how things are manifest within the perspective of each thinker.

In the process of concluding exposition, since the levels we have considered interpenetrate to form the total field of experience, it has been difficult to separate them completely. Consequently—and appropriately in a work dealing with aesthetic—this final exposition will be musical in structure. It will have three movements. And its development is not so much linear as spiral, returning again and again to the same themes, but each time at a higher level and consequently with varying emphases. In my execution I will bring in at different times different voices we have heard throughout this work: Heidegger, Plato, and Kant will take the main parts; but Aristotle, Nietzsche, Hegel, Dewey, and Albertus Magnus will join the chorus. And, indeed, at the deepest level we will from time to time hear from Martin Buber. At each level I will first review the fundamental features of that level and then link it to aesthetic considerations.

### *The Sensory Field*

Consider first the sensory field. It involves a bodily based presentation of the appearance of other bodily individuals in the surrounds of our own bodies within thresholds set up by our biological apparatus, mediated by the needs of our organisms and thus shot through with biological desire. Our body carves out a field of limited manifestness from the totality of influences impacting it from the environment for the purpose of fostering its own natural ends of growth, sustenance, and reproduction. Plato called such a field of appearance a Cave in which the intellectual soul was buried; Nietzsche called it a lie; Hegel considered it a hard rind that had to be penetrated with effort; Heidegger considered it, parallel to the work of intellect, both a revealing and concealing. What is shown is sufficient for our biological adjustment; what is concealed can, at one level, be progressively dug out by the tandem work of intellectual inference and active experimentation.

Vision displays an apparently empty space separating stable objects from the eye of the viewer, whereas reflection and experimentation show that the space is full and the objects significantly more dynamic at levels beyond immediate experience. The visual field appears as it does, first of all, in order to meet the organic needs of the perceiver, so that what appears visually is no epistemically neutral datum but is powerfully affect laden, immediately evoking organically based appetites. The visual field is, as it were, a luminous bubble blown by the nervous system, making a certain type of appearance possible so that an animal being can have a functional space available to meet its needs. Though vision is the lead sense, it plays in relation to the audile and olfactory fields and, most basically, the gustatory and tactual, for its mode of appearance aims at satisfying the desire for food or mate, which have to be tactually apprehended to fulfill such needs.[6] The field of the senses is thus, as I said, a synesthetic-kinesthetic whole of selective appearance shot through with desire and constructed to fulfill the needs of the perceiving organism. Its mode of revelation conceals the wholeness of what is encountered within that field, with the appearing things subserving organic need.

But in spite of the truth involved in Nietzsche's claim, the sensuous field cannot be entirely a lie, since it provides what the organism needs for its survival and prospering. And the organism itself is a functioning whole that constructs, from the materials available in its environment, a system of instruments for self-formation, self-sustenance, self-repair, and reproduction. Thus its mode of appearance *expresses* the inwardness of desire that surges up out of the organic base. For the perceiving animal, the sensory surface furnishes the basis for an organic dashboard knowledge, a mode of display sufficient to learn what to push, pull, and turn in order to get the required output.

Such a field of limited manifestness is the enduring biological pole of the field of awareness. Meditation on these considerations should lead to a sense of the strangeness of the taken-for-granted sensory givenness. Focused on this appetitively mediated surface, we live our lives within this cave, this internally luminous, externally opaque bubble. The sense of strangeness in the everyday opens up the field both for philosophic penetration and for artistic creation, the former seeking to comprehend, the latter to evoke the sense of strangeness in order to haunt the everyday with the awareness of that More which everydayness conceals.

This sensuous field is the field of operation of the arts and the basis of aesthetic experience in general. In discussing the aesthetic, Kant underscored the distinctive human capacity for disengaging the perceptual object within that field from organismic desire so as to provide a condition of what he called "unconstrained favoring." It culminates in a feeling of "disinterested satisfaction" in the epiphany of the beautiful beyond what is merely agreeable to our animal nature. Not coerced by biological desire, without interest in anything other than sheer sensory appearance, one is able to bring into focus the *form* of the display, the peculiar togetherness of sensory elements, where, in the first sense of the term, we have learned to find beauty.

Plato isolated certain features in the form of presentation in his *Republic* when he distinguished, in Socrates' purgation of the arts, between the referents of poetry—namely, gods and heroes—and its aesthetic features—namely, musical modes and instrumental timbres. In shifting attention to purely aesthetic considerations, Socrates pointed to two basic kinds of music, Apollonian and Dionysian. The Dionysian evokes the organismic desires. The Apollonian reveals harmony, order, proportion, and grace and produces those same properties in the emotions of the perceiver. The differentiation between those two modes turns, in the perceiver, upon the distinction between luxurious wallowing in good somatic feelings brought about by pleasing objects and a turning around of the soul so that its education at this level culminates in an appreciation of beautiful things themselves. Plato goes further in this direction, transferring the Apollonian aesthetic from the temporal arts of poetry and music to the spatial arts of architecture, painting, and design in the areas of clothing, furniture, and utensils. I must underscore painting here, since what is at stake is not the mirroring of surface alluded to in book 10 of the *Republic*, but the aesthetic features of composition. Surrounded visually and audilely from birth to death with an aesthetic ambiance characterized by order, proportion, harmony, and grace, the citizenry will have its dispositions so tuned as to supply a fit matrix for the emergence of nous opened to the harmonics of the larger cosmic order within which our sensory environment is located and to which we are by nature directed. What is crucial here is, as Nietzsche observed, "compelling the chaos within to take on form," becoming simple, holding opposites in tension without effort, achieving "the grand style."

Regarding the object of aesthetic focus, Kant spoke of form and Plato gave us a list of formal properties. Aristotle, in the restricted region of tragic art, presented us with what I regard as the most fundamental feature of aesthetic form, its organicity. Aristotle said that, just as an organism has in itself all that it needs for its functioning as a whole and nothing irrelevant to that functioning, so also a tragedy should be such that everything that needs to be there to produce the total effect is there and nothing that is there is irrelevant to that end. So the aesthetic character of a tragedy lies in a mean between aesthetic defect and aesthetic excess. This is one way in which art partly imitates and partly completes nature, conceived of here as what occurs outside art. The artist abstracts from all the details of what might actually occur in order to select and organize only what fits within the aesthetic whole. Of course, in focusing on tragic art, Aristotle has gone beyond the sensuous form of our immediate concern to the expression of the inwardness of character in the sensory forms of language and gesture. However, that observation of the organicity of a good tragic work can be generalized to cover every work of art. Organicity is *the* defining property of the work of art: the work functions as a whole and is thus fresh and live and not dead or mechanical. That links it back to the naturally organic. Indeed, the link between the organic and art is so close in Aristotle that, before Kant called attention to it, Aristotle used the causal factors in human artefaction to read the four causes back into nature. And as Plotinus noted—in this he was copied by Aquinas—art imitates nature in her mode of production. Two factors are linked in that observation: art operates like organic nature by shaping materials to reach a preconceived goal; but also, and more significant for our immediate purpose, the art product at its best has the character of organicity. We could consider "abstract" music here—non-text-accompanying, nonprogrammatic, nonreferentially titled music—a fugue, for example. Such music is an autonomous growth from the nature of the human being as culture-producing animal—an organism that freely creates organic objects. It refers immediately to nothing beyond itself. It is sheer sensuous display of an organic whole, resembling nothing externally presented in nature. And I should extend that along the lines of Walter Pater's by now oft cited claim that all art seeks the status of music (i.e., seeks the production of aesthetic form). Matisse observed similarly that photography freed painting to be painting, so that the latter would not simply be a mirroring of the pregiven but the production of visual form, the organized togetherness of visual elements that may or may not draw directly from previously observed natural form.[7] But whether painting does so draw or not, it is the organicity of the form that makes it good art.

However, Aristotle made another remark that puts even abstract art back into the orbit of mimesis and links up with Plato's focus on aesthetic form: it is the startling claim that music is the most imitative of art forms. What it imitates, Aristotle says, is *ethos,* usually translated as "character," but actually focused on what is most intimate to character, the wellsprings of action in felt proclivities to act. Shaping that is the chief task of ethics. Music produces states of mind, feelings akin to those aroused in encounter with nonartistic situations. (I hasten to add that the likeness also includes immense difference: sorrowful music like Ravel's *Pavane for a Dead Princess* is akin to, but also a world's remove from, sorrow at the death of one's own daughter.) The imitative character does not lie in the audile medium as such—or better, the character of the musically audile is not simply heard sound but the emotional tuning accompanying it, since sensation occurs in function of organic desire. Though we must note that such desire is transformed by rising into the full human field of culturally mediated, personally appropriated reference to the Whole that allows the unconstrained favoring of the form of sensuous display detached from physiological need.

Kant noted that the disinterested satisfaction brought about by concentration on the form of sensory presentation produces a certain quickening of the sense of distinctively human life, a life of the interplay between imagination rooted in the sensory and understanding that provides the basis for aesthetic distancing from biological desire. On the part of the artist, Kant noted that the aesthetic idea emerges from the animation of all the faculties and culminates in a work characterized by liveliness, freshness, organicity. For him the whole region of the aesthetic exhibits—in artist, work, and audience—an awakening, an animation, a quickening of the sense of the distinctive life of the rational animal. The region of beauty, located in the distinterested appreciation of the form of the sensuous, is, for Kant, *the* peculiarly human region, for animals have sensations and hypothetical pure intelligences would have thoughts; only humans can attend to the form of the sensuous display.

Thinking along these lines, Dewey worked the link between art and the organic further and more holistically. The organicity involved in the work of art is not simply derived from observing living things; it is also derived from the fact that artist and audience are themselves organic. That is, human beings, who both make and appreciate works of art, are organically functioning wholes. As such, our minds are not simply apart from the physiological—though there is obviously a sense in which they are apart, and thus our propensity to nonholistic, abstract forms of living; our minds are a significant aspect of our psychophysical totality. What we have come to call *reason* is *ratio*, or ratio, a matter of recognizing or becoming attuned to proportionate, harmonic relations, rooted in the biologically given environment, as they fit within the context of the harmonic totality, the ordered cosmos, to which mind is an aspiration. Organically functioning wholes—living forms which are organically formative processes—are such only because of their capacity to adjust to the totality of the environments within which alone they can live. So also, at the highest level of the organism, with reason as the capacity to apprehend and adjust to the total context of human existence.

It is in this direction that we could assimilate Feuerbach's criticism of Christian thinkers whose dream of being elsewhere distracts them from being here and makes them ashamed of being embodied.[8] We could also appreciate Nietzsche's observations about contempt for the earth exhibited by what became the mainline of Platonism and by Christianity insofar as it became Platonism for the masses. Being a psychophysical whole, an organism alive with a sense of the encompassing Whole or, in biblical terms, made from the clay or the slime of the earth and animated with a divine breath, the human being belongs to the earth. Art underscores the goodness of that belonging.

As Heidegger observed, in art earth rises up in sensuousness to bring the sensuous features to a mode of appearance they do not enjoy in our usual more pragmatic modes of disclosure. Color is most fully manifest as color in the painting. In our other modes of relation, the sensuous is strictly subsidiary. In ordinary language use, sound recedes from attention to bring the communicated into focus. This is the case in an audience's following what a speaker has to say, unless there are those who have lost interest and all that registers is the ongoing droning of the speaker's voice. But in poetic speech, sonority is part of the message and no mere vehicle. It is sonority that brings what is communicated into a more intensive mode of presence by entering into the communicated. And, indeed, it is a certain style of delivery that turns ordinary speech into a kind of art form that enhances the presence of what is communicated.

## The Cultural World

What I have attended to thus far is the sensuous field within which art works appear, and the functioning of art works within that field. But I had to move beyond that in several of my observations, and my last considerations introduced the larger whole of human awareness through the observation of language. Language bears witness to our essentially belonging to a tradition. It involves a peculiar capacity to attend differently than in an animal mode to the Now of sensory actuality and plenitude, relating that plenum to the nonsensory—ultimately and always horizonally to the emptily intended Whole. Language also allows one to absent oneself from the presently given in order to roam over the past in reverie, over the future in hope, over the purely fanciful in imagination, or over the abstract in thought. This enables the work of art to refer through the sensuous form to something beyond the sensuous.

Heidegger spoke of the work of art as a gestalt, a form appearing in the rift brought into being by what he referred to as "fighting the battle of Earth and World." We have considered Earth in the rising up of sensuousness to a new focus in the work of art; but as Earth interplays with World, it becomes native soil, suffused with a sense of belonging to a given, sensorily present place where people together inhabit the world of meaning brought into being by their tradition. World appears over time as the world of a people set on the earth. It comes into being as a requirement of the bipolar structure of the field of experience.

By nature the distinctively human pole, reference to Being, is vacuous, infinite in the sense of indeterminate, but also in the sense of emptily intending all determinations. The ontological reference hollows out a depth behind the animal surface but simultaneously opens up an indeterminate set of possibilities for interpretation and action. The guided circle of animal presentation, the security of instinctively following out natural purpose, is opened up in human beings to the precariousness of the possibilities for human choice. Ontological reference blows the lid off of human instinctual life. The ontological animal becomes the chaotic animal. So Nietzsche's admonition: "Compel the chaos that is within to take on form!" is the challenge to individuals and communities posed by the structure of human nature. The distinctively human task is to develop a coherent mode of understanding in relation to the totality of what is given, to provide a set of related choices for action, and to develop a sense of felt significance that can integrate an individual over a lifetime and a community over generations. Through those felt modes we learn to dwell in a world, to in-habit it. The choices that created those spontaneities are passed on to others as those who pass them on pass on. They become what Hegel called Objective Spirit, Spirit arising in subjectivity but enduring in objectivity beyond the lifetime of its originators. However, the choices of those long dead appear to those who are born into them, not as matters of choice at all, but as the way things are. Hence the tendency to resist any change in traditional forms. But the plurality of such worlds is the clearest proof that they are, in the broad sense in which Heidegger uses the expression, decisions, matters of choice.

Belonging to a world involves in-habitation, having patterns of interpretation and response developed that have become customary, habitual, and that allow things to draw near or to be set at a distance. Indwelling in a world articulates the heart of our personal being. Individual beings appear as endowed with a significance that corresponds to their meaningful place in that world. And such appearance can be located either in natural objects, in works of art, or, arguably, also in transcendent "objects."

One should stress creativity and adaptability in world construction, especially since the philosophic tradition has been dominated theoretically from early times by the notion of nonevolving species, more recently by the notion of sheer mechanism, and in the order of behavior by the idea of a fixed pattern.[9] If the organism furnishes the model of a rational system, exhibiting what existential coherence means, changes in its environment establish a disequilibrium that calls for flexible adaptability and leads to higher integrations. Human creativity introduces another level of disequilibrium, potentially and at times actually chaotic, but also potentially and at times actually fruitful in generating alternate forms of order in keeping with the spiral rather than circular repetitiveness of the ever-creative cosmos within which we are inserted.

By reason of the mediations of being formed within a world, our typical knowledge is, as in the animal mode, still "dashboard knowledge," but now extended beyond the functional circle of animal awareness by a tradition of interpretation and practice. Growing up is a matter of learning input and output correlations within the functional circle of our animal based, culturally mediated awareness. "Growing up" is largely a matter of learning to glance, stereotype, and respond in routinized ways that allow both for coordination of groups and for adjustment to the physical environment. Routinized attention defocuses sensory surface until it becomes subsidiary to our modes of adjustment. Furthermore, such attention also stands in tension between the disclosed and the merely passed on, so that it is replete with mere hearsay knowledge or claims to knowledge. This is precisely Plato's Cave of *doxa*, in which we are chained by nature to sensa and by culture to modes of interpretation. It is Heidegger's world of average everydayness, of *das Man*, the anonymous "one" or "they." It is Hegel's hard rind of everyday surface appearance, extended from the sensa to cultural interpretation, which covers up much more than it reveals and calls forth art to establish a more fully revelatory appearance of what underlies it. It is also related to Buber's "world of It," of experience and use, the relation to which he called *orientation*, knowing our way around in a region, be it pragmatic or intellectual.[10] Now it is absolutely crucial to see, as these various thinkers have seen, that this "real world" is precisely an appearance, constructed by our animal nature, our cultural upbringing, and our past modes of attention, functionally revealing, but more deeply concealing what is fully there. It is in this orientational world of It that one's awareness of the Thou as the hidden fullness that rises up to address us in nature and in art, as well as in other persons can disappear. In the It-world, as Buber noted, "morality" can come to hide the face of our fellowman and religion the face of God;[11] in it, from age to age religion takes the lead in perfecting the armor of invulnerability against the revelation that the Bible claims can speak to us in the everyday. But in the name of the Book, we look away from where we really are. We fail to read "the signs of the times." We fall in love with "the world," even and perhaps especially the world of Christendom.[12]

Born into a cultural world, every human individual is stamped in a peculiar way by genetic endowment and cultural upbringing, which together furnish the concrete possibilities for individual choices. Choices are made possible and necessary because, by reason of the founding reference to the Whole, each human being is an I, set at a distance from all determinations, from every objectifiable feature of its own total selfhood.[13] Hence emerges the distinction between the I and the Me. Genetic and cultural stamping furnishes the nonchosen Me. The history of choice based on this stamping furnishes a variation, the Me I have chosen to be from the possibilities afforded by my situation. The past sediments in the space provided by my nature between the sensuous plenum and empty reference to the Whole to form the historically constituted Me. At any given moment that peculiar Me is the artist's material given to the I to shape within the limits of its concrete possibilities.

The center of the Me is the heart, that which is closest to the I. And the I tends to move in the direction of the heart's desires. The heart is fixed on what is personally closest—though perhaps spatially far away—around which whatever else that appears falls into circles of decreasing relevance, shading off into indifference. Heart develops over time: anticipation and recall are governed automatically by that on which my heart is set. There are regions within me of anonymous functionings, beginning with my physiology; there are registrations of past experiences, development of motor skills—like being able to play a musical instrument—that may not lie close to my heart. Yet what is close is that which spontaneously solicits my attention.

To repeat, cultural formation opens up the concrete possibilities each I has for further determination of the stamp given it, without its asking, by genetics and culture. In the past, realization of this fact evoked *pietas*, a sense of gratitude for unpayable debts to parents, to country, and to God for allowing to come into being what would otherwise lay fallow within general human possibilities.[14] How many potentially great classical pianists roamed the jungles thousands of years ago, none of whom could actualize that potentiality prior to the development of the instrument, the technique, and the repertoire afforded by the tradition of classical piano? *Pietas* expresses what Hegel called *substantial freedom*, a certain fulfillment brought about by identification with what would otherwise seem to be simply other, alien to subjectivity. But the freedom provided by the primordial distance of the I—what Hegel called *formal* or *abstract freedom*—makes possible the deliberate abandonment of *pietas* and the deliberate attempt to repudiate as much as possible of the formation given to us by culture. Absolutized, it can dissolve most of the obvious external institutions. Today we see it expressed in the formlessness filling the contemporary sections of our museums of fine art. I choose to do with Me whatever I choose, for whatever reasons. The last two considerations have already moved us ahead to the aesthetic considerations of this part of my recapitulation.

Brought up in a cultural world, humans have regions of distinctive concerns: pragmatic, cognitive, and moral regions carved out by the tradition. And as these, along with biological need, absorb most of our attention, sensory surface is usually subsidiary to them, parallel to the way in which that surface functions in animal life. In opening up access to the aesthetic, Kant not only separated it from animal need, he also disengaged it from these other concerns that emerge in the course of cultural development. In the aesthetic mode one does not view an object in terms of the use to which it can be put or in terms of its providing occasion for some form of inference or explanation, or its giving us some form of moral instruction. Kant pushes very hard to achieve what Gadamer has called *aesthetic differentiation*, a complete lifting off of the form of sensory display from any other consideration, physiological or cultural.[15]

But for Kant, the defocusing of attention from any form of interest is only an initial, though quite important move. He himself viewed the appreciation of beauty more holistically. Disinterested focus on the form of sensory togetherness gives us the entrance ticket to the region of the beautiful. To this end, Kant isolated what he called *free beauty*, as found in bird plumage, seashells, arabesque drawings, or in purely instrumental music— in the appreciation of which, as he said, there is no antecedent notion of what the object ought to be, no concept governing our judgment, no other end than appreciation. Beauty is found in sheer sensory display. But such focus by itself gives us only what is for Kant ultimately trivial beauty.

Having established the entrance ticket to the realm of the beautiful in the form of sensuous display, Kant goes beyond that to the notion of *dependent beauty* and ultimately to the notion of *the ideal of beauty*. Most of what we consider beautiful is accompanied by some concept that refers us to a nonsensory content, articulated in the field of meaning of a given culture, of which the sensory display is an expression. In this case, the peculiar togetherness of the sensory features is governed by its suitability to what is being displayed. So, for example, Lawrence Welk's "champagne music" would be inappropriate accompaniment for the text of St. Matthew's Passion. The beauty of the music would here be dependent on what it brings to sensuous presence. The function of the sensuous form is to give to the referent a closeness it would not otherwise have in merely prosaic presentation.

For Kant the highest form of dependent beauty is what he calls "the ideal of beauty." It is found in an empirically derived archetype of the sensory presentation of the human form expressing moral qualities. In Kant's view of things, it is the moral that is the highest level of human experience, linking the phenomenal—the appearance of things relative to us—to the noumenal—being-in-itself beyond all appearance. But again, what makes the display of moral qualities in the human form beautiful is not the moral qualities; it is the *form* of the display. Now in this case, such display is expressive of something of what a noble human is as rising to presence in sensation, but simultaneously sinking back into unencompassable depth.

For Kant, in nature it is the organism that is a primary locus of such expressiveness. He calls this feature expressed in the sensory appearance of the organism "purposiveness" *(Zweckmäßigkeit)*, which he also claims to be basic to the aesthetic object. Even free beauty in nature expresses something of the belonging together of the display and the human capacity for perception of that display, as if the display were arranged for our aesthetic perception, intended by what underlies sensory surface. The deepest aspect of that belonging together lies in the founding human reference to the totality Kant terms *Vernunft*, a drive toward the totality of what-is, a drive realized most deeply in the moral disposition to act according to principle by arranging the empirically given to conform to our moral disposition.

Kant's initial disinterested focus on the form of sensory presentation, even as it operates in dependence on what it expresses, is the background to the nineteenth-century movement of art for art's sake, which appeared (for example) in France in Théophile Gautier and in England in Walter Pater. Pater's observation, often cited, that all art seeks the status of music is aligned with such aestheticism, the aim of which is to fill one's life as full as possible with a multiplicity of aesthetic experiences.[16] Artistically displayed form, whether in the free or dependent mode, becomes one's ultimate commitment. All life can be considered "aesthetically" in the sense of detached appreciation.

For Heidegger, on the contrary, art perishes in purely aesthetic experience.[17] And Kierkegaard leveled a powerful and persuasive attack on such an "aesthetic life."[18] Kant too recognized the problem of immoral artistic dilettantes.[19] We must distinguish between aestheticism and a more holistic mode of being moved. Art, seen in a larger perspective, requires participation, a holistic sharing both in what is communicated and in the mode of presentation as well. And as Hegel noted, it was in art that a people presented their deepest wisdom, their sense of what it means for humans to belong to the Whole.

The mode of presentation is originally meant to communicate not simply the content but also the proper mode of participative response. The work of art fuses sensory form and reference into a single gestalt wherein the sensory form brings about the disposition proper to the referent. The referent becomes a real presence instead of a merely intellectually intended or sensorily noted object. More than merely content, the artistic mode of presentation establishes a peculiar "feel" for the content, the way one is present to it. One does not only affirm the content; it becomes a living presence; it touches us; it moves our heart; we share in it. We can come to have not only what Newman would call a *notional assent,* but also something like a *real assent* (i.e., an assent that entails a realization).[20] A purely aesthetic approach will yield something like a real assent without a real assent. The aesthetic shows us something of what it is to live a belief, not in conduct alone but in the sense of realization, of attaining to significant presence, that lies at the basis of modes of conduct and belief—only art itself does this, not in the mode of belief, but in the mode of "as if." The problem is both in appreciatively distinguishing the aesthetic and in vitally relating it to the other aspects of human experience.

For Heidegger, the art work, within which Earth rises up in sensuousness as native soil, opens up simultaneously a World of inhabitance; it solicits the larger sense of indwelling in a world with its peculiar "feel" and is not simply a matter of isolated feelings aroused by isolated objects. The struggle between Earth and World, parallel to the struggle between closure and disclosure, creates the rift in the everyday surface, the lightning flash that creates the peculiar space for the form of the work. Art's isolation (e.g., through framing techniques) places the work outside ordinary experience—Plato's Cave, Hegel's hard rind of everyday appearance, Buber's world of It—but in order to bring us back to the whole of that experience in a different way. The work of art can bring about a transformation of one's general attunement, one's deep-seated way of holding oneself toward things, and thereby affect one's disposition to act. As Heidegger remarked, great art creates such world space that through it even the ordinary appears extraordinary. In Dewey's surprising way of putting it, art brings us from the focus of ordinary life to the fringe that always surrounds it. In so doing, it awakens what he calls "the mystical" as a sense of belonging to the universe, introducing us to a world beyond this world that is nonetheless the depth of this very world.

An artist may be interested in giving expression in his or her work to aesthetic surface or to the quotidian or the pornographic or the patriotic or the mystical or the idiosyncratic or whatever. What I want to emphasize is the founding structures that make that possible, whether or not they come to focal awareness in the artist or in the art produced. Indeed, those same structures make possible the observer's approach to the work of art, so that one could bring a superficial or a more or less reflective and encompassing awareness to bear on any given work. Nonetheless, from the point of view of art, the quality of treatment, the handling of aesthetic surface is what is crucial, even for an artisan wholly absorbed in that surface. And that can evoke appreciation from the most reflectively developed awareness, which has, so to speak, caught up with its own grounding in habitual lived direction toward the encompassing.

Aesthetic deepening depends on initiation into aesthetic community. As both Hume and Kant noted, the presentation of exemplars helps shape our ability to make meaningful discriminations among different types of aesthetic presentations. However, it may also tend to lock us into what has been unless we learn the lesson of essential plurality and novelty. As many dispositional conservatives never seem to learn, classics had to come into being; and when they did so, they were novelties. A study of the plurality of classics teaches us the perception of meaningful form in different arts, different genres, different styles. It frees us from our confining preconceptions and permits us the inner space to let the new work work upon us to show what it can do in comparison with previous forms. But as it does this, it also builds aesthetic community based on a distancing from our private selves and an adhesion to values sharable in principle by all properly attuned participants. For Kant this is the chief value of art. As civilization advances, people are given over more and more to communication rooted in the aesthetic, both in creating aesthetic forms and in verbally articulating and intellectually evaluating such experiences.

As I indicated in the beginning of this book, art works enter into a culture over the millennia following the articulation of the field of the senses. I laid out a preliminary system of the arts in terms of three parameters: the senses appealed to, the frameworks of space and time (separate and in their interrelations), and language, which situates the sensorily given within the culturally prearticulated Whole. I tried, within that preliminary division, to lay out some of the eidetic features of the different art forms. Plato and Aristotle advanced that endeavor, tying it to their own advancement in the understanding of the Whole that deepened and situated interpretively our preliminary descriptive presentation. Hegel extended that. But Dewey in particular warns against such divisions, calling attention to the concrete interplay of all the parameters of experience in each of the art forms. Heeding his warning, we nevertheless must note—as Dewey did—the focal priority of some parameters in certain art forms and in different styles. Thus, for example, the sculptural object is a spatial form appealing focally to vision, though it surely draws on associative values derived from the other senses, especially touch, and the other parameters in our division.

But our preliminary division paid no attention either to what is communicated or to a possible value hierarchy between the arts. Hegel in particular argued for a hierarchy based on the relative limitations in communicative possibilities among the art forms. Poetry ranked the highest because its linguistic medium had the greatest possible range. Music was second because it spans the whole range of emotional life—as Plato said, music sinks most deeply into the soul; and Aristotle claimed it the most imitative because most able to produce inner ethos. But in both cases this concerns the emotional life, or the "depths," of the soul. The "heights" are occupied by *nous*—or at least so it seems. But in Plato, Eros rises above *nous,* so that there is an emotional range in Plato that extends from the depths to the heights. Schopenhauer and Nietzsche argued for the priority of music over the apprehension of "Platonic Forms" or over the Apollonian. They both fall on this issue in the Platonic-Neoplatonic line of attending to that which exists *epekeina tes ousias,* beyond the correlate to nous in the Forms. In all cases, the visual arts stand lower in the hierarchy. Kant is an exception regarding the place of music: for him it is the least communicative, poised on the borderline between the agreeable and the beautiful.

Appearing within a world of communally constituted meaning, a work of art takes on form by drawing one from surface to depth and encompassment. But then, the world of meaning changes as time goes by or as the piece is approached by one who does not occupy the world from which it stems and to which it speaks. In the latter case it becomes a mere at-hand product and, as Heidegger said, a work that has been. In Buber's terms, it passes from form to object.[21] Apart from the purely aesthetic modality of a Walter Pater, the work of art can be studied in terms of the scientific aspects of the composition of its materials, in terms of the exhibition of techniques of construction, of its fitting within the history of the development of the artist's style, which can itself be located within a comparative schema of different artistic styles, in different epochs and cultures; it can further be considered in terms of autobiographical and sociological factors. It becomes an object of art history. In Dewey's way of putting it, it passes from work that effects the integration of the properly disposed viewer through disclosing a depth behind the surface, to become an art product, a sensorily present object in space and time, another mere thing accumulating dust for the cleaning personnel, which begins Heidegger's exposition of the thinghood of the work of art. But for those who learn to preserve the working of the work of art by standing in the space of its manifestness, it can bring about a sense of the ontological mystery.

## Transcendence

Mention of the ontological mystery leads into my final section. It is at this point that I want to focus more closely on the third feature of the context within which the aesthetic operates: that of our natural, empty reference to the Whole via the notion of being and its relation to the heart —though I could not help invoking it at other points in my exposition. The opposite pole to the sensory is that fundamental reference to the totality of what-is, expressed in the "is" of the judgment that articulates the notion of Being, outside of which there is nothing. By nature this reference is initially empty; but it provides, as an aspect of its anticipation of the totality, an anticipation of the whole of space and time that makes possible abstraction of universal forms and thus linguistic expression that refers an encountered form to all its instances wherever in space and whenever in time they might be found. It likewise furnishes the unrestricted generality of the principle of noncontradiction, which makes possible the development of inference and the building up of a progressively extended and consistent view of the Whole. Further, it raises the question of that which might exist beyond the finitude of our grasp. The grounding presence of this reference to the totality makes necessary our interpretatively locating whatever we encounter within that totality: what kinds of things appear in the sensory field and out of what depths do they appear? Pried loose from the Now by that reference, just as we are forced to interpret, so we are "condemned to choose" from the possibilities afforded by the givens of our biology and our reflective capacity. The congealing of interpretive and practical decisions settles into the initially empty space between the Now of sensation and the Whole of what is to constitute a cultural world that opens up pathways for acting, thinking, and feeling for those who have been assimilated to it as a second nature manifest most clearly in one's native language.

The notion of being is contracted in every judgment to the being on which we are focusing attention and to the peculiar manifest features in virtue of which we are attending. Nonetheless, it refers us beyond the limitation of the mode of manifestness—sensory and intellectual—to the underlying wholeness of the thing encountered. In the case of encounter with the expressivity of an organism or a person or a work of art where the way the sensory appears gives access to the nonsensory, which rises to manifestness, at the same time the unobserved powers and the underlying nature of a given organism recede into an ultimately unretrievable depth of which humans, distanced by nature from the dashboard surface of animal sensation and cultural mediation, can become aware. As Aquinas put it, "We do not know the essence of anything, not even of a simple fly."[22] But, beyond and essentially connected with that, the notion of being refers us to the encompassing whole surrounding the thing and ourselves as experiencing and passing judgment on it. This dual reference—to the wholeness of the encountered being within the encompassing wholeness of being itself—is the reason why we come to understand anything by fitting it into a world of meaning, the Whole as articulated by language. But language only emptily intends the ontological fullness of what in each case it partially delineates.[23]

Further, it is precisely because of our natural reference to the wholeness of each thing within the wholeness of all that we are each an I, a center referred beyond all objectification, even of the most intimate aspects of our own Me, beyond one's own heart. Each I is thus able to function as the center before which everything makes its distinctive mode of appearance and able—no, forced to take responsibility, to choose what I am to do with

Me. What I want to underscore at this point is that the reference to the Whole that founds the I is not simply neutral reference but fundamental Eros in the Platonic sense of poverty having passionate designs on plenty. If sensuous appearance occurs in function of organismic desire, the presence of the nonappearance of the plenitude of being is correlated with the peculiarity of ontological desire as passion for the absent totality. This gives the final depth dimension to the heart explored in a significant way by Augustine.[24]

Now one can make these observations, which I take to be true judgments. One might go on—bypassing contemporary dogmas about the impossibility of "onto-theo-logy"—and make responsible inferences as to the existence of an ever-present, ever-operative, and even personal Source Who is the Infinite Fullness of Being, *Ipsum esse subsistens,* imitated in finite ways by the works of His generosity, yet infinitely beyond any adequate comprehension on our part. But the modality of those judgments is impersonal. For the real life of the human being they sketch out the possibility of an all-encompassing Presence that may Itself flash through the cracks of our dashboard knowledge like lightning and transform our whole sense of things in the most radical way. If and when that happens, from then on it tends to hover in the background of all our wakefulness and may rise again from time to time in explicit presentness.

Buber reserves the term *presence* for the experience of the full gathering of the self in relation to the fullness of any encountered other, met but not comprehended, revealed as inexhaustible mystery and opening experientially to being heard as a word addressed by the Eternal Thou.[25] For Buber this is the core of biblical revelation: the world as spoken by God, the Presence Who will be present in whatever way He chooses, but whose Presence is announced in the speech that is creation.[26] If the world of It gives us orientation, the Thou is a matter of *realization*. But what is realized in meeting with the Thou is simultaneously threefold: first, the unencompassable fullness of what is encountered and second, the fullness of oneself—both standing beyond the partiality of what is available for our orientation, whether intellectually or practically, beyond the human dashboard; but the third aspect of ontological plenitude is the epiphany of the encompassing Mystery as personal address, which Buber calls the Eternal Thou. In this threefold display there is manifest a deep otherness rising to presence and receding into mystery to which we may refer intellectually—as I am now doing—but which is only available as a presence to the heart. Ontological reference gives the ultimate depth to the human heart—it reveals our heart of hearts, which is restless until its relation to the fullness of what manifests its deep otherness culminates in the coming to presence of the Eternal Thou.

We now move to our final aesthetic consideration, linked to the consideration of the deepest native concern of our hearts. Kant noted, as I have before, that in art we can give a new mode of presence to things already lying within our field of experience, like love, hate, and anger. But he also noted that it is in art that we are able to develop an imaginative-symbolic exploration of ideas deeply connected with the most fundamental interest of our reference to the Whole, ideas like the afterlife and the Four Last Things (judgment, heaven, hell, purgatory), such as we find instanced in the myths of Plato and in the works of Dante and Milton. Strictly speaking, we know virtually nothing about these things, even if we accept revelation. But the symbolic-imaginative extensions created by such poetic thinkers bring these matters close to us and bind them tightly to our mode of living as haunting presences.

However, the extended field of such exploration opens out to another kind of aesthetic experience. Kant put the aesthetic of the beautiful in contrast with the aesthetic of the sublime by setting the limited character of conceptuality exhibited in dependent beauty against the unlimited striving for totality characteristic of *Vernunft*. The contrast between the beautiful and the sublime deals with form and the transcendence of form respectively. In the latter, Kant hearkens back to the medievals and ultimately to Plotinus and Plato. Kant's own mode of philosophizing was underpinned by awe provoked by the moral law within, analyzed in the second critique. and by the starry skies above, whose exhibition of the principles of mechanical motion furnished the exemplary object of knowledge analyzed in the first critique. In the third critique, awe is presented as a peculiar aesthetic state: the simultaneous feeling of insignificance and exultation, rooted respectively in the animal and rational poles of our existence. Outside, "the starry skies above", the overwhelming character of whose vast spaces filled the pious Pascal with fear, play in relation to "the moral law within" which indicates the sublimity of our vocation as human beings. The combination of these two contrary dispositions yields awe as the sense of the sublime that transcends and locates the limited character of the appearance of the beautiful form. It is this awe that suffuses the otherwise seemingly dry and austere character of Kantian analysis and helps sustain his distinction between phenomenal surface and noumenal depth.

This hearkens back to Plato, for whom, as Heidegger noted,[27] philosophy has its pervasive and enduring principle in *thaumazein*, a state of astonishment attributed mythically to Iris, the messenger of the god Thaumas.[28] The mythic reference takes it out of the region of mere curiosity and links the philosophic enterprise to the divine. Precisely as the kind of philosopher he was, a philosopher of fully comprehensive reflectiveness, Plato wrote in such a way that the severity of conceptual elaboration always drew upon our peculiar Eros for the whole and returned his attentive readers to the world of our inhabitance through myths, imagery, and the concrete interchange between characters in dialogue. Philosophy for Plato is not simply curiosity about conceptual puzzles nor satisfaction in understanding the samenesses and differences exhibited in how things present themselves: it is rooted in ever-growing awe as the fuller context of our existence comes to light through inquiry aimed, as Socrates said, at the wholeness of each thing within the all-encompassing Whole of being.[29] Astonishment is deeply linked to the realization that we live in the cave of *doxa*, of animally grounded, culturally mediated appearance, complacently taking such appearance for reality. But it is also and simultaneously linked to the development of distinctively human Eros.[30]

Now Nietzsche saw Socrates, in his alleged influence on Euripides, to have defocused the erotic Dionysian in favor of the Apollonian and thus to have been the originator of that "aesthetic Socratism" which dominated Western existence and, in the form of science and technology, still dominates it. This focuses something important in understanding Western culture and things aesthetic, but it is one-sided. As Plato set the central focus of aesthetic consideration on beauty, Aristotle set it on the horrible presented in tragedy. Nonetheless, Platonic Eros was also Dionysiac, evoking the Dionysus of exultant creation, generating Apollonian forms. Aristotle, soberly nonerotic, won, from the objectification of the destructive Dionysus, purgation from the disorienting emotions of fear and pity, which the confrontation with destruction involves. A similar contrast between the Apollonian and the Dionysian appears in Kant's distinction between the beautiful and the sublime. What is central to a Platonic aesthetic is precisely the Dionysian, evoked by the beauty of form, but drawn beyond, ultimately toward the Whole and the Source of the Whole through the sublimation of erotic desire. For Plato art plays in the space between animal-like feelings and a sense of encompassing Beauty associated in his *Republic* with the Good, shaping such feelings into form, which ultimately gives expression to the epiphany of that encompassment. It is this that is announced in

Diotima's description of Beauty Itself as an overwhelming presence that suddenly bursts like lightning into the life of the aspirant. And in the *Phaedrus*, Socrates further claims that the privilege of this Beauty is that its presence is available through the eyes, expressed, that is, in the field of the sensuous as exceeding it. The character of that excess is indicated in the *Republic*, where the Source and End, the One/Good, is referred to as an incomparable Beauty beyond *ousia*. Here we see a move through form beyond form, whether "aesthetic" in the sensory sense or eidetic as correlate to intellect, toward that which we seek from the bottom or at the height or from the center of our psychophysical totality—all three metaphors appear in the tradition to focus on this feature. The move is in a direction laid out in Kant's notion of *Vernunft* as a drive toward totality and which I ground in the notion of Being. All form—sensory or intellectual, natural or artistic—points to a Beyond that it ultimately expresses to a psyche that is not fulfilled either in sensory or intellectual achievement, but only in dwelling with the fullness of one's being in relation to that ultimately mysterious Source of the all.

Kant and Plato clash over the limitation and extension of the notion of beauty. Plato follows out the structures of the field of experience in the *Symposium*, where Socrates presents Diotima's Ladder of Beauty. In the human case, the beauty of sensuous display stands in tension with the beauty of character. Kant places the ideal of beauty in their relationship, though *beauty* said of character is, for Kant, a metaphoric extension of the term, which applies properly to the form of sensuous display alone. Plato goes on to extend the term to the beauty of institutions and laws, since these are what shape the beauty of character. And both the beauty of sensuous display and the beauty of character, along with what shapes it, are measured by universal principles, whether in the mathematical sciences of material ordering or in the philosophic sciences of psychic structure grounding ethico-political shaping. Hence Plato goes on to speak of the beauty of the sciences. Kant employs the term *elegance* here and again repudiates the metaphoric extension of the term *beauty*. And yet what is displayed in the natural and human sciences provokes his awe, the subjective correlate to what he calls the sublime: the starry skies above, the moral law within. Kant reduces the being-drawn-out in this experience to an exalted mode of self-experience. What is sublime is, in relation to the vastness of nature's display, human thought's ability to exceed it, or, in relation to the power of nature's display, human moral destiny. This is linked to Kant's reduction of the *summum bonum* from its traditional location in the loving vision of God to the coincidence of happiness with deservedness to be happy in the just person. For Kant, God as omniscient, omnipotent, and just judge is the condition of the possibility of this coincidence. Platonic intoxication with the vision of Beauty Itself as the object of philosophic aspiration and the linkage of that Beauty to encounter with a divine Person in religious experience are repudiated by Kant as "enthusiasm," which generates the pretension of special insight and superstitious practices. Though one must admit the serious danger of self-deception in these matters, the tandem development of the rational and the mystical in the Platonic tradition furnishes the possibility of a corrective. And Augustine's "Beauty ever ancient, ever new" simply reverses the direction of Kant's sense of the sublime from its deflection back to the human.

As a long philosophical tradition maintains in common with primitive animism, everything gives expression to an underlying force, the depth beyond all depths, the center and ground of the whole, correlate to the human mind's reference to the Whole via the notion of Being. Plato sees it as the One/Good/Beautiful; Aristotle personifies it as Self-Thinking Thought; the Judeo-Christian tradition views it as the Creator-Redeemer-Judge, Whose glory is displayed in nature and in history. Indeed, as it attains philosophic expression in Hegel, the Christian view grounds the expressivity of things in the expressivity within God Himself: the Father expresses Himself in His Son, with Whom He unites in the Spirit of Love. Bonaventure locates beauty finally in the togetherness of the Trinity, wherein the Father is the One, the Son the True as mirror of the Father, the Spirit the Good as the Spirit of Love, and Beauty the seal on the transcendentals, the splendor of the Holy Trinity. Correlatively, the human relationship to the divine is being drawn out by ecstasy toward the divine Beauty expressed in all things. All things are traces of God; the human person is made in His image; the mature human, "returned to the Source" through contemplation and giving to others the fruits of contemplation, is the likeness of the divine.

Now it is this that was the special object of medieval aesthetic and which generated its theologies, culminating in the work of Bonaventure. But it was not something that became, in most thinkers, an object of extended attention, especially as it appears in works of art. As Umberto Eco noted and anyone can verify by searching around the writings of the scholastics, the medieval philosopher-theologians were severely deficient in reflection on the nature of art, for all the magnificence their artists and musicians produced and for all the efforts made by neo-Scholastic "fans" to make them appear otherwise.[31]

In Plotinus, the pagan source of the fundamental philosophic underpinning of much of patristic and medieval theology, that move beyond form appears in both the sensory and the intellectual mode through the distinction between harmonic properties on the one hand and in the shining of the One that makes those properties visible. And here he follows the direction laid out in Plato's notion of the Good. In modern times Schopenhauer reinvoked that distinction within the context of the arts by distinguishing between the art forms that exhibit Platonic Forms, or idealized types, and music, which gives expression to the ultimate Source of all (which he termed the Will). The attunement that music expresses is the underpinning of all aesthetic creation. Musical attunement generates form. Here Schopenhauer was also echoing Schiller, for whom the musical mood produced the poetic word, and anticipating Dewey, for whom all creativity is rooted in a felt aura in which ideas swim. It was this which Nietzsche picked up immediately from Schopenhauer in his analysis of the birth of tragedy from the spirit of music. For Schopenhauer and Nietzsche, such aesthetic creation became the fundamental cipher for world generation.

In medieval thought that distinction between form and a surplus giving a peculiar access to form reappears united in Albertus Magnus's expression *splendor formae*, a radiance beyond the objective recognizability of the form. In an otherwise severe scholastic presentation, he manufactures and piles up adjectives, laying stress on terms that describe the surplus of beauty over goodness as a light, a shining, a radiance, a splendor, a supersplendence, an incandescence, a resplendence, a lightning *(fulgor)*, a superfulgence, a *claritas* (understood, not as clarity but as glory, linked to the adjective *clarus*, famous). The property indicated is, nonetheless, rooted in the substantial form. In a typical scholastic presentation, this piling up and even manufacture of terms to describe a single property is indeed remarkable. Albertus was clearly struggling to give expression to a surplus in the experience of beauty beyond the intellectually analyzable properties to which it might otherwise be reduced. In the expression *splendor formae* this luminescence is linked to proportion and consonance, which are understood as a relation of aspects within the object. But whatever the identifiable ratios involved, *splendor* is a surplus property. And in the Dionysian context within which Albertus thought, that property is understood as the expression of the depth of divine mystery irradiating all things.

It was that sense of the divine light shining through proportionate form that created the splendor of the Gothic cathedral and that was suggested by the golden halo or the gilded background on the sacred icons. The silence of the cathedral's soaring spaces called forth the haunting sounds of the Gregorian chant, a music that arose out of the depths of its makers' silence and set its hearers back into the silence of our ultimate distance. For all the otherworldliness that currents of one-sided Neoplatonism tended to generate, the artists brought the other world here, into the field of sensuousness, where we as full human beings belong. That only spells out more fully the fundamentally incarnate character of Christian religion, rooted in the belief in God's own incarnation and culminating in the resurrection of the body.

❧ ❧ ❧

This brings us to the end of my presentation. I have set about to explore the major parameters of the field of experience. I have tried to show that at its center lies the heart. The heart is relation to being in the mode of significant presence. It is the core, the center of the self, the single root of the soul's powers, that from which everything in us arises and to which everything should return. The heart may be superficial or profound, it may be scattered or integrated. It is the center of the "Me," the sedimented resultant of the whole of my past—genetic, cultural, personal-psychological—which moves me spontaneously in certain directions. Yet, rooted in the ultimate distance from any determination afforded by my primordial reference to the whole, "I" am judging and choosing self in relation to the spontaneities of the heart, which I can follow or resist. The task of life is to align the spontaneous heart with the growing display of the whole context of existence. In this the arts work in tandem with intellectual development as they each in their own way disclose the Whole in more encompassing ways. The heart operates by an intuitive affinity with beings, situations, and regions based on the whole of our past dealings, bringing new directions to conceptual work; the intellect, based on a history of development in its own region, brings the intuitive to judgment by providing it with systematic context through explicit conceptualization. The arts explore the region of human dwelling, giving body and presence to intellectual apprehensions, but also providing direction for intellectual development as linked to the most comprehensive region of human dwelling. It is to the heart that the work of art appeals by establishing form as a charged presence appearing in the sensory field. By reason of the bipolar structure of humanness, the heart can be brought to its own fullness by being taken up into a mystical sense of the encompassing and even into a personal address by the Creative Source or it can slide down into the dissipation of sensory indulgence. Just so, art can make its appeal to the mystical in genuine religious art or to the prurient by creating the pornographic. But whether in nature or in art, the overall form of presence exhibits its arising into sensuousness out of the depth of mystery, into which it recedes. Correlated with the thrust of human awareness toward Being or toward the totality, or toward everything about everything, the depth of mystery in what is encountered is the mystery of the totality, within which everything is rooted and out of which all appearance—sensory and intellectual—occurs. Intellectual reference draws upon a significant aspect of ourselves in relation to whatever we apprehend of the objects that appear within our field of experience. Reference to being, which grounds both the thrust to understand and the requirement to choose in a manner consonant with understanding, calls us to holistic presence, to a recognition of the Not and the More than what is immediately revealed. The whole that encompasses everything can itself become a presence haunting the dashboard manifest in our usual modes of attention. The fullness calls to our hearts through the forms that arise in the between of appearance. But as reference to the Whole stemming from an organic base, our fully human response to it ought not to be simply a flight into the Beyond; it ought to be a renewed attentiveness set on the earth of sensuous presence that creates a world of inhabitance.

Throughout the ages, the call of the Mystery continually gives rise to new forms and leads to new formative institutions. In an epoch of the widespread dissolution of form, there opens up the possibility of a new epoch of form arising through attention to that which stands beyond and announces itself through all form as the object of our restless hearts' search.

# Appendix

## ON SCULPTURAL PRODUCTION

*Our aesthetics hitherto has been a woman's aesthetics to the extent that only the receivers of art have formulated their experience of "what is beautiful?" In all philosophy hitherto the artist is lacking.*

—Friedrich Nietzsche, *The Will to Power*

THE ATTEMPT TO UNDERSTAND art and beauty philosophically is usually developed on the experiential basis of the spectator as the philosopher watches or listens to aesthetic products. But one might be helped further by the actual practice of an art form. In what follows I will give an account of the process of following out particular lines of forms as they came to me while trying to develop as an amateur sculptor, as well as the process of assigning names and thus meanings to what I produced. This will furnish the basis for some more general remarks on the nature of sculpture.

### Descriptions

As a spatially oriented thinker who feels lost until conceptual relations can be given diagrammatic and thus spatial form, and as one who has scored very high in three-dimensional visualization tests, I decided to take up sculpture—or at least I think that is why I decided to take up sculpture. Actually, during a semester teaching in Rome I spent a good deal of time in museums throughout Europe and was attracted by sculptural pieces, especially by bronzes, and in particular by Phidias's Zeus-Poseidon in the Athens museum. As I wandered and wondered through the museum, I was drawn again and again to the power of presence in that work. It was as if it said to me, "I want you!" as a kind of command approaching irresistibility. I could understand a bit how one might consider such works the real presence of the divinity. Upon my return to the states, I decided to take up sculpture as a sideline while I continued my teaching and writing in aesthetics. It was my "aesthetics lab experience."

The old sculpture teacher, Heribert Bartscht, trained at the Academy of Art in Munich, started us out on eye-hand coordination exercises. The first assignment: a mask—like a death mask—of a human being. What astonished me was how little I knew of how the various parts of the human head related to one another. I found myself staring at other people during committee meetings. I had to learn not simply to glance and stereotype but really to *see* how heads actually appeared. I remember being especially astonished at how deeply the eyes were set into the head. There followed several other exercises: copying my left hand, copying live models. Old Heri once remarked, when looking at the works of the various students, how differently people see the same object. I remarked that it was not so much a matter of differently seeing at this point in Sculpture I; it was a matter of a different level of achievement of eye-hand coordination. "Seeing" would come later, if at all.

Then Heri asked us to do something "abstract." While I appreciated abstract painting and sculpture and played with elaboration of patterns in doodling, it took me a while before I had an abstract idea for sculpting. Why, I did not know, but I thought of drawing the letter C, then drawing its reverse and interrelating the two forms. I then determined that I would build up this simple drawing three-dimensionally by ascending to a high point and that I would work only with curved, not straight lines. Again, why, I do not know for sure. Perhaps it was a sense that staying consistently within certain parameters would give a kind of unity to the piece, much like holding oneself to certain rules, which will, as Nietzsche remarked, "compel the chaos that is within us to take on form."[1]

The clay we worked with fired pinkish and one of the ways we finished it was with brown shoe polish, which we then washed with turpentine to even the distribution and allow the color to settle into the grooves so as to bring out the texture of the surface. We completed the process with clear paste wax brought through buffing to a satin glow. But in the case of this abstract piece, I soon noticed that the shape it took, were it to be finished off with a brown patina, would strongly resemble feces. I therefore sprayed it white! (Knowing the reason why I did this, one of my students named it *Albino Feces*.) Because some of the subforms that appeared in this piece suggested other forms (which I shall shortly describe), I subsequently called this piece *The Matrix* (fig. a).

I found that, for the most part, as I followed out the lines of connected forms that emerged, I had to sit with the piece for quite a while after it was completed, sometimes waiting for months before I was able to assign a name that fit what I had produced. I became interested only in exploring related lines of shapes, not in "saying" something. Hence when a ceramics student once asked me what I was trying to say with a particular piece (she always had an "intellectual" message behind her pieces), I was a bit irritated and said, "What I want to say is: 'Look, this is an interesting form!' My own professional craft is with words, and if I want to say something, I *say* it!"

One part of the original piece resembled a leg in a squatting position, so I decided to follow with a human figure in such a position. For no apparent reason I thought to build the piece as if it were made out of potatoes of various sizes—though now it occurs to me that perhaps it was because the brownish patina of the first pieces I produced resembled the

Figure a. **The Matrix**

Figure b. **Melancholy**

surface of potatoes. As I worked with building such forms into a human figure, I saw that the one side of the chest area that was exposed required another round form to interrelate the parts in a way that satisfied my sense of spatial distribution, so I inserted a small, rounded "potato" and the figure became female! Because of the general mood of the piece, especially the way the head was tilted, I subsequently named it *Melancholy* (fig. b).

Another aspect of *The Matrix* resembled a peach. *The Matrix* was generating a fruit and vegetable period. I made three interlocking stylized pieces of fruit: a peach joined to an orange, which was joined to a pear, which, in turn, joined the peach again in a circular dance. The dividing line that I ran through the side of the peach facing the viewer tilted upward in such a way as to suggest prolongation into a spiral that culminated in the top of the pear. But here the choice of these particular fruits suggested a female peach and a male pear, with the orange their offspring. I called it *Fruit Family* (fig. c). It is this piece that has haunted me with a call to turn it into a large outside installation. There's even a peculiar opening in a wooded area outside the art department that beckons for this purpose. It would be a concrete piece, eight feet tall, with the same earth tones as the small original, only set on a square base, at least one and a half feet high. I see it again and again. Maybe I'll get the time and the cooperation to bring it into being.

Figure c. **Fruit Family**

Figure d. **Fruitfulness**

Figure e. *Dance of Life*

Figure f. *Empty Womb*

After the original *Fruit Family* I played with the possibility of developing a half-peeled orange and gave it up in favor of opening out the peach and the orange forms, peeling and emptying them. But the empty spaces called for some positive form and so I inserted an egg form in each. The result I called *Fruitfulness* (fig. d).

The next step along this line was to work with onion forms using a variation on the same triple motif. A small onion is linked, via a common base, to a larger onion that has developed a slit in its surface; and this is followed by a still larger onion that had opened up and out of which spilled several small onions, which joined the small one with which I had started. I called this piece *Dance of Life* (fig. e).

This led to a stylized peapod, opened and showing three peas. This picked up and orchestrated four formal elements that had been developing: the vegetable motif, the round, the opening motif, and the triad. Unfortunately it was dropped and smashed to pieces in a move into a new office.

Following out the peeling of the fruit forms in *Fruitfulness* and the onion forms in *Dance of Life*, I pulled a single onion form out of the *Dance of Life*, elongated it, opened it up, and hollowed it out. I attempted two variations on the same theme. Sometime later I entitled each of them *Empty Womb* (fig. f).

Figure g. *Couple*

Figure h. *Madonna without Child*

The same elongation of the onion I kept solid and joined two forms of differing sizes together. Both tops were finished off with a slightly concave oval top that opened upward. The figures faced one another, with the tops curved in such a way that extending the lines of their curves into the surrounding space created above the negative space of two intersecting parabolas opened upward, and created below another negative space between them that resembled a heart. I called the piece *Couple* (fig. f). I attempted a triple with the same motifs and called it *Family,* but I am not pleased with the resulting form, which looks like a three-legged person diving into a lake.

Going back to the *Empty Womb:* tipped over, this form resembled a bird's skull, so I tried to make a form that looked like such a skull. My first attempt I destroyed because of bad execution. But it was transitional to an interest in skulls and bones. I did a human skull and two cow skulls. I began at this time to collect several skull and bone specimens. Studying a pelvic bone, I saw the possibility of developing a female form out of one half of such a bone. This led to two versions of *Madonna without Child,* in which the form provides an empty cradle (fig. h).

I was next led to join the pelvic bone motif with a kind of stylized tree. Four trunks ascended from a single base, joined at the top and the middle to a central form. From the top the joinings create a cross. Viewed frontally the two opposing trunks are connected by an arching, cradling, bonelike structure with two symmetrical oval hollows on top and two symmetrical archways on the bottom. Viewed from the side, the two opposing trunks, which lean backward, are joined to the middle by a sloping connector, slightly suggesting a Cycladic figure connected with its lyre I had recently seen at an exhibition. After a while I named it, with Heideggerian connections in mind, *The Play of the Fourfold* (fig. i).

The next piece was my most complicated. It consisted of two intertwined forms, intended as male and female, though their stylization made it impossible to determine which was which. The curves and holes of *Madonna without Child* as well as the interior negative space of *Empty Womb* played throughout this work. The two forms are both joined in one continuous form and separated by complicated negative spaces. The curves are arranged so that following out their directions visually leads into the surrounding space in such a way that the space of the whole so prolonged curls back upon itself. I called it *Family* (fig. j).

Meanwhile, the skulls suggested a more stylized version of a symmetrical, hollowed form with the use of negative spaces suggested by the quasiovals of *Fruitfulness* and the bilateral symmetry of the skulls. I pushed these forms in the direction of geometrical exactitude. I was not satisfied with

Figure i. *The Play of the Fourfold*          Figure j. *Family*

the first such form and never gave it a name. What followed it was more interesting. I began with a round form from which I carved two symmetrical ovals, within which I carved two smaller ovals, within which, in turn, I located a third set of ovals. I further pierced the resultant divider between the two great oval hollows with another oval space at right angles with the other ovals. Behind the triple-carved sets I entered the round form from behind in order to let the light shine through. The head of the art department saw the piece at this time and suggested that I set the form on a column—which I proceeded to do, making the column three times the original form in height and slightly smaller in circumference. I mediated the column and the hollowed out figure with a double collar a bit larger than the width of the divider between the two sets of ovals and I continued the line of that divider, after the gap created by the collar, down the length of the column to the bottom. The top form had an owlish look, with austere, un-

Figure k.
*The Categorical Imperative*

blinking eyes, and the column made it appear lofty. I began to see it as the owl of Minerva, symbol of wisdom, applied to the moral order. I subsequently called it, following Kant, *The Categorical Imperative*. It says, in effect, "I don't care how you feel; you *must* do it!" (fig. k).

Bilaterally symmetrical shapes alternating negative and positive round shapes and playing out sets of ovals led to a mother goddess form with a frontal oval for a head and an oval base at right angles with the stylized head, two hollows for eyes, two cupped hollows for hands and corresponding full round forms for breasts and derriere, with a large bulging oval form for the stomach. I called it *Mother Goddess*. Unfortunately, someone stole it from my office before I had time to have it photographed!

The mother goddess form put me in mind of African Yoruba *akuaba*s, fertility dolls that expectant mothers carried. I made one from memory of those I had seen in the local museum (fig. l).

This, in turn, brought me to a kind of culmination of my attempts, reaching the form that would be worthy of being cast in bronze. As I developed the akuaba, I noted its cruciform shape and thought that I could flatten it and turn it into a male crucified figure. The eyes were the hollows I had introduced into the Mother Goddess. I bypassed the mouth and produced a set of male genitalia that corresponded to the eye-nose relationship

Figure l. *African Yoruba* (*made by author from memory of examples in local museum*)

Figure m. *Imago Dei*

on the head, only with the positive spaces below matching the negative spaces above. I slightly hollowed and divided the chest area and also hollowed the stomach area. In this move I was guided not only by the shapes, but also by what I sought to express: the marital relation between the Crucified and His Church, for the negative mold of this figure matched in its slightly protruding breasts and slightly distended abdomen, as well as in its recessed genitalia, the female forms corresponding to the male figure. The whole was perfectly symmetrical. The arms and legs, though half-rounds, were stiff and flattened on the ends, paralleling the stiff and flattened horizontal and vertical beams of the cross. The round head was located in the center of the lower half of a surrounding oval halo, while the stomach and breasts corresponded below to the oval halo above. While the arms were perfectly horizontal, the straight lines of the legs each deviated from verticality, imaginatively extending to embrace the bottom edge of the halo. It was a study in alternating straight lines and oval shapes, flats and rounds, concave, flat, and convex surfaces. I called the piece *Christus Africanus* because of its akuaban origin. (See the frontispiece of this book.) But I also saw that formally it paralleled the Egyptian ankh, an androgynous symbol of eternal life. Three symbolic traditions representing life came together, two by design, one by accident: the Yoruba fertility doll; the Christian Cross, source of eternal life; and the Egyptian ankh. I subsequently made the negative mold into a corresponding female figure and have exhibited the two of them together. I called the pair *Imago Dei*, the image of God, after the statement in Genesis: "In His image and likeness He made them; male and female He made them" (fig. m). This was for me a culmination: it was that toward which, unbeknown to me, I had been pressing from the beginning.

One more effort virtually closed the lines I had been pursuing. Inspired by the African antelope headdresses I had often admired in the local museum and following the skull motif, I began with a stylized antelope skull, which I prolonged from the top of the head to curl back upon itself. Along the curve I developed a rhythmically decorated mane using alternating negative ovals on the surface, creating a regularly undulating edge outside and set of alternating positive and negative flat toothlike spaces inside. The decorated curve was linked to a base continuous with both sides of the form, skull and curve. The whole somewhat resembled an ear. One art student said I had made a gear. Linking that to the antelope I eventually called it, playfully, *The Ear Gear Deer* (fig. n). Subsequently I thought of an appropriate quasi-poem.

Figure n.  *The Ear Gear Deer*

*List' to the sound of the Ear Gear Deer*
*Ground in the wheels of the earth.*
*Hark to the round of the near-fear tear*
*Bound in the seals of its birth.*

There were a few other works after this. There were circular plaques showing variations on the theme of trinity, with dominant focus on the Spirit in the form of a dove. The outer circle represents the Father, the origin; the smaller inner circle is the Son, like the Father but in some sense subordinate, derivative. The Spirit is larger because the focus is on the relation to us of the trinitarian Godhead. Specially interesting to me is what a colleague noted: that I had produced, unbeknown to me, a "tongue of flame" in the dove form. Later I noticed that the dove was also an exact replica of the "angel fish" doodles I frequently make. Dove and fire, symbols of the Spirit; fish, symbol of Christianity—and angel fish at that! Subsequently I made a medal of the form and cast it in silver.

There followed an undistinguished recollection of an African mask, two statues of Saint Francis of Assisi, and several portrait busts, which I regard as secondary to my main interest in sculpting. The busts I had done now and then from the beginning of my productive period. On commission from Cedric Messina, producer of the BBC Shakespeare series, who directed our university's production of *The Merchant of Venice,* I did a terra cotta bust of Portia's father, made to look like the sire of the woman who played Portia, but as a joke made it bald as counterpoint to the leonine mane of tight red curls that adorned the leading lady. It was wheeled in and out of the set as the centerpiece that dominated the action.

But administrative duties, the editing of a journal, and the authoring of a couple of books, including the present one, turned my energies away from sculptural production and on toward further reflection. Maybe I will be moved again to take up the sculptural task anew, maybe not. I sometimes feel the itch to get back to the clay. But I think I learned something important about the productive process and I did arrive at a form that satisfied me.

## Reflections

What has struck me most about this process is that it began with a random relation of shapes I found particularly attractive and went on to generate lines of shapes to which meanings later accumulated and suggested names. One shape would call forth others, moving in a certain direction; then the lines would crisscross and run in still other directions. It was the shapes rather than the meanings that occupied my deliberate attention, until I arrived at the idea for *Christus Africanus,* where meaning and shape emerged together. Fruitful forms, family forms, symbols of life and death, of fundamental human relations, sexual and familial, and basic religious forms, trinitarian and cruciform, all rooted firmly in earthiness, in vital embodiment: these were the symbolic meanings playing around in my pursuit of lines of shapes. Perhaps the interlocking Cs, one facing forward, one reversed, that was the basis of *The Matrix,* was an unconscious symbol of coupling, since the fertility-dominated shapes sprang forth from it. I came to see more clearly that the choice of shapes was tied deeply to the things that mattered most to me, the things that gripped my heart, even though my focal interest was initially in the shapes. Henry Moore remarked that certain natural shapes are spontaneously symbolic[2]—an observation Herbert Read exploited in his Jungian interpretation of Moore's work.[3] Though Moore found the human figure the object of deepest interest, nonetheless he found principles of form and rhythm in the study of pebbles, rocks, bones, trees, shells, and plants, thus linking the human to the natural order from which it has arisen.[4] I found natural affinities with Moore in my spontaneous attraction to the same natural forms. Unusually shaped pebbles with smooth surfaces and transitions, sprinkled with small pods of various sorts stand in front of me on my desk, while a collection of seashells peers at me from a display case. Vertebrae and half a pelvic bone from a horse stand on or below my bookshelves along with the skull of a racoon. Several plants surround me in my home and office, while five large oaks shade the front of the house. The combined formal properties of these natural objects give a sense of form and texture deeply relevant to what guides the eye and hand in sculptural production. As Herbert Read noted, "the eye of the artist feeds unconsciously on whatever formal motes come its way."[5]

The smooth transitions and the overall unity of the bones as well as the comprehensive structure and patterns of the seashells are linked to their being functional parts of organic wholes and teach us to produce organic wholes. Trees and plants, of course, *are* organic wholes. The stones, on the other hand, are not organic wholes. They have to be collected by an eye already sensitized to organic form from the overwhelming numbers of randomly generated forms produced by the grinding and washing process of the ocean and lake waves rubbing them against other stones. Having a visual understanding of the formal properties of such objects allows for the production of visual objects that do not necessarily represent or replicate the appearance of naturally produced objects appearing in the world of everyday attention.

Hence for Moore, Greco-Roman idealistic representation is but one conception. There is a broader conception, capable of doing justice to the whole range of differing styles of sculpture that have emerged historically, from the more primitive to the most modern. To see it, he said, one must remove the Greek spectacles.[6] Here he is less dogmatic than the Futurists, like Boccione, who speak of "the Phidian period and its decadence" and "Michaelangelesque [sic] sins."[7] Moore sees the great sculpture of the world in Sumerian, early Greek, Etruscan, Ancient Mexican, Fourth- and Twelfth-Dynasty Egyptian, Romanesque, and early Gothic styles.[8] What redeems Phidias for Moore is that he still maintained the fundamental sculptural principles of the archaic Greeks, which express an intense vitality, as certain figures of the Renaissance still remained close to primitive grandeur and simplicity. So-called "classical" periods arise on the basis of "primitive" art and then slowly fade into technical tricks and intellectual conceits.[9] Indeed, the realistic ideal of physical beauty in art was "only a digression from the main world tradition of sculpture, while . . . Romanesque and Early Gothic are in the main line."[10] Here Moore shares common ground with Brancusi, who said, "What is real is not the external form, but the essence of things. Starting with this truth it is impossible for anyone to express anything essentially real by imitating its exterior surface."[11] Along the same lines, Rodin makes a distinction between imitation of "form" and imitation of "life."[12] In this view, what is important is not beauty but vitality and power of expression.[13] The inclusivist conception Moore advances is sensitive to the intrinsic emotional significance of shapes and the importance of the materials employed.[14] Here Moore articulates a view identical with the architectural view of Frank Lloyd Wright[15] and parallel to the one advanced by Plotinus against Plato's (perhaps ironic) presentation of art as surface imitation. Unfortunately, it is Plato's overt view that has determined most people's expectation of the work of art. Moore sees the historical mission of Brancusi's work lying in a process of simplification that eliminated all surface distraction that has cluttered shape since the end of the Gothic. Brancusi's work thereby makes us more shape conscious.[16] In moving toward that consciousness, Wright, Brancusi, and Moore paid special attention to the nature of materials in their work.[17]

In my own work, at first asymmetrical organicity was the dominant formal motif, the belonging together of spatial configurations that ultimately harmonized, one with all the others, to compose a single whole. In sculpture the problem is much more complex than in painting, for in painting one has to satisfy "organistic" conditions only in two dimensions. The addition of the third dimension adds an indeterminate number of perspectives, each of which has to be respected to produce an integral piece. As Moore remarked, this makes sculpture the most difficult of all arts.[18] One has to learn how to perceive in three dimensions, so that today people are often more attracted to sculpture at first through photographic reproduction.[19] But to capture and express the vitality of the work, the sculptor has to occupy the center of gravity of the piece, which holds all the perspectives together.[20]

Producing works that are closer to relief is more like painting: the problem of organicity here is basically two-dimensional. But in the fully three-dimensional pieces, working the material from one perspective immediately modifies the other perspectives. This makes portrait busts particularly difficult. One has to capture the subject from all angles simultaneously. More freely creative work is easier because one does not have to attend to exactitude of resemblance with a given subject and is freer to pursue the aesthetic possibilities. Nonetheless, it is virtually impossible to conceive of a work from all angles simultaneously, so that one inevitably has to create as one goes along. And each decision one makes limits the possibilities for the next decision. Clay is easier in this respect, since one can always reverse a whole set of decisions—something that marble or wood does not allow. Furthermore, marble or wood does a lot more independent talking back by revealing the limits of the grain's ability to cooperate with the emerging form, for one ought not simply impose the form on the marble or the wood, but develop it in relation to the grain of the material. Michelangelo immortalized this relation between the material and the artist in the famous lines, "Non ha l'ottimo artista alcun concetto / Ch' un marmo solo in se non circonscriva." (The best artist has no concept that a piece of marble alone does not circumscribe within itself.) This is a notion that has passed into the fundamental character of twentieth-century sculpture.[21]

In my work, the process of production typically began with a rather vague idea that took on more determinate shape as I worked with the materials. Moore claims the creative process can begin from either of two ends of human experience, which he calls order and surprise, intellect and imagination, conscious and unconscious. One can have an expressed idea, after which one must figure out how to render it in the appropriate medium, or one can simply begin vaguely and let the idea come to fruition in the process of production.[22] The latter has been my typical mode of procedure.

In my own work, following the move from groups of vegetative forms to single animal and human forms via the interest in skulls, the dominant formal motif shifted for the most part from the belonging together of asymmetrical forms to bilateral symmetry, a subspecies of which is the vertebrate organic, involving a balance of two sides of a piece such that each side replicates the other. After the shift from vegetable and fruit to animal and human forms, the three-dimensional forms all display this. However, the plaques and medal maintain an asymmetrical internally organic preoccupation. What is tempting about bilateral symmetry is that it is an easy way to bring about a kind of harmony. It is the way followed by paper cutouts, kaleidoscopes, and Rorschach inkblots and also by Georgian architecture. The real aesthetic challenge, however, is the same in both forms, symmetrical or not: to create harmony or organic unity among the elements of either side so that a side could exist as a unity all its own. A human profile is an example of this challenge. Symmetry makes the elements correspond point by point with their symmetrical opposite and so adds balance to the piece. Either form displays wholeness.

The medium too has its own symbolic value. Bronze and stone, and to a lesser extent wood or ceramic clay fired at extreme temperatures, have a fixity, a solidity less subject to the decay of time than paint on canvas or plaster. A sculpted piece suggests an endurance, a hardness, a resistance and is particularly fit for memorializing. It renders its subject "immortal." The medium also determines treatment: modeling (e.g., with clay or wax, often linked with casting as a second step), carving (e.g., wood, stone, ivory), and, in more recent times, construction. Some dogmatic purists—and there are as many of them in the world of art as there are in religion—insist that carving is the only true form. R. H. Wilenski, for example, downplays modeling as more suited to Romanticism, which focuses on individualism and loses the more universal expressiveness involved in carving.[23] Others who claim "truth to materials" in too one-sided a way miss the sense of pleasant surprise involved in shifting from one medium to another in casting what is originally conceived in clay or wax or even in a hard (and thus carved) medium. Nonetheless, there is something important in Wilenski's observation that there is a formal meaning in each substance with which the true sculptor has to reckon.[24]

The sense of space is integral to sculpture, and not only the filling of space by mass. As Boccione notes, the different aspects of shapes interplay in such a way as to set up a dynamic relation between the parts and a kind of charge in the surrounding space.[25] The lines that determine a given form and the negative spaces within it suggest prolongation into that environing space. They make visible a translation into the sculptural medium of "those atmospheric planes that link and intersect things," giving "plastic form to the mysterious sympathies and affinities that the reciprocal formal influences of the planes of objects create."[26] Opening the forms provides a whole new dimension to a sculptural piece: a sense of inwardness and a sense of containment. The hole opens a third dimension, as, for example, in the work of Henry Moore and Barbara Hepworth (paralleled by the painting of her husband, Ben Nicholson, and the pelvic bone paintings of Georgia O'Keefe).[27] For Moore, the hole immediately creates the sense of the third dimension, while simultaneously evoking the mystery of the cave.[28] Together, external and internal space add, as it were, another dimension to traditional focus on mass.[29] Hollows and full forms of similar shape call out to one another; dissimilar shapes establish a counterpoint; and both play in relation to occupied space. In interplay with such shapes, the parts take on a kind of rhythm and harmony suggesting, as in every art form, a certain mood.[30] One might note here that the focus on space as a kind of material all its own is a peculiarity of modern art forms. The International Style in architecture for example, was dedicated to the shaping of space.[31]

My focus has been on free-standing sculpture. Mention of architecture calls attention to one of the dominant traditions, where sculpture is subservient to architecture. It was this tradition that almost wholly occupied the attention of John Ruskin, who claimed that "perfect sculpture must be a part of the severest architecture. . . . The first office of that sculpture is not to represent the things it imitates but to gather out of them those arrangements of form which shall be pleasing to the eye in their intended places."[32] Ruskin was particularly attentive to the medieval cathedrals, where the statuary was designed to fit into the niches provided by the architecture of the building, but where also sculpted decoration, often employing vegetative motifs, developed its own stylized rhythm. This entailed a play between representation and stylization that characterizes all good art, even the most "imitative."

In sculpture as well as in architecture, texture is particularly important. It sets up a play between light and shadow on the surface of the piece to help create the dominant mood of the work. An overly smooth piece might take on a boring character compared with the surface of one of Rodin's nudes which ripples and flashes as one moves around the work.

Though the ancient Greeks painted the surface of many of their statues, time has worn it off, presenting us today with naked marble or bronze. Schopenhauer, who should have known this fact, praised the Greeks for their "infallible good taste," as over against painted wax sculpture, since they are said to have left work for the imagination of the viewer.[33] Taste has largely moved in the direction dictated by the ravages of time: color, beyond that provided by the medium itself, with some addition of a patina, has usually not been associated with high-level sculpture. Of course, in contemporary times, no canons of taste are followed. Three-dimensional painted pieces, fusing painting and sculptural construction, are commonplace. And waxworks realism is found in many contemporary exhibitions. (In the Stuttgart museum I almost said "Pardon me" to the cleaning lady, until I noticed she did not move!)

In this regard, I am reminded of Hegel's remark regarding the legendary competition between Zeuxis and Parrhasios in which Zeuxis remarked that he had painted grapes so realistically that he deceived the birds, who tried to peck at them. Parrhasios then directed the braggart to pull back the drapes to see a real painting, only to have the grape painter discover that the drapes were painted! One who could fool humans is a greater painter than one who can fool birds![34] But, as Hegel remarked: So someone has such hand-eye coordination as to be able to fool perceivers into thinking the work of art is its real counterpart—so what? Where is the value of being able so to deceive? The invention of hammer and nails was much more significant to the development of humankind![35] Kant noted that the creation of illusion pleases for only a short time and we are soon bored with it.[36] Such illusionary art turns us back to the artist to admire his or her dexterity. It is an art of conspicuous display, much like the rich throwing money about to show their own ability to accumulate.

Of course, artists can do what they want. But art functions at a more profound level when it so transforms our ordinary "dashboard" relationship to things as to give us a sense of meaningful presence and of the underlying depths and encompassing wholeness, which are nonetheless anchored in the individual, sensorily present work. Art haunts us and has the ability to bring us both to an enhanced appreciation of sensory surface and, simultaneously, to a sense of lived meaning. And it can do this because it arises within and appeals to the field of human experience, which is anchored in the sensuous here and now and referred to the encompassing Whole through the mediations of cultural tradition. We have examined that structure throughout this work.

# Notes

## Preface

1. Robert E. Wood, *Martin Buber's Ontology: An Analysis of* I and Thou (Evanston, Ill.: Northwestern University Press, 1969).

2. Robert E. Wood, *A Path into Metaphysics: Phenomenological, Hermeneutical, and Dialogical Studies* (Albany: State University of New York Press, 1991).

3. I have presented a lengthy exposition of a seven-volume work (the first part of a trilogy on beauty, goodness, and truth) that advances that thesis against the background of the whole history of Western literature, philosophy, and theology in "Philosophy, Aesthetics, and Theology," *American Catholic Philosophical Quarterly* 67.3 (Summer 1993): 355–82.

## I. Introduction

1. I contend that this is exactly what is involved in Plato's Line of Knowledge. Cf. Robert E. Wood, "Plato's Line Revisited: The Pedagogy of Complete Reflection," *Review of Metaphysics* 44 (March 1991): 525–47.

2. Alfred North Whitehead, *Process and Reality: An Essay in Cosmology* (New York: Harper, 1960).

3. Edmund Husserl, *General Introduction to a Pure Phenomenology*, trans. F. Kersten, vol. 1 of *Ideas Pertaining to a Pure Phenomenology and to a Phenomenological Philosophy* (The Hague: Martinus Nijhoff, 1982), 21.

4. For an exposition of the major phenomenologists—Husserl, Scheler, Heidegger, Sartre, Merleau-Ponty—in relation to Plato's Line of Knowledge, see Robert E. Wood, "The Phenomenologists" in *Reading Philosophy for the Twenty-First Century*, ed. G. McLean (Lanham, Md.: University Press of America, 1989), 131–60.

5. On functioning intentionality, cf. Edmund Husserl, *The Crisis of European Sciences and Transcendental Phenomenology: An Introduction to Phenomenological Philosophy*, trans. D. Carr (Evanston, Ill.: Northwestern University Press, 1970), 109.

6. This is analogous to the threefold structure that governs Mikel Dufrenne's treatment in *The Phenomenology of Aesthetic Experience,* trans. E. Casey et al. (Evanston, Ill.: Northwestern University Press, 1973). Dufrenne distinguishes the sensous, the represented object, and the expressed world as aesthetic developments of presence, representation, and reflection (333ff.). It is in the relation between reflection and feeling that he locates what I am calling presence-to-being, as both distinguished from and found in the presence he locates as the sensuous component. I have explored these matters a bit more fully in *Path into Metaphysics,* especially in chapters 2 and 3.

7. Cf. Martin Heidegger, "The Origin of the Work of Art" (henceforth OWA), in *Poetry, Language, and Thought,* trans. A. Hofstadter (New York: Harper and Row, 1971), 26 (henceforth *PLT*).

8. Bernard Lonergan, *Insight: A Study of Human Understanding* (London: Longmans, Green, 1958), 416.

9. In what follows, I would claim fidelity to the acute observations of Aristotle throughout his *On the Soul* in close correlation with Hegel's work in *Philosophy of Mind,* where he claims direct descent from Aristotle's work. G. W. F. Hegel, *Hegel's Philosophy of Mind,* trans. W. Wallace (Oxford: Clarendon Press, 1971), 3 (henceforth *HPM*). For more recent accounts drawing upon contemporary research, see also Maurice Merleau-Ponty, *The Structure of Behavior,* trans. A. Fisher (Boston: Beacon Press, 1963), 59–114 and Errol Harris, in *Hypothesis and Perception: The Roots of Scientific Method* (London: George Allen and Unwin, 1970), 249–92 as well as *The Foundation of Metaphysics in Science* (Lanham, Md.: University Press of America, 1983), 388–419.

10. Cf. Friedrich Nietzsche, "On Truth and Lie in an Extra-moral Sense," in *The Portable Nietzsche,* ed. and trans. W. Kaufmann (New York: Viking, 1954), 42–47.

11. Cf. Aristotle, *On the Soul,* trans. W. Hett (Cambridge, Mass.: Harvard University Press, 1975), 3.12.434a23ff. (henceforth *OS*). Descartes understood this: see *Meditations on First Philosophy,* trans. D. Cress (Indianapolis: Hackett, 1979), 6.50ff.

12. Cf. Harris, *Foundation,* 163ff.

13. Cf. Robert E. Wood, "Being and Manifestness: Philosophy, Science, and Poetry in an Evolutionary Worldview," *International Philosophical Quarterly* 35.4 (December 1995): 437–47.

14. The recovery of natural form and teleology by Kant in the mode of "as if"— *Critique of Judgment,* trans. W. Pluhar (Indianapolis: Hackett, 1987), §§64–65.248–55 (henceforth *CJ*)—was made central to nonhypothetical expressivity in Schopenhauer, *The World as Will and Representation,* trans. E. Payne, 2 vols. (New York: Dover, 1966), vol. 1, bk. 2, §18, 99ff. (henceforth *WWR*). Cf. also Hans Urs von Balthasar, *Seeing the Form,* trans. E. Leiva-Merikakis, vol. 1 of *The Glory of the Lord* (San Francisco: Ignatius Press, 1982), 118, 151, 442, 444.

15. The felicitous metaphor of "dashboard knowledge" is Owen Barfield's in *Saving the Appearances: A Study in Idolatry* (New York: Harcourt, Brace and World, 1957), 28–35.

16. Aurelius Augustine, *Confessions,* trans. W. Watts, 2 vols. (Cambridge, Mass.: Harvard University Press, 1977), 3.6.

17. On the givenness of space and time as the framework of all experience, see Immanuel Kant, *Critique of Pure Reason,* trans. N. K. Smith (New York: St. Martin's Press, 1929), B 38/A 24f., 68–69 (henceforth *CPR*). There is the obvious question, made current in contemporary physics, of the real separability of space and time. Plato's notion

of the *receptacle (hupodoche)* interrelates the two; Plato, *Timaeus,* trans. R. Bury (Cambridge, Mass.: Harvard University Press, 1977), 49. For a correlation of time and space with subject and object, see Dufrenne, *Phenomenology,* 346ff.

18. Cf. Lonergan, *Insight,* 348ff.

19. For a treatment of the principle of noncontradiction, see Aristotle, *Metaphysics,* trans. H. Tredennick, 2 vols. (Cambridge, Mass.: Harvard University Press, 1967), bk. 4, 1005b ff. See Aristotle's *Organon* for the foundations of logic. Hegel's challenge to the principle in his *Logic* does not eliminate but only locates it: in fact, people do contradict one another and themselves, though they each remain what they are in spite of that. Existential contradiction in organisms becomes the motor for establishing an identity that strives to remove the contradiction. On contradiction, see *Hegel's Science of Logic,* trans. A.V. Miller (London: George Allen and Unwin, 1969), 431ff.; on the organism, 770 (henceforth *SL*).

20. Cf. Martin Heidegger, *Being and Time,* trans. J. Macquarrie and E. Robinson (New York: Harper, 1962), 32–35 (henceforth *BAT*).

21. Cf. Baruch Spinoza, *Ethics,* trans. R. Elwes (New York: Dover, 1955), pt. 2, prop. 44, cor. 2, 117.

22. On the notion of "decision" in this context, cf. Heidegger, OWA, 67. For a wider discussion of the nature of freedom see Robert E. Wood, "Aspects of Freedom," *Philosophy Today* 15.1 (Spring 1991): 106–15.

23. Cf. Lewis Mumford, *The Myth of the Machine: Technics and Human Development* (New York: Harcourt Brace Jovanovich, 1966), 51.

24. On the notion of the heart, see Stephen Strasser, *Phenomenology of Feeling: An Essay on the Phenomena of the Heart,* trans. and intro. R. Wood (Pittsburgh: Duquesne University Press, 1977).

25. For a systematic sketch of these meanings, see my introduction to Strasser, *Phenomenology,* 11–14.

26. Dufrenne, *Phenomenology,* 398, 402–7.

27. Søren Kierkegaard, *Either/Or,* vol. 1, trans. D. Swenson and L. M. Swenson (Garden City, N.Y.: Anchor Books, 1959).

28. Cf. Heidegger, *BAT,* 278–311.

29. Martin Buber, *Daniel: Dialogues on Realization,* trans. M. Friedman (New York: Mc-Graw-Hill, 1965), 91.

30. Schopenhauer, *WWR,* vol. 2, chap. 17, 161.

31. Cf. Dufrenne, *Phenomenology,* 137.

32. Ibid., 154.

33. Cf. Umberto Boccione, "The Futurist Manifesto" in *Theories of Modern Art,* ed. H. Chipp (Berkeley: University of California Press, 1968), 298–304.

34. Cf. Sigfried Giedion, *Space, Time, and Architecture: The Growth of a New Tradition* (Cambridge, Mass.: Harvard University Press, 1980), 385ff.; also Peter Collins, *Changing Ideals in Modern Architecture, 1750–1950* (Kingston, Ont.: McGill-Queen's University Press, 1984), 128ff.

35. Cf. Mark Taylor, *Disfiguring: Art, Architecture, Religion* (Chicago: University of Chicago Press, 1992), 242ff. Cf. Friedrich Nietzsche's suggestive comments on historical existence in *On the Uses and Disadvantages of History for Life,* in *Untimely Meditations,* trans. R. Hollingdale (London: Cambridge University Press, 1983).

36. Cf. Plato, *Politicus*, 259b, where *techne* and *episteme* are used interchangeably; *Politicus, Philebus, Ion*, trans. H. Fowler and W. Lamb (Cambridge, Mass.: Harvard University Press, 1975). See also Kant, *CJ*, §43.170; cf. also Aristotle, *Nichomachean Ethics*, trans. H. Rackham (Cambridge, Mass.: Harvard University Press, 1975), 4.3 (henceforth *NE*); and Paul Kristeller, "The Modern System of Fine Arts," in *Renaissance Thought and the Arts: Collected Essays* (Princeton, N.J.: Princeton University Press, 1990), 166.

37. Cf. Martin Heidegger, *The Question Concerning Technology, and Other Essays*, trans. W. Lovitt (New York: Harper and Row, 1977), 175 (henceforth *QCT*).

38. Plato, *Timaeus*, 28. As we will see below (chap. 10), Heidegger considers the West to have been dominated in its view of Being by the notion of production. Being is considered to lie in the enduring form, which is the goal of the production process. Cf. Martin Heidegger, *The Basic Problems of Phenomenology*, trans. A. Hofstadter (Bloomington: Indiana University Press, 1988), 99ff.

39. Cf. chap. 3.

40. As we will see below (chaps. 8, 9).

41. Aristotle, *NE*, 6.1140a.

42. *NE*, 1.2.1094a28.

43. *NE*, 10.1177a12ff.

44. Karl Marx, "From Excerpt—Notes of 1844," in *Writings of the Young Marx on Philosophy and Society*, ed. and trans. L. Easton and K. Guddat (Garden City, N.Y.: Doubleday, 1967), 281.

45. Cf. Kristeller, "Modern System," 163–227.

46. Plato, *The Republic*, trans. P. Shorey, 2 vols. (Cambridge, Mass.: Harvard University Press, 1969), 7.521b ff. (henceforth *Rep*).

47. See Plato's *Sophist* and *Politicus* for early illustrations of this insight into understanding as the display of samenesses and differences.

48. For a report on a more in-depth systematic treatment of the arts, see Robert E. Wood, "Metaphysics and Aesthetics," in *The Philosophy of Paul Weiss*, ed. L. Hahn, Library of Living Philosophers (Carbondale: Southern Illinois University Press, 1995), 615–35. Weiss's work appeared in *The World of Art* and *Nine Basic Arts* (Carbondale: Southern Illinois University Press, 1961).

49. Cf. Dufrenne, *Phenomenology*, 358; Umberto Eco, *Art and Beauty in the Middle Ages*, trans. H. Bredin (New Haven: Yale University Press, 1986), 66.

50. Thomas Aquinas, *Summa theologiae* (New York: Benziger Brothers, 1947), 1.78.3 (henceforth *ST*).

51. Cf. Robert E. Wood, "Heidegger on the Way to Language," in *Semiotics 1984*, ed. J. Deely (Lanham, Md.: University Press of America, 1985), 661–20 and "Martin Buber's Philosophy of the Word," *Philosophy Today* 30 (Winter 1986): 317–24.

52. Cf. Dufrenne, *Phenomenology*, 102.

53. Richard Wagner, *The Art-work of the Future*, trans. W. Ellis (London, 1892).

54. For a discussion of each of the art forms entailed, see Paul Weiss, *Cinematics* (Carbondale: Southern Illinois University Press, 1975).

55. For a penetrating treatment of film, see Stanley Cavell, *The World Viewed: Reflections on the Ontology of Film* (New York: Viking, 1971).

56. Cf. Dufrenne, *Phenomenology*, 77.

57. For a fuller discussion of architecture, see Robert E. Wood, "Architecture: Confluence of Art, Technology, Politics, and Nature" in *The Nature of Technology*, Proceedings of the American Catholic Philosophical Association (Washington, D.C.: The Catholic University of America, 1996), 79–93. One of the best books on the philosophy of architecture is Karsten Harries, *The Ethical Function of Architecture* (Cambridge, Mass.: MIT Press, 1997).

58. Cf. Constantin Brancusi, *Brancusi*, ed. Ionel Jianou (London: Adam, 1963), 69.

59. For the development of this concept, cf. Roman Ingarden, *The Cognition of the Literary Work of Art*, trans. R. Crowley and K. Olson (Evanston, Ill.: Northwestern University Press, 1973).

60. Schopenhauer makes much of this insight in *WWR*, 2, suppl. to bk. 3, chap. 34, 408.

61. Arthur Danto, *The Transfiguration of the Commonplace: A Philosophy of Art* (Cambridge, Mass.: Harvard University Press, 1983), 115ff.

62. Henry Moore, "A View of Sculpture," in *Henry Moore* (New York: George Wittenborn, 1968), 1:xxx.

63. Aristotle, *The Politics of Aristotle*, trans. E. Barker (Cambridge: Oxford University Press, 1970), 8.5.1340a1ff.

64. Heidegger, OWA, 73.

65. Walter Pater, *The Renaissance*, in *Selected Writings of Walter Pater*, ed. Harold Bloom (New York: Columbia University Press, 1974), 55–57.

66. For one of the major sources of modern hermeneutic thinking, see Hans Georg Gadamer, *Truth and Method*, trans. G. Barden and J. Comming (New York: Crossroad, 1982).

67. Thus there is a difference between a Platonic, an Aristotelian, a Cartesian, a Hobbesian, and a Whiteheadian body—even though all of them take their point of departure in some way from sensory presentation. See Wood, "Being and Manifestness."

68. Cf. Martin Buber, "Dialogue," in *Between Man and Man* (Boston: Beacon Press, 1961).

## II. Plato

1. For an illustration of how this works in Plato's central dialogue and for a general orientation in the *Republic*, see Robert E. Wood, "Image, Structure and Content: On a Passage in Plato's *Republic*," *Review of Metaphysics* 40 (March 1987): 495–514.

2. Alexander Pope, *An Essay on Man*, ed. F. Brady (Indianapolis: Bobbs-Merrill, 1965), 2.1.17.

3. Cf. *Theaetetus* (155c), in which Socrates says that the principle of philosophy is awe. Plato, *Theaetetus* and *Sophist*, trans. H. Fowler (Cambridge, Mass.: Harvard University Press, 1977). Heidegger picks that up again more recently in *What Is Philosophy?* trans. W. Kluback and J. Wilde (New York: Twayne, 1958), 78–85 (henceforth *WP*).

4. G. W. F. Hegel, *Phenomenology of Spirit*, trans. A. Miller (Oxford: Clarendon Press, 1977), preface, §20.11 (henceforth *PS*).

5. *Rep*, 2.268d.

6. *Rep*, 2.272b.

7. *Rep,* 2.272d.

8. Dufrenne, *Phenomenology,* 62–63: there are works that "flatter our subjectivity," but "authentic art turns us away from ourselves and toward itself."

9. *Rep,* 3.410d.

10. Plato, *The Laws of Plato,* trans. T. Pangle (New York: Basic Books, 1980), 2.672e (henceforth *Laws*).

11. *Rep,* 3.412d–e, 420e.

12. *Rep,* 3.401a.

13. *Rep,* 10.596d.

14. *Rep,* 10.601d.

15. We will see this discussed in some detail in chapter 9, on the aesthetics of John Dewey.

16. *Laws,* 2.698b f.

17. *Rep,* 3.399d.

18. See Carl Dahlhaus, *The Idea of Absolute Music,* trans. R. Lustig (Chicago: University of Chicago Press, 1989), 8. It is precisely this priority of the word that will be challenged in the emergence of "absolute music" and its metaphysical grounding in Schopenhauer.

19. *Laws,* 2.668a; cf. Aristotle, *Politics,* 1340a.

20. *Rep,* 3.400e.

21. *Rep,* 2.399c–d. It is not clear what *polyharmonic* means here, especially with regard to the flute.

22. *Laws,* 2.672a.

23. *Rep,* 4.424c.

24. *Rep,* 3.400e.

25. For the body as a harmonic whole, see, for example, *Rep,* 1.350a, where it is implicit, and *Rep,* 3.401a.

26. *Rep,* 3.402a.

27. *Rep,* 2.378a.

28. *Rep,* 3.386a ff.

29. *Rep,* 3.403c.

30. *Rep,* 3.415d; 4.124d.

31. *Rep,* 4.427e ff.

32. *Rep,* 4.433a ff.

33. *Rep,* 4.434d–37a.

34. Karl Popper, *The Open Society and Its Enemies* (Princeton, N.J.: Princeton University Press, 1950), 11ff. Cf. Thomas Thorson, ed., *Plato: Totalitarian or Democrat?* (Englewood Cliffs, N.J.: Prentice-Hall, 1963).

35. *Rep,* 5.449a.

36. On community of wives and children, see *Rep,* 4.423e; on property, see 416d.

37. On the equality of women and men, see *Rep,* 4.451c ff.; on the philosopher-king, see 473d ff.

38. *Rep,* 5.451c.

39. *Rep,* 5.459d, 461c; 6.490b, 499b; 7.540b.

40. *Rep,* 5.476a.

41. *Rep,* 7.540a.

42. *Rep*, 6.507d ff.

43. *Rep*, 6.509d. For a further elaboration of what follows, see Robert E. Wood, "Plato's Line Revisited: The Pedagogy of Complete Reflection," *Review of Metaphysics* 44 (March 1991): 525–47.

44. *Rep*, 6.508e.

45. *Rep*, 6.511b.

46. For a development of this theme see my "Self-reflexivity in The *Theaetetus:* On the Lifeworld of a Platonic Dialogue," *The Review of Metaphysics* [forthcoming].

47. *Rep*, 6.510b.

48. *Timaeus*, 49b–53c; cf. A. N. Whitehead, *Adventures of Ideas* (New York: Free Press, 1967), 150; for an exposition of Whitehead's Platonism, see Wood, *Path into Metaphysics*, chap. 15.

49. *Rep*, 6.509b.

50. *Rep*, 5.478e.

51. *Sophist*, 266c; cf. also *Rep*, 6.509e.

52. *Sophist*, 257a–59d.

53. *Rep*, 7.520c.

54. *Laws*, 10.897d.

55. *Sophist*, 264d f.

56. *Rep*, 3.392d.

57. *Rep*, 4.439d.

58. I tried to demonstrate that in "Image, Structure, and Content."

59. *Rep*, 10.607c.

60. *Rep*, 10.596d.

61. *Laws*, 2.669a.

62. *Rep*, 10.607c.

63. *Rep*, 10.597b f.

64. *Laws*, 2.668d.

65. Plotinus, *The Enneads*, trans. A. H. Armstrong, Loeb Classical bilingual edition (Cambridge, Mass.: Harvard University Press, 1989), 5.8.5 (henceforth *Enn*); Hegel, *Philosophy of Fine Art*, trans. F. Osmaston (London: G. Bell, 1920), 1:9–10; Schopenhauer, *WWR*, 2, suppl. to bk. 3, chap. 34, 408; Heidegger, OWA, 50.

66. Martin Buber, "Man and His Image Work," in *The Knowledge of Man: A Philosophy of the Interhuman*, trans. M. Friedman and R. G. Smith (New York: Harper and Row, 1965), 159.

67. Plato, *Parmenides*, trans. H. Fowler (Cambridge, Mass.: Harvard University Press, 1963), 130d.

68. *Rep*, 10.601c.

69. *Rep*, 10.597e.

70. *Sophist*, 465b.

71. Plato, *Gorgias*, in *Lysis, Symposium, Gorgias*, trans. W. Lamb (Cambridge, Mass.: Harvard University Press, 1975), 464b f.

72. Plato, *Phaedrus*, in *Euthyphro; Apology; Crito; Phaedo; Phaedrus*, trans. H. Fowler (Cambridge, Mass.: Harvard University Press, 1957), 248d.

73. Cf. also *Ion*, 533e ff.

74. *Rep*, 1.327a.

75. *Phaedrus,* 248d.
76. *Rep,* 2.372d.
77. *Rep,* 3.398c.
78. *Rep,* 6.506d.
79. *Symposium,* 201e (henceforth *Sym*).
80. *Rep,* 5.451c.
81. *Sym,* 206b.
82. *Sym,* 210a.
83. *Phaedrus,* 255c.
84. *Politicus,* 283b ff.
85. Aristotle, *Poetics,* trans. W. Fyfe (Cambridge, Mass.: Harvard University Press, 1973), 8.1451a30ff.; 23.1459a20.
86. *Sym,* 180c.
87. *Phaedrus,* 250d.
88. *Phaedrus,* 255c.
89. Plato, *Greater Hippias,* in *Cratylus; Parmenides; Greater Hippias; Lesser Hippias,* trans. H. Fowler (Cambridge, Mass.: Harvard University Press, 1963), 294c.
90. Ibid., 290c, 293e.
91. *Rep,* 10.601d.
92. I have attempted to lay out what I regard as the inescapable eidetic structures involved in all experience in "Taking the Universal Viewpoint: A Descriptive Approach," *Review of Metaphysics* 50 (June 1997): 69–78.
93. See Wood, *Path into Metaphysics,* chap. 6, for a treatment of this opening.
94. Dufrenne, *Phenomenology,* 117ff.
95. *Theaetetus,* 175a.
96. *Theaetetus,* 155c.
97. Frank Lloyd Wright, *The Future of Architecture* (New York: Mentor, 1953), 115. For a fuller treatment, see Wood, "Architecture."
98. Wright, *Future of Architecture,* 160, 206–8.
99. Ibid., 141.
100. Ibid., 156ff. On surface decoration, see 93.
101. Ibid., 33. Cf. the whole chapter "The Cardboard House," 143–62.
102. Ibid., 144, 152, 155.
103. Ibid., 94ff.
104. Ibid., 66.
105. Ibid., 60, 234.
106. Ibid., 70, 123.
107. Ibid., 221.
108. Ibid., 104. On 195, Wright calls for "ordered freedom" and an essential distinction between creative joy and mere pleasure seeking.
109. Ibid., 101.

## III. Aristotle

1. Aristotle, *The Physics,* trans. P. Wicksteed and F. Cornford (Cambridge, Mass.:

Harvard University Press, 1980), 2.1.192b8–19 and 4.195b31ff.; 9.199b34ff.; *Metaphysics,* 7.7.1032a13.

2. *NE,* 3.2.111b4ff.

3. *OS,* 3.425b27.

4. *OS,* 3.4.415b1.

5. *OS,* 3.425b27.

6. *NE,* 6.1.1139a7.

7. *NE,* 6.1141a.

8. *NE,* 1.2.1094a28.

9. *NE,* 2.1103a14.

10. See Wood, "Aspects of Freedom."

11. *NE,* 6.4.1140a1ff.

12. *Nicomachean Ethics,* W. D. Ross translation in R. McKeon (ed.), *The Basic Works of Aristotle* (New York: Random House, c. 1941), 1025

13. Aristotle, *Aristotle's Nicomachean Ethics,* trans. Hippocrates G. Apostle (Grinell, Iowa: Peripatetic Press, 1984), 104.

14. *NE* (Rackham trans.), 335.

15. Aquinas, *ST,* 1–2.57.3.

16. This is one of Heidegger's basic distinctions. See below, chap. 10, 5.

17. Elder Olson, "The Poetic Method in Aristotle," in *Aristotle's* Poetics *and English Literature,* ed. E. Olson (Toronto: University of Toronto Press, 1965), 181.

18. *NE,* 3.1118a21–3.

19. Cf. chap. 5.

20. Plato, *Timaeus,* 49.

21. *Physics,* 2.2-3.194a, 22–195b, 30. Cf. also my treatment of Aristotle in *Path into Metaphysics,* chap. 8.

22. *Physics,* 2.193a10 ff.

23. *OS,* 3.425b27.

24. *OS,* 2.1.412b.

25. *Metaphysics,* 12.1072b.

26. Cf. chaps. 7 and 8, below.

27. *Poetics,* 4.1448b.

28. Cf. chap. 2, above.

29. *Politics,* 8.5.1340a1ff.

30. *NE,* 2.1102a26.

31. *OS,* 3.2.425b26. For a similar position advanced by Socrates, see *Theaetetus,* 153d.

32. This seems to be a constant from Galileo and Kepler through Descartes, Locke, Hume, Kant, on up to Russell.

33. Heidegger, *BAT,* §29.172ff. Cf. also "What Is Metaphysics?" in *Martin Heidegger: Basic Writings,* ed. and trans. D. Krell (New York: Harper and Row, 1977), 101ff.

34. Walter Pater, *The Renaissance,* in *Selected Writings of Walter Pater,* ed. Harold Bloom (New York: Columbia University Press, 1974), 55–57.

35. *Physics,* 2.8.199a15.

36. *OS,* 3.432a1.

37. *Poetics,* 9.1451b.

38. *Poetics,* 25.1460b34.

39. For Polyclitus see Galen, *De placitis Hippocratis et Platonis,* 5, ed. Mueller, 425, and Quintilian, *Institutio oratoria,* 5.12.21, cited in J. J. Pollitt, *The Art of Ancient Greece: Sources and Documents* (Cambridge: Cambridge University Press, 1990), 76–77; for Schopenhauer see *WWR,* vol. 1, bk. 3, sec. 2, §45.222. Johann Winckelmann saw the Greek genius in the ability to depict nature in its visual ideality, "as it should be," in *Reflections on the Imitation of Greek Works in Painting and Sculpture,* trans. E. Heyer and R. Norton (LaSalle, Ill.: Open Court, 1987), 21–25.

40. Neither Polyclitus's treatise nor his *Doryphorus* are extant. See R. H. Wilenski, *The Meaning of Modern Sculpture* (Boston: Beacon Press, 1961), 37. For Kant, see below, chap. 7, n.88.

41. *Poetics,* 8.1451a30ff.; 23.1459a20.

42. Leon Battista Alberti, *The Ten Books of Architecture: The 1755 Leoni Edition* (New York: Dover, 1986), bk. 6, chap. 2.

43. *Poetics,* 6.1449b.25ff.

44. *Politics,* 8.5.1340a30.

45. *Poetics,* 1.1447a20.

46. *Poetics,* 4, 1448b, 24.

47. *Politics,* 8.5.1339a ff.

48. *Politics,* 8.5.1340a20.

49. *Politics,* 8.5.1341a15.

50. *Poetics,* 6.1449b24.

51. Cf. Jerome Schaefer, *The Philosophy of Mind* (Englewood Cliffs, N.J.: Prentice-Hall, 1968), 77ff.

52. Cf. Hegel, *PS,* §399ff., on action as communitarian.

53. *Poetics,* 7.1450b25.

54. Ibid.

55. Cf. chap. 5.

56. *Poetics,* 20.1457a ff.

57. *Poetics,* 22.1458a32.

58. *Poetics,* 22.1459a5.

59. *Politics,* 8.7.1342a5.

60. Plato, *Rep,* 10.606d.

61. *NE,* 1.1100b20.

62. *Poetics,* 4.1229a10ff.

63. *Poetics,* 24.1459b30.

64. *Politics,* 8.10.1329b24.

65. *Poetics,* 6.1450b1.

66. *Poetics,* 12.1452b16.

67. *Poetics,* 6.1450a37.

68. *Politicus,* 287b.

69. Erich Hertzmann, "Mozart's Creative Process," in *The Creative World of Mozart,* ed. Paul Henry Lang (New York: Norton, 1963), 17–30.

70. Cf. Dufrenne, *Phenomenology,* 34–35.

71. Paul Ricoeur, *The Rule of Metaphor,* trans. R. Czerny, K. McLaughlin, J. Costello (Toronto: University of Toronto Press, 1977), 35–41.

72. Sam Hunter and John Jacobus, *Modern Art: Painting, Sculpture, Architecture* (Englewood Cliffs, N.J.: Prentice-Hall, 1985), 112b.

73. Ibid., 112b, 118a.

74. Ibid., 55a.

75. Ibid., 110a.

76. Ibid., 110a.

77. Ibid., 56b.

78. This is attributed to Friedrich von Schlegel by G. W. F. Hegel, *Aesthetics: Lectures on Fine Art*, trans. T. Knox (Oxford: Clarendon Press, 1975), 2:662 (henceforth *ALFA*). In future citations, I will also refer to Hegel, *The Philosophy of Fine Art*, trans. F. Osmaston (London: G. Bell, 1920), following the Knox translation in parentheses with volume and page number, and thus here: (3:65). Schopenhauer traces it back to Goethe in Schopenhauer, *WWR*, 2, suppl. to bk. 3, chap. 35, 453–54.

79. Hunter and Jacobus, *Modern Art*, 28b; cf. Collins, *Changing Ideals*, 272.

80. *Rhetoric*, 1.1361b8.

81. *Metaphysics*, 13.1078b1.

## IV. Plotinus

1. Wladyslaw Tatarkiewicz, *History of Aesthetics*, vol. 2, *Medieval Aesthetics* (The Hague: Mouton, 1972).

2. In particular, Edgar le Bruyne in *The Aesthetics of the Middle Ages*, trans. E. Hennessey (New York: Ungar, 1969), and Umberto Eco in *Art and Beauty*, as well as in *The Aesthetics of Thomas Aquinas*, trans. H. Bredin (Cambridge, Mass.: Harvard University Press, 1988), have attempted to provide a continuous thematic and dialectical context for these scraps.

3. See chap. 2, n. 65.

4. Thomas Aquinas, *On the Truth of the Catholic Faith: Summa contra gentiles*, trans. A. Pegis et al. (Garden City, N.Y.: Doubleday, 1955), 4.29, 4.56, 4.79 ff.

5. On Avicenna, see Etienne Gilson, *History of Christian Philosophy in the Middle Ages* (New York: Random House, 1955), 204; on Averroës, 224–25.

6. *ST*, 1.84.5.

7. Schopenhauer, *WWR*, 1.3.§38.198.

8. Hegel, *HPM*, §564.298.

9. Cf. Gilson, *Christian Philosophy*, 76.

10. *Enn*, 5.3.

11. Emmanuel Levinas, *Totality and Infinity: An Essay on Exteriority*, trans. A. Lingis (Pittsburgh: Duquesne University Press, 1969), 102–5.

12. *Rep*, 6.518c–d.

13. *Rep*, 6.511b.

14. Cf. for example *Bṛhadāraṇyaka Upaniṣad*, 3.4.1 in S. Radhakrishnan and C. Moore, eds., *A Sourcebook in Indian Philosophy* (Princeton, N.J.: Princeton University Press, 1957), 83.

15. Porphyry, *The Life of Plotinus*, 23, in *Enn*, 71.

16. This is a constant theme: cf. *Enn*, 5.1.6; 6.7.34; 6.9.11.

17. The chief texts on beauty are *Enn*, 1.6; 5.8.

18. Cf. Hans Urs von Balthasar, *The Realm of Metaphysics in Antiquity*, trans. B. McNeil et al., vol. 4 of *The Glory of the Lord* (San Francisco: Ignatius Press, 1989), 307.

19. Actually Plotinus is ambivalent on this: the place of Beauty is the place of the Forms, with the Good beyond; *or* the Good and Beauty are on the same level, though Beauty is still also at the level of the Forms (cf. *Enn*, 1.6, 6 and 9).

20. *Enn*, 6.1.

21. *Enn*, 5.2.

22. *Enn*, 5.1.4.

23. *Enn*, 1.4.12–16. There is a line of texts that claims that all is form, including matter itself as the lowest level of form. (Cf. *Enn*, 5.8.7).

24. *Enn*, 4.8.4.

25. *Enn*, 1.6.9.

26. *Enn*, 5.8.11.

27. *Enn*, 2.9.16.

28. Cf. Huston Smith, *Forgotten Truth* (New York: Harper and Row, 1976), 19–33

29. Cf. Adolphe Tanquerey, *The Spiritual Life: A Treatise on Ascetical and Mystical Theology* (Belgium: Desclée, 1930), 297ff.

30. *Enn*, 5.8.10–11.

31. *Enn*, 2.9.16.

32. Cf. Paul Ricoeur, *Fallible Man*, trans. C. Kelbley (Chicago: Regnery, 1965), 103–5.

33. *Enn*, 5.8.1–5.

34. Cf. below, chap. 8.

35. *Enn*, 5.8.5.

36. *Enn*, 5.8.1.

37. *De institutione musica*, 1.34; *Medieval Aesthetics*, 2.86.

38. *Enn*, 5.8.1.

39. *Enn*, 4.3.30.

40. *Enn*, 5.8.5, 6.

41. Cf. Robert O'Connell, *Art and the Christian Intelligence in St. Augustine* (New York: Fordham University Press, 1978), 68, on the shift of accent in Plotinus from the earlier "On Beauty" (*Enn*, 1.6) to the later "On the Intelligible Beauty" (5.8).

42. Augustine, *Confessions*, 7.9.

43. *Confessions*, 9.10.

44. Hans Urs von Balthasar, *Studies in Theological Style: Clerical Styles*, trans. A. Louth, F. McDonagh, and B. McNeil, vol. 2 of *The Glory of the Lord* (San Francisco: Ignatius Press, 1984), 121.

45. *Confessions*, 10.33.

46. *De immortalitate animae*, 13; *On the Immortality of the Soul*, trans. G. Leckie in *Basic Writings of St. Augustine*, ed. Whitney Oates (New York: Random House, 1948), 313.

47. *De natura boni*, 3; *Medieval Aesthetics*, 2.60. Cf. Eco, *Aesthetics of Thomas Aquinas*, 66–67.

48. *De vera religione*, 30.55, 32.59, 40.76, MA, 2.59; *Confessions*, 4.13.

49. *De ordine*, 2.15.42, MA, 2.60.

50. *De civitate dei*, 11.18, MA, 2.61.

51. *De musica*, 6.12.38, MA, 2.61.

52. From *De ordine*, cited in Eco, *Aesthetics of Thomas Aquinas*, 50.

53. *De immortalitate*, 4, Basic Writings, 304.

54. *The Greatness of the Soul*, trans. J. Colleran (New York: Newman Press, 1950), 28.54.81.

55. *Greatness*, 33.76.104–6

56. O'Connell, *Art*, 88, commenting on *De musica*, 6.44.

57. O'Connell, *Art*, 78.

58. *Soliloquia*, 2.10.18, MA 2.65.

59. *De musica*, 1.12.

60. *Greatness of the Soul*, 33.72.100–101; 34.78.107–8.

61. Balthasar, *Clerical Styles*, 127, citing *De musica*, 6.20.

62. Cf. Eco, *Art and Beauty*, 18.

63. Dionysius, *On Divine Names*, in Pseudo-Dionysius, *Complete Works*, trans. C. Luibhead (New York: Paulist Press, 1987), 4.7.46.

64. Dionysius, *Mystical Theology, Works*, 4.141.

65. Dionysius, *Divine Names, Works*, 5.5.99 and 11.6.124.

66. Hans Urs von Balthasar, *The Realm of Metaphysics in the Modern Age*, trans. O. Davies, A. Louth, B. McNeil, J. Saward, and R. Williams, vol. 5 of *The Glory of the Lord* (San Francisco: Ignatius Press, 1991), 12–27.

67. Dionysius, *Divine Names, Works*, 4.9.78.

68. Cf. Balthasar, *Clerical Styles*, 164ff.

69. Cf. Eco, *Art and Beauty*, 84.

70. The expressions are scattered throughout the opusculum *De pulchro et bono*, a work originally attributed to Thomas Aquinas, but later discovered to be from the hand of Albert. Cf. Thomas Aquinas, *S. Thomae Aquinatis opera omnia: Aliorum medii aevi auctorum scripta* 61, ed. R. Busa (Stuttgart-Bad Cannstatt: Friedrich Frommann Verlag, 1980), 43–47.

71. Cf. Gilson, *Christian Philosophy*, 361ff. For a fuller presentation and the citation of texts pertinent to this exposition, see Wood, *Path into Metaphysics*, 177–203.

72. Aquinas, *ST*, 1.3.4; *Summa contra gentiles*, 2.52.

73. Augustine, *Confessions*, 3.6.

74. Thomas Aquinas, *On the Power of God* (Westminster: Newman Press, 1952), 7, 5, ad 14.

75. Thomas Aquinas, *On Being and Essence*, trans. A. Maurer (Toronto: Pontifical Institute of Medieval Studies, 1949), 4:43ff.

76. *ST*, 1-2.27.1, ad 3.

77. Cf. Augustine, *Confessions*, 10.27.

78. *ST*, 1.91.3, ad 3; 2-2.141.4, ad 3.

79. *ST*, 1.78.3.

80. Cf. below, chap. 6.

81. Le Bruyne, *Aesthetics*, 27.

82. *ST*, 1-2.27.1, ad 3.

83. Cf. Eco, *Art and Beauty*, 115.

84. *ST*, 1.39 ad 8. For an interpretation of these properties against the background of their development in Western thought before Aquinas, see Eco, *Aesthetics*, 64–121.

85. *ST*, 1.12.1, ad 4.

86. *ST*, 1.5.4, ad 1.

87. Jacques Maritain, *Art and Scholasticism* and *the Frontiers of Poetry* (New York: Scribners, 1962), 164.

88. *ST,* 1.5.4.

89. Maritain, *Art,* 132, 173. Eco does not find this notion of fusion in Aquinas: *Aesthetics of Thomas Aquinas,* 39.

90. *Disputed Questions On Truth,* vol. 3, trans. R. Schmitt (Chicago: Regenery, 1954), 22.1, ad 12.

91. Eco, *Aesthetics,* 37. Eco contradicts his own position here in the conclusion to the book, where the relation to the subject is what allows the transcendentality of beauty to show itself *(Aesthetics,* 191).

92. *ST,* 1.39.8.

93. *ST,* 1–2.57.4. Cf. my own translation of Aristotle's original phrase in chapter 3.

94. Eco, *Art and Beauty,* 92–95

95. *Commentary on the Physics of Aristotle,* trans. R. Blackwell, R. Spath, W. Thirlkel (New Haven: Yale University Press, 1963), 2.4.

96. *ST,* 1.77.1, ad. 7.

97. *ST,* 1–2.101.2, ad 2.

98. *ST,* 1–2.57.3, ad 3.

99. *De septem donis Spiritus Sancti,* 2.7.1, *Opera Omnia,* ed. A. Peltier (Paris: Vivès, 1866), 7.635b; for Balthasar, see *Clerical Styles,* 276-77.

100. Cf. Balthasar, *Clerical Styles,* 263.

101. *De sc. Chr.* q. 7 (Quaracchi edition, 5.43a–b), cited in Balthasar, *Clerical Styles,* 268.

102. Balthasar, *Clerical Styles,* 335.

103. Ibid., 283.

104. Bonaventure, *Itinerarium mentis in deum,* 1, *Opera,* 12.1.5–6; Balthasar, *Clerical Styles,* 346.

105. Balthasar, *Clerical Styles,* 318–19, 335.

106. Bonaventure, *In sententias,* 3.1, dubium 3, *Opera,* 4.7.

107. Bonaventure, *Breviloquium,* prologue, *Opera* 7.244.

108. Balthasar, *Clerical Styles,* 335.

109. Ibid.

110. See Hans Urs von Balthasar, *Studies in Theological Styles: Lay Styles,* A. Louth, J. Saward, M. Simon and R. Williams, vol. 3 of *The Glory of the Lord* (San Francisco: Ignatius Press, 1986), 406ff.

111. Francis of Assisi, "Canticle of Brother Son," in *The Little Flowers of St. Francis,* trans. R. Brown (Garden City, N.Y.: Image Books, 1958), 317–18.

112. Friedrich Nietzsche, *On the Genealogy of Morals,* trans. W. Kaufmann (New York: Vintage, c. 1967), 2.17.86 (henceforth *GM* ).

113. Cf. Hans Urs von Balthasar, *Theology: The Old Covenant,* trans. B. McNeil and E. Leiva-Merikakis, vol. 6 of *The Glory of the Lord* (San Francisco: Ignatius Press, 1991), 62; *Theology: The New Covenant,* trans. B. McNeil, vol. 7 of *The Glory of the Lord* (San Francisco: Ignatius Press, 1989), 239.

114. Hunter and Jacobus, *Modern Art,* 47a.

115. Balthasar, *Seeing the Form,* trans. E. Leiva-Merikakis, vol. 1 of *The Glory of the Lord* (San Francisco: Ignatius Press, 1982), 158.

116. Friedrich Nietzsche, *Twilight of the Idols,* trans. R. Hollingdale (Baltimore: Penguin, 1968), 37 (henceforth *TI*).

117. Martin Buber, "Man and His Image Work," in *Knowledge of Man*, 159.

118. Wassily Kandinsky, *Concerning the Spiritual in Art,* trans. M. Sadler (New York: Dover, 1977), 1ff.

119. Henry Moore, "The Sculptor's Aims," in *Henry Moore*, xxxi, b.

120. Cf. the discussion of Michelangelo in Wilenski, *Modern Sculpture*, 95. Michelangelo expresses the reverse in Plotinus's view here in a sonnet that begins, "Non ha l'ottimo artista alcun concetto / Ch' un marmo solo in se non circonscriva."

121. Plutarch, cited in Max Picard, *The World of Silence* (Chicago: Regnery, 1952), 154–55.

## V. Kant

1. Friedrich Paulsen, *Immanuel Kant: His Life and Doctrine,* trans. J. Creighton and A. Lefevre (New York: Ungar, 1972), 53.

2. Immanuel Kant, *Critique of Practical Reason,* trans. L. W. Beck (Indianapolis: Bobbs-Merrill, 1956).

3. For references to *CPR*, I will cite the Akademie edition references to the first and second editions of *CPR* as A or B, each followed by their respective page numbers in Akademie where the treatment begins. The reference will be completed by inclusive page numbers from the Smith translation: e.g., *CPR*, B 25/A 12, (59).

4. *CJ*, §§23–29.98ff. (244ff.). All references to *CJ* give the section number, followed by the page numbers of the Pluhar translation and, in parentheses, the Akademie edition.

5. *CPR*, preface to the 2d ed., B xv (22).

6. *CPR*, A 12/B 25, (59).

7. *CPR*, B 145 (161); A 671/B 699 (550). Cf. *CJ*, §77.408–9 (292–93).

8. *CPR*, B 45/A 30 (73). For three basic views of the nature of the sensa see Wood, *Path into Metaphysics*, 165.

9. *CPR*, A 22/B 37 (67ff.).

10. *CPR*, B 46/A 31 (74ff.).

11. *CPR*, A 24/B 39 (68ff.).

12. *CPR*, B 102/A 76 (111ff.).

13. *CPR*, A 70/B 95 (106ff.).

14. *CPR*, A 145/B (183ff.).

15. *CPR*, B 133ff.; A 341/B 399.

16. *CPR*, A 3212/B 377 (315–22).

17. Cf. Immanuel Kant, *Prolegomena to Any Future Metaphysics,* trans. P. Carus, rev. J. Ellington (Indianapolis: Hackett, 1977), 28off. (25ff.).

18. *CPR*, A 532/B 560 (464ff.).

19. *CPR*, A 57/B 75 (93).

20. *Prolegomena*, 1–2 (256).

21. Bonaventure, *II Sent*, 1.1.1.2.

22. Aristotle, *Metaphysics*, 2.1071b1; *Physics*, 251b12.

23. Aquinas, *ST*, 1.46, 2.

24. *CPR*, A 405/B 432 (384ff.).

25. *CPR*, A 590/B 618 ff. (499ff.).

26. *CPR*, A 592/B 620 ff. (500ff.); cf. Anselm, *Proslogion*, chap. 2–4, in *Opera omnia*, ed. F. Schmitt (Stuttgart: Friedrich Frommann, 1968), 1:101–4.

27. Aquinas, *ST*, 1.2.1, ad 2.

28. *CPR*, A 671/B 699 (550).

29. *CJ*, §91.468 (362), 474 (368).

30. *CPR*, A 542/B 570 (469).

31. Immanuel Kant, *Foundations of the Metaphysics of Morals*, trans. L. W. Beck (Indianapolis: Bobbs-Merrill, 1959), 64–67.

32. Ibid., 31ff.

33. Ibid., 39.

34. Ibid., 47.

35. Ibid., 49, 55.

36. Immanuel Kant, *The Metaphysical Principles of Virtue*, trans. J. Ellington (Indianapolis: Bobbs-Merrill, 1964), 50ff. (391ff.).

37. *Critique of Practical Reason*, 114, 126ff.

38. Ibid.; *CJ*, §86.444 (333).

39. *Critique of Practical Reason*, 37ff. (133ff.).

40. *CJ*, introduction, 2.174ff. (12ff.).

41. *CJ*, introduction, 4.179 (18–19).

42. *CJ*, introduction, 4.179ff. (18ff.).

43. *CJ*, introduction, 5.185 (24).

44. *CJ*, §43.303 (170).

45. *CJ*, §46.307 (174); cf. "First Introduction," 2.204 (393), 5.215 (403), 9.232 (421). This holds even though it seems that the consideration of art was a later addition to the Critique of Taste, projected in 1787. Zammito complains of the infelicity of its placement. John Zammito, *The Genesis of Kant's* Critique of Judgment (Chicago: University of Chicago Press, 1992), 4, 129.

46. *CJ*, §64.369-70 (248–49).

47. Aristotle, *Physics*, 2.3.194b16ff.

48. Cf. Aristotle, *OS*, 2.1.112a1ff.

49. David Hull, *Philosophy of Biological Science* (Englewood Cliffs, N.J.: Prentice-Hall, 1974), 103ff.

50. *CJ*, §10.220ff. (64ff.).

51. *CJ*, §46.307 (174).

52. *CJ*, §45.306 (174). Winckelmann, who seems to be in the background of Kant's discussion, suggests that Bernini, for example, was sensitized to the beauty of nature through the study of Greek statuary. Winckelmann, *Imitation of Greek Works*, 19.

53. Cf. *CJ*, introduction, 5-9.181ff. (20ff.); first introduction, 5.211ff. (399ff.). For a laying out of the underlying scheme of purposiveness in the third critique, see Robert E. Wood, "Aesthetics within the Kantian Project," in *Philosophy and Art*, ed. D. Dahlstrom (Washington, D.C.: Catholic University of America Press, 1991), esp. 176–80.

54. *CJ*, introduction, 6.187 (27); cf. also the comment following §29.266 (126). In the famous letter to Reinhold projecting a Critique of Taste, Kant paralleled the faculties of cognition, of feeling pleasure and pain, and of desire with theoretical philosophy,

*teleology*, and practical philosophy (cited in Zammito, *Genesis*, 46–47). Feeling and teleology are here thought together.

55. *CJ*, §86.442ff. (331ff.).

56. Friedrich Nietzsche, *Human, All Too Human: A Book for Free Spirits*, trans. M. Faber and S. Lehmann (Lincoln: University of Nebraska Press, 1984).

57. *CJ*, §16.229 (76).

58. *CJ*, §13.223 (68); §15.226 (73).

59. *CJ*, §4.207 (49); §16.229–30 (76–77).

60. *CJ*, §17.231ff. (79ff.).

61. Schopenhauer, *WWR*, 1, app., 528.

62. Jean-François Lyotard, *Lessons on the Analytic of the Sublime*, trans. E. Rottenberg (Stanford: Stanford University Press, 1994), 44–49.

63. *CJ*, §2.204 (45).

64. Aristotle, *NE*, 3.1118a21–23.

65. *CJ*, §5.209 (51).

66. *CJ*, §1.203 (44).

67. *CJ*, §13.223 (68–69).

68. *CJ*, §9.217–18 (62–63).

69. Cf. Zammito, *Genesis*, 131.

70. Cf. *CPR*, A72/B97 (108).

71. *CJ*, §6.212 (54).

72. Cf. Dufrenne, *Phenomenology*, 191.

73. *CPR*, A 70/B 95 (107). The corresponding pure concepts are unity, plurality, and totality (A 80/B 106, [113]), of which Kant does not seem to make even implicit use here.

74. *CJ*, §7.212 (55).

75. *CJ*, §8.213ff. (57ff.); §15.226ff. (73ff.).

76. *CJ*, introduction, 4.179 (18). He later identifies the indeterminate concept as that of the supersensible ground; *CJ*, §57.339ff. (211ff.).

77. *CJ*, §9.216ff. (61ff.); first introduction, 8, comment. 230 (419).

78. *CJ*, §20–21.238ff. (87ff.).

79. *CJ*, §35.287 (151): §38.289–90 (155–56); first introduction, 8.224 (413).

80. *CJ*, §49.314 (182).

81. *CJ*, §40.294 (160).

82. *CJ*, §14.225 (72).

83. *CJ*, §39–40.291ff. (157ff.).

84. *CJ*, §57.339ff. (211ff.).

85. *CJ*, §59.351ff. (225ff.).

86. *CJ*, n§57.339ff. (211ff.).

87. *CJ*, §56.338 (210).

88. *CJ*, §17.231ff. (79ff.).

89. Cf. *CJ*, general comment following §29.270 (130).

90. *CJ*, §17.234 (82–83). The Polyclitian canon seems to involve another element, namely a doctrine of harmonic proportions that need not necessarily be the kind of statistical average Kant suggests. Here we have a case of a kind of empirical-rational tension in arriving at a norm. Kant seem to have had in mind the descriptions of

Winckelmann in *Imitation of Greek Works* and *History of Ancient Art,* trans. G. Lodge, 4 vols. (Boston: Little, Brown, 1856–73). Cf. the discussion of Winckelmann in Alex Potts, *Flesh and the Ideal: Winckelmann and the Origins of Art History* (New Haven: Yale University Press, 1994), esp. 155ff.

91. *CJ,* §10.219ff. (64ff.).

92. *CPR,* A 80/B 106 (113).

93. *CJ,* §65.372ff. (251ff.).

94. *CPR,* A 80/B 106 (113).

95. *CJ,* §18.236ff. (85ff.).

96. *CJ,* §20–22.238ff. (87ff.); §40.293ff. (159ff.).

97. Aristotle, *OS,* 3.2.426b4ff.

98. *CJ,* §32.282ff. (145ff.).

99. Ibid.; *CJ,* §46.308 (175).

100. Cf. Dufrenne, *Phenomenology,* 416–18.

101. Zammito, *Genesis,* 269ff. Kant's notion of the sublime has received a great deal of attention recently. Significant essays have been gathered in Jean-François Courtine, *Of the Sublime: Presence in Question,* ed. and trans. J. Librett (Albany: State University of New York Press, 1993). I have already referred to Jean-François Lyotard's *Lessons on the Analytic of the Sublime,* which is a careful reading of pertinent sections of the third critique, leaning heavily on the concepts of reflection in the first critique.

102. *CJ,* §23.246 (100).

103. Lyotard, *Lessons,* 54–56.

104. Kant still has room for a transcendence beyond this world. It would seem that for Lyotard the door to such considerations has been definitively closed.

105. Immanuel Kant, *Observations on the Feeling of the Beautiful and Sublime,* trans. J. Goldthwait (Berkeley: University of California Press, 1960).

106. Psalms 8:3–5, New Revised Standard Edition.

107. Rudoph Otto, *The Idea of the Holy,* trans. J. Harvey (New York: Oxford University Press, 1964), 12–40.

108. *CJ,* §23.244ff. (97ff.).

109. *CJ,* general comment to §29.267–68 (127–28).

110. Lyotard, *Lessons,* 150.

111. Ibid., 123ff., 159, 214, 234; cf. also Lyotard, *The Differend: Phrases in Dispute* (Minneapolis: University of Minnesota Press, 1983) and *The Inhuman: Reflections on Time* (Stanford: Stanford University Press, 1988). For Derrida, see "Differance" in *Margins of Philosophy,* trans. A. Bass (Chicago: University of Chicago Press, 1982), 1–27.

112. Lyotard, *Lessons,* 129.

113. Ibid., 74, 76, 153–57.

114. Wing-tsit Chan, trans. and comp., *A Sourcebook in Chinese Philosophy* (Princeton, N.J.: Princeton University Press, 1963), 136–210.

115. G. W. F. Hegel, *The Encyclopaedia Logic,* trans. T. Geraets, W. Suchting, and H. Harris (Indianapolis: Hackett, 1991), §94.149 (henceforth *EL*).

116. Cf. Lyotard, *Lessons,* 111ff.

117. *CJ,* §24.247 (101).

118. Blaise Pascal, *Pensées* (New York: Modern Library, 1941), 6.§347.

119. *CJ,* general comment to §29.269 (129).

120. *CJ*, §26.256 (113).

121. *CJ*, general comment to §29.272ff. (132ff.).

122. *CJ*, §46.308 (175).

123. Cited in Katharine Gilbert and Helmut Kuhn, *A History of Aesthetics* (New York: Dover, 1972), 199.

124. Zammito, *Genesis*, 26–28.

125. Ibid., 34ff.

126. *CJ*, §49.313ff. (181ff.).

127. *CJ*, §43.304 (304).

128. *CJ*, §49.314 (182).

129. *CJ*, §53.328 (199).

130. See chaps. 8 and 9. Cf. Dahlhaus's detailed discussion of the full cultural context of this in *Absolute Music*.

131. *CJ*, §53.329 (199).

132. *CJ*, §53.326 (196ff.).

133. *CJ*, §49.314 (182–83).

134. See Lyotard, *Lessons*, 214.

135. *CPR*, A120 (144).

136. *CPR*, A137/B176ff. (180ff.); *CJ*, §59.351 (227).

137. *CJ*, §49.314 (182–83).

138. *CJ*, §51–52.320ff. (189ff.).

139. *CJ*, §59.354 (230).

140. *CJ*, §64.370ff. (248ff.).

141. *CJ*, §82.426 (313–14).

142. *CJ*, §83.429ff. (317ff.).

143. *CJ*, §84.434ff. (321ff.).

144. *CJ*, introduction, 9 (196), 37.

145. Ibid., 36–37.

146. *CJ*, general comment to §29.266ff. (126ff.).

147. Cf. the essays developing and criticizing this notion in George Dickie and Richard Sclafani, eds., *Aesthetics: A Critical Anthology* (New York: St. Martin's Press, 1977): Edward Bullough, "Psychical Distance as a Factor in Art and an Aesthetic Principle," 758–82; Allan Casebier, "The Concept of Aesthetic Distance," 783–99; and George Dickie, "All Aesthetic Attitude Theories Fail: The Myth of the Aesthetic Attitude," 800–15.

148. Cf. Nietzsche, *GM*, 3.6.104.

149. Dufrenne, *Phenomenology*, 55, 138–46.

150. Ibid., 231.

151. Hunter and Jacobus, *Modern Art*, 29a.

152. Ibid., 32a.

153. Ibid., 110a. Also see Dufrenne, *Phenomenology*, 284–85.

154. Augustine, *Confessions*, 10.27.

155. *CJ*, general comment to §29.272ff. (132ff.).

156. *CJ*, §28.263 (122).

157. Francesco Petrarca [Petrarch], "The Ascent of Mont Ventoux," in *The Renaissance Philosophy of Man*, ed. E. Cassirer, P. Kristeller, and J. Randall (Chicago: University of Chicago Press, 1971), 36–46.

158. Cf. Giedion, *Space*, 432.

159. Jean-Jacques Rousseau, *The Reveries of the Solitary Walker,* trans. C. Butterworth (New York: Harper and Row, 1979).

160. Dufrenne, *Phenomenology,* 357.

161. Peter Kivy, "Recent Scholarship and the British Tradition: A Logic of Taste—The First Fifty Years," in *Aesthetics,* ed. Dickie and Sclafani, 636.

162. David Hume, "Of the Standard of Taste," in *Aesthetics,* ed. Dickie and Sclafani, 592–606.

163. Alasdair MacIntyre, *Whose Justice? Which Rationality?* (Notre Dame, Ind.: University of Notre Dame Press, 1988).

164. Hume, "Taste," 592.

165. Ibid., 597.

166. Ibid., 597–600.

167. Ibid., 598.

168. Ibid., 601.

169. Ibid., 603.

170. Ibid., 597.

171. Ibid., 595.

172. Commenting on Hume's "ideal observer," Peter Kivy asks, "Should the ideal aesthetic observer be passionate or cold-blooded, emotional, or cerebral? Poet or peasant, of the elite or the masses? In the ivory tower, or in the ash can? Political or apolitical, moral or immoral? Sensitive to craftsmanship or aesthetic surface, technique or impression? Quick to judge or slow in judgment? All these questions have been part and parcel of the evolution of artistic and aesthetic movements and schools, just as much as have questions about the recommended aesthetic properties of works of art." "Logic of Taste," 639. Our reading of Plato and Hume would lead us to collapse some of the dichotomies, requiring passion and detachment, poet and peasant, inhabitance of the polis and its transcendence, an *Aufhebung* of conventional morality through critique rooted in the structures of experience, a holism that would appreciate surface and technique, but which would surely not advocate quick judgment over deliberation (who but a fool would?).

173. David Hume, *Dialogues Concerning Natural Religion,* ed. N. K. Smith (Indianapolis: Bobbs-Merrill, 1947), 2:148.

174. Cf. Joseph Lawrence, *Die ewige Anfang: Zum Verhältnis von Natur und Geschichte bei Schelling* (Tübingen: Köhler, 1984).

175. Cf. Le Corbusier, *Towards a New Architecture,* trans. F. Etchells (New York: Praeger, 1960), 32; Le Corbusier reports the judgment without sharing it.

176. Hegel, *ALFA,* 2:684 (3:89).

177. Eugène-Emmanuel Viollet-le-Duc, *The Foundations of Architecture: Selections from the* Dictionnaire Raisonné, trans. K. Whitehead (New York: George Braziller, 1990), 70ff., 163, 182ff., 259ff.

178. Wright, *Future of Architecture,* 51ff.

179. Umberto Boccione, "Technical Manifesto of Futurist Sculpture," in *Art and Its Significance: An Anthology of Aesthetic Theory,* ed. S. Ross (Albany: State University of New York Press, 1984), 537–38.

180. Henry Moore, "Mesopotamian Art," in *Henry Moore,* xxxii, a; "Primitive Art" (1941), in *Henry Moore,* xxxvi, a; xxxvii, b.

181. Cf. Hunter and Jacobus, *Modern Art,* 38b ff., 136a ff.

182. Meyer Shapiro, *Modern Art: Nineteenth and Twentieth Centuries* (New York: George Braziller, 1982), 135ff.

183. Carlo Carra, *La pittura dei suoni* (Rome: Archivi del Futurismo, 1958), 1:74, cited in Michael Benedikt, *Deconstructing the Kimbell* (New York: SITES/Lumen Books, 1991), 115, n. 44.

184. André Malraux, *Voices of Silence,* trans. S. Gilbert (Princeton, N.J.: Princeton University Press, 1978), 13ff.

185. Gadamer, *Truth and Method,* 33–39.

## *VI. Hegel*

1. Cf. *EL,* §128, ad, 198. For a general account see Preserved Smith, *A History of Modern Culture,* vol. 2, *The Enlightenment, 1687–1776* (New York: Collier, 1962), 410ff.

2. John Locke, *An Essay Concerning Human Understanding,* ed. P. Nidditch (Oxford: Clarendon Press, 1975), bk. 2, chap. 11, 17.

3. See, for example, Hume, *Dialogues,* 2:148.

4. John Locke, *The Second Treatise of Government* (Indianapolis: Bobbs-Merrill, 1952), bk. 2, chap. 2, 4; Thomas Hobbes, *Leviathan,* ed. M. Oakschott (New York: Collier, 1973), First Part, chap. 13.

5. Cf. the treatment of the issue in the Enlightenment by Ernst Cassirer, *The Philosophy of the Enlightenment,* trans. F. Koelln and J. Pettegrove (Boston: Beacon Press, 1951), 137–60.

6. Smith, *Enlightenment,* 202–11.

7. Ibid.

8. Cf. Hegel, *Lectures on the Philosophy of Religion,* ed. P. Hodgson, trans. R. Brown et al. (Berkeley: University of California Press, 1988), 458 (henceforth *LPR*).

9. *LPR,* 422.

10. *LPR,* 144ff.; cf. Gotthold Ephraim Lessing, *Die Erziehung des Menschengeschlechts und andere Schriften* (Stuttgart: Reclam, 1965), §72.

11. Aquinas, *ST,* 1.1.1.

12. Cf. *LPR,* 418.

13. Cf. Aquinas, *ST,* 1.27ff.

14. Cf. *HPM,* §566–70.299–301; also *LPR,* 418.

15. Plotinus, *Enn,* 6.1; Augustine, *On the Trinity,* bk. 15, 23ff.

16. Augustine, *Confessions,* 7.9.

17. Aquinas, *ST,* 3.2.

18. Cf. Karl Rahner, *Foundations of Christian Faith: An Introduction to the Idea of Christianity,* trans. W. Dych (New York: Seabury, 1978), 223ff.; cf. also Karl Rahner, ed., *Encyclopedia of Theology: The Concise Sacramentum mundi* (New York: Seabury, 1975), 1755ff.

19. Augustine, *Confessions,* 3.6.

20. For fuller exposition and references, see Wood, *Path into Metaphysics,* 9:187ff.

21. Cf. Rahner, *Encyclopedia of Theology,* 690ff.

22. Cf. Wood, *Path into Metaphysics,* chap. 2, 3.

23. Cf. Rahner, *Encyclopedia of Theology,* 1148ff.

24. Pius XII, *The Mystical Body of Christ,* trans. J. Bluett (New York: The America Press, 1943).

25. Aquinas, *ST,* 1.37.1 and 2.

26. *ST,* 1.46.1, ad 6.

27. *EL,* §212, ad. There is the enigmatic and undeveloped declaration in the *Encyclopedia of Logic* that "God is eternally complete and eternally completing Himself" that seems to give the lie to understanding the Trinity as "in itself" the realm of possibility and thus empty and requiring creation of nature as its own fulfillment. In the *Science of Logic* (50) logic is said to consider God in his eternal essence before creation. There is also the declaration in *The Philosophy of History* that "spirit is immortal; with it there is no past, no future, but an essential *now*. . .,. What Spirit is it has always been essentially." Trans. J. Sibree (New York: Dover, 1956), 79 (henceforth *PH*).

28. *Letter to the Ephesians* 3:6.

29. Aquinas, *ST,* 3.49.

30. G. W. F. Hegel, *Lectures on the History of Philosophy,* trans. E. Haldane (Lincoln: University of Nebraska Press, 1995), 1.73 (henceforth *LHP*).

31. Cf. Wood, *Path into Metaphysics,* 6:125–32.

32. *SL,* 82ff.; Nietzsche, *TI,* 37.

33. Cf. Aristotle, *Categories,* 5.2a11.

34. *SL,* 105ff.

35. *SL,* 479ff.

36. Cf. Dean Wooldridge, *Mechanical Man: The Physical Basis of Intelligent Life* (New York: McGraw-Hill, 1968).

37. Cf. Walter Kaufmann, "The Hegel Myth and Its Overcoming," in *From Shakespeare to Existentialism* (Garden City, N.Y.: Doubleday, 1960), 95ff.

38. *EL,* §96, ad.

39. Jacques Maritain, *The Degrees of Knowledge,* trans. G. Phelan (New York: Scribners, 1959), 112.

40. Cf. *Hegel's Philosophy of Nature,* ed. and trans. M. Petry, 3 vols. (London: George Allen and Unwin, 1970), 3:22. In spite of the rejection of evolution, Hegel's thought is so close to evolutionary thinking that it could readily pass over into such thinking when sufficient evidence had been gathered. That is precisely one of the major contentions of the lifework of Errol Harris. Cf. Harris, *Nature, Mind, and Modern Science* (London: George Allen and Unwin, 1958), 246.

41. *HPM* gives a short version Objective Spirit in §§483–552; it is elaborated in *Hegel's Philosophy of Right,* trans. T. Knox (London: Oxford University Press, 1952) (henceforth *PR*).

42. *SL,* 843–44.

43. *SL,* 50.

44. Cf. Plato, *Sophist,* 248b.

45. Aristotle, *Categories,* 5.2a11.

46. Aristotle, *OS,* 3.7.430a1–25; *Metaphysics,* 12.1072b22.

47. See note 28.

48. *SL,* 389ff.

49. *HPM,* §389.29–34.

50. *SL,* 576ff. See my "Being and Manifestness" for an attempt to articulate that notion in the contemporary context.

51. This is the basic outline of the level of subjective spirit in *HPM,* §387–482.25–240.

52. *HPM,* §465.224; §469.228; §481–82.238–40.

53. *PS,* §175ff. on self-consciousness.

54. See *PH,* 54ff., 69ff.

55. Preface to *PR,* 10; also 283; cf. also *EL,* §6.29; and *PH,* 36.

56. *PR,* §§34–104.37–74.

57. *PR,* §§105–41.75–104.

58. *PR,* §§142–360.106–223.

59. *PR,* §§158–81.110–22.

60. *PR,* §§182–256.122–55.

61. *PR,* §§257–360.155–223.

62. On freedom of property, cf. *PR,* §62.51; on freedom of the press, of speech, and of thought, §319.205–6; on freedom of conscience, §124.84, on freedom to choose a marriage partner, §162.111.

63. *PS,* §§641–71.

64. John 16:7–8; *PH,* 325; *ALFA,* 1:80 (1:108).

65. *HPM,* §§553–77.292–315.

66. G. W. F. Hegel, *Lectures on the Philosophy of Religion,* trans. E. Speirs and J. B. Sanderson (London: Kegan Paul, Trench, Trübner, 1895), 1:4. This is an alternative to the Hodgson version of Hegel's lectures, which was based on the 1827 series.

67. *LPR,* 146.

68. *LPR,* 144ff.; cf. *ALFA,* 1:108 (1:149): *Vorstellung* includes images but also abstract concepts like "man" and "the quality of blueness," while *Begriff* contains opposite factors in unity.

69. *LHP,* 1:249ff.

70. *PH,* 15; *ALFA,* 1:30 (1:40).

71. *LPR.* Cf. *ALFA,* 1:97 (1:133).

72. *ALFA,* 1:132 (1:182–83).

73. *ALFA,* 1:152 (1:208).

74. *ALFA,* 1:148–52 (1:203–8).

75. *ALFA,* 1:1 (1:2).

76. *ALFA,* 1:114 (1:157).

77. *ALFA,* 1:153 (1:209), 156 (1:213), 163 (1:222).

78. *ALFA,* 1:159 (1:217); cf. also 176–79 (1:238–41).

79. *ALFA,* 1:3–4 (1:8–9), 279 (1:377).

80. *ALFA,* 1:33–34 (1:45–46).

81. *ALFA,* 1:8–9 (1:10–11).

82. *ALFA,* 1:44 (1:60).

83. *ALFA,* 1:51 (1:70).

84. *ALFA,* 1:39 (1:53).

85. *ALFA,* 1:304 (2:9).

86. *ALFA,* 1:89 (1:120).

87. *ALFA,* 1:26ff. (1:35ff.), 283ff. (1:384ff.).

88. *ALFA,* 1:29–30 (1:39–40).

89. *ALFA,* 1:291–92 (1:395–96), 294–98 (1:400–405).

90. *ALFA,* 1:290 (1:394).

91. *ALFA,* 1:45 (1:62); cf. also 1:254–55 (1:342–43).

92. *ALFA,* 1:49 (1:68).

93. *ALFA,* 1:7 (1:9).

94. *ALFA,* 1:51 (1:70).

95. *ALFA,* 1:52–55 (1:72–77).

96. *ALFA,* 1:51 (1:70).

97. *ALFA,* 1:55 (1:77), 111 (1:154), 173 (1:235).

98. *ALFA,* 1:76ff. (1:103ff.), 81 (1:110).

99. *ALFA,* 1:76 (1:103–4), developed in 1:303–426 (2:8–168); on architecture, see 2:630–700 (3:25–108).

100. *ALFA,* 1:226–28 (1:300–303).

101. *ALFA,* 1:77–79 (1:104–6), developed in 1:427–516 (2:175–281); on sculpture, see 2:701–91 (3:109–216).

102. *ALFA,* 1:79–81 (1:106–10), developed in 1:517–611 (2:282–401).

103. *ALFA,* 1:9–11 (1:11–13); cf. 1:102–4 (1:141–42).

104. *ALFA,* 1:86 (1:116).

105. *ALFA,* 1:104 (1:142).

106. Pascal, *Pensées,* 4.§277.

107. *HPM,* §445.188.

108. *HPM,* §447.194.

109. *HPM,* §405.96.

110. *ALFA,* 1:87 (1:117–18); for further development see 2:797–958 (3:223–337).

111. *ALFA,* 1:87–88 (1:118–19); for further development see 2:888–958 (3:338–430).

112. *ALFA,* 1:254–55 (1:342). For a penetrating treatment of the development of the idea of absolute music in the time immediately preceding and following Hegel, see Dahlhaus, *Absolute Music.*

113. *ALFA,* 1:185ff. (1:249ff.), 263 (351ff.). Hegel sees such individuals as world-historical figures. In his own time, he reported his impressions on seeing Napoleon, "the world-spirit on horseback," riding triumphantly through the streets of Jena, as just such a figure in which the meaning of the whole is concentrated. Cited in Franz Wiedmann, *Hegel: An Illustrated Biography,* trans. J. Neugroschel (New York: Pegasus, 1968), 38.

114. *ALFA,* 2:966–7 (4:12–13), 977 (4:26).

115. *ALFA,* 2:964 (4:10), 968 (4:16).

116. Cf. *ALFA,* 1002 (4:58), 1011 (4:70), esp. 1036–37 (4:101–2), for the priority of sonorousness in poetry, which is like color to a mere outline.

117. On the general content of art, see *ALFA,* 1:177–298 (1:240–320), esp. 217–20 (289–91); on poetry, see the whole of *ALFA* 2:959–1238 (4:3–350).

118. *ALFA,* 1:204 (1:273).

119. *ALFA,* 2:1037–9 (4:102–4). For a development of the epic, see 2:1040–110 (4:106–192); of lyric, 2:111–57 (4:193–247); of drama, 2:1159–239 (4:248–347).

120. *ALFA,* 2:684–700 (3:89–108).

121. *ALFA,* 2:977 (4:27).

122. *ALFA,* 1:89 (1:120).

123. On epic see *ALFA,* 2:1114 (4:196); on lyric, 2:1152 (4:242.); on Shakespeare, 2:1227 (4:337) and 2:1235–36 (4:348).

124. *ALFA,* 2:976–7 (4:26).

125. *ALFA,* 1:83–86 (1:112–16).

126. *PH,* 61.

127. *PH,* 18.

128. *PH,* 340ff.; *HPM,* §482.239–40.

129. *ALFA,* 1:102–3 (1:141–42).

130. Cf. Wood, "Being and Manifestness."

131. Cf. Wood, *Martin Buber's Ontology,* 34ff.

132. Leonardo da Vinci, *Leonardo on Painting: An Anthology of Writings,* ed. Martin Kemp (New Haven: Yale University Press, 1989), 193.

133. Cf. Henry Moore, "The Sculptor's Aims," in *Henry Moore,* xxxi, b.

134. Cf. Wright, *Future of Architecture,* 221.

135. Kant, *CPR,* B xiii.

136. Cf. Giambattista Vico, *The New Science of Giambattista Vico,* trans. T. Bergin and M. Fisch (Ithaca, N.Y.: Cornell University Press, 1991), bk. 1, sect. 3, 1.331.96.

137. Cf. *ALFA,* 1:314–15 (2:23–24).

## VII. Schopenhauer

1. Arthur Schopenhauer, *On the Fourfold Root of the Principle of Sufficient Reason,* trans. E. Payne (LaSalle, Ill.: Open Court, 1974).

2. *WWR,* 1.2.§25.127.

3. *WWR,* 1.3.§30.169ff.

4. Auguste Comte, *Introduction to Positive Philosophy,* ed. and trans. Frederick Ferré (Indianapolis: Bobbs–Merrill, 1970).

5. Arthur Schopenhauer, *Essays and Aphorisms,* trans. R. Hollingdale (Harmondsworth: Penguin, 1986); 157 (henceforth *EA*).

6. *WWR,* 1.4.§28.153ff.; cf. also 2.3.§34.408.

7. *WWR,* 1.2.§18.99ff.

8. *WWR,* 1.3.§38.198.

9. *WWR,* 1.3.§53.274.

10. Alfred, Lord Tennyson, *In memoriam,* 56.15.

11. Peter Weiss, *Marat/Sade,* trans. G. Skelton (New York: Simon and Schuster, 1965), 53.

12. Tennessee Williams, *Suddenly Last Summer,* in *The Theatre of Tennessee Williams,* vol. 3 (New York: New Directions, 1971).

13. *WWR,* 2.4.50.645.

14. *WWR,* 2.4.46.373–88.

15. *WWR,* 1.4.§68.397.

16. *WWR,* 1.4.§68.381ff.

17. *WWR,* 1.3.§53.267.

18. *WWR,* 1.4.§67.375.

19. *WWR,* 1.4.§64.355.

20. *WWR,* 1.§66.372ff.

21. *WWR,* 2.47.623.

22. *WWR,* 1.§63.356; 2.608–9. See Radhakrishnan and Moore, *Sourcebook:* "The

Synopsis of Truth" (from *Majjhima-nikaāya*, in *Further Dialogues of the Buddha*, trans. Lord Chalmers), 275–78; and "Examination of Nirvana," (from the *Mādhyamika-śāstra* of Nāgārjuna, trans. Th. Stcherbatsky), 342–45.

23. *WWR*, 1.4.§68.378ff.

24. *EA*, 158.

25. Ibid.

26. *WWR*, 1.3.§36.185.

27. *WWR*, 1.3.§45.222

28. *WWR*, 2.3.34.408.

29. *WWR*, 1.2.§17.97.

30. *EA*, 158–59.

31. *WWR*, 1.2.§27.145ff.

32. *WWR*, 1.3.§39.200–207.

33. *WWR*, 1.3.§45.223ff.

34. Longinus, *On the Sublime*, trans. W. Hamilton Fyfe, in *Aristotle:* The Poetics, *"Longinus,"* On the Sublime, and *Demetrius:* On Style (Cambridge, Mass.: Harvard University Press, 1973), 119–254.

35. *EA*, 160.

36. *WWR*, 1.3.§43.214–18.

37. *EA*, 164.

38. *EA*, 165.

39. *WWR*, 1.3.§52.257.

40. *EA*, 162–63.

41. *WWR*, 2.3.34.407.

42. Edgar Allan Poe, "The Philosophy of Composition," in *Selected Poetry and Prose of Edgar Allan Poe*, ed. T. Mabbott (New York: Modern Library, 1951). On Schiller, see chap. 8, n. 111.

43. Dufrenne, *Phenomenology*, 187, 516.

44. *WWR*, 2.4.50.644.

45. Cf. Osmaston's remark in his translation of Hegel's *Philosophy of Fine Art*, 1:386, n. 1.

## VIII. Nietzsche

1. Friedrich Nietzsche, *The Gay Science*, 3.§125, trans. W. Kaufmann (New York: Vintage, 1974), 181–82 (henceforth *GS*).

2. Plato, *Rep*, 7.508C.

3. *GS*, 3.§151.196. Cf. Taylor, *Disfiguring*, for the playing out of this process in the interplay of the plastic arts, philosophy, and religion.

4. Kant, *Critique of Practical Reason*, 114, 126ff.

5. Kant, *CJ*, §28.120–21 (261–62).

6. Cf. Aquinas, *ST*, 1–2.3.8.

7. Ludwig Feuerbach, *The Essence of Christianity*, trans. G. Eliot (New York: Harper, 1957), 13ff., 155ff.

8. Friedrich Nietzsche, *The Will to Power*, trans. W. Kaufmann and R. Hollingdale (New York: Vintage, 1967), 1:9ff. (henceforth *WTP*).

9. *GS*, 3.§125.182.

10. "Toward a Hidden God: Is God Dead?" *Time* 87 (April 1966): 82–87.

11. *GS*, 5.§343–44.279–80.

12. *GS*, 4.§293–94.236; §320.254.

13. *GS*, §107.164.

14. *GS*, §§382–83.346–48.

15. Cf. the whole of Friedrich Nietzsche, *The Anti-Christ*, trans. R. Hollingdale (Baltimore: Penguin, 1968); on Plato, see *GM*, 3.25.153–54.

16. Friedrich Nietzsche, *Ecce Homo*, trans. W. Kaufmann (New York: Vintage, c. 1967), 334 (henceforth *EH*).

17. Gregory of Nyssa, *Hexaëmeron, Patrologia Graeca*, 44, 189 b–192 a. Cf. Nietzsche, *TI*, 110.

18. *GM*, 2.7.67.

19. *GM*, 1.8.34.

20. Friedrich Nietzsche, *Beyond Good and Evil: Prelude to a Philosophy of the Future*, trans. W. Kaufmann (New York: Vintage, 1966), 3 (henceforth *BGE*). Cf. *TI*, 106, where Nietzsche calls Plato an "antecedent Christian."

21. Friedrich Nietzsche, *The Birth of Tragedy*, W. Kaufmann (New York: Vintage, 1967) (henceforth *BT*), §5, 21; cf. also *GM*, 3.25.154.

22. *EH*, 273; *TI*, 109; *WTP*, 4.1.§1041.536.

23. *GM*, 1.3–5.27–31.

24. *GM*, 1.11.40.

25. Matthew 5.

26. *GM*, 1.10.36.

27. *GM*, 3.15.126.

28. *BGE*, §202–3.116–18; *WTP*, 4.§860.458; *WTP*, 1.2.§125.77.

29. Cf. the subtitle of *The Will to Power: Towards a Transvaluation of Values*.

30. *BGE*, §36.48.

31. *GM*, 2.12.78.

32. Friedrich Nietzsche, *Thus Spake Zarathustra*, in *The Portable Nietzsche*, ed. and trans. W. Kaufmann (New York: Viking, 1954), 3.278 (henceforth *TSZ*); *WTP*, 3.4.§797.419.

33. Eugen Fink, *Nietzsches Philosophie* (Stuttgart: Kohlhammer, c. 1960), 31, 108, 188.

34. Cf. Gadamer, *Truth and Method*, 9ff.

35. *GS*, 4.§276.223; *WTP*, §1041.536.

36. Fink, *Philosophie*, 189.

37. *BGE*, §19.25.

38. *BGE*, §3.11.

39. For an interpretation of Nietzsche's "physiology" see Martin Heidegger, *Nietzsche*, trans. D. Krell (San Francisco: Harper and Row, 1979–87), 3:39ff.

40. From 1872 in *The Birth of Tragedy*, where Nietzsche features Goethe's adage: "to live resolutely in wholeness and fullness," to 1886, where he repeats it in his "Attempt at Self-Criticism" (*BT*, 26), through *The Gay Science*, in which Goethe is presented as a supreme representative of authentic culture (§103.159), on to *Twilight of the Idols* (1889), where he refers to Goethe as the last German before whom he feels reverence (104) and as one who aspires to totality against the separation of reason, sensuality, feeling, and will (102), and on, finally, to *Will to Power*, where Goethe again is representative of one

who forms a totality of himself (§95.60), the spiritualizer of the senses (§118.70), an exemplar of "the grand style," of giving form to one's chaos (§842.444).

41. *BGE*, §211.137.

42. *BT*, §18.113; ASC (1886), §7.26. This is a quote from Goethe's *Generalbeichte* (cf. Kaufmann's note in *BT*, 113, n. 4).

43. *WTP*, 4.§957.503.

44. *WTP*, 4.§915.483.

45. *GM*, 2.17.86; *TI*, 93.

46. Cf. Friedrich Nietzsche, *Schopenhauer as Educator*, in *Untimely Meditations*, trans. R. Hollingdale (London: Cambridge University Press, 1983), 159ff.

47. *Uses and Disadvantages of History*, 63; cf. also *BGE*, 3.

48. *BT*, §23.135–37.

49. *TSZ*, 398.

50. *TSZ*, prologue, §5.129.

51. *GM*, 3.9.247; cf. *WTP*, 4.§912ff.482ff.

52. Cf. *BGE*, §5.12; *TSZ*, 2.198.225.

53. Friedrich Nietzsche, "Truth and Lie," 42–47; cf. also *Daybreak: Thoughts on the Prejudices of Morality*, trans. R. Hollingdale (Cambridge: Cambridge University Press, 1982), §117.73.

54. *GM*, 3.12.119; *BGE*, 3.

55. Plato, *Rep*, 2.377a.

56. *GM*, 3.25.153.

57. *WTP*, 3.4.§822.435.

58. *EH*, 218.

59. *GM*, 3.27.160; *GS*, 5.§357.507.

60. *GM*, 3.24.150.

61. *EH*, 334; *GM*, 3.24.150–53. Cf. *GS*, 4.§344.280–83.

62. *BGE*, preface, 2.

63. *GS*, preface, §4.38; *BGE*, §232.163; *WTP*, 3.4.§943.497.

64. *GS*, 4.§339.271–72.

65. *TSZ*, 3.336–43.

66. *WTP*, 4.§1011.523.

67. *WTP*, 3.4.§853.453.

68. *BGE*, §2.10; *WTP*, 5.§344.281.

69. *GS*, 1.§13.87; *BGE*, §211.136.

70. *BGE*, 9.

71. *Uses and Disadvantages of History*, §6.89.

72. *BT*, §23.137.

73. *BT*, §15.94.

74. *GS*, 4.§276.223.

75. *TSZ*, 1.126.

76. *TSZ*, 1.125.

77. *BGE*, §62.74–75.

78. *GM*, 3.§5.103.

79. *EH*, 334.

80. *EH*, 300–301.

81. *WTP,* 4.§983.513.
82. *TSZ,* 3.339ff.; *WTP,* 4.3.§1057–67.544ff.
83. *TSZ,* 3.329–30; 4.435–36.
84. Plato, *Sym,* 207a.
85. Aristotle, *Metaphysics,* 12.9.1074b.34.
86. Plato, *Rep,* 6.508e; 7.524d.
87. *WTP,* 4.3.1066.
88. Nancy Ross Wilson, *Three Ways of Asian Wisdom: Hinduism, Buddhism, Zen, and Their Significance for the West* (New York: Simon and Schuster, 1966), 65–66.
89. Pascal, *Pensées,* §206.
90. *GS,* §341.273–74.
91. Friedrich Nietzsche, "Aus dem Gedankenkreis der Geburt der Tragödie," in *Der griechische Staat* (1871; Stuttgart: Alfred Kroener, 1955), 206, 216–18.
92. *WTP,* 3.4.811.
93. Cf. Fink, *Philosophie,* 32. Fink makes the plausible case that his subsequent attraction to the Enlightenment, expressed in *The Gay Science* and *Daybreak,* merely cut him loose from his dependence on Schopenhauer and Wagner that dominates the first work. In *Thus Spake Zarathustra* and in the posthumously published *Will to Power* Nietzsche returns to elaborate the major insights of his *Birth of Tragedy.* The last parts of *Will to Power* (3.4, "Will to Power as Art," and 4.2, "Dionysus") fortify that case powerfully.
94. *BT,* §1.33ff.
95. Cf. Fink, *Philosophie,* 18.
96. *BT,* §25.143; 4.44ff.
97. *BT,* §16.99–100.
98. *BT,* §17.104–5.
99. *BT,* §3.41ff.
100. *BT,* §3.42.
101. *BT,* §3.43.
102. *BT,* §21.130.
103. Friedrich Schiller, *On the Aesthetic Education of Man in a Series of Letters,* trans. R. Snell (New York: Ungar, 1965), twelfth–sixteenth letter, 64–81.
104. *BT,* §18.109–10.
105. *WTP,* 3.4.§852.450.
106. *BT,* §5.49.
107. This is the burden of Richard Schacht's argument in "Nietzsche on Art in *The Birth of Tragedy,*" in *Aesthetics,* ed. Dickie and Sclafani, 269–312. Cf. esp. 301, 309.
108. *BT,* §3.43.
109. Schacht, "Nietzsche on Art," 289.
110. Ibid., 305.
111. *BGE,* §12.20.
112. *WTP,* 3.4.§809.428.
113. *BT,* §5.48.
114. *WTP,* 3.4.809.
115. *BT,* §5.48ff.
116. *BT,* 26.
117. *EH,* 300.

118. *BT*, §8.61ff.

119. *BT*, §§10–12.75ff.

120. *BT*, §15.94.

121. *BT*, §11.78.

122. Martin Heidegger, "The Will to Power as Art," in *Nietzsche*, part 4, 107ff.

123. *TI*, 24.81; *WTP*, 3.4.§802.422; §851.449; §853.453.

124. *GM*, 3.§5.105.

125. *BT*, §17.109.

126. Cf. M. S. Silk and J. P. Stern, *Nietzsche on Tragedy* (Cambridge: Cambridge University Press, 1981), 12ff. This work gives a comprehensive treatment of the general context and basic character of the *Birth of Tragedy*.

127. *BT*, §2.19.

128. *BT*, §19.119.

129. *BT*, §18.112.

130. *WTP*, 3.4.§796.419.

131. *TI*, 93.

132. *TI*, 39, 94.

133. *TI*, 37, 91.

134. *WTP*, 3.4.§842.444.

135. *GM*, 3.8.243.

136. *WTP*, 3.4.§803.422; §842.444.

137. *BGE*, §265.215.

138. *WTP*, 4.§983.513.

139. Plato, *Rep*, 2.367e.

140. For a consideration of rewards and punishments as a consequence but not as a motive for a just life, see Plato, *Rep*, 10.608c ff.

141. Plato, *Phaedo*, 82e

142. Plato, *Timaeus*, 41.

143. This is, of course, the familiar thesis advanced by Thomas Kuhn in *The Structure of Scientific Revolutions* (Chicago: University of Chicago Press, 1962).

144. John Dewey, *Reconstruction in Philosophy* (Boston: Beacon Press, 1957), ix (henceforth *RP*).

145. Martin Heidegger, *The End of Philosophy*, trans. J. Stambaugh (New York: Harper and Row, 1973), 4ff., 79 (henceforth *EP*).

146. Cf. *WTP*, 4.§883.471.

147. *Daybreak*, §296.126.

148. *BT*, §24.140.

## IX. Dewey

1. Elizabeth Flower and Murray Murphey, *A History of Philosophy in America*, 2 vols. (New York: Capricorn, 1977), 2:809–87.

2. John Dewey, *Art as Experience* (New York: Capricorn, c. 1934), 46 (henceforth *AE*).

3. John Dewey, "From Absolutism to Experimentalism" in *On Experience, Nature, and Freedom*, ed. R. Bernstein (Indianapolis: Bobbs-Merrill, 1960), 15 (henceforth FATE); *RP*.

4. *RP*, 159.

5. FATE, 10

6. *RP,* 107ff.

7. Cf. Plato, *Phaedo,* 67d.

8. Ibid., 86a. In this matter one should also recall the countervailing positions presented in other dialogues on the status of eros: the *Phaedrus* presents it as the wings of the soul, as a form of divine madness that allows the soul to ascend to the highest things (245b). Moreover, in that same dialogue the latter are discerned as really present in visible things under the aspect of the Beautiful Itself (250d); and the *Symposium* presents eros as occupying the same place as philosophy, in the mediating realm between being and becoming and thus implicitly between rational soul and body (202d).

9. *RP,* 109ff., 115.

10. *AE,* 20–21; *RP.*

11. Aquinas, *ST,* 2–2.182.1.

12. *RP,* 112ff., 145. This entails a view of reality as process, "the most revolutionary discovery yet made" (*RP,* xiii).

13. We should note that, in spite of these observations, Dewey remarked (in 1930) that Plato "still provides my favorite philosophic reading," but Plato as "dramatic, restless, co-operatively inquiring," "whose highest flight of metaphysics always terminated with a social and practical turn" (FATE, 12–13).

14. René Descartes, *Discourse on Method,* D. Cress (Indianapolis: Hackett, 1980), 4 (AT), 32–33; 5 (AT), 56.

15. Gilbert Ryle, *The Concept of Mind* (New York: Barnes and Noble, 1949), 15–16.

16. Galileo Galilei, *The Assayer,* in *Discoveries and Opinions of Galileo,* trans. S. Drake (New York: Doubleday, 1957), 274.

17. Descartes, *Discourse on Method,* 4 (AT), 32. For a general approach to Descartes, see Wood, *Path into Metaphysics,* chap. 10.

18. The *Chuang Tzu,* in Chan, *Sourcebook in Chinese Philosophy,* 190.

19. Cf. Descartes, *Discourse on Method,* 4 (AT), 32.

20. Gueroult claims that Descartes actually has a third notion of substance: the human composite of thinking and extended substance. Cf. Martial Gueroult, *Descartes' Philosophy Interpreted According to the Order of Reasons,* vol. 2, *The Soul and the Body,* trans. R. Ariew (Minneapolis: University of Minnesota Press, 1985), 116–17.

21. Descartes, *Meditations,* 3 (AT, Latin, 45ff.; French, 35ff.); 5 (AT, Latin, 65ff.; French, 52ff.).

22. Ibid., 6 (AT, Latin, 74ff.; French, 59ff.).

23. Ibid. (AT, Latin, 89; French, 71).

24. Descartes, *Discourse on Method,* 6 (AT), 65.

25. Reported in Diogenes Laertius 9.31, Kirk and Raven, 409–10.

26. Descartes, *Discourse on Method,* 6 (AT), 62.

27. FATE, 15–17; *RP,* 84, 91.

28. *RP,* 87.

29. John Dewey, *Experience and Nature* (New York: Dover, 1958), 303 (henceforth *ExN*).

30. *AE,* 19.

31. *AE,* 22, 58.

32. *AE,* 67–69.

33. Cf. *ExN,* 73–75, 110ff.

34. Friedrich Schelling, "System of Transcendental Idealism," in *Philosophies of Art and Beauty*, ed. A. Hofstadter and R. Kuhns (Chicago: University of Chicago Press, 1964), 5.1.359. Cf. my "Being and Manifestness" for a parallel approach.

35. *AE*, 14–15.

36. *ExN*, 48ff., 92ff.

37. *RP*, 187ff.

38. *AE*, 270.

39. *AE*, 32, 37, 73, 120.

40. Cf. Joseph Stalin, *Dialectical and Historical Materialism* (New York: International Publishers, 1940), 20–21.

41. Even Descartes did not escape from this process. Etienne Gilson, the prominent historian of medieval thought, began his life project by demonstrating the medieval bases of Descartes's thought (e.g. in *Index scolastico-cartésien*, Paris: Alcan, 1912–13). Though Descartes thought he was constructing things anew, the very way he went about his construction was a function of the distinctions and directions provided by his upbringing

42. Cf. *RP*, 183–86. Cf. also *The Child and the Curriculum* (c. 1900; rev. ed. 1915) and *The School and Society* (c. 1902; Chicago: University of Chicago Press, 1971).

43. *ExN*, 102ff.

44. *RP*, 176.

45. *RP*, 203.

46. *RP*, 209.

47. Cf. *RP*, ix.

48. *RP*, 177.

49. *RP*, 177, 186.

50. *RP*, 194, 203.

51. *ExN*, 401; *AE*, 144–46.

52. *RP*, 164–69.

53. The passive view of education is not Platonic, since interaction is the way learning goes on in a Socratic context, as indicated in a Platonic dialogue. Socrates calls upon his interlocutors to take their own position and then helps them work out the consequences. The dialogues are protreptic and proleptic, leading the reader on and suggesting, without following out convergent directions for the reader's thought. Even the *Republic*, which, after its first book, seems to present a teaching, does not simply hand out answers. The character of the imagery, the nature of the interlocutors, the dramatic movement, the general form, and all the apparent fallacies and strange turns and qualifications of claims are calculated to set up in the reader the attentiveness that allows him to follow the direction indicated proleptically, by way of hint, in the various features of the dialogue. There is no way to get what Plato is after in a direct way. (See Wood, "Image, Structure, and Content" for an illustration of these features in Plato's *Republic*.) Dewey himself calls for a return to the Platonic dialogues as instantiating a more active form of education than has all too often been the case in the modern curriculum: he calls for an interactional model of learning (FATE, 13).

54. *RP*, 183–86, 209.

55. *RP*, 105. Cf. also John Dewey, *A Common Faith* (New Haven: Yale University Press, 1934), 59–60, 87.

56. *AE*, 4–9.

57. *RP*, 170ff.

58. *AE*, 3, 337.

59. *AE*, 6–11, 131, 252ff.

60. *AE*, 3–4, 10, 150.

61. *ExN*, 358.

62. *AE*, 85.

63. *AE*, 14ff.

64. *AE*, 4–10.

65. *AE*, 26–7.

66. *AE*, 4.

67. *AE*, 14ff., 147ff., 162ff.

68. *AE*, 154, 164.

69. *AE*, 169.

70. *AE*, 13, 137ff.

71. *AE*, 150.

72. *AE*, 19.

73. *AE*, 22.

74. *AE*, 25.

75. *AE*, 17, 121.

76. *AE*, 125–26, 175. This is a notion that goes back to Plato's *Theaetetus* (184c) and Aristotle's *OS* (3.1.425).

77. *AE*, 29, 50, 53, 100, 121–22, 218.

78. *AE*, 25.

79. *AE*, 39.

80. *RP*, 212–13.

81. *AE*, 5.

82. *AE*, 36ff., 67, 192.

83. Cf. the parallel discussion in Dufrenne, *Phenomenology*, 327.

84. *AE*, 33, 37–38, 73, 120, 123.

85. *AE*, 129–30.

86. *AE*, 38, 119–20.

87. *AE*, 67–69, 192.

88. *AE*, 19.

89. *AE*, 84.

90. *AE*, 133.

91. *AE*, 93–94, 100ff., 151–52, 208, 313.

92. *AE*, 152.

93. *AE*, 173.

94. *AE*, 177.

95. *AE*, 137, 117. Emphasis Dewey's.

96. *AE*, 138, 145.

97. *AE*, 6off.

98. Ibid.

99. *AE*, 71, 89, 98, 155.

100. *AE*, 123. This is a notion underscored by Hegel in *HPM*, §447, 194 and, more

recently, by physicist-philosopher Michael Polanyi in *Personal Knowledge: Towards a Post-Critical Philosophy* (New York: Harper and Row, 1964), 134ff.

101. *AE,* 140ff.

102. *AE,* 143.

103. *AE,* 70. Dufrenne speaks in this connection of academic art in which the artist is "only a hand without a heart" (*Phenomenology,* 104).

104. *AE,* 70.

105. *AE,* 65.

106. *AE,* 74ff.

107. *AE,* 92.

108. *AE,* 95, 178.

109. *AE,* 162ff., 106–9, 139. This is a central theme in Dufrenne, *Phenomenology,* 15, 24ff.

110. *AE,* 108.

111. *AE,* 144ff., 182.

112. *AE,* 145.

113. *AE,* 180.

114. *AE,* 169. Dewey's emphasis.

115. *AE,* 109.

116. Percy Bysshe Shelley, *A Defence of Poetry,* in *The Complete Works of Percy Bysshe Shelley,* ed. R. Ingpen and W. Peck (New York: Gordian Press, 1965), 7:140.

117. *AE,* 348.

118. *ExN,* 41.

119. *AE,* 81.

120. *AE,* 92.

121. *AE,* 105, 270, 335.

122. *AE,* 194; cf. *Common Faith,* 18–19, 85.

123. *AE,* 195.

124. *AE,* 107, 184–85.

125. *AE,* 274.

126. Lonergan, *Insight,* 335–36.

## X. Heidegger

1. Cf. Edmund Husserl, *General Introduction* and *Studies in the Phenomenology of Constitution,* trans. R. Rojcewicz and A. Schuwer, *Ideas Pertaining to a Pure Phenomenology and to a Phenomenological Philosophy,* bk. 2 (Dordrecht: Kluwer, 1989). For a general approach from within the movement, see Heidegger's *History of the Concept of Time: Prolegomena,* trans. T. Kisiel (Bloomington: Indiana University Press, 1985), 13–134. For an approach that links phenomenology with Plato's Line, see Wood, "Phenomenologists," 130–60.

2. Cf. Husserl, *Cartesian Meditations: An Introduction to Phenomenology,* trans. D. Cairns (The Hague: Martinus Nijhoff, 1960), §50.109.

3. Cf. Husserl, *Crisis,* 26–27; Heidegger, *BAT,* 60–61.

4. Husserl, *Cartesian Meditations,* 7, 18–24; *Crisis,* 73ff. Cf. Descartes, *Meditations.*

5. Paul Ricoeur, *Husserl: An Analysis of His Phenomenology,* trans. E. Ballard and L. Embree (Evanston, Ill.: Northwestern University Press, 1967), 201; cf. Husserl, *General Introduction,* 183.

6. Martin Heidegger, *Kant and the Problem of Metaphysics*, trans. J. Churchill (Bloomington: Indiana University Press, 1965); *What Is a Thing?* trans. W. Barton and V. Deutsch (Chicago: Regnery, 1967); *Phenomenological Interpretation of Kant's Critique of Pure Reason*, trans. P. Emad and K. Maly (Bloomington: Indiana University Press, 1997).

7. *BAT,* 247ff.

8. Edmund Husserl, *Logical Investigations,* trans. J. Findlay, 2 vols. (New York: Humanities Press, 1970), 2:741–42.

9. Martin Heidegger, "The Way Back into the Ground of Metaphysics," trans. W. Kaufmann, in *Existentialism from Dostoevsky to Sartre,* ed. W. Kaufmann (Cleveland: World Publishing, 1956), 206–21.

10. *BAT,* 78ff.

11. *BAT,* 27, 67ff.

12. Cf. *BAT,* 61–62.

13. *NE* 1.4.1095b7. See Martin Heidegger, *Plato's Sophist,* trans. R. Rojcewicz and André Schuwer (Bloomington: Indiana University Press, 1997), 33–40, 91–123.

14. Martin Heidegger, "Memorial Address," in *Discourse on Thinking,* trans. J. Anderson and E. Freund (New York: Harper and Row, 1966), 54–56 (henceforth MA).

15. "Language," in *PLT,* 203.

16. *An Introduction to Metaphysics,* trans. R. Manheim (New Haven: Yale University Press, 1959), 37 (henceforth *IM*).

17. *IM,* 180ff.

18. *IM,* 194, 202; Martin Heidegger, *What Is Called Thinking?* trans. J. Glenn Gray (New York: Harper and Row, 1968), 102 (henceforth *WCT*).

19. *BAT,* 370ff. and 456ff.; Edmund Husserl, *Phenomenology of Internal Time-Consciousness,* trans. J. Churchill (Bloomington: Indiana University Press, 1964), 50ff., 76ff.

20. Martin Heidegger, *What Is a Thing?* trans. W. Barton and V. Deutsch (Chicago: Henry Regnery, 1967), 66ff. Cf. also *QCT,* 37.

21. *BAT,* 278–311.

22. *BAT,* 149ff.

23. Martin Heidegger, "On the Essence of Truth," in *Basic Writings from* Being and Time *(1927) to* The Task of Thinking *(1964),* ed. and trans. D. Krell (New York: Harper and Row, 1977), 132.

24. Hans-Georg Gadamer, *Heidegger's Ways,* trans. J. Stanley (Albany: State University of New York Press, 1994), 123.

25. MA, 46; cf. *WCT,* 139ff.; and "What Are Poets For?" (henceforth WPF), in *PLT,* 127ff.

26. Martin Heidegger, *On the Way to Language,* trans. P. Hertz (San Francisco: Harper and Row, 1971), 93 (henceforth *OWL*).

27. Cf. note 25.

28. "Essence of Truth," 132ff.

29. *OWL,* 95.

30. *QCT,* 175.

31. *QCT,* 17–20.

32. *QCT,* 27.

33. Cf. Wooldridge, *Mechanical Man,* 84–86, 158–62.

34. *IM,* 62–63.

35. *IM*, 38.
36. OWA, 17–87.
37. OWA, 78.
38. OWA, 19.
39. OWA, 74 ff.
40. OWA, 50.
41. OWA, 44.
42. Martin Heidegger, "What Is Metaphysics?" in *Basic Writings*, 99ff.
43. OWA, 62.
44. *IM*, 26; *WCT*, 131.
45. OWA, 73.
46. *PLT*, 165–82.
47. OWA, 22ff., 68.
48. Cf. *BAT*, 96ff.
49. Aristotle, *Physics*, 2.3.194b ff.
50. OWA, 42ff.
51. Meyer Shapiro challenged Heidegger's identification and claimed they were the painter's own shoes; Derrida undercuts the narrowness of Shapiro's observations in terms of Heidegger's basic concern in the essay. Cf. Jacques Derrida, *The Truth in Painting*, trans. G. Bennington and I. McLeod (Chicago: University of Chicago Press, 1987), 257ff.
52. *BAT*, 98.
53. Cf. Barfield, *Saving the Appearances*, 28–35.
54. Martin Heidegger, *The Principle of Reason*, trans. R. Lilly (Bloomington: Indiana University Press, 1991), 35ff. Cf. John Caputo, *The Mystical Element in Heidegger's Thought* (New York: Fordham University Press, 1986).
55. OWA, 46–47.
56. *IM*, 26
57. Martin Heidegger, "Building, Dwelling and Thinking" (henceforth *BDT*), in *PLT*, 49–51; cf. also "The Thing," in *PLT*, 172–82.
58. Cf. *EP*.
59. *IM*, 128.
60. Cf. "The Thing," in *PLT*, 181. "Wenn wir das Ding in seinem Dingen aus der weltenden Welt Wesen lassen, denken wir an das Ding als Ding." *Das Ding* in *Vorträge und Aufsätze*, p. 173.
61. This section is an adaptation of Robert E. Wood, "Six Heideggerian Figures," in *Martin Heidegger*, ed. John D. Caputo, special issue of *American Catholic Philosophical Quarterly*, Spring 1995, 311–31. For an approach that links Heidegger to two cognate twentieth-century thinkers, see Robert E. Wood, "Silence, Being, and the Between: Picard, Heidegger, and Buber," *Man and World* 27 (1994): 121–34.
62. Martin Heidegger, postscript to "What Is Metaphysics?" in *Existence and Being*, ed. and trans. W. Brock (South Bend, Ind.: Regnery, 1949), 360.
63. Martin Heidegger, "Why Do I Stay in the Provinces?" trans. T. Sheehan, *Listening* 12 (1977): 124. Unless otherwise indicated, all works referred to henceforth are those of Heidegger.
64. BDT, 146ff.

65. *BAT,* 95ff.

66. *QCT,* 15.

67. Martin Heidegger, "Hebel—Friend of the House," trans. B. Foltz and M. Heim, *Contemporary German Philosophy* 3 (1983): 93. Cf. also BDT, 160.

68. "Why Do I Stay?" 123.

69. BDT, 149 .

70. *QCT,* 153.

71. "Why Do I Stay?" 123.

72. MA, 55.

73. *EP,* 109.

74. "Hebel," 97.

75. Cf. *WCT,* 139–48 for what follows. Cf. also WPF, 127ff. and my introduction to Strasser's *Phenomenology of Feeling.*

76. "The Thing," in *PLT,* 181.

77. Hans-Georg Gadamer suggests the relation between *Andenken,* or remembrance, and *Andacht,* or devotion, though etymologically dubious, may have been intended to convey the proximity of such thinking to religious experience. See *Heidegger's Ways,* 27.

78. OWA, 36.

79. MA, 47.

80. "Why Do I Stay?" 123.

81. Gadamer, *Heidegger's Ways,* 117.

82. Cf. Aquinas, *ST,* 2-2.101.1. As antecedents he cites Aristotle, *NE,* 9.12.1162a4ff. and Cicero, *De Inv. Rhet, ii.*

83. Cf. Hegel's *Philosophy of Right.* The section on Ethical Life is divided into sections on Family, Civil Society, and State (§§142–340.105–216), in which the flanking notions— the loci of "substantial freedom"—set the limiting frame for the central section, which deals with modern freedoms—market, marriage, press, occupation, assembly, and the like.

84. Cf. Plato's *Phaedrus,* 245a5.

85. *BAT,* 149ff.

86. *IM,* 26.

87. Cf. OWA, 62, 74. Jacques Taminiaux points to a fundamental shift from the first version of the OWA lecture in November 1935 to the third, one year later. In the first two Heidegger was still in continuity with the contempt for everydayness evidenced in *Being and Time* and in *Introduction to Metaphysics;* in the third he shows a renewed appreciation for the strangeness of the familiar. See "The Origin of 'The Origin of the Work of Art,'" in *Reading Heidegger: Commemorations,* ed. J. Sallis (Bloomington: Indiana University Press, 1993), 392–404. This may dovetail with Gadamer's report (see note 20, above) on the transformation Heidegger experienced on his return to the Black Forest.

88. *IM,* 11, 63.

89. OWA, 63. On innerness, see WPF, 126–30. Cf. Michael Zimmerman, *Heidegger's Confrontation with Modernity: Technology, Politics, and Art* (Bloomington: Indiana University Press, 1990), 123; cf. 117 on the connection of Heidegger with *Innerlichkeit* as the center of Hölderlin's thought.

90. For a treatment of the notion of *Kampf* (struggle) in Heidegger, cf. John Caputo, *Demythologizing Heidegger* (Bloomington: Indiana University Press, 1993), 39–59.

91. *IM,* 61ff. Caputo claims that Heidegger moved from an early concern with the thematics of New Testament *kardia,* or the heart, to the *Kampf* of faith and thus to *polemos* as central orientation (*Demythologizing Heidegger,* 6, 39ff.). Need the two be incompatible? It seems to me that for Heidegger it is only through struggle with the tendency to settle down in surface appearances that beings draw near. In such drawing near, they speak to the heart. At any rate, it is clear that, for later Heidegger, the heart again becomes a focal notion (cf. above, n. 25).

92. Cf. Jean-François Mattéi, "The Heideggerian Chiasmus [*sic*]," in Dominique Janicaud and Jean-François Mattéi, *Heidegger: From Metaphysics to Thought,* trans. M. Gendre (Albany: State University of New York Press, 1995), 112. Leading humans in this way seems to be the sole locus, scarcely focused and developed, of *Mitdasein* in later Heidegger. Essentially following Levinas, Caputo notes Heidegger's predominant concern for things and not-so-predominant concern for people, and especially not for those other than fully functional adults (*Demythologizing Heidegger,* 65). But he notes further that what is required is more than an extension of "letting things be" from things to people, but a more radical openness to what is other (146).

93. "Language" in *PLT,* 199, 203.

94. Cf. Wood, "Heidegger on the Way to Language," 611–20.

95. OWA, 73–74.

96. Cf. Mattéi, "Heideggerian Chiasmos," 133.

97. *WCT,* 11.

98. Martin Heidegger, "Letter on Humanism" (henceforth LH), in *Basic Writings,* 230.

99. Martin Heidegger, "Way to Language," in *OWL,* 112–13.

100. Martin Heidegger, "Language," in *PLT,* 208.

101. Martin Heidegger, "The Nature of Language" (henceforth NL), in *OWL,* 97; "Way to Language," 115.

102. "Words," in *OWL,* 155.

103. NL, 66.

104. WPF, 91.

105. NL, 6off.; "Words," in *OWL,* 140ff.

106. *IM,* 70–73.

107. Cf. "Poetically Man Dwells . . . ," in *PLT,* 218; NL, 62.

108. LH, 230.

109. NL, 78.

110. *IM,* 152.

111. Martin Heidegger, "Language in the Poem," (henceforth LP), in *OWL,* 172.

112. LP, 160.

113. LP, 172.

114. BDT, 147; "The Thing," in *PLT,* 177–78; "A Dialogue on Language," in *OWL,* 12.

115. "A Dialogue on Language," in *OWL,* 10.

116. WPF, 93.

117. Nietzsche, *BAT,* 373.

118. *BAT,* 169ff.

119. LP, 196–97.

120. WPF, 94.

121. NL, 99.

122. Martin Heidegger, "The Thinker as Poet," in *PLT*, 13.

123. WPF, 97–128.

124. *WCT*, 224; *WP*, 31.

125. *WP*, 53.

126. *IM*, 14, 101. I find little ground for Zimmerman's contention that Heidegger did not adequately emphasize the first stem (*Confrontation*, 225). The text cited seems to me to make that transparent.

127. *WP*, 53.

128. *IM*, 18off.; *WCT*, 233, 238.

129. Dominique Janicaud, "Heideggeriana," in Janicaud and Mattéi, *Heidegger*, 16.

130. *WP*, 79. There is much in the Platonic dialogues that supports this way of reading *thaumazein*. However, when Aristotle explicitly treats it in his *Metaphysics* (1.1.982b12), it is not awe but curiosity as that which disappears when one can offer an explanation. I suspect Heidegger reads this into Aristotle because he had even greater respect for him than for Plato, whom, Gadamer suggests, Heidegger never really understood (*Heidegger's Ways*, 144). In general, Heidegger read Plato in the light of Aristotle, as is clearly indicated by his spending the first 237 pages of his 668-page *Platon: Sophistes (Gesamtausgabe*, vol. 2, Frankfurt am Main: Vittorio Klostermann, 1992) on Aristotle.

131. *IM*, 26; cf. also 120–21. We should underscore the "merely" since Heidegger is not repudiating but rather situating logic. When logic claims priority, it tends to dissolve the deeper sensitivity Heidegger is cultivating.

132. *WCT*, 103, 211.

133. *WCT*, 131; *WP*, 31–33.

134. *IM*, 26.

135. *On Time and Being*, trans. J. Stambaugh (New York: Harper and Row, 1972), 57.

136. *Time and Being*, 58.

137. LH, 232-33.

138. *QCT*, 75ff.

139. *What Is a Thing?* 8off.

140. *IM*, 62–63.

141. *Basic Problems*, 282-83. Cf. Reiner Schürrmann, *Heidegger on Being and Acting: From Principles to Anarchy* (Bloomington: Indiana University Press, 1990), 75: philosophy had its roots in Greek astonishment before things produced by man. This accounts for the dominance of "teleocracy" in all Western thinking (83). Metaphysics then becomes "the generalization of modes of thought appropriate to only *one* region of phenomena—artifacts" (105, Schürrmann's emphasis). For a critique of the Platonic origins of this notion, see Stanley Rosen, *The Question of Being: A Reversal of Heidegger* (New Haven: Yale University Press, 1993), 10–21, 43. Rosen thinks that, among other things, Heidegger fails to deal adequately with Platonic Eros, which operates in the crucial relation between mythos and logos (29). We noted above Gadamer's claim regarding Heidegger that the Platonic dialogues "remained inaccessible to this impatient questioner" (*Heidegger's Ways*, 144).

142. *QCT*, 17.

143. LH, 210; cf. Descartes, *Discourse on Method*, 33 (AT, 62).

144. *WCT*, 43.

145. *QCT*, 27.

146. *WCT*, 43.

147. *WCT,* 8. Schürmann suggests that this parallels Kant's distinction between thinking and knowing (*Being and Acting,* 291). This would seem to imply that science does not think because it knows—though it does not know what exceeds, situates and makes itself possible.

148. *WCT,* 32ff.

149. Cf. Zimmerman (*Confrontation,* 58–59) on Heidegger's relation to Jünger: human beings are viewed as standing reserve to be stamped with the gestalt of the worker. Meditation on Hölderlin led to the opposite view of drawing out of forms that are already there (76).

150. *BAT,* 219.

151. Cf. *WCT,* 57ff.

152. *WCT,* 30.

153. *IM,* 38.

154. *WCT,* 101.

155. LH, 230.

156. LH, 218.

157. MA, 48.

158. *OWL,* 58.

159. LH, 239.

160. LH, 195.

161. *WCT,* 21.

162. *WCT,* 17.

163. *WCT,* 50.

164. *WCT,* 77.

165. Cf. "Ground of Metaphysics."

166. Ibid., 276.

167. *BAT,* 44.

168. Martin Heidegger, *The Question of Being,* trans. W. Kluback and J. Wilde (New Haven: College and University Press, 1958), 92 (henceforth *QB*).

169. *WCT,* 103, 211.

170. *QB,* 92.

171. Dominique Janicaud, "Overcoming Metaphysics," in Janicaud and Mattéi, *Heidegger,* 5, 7. I agree completely with Mattéi's judgment that Heidegger is concerned with "displacing the metaphysical *point* of view on Being—not in order to cancel it, but to show its essential insufficiency in the absence of a premetaphysical *counterpoint*" ("Heideggerian Chiasmus" in *Heidegger,* 74). Janicaud correctly remarks: "At stake is the question of taking metaphysics upon oneself, and not leaving it aside" (Janicaud, "Heidegger in New York" in *Heidegger,* 197). I think then that Derrida is off the mark in claiming that Heidegger dealt with metaphysics in order to "send it packing" (*On Spirit,* trans. G. Bennington and R. Bowlby [Chicago: University of Chicago Press, 1989], 75).

172. *EP,* 87; cf. "Ground of Metaphysics," 267.

173. *Vorträge und Aufsätze,* 72.

174. *EP,* 84ff. Cf. Stambaugh's note 1. It seems to me that Gadamer is on firm ground when he claims that Heidegger's work gave metaphysics new strength and was calculated to do so (*Heidegger's Ways,* 82, 184–85).

175. *OWL,* 20.

176. Mattéi, "Heideggerian Chiasmus," *Heidegger,* 54.

177. LH, 231.

178. *EP,* 85.

179. Cf. WPF, 105ff.

180. On the notion of "sedimentation of concepts," cf. Husserl, *Crisis.* Gadamer notes the astonishment of himself and his fellow students as Heidegger demonstrated that, instead of charting out relations and formally linking judgments, thinking is showing and getting things to show themselves in and through the thinkers he examined, with whose horizons he fused his own (*Heidegger's Ways,* 61–62, 70, 141). He thus showed that the break with the tradition was "just as much an incomparable renewal of the tradition" (70).

181. WCT, 31.

182. In view of everything I have pointed out, I find it mind-boggling for Rosen to claim that Heidegger has detached philosophy from everyday life (*Reversal,* 272), only insofar as Rosen might understand that as not providing any guidance for living our lives except for "listening to the voice of Being," which Rosen regards as vacuous (217, 263).

183. *WP,* 75, 79.

184. If this interpretation is correct, Heidegger already circumvents Janicaud's objection that Heidegger creates a solidified dichotomy between metaphysics and the thought of being that disallows a "rational dwelling" in terms of a "non-techno-logical-scientific rational thinking . . . [which] reigned freely in the Medievals' theory of *analogia*" ("Heideggerian Chiasmus," *Heidegger,* 35, 29).

185. *WCT,* 163.

186. LH, 221.

187. LH, 192, 236.

188. *OWL,* 98ff.

189. *WCT,* 241.

190. *WCT,* 174. Heidegger spends the rest of the book (to 244) explicating this and the sentences that follow.

191. *WCT,* 202, 207; also WPF, 127ff.

192. *WCT,* 241.

193. *IM,* 141.

194. *WCT,* 208.

195. *WCT,* 209.

196. Cf. Dufrenne, *Phenomenology,* 427–30.

197. There's always been a problem with Heidegger's rhetoric, which may go deeper than rhetoric. For example, in the use of terms like *authentic* and *inauthentic,* surrounded in his own usage with high moral tone, Heidegger still denies any moral features to the notions involved. He seems to attack metaphysics and then to reinstate it; he does the same with technology.

198. "Hebel," 98.

199. Janicaud, "Heideggeriana," *Heidegger,* 22. I have tried to approach select high points in the history of metaphysics by leaning especially on Heidegger's notion of *aletheia* and developing a set of "secular meditations" that follow that lead in *Path into*

*Metaphysics.* Cf. especially chapter 1, on meditation, and chapter 16, on Heidegger. I have also linked Heidegger with the poet-essayist Max Picard and with Martin Buber in "Silence, Being, and the Between: Picard, Heidegger, and Buber," *Man and World* 27 (1994).

200. Wood, *Path into Metaphysics*, 190–98.

201. Ibid., 225. This is indeed the basic thesis of Balthasar's seven-volume *Glory of the Lord*, which he sees as an effort to appropriate Heidegger's project (vol. 5, *The Realm of Metaphysics in the Modern Age*, 449–50).

202. Hegel, *Philosophy of Fine Art*, 2.390; cf. also *PS*, §753.456.

203. Cf. Irving Singer, introduction to *The Last Puritan* by George Santayana (Cambridge, Mass.: MIT Press, 1994), xxii.

204. Walter Kaufmann, *Religions in Four Dimensions: Existential and Aesthetic, Historical and Comparative* (New York: Reader's Digest Press, 1976).

# XI. Conclusion

1. A variation on this concluding chapter has been presented as "Recovery of the Aesthetic Center," the 1994–95 presidential address to the American Catholic Philosophical Association. It appeared in *Recovery of Form*, Proceedings of the American Catholic Philosophical Association, Washington, D.C.: Catholic University of America, 1995, 1–25.

2. Cf. Gustavo Gutiérrez, *A Theology of Liberation: History, Politics, and Salvation*, trans. and ed. C. Inda and J. Eagleson (Maryknoll, N.Y.: Orbis, 1973).

3. For a development of this theme, drawing upon literature, philosophy, and theology from the early Greeks and Hebrews to the present, see his massive seven-volume *The Glory of the Lord: A Theological Aesthetics* to which I have several times referred. I have tried to indicate this direction earlier in "Art and the Sacred," *Listening* 18.1 (Winter 1983): 30–40.

4. Dewey, *AE;* on integral experience, see 46; on morality, 346–49; on depth, 193–95.

5. On the notions of earth and world, cf. Heidegger, OWA, 42ff.; on mystery, cf. "Essence of Truth," 132 ff. and MA, 55.; on the notion of the heart, *WCT*, 139–48 and WPF, 127ff.

6. Cf. Aristotle, *OS*, 3.12.434a23ff.

7. Henri Matisse, *Henri Matisse*, ed. Jack D. Flam (Berkeley: University of California Press, 1994), 48, 66, 92, 140.

8. Feuerbach, *The Essence of Christianity*, 12–32.

9. Cf. Peter Berger and Thomas Luckmann, *The Social Construction of Reality: A Treatise in the Sociology of Knowledge* (Garden City, N.Y.: Doubleday, 1966).

10. Martin Buber, *I and Thou*, trans. W. Kaufmann (New York: Scribners, 1970), 63–64, 73–74, 80–82, 87–88.

11. Buber, "Dialogue," *Between Man and Man*, 18.

12. This is, of course, a basic complaint of Kierkegaard, who strongly influenced Buber's thought. Cf. *Kierkegaard's Concluding Unscientific Postscript*, trans. D. Swenson (completed by W. Lowrie) (Princeton, N.J.: Princeton University Press, 1941), esp. 248–52. On Buber's relation to Kierkegaard, see Buber, *Between Man and Man*, 40ff., 161–63.

13. Cf. Hegel, *PM*, §381, *Zusatz* 11. Cf. also his *PR*, §7.21–24.

14. Cf. Aquinas, *ST,* 2.2.101, ad 1. As antecedents he cites Aristotle, *NE,* 9.12.1162a4ff. and Cicero, *De Inv. Rhet., ii.*

15. Gadamer, *Truth and Method,* 76.

16. Pater, *Renaissance,* 159.

17. OWA, 68, 79.

18. Cf. esp. Kierkegaard, *Either/Or.*

19. Kant, *CJ,* 42.165.

20. John Henry Newman, *An Essay in Aid of a Grammar of Assent* (Garden City, N.Y.: Doubleday, 1955), 49–92.

21. Buber, *I and Thou,* 117–19.

22. Thomas Aquinas, *Commentary on Aristotle's* De anima, 1.1, n. 15; *Disputed Questions on Spiritual Creatures,* 11, ad 3; *On Truth,* 4.1, ad 8. I have used this reference to mystery as a way of relating Aquinas and Heidegger in "Aquinas and Heidegger: Personal *Esse,* Truth, and Imagination," in *Postmodernism and Christian Philosophy,* ed. R. Ciapalo (Washington, D.C.: Catholic University of America Press, 1997), 268–80.

23. I have tried to delineate the fundamental phenomena here by triangulating through the work of three thinkers in "Silence, Being, and the Between."

24. Cf. Augustine's *Confessions,* beginning with the famous I I on the "restless heart," through the equally famous "tolle, lege" passage in 8.12, where his heart was suffused with light, to the "confessions of the heart" in book 10, culminating in the vision of "Beauty ever ancient ever new" of 10.27.

25. Buber, *I and Thou,* 44, 110;, cf. Wood, *Martin Buber's Ontology,* 54ff., 104–5.

26. Martin Buber, *Moses, The Revelation, and the Covenant* (New York: Harper, 1959), 52; cf. also *The Eclipse of God* (New York: Harper, 1952), 62.

27. Heidegger, *WP,* 78–85.

28. Plato, *Theaetetus,* 155c.

29. Ibid., 174a–175a.

30. For a different way of developing the link between metaphysics, the aesthetic, and the emotional, see Wood, "Metaphysics and Aesthetics," 615–35. For the way in which an enlarged sense of the aesthetic functions at the center of Weiss's thought, see Robert E. Wood, "Weiss on Adumbration," *Philosophy Today* 22 (Winter 1985): 339–48.

31. Eco, *Art and Beauty,* 92ff.

## Appendix

1. Nietzsche, *WTP,* 3.4.842.444.

2. Moore, "View of Sculpture," xxx.

3. Herbert Read, *A Concise History of Modern Sculpture* (New York: Praeger, 1964), 176ff. Read has a more extended work devoted entirely to this interpretation of Moore: *Henry Moore* (London: Zwemmer, 1934).

4. Moore, "View of Sculpture," xxxi, a. Cf. Naum Gabo on the emotional value of materials deriving from our own belonging to the material order. Naum Gabo, "Sculpture: Carving and Construction in Space," in *Theories of Modern Art: A Sourcebook by Artists and Critics,* ed. H. Chipp (Berkeley: University of California Press, 1968), 331.

5. Read, *Modern Sculpture,* 167.

6. Moore, "View of Sculpture," xxx, a.

7. Boccione, "Technical Manifesto," 537–38.

8. Moore, "Mesopotamian Art," in *Henry Moore*, xxxii, a.

9. Moore, "Primitive Art" (1941), in *Henry Moore*, xxxvi, a. In this observation Moore roughly follows a tradition represented by Winckelmann, for whom sculpture passes through several more primitive phases until it enters a classical culmination followed by decline, although Moore completely changes the evaluative perspective represented by Winckelmann, who had little sympathy for anything less than perfect idealized representation. Cf. Winckelmann's *History of Ancient Art*, 4 vols., trans. G. Lodge (Boston: Little, Brown, 1856–73).

10. Moore, "Primitive Art," xxxvii, b.

11. Cited in Hunter and Jacobus, *Modern Art*, 77a–78b.

12. Cited in ibid., 67a.

13. Moore, "The Sculptor's Aims," in *Henry Moore*, xxxi, b. Cf. Read, *Modern Sculpture*, 163. Cf. also R. H. Wilenski, *Modern Sculpture*, 162.

14. Moore, "View of Sculpture," in *Henry Moore*, xxx.

15. Wright, *Future of Architecture*, 104.

16. Moore, "Notes on Sculpture," in *Henry Moore*, xxxiv, a.

17. See Nicholas Penny, *The Materials of Sculpture* (New Haven: Yale University Press, 1993), for a detailed discussion of the significance of the use of various materials for sculpturing employed throughout history.

18. Ibid., xxxiii, b. Plato made the same observation about the indeterminate number of perspectives involved in sculpture in his *Laws* 2.

19. Moore, "Mesopotamian Art," xxxiii, a.

20. "Notes on Sculpture," xxxiv, a.

21. Cf. Wilenski, *Modern Sculpture*, 95, 101.

22. Moore, "Notes on Sculpture," xxxv, b.

23. Wilenski, *Modern Sculpture*, 25, 92–106.

24. Ibid., 100.

25. Boccione, "Technical Manifesto," 537.

26. Ibid.

27. Hunter and Jacobus, *Modern Art*, 240.

28. Moore, "Notes on Sculpture," xxxiv, b.

29. Cf. Gabo, "Sculpture," 332.

30. Cf. ibid., 336; Moore, "Notes on Sculpture," xxxv, b.

31. Cf. Giedion, *Space*, xlvii–lvi.

32. John Ruskin, *The Seven Lamps of Architecture* (New York: Dover, 1989).

33. Schopenhauer, *WWR*, 2, suppl. to book 3, chap. 34, 408.

34. Pliny, *Natural History*, 35.61–66, reported in Pollitt, *Art of Ancient Greece*, 150.

35. Hegel, *ALFA*, 1:42 (1:59).

36. Kant, *CJ*, 42.166 (299).

# Bibliography

Alberti, Leon Battista. *The Ten Books of Architecture: The 1755 Leoni Edition.* New York: Dover, 1986.

Albertus Magnus. *De pulchro et bono.* In *Aquinatis opera omnia: Aliorum medii aevi auctorum scripta* 61, ed. R. Busa, 43–47. Stuttgart: Friedrich Frommann, 1980.

Anselm. *Proslogion.* In *Opera omnia*, vol. 1, ed. F. Schmitt. Stuttgart: Friedrich Frommann, 1968.

Aquinas, Thomas. *Commentary on the Physics of Aristotle.* Trans. R. Bladewell, R. Spath, W. Thirlkel. New Haven: Yale University Press, 1963.

———. *Disputed Questions on Truth.* 3 vols. Trans. R. Mulligan, R. Schmitt, J. McGlynn. Chicago: Regnery, 1952–54.

———. *On Being and Essence.* Trans. A. Maurer. Toronto: Pontifical Institute of Medieval Studies, 1949.

———. *On the Power of God.* Westminster: Newman Press, 1952.

———. *On the Truth of the Catholic Faith: Summa contra gentiles.* 4 vols. Trans. V. Bourke, C. O'Neil, A. Pegis. Garden City, N.Y.: Doubleday, 1955.

———. *Summa theologiae.* 3 vols. New York: Benziger Brothers, 1947.

Aristotle. *Aristotle: The Art of Rhetoric.* Trans. J. Freese. Cambridge, Mass.: Harvard University Press, 1965.

———. *Aristotle's Nicomachean Ethics*, trans. Hippocrates G. Apostle (Grinell, Iowa: Peripatetic Press, 1984).

———. *The Basic Works of Aristotle.* Ed. R. McKeon; trans. W. D. Ross. New York: Random House, c. 1941.

———. *The Categories; On Interpretation.* Trans. H. Cooke. *Prior Analytics.* Trans. H. Tredennick. Cambridge, Mass.: Harvard University Press, 1962.

———. *Metaphysics*. 2 vols. Trans. H. Tredennick. Cambridge, Mass.: Harvard University Press, 1967.

———. *The Nicomachean Ethics*. Trans. H. Rackham. Cambridge, Mass.: Harvard University Press, 1975.

———. *On the Soul; Parva natura; On Breath*. Trans. W. Hett. Cambridge, Mass.: Harvard University Press, 1975.

———. *The Physics*. Trans. P. Wicksteed and F. Cornford. Cambridge, Mass.: Harvard University Press, 1980.

———. *The Poetics*. Trans. W. Fyfe. Cambridge, Mass.: Harvard University Press, 1973.

———. *The Politics of Aristotle*. Trans. E. Barker. Cambridge: Oxford University Press, 1970.

Augustine, Aurelius. *The City of God*. Trans. M. Dods. New York: Modern Library, 1950.

———. *The Greatness of the Soul*. Trans. J. Colleran. New York: Newman Press, 1950.

———. *On the Immortality of the Soul*. Trans. G. Leckie in *Basic Writings of St. Augustine*. Ed. Whitney Oates. New York: Random House, 1948.

———. *Saint Augustine's Confessions*. Trans. W. Watts. 2 vols. Cambridge, Mass.: Harvard University Press, 1977.

———. *The Trinity*. Trans. J. Rotelle. Brooklyn: New City Press, 1990.

Balthasar, Hans Urs von. *The Glory of the Lord: A Theological Aesthetics*. Vol. 1, *Seeing the Form*. Trans. E. Leiva-Merikakis. San Francisco: Ignatius Press, 1982.

———. *The Glory of the Lord*. Vol. 2, *Studies in Theological Style: Clerical Styles*. Trans. A. Louth, F. McDonagh, and B. McNeil. San Francisco: Ignatius Press, 1984.

———. *The Glory of the Lord*. Vol. 3, *Studies in Theological Style: Lay Styles*. Trans. A. Louth, J. Saward, M. Simon, and R. Williams. San Francisco: Ignatius Press, 1986.

———. *The Glory of the Lord*. Vol. 4, *The Realm of Metaphysics in Antiquity*. Trans. B. McNeil, A. Louth, J. Saward, R. Williams, and O. Davies. San Francisco: Ignatius Press, 1989.

———. *The Glory of the Lord*. Vol. 5, *The Realm of Metaphysics in the Modern Age*. Trans. O. Davies, A. Louth, B. McNeil, J. Saward, and R. Williams. San Francisco: Ignatius Press, 1991.

———. *The Glory of the Lord*. Vol. 6, *Theology: The Old Covenant*. Trans. B. McNeil and E. Leiva-Merikakis. San Francisco: Ignatius Press, 1991.

———. *The Glory of the Lord*. Vol. 7, *Theology: The New Covenant*. Trans. B. McNeil. San Francisco: Ignatius Press, 1989.

Barfield, Owen. *Saving the Appearances: A Study in Idolatry*. New York: Harcourt, Brace and World, 1957.

Benedikt, Michael. *Deconstructing the Kimbell: An Essay on Meaning and Architecture*. New York: SITES/Lumen Books, 1991.

Berger, Peter, and Thomas Luckmann. *The Social Construction of Reality: A Treatise in the Sociology of Knowledge*. Garden City, N.Y.: Doubleday, 1966.

Boccione, Umberto. "The Futurist Manifesto." In *Theories of Modern Art: A Sourcebook by Artists and Critics,* ed. H. Chipp, 298–304. Berkeley: University of California Press, 1968.

———. "Technical Manifesto of Futurist Sculpture." *Art and Its Significance: An Anthology of Aesthetic Theory,* ed. S. Ross. Albany: State University of New York Press, 1984.

Bonaventura. *Opera Omnia*. 15 vols. Paris: Vivès, 1876–.

Brancusi, Constantin. *Brancusi*. Ed. Ionel Jianou, ed. London: Adam, 1963.

Buber, Martin. *Between Man and Man*. Boston: Beacon Press, 1961.

———. *Daniel: Dialogues on Realization*. Trans. M. Friedman. New York: McGraw-Hill, 1965.

———. *Eclipse of God: Studies in the Relationship between Religion and Philosophy*. New York: Harper, 1952.

———. *I and Thou*. Trans. W. Kaufmann. New York: Scribners, 1970.

———. *The Knowledge of Man: A Philosophy of the Interhuman*. Trans. M. Friedman and R. G. Smith. New York: Harper and Row, 1965.

———. *Moses, The Revelation, and the Covenant*. New York: Harper, 1959.

Bullough, Edward. "Psychical Distance as a Factor in Art and an Aesthetic Principle." In *Aesthetics: A Critical Anthology,* ed. G. Dickie and R. Sclafani, 758–82. New York: St. Martin's Press, 1977.

Caputo, John. *Demythologizing Heidegger*. Bloomington: Indiana University Press, 1993.

———. *The Mystical Element in Heidegger's Thought*. New York: Fordham University Press, 1986.

Casebier, Allan. "The Concept of Aesthetic Distance." In *Aesthetics: A Critical Anthology,* ed. G. Dickie and R. Sclafani, 783–99. New York: St. Martin's Press, 1977.

Cassirer, Ernst. *The Philosophy of the Enlightenment*. Trans. F. Koelln and J. Pettegrove. Boston: Beacon Press, 1951.

Cavell, Stanley. *The World Viewed: Reflections on the Ontology of Film*. New York: Viking, 1971.

Chan, Wing-tsit, trans. and comp. *A Sourcebook in Chinese Philosophy*. Princeton, N.J.: Princeton University Press, 1963.

Collins, Peter. *Changing Ideals in Modern Architecture, 1750–1950.* Kingston, Ontario: McGill-Queen's University Press, 1984.

Comte, Auguste. *Introduction to Positive Philosophy.* Ed. and trans. Frederick Ferré. Indianapolis: Bobbs-Merrill, 1970.

Corbusier, Le. *Towards a New Architecture.* Trans. F. Etchells. New York: Praeger, 1960.

Courtine, Jean-François. *Of the Sublime: Presence in Question.* Ed. and trans. J. Librett. Albany: State University of New York Press, 1993.

Dahlhaus, Carl. *The Idea of Absolute Music.* Trans. R. Lustig. Chicago: University of Chicago Press, 1989.

Danto, Arthur. *The Transfiguration of the Commonplace: A Philosophy of Art.* Cambridge, Mass.: Harvard University Press, 1983.

Derrida, Jacques. "Differance." In *Margins of Philosophy,* trans. A. Bass. Chicago: University of Chicago Press, 1982.

———. *On Spirit.* Trans. G. Bennington and R. Bowlby. Chicago: University of Chicago Press, 1989.

———. *The Truth in Painting.* Trans. G. Bennington and I. McLeod. Chicago: University of Chicago Press, 1987.

Descartes, René. *Discourse on the Method of Rightly Conducting One's Reason and of Seeking Truth in the Sciences.* Trans. D. Cress. Indianapolis: Hackett, 1980.

———. *Meditations on First Philosophy.* Trans. D. Cress. Indianapolis: Hackett, 1979.

Dewey, John. *Art as Experience.* New York: Capricorn, c.1934.

———. *The Child and the Curriculum* and *The School and Society.* Chicago: University of Chicago Press, 1971.

———. *A Common Faith.* New Haven: Yale University Press, 1934.

———. *Experience and Nature.* New York: Dover, 1958.

———. "From Absolutism to Experimentalism." In *On Experience, Nature, and Freedom: Representative Selections,* ed. R. Bernstein. Indianapolis: Bobbs-Merrill, 1960.

———. *Reconstruction in Philosophy.* Boston: Beacon Press, 1957.

Dickie, George. "All Aesthetic Attitude Theories Fail: The Myth of the Aesthetic Attitude." In *Aesthetics: A Critical Anthology,* ed. G. Dickie and R. Sclafani, 800–815. New York: St. Martin's Press, 1977.

Dickie, George, and Richard Sclafani, eds. *Aesthetics: A Critical Anthology.* New York: St. Martin's Press, 1977.

Dufrenne, Mikel. *The Phenomenology of Aesthetic Experience.* Trans. E. Casey with A. Anderson, W. Domingo, L. Jacobson. Evanston, Ill.: Northwestern University Press, 1973.

Eco, Umberto. *The Aesthetics of Thomas Aquinas.* Trans. H. Bredin. Cambridge, Mass.: Harvard University Press, 1988.

———. *Art and Beauty in the Middle Ages.* Trans. H. Bredin. New Haven: Yale University Press, 1986.

Feuerbach, Ludwig. *The Essence of Christianity.* Trans. G. Eliot. New York: Harper, 1957.

Fink, Eugen. *Nietzsches Philosophie.* Stuttgart: Kohlhammer, c.1960.

Flower, Elizabeth, and Murray Murphey. *A History of Philosophy in America.* 2 vols. New York: Capricorn, 1977.

Gadamer, Hans Georg. *Heidegger's Ways.* Trans. J. Stanley. Albany: State University of New York Press, 1994.

———. *Truth and Method.* Trans. G. Barden and J. Comming. New York: Crossroad, 1982.

Galilei, Galileo. "Excerpts from *The Assayer.*" In *Discoveries and Opinions of Galileo,* trans. S. Drake. New York: Doubleday, 1957.

Giedion, Sigfried. *Space, Time, and Architecture: The Growth of a New Tradition.* 5th ed. Cambridge, Mass.: Harvard University Press, 1980.

Gilbert, Katharine, and Helmut Kuhn. *A History of Aesthetics.* Rev. ed. New York: Dover, 1972.

Gilson, Etienne. *History of Christian Philosophy in the Middle Ages.* New York: Random House, 1955.

———. *Index scolastico-cartésien.* Paris: Alcan, 1912–3.

Gueroult, Martial. *The Soul and the Body.* Vol. 2 of *Descartes' Philosophy Interpreted According to the Order of Reasons.* Trans. R. Ariew. 2 vols. Minneapolis: University of Minnesota Press, 1985.

Gutiérrez, Gustavo. *A Theology of Liberation: History, Politics, and Salvation.* Trans. and ed. C. Inda and J. Eagleson. Maryknoll, N.Y.: Orbis, 1973.

Harries, Karsten. *The Ethical Function of Architecture.* Cambridge, Mass.: MIT Press, 1997.

Harris, Errol. *The Foundation of Metaphysics in Science.* Lanham, Md.: University Press of America, 1983.

———. *Hypothesis and Perception: The Roots of Scientific Method.* London: George Allen and Unwin, 1970.

———. *Nature, Mind, and Modern Science.* London: Allen and Unwin, 1968.

Hegel, Georg Wilhelm Friedrich. *Aesthetics: Lectures on Fine Art.* Trans. T. Knox. Oxford: Clarendon Press, 1975.

———. *The Encyclopaedia of Logic.* Trans. T. Geraets, W. Suchting, and H. Harris. Indianapolis: Hackett, 1991.

————. *Hegel's Philosophy of Mind.* Trans. W. Wallace. Oxford: Clarendon Press, 1971.

————. *Hegel's Philosophy of Nature.* 3 vols. Ed. and trans. M. Petry. London: George Allen and Unwin, 1970.

————. *Hegel's Philosophy of Right.* Trans. T. Knox. London: Oxford University Press, 1952.

————. *Hegel's Science of Logic.* Trans. A. V. Miller. London: George Allen and Unwin, 1969.

————. *Lectures on the History of Philosophy.* Trans. E. Haldane. Lincoln: University of Nebraska Press, 1995.

————. *Lectures on the Philosophy of Religion.* Trans. E. Speirs and J. B. Sanderson. London: Kegan Paul, Trench, Trübner, 1895.

————. *Lectures on the Philosophy of Religion.* Ed. P. Hodgson. Trans. R. Brown, P. Hodgson, and J. Stewart. Berkeley: University of California Press, 1988.

————. *Phenomenology of Spirit.* Trans. A. Miller. Oxford: Clarendon Press, 1977.

————. *Philosophy of Fine Art.* 4 vols. Trans. F. Osmaston. London: G. Bell, 1920.

————. *The Philosophy of History.* Trans. J. Sibree. New York: Dover, 1956.

Heidegger, Martin. *The Basic Problems of Phenomenology.* Trans. A. Hofstadter. Bloomington: Indiana University Press, 1988.

————. *Being and Time.* Trans. J. Macquarrie and E. Robinson. New York: Harper, 1962.

————. *The End of Philosophy.* Trans. J. Stambaugh. New York: Harper and Row, 1973.

————. *Existence and Being.* Ed. and trans. W. Brock. South Bend, Ind.: Regnery, 1949.

————. "Hebel—Friend of the House." Trans. B. Foltz and M. Heim. *Contemporary German Philosophy* 3 (1983).

————. *History of the Concept of Time: Prolegomena.* Trans. T. Kisiel. Bloomington: Indiana University Press, 1985.

————. *An Introduction to Metaphysics.* Trans. R. Manheim. New Haven: Yale University Press, 1959.

————. *Kant and the Problem of Metaphysics.* Trans. J. Churchill. Bloomington: Indiana University Press, 1965.

————. "Memorial Address." In *Discourse on Thinking.* Trans. J. Anderson and E. Freund. New York: Harper and Row, 1966.

————. *Nietzsche.* Trans. D. Krell. 4 vols. San Francisco: Harper and Row, 1979–87.

————. "On the Essence of Truth." In *Basic Writings from* Being and Time *(1927) to*

The Task of Thinking *(1964)*. Ed. and trans. D. Krell. New York: Harper and Row, 1977.

———. *On the Way to Language*. Trans. P. Hertz. San Francisco: Harper and Row, 1971.

———. *On Time and Being*. Trans. J. Stambaugh. New York: Harper and Row, 1972.

———. "The Origin of the Work of Art." In *Poetry, Language, Thought*, trans. A. Hofstadter. New York: Harper and Row, 1971.

———. *Phenomenological Interpretation of Kant's Critique of Pure Reason*. Trans. P. Emad and K. Maly. Bloomington: Indiana University Press, 1997.

———. *Plato's Sophist*. Trans. R. Rojcewicz and André Schuwer. Bloomington: Indiana University Press, 1997.

———. *Poetry, Language, Thought*. Trans. A Hofstadter. New York: Harper and Row, 1971.

———. *The Principle of Reason*. Trans. R. Lilly. Bloomington: Indiana University Press, 1991.

———. *The Question Concerning Technology, and Other Essays*. Trans. W. Lovitt. New York: Harper and Row, 1977.

———. *The Question of Being*. Trans. W. Kluback and J. Wilde. New Haven: College and University Press, 1958.

———. "The Way Back into the Ground of Metaphysics." Trans. W. Kaufmann. In *Existentialism from Dostoevsky to Sartre*, ed. W. Kaufmann. Cleveland: World Publishing, 1956.

———. *What Is a Thing?* Trans. W. Barton and V. Deutsch. Chicago: Regnery, 1967.

———. *What Is Called Thinking?* Trans. J. Glenn Gray. New York: Harper and Row, 1968.

———. *What Is Philosophy?* Trans. W. Kluback and J. Wilde. New York: Twayne, 1958.

———. "Why Do I Stay in the Provinces?" Trans. T. Sheehan. *Listening* 12 (1977).

Hertzmann, Erich. "Mozart's Creative Process." In *The Creative World of Mozart*, ed. Paul Henry Lang, 17–30. New York: Norton, 1963.

Hobbes, Thomas. *Leviathan*. Ed. M. Oakschott. New York: Collier, 1973.

Hull, David. *Philosophy of Biological Science*. Englewood Cliffs, N.J.: Prentice-Hall, 1974.

Hume, David. *Dialogues Concerning Natural Religion*. Ed. N. K. Smith. Indianapolis: Bobbs-Merrill, 1947.

———. "Of the Standard of Taste." In *Aesthetics: A Critical Anthology*, ed. G. Dickie and R. Sclafani, 592–606. New York: St. Martin's Press, 1977.

Hunter, Sam, and John Jacobus, eds. *Modern Art: Painting, Sculpture, Architecture*. Englewood Cliffs, N.J.: Prentice-Hall, 1985.

Husserl, Edmund. *Cartesian Meditations: An Introduction to Phenomenology*. Trans. D. Cairns. The Hague: Martinus Nijhoff, 1960.

———. *The Crisis of European Sciences and Transcendental Phenomenology: An Introduction to Phenomenological Philosophy*. Trans. D. Carr. Evanston, Ill.: Northwestern University Press, 1970.

———. *General Introduction to a Pure Phenomenology*. Trans. F. Kersten. *Ideas Pertaining to a Pure Phenomenology and to a Phenomenological Philosophy*, book 1. The Hague: Nijhoff, 1982.

———. *Logical Investigations*, 2 vols. Trans. J. Findlay. New York: Humanities Press, 1970.

———. *The Phenomenology of Internal Time-Consciousness*. Trans. J. Churchill. Bloomington: Indiana University Press, 1964.

———. *Studies in the Phenomenology of Constitution*. Trans. R. Rojcewicz and A. Schuwer. *Ideas Pertaining to a Pure Phenomenology and to a Phenomenological Philosophy*, book 2. Dordrecht: Kluwer, 1989.

Ingarden, Roman. *The Cognition of the Literary Work of Art*. Trans. R. Crowley and K. Olson. Evanston, Ill.: Northwestern University Press, 1973.

Janicaud, Dominique, and Jean-François Mattéi. *Heidegger: From Metaphysics to Thought*. Trans. M. Gendre. Albany: State University of New York Press, 1995.

Kandinsky, Wassily. *Concerning the Spiritual in Art*. Trans. M. Sadler. New York: Dover, 1977.

Kant, Immanuel. *Critique of Judgment*. Trans. W. Pluhar. Indianapolis: Hackett, 1987.

———. *Critique of Practical Reason*. Trans. L. W. Beck. Indianapolis: Bobbs-Merrill, 1956.

———. *Critique of Pure Reason*. Trans. N. K. Smith. New York: St. Martin's Press, 1929.

———. *Foundations of the Metaphysics of Morals* and *What Is Enlightenment?* Trans. L. W. Beck. Indianapolis: Bobbs-Merrill, 1959.

———. *Kants Werke*, photocopied from the Preußishen Academie der Wissenschaften edition of *Kants Gesammelten Werken* of 1902. Berlin: Walter de Gruyter, 1968.

———. *The Metaphysical Principles of Virtue*. Trans. J. Ellington. Indianapolis: Bobbs-Merrill, 1964.

———. *Observations on the Feeling of the Beautiful and Sublime*. Trans. J. Goldthwait. Berkeley: University of California Press, 1960.

———. *Prolegomena to Any Future Metaphysics That Will Be Able to Come Forward as Science*. Trans. P. Carus; rev. J. Ellington. Indianapolis: Hackett, 1977.

Kaufmann, Walter. *From Shakespeare to Existentialism*. Garden City, N.Y.: Doubleday, 1960.

———. *Religions in Four Dimensions: Existential and Aesthetic, Historical and Comparative.* New York: Reader's Digest Press, 1976.

Kierkegaard, Søren. *Either/Or.* 2 vols. Vol. 1 trans. D. Swenson and L. M. Swenson; vol. 2 trans. W. Lowrie. Garden City, N.Y.: Anchor Books, 1959.

———. *Kierkegaard's Concluding Unscientific Postscript.* Trans. D. Swenson; completed by W. Lowrie. Princeton, N.J.: Princeton University Press, 1941.

Kivy, Peter. "Recent Scholarship and the British Tradition: A Logic of Taste—The First Fifty Years." In *Aesthetics: A Critical Anthology,* ed. G. Dickie and R. Sclafani, 626–42. New York: St. Martin's Press, 1977.

Kristeller, Paul. "The Modern System of Fine Arts." In *Renaissance Thought and the Arts: Collected Essays.* Princeton, N.J.: Princeton University Press, 1990.

Kuhn, Thomas. *The Structure of Scientific Revolutions.* Chicago: University of Chicago Press, 1962.

Lawrence, Joseph. *Die ewige Anfang: Zum Verhältnis von Natur und Geschichte bei Schelling.* Tübingen: Köhler, 1984.

Le Bruyne, Edgar. *The Aesthetics of the Middle Ages.* Trans. E. Hennessey. New York: Ungar, 1969.

Leonardo da Vinci. *Leonardo on Painting: An Anthology of Writings.* Ed. Martin Kemp. New Haven: Yale University Press, 1989.

Lessing, Gotthold Ephraim. *Die Erziehung des Menschengeschlechts und andere Schriften.* Stuttgart: Reclam, 1965.

Levinas, Emmanuel. *Totality and Infinity: An Essay on Exteriority.* Trans. A. Lingis. Pittsburgh: Duquesne University Press, 1969.

Locke, John. *An Essay Concerning Human Understanding.* Ed. P. Nidditch. Oxford: Clarendon Press, 1975.

———. *The Second Treatise of Government.* Indianapolis: Bobbs-Merrill, 1952.

Lonergan, Bernard. *Insight: A Study of Human Understanding.* London: Longmans, Green, 1958.

Longinus. *On the Sublime.* Trans. W. Hamilton Fyfe. In *Aristotle:* The Poetics, *"Longinus":* On the Sublime, and *Demetrius:* On Style. Cambridge, Mass.: Harvard University Press, 1973.

Lyotard, Jean-François. *The Differend: Phrases in Dispute.* Minneapolis: University of Minnesota Press, 1983.

———. *The Inhuman: Reflections on Time.* Stanford: Stanford University Press, 1988.

———. *Lessons on the Analytic of the Sublime: Kant's Critique of Judgment.* Trans. E. Rottenberg. Stanford: Stanford University Press, 1994.

MacIntyre, Alasdair. *Whose Justice? Which Rationality?* Notre Dame, Ind.: University of Notre Dame Press, 1988.

Malraux, André. *Voices of Silence.* Trans. S. Gilbert. Princeton, N.J.: Princeton University Press, 1978.

Maritain, Jacques. *Art and Scholasticism* and *The Frontiers of Poetry.* New York: Scribners, 1962.

———. *The Degrees of Knowledge.* Trans. G. Phelan. New York: Scribners, 1959.

Marx, Karl. *Writings of the Young Marx on Philosophy and Society.* Ed. and trans. L. Easton and K. Guddat. Garden City, N.Y.: Doubleday, 1967.

Matisse, Henri. *Henri Matisse.* Ed. J. Flam. Berkeley: University of California Press, 1994.

Merleau-Ponty, Maurice. *The Structure of Behavior.* Trans. A. Fisher. Boston: Beacon Press, 1963.

Moore, Henry. "A View of Sculpture." In *Henry Moore.* Vol. 1. New York: George Wittenborn, 1968.

Mumford, Lewis. *The Myth of the Machine: Technics and Human Development.* New York: Harcourt Brace Jovanovich, 1966.

Newman, John Henry. *An Essay in Aid of a Grammar of Assent.* Garden City, N.Y.: Doubleday, 1955.

Nietzsche, Friedrich. *The Anti-Christ.* Trans. R. Hollingdale. Baltimore: Penguin, 1968.

———. "Aus dem Gedankenkreis der Geburt der Tragödie." In *Der griechische Staat.* Stuttgart: Alfred Kröner, 1955.

———. *Beyond Good and Evil: Prelude to a Philosophy of the Future.* Trans. W. Kaufmann. New York: Vintage, 1966.

———. *The Birth of Tragedy.* Trans. and ed. W. Kaufmann. New York: Vintage, 1967.

———. *Daybreak: Thoughts on the Prejudices of Morality.* Trans. R. Hollingdale. Cambridge: Cambridge University Press, 1982.

———. *Ecce Homo.* Trans. W. Kaufmann. New York: Vintage, c. 1967.

———. *The Gay Science.* Trans. W. Kaufmann. New York: Vintage, 1974.

———. *Human, All Too Human: A Book for Free Spirits.* Trans. M. Faber and S. Lehmann. Lincoln: University of Nebraska Press, 1984.

———. *On the Genealogy of Morals.* Trans. W. Kaufmann. New York: Vintage, c. 1969.

———. *On the Uses and Disadvantages of History for Life.* In *Untimely Meditations.* Trans. R. Hollingdale. London: Cambridge University Press, 1983.

———. "On Truth and Lie in an Extra-Moral Sense." In *The Portable Nietzsche,* ed. and trans. W. Kaufmann. New York: Viking, 1954.

———. *Schopenhauer as Educator.* In *Untimely Meditations.* Trans. R. Hollingdale. London: Cambridge University Press, 1983.

———. *Thus Spake Zarathustra.* In *The Portable Nietzsche,* ed. and trans. W. Kaufmann. New York: Viking, 1954.

———. *Twilight of the Idols.* Trans. R. Hollingdale. Baltimore: Penguin, 1968.

———. *The Will to Power.* Trans. W. Kaufmann and R. Hollingdale. New York: Vintage, 1967.

O'Connell, Robert. *Art and the Christian Intelligence in St. Augustine.* New York: Fordham University Press, 1978.

Olson, Elder. "The Poetic Method in Aristotle," In *Aristotle's Poetics and English Literature: A Collection of Critical Essays,* ed. E. Olson. Toronto: University of Toronto Press, 1965.

Otto, Rudoph. *The Idea of the Holy.* Trans. J. Harvey. New York: Oxford University Press, 1964.

Pascal, Blaise. *Pensées.* New York: Modern Library, 1941.

Pater, Walter. *The Renaissance.* In *Selected Writings of Walter Pater,* ed. Harold Bloom. New York: Columbia University Press, 1974.

Paulsen, Friedrich. *Immanuel Kant: His Life and Doctrine.* Trans. J. Creighton and A. Lefevre. New York: Ungar, 1972.

Petrarca, Francesco [Petrarch]. "The Ascent of Mont Ventoux." In *The Renaissance Philosophy of Man,* ed. E. Cassirer, P. Kristeller, and J. Randall. Chicago: University of Chicago Press, 1971.

Picard, Max. *The World of Silence.* Chicago: Regnery, 1952.

Pius XII. *The Mystical Body of Christ.* Trans. J. Bluett. New York: The America Press, 1943.

Plato. *Cratylus; Parmenides; Greater Hippias; Lesser Hippias.* Trans. H. Fowler. Cambridge, Mass.: Harvard University Press, 1963.

———. *Euthyphro; Apology; Crito; Phaedo; Phaedrus.* Trans. H. Fowler. Cambridge, Mass.: Harvard University Press, 1957.

———. *The Laws of Plato.* Trans. T. Pangle. New York: Basic Books, 1980.

———. *Lysis, Symposium, Gorgias.* Trans. W. Lamb. Cambridge, Mass.: Harvard University Press, 1975.

———. *Politicus, Philebus, Ion.* Trans. H. Fowler and W. Lamb. Cambridge, Mass.: Harvard University Press, 1975.

———. *The Republic.* 2 vols. Trans. P. Shorey. Cambridge, Mass.: Harvard University Press, 1969.

————. *Theaetetus; Sophist.* Trans. H. Fowler. Cambridge, Mass.: Harvard University Press, 1977.

————. *Timaeus; Critias; Cleitophon; Menexenus; Epistles.* Trans. R. Bury. Cambridge, Mass.: Harvard University Press, 1977.

Plotinus. *The Enneads.* Trans. A. H. Armstrong. Loeb Classical bilingual edition. Cambridge, Mass.: Harvard University Press, 1989.

Poe, Edgar Allan. "The Philosophy of Composition." In *Selected Poetry and Prose of Edgar Allan Poe,* ed. T. Mabbott. New York: Modern Library, 1951.

Polanyi, Michael. *Personal Knowledge: Towards a Post-Critical Philosophy.* New York: Harper and Row, 1964.

Pollitt, J. J. *The Art of Ancient Greece: Sources and Documents.* Cambridge: Cambridge University Press, 1990.

Pope, Alexander. *An Essay on Man.* Ed. F. Brady. Indianapolis: Bobbs-Merrill, 1965.

Popper, Karl. *The Open Society and Its Enemies.* Princeton, N.J.: Princeton University Press, 1950.

Potts, Alex. *Flesh and the Ideal: Winckelmann and the Origins of Art History.* New Haven: Yale University Press, 1994.

Pseudo-Dionysius. *The Complete Works.* Trans. C. Luibhead. New York: Paulist Press, 1987.

Radhakrishnan, Sarvepalli, and Charles Moore, eds. *A Sourcebook in Indian Philosophy.* Princeton, N.J.: Princeton University Press, 1957.

Rahner, Karl. *The Foundations of Christian Faith: An Introduction to the Idea of Christianity.* Trans. W. Dych. New York: Seabury, 1978.

————, ed. *Encyclopedia of Theology: The Concise* Sacramentum mundi. New York: Seabury, 1975.

Ricoeur, Paul. *Fallible Man.* Trans. C. Kelbley. Chicago: Regnery, 1965.

————. *Husserl: An Analysis of His Phenomenology.* Trans. E. Ballard and L. Embree. Evanston, Ill.: Northwestern University Press, 1967.

————. *The Rule of Metaphor.* Trans. R. Czerny, K. McLaughlin, and J. Costello. Toronto: University of Toronto Press, 1977.

Rosen, Stanley. *The Question of Being: A Reversal of Heidegger.* New Haven: Yale University Press, 1993.

Rousseau, Jean-Jacques. *The Reveries of the Solitary Walker.* Trans. C. Butterworth. New York: Harper and Row, 1979.

Ryle, Gilbert. *The Concept of Mind.* New York: Barnes and Noble, 1949.

Schacht, Richard. "Nietzsche on Art in *The Birth of Tragedy.*" In *Aesthetics: A Critical An-*

*thology*, ed. G. Dickie and R. Sclafani, 269–312. New York: St. Martin's Press, 1977.

Schaefer, Jerome. *The Philosophy of Mind*. Englewood Cliffs, N.J.: Prentice-Hall, 1968.

Schelling, Friedrich. "A System of Transcendental Idealism." In *Philosophies of Art and Beauty*, ed. A. Hofstadter and R. Kuhns. Chicago: University of Chicago Press, 1964.

Schiller, Friedrich. *On the Aesthetic Education of Man in a Series of Letters*. Trans. R. Snell. New York: Ungar, 1965.

Schopenhauer, Arthur. *Essays and Aphorisms*. Trans. R. Hollingdale. Harmondsworth: Penguin, 1986.

———. *On the Fourfold Root of the Principle of Sufficient Reason*. Trans. E. Payne. LaSalle, Ill.: Open Court, 1974.

———. *The World as Will and Representation*. 2 vols. Trans. E. Payne. New York: Dover, 1966.

Schürrmann, Reiner. *Heidegger on Being and Acting: From Principles to Anarchy*. Bloomington: Indian University Press, 1990.

Shapiro, Meyer. *Modern Art: Nineteenth and Twentieth Centuries*. New York: George Braziller, 1982.

Shelley, Percy Bysshe. *A Defence of Poetry*. In *The Complete Works of Percy Bysshe Shelley*, ed. R. Ingpen and W. Peck, vol. 7. New York: Gordian Press, 1965.

Silk, M. S., and J. P. Stern. *Nietzsche on Tragedy*. Cambridge: Cambridge University Press, 1981.

Singer, Irving. Introduction to *The Last Puritan* by George Santayana. Cambridge, Mass.: MIT Press, 1994.

Smith, Huston. *Forgotten Truth: The Primordial Tradition*. New York: Harper and Row, 1976.

Smith, Preserved. *A History of Modern Culture*. Vol. 2, *The Enlightenment, 1687–1776*. New York: Collier, 1962.

Spinoza, Baruch. *Correspondence on the Improvement of the Understanding, The Ethics*. Trans. R. Elwes. New York: Dover, 1955.

Stalin, Joseph. *Dialectical and Historical Materialism*. New York: International Publishers, 1940.

Strasser, Stephen. *Phenomenology of Feeling: An Essay on the Phenomena of the Heart*. Trans. and intro. R. Wood. Pittsburgh: Duquesne University Press, 1977.

Taminiaux, Jacques. "The Origin of 'The Origin of the Work of Art.'" In *Reading Heidegger: Commemorations*, ed. J. Sallis. Bloomington: Indiana University Press, 1993.

Tanquerey, Adolphe. *The Spiritual Life: A Treatise on Ascetical and Mystical Theology.* Belgium: Desclée, 1930.

Tatarkiewicz, Wladyslaw. *History of Aesthetics.* Vol. 2, *Medieval Aesthetics.* The Hague: Mouton, 1972.

Taylor, Mark. *Disfiguring: Art, Architecture, Religion.* Chicago: University of Chicago Press, 1992.

Thorson, Thomas, ed. *Plato: Totalitarian or Democrat?* Englewood Cliffs, N.J.: Prentice-Hall, 1963.

Vico, Giambattista. *The New Science of Giambattista Vico.* Trans. T. Bergin and M. Fisch. Rev. ed. Ithaca, N.Y. : Cornell University Press, 1991.

Viollet-le-Duc, Eugène-Emmanuel. *The Foundations of Architecture: Selections from the* Dictionnaire raisonné. Trans. K. Whitehead. New York: George Braziller, 1990.

Wagner, Richard. *The Art-work of the Future.* Trans. W. Ellis. London, 1892.

Weiss, Paul. *Cinematics.* Carbondale: Southern Illinois University Press, 1975.

———. *Nine Basic Arts.* Carbondale: Southern Illinois University Press, 1961.

———. *The World of Art.* Carbondale: Southern Illinois University Press, 1961.

Weiss, Peter. *Marat/Sade.* Trans. G. Skelton. New York: Simon and Schuster, 1965.

Whitehead, Alfred North. *Adventures of Ideas.* New York: Free Press, 1967.

———. *Process and Reality: An Essay in Cosmology.* New York: Harper, 1960.

Wiedmann, Franz. *Hegel: An Illustrated Biography.* Trans. J. Neugroschel. New York: Pegasus, 1968.

Wilenski, R. H. *The Meaning of Modern Sculpture.* Boston: Beacon Press, 1961.

Williams, Tennessee. *Suddenly Last Summer.* In *The Theatre of Tennessee Williams,* vol. 3. New York: New Directions, 1971.

Wilson, Nancy Ross. *Three Ways of Asian Wisdom: Hinduism, Buddhism, Zen, and Their Significance for the West.* New York: Simon and Schuster, 1966.

Winckelmann, Johann Joachim. *The History of Ancient Art.* 4 vols. Trans. G. Lodge. Boston: Little, Brown, 1856–73.

———. *Reflections on the Imitation of Greek Works in Painting and Sculpture / Gedanken über die Nachahmung der griechischen Werke in der Malerei und Bildhauerkunst.* English and German texts. Trans. from the German by E. Heyer and R. Norton. LaSalle, Ill.: Open Court, 1987.

Wood, Robert E. "Aesthetics within the Kantian Project." In *Philosophy and Art,* ed. D. Dahlstrom. Washington, D.C.: Catholic University of America Press, 1991.

———. "Aquinas and Heidegger: Personal *Esse,* Truth, and Imagination." In *Postmod-*

*ernism and Christian Philosophy*, ed. R. Ciapalo, 268–80. Washington, D.C.: Catholic University of America Press, 1997.

———. "Architecture: The Confluence of Art, Technology, Politics, and Nature." In *The Nature of Technology*, Proceedings of the American Catholic Philosophical Association, 79–93. Washington, D.C.: Catholic University of America, 1996.

———. "Art and the Sacred." *Listening* 18.1 (Winter 1983): 30–40.

———. "Aspects of Freedom." *Philosophy Today* 15.1 (Spring 1991): 106–15.

———. "Being and Manifestness: Philosophy, Science, and Poetry in an Evolutionary Worldview." *International Philosophical Quarterly* 35.4 (December 1995): 437–47.

———. "Heidegger on the Way to Language." In *Semiotics 1984*, ed. J. Deely. Proceedings of the Ninth Annual Semiotic Society of America, 11–14 October, Bloomington, Ind. Lanham, Md.: University Press of America, 1985.

———. "Image, Structure and Content: On a Passage in Plato's *Republic*." *Review of Metaphysics* 40 (March 1987): 495–514.

———. Introduction to *Phenomenology of Feeling: An Essay on the Phenomena of the Heart* by Stephen Strasser, 3–39. Pittsburgh: Duquesne University Press, 1977.

———. *Martin Buber's Ontology: An Analysis of* I and Thou. Evanston, Ill.: Northwestern University Press, 1969.

———. "Martin Buber's Philosophy of the Word." *Philosophy Today* 30 (Winter 1986).

———. "Metaphysics and Aesthetics." In *The Philosophy of Paul Weiss*, ed. L. Hahn. Library of Living Philosophers. Carbondale: Southern Illinois University Press, 1995.

———. *A Path into Metaphysics: Phenomenological, Hermeneutical and Dialogical Studies*. Albany, N.Y.: State University of New York Press, 1990.

———. "The Phenomenologists." *Reading Philosophy for the Twenty-First Century*, ed. G. McLean, 131–60. Lanham, Md.: University Press of America, 1989.

———. "Philosophy, Aesthetics, and Theology: A Review of Hans Urs von Balthasar's *The Glory of the Lord*." *American Catholic Philosophical Quarterly* 67.3 (Summer 1993): 355–82.

———. "Plato's Line Revisited: The Pedagogy of Complete Reflection," *Review of Metaphysics* 44 (March 1991): 525–47.

———. "Recovery of the Aesthetic Center." *The Recovery of Form*, 1–25. Proceedings of the American Catholic Philosophical Association. Washington, D.C.: Catholic University of America, 1995.

———. "Silence, Being, and the Between: Picard, Heidegger and Buber." *Man and World* 27 (1994).

———. "Six Heideggerian Figures." *Martin Heidegger,* ed. John D. Caputo. Special issue of the *American Catholic Philosophical Quarterly,* Spring 1995.

———. "Taking the Universal Viewpoint: A Descriptive Approach." *Review of Metaphysics* 50 (June 1997): 69–78.

———. "Weiss on Adumbration." *Philosophy Today* 22 (Winter 1985): 339–48.

Wooldridge, Dean. *Mechanical Man: The Physical Basis of Intelligent Life.* New York: McGraw-Hill, 1968.

Wright, Frank Lloyd. *The Future of Architecture.* New York: Mentor, 1953.

Zammito, John. *The Genesis of Kant's* Critique of Judgment. Chicago: University of Chicago Press, 1992.

Zimmerman, Michael. *Heidegger's Confrontation with Modernity: Technology, Politics, and Art.* Bloomington: Indiana University Press, 1990.

# Index of Names

*Numbers in bold indicate places where an extended treatment of the thinker in question is found.*

Addison, Joseph, 157
Aeschylus, 87, 220
Alberti, Leon Battista, 81
Albertus Magnus, 33, 95, **105**, 108–9, 305, 326–27
Anaximander, 288
Angelus Silesius, 192, 277
Anselm of Canterbury, 123
Aquinas, Thomas, 19, 33, 95–96, 103, 104, **105–10**, 112, 113, 123, 160–61, 167, 233, 265, 282, 308, 320
Archimedes, 235–36
Ariosto, 154
Aristotle, 16, 29, 32–33, 40, 59, **71–94**, 103, 105–6, 107–8, 110, 112–14, 122, 127, 129, 135, 140–41, 146, 154, 161, 163–64, 167–68, 175, 177, 181, 201, 215, 218, 222, 231, 237–40, 243, 249–50, 256–58, 262, 266, 268, 275, 283, 285, 288–90, 292, 301, 305, 307–8, 318, 323, 325
Augustine, Aurelius, 6, 32–33, 63, 96, **102–4**, 106, 108, 110, 112, 149, 161–62, 167, 206, 278, 321, 325
Averroes, 96
Avicenna, 96, 106

Bach, Johann Sebastian, xiv, 40, 221, 301
Balthasar, Hans Urs von, 102, 104, 110, 113, 304
Barfield, Owen, 277
Baumgarten, Alexander, 33
Beethoven, Ludwig van, xiv, 221, 301
Bergman, Ingmar, 24
Bergson, Henri, xiv
Berkeley, George, 119, 239, 275
Bernard of Clairvaux, 114
Bernini, Gianlorenzo, 147
Blake, William, xiv, 22
Boccione, Umberto, 156, 341, 344

Böcklin, Arnold, xiii
Boethius, 101
Bonaventure, 33, 109, **110–11**, 113, 122, 192, 325
Brancusi, Constantin, 341–42
Brueghel, Peter, xiv, 29, 259
Bruno, Giordano, 140
Buber, Martin, xiv, 55, 114, 183, 261, 305, 312–13, 317, 319, 321

Carra, Carlo, 157
Cassiodorus, 108
Cervantes, 152
Cezanne, Paul, 147–48
Chuang Tzu, 235
Cicero, Marcus Tullius, 283
Comte, Auguste, 189
Confucius, 210
Copernicus, 118
Cummings, E. E., 22

Dante Alighieri, 54, 142, 151, 322
Danto, Arthur, 28, 259
Darwin, Charles, 238
Debussy, Claude, 29
Derrida, Jacques, 137
Descartes, 154, 163, 232, **234–40**, 257, 264–65, 271
Dewey, John, 33, 195, 227, **231–62**, 267, 272, 298–300, 304, 309, 317–19, 326
Diogenes, 203
Dionysius, 32–33, 95–96, 102, **104–5**, 106, 113
Dostoievski, Fyodor, 225
Dufrenne, Mikel, 11, 14, 66, 148, 151, 199, 298

Eckart, 192
Eco, Umberto, 109–10, 325
Endell, August, 93
Epicurus, 154
Euripides, 220, 323

Feininger, Lyonel, 93
Feuerbach, Ludwig, 204–5, 245, 310
Fichte, Johann Gottlieb, 165, 189
Ficino, Marsilio, 33
Fink, Eugen, 209
Flower, Elizabeth, 231
Francis of Assisi, 112, 183, 339
Franklin, Benjamin, 125

Gadamer, Hans-Georg, 157, 269, 283, 314
Galileo Galilei, 111, 235, 239, 289
Gallus, Thomas, 108
Gauguin, Paul, 93, 156
Gautier, Thèophile, 316
George, Stefan, 285–86
Gilson, Etienne, 105
Goethe, 156, 209–10
Gracian, Balthasar, 154
Gregory of Nyssa, 206
Gropius, Walter, 14
Guyon, Madame, 192

Hegel, Georg Wilhelm Friedrich, xiv, 5, 33, 36,
    55, 96, 114, 138, **159–86**, 197, 200, 202,
    204, 210, 222, 231, 240, 243, 245, 251,
    256–58, 284, 288, 299, 303, 305, 311, 314,
    316–17, 325, 345–46
Heidegger, Martin, xiv, 13, 29, 33, 55, 63, 78, 104,
    113, 151, 195, 209, 221, 227, 239, 241, 253,
    260. **263–301**, 304–5, 310–12, 316–17,
    319, 323, 335
Hepworth, Barbara, 344
Heraclitus, 209, 280, 284–85, 288, 292
Hobbes, Thomas, 160
Hölderlin, Friedrich, 285, 287
Homer, 214, 217–18
Hopkins, Gerard Manley, xiv
Hume, David, 33, 140, 151, **152–57**, 160, 189,
    239, 317
Husserl, Edmund, 3, 263–65, 268
Huxley, Aldous, 12

Innocent III, Pope, 206

James, William, 231, 238
Janicaud, Dominique, 288, 292, 296
John of the Cross, xiv
Johnson, Samuel, 157

Kandinsky, Wassily, 93, 114
Kant, Immanuel, 33, 63, 75, 80, 85, 93, 103, 108,
    **117–51**, 152, 173, 175–76, 182, 186–90,
    194–96, 198, 201–2, 204, 221–23, 236,
    239, 250, 257–60, 264, 279, 292, 305–9,
    314–18, 322–25, 337, 346
Kaufmann, Walter, 299
Keats, John, xiv

Kierkegaard, Søren, 13, 170, 184, 265, 270, 289,
    316
Kivy, Peter, 152

La Mettrie, 160
Lao-tzu, 210
Laplace, Pierre Simon, 168
Le Corbusier, 14
Leonardo, 185
Lessing, Gotthold Ephraim, 160
Levinas, Emmanuel, 96, 261
Locke, John, 160, 231, 239
Lonergan, Bernard, 4, 262
Longinus, 196
Luther, Martin, 221
Lyotard, Jean-François, 129, 136–37

MacIntyre, Alasdair, 152
Malraux, André, 157
Maritain, Jacques, 109
Marx, Karl, 16, 228, 241, 247
Mattéi, Jean-François, 293
Matisse, Henri, 93, 148, 308
Michelangelo Buonarroti, xiv, 14, 114, 147, 156,
    341–42
Milton, John, 54, 142, 151, 322
Moore, Henry, xiii, 29, 93, 156, 184, 340–44
Mozart, Wolfgang Amadeus, xiv, 90, 301
Muhammed, 210
Murphey, Murray, 231

Newman, John Henry, 316
Newton, Isaac, 117, 122, 186, 264, 289
Nicholson, Ben, 344
Nietzsche, Friedrich, 4, 16, 33, 63, 75, 76, 112, 113,
    141, 147, 163, 173, 200, 202, **203–29**,
    239–40, 254, 257–58, 261, 265–66, 286,
    289, 291–92, 299–300, 305–7, 310–11, 323,
    326, 329–30

O'Connell, Robert, 103
O'Keefe, Georgia, xiii, 344
Olson, Elder, 74
Origen, 206
Otto, Rudolf, 137

Parmenides, 63, 163–66, 172, 256, 266, 268, 286,
    288, 292, 294
Parrhasios, 345–46
Pascal, Blaise, 178, 216, 322
Pater, Walter, 30, 79, 93, 224, 254, 308, 316, 319
Peirce, Charles Sanders, 231
Petrarch, Francisco, 151
Phidias, xiv, 14, 156, 176, 330, 341
Picasso, 156
Plato, xiv, 16, 17–18, 29, 30, 32, **35–70**, 74, 75–80,
    83, 85, 88, 89, 91, 92, 94, 96, 97, 99, 100,

103, 106, 108, 111–14, 118, 120, 133,
141–42, 146, 148–51, 163–67, 172–73,
182–83, 187–88, 190, 194–98, 200, 202–4,
206–9, 211–12, 215, 217, 220–26, 228–29,
231–34, 237–38, 241, 243, 247, 251–52,
255–57, 259–61, 268–69, 271, 281,
288–90, 292, 299–301, 305, 307–8, 310,
312, 317–18, 321–26, 342
Plotinus, xiv, 32–33, 55, **95–102**, 110, 112–14, 121,
149, 161, 167, 187–88, 190, 194–95, 198,
200, 223, 225, 308, 322, 326, 342
Plutarch, 115
Poe, Edgar Allan, 199
Polyclitus, 80
Pope, Alexander, 36
Popper, Karl, 43
Porphyry, 97
Pythagoras, 233

Rachmaninoff, Sergei, xiii–xiv
Ravel, Maurice, 309
Read, Herbert, 340–41
Ricoeur, Paul, 92, 264
Rilke, Rainer Maria, 286–88
Rodin, Auguste, 342
Rousseau, Jean-Jacques, 151, 183
Ruskin, John, 345
Ryle, Gilbert, 235

Santayana, George, 299
Schacht, Richard, 219
Schelling, Friedrich, 75, 76, 156, 189, 231, 240
Schiller, Friedrich, 199, 218, 254, 326
Schlegel, Friedrich, 93
Schopenhauer, Arthur, 13, 16, 33, 55, 75, 76, 96,
101, 129, 130, 141, **187–202**, 205–6, 208,
211, 217–18, 221–23, 233, 253, 257–58, 272,
318, 326, 345
Scotus Eriugena, 95
Shakespeare, 157, 181, 210
Shelley, Percy Bysshe, 255

Shostakovich, xiv
Sibelius, Jan, xiv
Socrates, 36–60, 74, 85, 86, 96, 113, 210–11,
213–14, 220, 224, 233, 237, 292, 308,
323–24
Sophocles, 80, 87, 220, 286
Stambaugh, Joan, 293
Stravinsky, Igor, xiv, 156

Tatarkiewicz, Wyladislaw, 95
Tauler, John, 192
Tchaikovsky, Peter, xiv
Tennyson, Alfred Lord, 191
Terence, 154
Therese of Avila, xiv
Tolkien, J. R. R., 79
Trakl, Georg, 286

Ulrich of Strassburg, 95

Van Gogh, Vincent, 112, 276, 300
Vico, Giambattista, 186
Violet-le-Duc, EugÉne-Emmanuel, 156
Virgil, 54, 154
Vivaldi, Antonio, xiv, 301

Wagner, Richard, 23–24, 180, 197, 218, 221
Warton, Joseph, 140
Weiss, Peter, 191
Whitehead, Alfred North, 49, 188
Wilenski, R. H., 344
Williams, John, 24
Williams, Tennessee, 191
Winkelmann, Johann Joachim, 151, 221
Wordsworth, William, xiv, 253
Wright, Frank Lloyd, 14, 69–70, 93, 115, 156, 184,
342

Young, Edward, 140

Zeuxis, 174, 345

# Subject Index

Aesthetics (the Aesthetic), xv, 2, 17, 19, 31–32, 33, 35–36, 50, 61, 81, 91, 93, 94, 95, 113, 115, 117, 138, 141, 143, 147, 150–51 152, 174, 182, 186, 189, 193, 195–98, 216ff., 224, 227–28, 231–32, 237, 243, 245, 246ff., 272, 278, 287, 298, 300, 303ff., 329–30; Aesthetic Experience, 74, 102, 114, 118, 126–27, 129ff., 144, 174–76, 190, 194ff., 199–200, 204, 221, 306, 315–16, 322; Aesthetic Form, 21, 25, 29–30, 42, 56, 60, 65–67, 69, 75, 77, 78, 81, 90, 91, 93, 99, 101, 108, 109, 113, 114, 127, 130–35, 138, 140, 144, 146–49, 151, 153, 155, 201, 218, 251–53, 255–57, 261, 298, 303, 307–9, 311, 314–19, 322, 324, 326–29, 331ff.; Aesthetic Object, 11, 19, 39, 57, 59, 129, 145–46, 255, 257, 315

All. See Totality

Appearance (Disclosure, Display, Manifestness, Phenomena, Revealing), 2–6, 11, 31, 54, 55–56, 63, 64, 110, 112, 114, 118–19, 121–22, 124, 126, 129, 136, 143, 145–46, 150, 165–69, 173, 178, 182, 185–90, 192, 194, 202, 212–13, 217, 219–20, 222, 226, 229, 240, 256, 263–71, 273, 276, 278–81, 284–86, 288–91, 294–97, 305–7, 310, 312–14, 317, 319–22, 327–28, 341

Apollonian, 40, 59, 65–66, 77, 92, 216ff., 307, 318, 323

Architecture (Building, Cathedral), 26–28, 39, 51, 67, 69–70, 93, 95, 114, 143, 156, 171, 175–76, 180–81, 185, 196–97, 201, 213, 301, 307, 342–43, 345

Art (Artworks), 10–11, 12, 13–14, 14ff., 35, 36ff., 51, 52–56, 61, 62, 65–68, 71ff., 87, 88ff., 95, 101, 102–3, 109–10, 113–14, 126, 134, 138ff., 150ff., 165, 168–69, 171ff., 194ff., 208, 212, 216ff., 228–29, 233, 239, 242, 245, 246ff., 265, 270, 271ff., 285, 287–89, 291, 296, 298–301, 304, 306ff., 329, 341–42, 344–46; System of the Arts 18–30, 318

Artist (see also Genius), 76, 89, 101–2, 114, 127–28, 146, 148, 174, 195, 197, 200, 212, 215–17, 219, 221–22, 228, 253, 260, 281, 284–88, 294–95, 299, 306, 308–9, 317, 319, 326–27, 329, 343, 346

Autonomy. See Freedom

Beauty (the Beautiful), 32, 35, 37, 39, 42–45, 54, 56–61, 66–69, 74, 80, 85, 92, 94–95, 97ff., 102ff., 126ff., 140–43, 145–46, 148–51, 172–74, 180, 182–84, 188, 191, 194–95, 200, 202, 223–25, 249–50, 256, 258, 261–62, 299, 307, 309, 314–15, 319, 322–26, 329, 341–42

Being, xv, 6–11, 18, 31, 36, 38, 49, 54–55, 58, 60, 62–63, 72, 78, 97, 104, 106–7, 113–14, 121–23, 141, 150–51, 155, 161–67, 169, 171–72, 175–76, 182, 185, 188, 199, 206–7, 213–15, 217, 220, 222, 226–27, 232–33, 256–57, 260, 265ff., 303, 311, 319–21, 324–25, 327–28

Biology (the Biological). See Organism

Body. See Matter

Building. See Architecture

Catharsis, 86–87, 91–92, 99–100, 175

Cathedral. See Architecture

Choice (Decision), 8–9, 12, 15–16, 38, 71–72, 124, 145, 157, 169–71, 185, 201, 227, 243, 257, 259, 261, 275, 290, 303–4, 311, 313, 320, 327–28, 340, 343

Comedy, 83

Concept (Notion), 10, 15–16, 21, 31–32, 36, 59, 69, 72, 74, 77, 80, 82, 87–88, 91, 93, 95, 110, 112–15, 120–23, 125ff., 141–43, 145, 147ff., 160ff., 170, 172, 175–77, 183, 185–86, 189–90, 193–95, 197–98, 200–201, 204–5, 208–11, 215, 217, 220, 233–34, 236, 241–42, 244–45, 249–59, 252, 256–58, 261–62, 264, 268, 272, 275, 289, 292–95, 314, 322–23, 327, 329, 341, 343

Cosmos. *See* Totality
Creativity, 130, 169, 179, 185, 208, 210–11, 215,
　219, 221–22, 226–29, 242–44, 257, 261–62,
　272, 284, 286, 291, 306, 312, 321, 323,
　325–26, 328, 342, 346

Dance, 25, 38–39, 67, 82, 91, 180, 217–18, 220,
　223–25, 228, 259
Decision. *See* Choice
Democracy, 68, 70
Dialogue, xiv, xv, 25, 32, 96, 152–54, 171, 179, 229,
　285, 288, 323
Dialectic, xiv, 9, 96, 100, 169, 184, 241, 243,
　245–46, 258
Dionysian, 40, 59–60, 65–66, 87, 92, 216ff., 257,
　307, 323, 326
Disclosure. *See* Appearance
Divine. *See* God
Drama. *See* Theater
Dwelling. *See* Inhabitance

Eidetic Object. *See* Type
End. *See* Purpose
Epic, 83, 180, 217
Eros, xiv, 42, 44, 52, 54, 56ff., 62ff., 68, 92, 97,
　104, 113, 130, 150, 164–65, 183, 190, 215,
　223–25, 233, 321, 323
Essence. *See* Type
Ethics (Ethos). *See* Morality
Expressivity, 5, 82, 89, 97, 99–101, 110, 112–14,
　133, 141, 143, 148–49, 173–75, 189, 191,
　193, 199–201, 219, 246, 248, 250, 252–53,
　256, 264, 306, 315, 317, 320, 324–25,
　342

Field of Experience (of Awareness, of Con-
　sciousness), xv, 2–14, 32, 36, 46, 61, 88,
　91, 113, 229, 236, 249, 258–60, 266, 271,
　282, 303–5, 311, 322, 324, 327–28, 346
Film, 24, 301
Final Cause. *See* Purpose
Form. *See* Type; Aesthetic Form
Freedom (Autonomy), 68, 124–27, 138, 140,
　143–45, 150, 153, 157, 160, 169, 171, 179,
　181–82, 185, 190, 243, 256, 272, 283–84,
　290–91, 314

Genius, 86, 89, 126–28, 135, 140–43, 150, 174, 176,
　178, 194, 199, 214, 216, 222–23, 272
God (the Divine), 16, 63, 97, 102, 104, 106–7,
　110–12, 115, 118, 121, 123, 125, 128, 133,
　137, 139–11, 149–50, 160–63, 167, 171, 174,
　177–79, 181–82, 189, 191–92, 204–6, 214,
　219, 225, 236, 245, 257, 259, 279, 282–83,
　285–87, 290, 313–14, 321, 325, 327, 339;
　god(s), 37–38, 42, 54–56, 63, 76, 87, 177,
　181, 217, 220, 225, 245, 272, 279, 285, 287,
　290–91, 307, 323, 330, 337
Good, 44ff., 51, 56, 57, 59, 60, 62, 63–65, 89,

96–97, 105, 107, 109, 111, 188, 191, 204–6,
　215, 225–26, 241, 249, 255, 261–62,
　324–26

Heart, 10–13, 35, 62–63, 114–15, 117, 125, 172, 175,
　178–79, 184–86, 197, 270, 280, 282, 285ff.,
　291, 294ff., 303–4, 312–13, 317, 319ff.,
　327–28, 340
Hermeneutics (Interpretation), 31–32, 64, 94, 123,
　174, 237, 265–66, 299, 304, 311–12, 318–19
History, 58–59, 79–80, 99, 157, 162–63, 166,
　168ff., 176, 184–86, 191, 204, 218, 223,
　264, 269ff., 279, 287, 289, 292–93, 295,
　313, 319, 325, 327, 346

Idea. *See* Type
Image, 47, 49ff., 54–55, 63–64, 97, 101–3, 111, 119,
　282, 323, 325
Imagination, 22–23, 28, 101, 121–22, 130–32, 134,
　136–38, 141–43, 147–18, 151, 179, 181,
　195–97, 223, 254–56, 258, 263, 265,
　309–11, 322, 343, 345
Imitation (*Mimesis*), 39, 50–52, 69, 77ff., 83–84,
　92, 100–101, 103, 110, 114, 174–75, 179,
　194, 308–9, 342, 345
Incarnation, 102, 111, 161, 163, 300, 327
Inhabitance (Dwelling), 11, 15, 51, 90–91, 185,
　264, 266–67, 270–74, 277–78, 280–81,
　283ff., 295, 297–98, 300–301, 311–12, 316,
　323, 327–28
Intellect. *See* Reason
Intentionality, 2–3, 166, 250, 260, 263, 265
Interpretation. *See* Hermeneutics
Intuition, xiv

Kind. *See* Type

Language, 9–10, 14–15, 20–21, 23, 28–29, 62, 82,
　85–86, 91, 99, 111, 154, 166, 169, 180, 195,
　197–98, 219, 241, 256, 259–60, 270–71,
　274–75, 278–79, 285–86, 291, 293–94,
　298, 301, 308, 310, 318–20
Life. *See* Organism
Lifeworld (*Lebenswelt*, World of Meaning, World-
　Space), xv, 7, 11–12, 105, 173, 264–65,
　267, 269ff., 276–78, 280, 282–84, 286,
　288–91, 293–99, 301, 304, 310–20, 323,
　328
*Logos* (Word), 39, 54, 62, 73, 75, 85–86, 96, 98–99,
　102, 109, 127, 148, 161–62, 167–68, 171,
　182, 198, 280, 285

Manifestness. *See* Appearance
Mathematics (Geometry), 1, 6, 20, 31, 45–46,
　48–50, 67, 69, 79–80, 96, 101, 119–20,
　122, 138, 141, 149, 187, 196, 222, 232,
　235–36, 297, 324
Matter (Body, the Receptacle), 3, 5, 16, 49–50,
　67–68, 75–76, 90, 98–99, 100ff., 110–14,

Matter (Body, the Receptacle) *cont.*,
141, 151, 161–62, 164, 168–69, 171, 175,
177–78, 181, 188–89, 194–95, 204, 206,
208–10, 212, 218, 220, 222–23, 225–26,
232ff., 245–46, 248, 251–53, 257, 260, 271,
275, 278, 299–300, 305, 308, 310, 319,
324, 327, 342–44

Meaning, 7, 9–10, 12–14, 20, 23, 32, 35, 37, 45, 49,
72, 84–86, 91, 142, 148, 174, 180, 183, 185,
188, 203, 205–6, 210–11, 213–15, 221–22,
227–28, 248–50, 252, 255–56, 259–60,
264–65, 267, 270–72, 277–78, 280–81,
285, 294, 298–300, 312, 315, 317, 319, 329,
340, 344, 346; World of Meaning. *See*
Lifeworld

Metaphor, 16, 23, 90, 100, 134, 149, 162, 253, 261,
293, 324

Mime, 25

*Mimesis. See* Imitation

Morality (Ethics, Ethos, Mores; *see also Phronesis*),
61, 78, 124–26, 129, 133–34, 145, 170–71,
173, 175–76, 179, 184, 199, 207–8, 218,
224–26, 227, 242–43, 249, 255, 258, 260,
266, 274, 301, 304, 308, 313–16, 322, 324

Music, 23, 37, 38ff., 66, 74, 77–79, 81, 83, 85–86,
91, 92–93, 101–3, 114, 141–43, 146, 148,
175, 178–81, 196–99, 201–2, 217–18,
221, 224–25, 252, 254–55, 259, 285,
300–301, 305, 307–9, 314–15, 318–19,
326–27

Mysticism, xiv, xvi

Nature, 8–9, 14–16, 36, 38, 50, 58–59, 61, 71–73,
74–77, 79ff., 87, 89, 91, 111, 119, 126–27,
134, 136, 138–40, 143–46, 149–51, 155,
157, 160, 162, 166–69, 171–73, 175,
182–85, 189–91, 194–96, 204–5, 207–8,
214, 216–18, 220, 222, 226, 228, 232, 235,
237, 240, 246, 248, 251, 257, 259, 266,
268–69, 287, 289–92, 295, 300, 303, 308,
311–13, 315, 319–20, 324–25, 328, 340–41

Notion. *See* Concept

Novel, 22, 28, 30, 90, 197, 254

One (Unity), 48–50, 59, 62, 64–65, 89, 97–99,
100, 102, 105, 107, 109, 111, 113, 121, 161,
167, 188, 190–91, 193, 198, 200, 204, 215,
225, 241, 256, 324–26

Opera, 23–24, 143, 197, 218

Organicity, 80–81, 90, 92, 93, 98, 110, 307–9, 342

Organism (Biology, Life, Physiology), 5–6, 11, 14,
37–38, 41, 57, 62, 64, 76, 80, 86, 88, 94,
101, 113, 119, 126–27, 134, 137, 143–48,
164, 166, 168, 182, 185–86, 189, 196,
206–8, 210–16, 218–19, 221–29, 233–34,
237–40, 242–48, 250–52, 255–61, 266,
276–77, 298, 303, 305–10, 312–15, 320–21,
328, 341, 343

Painting, 27–28, 39, 53–55, 66–67, 74, 81–82, 90,

92, 103, 114, 129, 134, 143, 146, 148,
178–79, 180–81, 196, 224, 254, 258, 275,
307–8, 310, 330, 342, 345–46

Participation, 50, 63–64, 98, 99–100, 104–6,
162, 225, 239, 247–48, 296–97, 316,
318

Phenomena. *See* Appearance

Phenomenology, xv, 3, 30–31, 145, 263–64, 269,
273, 305

Philosophy, 1–2, 31–32, 35–36, 44, 46, 51, 61, 63,
65–66, 79, 87, 91, 157, 161, 172, 181–83,
185, 197–98, 213, 218, 220, 225, 227, 241,
246, 258, 260–61, 265, 271, 278, 280–83,
286, 288–90, 292–98, 300, 304, 306, 312,
322–25, 329

*Phronesis* (Prudence) 10, 16–17, 58, 73, 83, 140,
249, 262

Physiology (the Physiological). *See* Organism

Poetry, 22–23, 29, 39ff., 51, 53ff., 61, 65, 80, 82,
89, 91, 93–94, 110, 114, 141–43, 179–81,
196, 198–99, 218, 249, 254–55, 259, 271,
278–82, 284–88, 291, 294–95, 297–300,
307, 310, 318, 322, 326

Potentiality (Potency, Possibility), 74, 76, 89, 107,
134, 155, 167–69, 171, 194, 228, 237,
239–40, 243, 278, 282–83, 292, 296, 303,
311–14, 320–21, 325, 342

Presence (Presentation, *see also* Participation), xiv,
10–11, 13, 15, 23, 26, 60, 62, 66, 82, 86,
89, 94, 97–98, 100, 104–7, 111–12, 133,
137–38, 142, 148–49, 151, 155, 174, 183,
186, 260–61, 263–64, 266, 268–71,
276–82, 284–85, 287–89, 292–99, 303–4,
309–10, 315–16, 319, 321–22, 324, 327–28,
330, 346

Principle of Noncontradiction, 7, 48

Prose, 21–22, 82

*Psyche. See* Soul

Purgation. *See* Catharsis

Purpose (End, Final Cause, Teleology, *Telos*),
75–76, 84, 86–87, 89, 103–4, 106, 110, 123,
124–28, 132, 134, 136, 143–45, 148, 150,
153, 166, 168–70, 173, 175–76, 179,
182–84, 216, 237–38, 240–47, 256, 258,
261–62, 271, 277, 289, 305, 307–8, 311,
315, 324

Reason (Rationality, Intellect), 41–43, 45ff.,
53–54, 58, 60, 62–65, 66–68, 73, 78,
96–97, 99, 101, 106–7, 109, 118, 121–23,
128–29, 133, 136–42, 149–51, 156, 160–61,
163, 167, 169–70, 172, 175, 178, 185,
187–89, 195, 202, 205, 209, 212, 220, 223,
225–26, 228–29, 232–33, 237, 240–45,
247–49, 250–51, 254, 258–59, 262, 265,
267, 270, 276–77, 280, 288–89, 296–98,
303–5, 309–10, 312, 318, 320–22, 324–28,
331, 343

Receptacle. *See* Matter

Reference, 20–23, 25, 28–30, 39, 41, 57, 65–66, 72, 77, 81–82, 93, 120–21, 133, 139, 148, 155, 169, 201, 255, 259–61, 304, 307–8, 311, 313, 315–16, 319–23, 327–28

Religion, 7, 61, 69, 154, 171–72, 177–78, 181, 183, 210, 217, 220, 227, 234, 241, 245, 247, 249, 256, 258, 282, 298–300, 313, 325, 327–28, 340, 344

Representation (*see also* Imitation), 27, 39, 66, 81, 92–93, 189ff., 199, 223–24, 270–71, 292, 296–97, 341, 345

Revealing. *See* Appearance

Science (*Theoria*, the Theoretical), 15–16, 72–73, 87, 89, 91, 117–19, 122–23, 125–26, 138, 145, 149, 165, 167, 182, 187–88, 190, 195, 203, 215, 219, 221, 226–28, 232–34, 236, 238, 242, 245–247, 258, 260, 264, 267, 271, 273–74, 276, 278, 280–81, 283, 286, 288, 289–97, 312, 324

Sculpture, 26–28, 51, 66–67, 74, 80–81, 90, 95, 114, 134, 177, 180, 196, 318, 329–46

Sensing, 3–6, 18–21, 31, 46–47, 50, 54, 60–62, 63–64, 71–72, 77, 82, 88, 97, 99–101, 103, 106–10, 113, 118–22, 132, 134–35, 137, 146–49, 155, 160, 166, 168, 174, 176–77, 179–80, 183–84, 186–87, 191, 194–95, 200, 228–29, 235–36, 238–40, 247–50, 255–57, 259–61, 263–64, 266, 273, 275–78, 280, 287, 295, 297–98, 300, 303–4, 305ff., 346

Sexuality, 8

Soul (*Psyche*), 42–44, 52–53, 56, 58–59, 64–68, 71–72, 76–77, 83, 86–88, 93, 98, 100–101, 103, 105–6, 113, 121, 125, 127, 133, 139, 141, 146, 179, 192, 210, 222–25, 226, 233, 240, 248, 255, 257, 266, 301, 307, 324

Space, 26–28, 69, 114, 119–20, 122, 132, 137, 139, 144, 175, 216, 220, 239, 242, 244, 249, 259, 278, 284, 288–89, 297–98, 300, 305–6, 313, 317–19, 322–23, 329, 332ff.

Space-time, 6, 8, 16, 18, 21, 25, 28–29, 36, 47–50, 58–59, 62, 72, 78, 98, 122, 155, 164, 167–68, 187–88, 196, 254, 289, 318, 319

Spirit, 69, 93, 98, 102, 105, 114, 140–41, 161–62, 165ff., 206, 208, 214, 223, 248, 299, 303, 311, 325, 339

Sublime, 85, 117, 126, 136–40, 144–46, 149–50, 195–96, 201–2, 204, 219, 223, 258, 322–24

Symbol, 142, 176–77, 179–81, 204, 322, 340, 344

Taste, 1, 129ff., 140–41, 145, 147, 151, 152–57, 173

*Techne*, 73–75, 79, 89

*Telos* (Teleology). *See* Purpose

Theater (Drama), 23–24, 81–82, 103, 143, 180, 197, 218, 220

*Theoria* (the Theoretical). *See* Science

Time, 12, 25, 27, 85, 101, 103, 119–22, 132, 142, 169–70, 175, 187, 190, 215–16, 223, 225, 234, 244, 249–50, 253, 263–66, 268–69, 276, 279, 282, 287, 300–301, 311, 313

Totality (the All, Cosmos, the Universe, the Whole, World), xv, 7–11, 13, 15, 29, 31–32, 36–37, 42, 47, 52, 58–59, 61, 66–69, 71, 78–79, 88, 91, 93–94, 97, 104, 114, 121, 133, 136–39, 141, 155, 162, 167–70, 172, 176, 178–79, 181–86, 187, 189, 204, 213, 217, 222, 224–25, 228, 229, 241, 256–60, 262, 265–69, 273, 279–86, 288, 291, 293–96, 298, 300, 303–4, 309–13, 315–28, 346

Tragedy, 83ff., 92, 146, 197, 201, 217ff., 250, 307–9, 323, 326

Truth, 41–42, 49, 53, 57, 73, 107, 109–11, 120, 161, 171, 175, 182, 190–91, 211–12, 220, 226, 228–29, 236, 270–75, 285, 306, 325, 344

Type (Eidetic Feature, Essence, Form, Idea, Kind), 10, 18, 31, 49–50, 54–56, 58, 59, 60–62, 64–65, 67, 76, 89, 91, 97, 100–101, 103, 106, 110, 113, 120–22, 126–27, 131, 134, 139–44, 148–49, 151, 155, 162, 167–68, 174, 182–85, 187–90, 194–98, 200–201, 204, 208–9, 211–13, 215–20, 222–23, 225–28, 231–34, 237–38, 240, 242, 244, 246, 248–49, 250, 252, 258, 262–64, 268–71, 275, 277–78, 288–93, 297, 299, 301, 303, 307–9, 311–12, 315, 318–20, 322, 324, 326, 329–30, 333, 341–43

Unity. *See* One

Whole. *See* Totality

Word. *See* *Logos*

World. *See* Totality